Inequality
Matters

Inequality Matters

Diversity and Exclusion in Canada

Augie Fleras

Oxford University Press is a department of the University of Oxford.
It furthers the University's objective of excellence in research, scholarship,
and education by publishing worldwide. Oxford is a registered trade mark of
Oxford University Press in the UK and in certain other countries.

Published in Canada by
Oxford University Press
8 Sampson Mews, Suite 204,
Don Mills, Ontario M3C 0H5 Canada

www.oupcanada.com

Library and Archives Canada Cataloguing in Publication
Fleras, Augie, 1947–, author
Inequality matters : diversity and exclusion in Canada / Augie Fleras.

Includes bibliographical references and index.
ISBN 978–0–19–544751–4 (paperback)

1. Equality—Canada. 2. Marginality, Social—Canada. 3. Cultural
pluralism—Canada. 4. Canada—Social conditions. I. Title.

HN110.Z9S6 2016   305.0971   C2016-901537-8

Oxford University Press is committed to our environment.
This book is printed on Forest Stewardship Council® certified paper
and comes from responsible sources.

Printed and bound in the United States of America

1 2 3 4 — 20 19 18 17

Contents

Chapter 5 The Politics of Poverty

Part III   Status Inequalities: Gender, Race, Aboriginality

Chapter 6 Gendered Inequality, Engendered Exclusions

Chapter 7 Racialized Inequalities, Immigrant Exclusions

Chapter 8 Aboriginal Peoples: Canada's First Inequality

Part IV   Institutional Exclusions

Chapter 9 The New Economy, New Exclusions: Work, Working, Workplaces

Preface

As far as clichés go, the politics of inequality resonate powerfully as an idea whose time is now. As recently as 2011, inequality as a concept was a relatively obscure topic, one that rarely elicited much political attention or public concern (Carney 2012). But no more: inequality has proven a timely and contentious issue since late 2011 when the Occupy movement leapt into public prominence. President Obama (and Pope Francis, among others) has repeatedly singled out growing income inequality as "the defining issue of our time." The annual meeting of the World Economic Forum in January 2015 identified gross income inequality as "a top global risk" whose disruptive consequences put it on par with global crises such as cyber-terrorism and global warming (also Dorling 2014). Social inequality is also riding the crest of a powerful media wave, judging by the massive coverage of populist uprisings in Arab countries during 2010–11; the "anarchy in the UK" riots later that summer; the Occupying Wall Street movement that pitted the "unruly" 99 per cent against the ruling 1 per cent; the prolonged resistance of Quebec students (dubbed the "Maple Spring") over proposed tuition increases; and the Idle No More resistance that drew national (and international) attention to aboriginal grievances (Kino-nda-niimi Collective 2014). The film industry, too, has hopped aboard the inequality bandwagon (Crooks 2014): a 2013 documentary entitled *Inequality for All* (narrated by Robert Reich, a former Clinton cabinet member) lamented the middle class, calling its demise a looming inequality disaster (also Graves 2014a). Even *The Economist* (2013)—no friend of an interventionist economy—has entered the fray. Yes, some degree of inequality is good for the economy since it fosters incentives, spurs risk-taking, and increases productivity. Yet recent concentrations of income and wealth are proving both politically toxic and economically catastrophic. Finally, if proof is required that inequality looms as a provocation whose time has come, consider the extraordinary popularity of Thomas Piketty's 2014 book *Capital in the Twenty-First Century*—a 700-page door-stopper that deconstructs the logic and consequences behind capitalist inequality.

Canada is no exception to this escalating trend and rallying cry (Gutstein 2014; OECD 2014; Alexander and Fong 2014; United Way 2015). Polls in Canada point to public worry and political criticism over accelerating gaps in power, privilege, and income (Broadbent 2012). Resentment is directed at a neo-liberal experiment that has unfolded according to plan, with governments pursuing market-friendly (neo-liberal) policies at the expense of the environment, the public good, and the economically vulnerable (McGrane 2015). Canadians are increasingly concerned over the gap between the haves and the have-nots—from the exorbitant pay packages of high-flying executives to the relatively stagnant incomes of middle-class households whose wages have flat-lined (Mackenzie 2015). They also worry about how this disparity generates an adverse effect that puts people behind while pulling society apart (Citizens for Public Justice 2013). Unacceptably high levels of poverty and homelessness in a resource-rich Canada constitute a source of national embarrassment that bodes poorly for its international reputation. No less embarrassing is the reality that highly skilled immigrants are stuck in survival jobs or that women in full-time employment continue to earn just over 70 cents for every male dollar earned (though it's a bit more complex than that), as well as the spectre of highly educated youth wallowing in the quintessential contradiction of a twenty-first-century workplace—namely, a jobless economy of high unemployment yet crippling labour shortages and precarious employment options: a world of workers without work, work without workers. Of particular note is mounting dismay over the dreary conditions in many aboriginal communities (Frideres and Gadacz 2012; Anaya 2014). That many Aboriginal peoples across Canada continue to be mired in developing world conditions is a scathing indictment of an unequal Canada (the inconvenient truth) that smugly professes otherwise (polite fictions).

Clearly then, Canada is an inequality paradox (Gaetz 2010). The paradox can be captured by paraphrasing Charles Dickens: it is the best of times; it is the worst of times. To one side, Canada commits to the principles and practices of equality and inclusion (EKOS 2013c). This commitment has paid off handsomely, with lofty socio-economic indicators that generally put Canada at or near the top of international rankings. Of the 34 leading countries surveyed by the OECD's Better Life Index (2011), Canada ranks second to Australia as a go-to destination, based on 11 factors ranging from material living standards to quality-of-life indicators, including health, life satisfaction, and work-life balance. Canada has also earned top marks from the Reputation Institute's 2014 Country RepTrak for the fourth time in six years (Reputation Institute 2015), an annual study that measured the public perceptions of 42,000 respondents across 50 countries along 16 different attributes. To the other side is a decidedly different picture. Canada may be one of the richest countries in the world, yet it remains deeply stratified, with layers of affluence superimposed upon levels of poverty. Structures of exclusion and inequality remain institutionally embedded, beyond most people's awareness, harmful to the most vulnerable of society, and resistant to change. The recent economic meltdown simply exposed yet another harsh new reality involving a toxic mix of chronic joblessness, job insecurity, rampant automation, and declining living standards—that is, a fearsome world of "work without workers" and "workers without work" (Citizens for Public Justice 2013). To yet another side, a more mixed picture appears. Canadians seemingly endorse the principle of progressive policies and inclusionary programs, yet many appear indifferent or unwilling to put principles into practice for transformative change. Or they are flummoxed by the feasibility of creating a Canada that puts people and the planet on par with profits, co-operation before competition, coexistence before violence, and sustainability before destruction. The consequences of such procrastination—talking the talk but not walking the walk—are unnerving, though there may be little danger of Canada backsliding into a dystopian Hobbesian nightmare where life is "nasty, brutish, and short." Nevertheless, the factors that once propelled progress and productivity don't seem to be working anymore, especially as we move down the generational ladder (Graves 2014a).

The politics of social inequality are as controversial an issue in Canada as they are a contested a topic in sociology. As John Porter (1965) concluded a half century ago in his landmark book *The Vertical Mosaic*, Canada is not a classless, egalitarian, and democratic society of equal opportunity or equitable outcomes. More accurately, it's a "steeply hierarchical patchwork" of classes and ethnicities, with power, opportunity, and mobility dominated by a WASP elite (Clement and Helmes-Hayes 2015; Jedwab and Satzewich 2015). The centrality and interplay of spiralling gaps, structural exclusions, and polarized communities continue to blur perceptions of Canada as a kinder and more caring society. Reactions to this inequitable state of affairs are varied. For some, the unequal distribution of income and wealth possesses redeeming value by virtue of creating richer lives, accelerated innovation and entrepreneurship, increased productivity, and improved overall prosperity (Sarlo, Clemens, Emes 2015; Noah 2012). Its pervasiveness and persistence in Canada is rationalized as the price Canadians pay for living in a dynamic and complex economy, with avenues to advancement that tradition-bound societies can only dream about (Noah 2012). For others, social inequality is an abomination that casts a blight on society (Campaign 2000 2013). Sharp spikes in social inequality compromise the prospects for co-operative coexistence, sustained economic growth, and vibrant democracy. They also trigger a raft of societal problems pertaining to societal cohesion, environmental sustainability, individual life chances and social well-being, and socio-economic gaps (Broadbent Institute 2012; Finn 2011; Wilkinson and Pickett 2009). Sharply unequal societies impose a punishingly high premium on acquiring money and possessions; consuming conspicuously; preening over physical appearances instead of nurturing inner growth; extracting resources regardless of environmental costs; and resorting to antisocial (illegal) behaviour in pursuit of fortune and fame. These misguided priorities exact a cost since they put people at greater risk of depression, anxiety, personality disorders, resentment, and shame and humiliation.

They also intensify the risk of anomie or a loss of solidarity when societal members become so alienated they no longer have any sense of belonging, connection, or fulfilment (Bland 2009). Wilkinson and Pickett (2009:3) capture the irony of emotional bankruptcy at a time of material abundance:

> It is a remarkable paradox that, at the pinnacle of human material and technological achievement, we find ourselves anxiety-ridden, prone to depression, worried about how others see us, unsure of our friendships, driven to consume, and with little or no community life. . . . [W]e seek comfort in over-eating, obsessive shopping and spending, or become prey to excessive alcohol, psychoactive medicines, and illegal drugs.

No matter how the inequality of exclusions is evaluated—good, bad, or a necessary evil—one theme is constant. We now live in a polarizing era in which the super-rich are pulling away while low income households are slipping further behind (OECD 2014b). The vast majority of citizens have barely improved their socio-economic status over the past 25 years, whereas a small cohort of uber-rich have monopolized most financial gains, prompting Frank Graves (2014a:1) to assert that "this new crisis of the middle class is possibly the defining issue of our time. . . ." Gaping social inequalities may prove unsettling enough to destabilize any society eroded by trust in democracy and the public institutions that constitute the core of community well-being and cohesion (Osberg 2012; Jones 2012; Canadian Index of Wellbeing 2012; Graves 2014b). Worse still, those policies and institutions that once generated prosperity and progress are no longer as effective in providing a balance of incentives and fairness for growing the economy. No less worrying is failure to stanch deepening worldwide inequities. Consider only the wealth gap: the world's richest 1 per cent now own more wealth than the other 99 per cent combined or, more specifically, 62 individuals possess as much wealth as the world's poorest 3.5 billion (Oxfam International 2016). The spectre of material deprivation, resource competition, corporate globalism, sectarian violence, environmental disasters, and international migration may well torpedo the possibility of co-operative coexistence on a sustainable planet.

Inequality Matters engages with this troubling reality by offering a critically informed and sociologically rich analysis of social inequality in a Canada that should know better—and do better. Emphasizing both the politics and paradoxes of social inequality as well as their patterns and practices, *Inequality Matters* begins with the premise that complex human societies are sites of unequal relations in allocating wealth/income, power, and privilege; within contexts of power and control; along the status and identity lines of race, aboriginality, gender, and class (in addition to other identity markers such as age or sexuality); across those institutional domains undergoing an identity crisis of confidence; and at the global level as competition for valued resources intensifies. Patterns of social inequality are known to be socially constructed and ideologically infused rather than anything natural or normal or neutral, and fundamentally inconsistent with the principle of a so-called level playing field. Yet these inequalities of exclusion are expertly concealed or normalized by way of comforting fictions that politely mask a host of inconvenient truths, internal contradictions, vested interests, and hidden agendas (Hacker and Pierson 2010; OECD 2011). Not surprisingly, Canadians and Americans display ambivalence in embracing contradictory beliefs over who gets what and what goes where (also McNamee 2014). The overarching theme of this book revolves around the politics and paradoxes of social inequalities of exclusion: that is, despite its vast abundance, *Canada remains an unequal society in terms of how exclusions of power, privilege, and property (wealth and income) are distributed across individual, institutional, and national levels. The persistence and pervasiveness of these inequalities of exclusion reinforce the importance of explaining how patterns of inequality are created, expressed, and sustained, in addition to how they are challenged and transformed by way of government policy, institutional reforms, ideological shifts, and minority resistance.* In putting the theme "inequalities matter" to the analytical test, Canada remains the focal point of interest. Nevertheless, its placement within a broader framework of globalization and global inequalities demonstrates the value of shifting the frame of reference beyond national boundaries (Korzeniewicz and Moran 2009).

Reference to social inequality as concept and reality has long informed the sociological analyses of society and its constituents (Porter 1965; Sernau 2011). Or as Wallace Clement (1988:6) once claimed, "The study of inequality has been the bread and butter of sociology." Virtually every topic within sociology—from the introductory to the study of institutions (i.e., family, media, criminal justice), from the macro to the micro—entails the domain of inequality either as a topic in its own right or as complicit in reproducing an unequal society. Sociology has much to offer in unpacking the politics, patterns, and paradoxes of social inequality. Of particular sociological value is a commitment to reframing inequality in terms of social exclusions that deny, exploit, or oppress, in the process shifting the focus of analysis from income distribution to participation, connections, empowerment, and contribution. Coaxing fresh insight into the politics and paradoxes of social inequality demonstrates the discipline's knack for moving beyond stale conventions and tired formulas. Nor does sociology as a discipline flinch from asking some tough questions about who gets what and what goes where. Not surprisingly, debates over the inequality of exclusions rarely question its existence per se. Controversies are driven instead by those patterns of inequality and exclusion thought to be unjustified because they draw on irrelevant characteristics; are persistent over time or space; are entrenched within institutional structures and foundational principles; are supported by ideological beliefs; are rooted in the exploitation of others and restrictive of their life chances; and are unresponsive to interventions. That each of these dimensions continues to baffle and infuriate sociologists reinforces the elusiveness of answers or solutions. Still, much can be gained from applying a sociological lens to see the world of social inequality differently.

An introductory text is mindful of the need to inform, enlighten, and inspire. This introduction to the inequalities of exclusion in Canada offers the necessary building blocks—from definitions and relevant concepts to theories and recurrent debates—for analysis, assessment, and action at a time when ambiguity or contestation are displacing the certainties of the past (Gratton 2010; Kimmel 2013). Instead of simply exhuming dry treatises or reciting sterile facts with respect to the what, why, where, and how, *Inequality Matters* enlightens and energizes by juxtaposing polite fictions with inconvenient truths in hopes of debunking the myths and misconceptions that not only distort students' lived experiences and inflate Canada's collective image, but also underplay the cost of escalating inequality patterns (Heath 2009; Feagin 2011; Bush 2011). A range of questions should immediately come to mind that concede the corrosive effect of those hyper-inequalities that disrupt the stability of Canada's democracy, the resiliency of its social fabric, and the prosperity of its economy (Broadbent Institute 2014): Why do inequalities of exclusions persist and proliferate in a bountiful Canada that many see as a "solution in search of a problem" (Fleras 2012)? Why are patterns of social inequality escalating to levels unseen since the "Dirty Thirties"? Is it possible to attain an equal society (if one were even desirable), or is this goal essentially a pipedream? Can a more equitable society be constructed through a series of reforms (i.e., "tweaking the conventions defined by the rules") or must the focus of change be transformative ("changing the rules that inform conventions")? Answers to these questions are critical but elusive: both equality and inequality are more complex than people realize since the concepts are sharply contested, references to causality are convoluted and contradictory, and the embeddedness of structural biases preclude easy detection or simple explanations (Jackson 2010).

The rationale behind *Inequality Matters* draws on this simple yet salient fact: the inequalities of exclusions matter in their own right beyond a preoccupation with poverty levels or income polarization (Cameron 2011). People's lives and life-chances are profoundly influenced by patterns of inequality that also shape opportunities and outcomes with respect to social engagement and societal participation. Yet the centrality of social inequality in people's daily experiences and life chances is so quietly pervasive that few acknowledge their complicity in reproducing inequality or their vulnerability to its consequences (Schwalbe 2008; Sernau 2011). Inequalities also matter because of a strong relationship between low socio-economic status and social exclusion, even if their effects are mediated (and masked) by a host of intervening variables that complicate the search for cause–effect relations (Piketty 2014). Extremes in social exclusion and income inequality tend to foster contexts that are economically inefficient (OECD 2015a); politically corrosive; socially divisive; morally unethical; culturally unsettling; psychologically distressing; and environmentally destructive (Oxfam 2013). Societies with glaring income inequalities trend toward higher rates of mental illness, violent crime, teenage pregnancy, imprisonment rates, and medical issues from substance dependence to eating disorders and obesity (Lee 2011). Or as bluntly put by Wilkinson and Pickett (2009) in their best-selling book *The Spirit Level*, persistently high levels of social inequality exact social costs that create or intensify existing social problems, despite the trickiness of proving a causal relationship. Conversely, the more equal a society, the better the range of positive social outcomes across a wide spectrum of measures.

The title of this book is neither random nor arbitrary. Reference to the "matters" in *Inequality Matters* is a reminder that inequality is consequential because it increases the possibility that something will happen—or not (also Krugman 2013). Inequalities constitute a difference that often makes a difference (variable) in shaping outcomes, for richer or poorer, better or worse, at both personal and collective levels, and across Canada and beyond. By the same token, social equality matters in constructing a more inclusive and egalitarian Canada, one in which no one is excluded because of their race, aboriginality, class, or gender. Admittedly debates over the attainment of social equality—from what it is to how to get there—rarely achieve consensus in light of competing explanatory frameworks. And while spiralling income and wealth gaps are worrying in their own right, no less detrimental to attaining equality are growing inequalities of exclusions that preclude people from an active and positive contribution to society. Nevertheless, visions of a more equitable Canada are not beyond the realm of the impossible, as the late Jack Layton, leader of the New Democratic Party, movingly implored in a two-page letter written to both New Democrats and Canadians on Saturday 20 August 2011—less than 48 hours before he died.

> Canada is a great country, one of the hopes of the world. We can be a better one—a country of greater equality, justice, and opportunity. We can build a prosperous economy and a society that shares its benefits more fairly. We can look after our seniors. We can offer better futures for our children. We can do our part to save the world's environment. . . . [W]e can be a better, fairer, and more equal country by working together. Don't let them tell you it can't be done.

> My friend, love is better than anger. Hope is better than fear. Optimism is better than despair. So let us be loving, hopeful, and optimistic. And we'll change the world.

Let's put Layton's plea into perspective. Compared to other parts of the world, Canadians are much better off in terms of incomes, job creation, health care and education levels, a commitment to diversity as a strength, levels of happiness and life satisfaction, and a belief they live in the best country in the world (Martin and Milway 2012). But in contrast to Canada's commitments and abundant resources, we can do better, and Layton's parting words provide the stimulus and rationale for *Inequality Matters*. Perhaps a Canada of perfect equality is neither attainable nor even desirable. But the persistence of extreme inequalities and punishing exclusions in one of the world's luckiest societies is an affront to those ideals that Canada endorses and Canadians aspire to.

Inequality
Matters

I Conceptualizing Social Inequality

Canada presents a paradox: it may be one of the luckiest countries in the world when it comes to living well, thanks to its vast resources and the resourcefulness of its population (The Economist Intelligence Unit, 2015). A 2016 World Economic Forum survey of 60 countries across 24 categories, prepared by U.S. News and World Report, University of Pennsylvania's Wharton School of Business, and global brand consultants BAV Consulting, put Canada second (behind Germany) in a ranking of the best countries in the world. Yet **social inequality** and inequalities of exclusion are deeply entrenched in a country that aspires to doing things differently. Canada is hardly immune to the harsh realities of **inequality** that privileges the supernova few by marginalizing the many. The stalled (inflation-adjusted) salaries that many Canadians have endured over the past 30 years pale by comparison to the mind-boggling incomes of pampered sports figures, Hollywood A-list stars, chief executive officers (CEOs), and financial wizards (Mackenzie 2015). Some see the pervasiveness and persistence of these income-based inequalities as a regrettable necessity if this lucky country is to stay competitive. For others, the disparities of social inequality represent a disgraceful blot at odds with an ostensibly kinder and gentler Canada. The inequalities of exclusion not only contradict national ideals, tarnish Canada's international reputation, and sow the seeds of anti-social behaviour—the politics of social inequality also possess the menacing potential to destabilize Canada to the point of incoherence and chaos (Canada 2020 2011).

Concern is also mounting over Canada's future as a progressive society (Killian 2015). In recent years, Canadian governments have followed an agenda based on austerity and a commitment to lower taxes and gut social programs in order to balance budgets and foster national growth through "trickle-down" economics (Hurtig 2015). People's lives and life chances are negatively impacted by the centralization of power and resources in the hands of a power elite who prosper from the very dynamics that marginalize others (Gutstein 2014; Grabb and Guppy 2009). The poor, asylum-seekers, and the unemployed may be labelled as freeloading parasites or conveniently demonized as scapegoats when things go bad. Their potential as individuals is also adversely compromised when they are denied (a) access to emotional and physical health; (b) a personal sense of well-being, belonging, and security; (c) meaningful levels of involvement within the local community, connections to others, and participation in society; and (d) recognition of their contributions as valued members (Wilkinson and Pickett 2009). The bonds of mutual trust and social solidarity are further eroded when the pampered rich further isolate themselves—both physically and psychologically—from the precarious poor (see also Freeland 2011). Social costs, from dissension and jealousy to cynicism and mistrust, are particularly worrisome if socio-economic gaps are perceived as unfair or excessive (Cameron 2011; Reich 2012). The following indictment of social inequality captures how and why inequalities matter:

Inequality divides us from one another in schools, in neighborhoods. . . . Inequality makes it harder to imagine the lives of others—which is one reason why the fate of over 14 million more or less permanently unemployed Americans leaves so little impression in the country's political and media capitals. Inequality corrodes trust among fellow citizens, making it seem as if the game is rigged. Inequality provokes a generalized anger that finds targets where it can—immigrants, foreign countries, American elites, government in all forms. . . . Inequality saps the will to conceive of ambitious solutions to large collective problems, because these problems no longer seem very collective. Inequality undermines democracy. (Packer 2011)

Inequalities in income and wealth are now ranked alongside terrorism, climate change, and pandemics as the most critical issues on the international policy agenda. Yet, despite progress on some fronts, few potentially effective solutions have been proposed and finding the best policies for reducing inequalities remains a puzzle (Moyo 2016). Furthermore, references to social inequality are prone to misunderstanding (see also Tilly 2005). Misconceptions reflect a tendency to frame inequality as an aberration to an otherwise healthy and meritocratic society; a largely individual phenomenon in terms of causal factors; synonymous with income differences and financial rewards; and amenable to reform through quick-fix solutions. For sociologists, however, the inequalities of exclusion are often differently framed as:

1. an inevitable and enduring component of any human society organized along lines of **class**, race, aboriginality, or gender;
2. embedded within the institutional structures of society;
3. focused on a range of social exclusions beyond income differences only (Levitas et al. 2007);
4. derived from the principles of organization that inform social relations (Clement 1988);
5. based on biases largely impervious to detection while stubbornly resistant to reform (Wallis and Kwok 2008); and
6. involving a process that enriches some at the expense of impoverishing others.

Sociology as a discipline tends to frame inequality as *structural and social. Structural,* because ideas about power, privilege, and property, as well as *ideals* about what is normal, desirable, and acceptable with respect to who gets what and what goes where are deeply embedded (structured) within the founding assumptions and foundational principles of a society's **constitutional order.** *Social,* because sociology emphasizes the social dimensions of inequality—namely, the mutually reciprocating relation between society and inequality that draws attention to the impact of inequality on society, and vice versa. Reference to the social also addresses how the inequalities of exclusion are created, expressed, and sustained through principle and practice, as well as how exclusions of inequality related to powerlessness, resource allocation, and quality of life indicators are challenged and changed by means of resistance and reforms.

Part I applies a sociological perspective for conceptualizing the politics and paradoxes of social inequality. Chapter 1 begins by pointing out how and why social inequality matters since it increases the chances of making things happen. The chapter provides an overview of social inequality and the inequalities of exclusion in Canada (and the United States for comparative purposes) at the level of income and wealth in addition to power and privilege. An analysis of core themes that underpin *Inequality Matters* reinforces the value of analyzing social inequality on sociological grounds. Chapter 2 **problematizes** the concept of social inequality in terms of its constituent components: *social* and *inequality.* An examination of these constituents demonstrates how deconstructing social inequalities along sociological lines secures the basis for understanding who gets what (*differential access*) and what goes where (*differential distribution*). Chapter 3 addresses those sociologically based explanatory frameworks that account for the prevalence, pervasiveness, and persistence of inequalities and exclusions at different levels and across diverse domains, from the personal and the institutional to the national and the global. A sociological lens not only provides insight into social inequality as social exclusion whose roots reflect structural arrangements within society. The myths and misconceptions that get in the way of proposed solutions are debunked as well, in hopes of separating comforting fictions from uncomfortable truths.

1 The Iniquities of Inequality

Learning Objectives

1. To provide a general overview of social inequality in terms of power, privilege, and property.

2. To point out why separating polite fictions from inconvenient facts informs debates over social inequality and the inequalities of exclusion.

3. To identify how patterns of social inequality in a bountiful Canada are prone to paradox and controversy.

4. To demonstrate Canada's complicity in reinforcing global exploitation.

5. To instill an awareness of income disparities among Canadians, and why this matters in establishing the inequalities of exclusion.

Introduction: Surveying the Damage

Canada is a good place to be born and raised. The collapse of the financial system may have triggered the onset of the great global recession in 2008, but Canada weathered the collapse better than most other countries (at least until recently), thanks in part to its solid economic infrastructure, regulated bank systems, and financial incentives (such as low interest rates) to stimulate consumer spending (*The Economist*, March 30, 2013). The Paris-based Organisation for Economic Co-operation and Development (OECD) predicts Canada will continue to lead the Group of Seven (G7) industrialized economies in economic growth over the next 50 years. The OECD ranks Canada a solid ninth overall (with Switzerland first), a figure calculated on a mix of factors related to wealth, crime rates, job security, unemployment rates, gender parity in Parliament, trust in public institutions, and health of family unit

(OECD 2015b, c). Another report by the Conference Board of Canada (2013b; Grant 2013) put Canada seventh (a B ranking) among 17 peer countries. Canada performed splendidly on some measures such as low murder rate, high levels of life satisfaction, income for persons with disabilities, low levels of elderly poverty (despite a modest increase in recent years), intergenerational income mobility, and tolerance toward diversity. It scored poorly on rates of child poverty (15.1 per cent, up 2.3 percentage points since the mid-1990s), working poor (11.1 per cent, up 1.7 per cent), gender income gaps, poor voter turnout, and public confidence in Parliament. The countries of Fennoscandia, as well as the Netherlands and Austria, scored As in this assessment; by contrast, the USA and Japan posted Ds.

But signs point to a meaner and leaner Canada (Himmelfarb 2013; Alexander and Fong 2014; Gutstein 2014; Mackenzie 2015; United Way 2015). Compared to its utopian ideals, Canada falls short of its self-appointed benchmark as a happy medium, neither too rich nor too poor. Canada may bask in the limelight as one of the world's premier places to live, but too many congratulations run the risk of fostering indifference or complacency. Allusions to a "caring" and "kinder" Canada are gradually being whittled away by political agendas that bifurcate Canadians into the "haves" and "have-nots" (Banting and Myles 2013; Gutstein 2014). The erosion of full-time jobs in favour of part-time work, precarious jobs, and self-employment have had a dampening effect on wages. Yes, average wages have increased, drawn up by the high end, yet there has been no real change in the median wage since the mid-2000s (Tal 2015). The primacy of neo-liberalism as a more-market/less-government ideology continues to rule the economic roost, in the process putting pressure on individuals to manage their lives and life-chances. Short-term economic growth resulting from, for example, massive resource extraction endangers the viability of an already plundered environment. Aboriginal people's rights are compromised as well in the headlong rush to protect vested interests and promote wealth creation, regardless of consequences (but see Coates and Crowley 2013). Even the spectacular failures of the great recession do not appear to have dislodged a neo-liberal mentality from its premier perch as the dominating political vision and overriding rationale for wealth creation and income distribution (Shantz and Macdonald 2013).

Most Canadians know that disparities exist. But few comprehend the depth and scope of these inequities, much less their impact and implications for Canada and Canadians. Mainstream calculations of inequality tend to be skewed because both the very wealthy and the very poor tend to be excluded or underrepresented, while statistics on income and wealth hidden in tax havens underestimate the problem (Lansley 2012; Stewart 2012). Billions of dollars of income acquired by the richest Canadians are excluded from calculations of their assets because these vast sums are funnelled into private corporations for tax reduction purposes (Woolfson et al. 2014). Notwithstanding these caveats, the following range of inequalities and exclusions involving Canadians at home and abroad paints a baffling picture of extremes of power, privilege, and income/wealth

whose rationale may be difficult to defend or rationalize:

1. Celine Dion earned just under $75 million per year during the 2000–2010 decade, largely from concert ticket sales and CD sales, putting her at the top of the Ultimate Decade list, just ahead of country singer Kenny Chesney and the jazz-rock fusion group, The Dave Matthews Band. According to annual rankings by Forbes.com, Robert Downey Jr. was Hollywood's highest paid actor in 2014 (and again in 2015) with earnings of $75 million; Sandra Bullock topped the list for female actors at $51 million.

2. In 1972, the average NHL salary was about $25,000; by the beginning of the 2013–14 season, the average had soared to $2.58 million. Let's put this $2.58 million into perspective: *It would take most Canadian workers with a university degree an entire lifetime to earn this amount* (inflation adjusted [see Singer 2012]). In August 2014, P.K. Subban, star defenceman for the Montreal Canadiens, signed an eight-year, $72 million contract. He will earn $109,752 per regular season game, or $4,573 per minute, based on an average 24 minutes of ice time each game, excluding practices and conditioning. Shea Weber of the Nashville Predators is the highest paid puckster at $14 million per year.

3. Unlike NHLers, the 450 players in Ontario's Junior Hockey League (OHL) are paid as little as $35 a week, yet must endure up to 60 hours of travel, training, and playing time. The 58 cents per hour they receive is well below Ontario's minimum wage threshold of $11.25. These amateur players aren't entitled to overtime, vacation, or severance pay (as mandated by Ontario law) (Gillespie 2012), in effect making them little more than indentured labourers who hope to strike it rich one day (but see the Spotlight box in this chapter).

4. The prime minister of Canada received a salary of $327,400 in 2014, including an annual car allowance of $2,112 in addition to other perks of the office. By contrast, the minimum salary for an NHL player in the 2014–15 season was $550,000. An awkward question is inescapable: *Why is the office of prime minister—arguably the*

most important position in Canada—underpaid in comparison to the earnings of entertainers or sports figures? Similarly, US President Obama earns $400,000 per year, in addition to $169,000 tax-free dollars to spend on travel, expenses, and entertainment. Compare this with the minimum entry level salary for a major league baseball player which increased from $414,000 in 2011 to $480,000 in 2012 (the average major league baseball MLB salary in 2015 was in the $4.5 million bracket).

5. The rich keep getter richer. The richest 1 per cent of Canadians, whose average income exceeds $405,000 ($320,000 according to Lemieux and Riddell 2015), continue to monopolize the economic pie. Income for the richest 1 per cent of Canadians has *doubled* since the 1970s from an extremely high base rate, *tripled* for the richest 0.1 percent, and *quintupled* for the richest 0.01 percent. CEOs in the top 100 earn 195 times more than the average Canadian—up from 105 times in 1998 and about 40 times the total in the 1980s. (The AFL-CIO labour federation calculates that a typical CEO at a large American company earned 354 times more than the average worker, compared to 84 more times in the UK and 67 in Japan). In other words, by 12:18 of the first working day after New Year's, Canada's top corporate executives will have out-waged an average worker's earnings for the entire year (Mackenzie 2016). A combination of weak corporate governance, ineffective government regulation, lax tax rules and loopholes, and growing pressure to deliver maximum short-term profits (or what Dominic Barton [2011] calls "quarterly capitalism") has paid off in outsized rewards for senior managers and executives especially in the financial sector (Broadbent Institute 2012).

6. The top 10 per cent of earners in Canada receive 28.1 per cent of income and pay 42.1 per cent of Canada's income tax. But income disparities are one thing; **wealth** gaps are something different. Based on a study by the Broadbent Institute (2014), the top 10 per cent of Canadians have seen their net worth increase by 42 per cent since 2005, or 47.9 per cent of all Canada's wealth. By contrast, the bottom 10 per cent saw

their median wealth shrink by 150 per cent; as a result, they owned less than 0 per cent of Canada's wealth, since their debts outweighed their assets by $5,100 (Flavelle 2014). The level of wealth inequality in Canada has reached such an extreme that, in 2012, the 86 wealthiest Canadian resident families (or 0.002 per cent of the population) owned as much wealth as the poorest 11.4 million Canadians combined (or 34 per cent of the total population) (MacDonald, 2014). The two wealthiest families in Canada, the Thomson and Weston families, experienced double-digit growth in their net worth between 2012 and 2013—$26.1 billion (up 30 per cent), and $10.4 billion (up 24 per cent), respectively.

7. The collective profits of Canada's Big Five banks hit a record $35 billion in 2015 (for the fiscal year that ended 31 October); meanwhile, the banks also eliminated 4,664 jobs in the fourth quarter as part of a move to streamline operations in the face of technological changes (Freeman 2015; Wong 2013). Income disparities continue to astonish: according to the 2 September 2013 issue of *Maclean's*, the CEO of RBC earned $12.6 million per year, whereas a bank teller for RBC earned $32,000, and an India-based IT worker for RBC (employed by iGATE) earned around $12,000.

8. Data from the 2011 National Household Survey and published by Statistics Canada shows that the median individual income for full-time work is $50,699 (although the highest annual income in Canada is found around the Fort McMurray area where the median family income is $186,782), whereas median individual income for all workers (both part-time and full-time) is $27,600. The median income for racialized minority individuals in full-time work is $45,128 and $41,684 for aboriginal individuals in full-time employment (Scoffield 2014).

9. How does income inequality in Canada compare to that of other advanced industrial societies? The **Gini Coefficient** (a measure of income equality in which 0.0 indicates perfect equality of income, and 1.0 indicates absolute inequality, wherein one person owns all the income) places Nordic countries at between 0.25 and

0.26; Western European countries between 0.26 (Belgium) and 0.30 (Germany); and Anglo Saxon countries between 0.29 (Ireland) and 0.38 (United States). Canada's score is 0.32 (Rajotte 2013). Other studies, including one by Janet Gornick, director of the CUNY Research Center of International Inequality, put Canada's Gini coefficient of income at 0.38 after taxes and transfers (0.55 before taxes and transfers) (Gornick and Jantti 2013).

This admittedly selective review is both informative and disturbing. It demonstrates how comparisons in income and wealth expose the paradoxes of inequality in a Canada that aspires to be otherwise. Economic growth tends to disproportionately benefit a small group of uber-rich whose interests and agendas do not necessarily dovetail with the welfare of society or the well-being of the disenfranchised poor. Nor do many appreciate how massive income disparities may well represent the foremost risk in eroding this planet's survival scenario. The magnitude of the challenge raises a number of questions that must be addressed in whole or in part. Why is there so much income inequality in a resource-rich Canada with one of the world's highest standards of living, a robust economy whose performance outpoints much of the industrial world, a constitutional commitment to equality as a core Canadian value, and a raft of government programs to alleviate economic disparities? Why is Canada, of all OECD countries, experiencing one of the most rapid increases in rates of income and wealth inequality (OECD 2014; Conference Board of Canada 2011b)? Does a connection exist between the enrichment of the rich and the impoverishment of the poor? Are these discrepancies a social anomaly at odds with Canadian values or are they consistent with the free-market principles of supply and demand? Does any theory of distributive justice justify the exorbitant salaries of executives, athletes, and entertainers, yet miserly wages for those in the caring professions? Disparities of such magnitude may be immoral, conclude McQuaig and Brooks (2010), but no political party seems interested in pitching social inequality as an electoral platform except as middle-class wedge politics.

Of these questions, three are uppermost. First, why have income/wealth gaps expanded exponentially, despite Canada's reputation as the "un-USA" in terms of extreme income inequality (EKOS 2013a; but see Lamman, Karabegovic, and Veldhuis 2012; and Sarlo, Clemens, Emes 2015 for counterargument)? What is it about Canadian society that emboldens a greedy few to accumulate vast amounts of income, wealth, and power, while many languish in poverty or at the margins (McQuaig and Brooks 2010)? Should anyone have to live in poverty in a bountiful Canada, rely on food banks or experience food scarcity, default into unwanted homelessness, or feel excluded or unwanted? Second, why have Canadians generally accepted these realities instead of rioting in the streets in protest over the injustices? (Quebec's Maple Spring movement and Aboriginal peoples' Idle No More movement are exceptions, of course.) The dazzling lives and profligate lifestyles of billionaires are not simply an inconsequential statistical aberration. The lavish standards of living of the extremely wealthy constitute an affront to the very concept of Canada as an egalitarian society, while sowing the society-sapping seeds of distrust, cynicism, and divisiveness. Third, does it matter? For some, inequality doesn't matter because it's irrelevant as long as everyone plays by the rules, competition is fair, and a safety net cushions the blow for those less fortunate. Moreover, rather than emphasizing income inequality and aiming to reduce the gap between rich and poor, public policy should focus on ensuring that all citizens enjoy basic living standards, including full and equal participation in society (Moyo 2016). For others, inequality is critical in creating a complex and creative society, one that differently rewards hard work and risk-taking. For still others, inequality matters because it reverberates through society by unsettling the social order, eroding standards of living, dampening economic performance, and hollowing out democratic foundations (Broadbent Institute 2012; McQuaig and Brooks 2010). That these patterns of inequality beget yet more inequality is captured in this Spotlight box on the economics of novice hockey.

Spotlight Playing Hockey Lottery: An Expensive Illusion

How does income inequality affect Canadians? In one of the more curious ironies at present, Canada's national game is becoming an increasingly expensive proposition that prices out many working-class families. According to Hockey Canada (cited in Mirtle 2013), the average hockey parent spent just under $3,000 on minor hockey in the 2011–12 season (approximately $1,200 for registration, $900 for travel and accommodations, $600 for skates and equipment, and the rest on incidentals). Costs can quickly spiral upwards: the parents of one of the most successful hockey families in Canada, the Subbans (three sons have been drafted by the NHL), shelled out $5,000 per year for each son to play in the Greater Toronto (Minor) Hockey League. At the highest levels of Triple A minor hockey, from novice up, the annual cost soars to between $10,000 and $15,000 per year (and higher), reflecting escalating costs related to ice rental time (which can consume up to seven days a week); "rep" or elite hockey players competing with elite players from out of town; skills development programs; and off-season training regimes (Parcels 2013). Or as the father of Matt Duchene (star forward for Colorado Avalanche) put it, he invested more than $300,000 in his son's 13-year minor hockey career (Traikos 2015). The conclusion is inescapable: Canada's national game is beyond the reach of many young Canadians. A game that once represented a true meritocracy by rewarding the skilled and dedicated is increasingly the exclusive preserve of wealthy families.

One additional irony: the extremes that parents endure in chasing the dream masks a sobering reality. In general, less than one per cent of Canadian kids who are registered to play hockey in any given birth year will play even one game in the NHL (Campbell and Parcels 2013). More specifically, a study of 25,000 males from Ontario's minor hockey ranks born in 1975 indicated that only 34 played a single game in the NHL, 16 played for less than a season, and only 5 played more than 400 games (about five full seasons) (Parcels 2013). In other words, Parcels explains, the chances of making it to the "bigs" is a crapshoot. If a parent took the cost of putting a player through AAA hockey and instead purchased $100,000 worth of 6/49 tickets, the odds of winning the lottery and playing a single game in the NHL would be about the same.

Put bluntly, inequality matters, although its impact and relevance are often undertheorized or underappreciated (Tilley 2005). Inequalities matter because inequities based on the interrelationship of gender, race, and class are instrumental in shaping people's life chances in their working years and in later life (Abramson 2015). Admittedly, much of what passes for social inequality as a cause and consequence of social exclusions pivots around income differences and financial considerations. Income inequalities are one of the more visible aspects of broader and more complex issues that encompass everything from inequality of opportunity to social exclusions based on gender, race, and social class, among others (World Economic Forum 2015). However important income gaps are as predictors and proxies, a sociology of social inequality attends to those social exclusions involving power and privilege as well as social capital and social citizenship. For far too many Canadians, the sting of inequality is sharpest when they are excluded from full and equal participation, a connectedness to community and its members, and the exercise of their democratic rights. The costs and consequences of exclusionary inequalities not only impact those who least can afford it. Social costs also apply to society at large. A perception of income polarization as extreme or unjustified has the potential to undermine shared commonalities, mutual trust, and social cohesion. The words of the prominent American sociologist Jonathan H. Turner (2000:62) are chillingly prophetic in light of populist upheavals around the world from North Africa and England, to the United States and Canada:

> Inequality is a tension-generating dynamo; it sets into motion individual misery and social pathologies, such as high crime rates, unstable families, dependence on drugs, domestic and civil violence, and ethnic and racial conflicts, which become difficult to contain.

In short, it's time to coax critically informed responses from these admittedly vexing dilemmas. The lives and life chances of many Canadians depend on such clarification, and this introductory chapter explores patterns, politics, and paradoxes of social inequality in Canada. Surveying the damage by reframing social inequality against the backdrop of a bountiful Canada provides insight into those lively debates over who gets what and what goes where. The chapter also delves into those key themes and foundational assumptions that inform *Inequality Matters*. A detailed analysis and assessment of the Rana Plaza tragedy later in the chapter reinforces the complexities of blame by implicating Canadian consumers as part of the problem.

Paradoxes of Inequality in a Bountiful Canada

Canadians possess an enviable reputation at home and abroad as a kind and compassionate people. Instead of jarring extremes of conspicuous wealth and abject poverty that enrich some while pauperizing others (Lardner and Smith 2007; Hodgson 2010; Courchene 2011), Canada is perceived as a generally egalitarian society whose citizens ostensibly bristle at the prospect of extremes in wealth, status, or power (MacKinnon 2008; see McGrane 2015). This portrayal of an egalitarian Canada is arguably true in a relative sense. Compared to the magnitude of inequities and racial oppression

elsewhere, Canada sparkles; in contrast to its history as an openly white supremacist society, it soars as a beacon of enlightenment and a path to progress, thanks to its widely lauded endorsement of liberal universalism, institutional inclusion, multicultural tolerance, and social equality (Adams 2007). To be sure, the ideals enshrined in the Constitution and Charter of Rights and Freedoms are too often dishonoured in the breach. The inequities confronting women, racialized minorities, Aboriginal peoples, immigrants to Canada, and working Canadians will attest to that. Nevertheless, Canada's standard of living and quality of life are globally admired and often envied. As proof, consider the results of a poll commissioned in 2010 by the Historica-Dominion Institute and the Munk School of Global Affairs. More than half of the adults (54 per cent) of the world's 24 leading economies, including 77 per cent of Chinese respondents, agreed with the statement, "If I had a choice to live in Canada or stay in my current country, I would move to Canada." High praise indeed.

In theory, all parts of Canada's much ballyhooed "mosaic" are envisaged as contributing equally to the whole. Each of these diverse components is viewed as deserving a fair share of the entitlements pertaining to property, privilege, or power. Robust government intervention ensures that few Canadians are denied the basic physical necessities of food, clothing, and shelter, although some may lack a few of the creature comforts (e.g., smartphones) that many take for granted. Older Canadians are healthier, wealthier, and living longer, largely because of improvements in pension plans and Old Age Security payments. Also unvarnished is Canada's stature as a global pacesetter and role model in accommodating differences as dissimilar yet equal. Canada was the first (and remains the only) country in the world to constitutionally entrench Aboriginal rights; establish official multiculturalism as a platform for living together with differences; facilitate immigrant admission into Canada by disregarding national and racial origins; and receive the coveted Nansen Refugee Award for humanitarian work with overseas refugees (Fleras 2012). Evidence of Canada's "rock star" status is bolstered by UN quality-of-life surveys that consistently rank it among the world's top countries, with one of the highest standards of living when measured by income, education, and life expectancy. And while Canada no longer retains its lustre as the best country in the world to live (which it did for eight consecutive years during the 1990s, according to a UN developmental agency), eight in ten Canadians believe it's the best country in the world, according to a Leger survey of 1,500 Canadians commissioned by the Association for Canadian Studies and released to the QMI Agency in February 2015. Canada's exalted status is further attested to by the fact that Canadians are reputed to be the world's fifth happiest population while the Social Progress Index (2015) ranks Canada as the sixth most socially advanced country.

Not everyone endorses this benign portrayal of Canada as an egalitarian utopia. On closer inspection, Canada's reputation as egalitarian or utopian is blemished by gaping levels of inequality that expose glaring gaps between the haves and the have-nots (Curtis and Tepperman 2004). Canadians may like to think of themselves as relatively equal and inclusive, notwithstanding a few exceptions at the extreme. The data tell us otherwise, although critics of the income inequality perspective argue that how you measure it matters—that is, a lot depends on the definition of income and the choice of economic units (individuals or families) (Sarlo, Clemens, and Emes 2015). Canada pales by comparison to Fennoscandia (or Nordic) countries along a broad range of socio-economic fronts pertaining to equality and justice (Olsen 2011). Patterns of property (wealth and income), power, and privilege in Canada are unequally distributed across the categories of class, gender, race, and aboriginality. Aboriginal peoples, racialized minorities, new Canadians, and women, among others (including the elderly, people with disabilities, and single female parents) endure pockets of inequality and exclusion that, frankly, pose an embarrassment to Canada's international reputation (Block and Galabuzi 2011). The fact that inequities based on these identity markers intersect with each other to amplify the inequalities of exclusion compound the marginalization. The complexities of these intersections also reinforce the futility of applying quick-fix solutions to the equalities of complex diversities and diverse complexities (Fleras 2015).

Social institutions are no less exempt from the politics of inequality. In a society of rapid changes, increased diversity, and more uncertainty, institutions are buckling under pressure to become more accommodative without abandoning their integrity or the bottom line. The goal lies in creating an institutional workplace that reflects, respects, and responds to the needs of the historically disadvantaged, while providing a service that is available, accessible, and appropriate for an increasingly diverse and demanding public. But moves toward institutional accommodation are easier said than done, even in a Canada that recoils from the smear of social exclusion for fear of blowing its cover. Resistance to accommodation prevails in organizational design, bureaucratic barriers, corporate values, occupational subcultures, and prejudicial discrimination, all of which are proving more durable than many had anticipated. In too many institutions inequality persists with respect to distribution of power and privilege, hierarchies of stratification involving management–labour relations, and the endorsement of downsizing or outsourcing of jobs. Discriminatory barriers continue to be deeply (systemically) entrenched in the infrastructure of institutions, namely, in the founding assumptions and foundational principles that reflect, reinforce, and advance a racialized, gendered, and classed constitutional order. That social institutions are experiencing an identity crisis of confidence in responding to the challenge of balancing inclusiveness with productivity or service creates a churning effect at odds with a business-as-usual mindset.

The political sector often exemplifies the inequality problem rather than an equality solution. Consider the "mean streets" agenda of consecutive federal governments (Gutstein 2014; McGrane 2015; Black 2011). Canadian society is increasingly organized around market demands and corporate interests at the expense of the public good, the average Canadian, and the environment. Provincial and federal policies since 1990 appear to have had the intent or effect of enriching the already rich through de-industrialization via free trade and off-shoring, low wages by deregulating the labour market, tax benefits for the rich, cuts in social spending and social program transfers, and off-shoring of corporate profits to avoid Canadian taxation (Hulchanksi 2010; Rider 2015). The subordination of people and the planet to the pursuit of profits dovetails with neo-liberal (*free market*) principles, including substantial tax concessions for perhaps no compelling reason except to prove how ideology can trump reality (Rosenblum and Frankel 2011). The Canadian economy may have enjoyed a robust period of growth between 1997 and 2007; nevertheless, levels of poverty remained persistently high, the number of homeless spiraled upwards as did the number of food banks, and income inequality spun out of control (Sharpe and Ross 2011). Yes, Canadians are, on average, better off in terms of income and assets than they were 30 years ago, but income growth has not been equally shared among Canadians, and the rich hoard a disproportionate portion of the gains. As a result, almost 1.5 million Canadians are unemployed, about 20 per cent work in part-time or insecure jobs, nearly one in ten live in poverty (including 600,000 children), and up to one-third of Canadians have trouble making ends—from housing to nutrition—meet (Klein 2011). The consequences are costly not only for the poor, as Armine Yalnizyan (2011) says, but also for everyone else and for Canada at large:

> High inequality can diminish economic growth if it means the country is not fully using the skills and capabilities of all its citizens or if it undermines social cohesion, leading to increased social tensions. . . . High inequality raises a moral question about fairness and social justice.

Despite a looming catastrophe, the state's historical commitment to building a better Canada through social engineering is showing its age. The primacy of neo-liberal values in measuring success and progress puts Canada on the path to spending less on social programs than many OECD countries. These proposed austerity measures and the hollowing out of public spending will invariably inflict additional hardship on many Canadians—from steeper university tuition to inadequate child care to lack of timely and accessible health care—while eroding the incentive or rationale for collective action that advances the common

good and national interests (Finn 2011). Errol Black (2011) speculated on the pending disaster if government remained indifferent to issues of concern to Canadians:

> Environmental problems will not be tackled in a meaningful way, because to do so requires challenging corporate powers; inequality and its attendant damage will continue to grow; the deep, complex, and racialized poverty that now grips most of Canada's cities and that produces so much human damage will remain unaddressed, save that more and more young people will be incarcerated in the prisons that the Conservatives are committed to building; the shameful conditions of so many rural and northern Aboriginal communities will remain unaddressed. More of the poor will remain imprisoned, and for a longer time. These measures . . . have already diminished us in the eyes of the world.[1]

Put candidly, allowing the fabulously rich to do as they like while the majority struggle just to stay afloat is a recipe for an unsustainable future in Canada. Failure to act bolsters the likelihood of mutual incomprehension as the *have-it-alls* circle the wagons of power to preserve their privilege, while the *have-nots* struggle for a more equitable share of the economic pie.

The persistence and pervasiveness of social inequality in Canada does not necessarily reflect a revenue shortage or lack of productivity. Contrary to widespread belief, the politics and patterns of social inequality entail a set of political choices over the allocation of valued resources, with more of it shoveled into fewer pockets, but less of it for shoring up a fraying social safety net (Finn 2011). For example, commitment to an austerity discourse is not just an economic tool but also a political calculus and a manufactured crisis based on the principle that taxes are bad, that everything can be measured in terms of the bottom line, and that as little as possible (such as costly services) should be drawn from a dwindling public purse (Vose 2015). The resultant equality gap reinforces those neo-liberal ideologies that extol the value and necessity of an unfettered market to create and distribute wealth. Of particular salience under a neo-liberal doctrine are the ideals that elitism must rule, inequality is necessary, competition is natural, greed is good, and losers are inevitable (Dorling 2010). The dearth of checks and balances to keep inequality at bay aborts the possibility of challenging a steeply unequal status quo, especially with the hollowing out of the middle class and the decline of labour unions. Membership in the Canadian labour movement continues to dwindle, from 33.7 per cent of all workers in 1997 to 31.5 per cent in 2012, with almost all of the decline in the private sector (Keenan 2012). Economic power remains concentrated in the executive suites, while senior management hoards monetary pickings at levels deemed to be reckless or shameful just a generation ago (Reich 2013).

Clearly then, Canada is not more just, caring, kind, equal, or fair. More accurately, it's increasingly leaner, meaner, and greedier (Yalnizyan 2010; Himmelfarb 2013). Just as the great recession unleashed a fury of devastation in the United States (Peck 2010; 2011), so too have patterns of inequality in Canada spiked to levels unseen since the 1920s. Such levels are *reversing* a long-term trend: A post–World War Two era of incremental increases toward equality is now eclipsed by a regime of gaping inequalities that exponentially concentrate income in the pockets of elite few, in good times or bad, deservedly or not. The post-war contract between capital and labour mediated by an activist state is rapidly disintegrating. Worse still, economic gaps and social exclusions have intensified in the midst of what was until recently a generally buoyant economy. For example, wealth inequality unfolds over the course of a Canadian family's lifetime, but the wealth accumulation for Canada's most affluent families in their twenties provides a half-million-dollar head start over middle-class Canadian families in the same age group (MacDonald 2015a). The end result of this inequality inflation is a "trichotomizing" of Canada into three layers: one is growing more prosperous and powerful, the second is squeezed by modest income increases, and a third appears to be drifting downward into depths that preclude recovery (Hulchanski 2010).

Status differences related to identity groups also sway who gets what and what goes where. In the same way class matters, so too does gender influence outcomes (Nelson 2010). With the possible exception of single, university-educated, never-married women (Turcotte 2010), females in full-time employment continue to be outpointed by men in moving up the escalator of corporate payoff. The presence of women in the workplace may be routinely accepted and sometimes rewarded, nonetheless women in general continue to earn less than male counterparts despite pay and employment equity initiatives (the picture is somewhat more complex than suggested by polemics). Many continue to bump into glass ceilings or exit through revolving doors when attempting to scale the institutional ladder of corporate success, while immigrant and racialized minority women remain stuck on the sticky floors of entry level jobs (Sandberg 2013; also Reitz, Phan, and Banerjee 2015). To compound and amplify the impact of exclusion, women's experiences with gendered discrimination usually intersect with other negatively defined identity markers related to age, race, aboriginality, and class (Zawilski 2016). Worse still, women from all social classes and ethnocultural backgrounds remain vulnerable to punishing patterns of harassment and violence—the persistence of which, in a more enlightened era, makes mockery of any claim to female empowerment (Bates 2014). For example, a scathing report on the Canadian Armed Forces by Marie Deschamps (2015) drew attention to a deeply embedded sexualized culture that was hostile to lower-ranking women and LGBT members of the military; rampant incidents of abuse, sexual harassment, sexism, and assault, despite a zero tolerance policy; and a perception that this toxic work environment is condoned or ignored by senior officials—making it difficult for victims to come forward. The military's refusal to acknowledge the seriousness of the problem not only complicates a search for solutions, but also suggests the pervasiveness of systemic sexism across other male-dominated institutions.

Racialized minorities and new Canadians routinely encounter income inequalities and blocked opportunity structures first exposed by the eminent Canadian scholar John Porter in his groundbreaking book, *The Vertical Mosaic*

Spotlight   Unsettling Canada: Will Push Come to Shove?

It's no secret Aboriginal peoples endure grinding levels of poverty and powerlessness that chafe in a seemingly progressive Canada. Too many individuals are disadvantaged, marginalized, poorly educated and unemployed, and unhealthy. Homicide rates in "Indian" country are about seven times those in the non-aboriginal population; so too is the incarceration rate in federal penitentiaries (Sapers 2013a, b). Aboriginal youth unemployment is about three times the national rate in contrast to high school graduation rates at about one-third of mainstream Canada's. Not surprisingly, a growing number of aboriginal activists are seething with anger and frustration and opting for acts of civil disobedience to express their indignation (Kino-nda-niimi Collective 2014). Even more disturbing is the prospect that this barely suppressed hostility could erupt into open defiance and confrontations. According to Douglas Bland (2013; 2014), Canada possesses all the necessary so-called feasibility conditions (rather than root causes[1]) conducive to a violent challenge to civil authority, including:

a. a significant cohort of aboriginal activists or "warriors";
b. an economy vulnerable to crippling disruption by sabotage;
c. timidity on the part of the government to enforce the letter of the law;
d. a small police presence for protecting energy sources and transportation infrastructures; and
e. vast geographical expanses nearly impossible to defend against guerilla strikes.

Aboriginal peoples are now in the driver's seat: a series of successful court challenges has seen to that. So too has a series of comprehensive land and specific treaty claims secured unprecedented access to power and authority over the extraction and transportation of natural resources across traditional aboriginal land (Coates and Crowley 2013). Aboriginal peoples also possess the potential to cripple wealth production in Canada (Bland 2013), for example by challenging the proposed energy corridor across those parts of British Columbia with unresolved land claims (Hunter 2013). Consider the vastness of the 4,000 km path of TransCanada Corporation's proposed Energy East pipeline to transport western crude oil to eastern Canada refineries and export terminals. The pipeline would traverse the traditional territories of 180 different aboriginal communities, each of which must be consulted as partners (not just stakeholders), from whom consent must be acquired, and who must receive compensation (Coates and Crowley, 2013). Without engagement or accommodation of aboriginal interests, the Canadian economy could grind to a standstill in the event of widespread opposition, blockades and occupations, sabotage, and aboriginal insurgency, quickly bringing the country to its knees. A handful of leaders and activists is all that is needed to pull off lightning-quick strikes and foment public panic, then melt into the landscape beyond the reach of conventional forces. Precedents for such guerilla tactics are

(1965). They continue to be sorted out unequally against a mosaic of raised (dominant) and lowered (subordinate) tiles that favour some but disqualify others (Tepper 1988; Helmes-Hayes and Curtis 1998; Clement and Helmes-Hayes 2015; Jedwab and Satzewich 2015). References to Canada as a *vertical mosaic* reflect pyramids of privilege that elevate "pale males" to the top of the socio-economic heap, whereas others flounder at the bottom (Block and Galabuzi 2011;

Galabuzi 2006; Nakhaie and Kazemipur 2013). Neither the inception of official multiculturalism nor the introduction of employment equity appear to have appreciably altered this vertical hierarchy, despite good intentions. Nowhere is an "illusion of inclusion" more damaging than in many aboriginal communities. The interplay of historical dependencies, with debilitating levels of underdevelopment because of an aggressive colonialism and its aftermath, have hardly unknown. As Bland (2013) likes to remind, it took only about 500 dedicated IRA members to pin down a massive British army presence in Ireland for 25 years.

This seemingly exaggerated scenario for crippling Canada as we know it is not as far-fetched as it might appear (Cooper 2010). However foreboding, this doomsday scenario has already been described by Douglas Bland in his 2009 apocalyptic novel *Uprising*. A charismatic female leader (Molly Grace) mobilizes a group of loosely connected cells into a full-blown rebellion by embracing a unifying narrative of injustices, betrayed promises, and denied rights. An armed insurrection is incited (from open gun battles to bombings to a takeover of strategic sites with casualties on all sides) by disaffected aboriginal youth trained by a disciplined cadre of aboriginal veterans of the Canadian army who are hostile to the very idea of Canada as ". . . an artificial nation . . . a multicultural blob held together by little self-interested mobs of foreigners" (Bland 2009; Blatchford 2013). In Molly's view, the point of this revolution is not to negotiate with Canada but to destroy it.

This chilling prognosis resonates with potential because of Canada's vulnerability as a country without a domestic national security program. The situation in many parts of Canada is so susceptible to sabotage that a security specialist conceded to Bland "the reality is that the security of Manitoba now and in the future is whatever the First Nations allow it to be." Nor is there much inspiration to be gained from this tepid response by former prime minister Paul

Martin to the threat of a revolution by unruly aboriginal youth: ". . . We would hope not." Not only do militant warriors possess the capacity to wreak domestic terror of a magnitude that dwarfs the stealth tactics of Al Qaeda or Islamist jihadists (Kay 2013), even aboriginal elders concede an inability to control increasingly restless youth. As one elder said to Bland, "I don't think we elders can control the young ones much longer. . . . They're listening to outsiders and those ones are bad people." As recently as fall 2012, such speculation and questions might have been dismissed as unrealistic. By January of 2013, however, the Idle No More movement had made abundantly clear that disruptive confrontations across Canada are indeed a feasibility whose time has come (Kino-nda-niimi Collective 2014).

Endnote

1. Conventional wisdom argues that insurgencies are created by a combination of factors, from pent up grief and ongoing grievances. Address the root causes, it is argued, and avert insurgency. The new wisdom disagrees, arguing that insurgencies occur when the feasibility factors are properly aligned for making a revolt feasible. In Canada's case, young aboriginal men are aware of Canada's economic dependence on natural resources and the transportation of these commodities through difficult-to-defend aboriginal land (Bland 2013). The irony is unmistakable in exposing how weaknesses can morph into strengths. As menacingly put by the leader of a group who closed the railway between Montreal and Toronto as well as Highway 401 near Belleville, "the white man made a mistake when they built their infrastructure on our land. Now we have the power" (Bland 2013).

combined to deny, demean, and destroy (Helin 2006, 2010; Coulthard 2014; Czyzewski 2011). Notwithstanding an expanding inventory of success stories, Aboriginal peoples continue to do poorly based on almost any indicator of socio-economic success. Escalating patterns of violence (both inward [suicide] and outward [abuse]), coupled with poverty and health issues, remain impervious to quick-fix solutions (Frideres and Gadacz 2012). The

fact that many aboriginal communities must endure a standard of living that would embarrass some developing countries is surely a blistering indictment of Canada's priorities and self-delusions (Royal Commission 1996; Maaka and Fleras 2005; Long and Dickason 2011). The consequences of this disenfranchisement should not be taken lightly and may prove both disruptive and deadly, as the Spotlight box demonstrates.

Illusions aside, all the deeply ingrained myths ("polite fictions") in the country cannot paper over the inconvenient ("uncomfortable truths") and inescapable ("awkward paradoxes"). Canada may be a bountiful country whose resources and the resourcefulness of its peoples are admired and envied, yet it remains a fundamentally unequal and exclusionary society where far too many citizens are denied, excluded, or exploited for reasons often beyond their control (also Macleod 2015). Socially defined yet devalued exclusions because of race or nationality or gender and class continue to make a difference on a persistent and predictable basis. Worse still, patterns of inequality are neither temporary nor randomly distributed. To the contrary, they tend to coalesce around the poles of race, gender, aboriginality, and class. These often devalued identity markers also have a tendency to intersect with one another in ways that intensify the exclusion or exploitation (Sernau 2011; McMullin 2010; Zawilski 2010; Olsen 2011). The intensity and outcomes of socio-economic disparities is further sharpened by the dynamics of a capitalist global economy. A few may prosper under freewheeling globalization (Fortin et al. 2012), yet many suffer from the deficit-pruning obsession of government agendas (with their austere focus on slashing services rather than hiking taxes or fostering job creation) and the cost-cutting measures of a corporate-driven global economy (from off-shoring to out-sourcing).

The consequences of this deepening inequality are hardly trifling: those at the top enjoy privileges and fabled lifestyles, indulging in an endless spree of greed, accumulation, and patterns of conspicuous consumption that the disenfranchised can only fantasize about from afar. Top earners exert disproportionate influence on politics, public opinion, and policy, yet become increasingly estranged in outlook and experience from the average person. Such social polarization poses a predicament to a functioning democracy whose viability may depend on all citizens sharing a common commitment. Such polarity also hurts those at the bottom who are more likely to suffer from poor health or be denied access to proper medical attention, endure lower levels of education and revolving cycles of poverty, reside in substandard housing, relinquish prospects for career advancement, and be treated more harshly by the justice system (Sapers 2013b; Town Hall Report 2013). Income inequality matters in shaping health outcomes, life expectancy, higher levels of destructive behaviour from drinking and smoking to violence, and psycho-social stress caused by feelings of insecurity, resulting in higher rates of disease such as diabetes. It can also depress levels of social capital because people don't trust each other (Wilkinson and Pickett 2009). In response to the 2011 riots that originated in London and spread to Liverpool and beyond, Dan Leighton of the political think tank Demos writes:

> You have the top 1 percent who continue to earn unimaginable money in the midst of austerity, then the squeezed middle classes, and the "stakelessness" of young people who are excluded from and have no respect for the norms of society. (in Ward 2011:A-6)

There is a price to pay for this exclusionary inequality. Wealth may beget wealth in a spiralling process that consolidates the privileges of those few who have hijacked the economy at the expense of the many and to the detriment of everybody. But any society that condones instant billionaires while tolerating grinding poverty must invariably confront its demons and dissenters.

Debating Social Inequality

Historically, Canada saw itself as a white man's society that revered its exalted status (Thobani 2007; Day 2000). From restrictive immigration programs to discriminatory legislation, Canada was constructed in ways that reflected, reinforced, and advanced pale male power and Eurocentric priorities in defining normalcy, acceptability, and desirability. Insofar as Canada was organized by, for, and about the realities and aspirations of "pale stream" elites, the founding assumptions and foundational principles of its constitutional order were gendered, raced, and classed. Of course, the most egregious forms of social inequality related to pale male privilege, power, and injustice no longer prevail. But remaining intact are those founding assumptions and foundational principles of Canada's **constitutional order** regarding what is acceptable, normal, or desirable as they apply to race, gender, class, and aboriginality. The assumptions and principles of a gendered, racialized, colonialized, and classed constitutional order not only dislodge any pretense of a level playing field. They also undermine minority moves toward equality since members of historically disadvantaged groups must compete for success and acceptance in a tilted social system (i.e., an *unlevel* playing field) that is neither designed to reflect their realities or experiences nor constructed to advance their interests or ambitions.

Most Canadians are superficially acquainted with Canada's socio-economic disparities, but their perceptions and understanding are imbued with an air of false consciousness. Too many Canadians accept an ideologically slanted and elite-lensed view of the world in which vested interests do not necessarily coincide with those of the public or the planet (Feagin 2011). The image that many possess of Canada as a land of equal opportunity is idyllic and idealistic (ACS History 2015)—an inclusive and egalitarian society where extremes of inequality are thought to be the exception rather than the rule. Yet the reality of inconvenient truth rattles the complacency of comforting fictions. Canada is a steeply unequal society with sometimes shocking patterns of exclusion at odds with our collective self-image as progressive and egalitarian. Even the *study* of inequality in terms of patterns, politics, and paradoxes has proven perplexing and inconclusive. Disagreements proliferate over its causes, characteristics, consequences, and cures. Consensus is elusive on the problem–solution nexus to social inequalities because of competing perspectives, underlying assumptions, causal connections, and proposed outcomes. To attend to these puzzles of social inequality, sociology as a discipline and perspective originated at the turn of the twentieth century in hopes of explaining the social dislocations unleashed by urban–industrial transformations. Early sociologists focused on how best to ameliorate dysfunctional social conditions associated with rapid social change. The fact that questions about social inequality remain

as relevant today as they did then—*and as paradoxical and prone to sharp disagreements*—reinforces their timeliness and tenacity. Consider these points of contention between the ideals of equality (however defined) versus the reality of inequality (however measured) that elicits debate over the concept of social inequality and the inequalities of exclusion:

1. How much social inequality is tolerable? Too much social inequality may destabilize a society by unraveling the bonds of social trust to ungovernable proportions; too little inequality may rob a society of its initiative or creativity (Sheppard 2010). What balance of inequality and equality does a complex society require to operate at peak efficiency? Who decides and on what basis?
2. Why is social inequality perceived to be a social problem? Who says so? On what grounds (Sarlo 2013)? If social inequality is a pervasive element in all human relationships and inherent in all societies, why bother tampering with what comes "naturally"? Why do inequalities of exclusion persist in the midst of affluence despite initiatives to reduce its scope and sting (Dorling 2010)?
3. Who is to blame? Should individuals or structures or situations be blamed for the social inequality predicament? Or must the focus be reframed toward the interplay of structure with individuals and situations? Sociologists argue that individuals must take responsibility for their actions; they also acknowledge that personal choices do not exist outside a broader and unequal context beyond people's control. Yes, individuals must learn to take control of their lives by "pulling themselves up by their bootstraps," but conditions must be created that equip people with bootstraps in the first place.
4. How is inequality structured across space? Inequality may be a defining and inherent feature of all capitalist societies, but some capitalist societies, such as Fennoscandia, have ameliorated levels of inequality (from lower rates of poverty to a more comprehensive range of social programs and supports) without sacrificing high and widely shared standards of living. By contrast, inequality gaps are escalating

in those capitalist countries in the throes of a robust neo-liberalism (less government, more market, more self-responsibility), including Canada, the United Kingdom, and the United States. The end result of a neo-liberal economy is affluence for some, but immiseration for others, including austerity reductions that further punish the already peripheral (OECD 2015a; Olsen 2011).

5. Is income inequality justified (Banting and Myles 2015)? Do those in the higher echelon merit their largesse because of ability, risk-taking, or talent (McNamee 2014)? Or have the turbo-driven rich prospered by rigging the rules of the economic game through control of the political agenda (Schwalbe 2008)?

6. How are the politics of inequality played out within and between groups? Is there any truth to the belief that high wages and tax breaks for the rich will generate a trickle-down effect (rising tides lifts all ships)? As a student once quipped in assessing the merits of a trickle-down effect, the effect is closer to that of being "pissed" on, and subsequently "pissed off." Perhaps, as noted by others, a more fitting metaphor is the "lock and dam" operation: raising the water in one compartment lifts the yachts but lowers the water levels in another compartment, which sinks the rowboats. In short, any analysis of social inequality must acknowledge the process by which the enrichment of the haves comes at the expense of impoverishing the have-nots.

7. How can social inequality be analyzed? Sociologists may prefer to study social inequality in terms of mutually exclusive categories of race or gender or class. Convenient, yes, but not necessarily reflective of how reality works. Analytical focus has shifted to how patterns of inequality and stratification—class, race and ethnicity, and gender—intersect to generate overlapping patterns of inequality that intensify the exclusion (Signs 2013; Zawilski 2016; McMullin 2010).

8. How and why does inequality matter? It is widely acknowledged that social inequality negatively effects individuals; it also exerts a costly impact on society at large (Gordon 2015; OECD 2015a). Similarly, while many assume that reducing inequality improves the lives and life chances of the poorest in society, others such as Wilkinson and Pickett (2009) argue that more equality is beneficial for society as a whole.

9. What would a society based on perfect equality look like? Does true equality arise from treating people exactly the same regardless of their differences? Or is it attainable only by recognizing people's differences and treating them differently according to their rights or needs?

Answers to these questions are unlikely to yield consensus, but the conclusion seems obvious. Attaining the ideal of equality is as elusive as solving the problem of inequality.

A Working Framework: Themes and Assumptions

That debates over social inequality rarely yield consensus or commitment is hardly surprising, given the complexity of the issue. To unlock the paradoxes of social inequality, sociologists embrace certain assumptions that presumably distinguish sociology from other disciplines. Social inequality is addressed as *exclusion* related to power and privilege as well as to property, income, and wealth. It is also framed as *structural exclusion*: *structural* because inequalities are so deeply embedded in the foundations of society that notions of intent or awareness rarely apply; *exclusions* because they encompass multidimensional processes related to a lack of resources and social capital (social, cultural, and human); the right to participate economically, politically, and socially on equal terms; and access to quality of life, from health and well-being to protection from crime (Percy-Smith 2000; Peace 2001; Levitas et al. 2007).

Social inequality is also taken seriously because it's patterned, pervasive, persistent, harmful, and resistant to reform. A marked preference exists for analyzing the **social** dimensions of inequality—that is, those inequalities of exclusion that are social in origin, that are defined as social problems, that exert a negative impact on society or members, and that are amenable to reform through social activity. Or put in a slightly different way, the relationship of social inequality to society is a mutually reciprocating one—namely, social inequality has an impact on society, and the impact of societal change has an impact on patterns of social inequality.

Inequality Matters is framed by a set of underlying assumptions that inform content, argument, organization, levels of proof, and conclusions. Nine key assumptions prevail, drawn from a critically informed approach that challenges conventional ways of framing social inequality.

Social Inequalities as Socially Constructed

Most sociology begins with the assumption there is nothing natural or inherently normal about society or its constituent components such as institutions and values. Societies are framed instead as socially constructed conventions whose re-constructedness is carefully concealed to convey the impression of inevitability and invincibility. Two inequality implications follow: first, any social construction will invariably reflect, reinforce, and advance the interests and realities of those who create, own, or control the conventions. Societies are subsequently designed and organized along gendered, raced, and classed lines in terms of who gets what and what goes where. Second, a racialized, gendered, and classed society is, by definition, inherently unequal insofar as ideas and ideals about the desirable, normal, and acceptable are wired (structured) into the founding assumptions and foundational structures of a society's constitutional order. The ideological basis of societies (Canada included) is thus infused with principles and priorities that privilege and empower the rich and powerful at the expense of others because of how the system is designed and organized. According to a line of thinking that debunks the notion of a level playing field, women, minorities, Aboriginal peoples, and working classes may be equal before the law. Yet the exercise of their rights is compromised by their placement in contexts that neither reflect their realities nor advance their interests.

The Universality of Social Inequality

This book capitalizes on a core sociological axiom: inequality is neither incidental to society nor the reflection of greedy capitalism. As far as sociologists can tell, all human societies are informed by the inequalities of exclusions, although expression is relative to time and place. No matter how small or shifting, all human groups are stratified (ranked) with respect to gender (males tending to dominate in the public sphere) and age (older adults dominating, although the highly skilled in hunting or fighting might also prevail). All human groups also make a distinction between women and men as well as the younger and older; assign a corresponding division of labour based on gender and age; and devalue the activities of those on the wrong side of the status divide. This devaluation filters down and becomes lodged in the founding assumptions and foundational principles of a society's constitutional or moral order. The implications are far reaching: just as society and its assemblage of institutions are neither neutral nor passive, so too is social inequality neither an accident nor an anomaly, but rather a structural (patterned, pervasive, and persistent) feature of society (Olsen 2011; Schwalbe 2008). Furthermore, acknowledging the universality of social inequalities is not always the issue. What has evolved are people's perceptions and evaluations of social inequality; as a result, what once was seen as normal and inescapable is now criticized as arbitrary and unacceptable (see the study on social class and the *Titanic* in Chapter 4).

Normalizing Inequality

The relationship between society and social inequality is frequently misunderstood. Too often this relationship is framed as if inequality were an aberration at odds with an otherwise egalitarian human condition. In reality, patterns of inequality are inherent in most if not all human relationships, from the interpersonal to the intergroup, from the institutional to the national. That is, all human relations are fundamentally unequal, given the inevitability of distinctions and rankings in power, privilege, status, and wealth. Moreover, if society is defined as a network of unequal relations in the broadest sense of the term, social inequality cannot exist outside the framework of human existence. More accurately, social inequality is intrinsic to society and its relational components, although the range and magnitude of these inequalities of exclusions can vary in time and across space (Olsen 2011).

Social Inequality as a Problematic

Sociologists routinely frame social inequality as a social problem when linked to those exclusionary outcomes that are patterned, pervasive, resistant to change, and harmful to society or its members. The framing of social equality from a problematic paradigm points to questions of why it exists (origins/causes), who's to blame, what it looks like (characteristics), where it's expressed, how it inflicts personal harm or intensifies existing social exclusions (consequences), and what must be done to minimize this problem (cures) (Jones 2012). Normative and ethical issues are raised as well since equality constitutes a core democratic value (Broadbent 2011). Is social inequality good or bad? Right or wrong? Necessary or superfluous?

Reframing Inequality as Social Exclusion

Most of the discussion in inequality discourse revolves around income differences, economic privilege, financial resources, or material distribution (Grabb 2006; Saloojee 2003). There is no doubt that income matters since it remains one of the better predictors of life satisfaction, social inclusion, and societal cohesion (Cameron 2011; Canada 2020 2011; Meili 2012; Jedwab and Satzewich 2015). But income inequality may not tell us much about the living conditions of the poor, their health and well-being, the overall disadvantages they face, or their access to economic opportunity (Rohac 2012). Clearly, then, an emphasis on the exclusionary dimensions of social inequality must go beyond the size of the wallet. Income differences are important, but often as a proxy for those social conditions that disadvantage and marginalize by denying access to the powers, resources, networks, rights, and opportunities that forge a sense of citizenship (membership, acceptance and self-fulfillment); quality of life (access to necessary material goods and services); and functioning level of integration (participation, trust, and connections)

(Wynne and Currie 2011; Saloojee n.d.; MacKinnon 2008). In other words, *inequalities matter because they create social exclusions—that is, the interplay of differential access to and differential distribution of valued resources related to power, privilege, and productive property reflect, reinforce, and advance the exclusions of participation, entitlement, and quality of life.* Finally, just as social inequalities such as income disparity leads to multiple non-material dimensions of social exclusion, so too do social exclusions produce income gaps and poverty patterns. In short, social inequality and social exclusions should be seen as a mutually reinforcing process. (See the more detailed discussion of social exclusion in Chapter 2.)

Inequality as Interplay of Agency + Structure + Context

Social inequality is inescapably linked to structural exclusions. Inequality is structured when social exclusions become institutionalized: entrenched because of their embeddedness in those social, economic, and political spheres that sustain the power, advantage, and privilege of some at the expense of others (Olsen 2011). To be sure, the structural arrangements that produce and reproduce material inequality do not materialize out of nothing. Rather, they are created by and perpetuated through routine social practices and everyday actions (Essed 1991; Schwalbe 2008). Individuals are not necessarily the cause of social inequality; nevertheless, they are framed and blamed as carriers who—however unwittingly—sustain, modify, or challenge unequal patterns. Admittedly, there is some validity in assigning blame and responsibility to individuals for their actions and outcomes. However valid, though, people's lives and life chances may be seriously constrained by circumstances that circumscribe their options and experiences. Initiatives to reduce inequities must recognize this sociological truism: inequality reflects the interplay of structure, context, and agency so that individual responsibility for any predicament must be situated within a broader context often beyond a person's control.

Multiple Social Locations as Intersecting Inequalities

What you get, and why, depends on where you stand. The concept of **social location** is a reminder that where people are socially located in society (standpoint) with respect to gender, race, class, or aboriginality will profoundly influence access to opportunities and outcomes. But these often devalued identity markers are no longer treated as discrete attributes that mechanically yield to social inequality. Traditional approaches often splintered vulnerabilities into distinct categories (race, class, or gender), prioritized one over the other, failed to fully consider the context of social power inequalities, and ignored the interaction of numerous characteristics of vulnerable populations at individual and structural levels (Dhamoon and Hankivsky 2011). The study of inequality in Canada increasingly recognizes the centrality of interlocking axes of gender, race, ethnicity, and class, in addition to social fault lines pertaining to age, sexuality, and ability (Olsen 2011). The interplay of race, gender, class, and aboriginality creates interlocking systems of oppression that not only intersect to amplify the exclusion and exploitation of the historically disadvantaged (Zawilski 2016; McMullin 2010). This interplay of oppressions also highlights the complexity and multidimensionality of multiple identity markers as they overlap, interact, and intersect in perpetuating social inequalities (Signs 2013; Hankivsky 2011).

Challenging Social Inequality: Reconstructing the Deconstructed

Social inequality is often seen as something natural and normal and beyond human agency to change. Alternatively, inequality is defended or promoted as beneficial to human progress or as regrettable but inevitable in any merit-based, market-driven society. For example, the emergence of neo-liberalism as a defender of market supremacy and government retreat has had the effect of establishing inequality as normal, necessary, and beneficial (see Olsen 2011 for critique). *Inequality Matters* takes a fundamentally different tack. There is nothing natural or inevitable about the **structural exclusions** that inform social inequalities, despite vested interests to render them otherwise. Instead of something biologically inherent or psychologically inescapable, social inequality is framed as a socially constructed convention created by those in positions of power with the resources and resourcefulness to conceal the constructedness and conventionality behind a veneer of respectability, neutrality, or inevitability. But consider the implications in reframing social inequality as a human accomplishment rather than an immutable fact of human existence. What has been constructed in terms of who gets what and what goes where is amenable to challenge (deconstruction) and transformation (reconstruction)—even when inconvenient truths are skilfully concealed behind a smokescreen of comforting myths and polite fictions. After all, what humans have constructed in creating the inequality of exclusions can be deconstructed and reconstructed along more humane and inclusive lines.

Globalizing Inequalities, a Global Perspective

Nation-states have historically served as the focus of analysis when examining social inequality. Such a restricted focus spawns distortions and omissions that downplay the interconnectedness of the global with the national and the local. But patterns of social inequality have unfolded globally, thus necessitating a world perspective that recognizes the interplay of the national with the international in creating and sustaining exclusionary structures. This dynamic acknowledges the need for concepts that capture the new global realities of interconnectedness, plurality, and multi-locality, without sacrificing the salience of the national and the local. The concept of *glocalization* captures this connection between the local and the national with the global in a way that particularizes the universal (micro-globalization) yet universalizes the particular (macro-location) (Khondker 2004). In the process, the scope of analysis is expanded to incorporate the global/national/local nexus (Beck 2007). The following Spotlight box demonstrates how the new economy forges global inequalities that render human lives expendable and leave no one untouched.

Spotlight "The Price of Cheap Is Bangladesh"[1]: Implicating Canada

A worker in Bangladesh receives 12 cents for a polo shirt that retails for $14 (Westwood 2013).

The true cost of inexpensive clothes hit home in late April 2013 when over 1,100 garment workers were crushed to death following the collapse of an illegal and unsafe eight-story factory building in Dhaka. The world's greatest industrial tragedy was not an isolated incident that captivated global attention. Several months earlier, a fire at a nearby garment factory had killed 112 workers; yet another 300 workers died in a garment factory fire in Pakistan in 2012 because locked exits and barred windows prevented escape (Ward 2013). These deaths have focused worldwide attention not only on workplace regulations in Bangladesh but also on the responsibilities of Western companies that rely on cheaply produced apparel for budget conscious consumers (Human Rights Watch 2015). Admittedly, everyone agrees the human cost for producing low-priced garments for high-end markets is unacceptable. But agreement falters in responding to the following questions: What is the cause of the crisis? Who is to blame for the tragedy? How can the situation be remedied in ways that maximize benefits for everyone (MacKinnon and Strauss 2013; Chakma 2013)?

1. Who is to blame for the disaster (Seabrook 2014)? Let's begin by pointing fingers at the factory owner of the Rana Plaza who ignored warnings of a pending building collapse (Yardley 2013). Mohammed Sohel Rana illegally added three additional floors to a building never intended for heavy garment machinery. The police ordered an evacuation when infrastructural cracks first appeared, but bosses insisted that workers return. Lacking union protection and fearful of losing their jobs, 3,000 workers complied—and paid the price (also Human Rights Watch 2015).
2. Murder in the name of profit (Seabrook 2014). Collectively, factory owners possess the political clout (it is estimated that about 10 per cent of parliamentarians and lawmakers are garment factory owners) to bring about changes in worker wages and deplorable working conditions. Wages are so low (and declining, including a 3 per cent drop in Bangladesh over the last decade) that a Bangladeshi garment worker earns only a fraction of a living wage, making it impossible to afford the necessities of daily subsistence, let alone to take a path out of poverty or to cobble together a decent standard of living (Peters 2013). But pressure to keep costs down (by suppressing wages) induces a blind eye to safety infractions and shoddy building codes. The end result of erratic government inspection and non-enforcement of labour laws reduces working conditions to the level of slave labour in industrial-era sweatshops. Furthermore, it is difficult for workers to assert their rights when exploitative labour conditions combine with short term contracts make it easy to control or fire workers (also Human Rights Watch 2015a, b, c). Factory owners also conspire with the Bangladesh Industrial Police force to crush dissent and union activism, thereby securing the lowest minimum wages in the world—about $40(US) a month (Chalmers 2013).
3. The Bangladesh government is lax about implementation and enforcement of worker rights and labour laws. For many such poor countries, cheap labour is the principal comparative advantage; as a result, labour laws are flouted and workers are poorly paid to ensure the sale of goods in a global market (Farrell 2004). In Bangladesh, increased regulations and safety standards run the risk of disrupting a multi-billion-dollar industry (amounting to about 75 per cent of the country's GDP [Strauss and Slater 2013; Olive 2013a]). The ready-made garment industry generates $20 billion a year in clothing exports, while employing about 4 million workers, many of them women. According to Human Rights Watch (2015), only

18 inspectors monitor the 100,000 factories in the Dhaka region, resulting in a pervasive flouting of safety rules, rampant corruption, and cursory inspections. To be sure, the law allows labour unions to negotiate for better wages and working conditions (unions can make a difference), but the government rarely defends these rights, even suppressing labour activism to the point where workers who try to organize unions are fired or beaten (Human Rights Watch 2015c). To no one's surprise, only 11 collective bargaining agreements exist in a country of 150 million people.

4. A cultural bias devalues the worth and work of women (Human Rights Watch 2015). Bangladeshi women are put at risk in hazardous conditions because of widespread stereotypes. Women are perceived as more nimble for the garment work, more docile and desperate, and less likely to agitate over precarious working conditions. Others argue that no one coerces female workers to work for 20 cents an hour ($2 a day) to feed their extended families. Moreover, as both Saunders (2013) and Nolen (2013) and others point out, the garment boom has empowered women by raising living standards, reducing poverty, and uplifting the status for millions of Bangladeshi women, including significant reductions in maternal and child mortality (Chakma 2013). In short, Bangladeshi women should not be seen as victims but as active agents who want to take control of their lives through employment in a context of few options (Nolen 2013; Saunders 2013).

5. Should the Canadian government be blamed for allowing duty-free access on most Bangladeshi goods? In a bid to bolster that country's development through trade, Ottawa dropped its 18 per cent duty on Bangladeshi clothing in 2003, then removed restrictions on the volume shipped to Canada (Strauss and Slater, 2013). In 2004, the global Multifibre Arrangement lifted imposed quotas on developing countries' textile and garment exports to rich countries (Chalmers 2013). The end result? Producers and retailers embraced Bangladesh to get the best "bang for their buck," to the detriment of Canadian garment makers who went out of business (Strauss 2013). The Bangladeshi garment industry has staked its competitiveness on low wages made possible by a massive and disposable labour force (Bangladesh's minimum pay remains the lowest in the world even with a proposed increase to $66 a month [Associated Press 2013]). Its competitive edge is further secured through high levels of unemployment, a dearth of formal sector work, and poverty so extreme that even a 12-hour-a-day sweatshop job appeals to the masses of rural poor who flooded the export-processing zones at the edge of Dhaka.

6. Flawed business model 1: Corporate brands such as Walmart, Sears or Loblaws (Joe Fresh clothing line) are continually on the hunt for expanding profits and shrinking costs, even if this launches a race to the bottom for wages, working conditions, and worker safety (Ward 2013). A subcontracting business model prevails: retailers such as Walmart and brands such as Tommy Hilfiger do not manufacture the goods themselves; rather they contract out production to overseas manufactures who in turn subcontract to others and so on down the line. These brands source their products from factories in poor countries with inadequate labour laws and non-existent safety regulations—because it's cheaper to do so—and move from one country to another when costs rise (Seabrook 2014). The production process comprises many layers, with each layer thriving on the ability to hire ever-cheaper labour to generate profitability (Greenwald 2013). Not surprisingly, First World retailers are known to play factory owners off each other to secure the lowest price (Chalmers 2013). When the cost of production is no longer competitive (cheap production is the business model), owners pack up and move to another country (Strauss and Slater 2013). For example, China is no longer the go-to place for the garment trade because of improved working conditions and wages that have risen between 5 to 15 per cent each year for the past five years

continued

(up to nearly $1 per hour) (Saunders 2013). In short, as garment factories search for ever cheaper labour, the apparel industry may well represent the quintessential symbol—for better and worse—of neo-liberal globalization (MacKinnon and Strauss 2013).

7. Flawed business model 2: Factory owners have little incentive or resources to improve plant safety. Most American and European brands and retailers do not establish long-term working relationships with factory owners, instead relying on a rotating cast of numerous Third World suppliers who must submit competitive bids for each bulk order. Factory owners are ensnared in a paradox if costs are to be reined in: Those who want to improve conditions may find themselves out of business, since overseas customers have no obligation to provide either more work or compensation for safety renovations. Those who make upgrades may have to raise their costs to the point where they cannot compete with more ruthless suppliers. Clearly then, a new outsourcing business model is required that involves something of a paradigm shift in "how we do things around here" (Human Rights Watch 2015).

8. Perhaps the real culprits are the global apparel industry and penny-pinching consumers. Both are complicit in supporting a system of trade designed to bypass regulatory protocols while maximizing profits (Greenwald 2013). Offshore suppliers in Bangladesh cope with relentless consumer demand for designer-style yet disposable clothing at rock bottom prices—in large part by cutting corners to maintain slender profit margins, even at the expense of worker safety (Olive 2013). Consumers who want the cheapest in fast-fashion trends or discounted T-shirts and underwear should be aware of consequences. Their preferences cost workers their lives.

What to Do?

This indictment of sweatshop labour raises some key questions. Is our fetish for bargain clothing generating misery and inflicting suffering in poor countries? Is there blood on your hands if you wear a Joe Fresh T-shirt? Would Canada be a better place if Canadians didn't buy made-in-Bangladesh (Saunders 2013)? Are Canadians willing to buy more expensive made-in-Canada clothing (see Kimeldorf et al. 2006)? If fair-trade coffee and chocolates are available (meaning workers are paid a "fair" price and work in safe environs—although there is no *guarantee* of fairness without monitoring or inspections), why not fair-trade clothing? How do Canadians negotiate the challenge of living ethically in a connected world of increasingly unfettered trade (Straw and Glennie 2012)? What are the limits to improving conditions (changing the conventions that refer to the rules) without changing how the industry does business (changing the rules that inform the conventions)?

Much of the challenge in addressing unsafe working conditions and miserly wages depends on framing the problem–solution nexus. One option is to put pressure on improving the terms of the trade conditions. Freer trade links between north and south may have lifted millions of workers out of abject poverty, yet new, precarious conditions are created that generate new forms of exploitation and social exclusion. More responsible and legal trade guarantees are required. For example, the Retail Council of Canada could insist that manufacturing plants conduct business in a socially responsible way (Chakma 2013). The fact that Bangladesh depends on $20 billion in export trade (including $1 billion with Canada) provides Ottawa with leverage in securing worker rights and workplace safety.

A second option is for consumers to boycott companies that buy Bangladesh ready-made garments from factories that violate worker rights and factory safety standards. Admittedly, punishing those derelict in their responsibilities runs the risk of inflicting collateral damage. Millions of workers could lose their jobs, with no real options for pursuing better work elsewhere—in the same way that a consumer boycott of South African wines to protest apartheid resulted in mass unemployment for workers. Predictably perhaps, while Bangladeshi workers have taken to the streets in protest of deplorable working conditions, they stop short of calling for expelling foreign companies to leave or for consumer boy-cotts (Frazer 2013). Countries and companies have promised to introduce ethical standards to improve the appalling conditions for women (Mukherjee and Reed 2014; but see Human Rights Watch 2015b; Wells 2016). A slight modification in consumer behaviour with respect to eth-ical clothing and significant workplace reforms would not only meaningfully improve the lives of Bangladeshi garment workers, it would also pro-vide a lasting legacy for the hundreds who have lost their lives in modern day sweatshops that practise what appallingly might be called "indus-trial terrorism" (Seabrook 2014).

Endnote

1. Borrowed from Armine Yalnizyan, economist, Canadian Centre for Policy Alternatives, cited in Ward 2013.

Prioritizing Social Inequality: The Defining Issue of Our Time

Sociologists have successfully primed the con-cept of inequality for study and analysis (Porter 1965). Emphasis spans the spectrum from defining inequality and exploring its genesis and persistence to explaining its magnitude and scope to exam-ining its impact on individuals and consequences for society. But as a rule, sociologists have been less successful in conveying the excitement and dismay of this discovery to students. *Inequality Matters* hopes to overcome this lacuna by analyz-ing the politics and paradoxes of social inequality in Canada as an evolving yet contested dynamic. Attention is devoted to the social dimensions of inequality through five prevailing themes: expres-sions of inequality as socially constructed rather than anything inherent in human hardwiring; inequality as exclusion (both social and struc-tural) amenable to sociological analysis and meas-urement; patterns of inequality derived from the intersecting axes of race, ethnicity, gender, class, and location; the primacy of social location theory in not only shaping opportunity and outcome but also in framing debates over causes and blame; and the proposition that equality is preferable, possibly attainable, even if few can concur on its meaning or attainment. *Inequality Matters* is predicated on the premise that unequal relations constitute relations of social power, dynamics of domination and sub-domination, and sites of contestation and struggle, despite acknowledgement that the game is rigged in favour of the affluent (Schwalbe 2008). Moves to "naturalize" these inequities as normal or common sense by papering over ugly truths with polite fic-tions ramps up the onus to deconstruct how these inequalities of exclusion are constructed and main-tained as well as challenged and changed.

The notion that peoples' life chances are socially conditioned and structurally constrained is not a popular sell in Canada. Canadians are rarely encouraged to think of their own experiences in terms of structure or exclusion except, of course, when someone rationalizes the loss of a job or pro-motion. Many also believe that the removal of dis-criminatory barriers, the introduction of positive initiatives, and the expansion of enlightened atti-tudes catapulted Canada into an egalitarian uto-pia of free choice, unrestricted social mobility, and equal opportunity. Based on a March 2015 survey by Leger Marketing for the Association for Canadian Studies, 50 years after John Porter debunked the idea of Canada as a land of equal opportunity in his *The Vertical Mosaic*, an overwhelming majority of Canadians continue to believe in Canada as a coun-try of equal opportunity for all. But the inequalities of exclusion that pervade Canada are not simply the result of market imperfections that can be resolved through cosmetic reform. Nor is it accurate to pin the blame on individuals as the architects of their inequality misfortune. The focus instead must shift to systemic biases and social exclusions that reflect an interplay of structure and agency, are chronic and persistent over time, firmly embedded within the political and economic structures of a capitalist society, and resistant to even well-intentioned and carefully crafted solutions. Admittedly, it may be excessively harsh to downgrade Canada to the level of a twenty-first-century plutocracy (a society by, for, and about the rich). *Nevertheless, there is something deeply unsettling about the persistence of haves and have-nots in a Canada of bountiful resources and boundless resourcefulness.*

A plea for critically informed understanding cannot come too soon. As many have noted (Wilkinson and Pickett 2009), including the Occupy Wall Street and Idle No More movements, Canada's long-term interests are best secured by reducing inequality to ensure everyone shares in the largesse this country has to offer. Canada is more than a collection of isolated communities. Rather, it consists of a community of individuals and groups coexisting in a common framework of trust and collective responsibility for the public good (Clarkson 2014; Canadian Race Relations Foundation 2014). Schwalbe (2008:4) writes to this effect:

[I]nequality is perhaps the most consequential feature of our society. It matters for every aspect of our individual lives: comfort, safety, health, education, stress, dignity, pleasure, longevity, opportunity to fulfill our potentials. It also matters for our collective life, since inequality affects the workings of democracy, community, and relations between nations. So if there is any feature of the social world that deserves serious analytical attention, it's inequality. Not only is it at the center of things, but it matters, we could say, right down to our bones.

Taking a cue from this quote, *Inequality Matters* focuses on deconstructing the logic and dynamics of *social inequality* as social *exclusions* with regards to what they are; why they exist, persist, and expand; how they are expressed; where and when they negatively impact vulnerable populations; and what (if anything) can rein in these inequities to livable proportions. The focus on exclusions serves to remind us that inequality goes beyond income differences and financial considerations.

Ultimately, it is about powerlessness in shaping disparities in social capital, material resources, community engagement, valued contributions, and quality-of-life indicators. The centrality of the structural to social inequality draws attention to how patterns of power, privilege, and property are entrenched within the design of society and its institutions, from founding assumptions and foundational principles to those unwritten rules that define conventions regarding opportunities (who gets what) and outcomes (what goes where). The *social* in social inequality also reinforces the notion that socially constructed conventions are not cast in stone; rather, they are human accomplishments amenable to reform.

Once fortified with both insight and incentive, Canadians can begin to critically reflect on their own positions and how they might be complicit in perpetuating the inequalities of exclusion (Tang and Browne 2008). Individuals who commit to the struggle of advancing a more just and fair Canada *must begin by painting themselves into the picture.* For those casting about for role models to emulate, all Canadians can take inspiration from the creativity of Brigette Marcelle DePape, a young Senate page who disrupted the opening of the 2011 parliamentary session by brandishing a simulated sign that read, "Stop Harper." In a prepared statement in defending her defiance, DePape declared, "Harper's agenda is disastrous for this country and my generation. We have to stop him from wasting billions on fighter jets, military bases and corporate tax cuts while cutting social programs and destroying the climate." Not everyone would concur with the theatrics of DePape in drawing attention to growing socio-economic inequality and reckless environmental destruction. But many may applaud the courage of her convictions in powerfully yet non-violently challenging the drift away from what Canadians value: freedom, equality, loyalty, civility, and respect (Canadian Race Relations Foundation 2014; also McGrane 2015). As John F. Kennedy once said, "Those who make peaceful revolution impossible, will make violent revolution inevitable."

Summary

1. A general overview of social inequality is framed in terms of patterns, politics, and paradoxes against the backdrop of a changing and diverse, yet still bountiful, Canada.
2. Income disparity among Canadians matters in establishing the inequalities of exclusion at odds with Canada's constitutional commitment to equality and inclusion.
3. Debates over social inequality reflect the gap between polite fictions (Canada as land of opportunity) and inconvenient truths (Canada as racialized, gendered, and classed).
4. Canada is complicit in reinforcing global inequalities, sometimes deliberately, often inadvertently, as demonstrated in the Rana Plaza tragedy.
5. Social inequality matters because it increases the probability of making negative things happen that are related to exclusions or exploitation.
6. The value of analyzing social inequality by exploring how inequalities are constructed, expressed, and maintained, in addition to how they are challenged and transformed by institutional reform, government policy, ideological shifts, and minority protest, was reinforced.
7. Core themes that inform *Inequality Matters* focused on demonstrating the prevalence, pervasiveness, and persistence of inequalities and exclusions at different levels and across diverse domains, from the personal and the institutional to the national and the global.

Review Questions

1. The theme of this book is expressed by the title, *Inequality Matters*. Indicate how and why inequalities matter in a Canada that aspires to do better.
2. Are patterns of inequality necessary, inevitable, or justified in a Canada that is informed by market principles and the principle of meritocracy, yet simultaneously committed to inclusion and equality?
3. *Inequality Matters* is predicated on the assumption that inequalities are universal yet socially constructed. Explain this seeming contradiction.
4. Is the *system* or are *individuals* responsible for the deaths of over 1,100 garment workers in the Rana Plaza disaster? Justify your response.
5. Discuss some of the issues that need to be addressed (i.e., *problematized*) in studying social inequality and the inequalities of exclusion.

Note

1. © Black, Errol 2011. "Fast Facts: 'Mean Streets' Society Coming". Canadian Centre for Policy Alternatives. 19 May. This work is protected by copyright and the making of this copy was with the permission of Access Copyright. Any alteration of its content or further copying in any form whatsoever is strictly prohibited unless otherwise permitted by law.

2 Problematizing Social Inequality

Learning Objectives

1. To demonstrate how references to social inequality are not self-explanatory but require clarification.
2. To problematize the concept of social inequality by unpacking the terms *social* and *inequality*.
3. To assess the value of reframing social inequality as social exclusion.
4. To point out how sociology provides a distinct and interpretive lens for studying the inequalities of exclusion.
5. To explain how the ideology of neo-liberalism is pivotal in remaking Canada along more antisocial lines.

Introduction: Establishing the Parameters

We live in a world where patterns of inequality involving the exclusions of **power**, privilege, or property (income and wealth) are the rule rather than exception (Tilly 2005). But not all inequalities are the same in attracting the interest of sociologists or of relevance to sociology as a discipline. Nor do all expressions of inequality qualify as problematic for sociological analysis. For instance, the following examples are rarely regarded as grist for the sociology analysis mill: Those with seniority in full-time jobs will earn more than part-time workers who have just entered the workforce. New Canadians initially earn less than the Canadian-born because newcomers lack experience and seniority in Canada. University professors are better paid than support staff because of their educational credentials and onerous responsibilities. Senior corporate management are more amply rewarded than shop-floor workers since the talents of senior managers are in higher demand but in shorter supply. High flying sports figures and movie stars out-earn factory workers because their uncommon skills (or looks) generate additional revenue for the moneyed.

Many Canadians regard these income disparities as normal and necessary—even laudable—in terms of fairness and justification. People ought to be rewarded accordingly in a free market economy whose complexities put a premium on attracting and keeping the brightest and best (see also Johnson 2013). Those with exceptional talent or skills should be better paid than a menial labourer, according to the principle of supply and demand. Those who work hard and apply themselves are more deserving than others in a society that commits to the principle of meritocracy. But closer inspection reveals more puzzles in these payoffs. University professors may be entitled to more pay than custodial and support staff, although how much more is open for debate. On what principled grounds can income differences be justified? On the basis of responsibility or workload or levels of education or merit? Or perhaps there should be no difference in remuneration since taxpayers ultimately defray much of the cost of educating a university professor. How about this incongruity: the prime minister of Canada may deserve a hefty pay packet in light of onerous responsibilities and punishing work schedules, but questions remain over how much he or she deserves compared to other Canadians. For example, what is the rationale in paying Canada's prime minister a salary of about $327,000 per year (plus benefits) when the minimum entry-level hockey salary in the NHL is $550,000? Clearly, explaining the how and why behind income distribution is not nearly as straightforward as appearances would suggest.

Social inequality is an established fact of human life. Inequalities are known to reflect patterns of stratification that partition society into unequal *strata* (layers), based on criteria such as class, race and ethnicity, aboriginality, gender, age, sexual orientation, or disability. Less well-known are the reasons for the origin and persistence of social inequalities in stratified society. What is it about living in a society that creates those inequalities of **exclusion** that deny or diminish? Should individuals be held responsible for their predicament (blame the victim)? Or are they victims of **structural exclusions** beyond individual control (blame the system) (Royce 2015)? Does the answer lie in the interplay of agency and structure within the interactional context of a specific situation (blame the situation)? Who is at fault if governments pursue austerity measures that target the already marginalized? Where should blame be affixed when corporations downsize, outsource jobs, or move operations offshore to stay competitive and reward shareholders? However urgent or overdue, responses to these difficult questions are not readily forthcoming. No one should be surprised by the failure to agree or finalize since (a) the subject matter of social inequality is expansive; (b) different perspectives yield diverse answers; (c) inequality itself hides behind those polite fictions that paper over inconvenient truths and awkward contradictions; and (d) nobody is quite sure of what an equal society would look like, even if one were desirable or attainable. The range of responses will depend on a variety of factors and perspectives, including:

1. Debate over *what society is for*. Does society exist to reward the rich and powerful, to advance a freewheeling economy of winners and losers, or to exercise control over those who dare to challenge the system? Or should the economy be serving the public good by advancing an inclusive and egalitarian society, one that ensures no one is excluded from material resources and social services, access to active participation within the community, and quality-of-life indicators such as health care? Is society (to the extent it even exists) little more than a rabble of competitive and self-serving individuals? Or does society comprise a community of concerned citizens with some degree of commitment to those less fortunate?

2. A preferred *model of society*—functionalist, radical conflict (Marxism, structuralism, and feminism), or symbolic interactionist—will temper the analysis of social inequality. Those inclined to see society as fundamentally sound and a relatively neutral playing field (functionalism) will interpret patterns of social inequality differently than those who define society as an unequal site of domination, control, and exploitation (radical conflict theories). Neither of these approaches will please those who frame society as a socially constructed process of definition, negotiation, and accomplishment (symbolic interactionism).

3. Responses will also reflect people's *social location* in society. Phrased alternatively in the language of standpoint theory, what people see and how they interpret it depends on where they stand or who they are. That is, where individuals are socially located with respect to the interlocking identities of gender, age, race, class, and so on will profoundly influence their assessment of social inequality as good or bad, natural or constructed, attitudinal or structural, or permanent or transitory. Men see things differently than women, the young differently than the old, the "whitestream" differently than racialized minorities, and the rich differently from the poor.

4. Assessments will vary according to different definitions of social inequality. Is inequality about unfair opportunity or unequal outcomes? Is it about treating everyone the same regardless of race or gender? Or does it entail treating people differently precisely because of their differences? Is it about similar treatment as a matter of course but different treatment (such as exemptions from the general rule) when the situation arises?

This chapter explores the different ways of conceptualizing (i.e., framing, describing, defining, comparing, assessing, explaining, and problematizing) the politics and paradoxes of social inequality and the inequalities of exclusion. The magnitude and tenacity of social inequalities in an otherwise bountiful Canada calls for examination of the realities that maintain these disparities and exclusions and how these inequalities of exclusion are challenged and transformed by way of institutional reform, government policy, ideological shifts, and minority protest (including social movements). Assuming the concept of social inequality is not necessarily self-evident but problematic and in need of unpacking (deconstructing), the chapter begins by looking at how sociological principles inform the study of social inequality and the inequalities of exclusion. The chapter then provides a working definition of *social inequality* and its relationship to stratification. Of particular use in advancing a sociological lens is the reframing of social inequality along the lines of **social exclusions**. The core features of social inequality are examined next, with emphasis on deconstructing its constituent elements, namely, the *social* and the *inequality*. This examination is followed by a detailed look at the four key dimensions of inequality in social inequality (material, ideological, power, and reform). The chapter concludes with discussions of neo-liberalism in Canada, the power of media communication, and the Idle No More movement that focused national attention on the fact that aboriginal inequalities do matter.

A Sociology of Social Inequality

Social inequality's centrality to sociology confirms what many know. Much of what passes for sociological inquiry is devoted to the task of discovering, analyzing, and reducing the inequities of exclusion wherever they are found (Cancian 1995). Conversely, sociology as a discipline has long claimed social inequality (especially the inequalities of exclusion) as a preferred domain. A cursory look through any introductory sociology text attests to the importance and pervasiveness of inequality as a preferred frame. This chapter (as well as the book in its entirety) is predicated on the premise that sociological principles provide a distinct perspective for analyzing social inequality. What does sociology bring to the table that enhances our understanding of social life in general and the inequalities of exclusion in particular?

1. *Data-driven/research-based.* The study of social inequality is grounded in information drawn from the systematic (scientific) collection of empirical data. A commitment to research-based data as a basis for analysis and assessment is preferred over interpretations or arguments involving first principles, ethical puzzles, or abstract theories.

2. *Complexity/contextuality of human behaviour.* A society that emphasizes individuality too often frames inequality along individualist lines and personal choices. Sociology proposes a critically informed approach that goes beyond the individualistic by proposing both social inequality and human behaviour as an interplay of *agency, structure, context, and power* (also Antony and Samuelson 2012). Humans are framed as social actors (i.e., they occupy statuses and play roles within specific contexts) who produce and reproduce the structures of society (from values to institutions) which, in turn, impact on people's thoughts and behaviour. In theory, individuals must assume responsibility for their choices; in reality, their actions are informed by and constrained within those contexts of power and exclusion of interest to sociologists. The concept of **intersectionality** further reinforces the complexity and contextuality of people's behaviour and group life. People are differently situated (socially located) so that they experience reality simultaneously through the prism of race, aboriginality, gender, and class.

The interplay of these often devalued identity markers creates overlapping hierarchies that amplify the inequalities of exclusion (Ferguson 2012; Hankivsky 2011; Goswami, O'Donovan, and Yount 2014).

3. *Human realities as socially constructed.* Sociology tends to focus on society as the primary frame of reference, with particular attention paid to how social realities are created and maintained as well as challenged and changed. It acknowledges the arbitrariness of society and its constituent elements (from structures to values to groups), despite vested interests to convey a different impression. Rather, social realities are defined as socially constructed and ideologically loaded human accomplishments whose conventionality is often concealed behind a façade of common sense truths (polite fictions). Sociologists also claim that societies as social constructions are neither neutral nor value free. More accurately, the founding assumptions and foundational principles of society's unwritten constitutional order are deeply ingrained along gender, race, and class lines in defining what is normal, acceptable, and desirable as they apply to societal design, institutional organization, cultural values, and everyday interactions.

4. *Critical orientation/debunking.* Sociology as a discipline tends toward the critical—not in the sense of carping negativity, but more in a commitment to challenge the obvious, to interrogate the taken-for-granted, and to concede how appearances may be deceiving since things are not always what they appear to be. This commitment to debunking the commonsensical and taken-for-granted puts an emphasis on unearthing the root (structural or systemic) causes of social phenomena or the feasibility (or risk) factors that increase the likelihood of certain outcomes.

5. *Root causes.* In explaining behaviour or outcomes, sociologists acknowledge the importance of precipitating or immediate causes. But precipitating causes are often the symptom of a deeper logic or root cause—related in part to **social structures**, cultural values, institutional frameworks, or group affiliation. No less important are those risk factors that increase the

possibility of making something happen. For example, while some might dismiss the deaths of aboriginal women, saying they are a crime in need of law enforcement, sociologists would argue that Tina Fontaine's death and the deaths of hundreds of aboriginal women represent a sociological phenomenon whose root causes include a series of risk factors related to colonial legacies, structural barriers, systemic failures, and institutionalized racism (Singh 2014). A commitment to highlighting root causes reinforces sociology's critical dimension as an explanatory framework that situates human behaviour within the context of a wider framework.

6. *Generalizing orientation: The bigger picture as a sociological imagination.* Sociology is interested in extracting broader patterns of society in and from the lives of individual people or social actions. This orientation is predicated on the principle that human behaviour, intergroup relations, and institutional outcomes are patterned, pervasive, and predictable, and amenable to sociological analysis. Admittedly, formulating universals of human behaviour might not be possible, given the complexity of human behaviour. Nevertheless, sociologists continue to search for generalizations (explanations) without resorting to the individualistic or obsessing with the idiosyncratic. In other words, much sociology is animated by the principle of a sociological imagination—that is, to frame private troubles as public issues by linking the personal with the political, the micro with the macro, the local with the global and national.

7. *Social dimensions.* For sociologists, the social dimensions of human life are a primary focus of study, in effect reinforcing a sociological dictum that only social facts can explain social facts. Focusing on the social dimensions of inequality yields the inevitability of a mutually reciprocating relationship: how do inequality discourses and unequal realities impact on social reality and people's lives and life chances? Conversely, how do society and societal changes influence shifting patterns of social inequality regarding who gets what and what goes where (Therborn 2013)? Sociologists also emphasize the *what is*

over the *what was* (without neglecting history in understanding the present) or the *what ought to be* (without ignoring the normative as basis for debate).

8. *Multiperspectival.* Sociologists operate on the assumption that the interacting trifecta of society, social reality, and social behaviour are *framable* from a variety of different perspectives, including functionalism, radical conflict theories (including Marxism, structuralism, and feminism), and symbolic interactionist approaches. Each of these models of society/social reality/social behaviour begins with a different set of assumptions about the human conditions, utilizes different explanatory frameworks to account for human behaviour, and arrives at different generalizations related to patterns of social inequality (see next chapter.)

Reframing Inequality as Exclusion

Sometimes the most routine things are the most difficult to define or explain. The concept of *social inequality* is no exception, despite its popular public use. It has long been a challenge to define because of its contested and convoluted nature (Warwick-Booth 2013). Definitions vary on points of emphasis that apply to a preferred frame of reference. Should definitions focus on what something looks like? What the phenomenon in question says it does? What it should be doing? What it's really saying or doing? Definitions will depend, to some extent, on the desired level of analysis—deep or broad, superficial or complex, micro or macro (Bastia 2013). However elusive or complex this challenge, a commitment to defining an issue is more than an analytical exercise. The politics of definition are critical in shaping responses and crafting solutions; after all, people act on the basis of how an issue is defined, how issues are framed for public debate, and what kind of solutions are permissible.

A similar line of reasoning applies to definitions of *social equality*. Many definitions lean toward a narrow economist perspective (economic inequality), with its focus on income or wealth

that is relatively easy to quantify and measure (see Fortin et al. 2012). And yet difficulties prevail since references to income inequality may invoke different meanings—as poverty, as median and mean, as top-end concentration (the 1 per cent)—each involving a different discourse, data sets, and problem–solution nexus (Gordon 2015). For sociologists, inequality is more related to its social dimensions, most notably around the concept of social exclusion (Bastia 2013). The concept of social exclusion has entered social science circles, enjoying considerable popularity and acclaim as well as criticism and concern (Winlow and Hall 2013; Teelucksingh and Galabuzi 2010; Popay et al. 2008). For some, social exclusion lacks a clear definition and a coherent theoretical core, thus rendering it inapplicable for analysis (Mathieson et al. 2008). Its semantic flexibility allows it to mean different things to different people at different times; not surprisingly, the concept is dismissed by some as little more than a slogan of limited value (Buckmaster and Thomas 2009). Others see its usefulness as a theoretical framework—even a new paradigm—for interpreting social inequality through a distinctive lens (Labonte, Hadi, and Kauffmann 2011; Mathieson et al. 2008). Social inequality, reframed through the prism of exclusion, points to a wide range of disadvantages and deprivations above and beyond income differences: powerlessness, discrimination, hampering political participation, institutional involvement, health and quality of life, and including vulnerability to **violence** and violations of rights (Saloojee 2003; Green and Kesselman 2006; Levitas et al. 2007; Wilkinson and Pickett 2009).

The concept of social exclusion consists of several key components. First are the *unequal conditions* that preclude opportunity and *access* to social citizenship (notions of belonging, engagement, and identity); unequal allocation of services and resources as well as rights and capabilities that culminate in material deprivation and social alienation; barriers to active *participation* in social, cultural, political and economic activities along normative lines; and an inability to meaningfully *contribute* as valued, recognized, and respected members of a community of shared experiences, mutual understandings, and reciprocal respect (Saloojee 2003; Teelucksingh and Galabuzi 2010; Labonte, Hadi, and Kauffmann 2011). Second, social exclusion entails *membership in groups* that suffer real deprivation due to lack of food, shelter, and clothing; are precluded from full and equal participation owing to a lack of social capital; trend toward powerlessness, helplessness, and marginalization; are underappreciated and undervalued; and may be prone to anti-social behaviour because of early childhood dysfunctionalities and restricted opportunities (Sarlo 2013; Crouch 2011; also Kristol 2011). Third, it also emphasizes those *denials and discriminations* (from structural exclusions [systemic bias] to exclusionary structures [systematic barriers]) that pre-empt a person's full potential as a human (self-actualization) and full participation as a citizen, with its attendant notion of belonging and recognition (Therborn 2013; Winlow and Hall 2013; Saloojee 2003; Richmond and Saloojee 2005; Fraser 2008).

Despite criticism, much commends social exclusion as an explanatory framework. First, reference to social exclusion offers more of a multi-dimensional perspective on social inequality than is conveyed by the concepts of poverty or income deprivation. Too often, references to inequality tend to be synonymous with income redistribution (quantity of goods) (Fortin et al. 2012). Yet emphasis on income as the quintessential indicator of material inequality may be misleading. Income levels can prove meaningless in places like northern Canada, where the cost of living is high. By contrast, referencing the inequalities of exclusion acknowledges a combination of linked problems, from family breakdown to unemployment, that impede membership, access, and contribution (quality of life) (Teelucksingh and Galabuzi 2010; Mathieson et al. 2008). Unlike the singularity of the income-based inequality framework, social exclusions are experienced in multiple and reinforcing ways; after all, individuals and groups who are structurally excluded from the labour market tend to be additionally marginalized by lack of adequate housing, education, health care, and social services. The position of this framework is not intended to dismiss the value of income and wealth as indicators and drivers of inequality (United Way 2015). Income inequality remains an important signifier of exclusion since it denies the material benefits that allow full and equal inclusion (Winlow and Hall 2013).

Second, the concept of social exclusion appears less concerned with the status of inequality per se (Mathieson et al. 2008). Rather it is more attuned to:

- the *processes, relations, and barriers* that present fewer opportunities to fully and equally participate (Labonte, Hadi, and Kauffmann 2011);
- the diminishing of individuals' full potential to function as complete human beings (self-actualization), with a corresponding sense of belonging, recognition, representation, and respect (Therborn 2013; Winlow and Hall 2013; Saloojee 2003; Richmond and Saloojee 2005; Fraser 2008); and
- highlighting quality-of-life indicators ranging from a sustainable environment to violence-free relationships (Senate 2013; Warwick-Booth 2013).

A relational approach to defining social exclusions points to those dynamic processes and multi-dimensional barriers that amplify the inequalities of exclusion along four main dimensions (economic, social, political, and cultural), at different levels (individual, household, group, and community), and across intersecting identity domains of class, gender, race, and aboriginality (also Popay et al. 2008). References to the inequalities of exclusion also convey different meanings to differently disadvantaged groups. For immigrants, for example, the domain of exclusion is focused on the challenges of getting in, settling down, fitting in, and moving up. The dominant concern of refugees (in addition to material deprivation) is the psychological cost of uncertainty, precarious status, and confusion, as well as the uneven distribution of hope, respect, and dignity (Marston 2003).

Third, emphasis is aimed at the structural dimensions of disadvantage, alienation, and deprivation (Winlow and Hall 2013). That is, social exclusion is reflected in, reinforced by, and advanced through system-based inequalities that preclude access to resources and resourcefulness. An ideal-typical distinction between structural exclusions and exclusionary structures may be helpful: *structural exclusions* refers to institutional barriers that inadvertently exclude because of

systemic bias ("the logical consequences of deeply entrenched rules that treat everyone the same when differences need to be taken into account to make any difference"[Fleras 2014b]). **Exclusionary structures** refers to deprivation that results from more open and *systematic* forms of closure and discrimination (treating people differently when similar treatment is expected or obligatory). In both cases, the issue is one of power in the narrow sense (preventing someone from doing or making someone do something they otherwise would or wouldn't do) or, in the broader sense, a capacity to influence outcomes without seemingly trying to.

Finally, framing social inequality as exclusion reinforces the centrality of *inclusiveness* as a necessary discourse. With its commitment to community engagement, access to necessary resources and services, a framework for self-fulfillment and acceptance, and quality of life indicators (from a sustainable environment to violence-free lifestyles), the concept of inclusiveness represents an increasingly popular perspective—even a dominant paradigm—for thinking about disadvantage and poverty (Senate 2013; Warwick-Booth 2013). A later chapter draws attention to inclusion (fitting in) and inclusivity (adjusting the system) as analytically distinct subsets of inclusiveness.

A brief comparison of the competing discourse between *social inequality* and *social exclusion* reveals the following ideal-typical contrasts:

Social Inequality	Social Exclusion
Is one-dimensional	Is multi-dimensional
Affects material needs	Affects access + participation + contribution
Is monetary	Affects membership
Is income-focused	Is inclusiveness-focused
Concerns quantity-of-goods factors	Concerns quality-of-life factors
Concerns poverty	Reflects and reinforces powerlessness
Is distributional	Is relational
Is static	Is dynamic
Reflects a state of inequality	Focuses on barriers to equality

In short, any definition of inequality implies two dimensions: first, inequality can be framed as the condition involving people's *differential* (unequal) *access* to the good things (power, privilege, property) in life because of their differently positioned location in society related to class, gender, race, and ethnicity. Second, it can be framed as *differential distribution* of these valued resources among socially defined categories of persons according to characteristics such as class, gender, race, and ethnicity (i.e., social location). Defining inequality as both *differential access* (who gets what) and differential distribution (what goes where) draws attention to *inequality as differential access to valued resources resulting in unequal distribution of power, privilege, and property.* Or to put it more succinctly:

> [Inequality] refers to the unequal access people have to a wide range of material and non-material resources, supports, provisions, and opportunities that are widely held as valued and desirable in society and are consequential to our lives. It also refers to the asymmetrical distributions that this unequal access fosters and perpetuates across many sites (such as the family . . .) and spheres (economic . . .) (Olsen 2011:13).

Phrased in a different way, *inequality is about entitlement patterns in regards to who gets what, and how and why they get it (differential access), in addition to patterns of distribution with respect to what goes where, and when and how it goes (differential distribution).* Reference to inequality entails those conditions and opportunities in which preferential access to valued goods is not randomly distributed but is stratified in ascending and descending order and aligned around those human differences defined as socially significant (Grabb and Guppy 2009). Of necessity, then, any analysis of either society or social inequality must begin tapping into the concept of social stratification.

Inequality as Social Stratification

It is widely conceded that a society of perfect equality is a contradiction in terms. No human society is "equal" in the sense that everyone is equally ranked in accessing valued resources (Tepperman 2012). All human societies are unequal and stratified to some extent. Some individuals are higher ranked than others because they have more of what is prized: valued resource distribution, biological traits that are imbued with cultural meanings, and groupings and rankings of persons based on shared characteristics. Both simple and complex societies are ranked/stratified along the lines of age or gender. Yet only agricultural–industrial societies possess the technology and organization to support extremes of stratified inequality. The concept of **stratification** refers to a division of society into unequal vertical layers of inequality known as strata. Stratification entails an arrangement by which categories of persons are grouped together into different statuses (positions) according to shared commonalities in occupation, income, wealth, class, and race or ethnicity (Olsen 2011). These categories are then hierarchically ranked (stratified) into layers of unequal worth and arranged in ascending and descending orders of recognition, reward, or significance (see also Steckley and Letts 2007). Patterns of stratification are not only persistent, patterned, and resistant to change, they are also supported by a legitimating ideology that rationalizes the alignment of persons or the allocation of goods (Breen and Rottman 1995).

Class and caste systems provide two popular and ideal-typical expressions of social stratification. A person's status in a caste system is ascribed (assigned at birth), whereas status in class systems is generally acquired through achievement and social mobility in what is commonly called a meritocracy (McNamee 2014; Crompton 2008) (see Spotlight box below). For Marxists, stratification systems embody an economic dimension involving positioning of class relationships (from workers to owners, with fractions in between) to the means of production. For Weberians (followers of the German sociologist, Max Weber), a person's position in a stratified system is more reflective of his or her "market situation" (from family background to education levels to political affiliation) than of a specific relationship to productive property (Breen and Rottman 1995). According to Weberians, systems of stratification are multi-dimensional and overlapping rather than comprising a single factor (as posited by Marx). The concept of *socio-economic status hierarchy* best describes this composite social stratification based on the following metrics of social inequality: family background, access to political authority, power to make things happen, varying levels of prestige, and the status of identity groups related to race or gender (see also Kerbo 2012; Perucci and Wysong 2008; Macionis and Gerber 2010).

Spotlight Social Stratification and Income Mobility in Canada: Polite Fiction or Inconvenient Truth?

One common assertion about Canada reflects its commitment to the principle of **meritocracy**. Meritocratic principles are built on the belief that society is essentially a level playing field where people are judged and rewarded on the basis of talent and hard work (i.e., individuals deserve what they get). Accordingly, anyone who works hard can "make it" through effort and risk-taking (McNamee 2014; Johnson 2015; but see Wotherspoon and Hansen 2013). Central to any meritocracy is a commitment to the principle of income-based social mobility (Corak 2010). Canada is often praised as

a socially mobile society since the relationship between family background and adult incomes is thought to be relatively weaker here—that is, adult children are thought to fare better than their parents thanks to more intergenerational income mobility (Conference Board 2013b; also Corak and Stabile 2013). Not surprisingly, Canadians may be less concerned with income gaps but more interested in the principle of equal opportunity so that they and their children have a fair chance to scale the socio-economic ladder (Gordon 2015; ACS History 2015).

continued

A study by Lammam, Karabegovic, and Veldhuis (2012) for the Fraser Institute put this principle to test by measuring income mobility over a 10-year period (1990–2000) and a 19-year period (1990–2009). According to their data, between 1990 and 2009, the lowest quintile of Canadians (the bottom 20 per cent) experienced the highest relative income increase, including 87 per cent who moved into a higher income group, with 21 per cent making it into the top income quintile group. (By comparison *The Economist* (2014) notes, the United States is not a particularly mobile place: a child born in the poorest fifth of society only has a 9 per cent chance of making it to the top fifth.) The same study also pointed out that 36 per cent of Canadians experienced a relative decline in income and dropped at least one income bracket over the 19-year period. As well, the average income of those in the bottom 20 per cent in 1990 grew by 635 per cent by the end of 2009 (from $6,000 to $44,100). By contrast, the average income of those initially in the top 20 per cent grew by 23 per cent during the same period, with the result that the average income ratio between the top 20 per cent and the bottom 20 per cent (which was 13 times in 1990—$77,200 vs. $6,000) dropped to about twice that amount in 2009 ($94,900 vs. $44,100).

The authors of the study concluded accordingly: Canadians do experience income mobility since they are not stuck in fixed income brackets but move up and down the socio-economic ladder over the course of their lives. Most Canadians begin with a low income, but income levels typically increase with age (seniority), experience, education, and enhanced skills. Furthermore, the poor are not getting poorer, but experiencing marked increases in their income (Veldhuis and Lammam 2012), depending on the measures employed (Banting and Myles 2013). Others paint a gloomier picture, challenging both the methodology and the interpretations. Movement to the top of the income ladder is uncommon (Conference Board 2013b). As critics note, 64 per cent of those in the top bracket didn't budge, suggesting the rich tend to stay put, whereas other categories are churning about near the bottom (MacDonald 2012). Moreover, the numbers cannot disguise the obvious: in a world of globalization and a global economy, digital and automation technologies, and public austerity programs that cut back on services, many Canadians will remain poor at some point of their lives—if not permanently then at least temporarily (MacDonald 2012).

But social mobility is not nearly as extensive as myth-making implies (Corak 2010). More income inequality in one generation means fewer opportunities and less income mobility for the next generation (Corak and Stabile 2013). As it stands, Canada sits in the middle of a curve among developed countries: more equal and mobile than countries at the extreme (US), yet trailing Fennoscandia (McKenna 2014). Canada's status as more economically mobile than the US yields an interesting insight: if you are rich and want to stay that way, it is better to be born in the US. Canada is a better bet if you are poor and anxious to move up (Corak 2012; Pew Charitable Trusts 2010). And while rates of mobility can increase during periods of economic expansion and technological growth, a rags-to-riches fairy tale is rare. No society—Canada included—can afford unrestricted movement up and down the class ladder without unsettling the social order. The fact that rags-to-riches tales of social mobility occasionally happen (for example with highly publicized payoffs for internet start-ups and mobile applications [apps]) appears sufficient to substantiate people's faith in the virtues of an open and meritocratic system.

Stratification as a hierarchical ranking of statuses can be aligned along two analytically separate yet mutually overlapping tracks (Ferguson 2012). First, just as inequality can be conceptualized as differential distribution (what goes where), so too can stratification refer to the differential (i.e., unequal) allocation of scarce resources among socially significant groups based on class, race, gender, ethnicity, aboriginality and so on. Second, in the same way inequality can refer to differential access (who gets what), so too does stratification embody the differential alignment of persons or groups in relation to scarce resources such as power, privilege, and property. Society is said to be stratified when socially defined categories of individuals differ from other groups in the amount of valued resources they possess or can access. The resulting stratified access is not randomly distributed. Differential access to and distribution of valued goods tends to cluster around the status of social categories such as social class, with its basis in material wealth; race (inequality due to visibility); ethnicity (inequality from culture and symbols); gender (inequality based on perceived sex differences); and aboriginality (inequality reflecting the logic and legacy of colonialism). The interplay of these hierarchically ranked strata intersect and overlap to intensify patterns of power, privilege, and property (Ferguson 2012).

Deconstructing Social Inequality

What's So *Social* about Social Inequality?

What is meant by the *social* in social inequality? Why is the concept of equality prefaced by the word *social* when logic dictates inequality should be framed as *anti-social*? What distinguishes social inequality from the kind of inequality studied by, say, economists who might be more inclined to frame it along income lines (Fortin et al. 2012)? For sociologists, social inequality goes beyond income differences, although the latter may serve as a shorthand (or proxy) for broader socio-economic disparities. The *social* in *social inequality* incorporates the concept of *exclusion* with its attendant notion that people should not be excluded from full and equal participation in society through no fault of their own: discrimination based on race, gender, ability, and so on; violation of individual rights including exposure to violence; patterns of poverty and powerlessness; denial of valued goods and services of necessity; lack of social capital to engage

and connect; inadequate opportunities for making a contribution to society; and a host of quality-of-life features from health to safety (Saloojee 2003; Levitas et al. 2007). In other words, if inequality refers to differential access and differential distribution, social inequality moves positively beyond these dimensions by emphasizing those exclusions that preclude full, equal, and meaningful participation. References to the social also point to the placement of inequality within a broader context of society, namely, the impact of social inequality on society and vice versa. Finally, inequality is deemed to be social and amenable to sociological analysis on the basis of four criteria: origin/cause, definition, impact, and treatment (Fleras 2005).

First, inequality is defined as social when it's perceived to *originate* in a society or within a social context (including values, institutions, and structures). The *social* takes the blame as the *cause* of social inequities instead of attributing inequality to biology or psychology, or morality. True, both Canadians and Americans may well embrace more ambivalent views and contradictory beliefs about the distribution of income and wealth (McNamee 2014). Nevertheless, they tend to endorse the meritocratic belief that individual characteristics and choices (from hard work to ambition) account for economic mobility and material success (Corak 2010; Pew Charitable Trusts 2011; Johnson 2015). For many sociologists, however, social inequalities are deeply social because they are socially constructed, structurally embedded, and ideologically maintained. That is, there is nothing natural or normal about social inequalities, despite concerted efforts by vested interests to make them appear so ("polite fictions"). They are conventions constructed and imposed by those with the power to create "inconvenient realities."

Second, inequality is social when *defined* as an issue or concern to society (or sector thereof). Consider how the existence of billionaires in society is not necessarily a problem of social inequality, unless defined as such because their fortunes were illegally accumulated, based on blatant forms of exploitation, hoarded at the expense of a common good, or manipulated to rig the political economy. Or consider how, until recently, neither sexism nor racialized discrimination were perceived as a problem (for example, the term *racism* did not enter the English language until the early 1930s). Both exclusions were defined as a normal and inescapable—even desirable—part of the human condition. A closer look at the politics and probabilities of dying on the doomed *Titanic* also demonstrates how Edwardian society did not regard inequality-based entitlements as a problem (see Chapter 4).

Third, inequality is social because, in theory, it's amenable to *reform* through government action or institutional reform. For sociologists, solving the problem of social inequalities must go beyond modifying attitudes or behavioural modification, even though the problem itself is expressed in and through individual choices and actions. The focus of reform is aimed at those root causes or feasibility factors that generate patterns of exclusions beyond individual control. Admittedly, a commitment to reform is one thing; it's quite another to change those deeply embedded founding assumptions and foundational principles of a society's unwritten constitutional norms.

Finally, inequality becomes social when it exerts a negative *impact* on society or inflicts harm on segments thereof. Extreme patterns of social inequality may threaten to undermine the social fabric of society by eroding the trust at the heart of a co-operative co-existence (Wilkinson and Pickett 2009). The *social* matters at individual levels as well. For example, in calculating how many deaths in the US are attributable to social factors, a research team from Columbia University has estimated that, of the 2.4 million Americans who died in 2000, nearly 900,000 of those deaths (or 36 per cent of the country's total) could be attributed to poverty and income inequality (Galea et al. 2011). The number of deaths attributed to low education attainment was 245,000; to racial segregation, 176,000; to low social support, 162,000; and to income inequality, 119,000. By comparison, approximately 193,000 died from heart attacks, 119,000 from accidents, and 156,000 from lung cancer.

In short, the *social* in social inequality refers to the social dimensions of a stratified human reality. It draws attention to how the mutually reciprocal relationship between social inequality and society is constructed, challenged, and transformed.

Focusing on the social dimensions of inequality pays homage to Durkheim's prescient insight of a century ago: only a social fact can explain another social fact. Similarly, social inequalities are best explained by other social factors, thus justifying the importance of sociological models and structural perspectives. Admittedly, the *social* is under pressure in this neo-liberal era of market rule. What becomes of the social, ask Winlow and Hall (2013), if people are cut adrift from its organizational logic, resulting in its exclusion from the core of human existence?

> [S]ocial exclusion is not simply a problem, an aberration in an otherwise progressive socio-economic system, an ailment whose micro-causes and effects can be easily identified, isolated, and "fixed" by a sympathetic and benevolent government elite. Rather the problem of "social exclusion" reflects a broader "problem of the social" during a period characterised by the restoration by liberal capitalism and its marketisation of the social world . . . .

In sum, inequalities that do qualify for sociological analysis originate in human interaction; are defined through intergroup dynamics; respond (theoretically) to collective treatment yet remain resistant to change; and negatively impact on society or its members. Sociologists also respond to those social inequalities embodied in structural exclusions—that is, those deprivations and institutionalized biases that block people's access to full and equal participation and integration into society because of barriers to material necessities and the rights to social citizenship. The inequalities of health outcomes and health care reinforce the centrality of the social in understanding the inequalities of exclusion.

"Wealth as Health": The Social Determinants of Health and Health Care Inequality

Popular references to health and health care are normally couched along biomedical lines (Adelson 2005). The focus is on genes (genetic dispositions), disease (germs and viruses), and technology (gadgets and innovations for improving health care). According to this model, inequalities in health outcomes arise when one or all of these dimensions are out of whack. Not surprisingly, a widespread conviction exists that health is dictated by individual choices within the framework of the health care system. Canadians like to think they possess a world-class health care system; in reality, Canada is a middle-of-the-pack performer, achieving admirably in some areas, but poorly in others (Picard 2013). For example, Canada spends more than many developed countries (the US excepted) on health care. Yet Canadians routinely experience lower levels of quality care. For example, the median wait time for treatment by a specialist was 17.7 weeks in 2012 compared to 11.9 weeks in 1997, despite substantial spending increases to alleviate the problem (Esmail 2013). The Canadian Institute for Health Information (2015) put Canada dead last among 11 wealthy countries when it comes to timely access to health care, especially for older Canadians.

In theory, Canada may have a universal health care system that entitles everyone to basic health care (doctors and hospitalization) within a reasonable time frame and without incurring catastrophic financial obligations in the process. The reality of basic health care differs: many Canadians do not have access to a family physician, relying instead on walk-in clinics or hospital emergency wards. Frail, frightened, and non-ambulatory elderly people awaiting treatment are known to spend hours, even days, on gurneys in emergency departments, sometimes dying before receiving appropriate care (Picard 2014). Millions of Canadians without access to dental insurance suffer dental decay and health problems, from gum diseases to diabetes, because they cannot afford to see a dentist (CAHS 2014). Large numbers of Canadians, from newcomers to Aboriginal peoples to rural Canadians, lack access to high-quality health care because of who they are (cultural differences, language barriers) or where they live (regional disparities in the calibre of health care and health outcomes). Admittedly, danger lurks in overemphasizing the health care system as a solution to improving health outcomes. According to Senator Michael Kirby, health care per se accounts for only 25 per cent of a population's health; the remaining 75 per cent reflects socio-economic conditions, biology,

prevention, and the physical environment. Still, the fact that an estimated 42,000 Canadians (based largely on Fraser Institute data) sought medical care outside of Canada points to a problem in need of a solution (Esmail and Barua 2013; Esmail 2013).

Inequities in the health care system contribute to an individual's health status. More important still are those social and environmental factors that influence health, including the degree to which material resources and social circumstances restrict an individual's options. Sociologists criticize and challenge a highly individualistic approach to health that neglects social influences (Armstrong 2012). For example, health sociologist Dennis Raphael (2011) has accused mainstream media of ignoring the social determinants of health, especially the connection between adverse health effects and social inequality. He and others propose the value of a social lens for framing and interpreting inequalities in health and health care within the context of political, economic, cultural, and environmental factors (Raphael 2002; Adelson 2005; Trovato and Romaniuk 2014). Social determinants such as social exclusion and income inequality (and its correlates, poverty, housing, nutrition and food/job security, and early childhood development) not only account for the inequality of health care Canadians receive, but also contribute to the premature death of 40,000 Canadians each year (Tjepkema et al. 2013). Racism is increasingly recognized as a barrier to good health and accessible health care services for aboriginal women, women of colour, and immigrant and refugee women (Nestel 2012). Health outcomes are also generated by the intersection of interlocking yet devalued identity markers such as gender, race, and class (Tang and Browne 2008; Hankivsky 2011; Gee, Kobayashi, and Prus 2007). Social factors behind health and health care are relational and interact in complex ways, with some determinants playing a more prominent role in generating options and outcomes (Spence, N. 2011). The logic is impeccable: if social and economic factors influence health outcomes, it stands to reason that only socio-economic policies can modify unequal health outcomes that impose both direct and indirect costs.

Health (and health care) inequalities are a stain on Canada and its global reputation. These inequities not only strain Canada's health care system but also subvert those collective values that bind Canadians into a national community. Nowhere is this inconvenient truth more evident than with Aboriginal peoples who may well constitute Canada's least healthy population (Boyer 2014; McMahon 2014; Trovato and Romaniuk 2014; Sinha and Blumenthal 2014; Reading and Wien 2009). Health indicators continue to spiral downward—an appalling state of affairs for a country that trumpets its much-vaunted health care system as the cornerstone of national identity (Cooke and Long 2016; Cooke et al. 2014; Picard 2012; Nestel 2012). Aboriginal peoples live, on average, a decade less than other Canadians. They experience degenerative diseases such as heart problems at twice the rate of non-aboriginal persons, are twice as likely to have cancer, and are five times more likely to have diabetes. Parasitic and infectious diseases maintain a pernicious grip, including TB, the rate of which is 16 times higher than in the rest of Canada. Infant mortality rates are about three times higher than the national average, while aboriginal children are more likely to be born with severe birth defects and debilitating conditions such as fetal alcohol syndrome. Alcohol and substance abuse are widely regarded as the foremost problem on most reserves, with alcohol-related injuries from suicides to sexual violence accounting for up to 80 per cent of the fatalities on some reserves.

How can we account for these massive disparities in health between Aboriginal peoples and non-aboriginal Canadians? These dismal figures reflect a range of contributing factors, including poverty and powerlessness, that reflect the legacy and ongoing consequences of genocide and colonialism, both systemic and deliberate (Adelson 2005; Czyzewski 2011). The roots of aboriginal health disparities reflect government policies and programs that sometimes inadvertently (from loss of traditional food sources to the introduction of European diseases)—but often deliberately (from forced relocation to withholding food supplies)—sought to dislodge those aboriginal communities that stood in the way of Canada-building (Daschuk 2013). Improving health outcomes is contingent on eliminating those systemic barriers, from colonialist structures and legacies of genocide to institutional racism, that continue to distort Aboriginal people's health (Allan and Smylie 2015; Boyer 2014; Tang and Browne 2008; Czyzewski 2011; Nestel 2012). Any improvement to health disparities must acknowledge a multi-dimensional approach around a complex range of socio-historical factors, from forced relocation and coercive assimilation, to the loss of land, identity, and political voice (de Leeuw and Greenwood 2011; Adelson 2005; Dhamoon and Hankivsky 2011). Finally, improvements must acknowledge a conflict of interest: to one side, prevailing biomedical models of health and healing (based on the model of a passive patient who is prescribed treatment); to the other side, a more holistic aboriginal model of well-being with its focus on the whole person (emotional, mental, spiritual, physical), the individual's placement within family and the relationship to community (Adelson 2005), and the centrality of culture as it relates to land, tradition, and language (McGavock 2016). Failure to bridge this (mis)communication gap invariably generates a "talking past each other," as demonstrated by the decision of two aboriginal families to forego conventional chemotherapy and rely instead on traditional/naturalistic/less invasive remedies for their cancer-stricken children (Frketich 2015).

Socially determined health inequities are equally evident in the mainstream population (Meili 2012). For example, consider how poverty is killing Canadians prematurely (Town Hall Report 2013). A collaborative study entitled *Code Red*, by *The Hamilton Spectator* and McMaster University, found staggering disparities in the mortality of rates of Hamiltonians based on income and education (Buist 2010). Data sets from two neighbourhoods just kilometres apart concluded that life expectancy in the rich west-mountain neighbourhoods was 86.3 years (five years longer than Canadian average). By comparison, the figure for a poor north-end neighbourhood was 65 years—a gap of 21 years (Town Hall Report 2013)! Or put another way, if disaggregated and assessed independently, the poor Hamilton neighbourhood would rank 165th in the world for life expectancy, tying with Nepal but behind Mongolia and Turkmenistan. This figure is all the more shocking in a country with universal, publicly funded health care and a city with a major medical school and a top teaching hospital (Buist 2010). Studies have further cemented the link between socio-economic inequality and life expectancies in Montreal, where six years separated the overall life expectancy between all males from the wealthier parts of the city and those from poorer neighbourhoods (Denney et al. 2012).

A "wealth as health" nexus is unmistakable (Picard 2004; 2013; Abramson 2015). The top 20 per cent of income earners in Canada not only live on average about five years longer than the lowest 20 per cent. The rich are also healthier, and the health gap is growing between low- and high-income Canadians. A survey conducted by Ipsos Reid found that, among people with salaries in excess of $60,000, about 70 per cent reported their health as excellent or very good, compared to only 40 per cent of those who earned less than $30,000 (Town Hall Report 2013). A decade after a heart attack, twice as many low-income patients (below $30,000) die, unlike those in the $60,000 income bracket (35 per cent vs. 15 per cent), regardless of the level of health care (Picard 2013). Finally, those defined as working poor (earning wages that fall below the poverty line) in Ontario report having worse health indicators than those working but not poor (Block 2013).

These figures reinforce what many have cautioned (Wilkinson and Pickett 2010): societies with greater gaps in income between rich and poor show poorer health outcomes, especially for those at the bottom of the socio-economic ladder. Those with low incomes or living in poverty tend to have worse health and health-care outcomes, in part because of unequal health care access, lack of information, higher stress levels yet poorer coping skills, increased exposure to workplace risks because of precarious jobs, riskier lifestyle options, and low socio-economic status resulting in malnutrition or food scarcity (Raphael 2002). Evidence also demonstrates how socio-economic inequalities may exert an impact on the expression of genes and specific biological processes that, in turn, affect health outcomes (Wolfe, Evans, and Seeman 2012). In other words, poverty and health are inextricably linked. For example, 40 per cent of aboriginal children in urban areas live in poverty, a figure that resembles a Third World statistic at odds with a prosperous and progressive Canada. Or to put it another way, as Michael Kirby concluded in his Senate report on Health (2002), "if aboriginal people had the same health outcomes of the overall population, Canada would probably stand as the healthiest country in the world."

The conclusion is inescapable: health and health care must be situated within the broader context of Canadian society. Social factors define the determinants of good health above and beyond the parameters of health care access and timely treatment (Meili 2012). They include income and standard of living, social support networks, levels of education, employment and working conditions, a clean physical environment, safe neighbourhoods, lifestyle choices, socio-economic status, and levels of wealth and income distribution in society. Furthermore, the best way to improve health is to attack inequality at its roots by devoting resources to jobs, early childhood education, and affordable housing. Still, it is important not to isolate these contributing factors by treating them independently of each other. Health and health care are complex and multi-dimensional phenomena within social, spatial, and temporal contexts. An analytical framework must recognize the interplay of people's identities, their relationship to asymmetries of power, and patterns of interactions with others. The concept of intersectionality offers a framework for understanding and improving matters of health and health care, primarily by examining how race, gender, class (and other markers of identity or devaluation) intersect and interlock to amplify "unhealthiness" (Hankivsky 2011).

Deconstructing the *Inequality* in Social Inequality

The *inequality* in social inequality is no less an analytic puzzle. In general, inequality revolves around the notion of who gets what and why (differential access) and what goes where and how (differential distribution). Descriptive references to inequality merely assert the prevalence of disparities in the placement of individuals within a stratified society vis-à-vis the distribution of valued goods. More evaluative references acknowledge how inequality becomes a problem if the gaps are perceived as too extreme, illegally produced, mobility-stifling, deeply entrenched, arbitrarily defined, hardship-creating, and resistant to reform. A distinction between *gradual* and *categorical* inequalities is useful. Gradual inequalities consist of degrees of socio-economic disparities that theoretically do not constitute insurmountable barriers to social mobility and are justifiable in a free market system. By contrast, categorical inequalities reflect mechanisms of vertical differentiation that divide society into self-contained silos with little interaction, except, perhaps, in the marketplace (Schmidt 2013). Clearly then, not all inequalities between individuals or among groups are socially significant, a cause for concern, or worthy of sociological investigation. Rather, inequality becomes analytically interesting under five sets of circumstances, namely, when they are:

- socially constructed, a convention created by human interactivity rather than an inevitability both natural or inherent;
- patterned, persistent, and pervasive;
- arbitrary or unjustified;
- harmful to some demographic in society; and
- resistant to reform.

The concept of inequality also encompasses four dimensions: objective conditions, ideological supports, social power, and social reforms (Curtis and Tepperman, 2004).

Material/Objective

The *material dimension* refers to the expression of social inequality with respect to socially constructed variations in power, privilege, and resources (wealth/income). The Introduction to Chapter 1, "Surveying the Damage," provides examples of income-based inequalities. But the material also extends to deprivation of power. For example, despite Toronto's slogan, "Diversity, Our Strength," racialized minorities account for only 7 per cent of councillors in the 25 municipal regions comprising the Greater Toronto Area (GTA) (Omidvar and Tory 2012), even though nearly 50 per cent of greater Toronto's population consists of racialized minorities. A review of **diversity** on

Canadian corporate boards yields mixed results. According to Pamela Jeffrey of the Canadian Board Diversity Council (2014), women accounted for 17.1 per cent of board seats at the FP500 companies in 2012, up from 15.6 per cent in the previous year. But racialized minorities held only 2 per cent of board seats, down from 5.3 per cent in 2010—despite constituting nearly 20 per cent of Canada's population. Representation of Aboriginal peoples (just over 4 per cent of the population) remained at 0.8 percent, unchanged from 2010.

Or consider how Aboriginal peoples rank at or near the bottom of all socio-economic indicators, from income to health. Pikangikum, a fly-in reserve community of 2,400 people, situated 300 km northeast of Winnipeg, is dubbed the suicide capital of the world (Patriquin 2012). In 2011, Pikangikum's suicide rate was equivalent to 250 per 100,000 of population, or 20 times that of Canadians in general (based on a small sample that can inflate ratios). This figure is perhaps not surprising in a community where 80 per cent of homes have no running water or sewage outlet, only two students graduated from high school in 2011, and 3,600 lockups occurred in response to 5,000 calls for police services (Patriquin 2012). And despite a "dry" bylaw in force since 1986, a 26-oz bottle of rye whisky, which sells for about $25 at LCBO outlets, fetches upwards of $200 a bottle when bootlegged in Pikangikum (Patriquin 2012). Finally, Canada's prisons, like those in the US, are becoming increasing colour-coded (Sapers 2013b). Howard Sapers, Canada's Correctional Investigator (2016), concludes that, of the 14,624 federal prisoners serving sentences of two or more years, 25.4 per cent are aboriginal persons (who constitute just over 4 per cent of the population), including 48 per cent of federal inmates in the Prairie provinces. The numbers are even higher for aboriginal women: 36 per cent of women in prison are of aboriginal descent. Thirty years ago, just 10 per cent of federal inmates were aboriginal, clearly indicating a rapidly growing problem. To add injury to insult, those with prison records will have difficulty finding a job, making them vulnerable to recidivism and re-incarceration (Pager 2007). In short, Canadians should be worried if there is value to the late Nelson Mandela's admonition that "...no one really knows a nation until one has been inside its jails. A nation should not be judged by how it treats its highest citizens, but its lowest" (cited in Sapers 2013b:1).

Ideological Support

Patterns of material inequality are justified and secured by the ideas and ideals (**ideology**) situated in and expressed by formal laws, public policies, and dominant discourses (Grabb and Guppy 2009). Ideologies serve three functions: first, to conceal the social constructedness of inequality; second, to rationalize or justify the prevailing patterns of power and privilege; and third, to secure the dominant group's supremacy over the less fortunate. Those in positions of power and privilege have a vested interest in promoting the ideology of inequality as natural and normal, beneficial and fair. Consider those self-serving clichés (comforting fictions) that reflect a highly individualistic ideology for explaining away inconvenient truths. These polite fictions also distort people's perception of what is really going on by camouflaging the reality of uncomfortable truths (Grabb and Guppy 2009; Wotherspoon and Hansen 2013; also, for the United States, Iceland 2012):

- Canada is a classless society with everyone bunched into the middle.
- Hard work and initiative will deliver material success (the "American dream").
- People who are poor or failures have only themselves to blame.
- Individuals are judged and rewarded on the basis of merit only.
- Racism no longer exists as a problem of inequality in post-racial Canada.
- The feminist movement and equality guarantees have rendered sexism obsolete.
- Inequality is natural and normal, and there isn't much we can do about it.
- A free market eventually creates greater overall prosperity (the "trickle-down effect").
- Too much government spending and market regulation will damage the economy and jobs (Jackson 2015).
- People will accept inequality as long as it's acquired through fair competition.
- As a land of equal opportunity, Canada is an open and socially mobile society.

Ideologies also exist to co-opt non-dominant groups into co-operating with an unequal status quo. Reference to ideology as hegemony helps to explain the process by which the powerful can secure consensus and co-operation—not through coercion, but by consent—so that people's attitudes change without their awareness of what is happening. For example, the combination of technological changes and the emergence of a knowledge-based economy has yielded a profound ideological shift entitled neo-liberalism, which challenges the very notion of how social inequality is defined, rationalized, and expressed. Initially endorsed by Prime Minister Margaret Thatcher in the United Kingdom in 1979, then in the United States by President Ronald Reagan, and later in Canada by Prime Minister Stephen Harper, neo-liberalism reflects an ideological shift with a corresponding set of structural adjustments and far-reaching social implications. **Neo-liberalism** is an umbrella term that reflects a belief (ideology) and a set of principles (structural adjustments) about wealth creation and distribution based on the virtues of and commitment to more (unfettered) markets, less (smaller) government, hyper-individualism (a responsibilized and competitive self), and an inequality-is-good ethic. David Harvey (2005) defines neo-liberalism as:

> . . . a theory of political economic practices that proposes that human well-being can best be advanced by liberating individual entrepreneurial freedoms and skills within an institutional framework characterized by strong private property rights, free markets, and free trade.

Neo-liberalism as ideology can also be interpreted as a "governing rationality" (Brown 2015) through which everything becomes economized: humans become market actors; every field of activity (even non-wealth-producing domains such as learning or dating) is defined by market metrics; every entity from the public to the private is governed as a firm and on market terms and techniques; the meaning of democratic values is transformed from a political to an economic register; and people are cast as human capital who must pay for the use of services ("user pays"). A belief in market fundamentalism—in marketizing, commodifying, and consumerizing all aspects of society—is central to neo-liberalism; that is, the superiority of free-market enterprise and market competitiveness as a vehicle for economic efficiencies and societal growth (Standing 2012; Gutstein 2014). Moves to "recapitalize capital" along neo-liberal lines entail a series of structural adjustments founded on market-driven principles that justify deregulating investment rules for the advantage of economic elites, liberalizing trade in a so-called borderless world, suppressing organized labour (unions) in favour of corporate interests while promoting more flexible labour availability for the demands of a just-in-time economy, cutting taxes for the rich and corporations, implementing austerity measures that slash government and social services, promoting diversity as a commercial good, privatizing public services, and hollowing out the welfare state for fear that overgenerous payments could undermine the work ethic and generate social ills such as the demise of the nuclear family (Winlow and Hall 2013; Monbiot 2012a; Wallis et al. 2010; Shields 2003; Shantz and Macdonald 2013). The prescription for growing the economy calls for incentives for top performers, low taxes on capital and income, balanced budgets, low debt and inflation, and a light regulatory touch (cutting back on expensive social programs or restricting legal protections of low earners) to ensure a free-wheeling market works its trickle-down magic in stimulating economic growth (Ciuriak and Curtis 2013).

One of the major tenets of neo-liberalism is the idea that smaller government unfetters a free market. Neo-liberals attack the state (from bureaucracy to labour unions) as equivalent to centralized (Soviet Union-style) government whose planning and regulatory apparatus stifled productivity and competition and individualism. Preferred instead is an open marketplace in which investment, employment, and income should flow without undue interference to where it was most welcome (Standing 2012). References to nationalistic programs or industrial policies are rejected, as is the belief in government intervention through tariffs or subsidies to nurture the competitiveness of select industries. Economic efficiencies are thought

to flow from establishing fiscal austerity over government spending to reduce debt and stimulate a sluggish economy. Introduction of austerity measures reinforces the perception that individuals are morally autonomous entities who are responsible for their own security and who must invest in their future value as a life-long learning process (Brown 2015; Green and Kesselman 2006). They also are gratification-seeking and inherently competitive persons largely indifferent to acting collectively for the greater good and incapable of responding collectively to any existential crises (Klein 2014). The privatization of risk under neo-liberalism is inseparable from the marketization of the social and its elimination from the public domain in what amounts to a post-social world, one in which the structuring reality of public life and social institutions is displaced by a milieu of atomized and self-seeking individuals (Winlow and Hall 2013).

In short, the best a government can do under neo-liberalism is stand aside and let the market take care of itself—except to implement economic fundamentals such as debt reduction, enforce property rights, remove barriers to business, provide infrastructure for trade and commerce, create incentives for growing human capital, and secure a climate for investment. In reality, critics argue, neo-liberalism increasingly looks more like a rationale (or smokescreen) to advance corporate interests, especially when applying the principle of less government to themselves. The theory of state non-intervention was simply hijacked by the elites to fleece the system—bailing out the financial sector with billions of taxpayer dollars while gutting labour and environmental regulation (Harvey 2005). For example, corporate welfare is alive and well in Canada (Milke 2012; 2013b). Between 1982 and 2012, the federal department of industry spent $13.7 billion on subsidies to business, with 44.3 per cent disbursed without expectation of repayment. And yet the average Canadian corporate profit margin, 8.2 per cent in 2014, reached a 27-year high (Tal 2015b). In early January 2013, the Ontario and federal governments offered Japan's Toyota Motor Corporation up to $34 million to build a hybrid car in the Cambridge, Ontario, plant (and another $100 million grant in late July 2015 [Owram 2015])—bringing the total amount of bailout cash between 2003 and 2013 to various automotive companies to $17.2 billion courtesy of taxpayers (Milke 2014). Clearly then, a double standard exists that reinforces the perception of a system rigged to mask the power of moneyed interests to manipulate the market to their benefit (Reich 2015).

The impact of neo-liberalism's transformation of society is widely recognized (Lamont and Hall 2013; OECD 2014). Neo-liberalism may have limited effectiveness as an engine of economic growth; nevertheless, it has excelled in transferring vast amounts of wealth to dominant classes and restoring class fortunes to sectors threatened by the ascent of social democratic endeavours, in part by dismantling those institutions and narratives that promoted more egalitarian distribution patterns (Harvey 2007). The doctrine of neo-liberalism

asserts that both economies and societies operate most effectively when allocating resources along market lines without public input or government intervention (Lamont and Hall 2013; Vallas 2011). A neo-liberal commitment does not ask if a public policy initiative is good or just. Justification under neo-liberalism is based on whether an initiative improves economic competitiveness, spurs investment, or enhances present and future value, even at the expense of democratic principles (Brown 2015; Fallis 2013). But as the Occupy Wall Street movement demonstrated all too clearly, the act of excising the social from society because of this neo-liberal logic (from deregulation to marketization) tends to erode the very fabric that makes us social and human (also Winlow and Hall 2013)—as demonstrated below.

Spotlight Harperism as Neo-liberalism: Creating a More Unequal Canada

Did Stephen Harper attempt to reinvent Canada and make it more unequal and exclusionary by unleashing neo-liberal market forces, regardless of the social costs (Hurtig 2015)? Was the prime minister, in his resolve to reconstruct Canada as an energy superpower, undermining traditional Canadian values by gutting environmental regulation, fast-tracking dirty oil projects, targeting and vilifying any opposition to aggressive expansion, and slashing corporate taxes (Dickinson 2015)? For some, Harperism was reverting Canada back to its pre-World War Two status as a society of sharp class divisions, widespread economic hardship, and meagre social assistance programs (Gutstein 2014). According to a study of the 2015 budget by the Royal Bank, federal government revenues as a percentage of the GNP declined to 14.5 percent because of tax cuts, down from 18.4 percent in 1980–81, while federal program spending dropped to 13 per cent of the GNP compared to 16 per cent in 1990 (Axworthy 2015). Others believed this assessment was too simplistic (Ibbitson 2015). Yes, there was no denying Harper's

dream of transforming Canada into a resource-based economic power and ultra-conservative (far right) society, in part by radically restructuring existing social arrangements while incorporating unregulated market freedoms into the social and political domains. A populist ideology prevailed, one in which majority rule reigned over minority rights or provisions of the Charter of Rights and Freedoms (Brison 2015). Yet not all Canadians hopped aboard his neo-liberal social, political, and economic agenda (Adams 2015; Northrup and Jacobs 2014). Nor did Canadians automatically buy into the ruling government's pandering to people's dark side and their fears of the diverse and changing (Brison 2015). Strong support remained for continuing Canada's reputation as a social democratic society of decent, caring, and tolerant people, with a corresponding commitment to the principles of **multiculturalism** and immigration.

In his 2014 book on Harperism, Donald Gutstein argued that Harper's business-friendly world view was obsessed with promoting a neo-liberal, market-driven Canada at the expense of all

continued

other societal considerations, including a restriction of the social as space for human existence (Winlow and Hall 2013). This ideology represented a working blend of neo-liberalism and conservative socio-cultural values as famously espoused by Margaret Thatcher and Ronald Reagan, based on the principles of individualism, inequality, and competition, and a market philosophy that trumps all other priorities. A market displacement of the social (a "marketization of society") is hostile toward anything "social" that questions or criticizes the organizing logic of liberal capitalism. Such an outlook may explain the former prime minister's resistance to a national inquiry into murdered and missing aboriginal women, based on his insistence that there was nothing sociological about these crimes. Rather, he argued, they represented a series of isolated, family-based crimes by aboriginal men on reserves, crimes that were best addressed through law enforcement and police investigation (Singh 2014). In other words, Harper's market agenda was an assault on the social as the organizing logic of society (see also Winlow and Hall 2013). In advancing a no-holds-barred economy that ruthlessly sorts out winners from losers, regardless of the human costs, Harper tilted the system to accommodate pro-rich and anti-public measures, including lowering taxes (hence less revenue for social programs); imposing austerity moves by cutting back on assistance and promoting freer trade at the expense of national governments to protect local interests; removing any commitments or regulatory mechanisms that stood in the way of free-wheeling capitalism, such as environmental protection, labour unions, and collective bargaining protocols; eliminating any database (from scrapping the long-form census to muzzling government scientists) that could compromise a commodity-based economy; and

refashioning Canada's national identity along more militaristic lines, including remnants of its British colonial past such as the Crown, "royal" titles, and celebrating the War of 1812.

Harper's vision of Canada was a dangerously undemocratic one (Gutstein 2014). Canada is less democratic when power is marshalled into the government sector without much degree of accountability and transparency. But this marketization of Canada—at least in its totality—did not resonate with Canadians (Northrup and Jacobs 2014), most notably at the Supreme Court level, where a series of socially progressive rulings related to personal rights and freedoms, from same-sex marriage to physician assisted dying, were largely inconsistent with Harper's attempt to move Canada in a different direction (Tieleman 2015). His Commonwealth version of Canadian nationhood did not sit well with Canada's increasingly diverse population, robust immigration program, and commitment to multiculturalism. As well, younger Canadians (aged 35 and under) appeared to be more socially progressive than the positions espoused by Harper (and that of older Canadians too). According to a data set of 8,121 respondents (McGrane 2015), their left-of-centre attitudes endorsed a belief in activist government intervention in advancing social justice and social inclusion, a government willing to modify moral views in adjusting to changes in society, an attachment to national welfare programs such as health care and education, an abiding respect for human rights, environmental stewardship, peacekeeping and international collaboration, and scientific advancement. In light of these conflicting agendas and clashing world views, perhaps it is not surprising the Harper Government was voted out of office in October 2015 and replaced by a Liberal government that promised "sunnier ways" and a resumption of the social.

Social Power

Power is central to all systems of inequality and stratification (Olsen 2011; Lukes 2005). Put differently, inequality is about power (Schutz 2011). Differences in power relations not only generate

social inequalities by ensuring preferential access to valued resources along class lines (Porter 1965), they also justify these inequities through ideologies that protect and promote ruling class interests (Antony and Samuelson 2012). Thus, inequality is ultimately a function of power since the power-less may be unable to resist or reject, whereas the powerful can manipulate the system to establish agendas and eviscerate unwanted reforms (Hacker and Pierson 2010). Not surprisingly, contemporary Canadian sociologists have long addressed the primacy of power in understanding social inequality (Zawilski 2010; Grabb and Guppy 2009). Max Weber and Karl Marx also emphasized the centrality of power in generating unequal relations. For both, power as a valued resource was unevenly distributed across society, typically acquired through command over resources, wielded in a way that improved access and control over other valued good and resources, and manipulated to justify unequal dispersal of resources between groups. Their different views lay in defining the source of power and inequality: for Marx, power reflected class relations, whereas for Weber, the interlinkage of class/status/party was the basis for power. A third approach differs from both by framing power along more systemic lines.

Marx argued that power flowed from the ownership of productive property and resources (class), with a corresponding ideology as a form of social control. Inequality as power (and vice versa) arose from structural and systemic sources related to exploitation and class differences between the exploiter and the exploited. Patterns of inequality were then bolstered by ruling-class control over the state (including law and police) and its imposition of a capitalist ideology (ideas and ideals about what is desirable and acceptable reflect the values of the ruling class, yet evolve into common sense notions in society [hegemony]). For Marx, then, the essence of capitalism was neither physical nor financial. It was rooted in the power and authority of capital/capitalists to make decisions, especially in extracting surplus from workers (Galbraith 2014). In contrast to Marx, for whom power lay in ownership, Weber tended to frame power as the ability to command resources and people. He defined power along multi-dimensional lines pertaining to status (social position) and party (goal-oriented groups such as political parties) as well as to class (family background) as it pertains to market placement and life chances. Power itself was defined as

a person's ability to command resources and influence others' behaviour with or without their consent. Or to paraphrase Sherrow O. Pinder (2013:ix) who captured the Weberian notion of power as the ability to compel others even against their resistance, "power is despotic," since it positions marginalized "others" within and across multiple and overlapping lines of social stratification.

Post-structural notions of power have shifted the intellectual yardsticks. Reference to power is framed in systemic and situational terms. Instead of focusing on individuals (agency) or institutions (structure) who manipulate power as an instrument of coercion or domination (or what Lukes 2005 calls "power over"), power is defined as a capacity or ability to influence favourable outcomes (or "power to") through willing compliance to domination (**hegemony**) (also Swartz 2007). For Michel Foucault (1991; 1998), power is not necessarily something possessed by sovereigns or located in law or emanating outward from a hierarchical centre. Rather it constitutes a set of capacities, discourses, expert knowledge, or network of relationships that are pervasive and dispersed throughout society (Foucault 1980; Dhamoon 2009). Power is everywhere yet nowhere insofar as it is diffused (rather than concentrated); fragmented and contradictory (rather than monolithic); discursive (rather than coercive); subjective and objective, as individuals are both subject to rules and yet active agents (subjects) in enforcing them; and implicated (rather than possessed) in symbols, representations, arrangements and allocations. The intimate connection between (expert) knowledge and power is not wielded in the conventional (Weberian) sense of control or domination; rather, people discipline themselves (and others) without any willful external coercion because of internalized yet shared values, beliefs, and norms to judge, compare, criticize, and comply (see Spotlight on micro-aggression in Chapter 3). Nor should references to power be framed exclusively as negative or coercive. Power can be reframed instead as a social dynamic in constructing tacitly assumed "truths" about what is normal, desirable or acceptable—in the main by rewarding or rejecting others on the basis of the others' proximity to the norm. In other words, as demonstrated below, power is expressed through the process of normalization, since the "normal" is, as Bourdieu asserts, a form of social regulation and cultural obligation that quietly infuses everyday practices at institutional and individual levels (Brock, Raby, and Thomas 2012; Swartz 2007).

The Language of Media Representations: Framing as Power

Mainstream news media have long been accused of doing a disservice to "migrants," "peoples," and "minorities" (Hall 1997; Mahtani 2002; Henry and Tator 2002; Larrazet and Rigoni 2014). **Representations** are known to underrepresent Aboriginal peoples, racialized minorities, and immigrant and asylum seekers in areas that "count" (success) but overrepresent in areas that "don't count" (failure), with a range of *mis*representations (flaws) in between (Fleras 2011a; Journalists for Human Rights 2013). Pressure to improve coverage, notwithstanding, migrants, minorities, and peoples continue to be negatively **framed** as invisible, problem people, stereotypes, whitewashed, ornamental, and the "other" (Fleras and Kunz 2001). By contrast, so-called whitestream identities, experiences, and interests are positively framed as a tacitly assumed universal benchmark that normalizes as it privileges (Aleman 2014). Efforts to explain these misrepresentational tropes have varied: to one side are prejudicial attitudes, implicit biases, and discriminatory practices; to the other side are institutional routines, workplace practices, and commercial imperatives related to audience ratings and advertising revenues; to yet another side are those systemic biases whose one-sidedness perpetuates an exclusionary effect. Of particular sociological salience are those explanations that frame news media as Eurocentric discourses in defence of dominant ideology. This explanation effectively exposes the representational biases of migrants/minorities/peoples as racialized rather than racist, structural rather than attitudinal, institutional rather than individual, patterned rather than random, and systemic (normalized) rather than deliberate (systematic).

To be sure, changes are discernible (Lehrman 2014). An exclusive diet of monocultural representation frames is gradually giving way to mediated images more reflective of, respectful of, and responsive to diversity and differences (Fleras 2011a). More nuanced discourses are increasingly rejecting the one-dimensional caricatures of the past (Alsultany 2012), if only to avoid being branded as racists or reactionary (McGowan 2001). Mainstream media in Canada are loathe to openly criticize migrants or government minority policy for fear of disturbing a national consensus or inciting a frosty consumer reaction. They also take pains to avoid explicitly vilifying immigrants by stripping from stories unnecessary references to race or religion (race-tagging) or, alternatively, emphasizing the loyalty and law-abidingness of most new Canadians (Silk 2008). Yet negativity persists, albeit in a more oblique manner. For example, minorities, peoples and migrants are rarely criticized on the basis of physical inferiority (race). A categorical dislike is replaced by a situational antipathy predicated on the premise of migrants/minorities/peoples as culturally incompatible or socially deviant (Pottie-Sherman and Wilkes 2014). Migrants, peoples, and minorities are inferiorized by association with *negative news contexts*, including moral panics related to crime, public disorder, and deviance; so-called reverse discrimination against whites; religious fundamentalism; home country troubles; and security or medical risks (Cottle 2005). This tainted-by-association frame tends to essentialize (homogenize) all group members, despite the complexity of their lived realities (Fleras 2014a).

Widespread criticism and advocacy notwithstanding, news media appear incapable of improving the quality of minority representations—either they don't know how or they don't care (Clark 2014; Journalists for Human Rights 2013). News media continue to process information by utilizing a whiteframe that whitewashes race, ethnicity, and aboriginality without openly denigrating diversity and differences (Race Forward 2014). A racialized whiteframe frames whiteness as culturally superior in achievement compared to racialized non-whiteness; insinuates white-dominated institutions and white privilege as unremarkable; perpetuates stereotypes by essentializing the lived realities of minorities; and endorses the principle of diversity as long as it doesn't cost or inconvenience, in the process confirming a mainstream right to define what counts as differences, and what differences count (Feagin 2010). Not surprisingly, media decision-makers and gatekeepers may not be consciously biased towards the "other" in accord with the sedimented nature of **systemic whiteness**. Seemingly race-neutral representations that appear to treat everyone the same may be deeply racialized when whites and non-whites alike are shoe-horned into Eurocentric language and imagery, consistently whitewashed ideals, and normative expectations (see Goodyear-Grant 2013). Relying on white Eurocentrism as the universal norm by which to compare, judge, and evaluate tends to frame migrants/minorities/peoples as beings both novel and foreign ("fish-out-of-water stories") as well as inferior or irrelevant, rather than normal and equal. Who then can be surprised when whites and non-whites relate differently to mainstream media? Whites see themselves painted into the media picture as normal or exceptional, whereas visible minorities find themselves racialized and excluded by discursive frames that prejudge without the prejudice.

Even a news media commitment to diversity and inclusion is thought to perpetuate a pro-whiteness as the tacitly assumed norm; after all, framing race, ethnicity, and aboriginality in the language of the whitestream—even with the best intentions—tends to discipline diversities and whitewash diversity. The discursive frames that follow reflect a white-frame reading of reality in which systemic whiteness distorts or denies the experiences and realities of those on the "wrong" side of the racialized divide:

- Blaming the victim: a belief that every individual in a meritocratic society can make it if they work hard, play by the rules, take advantage of opportunities, and assume personal responsibility. This frame makes invisible the structural barriers that confront racialized minorities who must achieve success in a system designed neither to reflect

their realities nor advance their interests (Gemi, Ulasiuk, and Triandafyllidou 2013);
- Individualizing racism: racism as personal prejudice or as randomly isolated rather than routinized as power that is systemically embedded in structure and institutionalized;
- An a-historical perspective: dismissing cumulative inequalities or the persistence of colonialism as an ongoing project on the grounds the past is the past and it is time to move on (Race Forward 2014);
- De-contextualizing reality: framing newsworthiness as episodic and sensationalistic, rather than thematic and situational. This frame reinforces victim-blaming while ignoring root causes (Race Forward 2014);
- Problematizing deep diversity: the primacy of liberal universalism (our commonalities as freewheeling individuals supersede the differences between groups) as the basis for entitlement and recognition (Fleras 2012). This inability to frame diversity and differences except as superficial or abnormal or as conflict or carnival is consequential. It undermines the interests of those migrants/minorities/peoples who want their differences (from religion to race) to be taken seriously.
- A post-racial Canada: this frame criticizes those who insist on playing the "racism card" in a supposedly race-blind society where neither race nor racism allegedly matter in defining who gets what (see Race Forward 2014; Bonilla-Silva 2006);
- White normativity as universal standard: this frame pounces on any minority belief or practice at odds with core values related to freedom, democracy, reason, and tolerance. Minorities are judged on the basis of their commitment and conformity to the whitestream or, alternatively, on whether their creativity and achievement are aligned along dominant lines (Spoonley and Butcher 2009).

In short, mediated images approvingly endorse "good" (model) immigrants who fit the image of the white ideal, are thought to embrace capitalist and liberal values, and establish productive families that contribute to growing the economy. After all, model minorities legitimize myths and virtues of meritocracy, in effect "superiorizing" the virtues of white tolerance and a universal Eurocentrism (DeVega 2014). By contrast, "bad" minorities are framed as "troublesome constituents" who pose security risks; steal jobs from "real" Canadians; destabilize the labour market; cheat on the welfare system; clog up resource-starved social, medical, and municipal services; create congestion and crowding; compromise Canada's highly touted quality of life; take advantage of educational opportunities without making a corresponding commitment to Canada; engage in illegal activities such as drugs or smuggling; and imperil Canada's national unity by refusing to conform or participate (Chan 2014). Their labelling as *problem people* is compounded by a fixation on illegal entries via queue-jumping or human smuggling rings; anxieties over security; anger over the cost of processing and settlement; and resentment over those asylum seekers who self-select themselves for entry into Canada on the basis of *their* needs instead of Canadian priorities (Hier and Greenberg 2002; Bauder 2008). Their unannounced and sometimes massed arrival poses an unforgiveable slight in compromising Canada's sovereign right to determine who to admit and how many (Simmons 2010; Wilkes, Corrigall-Brown, and Ricard 2010).

The paradox is unmistakable: *a commitment to more inclusive media representations of migrants/minorities/peoples may ironically perpetuate the exclusionary discourse when mediated images of race, ethnicity, and aboriginality are coded (framed) in the language of white Eurocentrism as the preferred norm.* To be sure, the language of *representation as power* is lost on those who reduce language to the level of a postal system, namely, a relatively neutral system of conveyance between sender and receiver for the transmission of messages independently created through a process called *thinking.* Nothing could be further from the truth: language (or speech) is intimately bound up with people's experiences of the world, together

with efforts to convey that experience to others. It is neither neutral nor value-free nor a passive or mechanical transmitter of information. Language as a socially constructed convention is *loaded* with values and priorities that encourage a preferred reading of reality, while dismissing other renditions as inconsequential or incompatible. Clearly, there is much of value in acknowledging language as a powerful force of reference for defining what is desirable and acceptable, normal and important. But as Bourdieu (1991) might say, the power implicit within the context of language is not about words that hurt. More importantly, it is about *the hidden patterns of power relations that are reflected, reinforced, and advanced through the use of language in everyday discourses and practices.* That alone makes doubly important the awareness of language as a regime of power and control in defense of dominant ideology.

Power then is a complex and contentious concept that defies simple definition or any list of attributes (Olsen 2011). Many like to think of power as the capacity of A to get B to do something that B otherwise would not do. This largely Weberian approach characterizes power as something systematic: possessed by individuals or actors; intentionally and visibly exercised; manifested in open competition or conflicts; and directly observable through interaction. But such a conceptualization is too narrow because it ignores the logic behind systemic power. Systemic power refers to the powers embedded in the structures of a complex system, with corresponding control over resources and production (economic power), control over ideas and ideals (ideological power), and control over decision-making (political power). A neo-Marxist/Foucauldian orientation contends that power in its ability to influence outcomes is disciplinary because:

- it is deeply embedded in the founding assumptions and foundational principles of a society's constitutional order, the structure of social institutions, and ideological values;
- it may exert unintended rather than deliberate effects that reflect the normal functioning of the system;

- it focuses on the minds of the subjects through dominant discourses (for example, media) that divert attention from points of conflict yet sustain discriminatory social structures and unequal social relations (Brunon-Ernst 2012; Henry and Tator 2002); and
- it may assume a latent form rather than a visibly manifested form when setting rules, shaping the parameters of debate and defining situations and options in self-serving ways (Grabb 2007). This systemic approach reinforces the cliché that power is most powerful when least visible and most imprecise (Pinder 2013:ix).

Social Reforms

Social reforms contain both formal and informal strategies for challenging inequality through government initiatives, ideological shifts, minority protest, and institutional reform. (State-intervention policies such as employment equity will be examined in Chapter 12 of this book, whereas issues of institutional reform are addressed in Part III). Moves to bring about equality may also be expressed through the proliferation of organized resistance, counter ideologies, and protest groups involving the historically disadvantaged—women, racial minorities, gays and lesbians, people with disabilities, and the poor and the homeless. These counter ideologies often assume the form of social movements that challenge the status quo.

The concept of **social movements** has long been a staple of sociological study (Carroll 1997; Smith 2007). This is hardly surprising since Canada (and the US) are renowned for their many social movements, ranging in scope from the 1960s civil rights, environmental, human rights, and feminist movements, to the AIDS and breast cancer advocacy groups of the 1980s, to the identity politics of gays and lesbians in the 1990s, to the recent rise of disability and quality-of-life movements as markers for the early 2000s (Clement 2009). Such diversity may be a healthy sign. Yet such popularity hampers the creation of a coherent body of thought for theorizing the nature of social movements. The prospect of conceptualizing social movements may appear daunting, especially when the phenomena span everything from well-financed international organizations such as Greenpeace to the spontaneity of street activists such as the Occupy Movements of 2011. Nevertheless, social movements can be defined as a collective effort by aggrieved individuals who initiate (or resist) social change through actions that fall outside institutional frameworks or conventional political channels. Such movements arise when individuals become disenchanted with disreputable aspects of society and experience a corresponding willingness to do something constructive about their disenchantment. Involvement comes about not only because people know something is wrong and they are willing to do something about it. People must also be mobilized into action groups under recognizable leadership in pursuit of shared goals. A focus on claims-making activities aligns the concept of social movements with a sociological perspective (Spector and Kitsuse 1977).

Social movements vary in scope, organization, and style (Smith 2007). Some are concerned with partial change (reform), others with a complete overhaul (revolution), still others with reversing current trends by reasserting conventional values or traditional structures (reaction). "Older" social movements often focused on labour issues; by contrast, "new" social movements invoke the politics of identity or community renewal in light of rampant urbanism, overwhelming globalization, innovations in telecommunications and technology, and the tide of modernization. Tactics and strategies may also vary. Certain social movements advocate peaceful change (conventional channels and behind-the-scenes negotiations); others involve civil disobedience or flamboyant, media-catching actions. Still others endorse violence as the preferred course of action for achieving visionary goals. Finally, most social movements combine a variety of organizational forms and spaces, from the local to the international, often co-operating with other groups when strategically useful to do so (Smith 2007). The multi-dimensional dynamics of social movements are captured in a Spotlight box that deconstructs the logic behind the Idle No More movement along different vantage points.

Spotlight IDYLL no More/Idle No More: Unsettling the Governance of the Canada–Aboriginal Peoples Relationship

The Occupy Wall Street Movement made it abundantly clear: a relatively small number of media-savvy folk possess the power not only to mobilize the masses into action but also to galvanize public awareness of social injustices. A similar logic applies to the Idle No More movement that originated in late 2012, then accelerated into prominence in 2013 (but see Barker 2012). A pan-aboriginal grassroots movement was ignited that, unlike more localized struggles with definable leadership, reflected a nationwide constituency whose concerns generated a critical mass of energy that capitalized on the revolution of rising expectations, especially among aboriginal youth and women (Kino-nda-niimi Collective 2014). Beyond a general frustration with the status quo (Coates 2013), a shifting package of demands and diffuse grievances prevailed over a clearly articulated policy framework. The mainstream media and political pundits might have lamented the dearth of consensus as problematic (it complicates the challenge of determining who speaks for Aboriginal Canadians); however, the diversity of aboriginal voice—both young and female, thanks to the movement's fluidity in content and organization—could just as easily be interpreted as a healthy sign of a deep democracy from below (Kino-nda-niimi Collective 2014). If nothing else, the Idle No More movement drew attention to the complexities and contradictions that infuse aboriginal issues and the fault lines that complicate politics of aboriginality (Wotherspoon and Hansen 2013). And like the Occupy Wall Street movement, Idle No More was hash-tagged by social media, in the process bypassing the corporate media as the primary source of representation and dissemination (Simpson 2013; Coates 2015a).

Idle No More originated in Saskatchewan when four Aboriginal women challenged the federal government's omnibus budget bill that bundled together a large number of changes, including reduced environmental protection for waterways across traditional lands. The proposed Omnibus Bill C-45 dismantled a 130-year-old environmental statute by removing federal oversight of over 99 per cent of Canada's 32,000 major lakes and 2.25 million rivers. Bill C-45 also made changes to the Indian Act to streamline the leasing of federally protected reserve lands to resource-hungry development companies without community consent or majority support, thus empowering the minister in charge of aboriginal affairs (an agent of the federal government) to circumvent community opposition to leasing land without adequate safeguards (Douglas and Lenon 2014). Passage of a bill in December (the Jobs and Growth Act 2012) that proposed legislative changes to ramp up federal plans for gas and oil extraction on reserve land by bypassing aboriginal rights did little to quell the outrage. The Idle No More movement was fueled by anger over the perception that Stephen Harper's government was a dismissive and assimilationist colonial power (Palmater 2014). In an effort to encourage solidarity, activism, and education, Idle No More coalesced around several broad motivations or objectives (Kino-nda-niimi Collective 2014; Coates 2015), most notably, a rejection of the colonial state that suppressed Indigenous peoples' rights, while insisting on a nation-to-nation partnership anchored in the spirit and intent of treaties (i.e., including control over traditional territories and sharing of resources). The movement eventually gravitated to more specific concerns: the squalid state of many aboriginal communities, government intransigence toward fulfilling treaty agreements, legislative erosion of aboriginal rights, and demands for more equitable sharing of resource development proceeds across traditional aboriginal lands. But the most recurrent theme focused on the principle of repairing a broken relationship—changing from one rooted in a colonial mentality of co-optation and control to that of a post-colonial model for living together differently as power-sharing partners (Kino-nda-niimi Collective 2014; Smith and Campion-Smith 2013).

It is too early to gauge the success, consequences, and implications of the Idle No More movement. Despite its profile and persistence, the movement does not appear to have gained much traction with the Canadian population. An Ipsos Reid poll in mid-January 2013 indicated that most Canadians reject the legitimacy of Idle No More, agreeing in principle with the grievances raised but objecting to the means used (from blockades to traffic disruptions) to resolve the issues. But another perspective is helpful as well. As perhaps the largest and most important outpouring of grassroots aboriginal anger since the late 1960s (Dobbin 2013b), the cumulative impact of Idle No More promises to be transformative (Coates 2015; Wotherspoon and Hansen 2013) in curbing corporate Canada's headlong rush to extract natural resources without appropriate pause for long-term consequences. Pam Palmater (2013) put it aptly in defending the benefit of Idle No More for Canada, especially in protecting Canadians from Harper's destructive environmental agenda: "Canadians need to realize that we are their last best hope at saving the lands, waters, plants, animals and resources for future generations because our Aboriginal and treaty rights are constitutionally protected" (cited in Rebick 2013b). Finally, the Idle No More movement shares much in common with the civil rights and feminist movements that were also ridiculed or dismissed by mainstream media and politicians as idealistic and misguided (see Killian 2013; Rebick 2013b). In the end they ushered in fundamental changes by linking the personal with the socio-political, while empowering the once powerless to challenge, resist, and change. To be sure, there are differences between these movements. The more recent are deeply anarchistic—that is, driven by grassroots democracy from below (anarchy). They also are propelled by the historically disenfranchised—young people and aboriginal women—who increasingly dismiss both mainstream politics (Kurlantzick 2012) and traditional leadership (such as the AFN) as being co-opted and too establishment-friendly (Kino-nda-niimi Collective 2014; Dobbin 2013b). The lesson is clear: as Franz Fanon recognized many years ago, colonization and oppression work best when the colonized have internalized a sense of helplessness and inferiority. Shatter that ideology, it is argued, and people will no longer sit by idly.

Summary

1. References to the concept of social inequality are not self-explanatory but must be problematized.
2. Inequality can be defined in terms of who gets what (differential access) and what goes where (differential distribution).
3. The concept of social inequality can be deconstructed by unpacking its constituent components, *social* and *inequality*.
4. The importance of framing social inequality as social exclusions pertaining to powerlessness, disengagement from society, and inability to positively contribute should be reinforced.
5. Sociology is a distinctive lens for studying the inequalities of exclusion, the roots of which reflect the social and the structural.
6. Four key dimensions are associated with the concept of inequality: the material, ideology, power, and reform through social movements.
7. The ideology of neo-liberalism remakes Canada along more exclusionary lines.

8. The systemic nature of power is demonstrated in the ability of media communication to construct distorted images (representations) of class and class relations that reinforce patterns of inequality.

9. The Idle No More movement promoted the idea that aboriginality matters in reconstructing a new post-colonial relationship between Canada and Aboriginal peoples.

Review Questions

1. Explain why references to the *social* and *inequality* continue to pose challenges in analyzing social inequality.
2. Explain what sociology as a discipline can bring to the study of social inequality.
3. This chapter argues that the concept of social inequality should be seen within the context of social exclusions. Explain why reference to the *inequalities of exclusion* provides a more sociological and comprehensive approach to the study of social inequality.
4. Discuss why the determinants of health outcomes and access to health care are largely social phenomena and amenable to analysis by sociology.
5. Explain what is meant by *neo-liberalism*. How do the principles of neo-liberalism create the potential to intensify the inequalities of exclusion?

3 Framing Inequality Sociologically

Learning Objectives

1. To show how philosophical insights into the human condition serve as prototypes for a sociological study of social inequality.

2. To point out how debates over social inequality are informed by three blaming paradigms each of which generally aligns with sociological models of society.

3. To appreciate how functionalism, symbolic interactionism, and radical conflict theories of society encapsulate different approaches to social inequality.

4. To illustrate how the concept of social inequality as structural exclusions is reflected in Kanter's landmark study on gendered corporations.

5. To demonstrate how the concept of micro-aggression as "Racism 3.0" provides insights into a symbolic interactionist approach to social inequality.

Introduction: What's the Cause? Where's the Source? Who's to Blame?

Man is born free, and he is everywhere in chains. — Jean-Jacques Rousseau

And the life of man, solitary, poor, nasty, brutish and short. — Thomas Hobbes

No man's knowledge here can go beyond his experience. — John Locke

The above insights into the human condition strike at the core of debates over social equality. A lack of gender inclusiveness notwithstanding, Rousseau's indictment of the human condition captures the ambiguity inherent in society as a moral community. For Rousseau, society had betrayed "man's" natural liberty, equality, and "fraternity." The societal forces of domination and exploitation had subverted "his" innate goodness by transforming "him" into an oppressed being. The legacy of Rousseau persists in Marxist interpretations of inequality as an aberration from human "nature." But not everyone concurred with Rousseau's observations. The previous century saw the English philosopher Thomas Hobbes conclude differently when he challenged the essence of human nature. For Hobbes, "man's" natural inclination to maximize self-interest put a premium on imposing constraints if only to neutralize people's acquisitive and self-serving impulses. Unfettered individualism had to be curtailed for the safety and survival of the collective whole; accordingly, society represented a collective agreement (social contract) to protect individuals from the predations of others. Finally, John Locke, another seventeenth-century philosopher, disagreed with both Rousseau and Hobbes (although he came somewhat closer to Rousseau's position). Locke argued that humans were neither innately good nor inherently evil; they just were. People were born as blank slates (tabula rasa), with the result that their thoughts and actions reflected their realities, experiences, and engagement with the world at large.

The significance of these proto-sociological observations should be clear by now. If Rousseau was right, then the inequality and the chains that historically have shackled women and men represent a societal artifice perpetuated by vested interests for self-serving reasons. If Hobbes is correct and individuals are willing to sacrifice some of their natural liberty to a sovereign state (Leviathan) to control anti-social behaviour, then inequality and stratification are an inevitable counterpoint to a dystopian human coexistence. If Locke is right, social inequality is neither an imposition nor a necessity but a human accomplishment (or convention) created through socially constructed activity. For those of a Hobbesian persuasion (including **functionalists**), inequality per se is not a problem. Inequality becomes a problem when it is enduring and permanent; unfairly acquired; based on irrelevant criteria such as skin colour rather than on merit; rooted in the exploitation of others; entrenched in the institutional structures of society; and seemingly impervious to reform. For the Rousseauians and **conflict/Marxist/feminist** theorists, extremes in inequality are endemic only in those societies organized around the unholy troika of private property, class relations, and profit-making. Conflict and instability are inevitable in a highly competitive class-based system as each group struggles to preserve or enhance its privilege, power, or wealth. Rationalizations that justify these gaps as necessary or inevitable are dismissed as ideological ploys (false consciousness) that cushion the blows of inequality and exploitation. For Locke and symbolic interactionists, social inequality is neither inherently natural or normal nor intrinsically good or evil—it just is, as a social construct created through a jointly linked process of intersubjective activity.

To assist in responding to these optics and oppositions, three explanatory models of social inequality are employed—*blaming the individual*

(victim); *blaming the system*; and *blaming the situation*. Blaming-the-victim models that classify the individual as the problem are generally consistent with Hobbesian world views. By contrast, a Rousseauian world view endorses a blaming-the-system model by castigating the structures of society, its values and institutions. A Lockean perspective pins the blame on those situations (or contexts) and patterns of meaningful interaction that socially construct conventions known as social inequality. Sociological models of society also align (more or less) with the observations of Rousseau, Hobbes, and Locke. Functionalism conforms to a blaming-the-victim (Hobbes) model; radical conflict models such as Marxism, feminism, and structuralism endorse a blaming-the-system (Rousseau) approach; and symbolic interactionism dovetails with a blame-the-situation approach (Locke). The introduction of symbolic interactionism as an explanatory framework provides an intermediate position that balances both agency (victim) and structure (system), in large part by situating people's lived experiences within an interactional context. A blaming-the-situation framework acknowledges that inequality is not inherent to reality; rather it is socially constructed through negotiated engagement and interpretative practices, relative to time and place, and best understood by tapping into how social actors define situations and act upon these definitions. Table 3.1 constructs a matrix that links inequality explanatory frameworks with sociological models of society.

This chapter addresses how sociology offers an insightful lens for analyzing the how and why behind social inequality. It examines those competing explanatory frameworks that approximate the perspectives on the human condition espoused by Hobbes, Rousseau, and Locke—that is, systemic (blame the system) models, individualistic (blame the individual) models, and situational (blame the context) models. These explanatory frameworks are then aligned with the three major sociological models of society, namely, functionalism, radical conflict, and symbolic interactionism. The chapter also provides a sociologically inspired analysis of social inequality by demonstrating how structural exclusions negatively impact both

Table 3.1: Explanatory Frameworks, Sociological Models

	Blame the Individual (or Victim)	Blame the System	Blame the Situation
Sociological models of society	Functionalism	Radical conflict	Symbolic interactionism
Approaches consistent with sociological models	Biological Psychological Anthropological (cultural)	Marxist Feminist Structural	
Philosophical underpinnings on the human condition	Hobbes	Rousseau	Locke

organizational behaviour and corporate entitlements along gender lines. It concludes by looking at how the concept of micro-aggression as Racism 3.0 represents a shift in how we think about racism, consistent with the principles of symbolic interactionism.

Blame-the-Individual/ Victim Model

A blaming-the-individual/victim model identifies individual failure as the prime cause of social inequality, with retraining or removal as the cure. Individuals who lack human capital (skills) or cultural capital (values) are responsible for social inequality because they lack skills or possess attributes that contribute to their marginalization or oppression. This view is hardly surprising in a culture whose dominant ideology believes success is proportional to individual effort, with the result that patterns of inequality are perceived as inevitable and fair (Gandy Jr. and Baron 1998). For example, London mayor Boris Johnson (2013) provoked controversy when he argued that economic inequalities reflected how some individuals are smarter (the top "cornflakes") than others. The poor are to blame for their poverty because of their psychological dispositions, cultural deprivation, faulty socialization, moral shortcomings, or circumstances of their own making (see Royce 2015 for debates). A

blaming-the-individual approach is closely aligned with a blaming-the-other approach: social inequalities are attributed to some non-mainstream group. Immigrants, for example, may be blamed (scapegoated) for taking jobs from ordinary Canadians and adding to this country's unemployment woes. But such labelling detracts from the possibility of looking at the broader picture of power, profit, and privilege as a primary problem source. Solutions to the blaming-the-victim inequality problem involve changing the person (behaviour modification) rather than addressing the broader context. This victim-blaming framework that views individuals as being primarily responsible for social inequality aligns it with the principles of functionalism (and neo-liberalism) as an explanatory framework (see Chapter 5, The Politics of Poverty, for more analysis).

Functionalism

Functionalist models portray society as the metaphorical equivalent of a biological organism. That is, like a non-human organism, society can be interpreted as an integrated system of interrelated and interdependent parts, each of which contributes to the "needs" of the organism, even if superficially they do not appear to do so. With respect to society, all of these components (such as institutions, values, and practices) are properly understood in terms of their contributions to survival and stability.

By definition then, if inequality exists in society, it must be functional, making a positive contribution that solves some societal need or problem. Or as London Mayor Boris Johnson (2013) contended at a Margaret Thatcher lecture series:

> I don't believe economic equality is possible: indeed, some measure of inequality is essential for the spirit of envy and keeping up with the Joneses that is, like greed, a valuable spur to economic activity.

For functionalists then, inequality is integral to a complex and productive society (although too much inequality can prove exploitative or dysfunctional). All societies must devise some method (incentives) for motivating the best individuals to occupy the most important and difficult positions. A sophisticated division of labour in an urban, post-industrial society demands a high level of skill and training. A hierarchy of rewards entices skilled individuals to compete for positions in short supply. Differences in the rates of reward are rationalized as the solution to this problem. Skilled personnel are attracted to key positions if adequate levels of compensation provide an incentive for recruitment. Failure to provide incentives dilutes or disperses the pool of talent, with disastrous consequences for society as a whole. Reward structures under this model are supported by the "law" of supply and demand. Premier hockey players such as Sidney Crosby or P.K. Subban are remunerated more generously than unskilled labourers not because hockey players are more important to society but because, compared to demand, crowd-pleasing pucksters (unlike manual labourers) are in short supply. Their value is further enhanced since they possess a talent for directly generating more revenue for team owners, either by putting more spectators in seats or by moving merchandizing. A similar line of reasoning (supply and demand) applies to different occupations and incomes. Physicians are compensated more for their services than are childcare workers, even though, arguably, both are socially important for society's survival.

A functionalist perspective interprets inequality as normal and necessary: necessary, because of the need to fill critical positions in society with skilled but scarce personnel; normal, because a sorting-out process reflects and reinforces a complex division of labour—that is, unequal rewards stimulate economic productivity by making people work harder and smarter (Noah 2012). Inequality is condoned when the rules of the game are applied fairly and according to market principles. In an open and democratic society, people will invariably re-distribute themselves unequally, provided the competition isn't rigged, but based on merit and open competition. Inequality is healthy in properly functioning and complex societies, especially if it encourages competition and achievement, although extremes must be held in check to foster stability and co-operation. That some individuals suffer more than others in an open competition is unfortunate, even regrettable, but pivotal in maximizing outputs.

In other words, inequality is not a problem per se as long as the system is allowed unfettered play (equal opportunity), people play by the rules, and those who can't compete are cared for through safety nets. This orientation is consistent with the neo-liberal principles of more market, less government, greater individual responsibility, and an inequality-is-good mantra. Admittedly, a minimum degree of government intervention may be required to ensure everyone has a "fair go," including special assistance for those incapable of competing for reasons beyond their control (Johnson 2013). Imperfections in the system, such as unfair trading practices or monopolies, may interfere with the proper functioning of the system, putting pressure on governments to curb these market impediments. But such interventions should be kept to a minimum. Excessive interference not only rewards dullness and encourages apathy, while stifling the creativity and initiative necessary for progress and prosperity, but also runs the risk of distorting free market dynamics.

Functionalism-Friendly Approaches

A blame-the-victim approach to social inequality yields additional perspectives consistent with functionalist principles. These perspectives—biological, psychological, and anthropological—differ in terms of specific argument. Nevertheless, they seem to share a number of common beliefs, namely, society is basically good, inequalities are rooted in individuals, and reforms must focus on changing individuals rather than modifying an ostensibly sound social system.

Biology

Some prefer to blame social inequalities on inherited genetic characteristics (Sayenga 2014). Those who subscribe to the theory of biological determinism portray certain groups as genetically and intellectually inferior. The invoking of evolutionary principles argues that certain individuals are better adapted for success in the competitive struggle for survival (Herrnstein and Murray 1994; Rushton 2004). Individuals of "superior stock" will prevail and succeed, in keeping with the so-called Darwinian doctrine of struggle for survival—"survival of the fittest." Similar positions attribute inequality to genetic difference (Raine 2013). For example, Leonard Sax (2006) argues that gender matters because sex differences are real, biologically programmed, and play a significant role in how men and women think and act.

Psychology

Others believe the origin of inequality taps into the human psyche. To one side are those evolutionary psychologists who posit that inequality is an instinctual adaptation to the challenges of survival and perpetuation of the group. Another side identifies those psychological attributes people acquire—or don't—as they mature. For various reasons, some individuals do not develop "normally"; instead, they internalize a host of attitudes contrary to commonly accepted definitions of success. This thinking blames the victims of poverty and discrimination for their plight. Under this approach, victims are blamed for (i.e., they cause) their predicament because of poor moral fibre or personality flaws for which they alone are responsible. The proposed solution is consistent with this assessment: with hard work and dedication to the task at hand, anyone can succeed in a society organized around the virtues of merit, equal opportunity, and competition.

Anthropology/Culture

Another perspective on inequality focuses on the primacy of culture (and socialization to a lesser extent) as an explanatory variable. Inequalities are resistant to solutions because of the self-perpetuating cultural lifestyles of the poor and marginal. The emphasis on kinship, sharing, and generosity characteristic of poor families may be commendable; nevertheless, such lifestyles may be an anachronism from the past, at odds with a competitive and consumerist present, and inimical to success in the future (Widdowson and Howard 2009). The interplay of welfare dependency with female-headed households and lack of ambition and resourcefulness contribute to the perpetuation of intergenerational poverty. Oscar Lewis's (1964; 1998) work on the culture of poverty follows this line of thinking (see the Spotlight box, Cultures Matter, in Chapter 5). For Lewis, living in poverty elicits a cultural response to marginal conditions. This attitudinal response is characterized by low levels of organization, resentment towards authority, hostility to mainstream institutions, and feelings of hopelessness and despair. Once immersed in this culture, a self-fulfilling prophecy is set in motion (a belief that leads to behaviour that confirms the original belief), which further amplifies those very behaviours and beliefs that inhibit mobility and advancement.

Not everyone concedes the validity of a cultural interpretation. Using culture as an explanation is perceived as yet another version of the victim-blame approach. Social inequalities are "individualized" by situating their cause in the culture of the victims themselves. A culturalist explanation tends to ignore the external environment of structural constraints and systemic barriers. Even the very status of a culture of poverty is challenged. What passes for a "poverty culture" is not necessarily a coherent lifestyle in the anthropological sense. A strategic response to destitute conditions is a more likely explanation. Nor is the cultural-as-deprivation the problem. Cultures themselves are neither inferior nor deprived in the absolute sense of the word; more accurately, certain cultures are demeaned as such by the powerful and deemed to be unworthy of equitable treatment.

To sum up: Do bio-psychological explanations of social inequality meet the sociological test? Most sociologists have difficulty condoning biological-based arguments, in part because of a reluctance to accept reductionist explanations of social differences and human similarities, in part because most sociologists are unqualified to judge the quality of research in this area. Nor is there much enthusiasm for individualistic explanations that magnify a person's predicament as personal responsibility or one of morality. According to most sociologists, people are deprived because of their social circumstances rather than depraved because of moral blemishes. In their words, individuals may appear to be lazy and unmotivated but sociologists prefer to set their sights on the social circumstances that created or sustain these personal attributes. Finally, cultural explanations pose a problem for many sociologists since this approach blames victims of a particular culture for their victimization. Sociologists are moving away from conceptualizing culture in such essentialistic terms—fixed, homogeneous, and determinative of thought and behaviour. Preference instead is focused on the concept of culture as a fluid, contested, and negotiable phenomena that provides sociologists with a heuristic tool (or analytic construct) for navigating the complex diversities and diverse complexities of contemporary societies.

Blame-the-System Model

A blame-the-system approach holds society accountable for social inequalities. Several variants can be discerned. Blaming institutions acknowledges how problems of social inequality are situated within the institutional structures and ideological arrangements. Institutions are criticized for discriminatory barriers and systemic biases that have the intent or the effect of denying, excluding, or exploiting others because of race, ethnicity, gender, class, sexual preference, ability, or age. Part IV of this book points out how institutions such as post-secondary school or the workplace are often sites of inequality that wilfully deny or inadvertently exclude those who don't fit into a mainstream profile (Henry and Tator 2010). A blaming-the-system framework looks at the structures and values of society as the source of social inequality problems. The problem of social inequities is often framed as systemic; that is, the rules, roles, and relationships within society are not openly discriminatory or exploitative. Rather, inequalities stem from the logical yet negative consequences of seemingly neutral rules, routines, and protocols that, when equally and evenly applied, exert a discriminatory effect by virtue of not taking into account people's differences, needs, or rights. Yes, everyone may be formally equal before the law, yet the rights of the vulnerable are compromised in an inherently biased system that neither reflects their realities nor advances their interests.

In general, a blame-the-system approach is consistent with variations of the radical conflict perspective. As noted, functionalism as a blaming-the-victim approach sees society as fundamentally sound while assigning blame on individual shortcomings. Radical conflict theorists tend to view societies and their corresponding institutional frameworks as fundamentally unequal because of their exploitative, confrontational, and controlling nature. Individuals are not necessarily to blame since a system slanted toward the rich and powerful is the real culprit. Radical conflict theorists also reject the dominant neo-liberal/functionalist view that inequality provides benefits for society as a whole (Olsen 2011). Inequality for radical conflict theorists is perpetuated by powerful groups who exert power and influence in advancing their interests and priorities. Conflict theorists locate inequality within the context of group competition for scarce and valued resources. For conflict theorists, extremes in inequality are neither natural nor necessary; rather they are relative to a particular place and time as competing groups struggle to preserve their privilege, power, and advantages. Efforts to justify these inequality gaps as natural and necessary are dismissed as ideological ploys for shoring up the status quo, largely by cushioning the blows of exploitation, creating internal divisions within exploited groups, and fostering false consciousness. Three versions of radical conflict can be discerned: Marxist, feminist, and structuralist.

Radical Conflict: Marxism

Inequality is embedded within the capitalist framework of private property, class relations, and profit-making according to an observation popularized by Karl Marx in the nineteenth century and subsequently promulgated by legions of followers since then. Capitalist societies such as Canada condone the ownership of property and control over economic processes as critical criteria in sorting out who gets what and what goes where. A capitalist system by its nature is riddled with social contradictions that culminate in competition, conflict, and change. The owners of the means of production (the ruling class) are constantly on guard to reduce labour costs and protect private property (see Chapter 9, The New Economy, New Exclusions). In turn, the working class is locked in a struggle with the capitalist class to push this inequality towards more equitable outcomes. The clash of these competing interests in this cutthroat game of winners and losers generates intergroup conflicts over scarce resources. Under capitalism, moreover, repressive structures may extend to those cultural practices that seek domination and control over individuals on the basis of race (racism) and gender (sexism). Unlike neo-liberals who put their trust in an open economy, Marxists reject the principle of an unfettered market as a solution to inequality. Instead, a market economy is vilified as contributing to inequality through such entrenched barriers as segmented labour fields, racial division of labour, dual labour markets, and systemic structures of discrimination. Worse still, the past few decades have been marred by growing inequalities, especially glaring in the United States and Canada, with their zealous embrace of free-market neo-liberalism as the basis for wealth creation and income distribution (Gutstein 2014; Olsen 2011).

Radical Conflict: Feminism

A feminist conflict perspective also acknowledges the centrality of inequality and domination. Society is perceived as a patriarchal site of domination—that is, institutions, agendas, and values are designed and organized to reflect, reinforce, and advance male interests and priorities. This perspective also begins with the assumption that there is nothing natural or normal about patriarchal (male) domination with respect to power, privilege, and property. Patterns of domination, control, and inequality are socially constructed and ideologically infused with the founding assumptions and foundational principles of a gendered (patriarchal) constitutional order. And just as gendered (male-stream) society tended to construct demeaning and debilitating images of women, so too are minority women (including aboriginal women, immigrant and refugee women, and racialized women of colour) defined and dismissed as irrelevant, inferior, or a threat. Paradoxically, however, the social construction of this reality points to the possibility of a solution: what has been socially constructed can also be deconstructed, then reconstructed to create patterns of gender parity. (See Chapter 6 for a fuller explanation.)

Radical Conflict: Structuralism

For sociologists of a radical-conflict persuasion, individuals are neither the cause of social inequality nor should they be blamed for its persistence. Inequality patterns are not necessarily reflective of cultural deprivation (a culture of poverty). Rather, the inequities of power, wealth, and status are anchored in the institutional **structures** of society. Social structures refer to those repetitive and systemic patterns that are external to individual behaviour, often outside people's awareness and not reducible to the sum of individual meanings or actions (Weinberg 2008). These patterned regularities (for example, the concept of *status* and *roles*) may be seen as structures in their own right or, alternatively, as manifestations of deeper structures that regulate thought and behaviour. Structures may include the following exclusionary patterns: institutionalized arrangements, economic imperatives and opportunities, class entitlements, racist/sexist ideologies, discriminatory practices, intersecting social locations, core cultural values, and unwritten constitutional principles. The expression and interplay of these patterns in roles, institutions, classes, and values provide social structures with the power to shape people's lives and life chances.

Structural explanations of inequality do not necessarily reflect a specific theoretical framework. They draw on several theoretical strands that link individual inequality problems to a broader (structural) context of root causes (Weinberg 2008). Inequality and barriers to advancement are blocked by institutionalized constraints, many of which are largely systemic and consistent with a job market constructed around "male-stream" interests. A structural inequality is predicated on the premise that the very foundations of society's unwritten constitutional framework are neither neutral nor value-free. To the contrary, these founding assumptions and foundational principles are ideologically loaded with a tacitly assumed set of Eurocentric-based values and beliefs that racialize and sexualize society in terms of what is good, right, or normal (Fleras 2014a). Their persistence has led societies to be described as racialized because design, organization, and operations are informed, influenced, and supported by socially defined race categories, racial ideologies, and racist language (Fleras 2012). Inasmuch as the Eurocentric foundational principles of a racialized constitutional order continue to be organized in ways that advance white interests at minority expenses, the expression of social inequality as structural exclusions is real and powerful, yet difficult to detect or eradicate. A similar line of argument but applied to gender is discussed in the Spotlight box below.

Spotlight Incorporating Women: Corporate Inequality as Structural Exclusions

In 1977, Rosabeth Moss Kanter published what is now considered a modern-day classic in sociology. *Men and Women of the Corporation* garnered countless accolades, including the coveted C. Wright Mills Prize for its contribution to a critically informed sociology (Puffer 2004; Fleras 2005). The significance of Kanter's book went beyond exploring gender-based disparities within corporate America. The book aimed to apply a sociological lens to how social structures impacted on human behaviour since organizational actors tended to respond predictably when confronted by similar structural circumstances. Women and men display different patterns of organizational behaviour not because of gender, either innate or acquired, but because of different cultural expectations, opportunity structures, and systemic bias. The case study serves as a primer for thinking sociologically about social inequality as structural exclusion by reinforcing a key assumption: women as women are not the cause of corporate gender inequalities (see Toller 2013). More to the point, women are differently located within the corporation, resulting in different mindsets, diverse reactions, and differential outcomes. Phrased alternatively, gender (or social) location in a gendered society will profoundly yet negatively influence opportunities and outcomes for women. Or as Sandra Bem (1994) once noted, in a society dominated by men (a gendered or patriarchal society), female differences are invariably defined as female inferiorities and used against women.

Kanter focused on the structural determinants of organizational behaviour. The process in a corporate setting by which some prosper while others falter reflected an interplay of variable access to opportunity structures, the prevalence of ingrained cultural values, hidden agendas that bias without prejudice, situational adjustments, and the unconscious responses of actors to their status (or "location") within corporate structures. More than a passive backdrop for corporate games, these structures were shown to be logically prior and external to the individual, insofar as they reflected the values, interests, experiences, and aspirations of those who created and controlled the corporation. As a group, men ruled corporate settings, not necessarily because of male personality features or predispositions. They prevailed because of an advantageous placement vis-à-vis preferential opportunity structures, access to power, and numerical superiority. Women, by contrast, were often excluded or put down for precisely those reasons that groomed men for success. For example, whereas assertiveness in males is valued (in control, confident, focused), the display of assertiveness in women may be interpreted as bossy, combative, or arrogant. Behaviour differences also arose from confinement of women to the velvet ghetto of public relations, advertising, staff support, and personnel, in part because of a patriarchal legacy whereby women were perceived to excel in people-handling and emotional fine tuning, while men took care of business. In other words, Kanter seemed to argue, it was not gender differences that created structural inequalities; rather structural inequalities tended to accentuate gender differences that, in turn, reinforced sexist patterns of exclusion.

Opportunity Structures: "Nothing Succeeds Like Success"

The behaviour of corporate actors reflected their position within an institution's opportunity structures (Fleras 2005). Those who were labelled as having potential by virtue of being streamed into the fast-track behaved differently from those with limited opportunities. Those on the fast track of opportunity acted in a competitive, dedicated, and instrumental manner, that is, in a manner that articulated a commitment to the corporation, with sights firmly locked on entry into the upper echelons. Their confidence and assertiveness reinforced people's expectations in a kind of self-fulfilling prophecy, subsequently opening even more corporate doors for advancement. Those without high expectations acted accordingly. Corporate actors slotted into the slow track to nowhere were inclined to be peer-oriented, to exhibit signs of complacency and resignation, and appeared bereft of ambition, thereby reinforcing their peripheral status, both real and perceived. They related to the corporation with hostility to management, displayed an unwillingness to commit to the company, refused to take risks for upward mobility, and conducted themselves accordingly, with an air of resignation and defeat as might be expected of life at the margins.

The significance of structures for corporate-based gender behaviour is critical. Gender matters, albeit not in the way most expect. Men do not necessarily monopolize these fast opportunity tracks because of superior work habits or heightened ambition. Nor are women shunted aside because of their skills or lack thereof. Rather, men find themselves in positions (i.e., social location) where they are encouraged and rewarded to move upwards, whereas women are located in statuses and roles that inhibit career enhancement. As proof, Kanter argued, men who were derailed from the fast-tracking express tended to exhibit many of the same gendered symptoms—from passivity to fatalism—as women on the track to nowhere. In sum, individuals are successful not necessarily because they have the "right stuff" (although that is obviously important). The fact they have been singled out for success because of prevailing opportunity structures tends to elicit the right corporate stuff. The person, in other words, does not make the job; more to the point, the job makes over the person.

Structural Power: The Power of Authority, the Authority of Power

Those who possessed power tended to act in a powerful fashion. They could take advantage of power to get things done, define situations, propose solutions, establish agendas, draw on resources when necessary, enhance performance, and improve productivity. These objectives were often achieved through discretionary decisions that went beyond the "rulebook." Powerful individuals also knew how to delegate responsibility or make decisions to influence outcomes without having to check with superiors. They were in a position to take chances or run risks, yet were rarely victimized by second-guessing, thereby reinforcing the idea that power is most powerful in the hands of the empowered.

Conversely, those without power displayed disempowering behaviour patterns at odds with corporate goals. Powerless people concentrated on what little residual power they had over subordinates by taking refuge in rigid, coercive, and vindictive displays. Throwing this "weight" around may have achieved the goal of compliance and ritual subordination, but ultimately sabotaged

continued

productivity while eroding co-operative manager–labour relations. Even when occupying positions of formal authority within the corporate chain of command, the powerless resorted to excessive authoritarianism or displaced aggression, reinforcing yet again the observation that the most powerful are those least inclined to flaunt it. Without the authority of power, a person's credibility was in doubt and openly contested, making it doubly difficult to receive deference, ensure compliance, and impress superiors. In brief, as Kanter asserts, power does not necessarily corrupt; rather, powerlessness is corrupting because it diminishes.

The Structure of Relative Numbers: Token Effects

Relative numbers refer to the proportional distribution of certain categories of persons within corporations. The behaviour of those who constituted the majority differed from members cast as minorities. The majority did not have to worry about being excluded; after all, they set the norm and established the standard that judges others. Majority members were exempt from prejudices and stereotypes that plagued minorities. Conversely, minorities and women of the organization behaved differently because of their marginal status. Differences in behaviour did not necessarily reflect corporate acumen or the human capital they brought to the company (although these attributes may have been important). They resulted from different expectations and diverse pressures brought to bear on the margins. Minorities such as women were likely to be treated as tokens, a situation that culminated in double standards and double binds regardless of what they did or did not do, including:

1. Tokens are viewed as typical representatives of their race or gender when they fail, but exceptions when they succeed.
2. Tokens are constantly reminded of their differences, but must conduct themselves as if these differences were immaterial even as dynamics conspire to exaggerate their uniqueness yet depersonalize their individuality.
3. Tokens tend to be thoroughly scrutinized and evaluated for any weaknesses, yet strengths and contributions may be ignored or assumed as a given. Token failures are used to indict the entire community, whereas token successes are attributed to the openness and tolerance of the mainstream.
4. Tokens are extremely visible and the most dramatized of corporate performers, yet they are rendered invisible by exclusion from centre stage where props are set, scripts are rehearsed, and casts are assembled.
5. Tokens find the organizational settings stressful and constraining, even more so during times of relaxation or socializing (from coffee breaks to office parties), due to more intense scrutiny.
6. Tokens are undervalued as potentially disruptive to the firm, although this perceived disruptiveness reflects their exclusion from meaningful participation within the organization.

The repercussions of this token effect should be obvious, argues Kanter, although others dispute the potency of numbers as a social-change strategy without taking into account contextual factors (Yoder 1991). Constant exposure to scrutiny and monitoring because of performance pressures, social isolation, and role stereotyping inevitably takes a toll on those hand-picked as standard-bearers for their "kind." Their imposed status as ambassadors and role models practically guarantees that any missteps will reinforce negative stereotypes as self-fulfilling prophecies. Worse still, these tokens carry the burden of knowing that the future of others falls on their failing shoulders. The combined impact of this token effect, Kanter explains, is anything but tokenistic in its impact and implications.

Structures Matter: Glass Ceilings, Brick Walls, Slippery Steps, and Sticky Surfaces

What can we conclude from Kanter's work? First, organizational structures are important in shaping differences in behaviour between men and women. Maleness or femaleness is not the determining factor in defining who gets what. Personality characteristics or attitudinal predispositions are not nearly as important as many believe. What appears to be critical is the structural (or social) location of individuals that shape people's expectations, interactions, and responses. Women and minorities occupy the lower echelons of a corporate hierarchy not because of personal deficiencies that make them a liability to the organization. The passivity and noncommittal orientation displayed by the devalued is largely a behavioural response to structural exclusions that involve denied opportunity, an inadequate power base, and numerically induced tokenism (also Randstad 2014). To be sure, cultural factors are also important. For example, the pigeonholing of women and minorities into preconceived cultural slots may influence who is eligible for access to organizational opportunity or rewards. Organizational behaviour is also derived from situational circumstances, including personality differences among the social actors. But structural limitations restrict the range of behavioural options, primarily because the system ". . . set limits on behavioural possibilities and defined the context for peer interaction" (Kanter, 1977:239). These structures were systematic and deliberate in some cases; otherwise, they were systemic and unintended. Nevertheless, they had a controlling effect by incorporating historical social practices that assumed women would be marginal workers and occupy subordinate roles (Albiston 2010).

Second, Kanter drew attention to the unmistakably androcentric logic at the core of organizational cultures. Corporate culture matters: Corporations remain a "man's world," with masculine values and male priorities systemically embedded into organizational agendas, including managerial styles and standards for appointments, entitlements, and conduct (McKinsey & Company 2013). Workplace norms reflect and privilege male ways of living and working predicated on a stay-at-home partner to handle the non-paid work aspects of everyday life, including child care and home maintenance (Albiston 2010; Slaughter 2012). Core organizational values are typically male-linked, including a commitment to aggressiveness, competitiveness, achievement orientation, individualism, and analysis, and

an emphasis on rationality and logic, toughness, and emotional neutrality. Values pertaining to connectedness and other-directedness are shuffled aside in the rush for success at all costs. Even organizational conduct is unmistakably androcentric. Survival techniques focus on the need to be unemotional (avoid feelings); depersonalize issues (never point the finger at anyone); be subordinate (never challenge authority); be conservative (better the devil you know); be isolated (mind your own business); and be competitive (people prefer to compete). Routinely dismissed as career-limiting (at least until recently) are female styles of discourse, with their adherence to consensus, accommodation, and communication, supportiveness, deference, and approval-seeking—all of which may be perceived as an inability to make decisions (McKinsey & Company 2013). Who then can be surprised that women and minorities have found corporations user-unfriendly when navigating their way through the cultural minefields of male-dominated institutions?

Third, Kanter's work was directed at dissecting organizational behaviour patterns. She was not interested in gender inequalities per se as much as how structures of inequality influenced patterns of gender behaviour within institutional settings. Much of her analysis is equally applicable to understanding the behaviour of women and minorities in society at large. For example, just as corporate dynamics are unmistakably male in structure and ethos (men are the prime beneficiaries of continuous employment and minimal domestic responsibilities), so too is society an essentially "pale male" construction. (See Chapter 6.) A commitment to inclusiveness, notwithstanding, those who fall outside the pale-male mould are subject to criticism or second guessing, yet rarely accorded the benefit of the doubt. Pressures for conformity lead to frustration and despair, as well as disinterest and indifference, given the **androcentric** demands of contemporary institutions. A seeming lack of ambition and commitment among minorities is not necessarily a sign of inferiority or apathy. Unproductive responses reflect minority perceptions of themselves as undervalued and irrelevant to society. Behavioural responses, from deviant acts

continued

to passive resignation, appear to be consistent with the structural location of the devalued.

Fourth, what can be done about transforming organizations along more gender-friendly lines? Two ideal–typical options prevail: change the conventions that refer to the rules or change the rules that generate conventions. Change the incumbents that play by the rules or change the rules that incumbents must abide by. Programs and policies that focus on attitudinal or personality modifications rarely get to the root of the problem. Proposing to replace pale males with minorities or women without any corresponding structural changes is unlikely to alter the status quo. Only the players would change, while the corporate game would merrily roll along.

Postscript: "Business as Usual"

Ten years after the publication of her book, Rosabeth Kanter provided an update in the journal *Management Review* (1987). Modest organizational reforms had materialized, Kanter concluded, some of which came about because of her book. Women and minorities began to chip away at the glass ceiling that had inhibited upward mobility. Yet it was largely "business as usual." As far as Kanter was concerned, the interplay of power, lack of opportunity, and relative numbers remained as formidable as ever as exclusionary structures. Male stereotypes continued to extol deeply held values about a woman's "rightful place" that pigeonholed women into communications, human resources, and corporate cheerleader jobs, thus denying them the core experience required for accelerated promotions (also Sandberg 2013; Barreto, Ryan, and Schmitt 2009). The situation in the second decade of the twenty-first century does not appear to have appreciably altered patriarchal structures that inform a gendered status quo. Anne-Marie Slaughter (2012) (a former state department official under Hillary Clinton) wrote about her experiences of "having it all" when trying to balance family life with an insane work world and a pervasive sense of guilt—in spite of a supportive husband and enough wealth to hire domestic help and child care (Rosen 2012). Her

indictment of women striving to "have it all" by excelling both as moms and high-powered executives drew attention to the systemic biases associated with a "time macho workaholic world" (Beckiempis 2012) designed to reflect, reinforce, and advance male interests and androcentric realities.

Admittedly, a loosening of the corporate structures had encouraged upward mobility among women and minorities. Beyond a certain point, however, movement upward had ground to a halt, leaving women to ponder whether to persist or resign in the face of subtle and not-so-subtle pressures (Randstad 2014). Women continued to be excluded from the top ranks of the biggest companies, aside from some high-profile successes such Marissa Mayer (Yahoo Inc.) and Mary T. Barra (General Motors) (Catalyst 2015b). But despite efforts to recruit more women into higher management echelons, the number of women dwindles the closer one gets to the top. According to women's advocacy group Catalyst, women comprised 20.8 per cent of Canadian corporate board members in 2014 (19.2 per cent of the American-based S&P 500), but just 4.8 per cent of CEOs in Forbes 500 companies and 4.6 per cent of CEOs in S&P 500, compared to 25.1 per cent as executives and senior management. The situation is tougher still for racialized women in the United States: for CEOs, Latino women—0.0 per cent; black women—0.2 per cent; and Asian women—0.2 per cent. For executive and senior level management, the respective figures are 1.0 per cent, 1.2 per cent, and 1.7 per cent (Catalyst 2015a). Modest improvements notwithstanding, women continue to encounter mobility patterns that hit a "brick wall" because of male refusal to take them seriously or an inability to fit into a competitive corporate mould. A study by Randstad Women Shaping Business released on 15 October 2013 found that 93 per cent of female managers and executives said they were overworked yet paid less than men doing the same job. Many also believed that image and appearance played a more important role for women than men in any advancement. Burnout from the conflicting and impossible demands of the double shift (a reminder that unco-operative partners are as much of an impediment as bullying bosses) constituted additional contributing factors. To the surprise of no one, women and minorities are fleeing corporate cut-throat competition for the friendlier confines of small business and individual entrepreneurship.

Blame-the-Situation Model

What's the cause of social inequality in society? Is it human agency or social structures? Who should shoulder the blame? Are individuals entirely to blame for what they do and where they stand regardless of the social context? Most sociologists would say no to this assessment. Or as Parenti (1978) shrewdly observed, "blaming the poor for being poor while ignoring the system of power, privilege, and wealth that creates poverty, is a little bit like blaming the corpse for its murder." Should the system take the blame but run the risk of removing all traces of individual agency or responsibility? Such a level of determinism sits uneasily with those who prefer an intermediate position. People are ultimately responsible for their actions, but these actions cannot be divorced from their social location and broader context. People must take ownership of their predicament in the social inequality debate without ignoring how social contexts and situational circumstances can make some choices more likely than others.

According to a blame-the-situation approach, neither the individual nor the system are entirely to blame. Both are blameworthy in constructing realities or outcomes: individuals must take responsibility for their actions, although their choices and options are restricted by the context in which they are socially located. This approach, which acknowledges the interplay of agency with structure, context, and power is largely consistent with the principles of symbolic interactionism. Both functionalist and conflict perspectives define society as taken for granted. Society is portrayed as durable and real, existing above and beyond the individual, yet exerting vast leverage over people's behaviour. By contrast, symbolic interactionist perspectives begin with the notion of society as an ongoing human accomplishment. Instead of something "out there" and determinative, society is perceived as social convention constructed through meaningful interaction. People do not live in a predetermined world of objective phenomena or mechanistic outcomes. Rather, reality is constructed by applying provisional meanings to particular situations. Once a situation has been defined and redefined, jointly linked lines of action are constructed and reconstructed. Society constitutes the sum total of these personal and group interactions at a given point in time and space. For symbolic interactionists, then, social reality and intergroup dynamics are properly situated against the backdrop of constant flux, dynamic tension, mutual adjustment, negotiated compromise, and ongoing movement.

Applied to social inequality, symbolic interactionists contend there is nothing natural, normal, inevitable, or objective about the inequalities of exclusions. More accurately, inequalities of exclusions are brought into existence through meaningful interaction and interpretive practices that creatively make sense of the world within the context of specific situations. To be sure, interactionists do not dismiss the salience of individuals as relevant social actors in shaping patterns of social inequality. On the contrary, individual people are ultimately responsible for their actions. But human behaviour does not materialize in a vacuum; rather, actions are embedded within specific social contexts that influence and constrain without being coercive or deterministic. Individuals are free to choose, although they must make selections on the basis of situationally specific and culturally prescribed options. This focus on the social construction of people's lived experiences requires understanding the perceptions and perspectives of those affected by the realities of inequality. The Spotlight box on the next page provides insight into the view of racism as a situationally defined and intersubjective activity consistent with a symbolic interactionist perspective.

Spotlight Situating Racism as Lived Micro-aggression

The concept of racism may be framed in different ways, although references to exclusion and disadvantage are fundamental to most definitions (Stanley 2012). Both functionalist and conflict theories tend to focus on defining racism, measuring it, and uncovering those variables or factors that create or inhibit its existence. By contrast, symbolic interactionism prefers to "de-reify" racism as a thing amenable to analysis through official definition, formal measurement, and explanatory frameworks (Harris 2001). Racism is framed instead as a set of subjective meanings and lived experiences constructed by individuals in the course of their daily lives and interactions. For symbolic interactionists, nothing is inherently racist even though most people take for granted racism's objective existence. To the contrary, an activity becomes defined (interpreted or labelled) as racist depending on how the situation is defined through interaction and interpretation. Consider the following case study, adapted from an actual incident, as an example of situationally defined racism (Sue et al. 2007).

Two colleagues, one African American, the other Asian American, board a small plane (a "hopper" with a single row of seats on one side, a double row on the other) for a flight from Boston to New York. A flight attendant tells them they can sit anywhere they want in the uncrowded plane; accordingly, they choose seats near the front and across the aisle from each other so they can freely converse. At the last minute, three white males in suits enter the plane and take the seats in front of them. Just before take-off, the flight attendant (who is white) asks the two colleagues if they would mind moving to the back of the plane to better balance the plane's load. Both react with anger at the request to symbolically "sit at the back of the bus." They eventually express their outrage over treatment as second-class citizens to the flight attendant; after all, they had boarded the plane prior to the white males. But the flight attendant reacts indignantly to these charges, claiming it was her responsibility to ensure flight safety by redistributing the weight on the plane. She also claims to have their best interests in mind by providing them with more space and privacy (DeAngelis 2009). Repeated efforts to explain their perceptions and concerns simply generate more defensiveness and dismissals.

What's going on? Is this the new face of racism or is it making a mountain out of molehill (Mitra 2014)? Were the colleagues overly sensitive to a legitimate request, thereby misinterpreting an action that lacked racist intent? (One of the colleagues acknowledged the probable sincerity of the attendant in her belief she acted in good faith and without racial bias [Sue et al. 2007].) Or was the attendant acting out a hidden and unconscious (subliminal) animus towards blacks, albeit behind the pretext of concerns over safety and comfort? Was the offer to move them a thinly veiled dislike of blacks in yet another ambiguous interaction informed by an implicit bias (Sue 2011)? Is the attendant guilty of what is known as racial micro-aggression, namely, insults and slights directed at racialized minorities by seemingly well intentioned yet woefully naive individuals (Caplan and Ford 2014)? Does reference to micro-aggression represent a new face of racism consistent with the post-racial sensitivities of the twenty-first century (Pierce 1974)? Or is the theoretical value of the concept outweighed by the practical problems posed by racializing all snubs or politicizing every criticism (Pettigrew 2014)?

Welcome to the new world of racialized discourses that promises to profoundly challenge and change how we see, think, and talk about racisms. If old-fashioned macro-racism 1.0 and 2.0 played up the contours of a colour-conscious Canada, reference to a so-called colour-blind and post-racial Canada creates a context for a new kind of micro-racism at odds with conventional theorizing. The concept of Racism 3.0 secures a new discursive framework that unapologetically situates racism within the lived experiences and world view of the micro-aggressed. In realigning the conceptual focus of racism from that of the "doer" (sender-oriented) to the "done-to" (receiver-dependent), a paradigm shift is proposed, one that not only centralizes the lived experiences of racialized minorities but also bolsters a new explanatory framework in redefining the politics of *who decides what counts as racism and what racisms count*.

Creating a Context: Racisms 1.0, 2.0, 3.0

For purposes of analysis, the concept of racism divides into two camps. Racism 1.0 could be described as overt, blunt, direct, and deliberate. It drew its inspiration from earliest definitions of racism based on the dogma that race was real insofar as it determined people's lives and life chances. In assigning explanatory priority to objective reality, Racism 1.0 was informed by a specific set of beliefs and actions, with clearly marked victims and victimizers. Racism 2.0 differs from its 1.0 counterpart in the degree of bluntness, directness, and awareness levels. In opposition to overt and highly aggressive forms of racism involving open dislike or institutional discrimination, neither of which is acceptable in today's political ("correct") climate, Racism 2.0 is conveyed systemically at institutional levels or subliminally through the subtleties of interaction (Riggins 1991). Explicit racist practices have yielded ground to racially coded subtexts that operate through "inaction, silence, neglect and indifference" (Battiste 2009), yet are no less controlling or exclusionary. People speak in code by employing proxies to hide their bigotry from others (polite) and from themselves (subliminal), especially in those ambiguous contexts when individuals can camouflage their racism behind a principled excuse (Fleras 2014a; Freshley 2014).

Despite diametrically opposed differences, Racism 1.0 and 2.0 share commonalities. Both perspectives assume that racism exists out there, that certain actions are inherently racist, and that it is their responsibility to identify, define, and explain them (Harris 2001). Questions asked of Racism 1.0 and 2.0 emphasize causation behind individual prejudice and institutional discrimination. The emphasis is on how and why individuals and institutions continue to deny or exclude, however inadvertently and by consequences rather than intent, especially when doing so is illegal or socially unacceptable. In contrast to the direct racism of 1.0 and indirect racism of 2.0, Racism 3.0 acknowledges the *lived subjectivities* of racialized minorities as central to any analysis. Moving the frame of reference from doer to done-to shines the spotlight on those demeaning slights and subtle indignities (known as micro-aggressions) that racialized minorities *experience* on a daily basis, albeit without evidence of any explicit offence. The defining feature of Racism 3.0 is neither the subtlety of the slur nor the seeming innocence of the perpetrator. Its definitive aspect resides in prioritizing the victim's lived experience in terms of how *he or she* sees, assesses, is affected by, and reacts to these covert micro-aggressions. The cumulative weight of these numerous small slights (akin to "a ton of feathers") establishes a context (or "chilly climate") that renders minorities uncomfortable, marginal, fearful, or socially impotent—the symbolic equivalent of death by a thousand cuts. In other words, the paradigmatic core of a Racism 3.0 embraces the subjectivity of racism as a lived experience from the perspective of those being victimized (Sue et al. 2007; DeAngelis 2009). It also repudiates those frameworks that reify racism as a thing or object based on what the mainstream elite identify as definitive (see also Hier and Walby 2006; Henry 2006).

Racial Micro-aggression as Racism 3.0

Racism 3.0 and the concept of racial micro-aggressions have much in common. Derald Wing Sue (2010) defines micro-aggressions as those commonplace interactions, both verbal and non-verbal, intentional or not, that racialized minorities experience as putdowns without overt prejudice. These brief daily exchanges are imbued with coded negative messages, from confirming stereotypes to privileging the dominant group as the normative standard and others as aberrant, to essentializing all group members as undifferentiated, to denying the pervasiveness of both discrimination in society or the perpetrator's own bias. More specifically (Sue 2010:5):

> Microaggressions are the brief and commonplace daily verbal, behavioral, and environmental indignities, whether intentional or unintentional, that communicate hostile, derogatory, or negative racial, gender, sexual orientation and religious slights and insults to the target person or group.

The following list provides expressions of micro-aggressions that are woven into the fabric of everyday social life (Sue et al. 2007):

continued

Examples of Racialized Micro-Aggressions

Expression/Action	Interpretation
Where are you really from?	You are foreign/alien/not really Canadian.
Those people	You are being "otherized."
You speak good English (compliment?).	Who would have thought you could be so articulate (offence)?
You are a credit to your race.	Your group is usually not as intelligent as whites. You are not like the inferior others in your group.
When I look at you, I don't see race.	We deny your identity and lived experiences.
There is only one race—the human race.	We deny your racial/cultural identity.
Clutching purse more tightly.	You are a criminal.
Following a customer of colour in a store.	You are a stereotype.
Ignoring customer at a counter.	You are less valued/whites get preferential treatment.
Taxi passing a racialized person for a white fare.	You are dangerous, cannot be trusted.
I'm not racist—I have black friends.	Friendships do not exclude micro-aggressions.
As a woman, I know what you are experiencing.	I can't be a racist because I'm like you.
Choosing the "most qualified" person for a job.	Minorities always get preferential treatment.
Everyone can succeed if they work hard enough.	Minorities are lazy or incompetent.
It's a post-racial society.	Race is irrelevant to success (you have only yourself to blame).
Asking minority person to settle down, be quiet.	Do as you are told by assimilating into the mainstream.
Mistaking a racialized minority for service worker.	Minorities occupy menial jobs.
Naming university buildings after white males.	You don't belong.
Using your cultural privilege to assume another identity (Halloween).	It's OK to mock or trivialize cultural identities.

Source: Sue et al. 2007. Adapted with permission from the American Psychological Association.

Do micro-aggressions matter? Unlike the "macros" and "metas" of racism 1.0/2.0, the micro-aggressions of Racism 3.0 embody the banalities of everyday language and the seemingly petty gestures of daily interaction. The *micro* in micro-aggressions may imply an informality that makes it sound trivial and harmless; nevertheless, the cumulative effects pose a risk to the physical, social, and mental health of the micro-aggressed (Alvarez and Juang 2010). Comments that might seem innocent at first glance can cause emotional distress so that even small slights can carry a lot of clout (Mitra 2014). For example, the intent of saying, "So where are you really from?" might not be racist, but its use in everyday social interaction has the effect of positioning racialized minorities or migrants as the "other" and excluded from mainstream identity. The totality of micro-aggressive incidents exerts a chronic adverse effect—even more powerful than open bigotry—in fostering personal strife, in part because the invisibility or ambiguity of these incidents are easy to dismiss or downplay (Essed 1991; Sue 2011). These micro-aggressions instil a sense of confusion that hampers performance and erodes self-esteem, in large part because the unspoken messages are tricky to interpret or assess (Sue et al. 2007). Victims often struggle to determine if bigotry is at play or whether to dismiss the experience by blaming themselves as hypersensitive (Sue 2010; Caplan and Ford 2014). The micro-aggressed expresses a degree of self-doubt rather than justified anger—of isolation instead of support—in trying to sort out what is going on. This passage from Caplan and Ford (2014:54) captures the confusion and uncertainty racialized students experience at the receiving end of micro-aggressions:

> Much of the mistreatment comes in the form of microaggressions, so that people who are its targets spend a great deal of time in internal dialogue, asking themselves whether they imagined or misinterpreted what the other person said or did and, given the less than blatant form of the mistreatment, feeling apprehension and anguish about whether, if they try to name and object what was done to

them, they will only be told that they are overly sensitive or even that they are imagining it. They worry that speaking up to protest such treatment carries the risk of creating still more problems for themselves and other members of their respective group.

To be sure, the *micro* in micro-aggressions does not invalidate the broader context of power, injustice, and inequality. Reference to micro-aggression as *micro-management* is reflective of and mediated by institutional racism and systemic barriers. The salience of micro-aggressions perpetuates and is perpetuated by those foundational ideologies that bolster **white supremacy** and dominant power structures (Huber and Solorzano 2015). In acknowledging that the micro matters because the macro exists, the relevance of a racialized framework ups the ante in redefining micro-aggression " . . . *as a set of beliefs and/or ideologies that justify actual or potential social arrangements that legitimate the interests and/or positions of a dominant group over non-dominant groups, that in turn lead to related structures and acts of subordination*" (Huber and Solorzano 2014:7 [emphasis mine]). In other words, references to the *micro* in micro-aggression allude to its brevity and nuance ("micro in name only") rather than a denial of its potency, scope, and consequences—perhaps more powerful than open bigotry (Caplan and Ford 2014).

Putting It into Perspective

Which sociological models of society provide the best reading of social reality? Which one provides the best explanatory framework for social inequality? Is it even possible to isolate one model from another when the domain of social inequality reflects a series of complex and interrelated social, economic, and political factors (Broadbent Institute 2012)? Functionalists tend to endorse the principle of equal opportunity and meritocracy, in which individuals get ahead because of talent and

hard work, as the primary determinant of social inequality. Radical conflict theorists point to a fundamentally un-level playing in which people's lives and life chances are sharply determined by their starting point (for example, non-merit factors such as inheritance or discrimination) within an existing structure of inequality as primary determinants (see also McNamee 2014:11). Neither functionalism (blaming the individual) nor radical conflict models (blaming the system) are more correct, although this book certainly leans toward the latter. And the blaming-the-situation focus of

Table 3.2: Explaining Social Inequality: Sociological Models of Society

	Functionalist model	Radical conflict theory— Marxist model/ class-based	Radical conflict theory— Feminist model/ gender-based	Symbolic interactionist model
Nature of society	Integrated whole of interrelated parts	Site of class inequality	Site of male domination	Ongoing human accomplishment
Normal state of society	Stability, order, consensus, co-operation	Competition, conflict, control, change	Domination, conflict, control, change	Dynamic interactional process
Key question	How is order achieved?	How does inequality persist?	How is domination maintained?	How is reality socially constructed?
What holds society together	Shared consensus	Hegemony + threat of force + power	Hegemony + threat of force + power	Negotiation, compromise, and self-interest
Assessment of society	Society is good	Society is exploitative	Society is dominating	Society just is—a blank slate
Assessment of inequality	Functional, necessary, inevitable, beneficial	Exploitative	Controlling	Depends on the context (i.e., how the situation is defined)
What is the cause? Who is to blame?	Blame the individual/victim	Blame the capitalist system	Blame the patriarchal system	Blame the situation
Proposed solution to inequality	Change the person	Change the system	Change the system	Redefine the situation

symbolic interactionism provides a useful corrective to functionalism and conflict theories by anchoring social inequality in the lived experiences of people relative to time, place, and situation. In short, each model appears to be trapped within the framework of its own truths, in the process illuminating different aspects of social inequality. For these reasons, most sociologists prefer to couch human behaviour in social terms by looking for causal explanations within the social (situational) and structural. Such an approach recognizes the constraining influence of social structure and social context without denying the relevance of individual agency.

Table 3.2 compares how each of these perspectives explains social inequality (blame the individual/system/situation) by way of competing sociological models of society (functionalist, radical conflict [class + gender], and symbolic interactionism). In the interests of simplifying the table, reference to structuralism is excluded since it entails both Marxist and feminist versions of **radical conflict theory**.

Summary

1. The philosophical insights of Hobbes, Rousseau, and Locke into the human condition as prototypes for studying the nature and characteristics of social inequality were discussed.
2. The debate over social inequality was framed around three blaming models (blame the individual, blame the system, blame the situation), each of which generally aligns with positions endorsed by Hobbes, Rousseau, and Locke.
3. The three blaming models were aligned with the three major sociological models of society for explaining the causes of social inequality.
4. Functionalism, radical conflict theories, and symbolic interactionist models of society were discussed as fundamentally different approaches to social inequality.
5. Social inequality as structural exclusions was examined, reflected in Kanter's landmark study on gendered corporations.
6. The concept of micro-aggression as Racism 3.0 exemplified a symbolic interactionist approach to social inequality.

Review Questions

1. Explain social inequality from a *functionalist/blame-the-individual* model.
2. Compare the different approaches to social inequality that are encompassed by a radical *conflict/blame-the-system* model of social inequality.
3. Demonstrate why a structural approach has proven useful in explaining patterns of inequalities and exclusions as they apply to gender in the corporation.
4. How does the concept of Racism 3.0 provide a good example of the *symbolic interactionist/blame-the-situation* model of social inequality?
5. Discuss how the ideas of the social philosophers Hobbes, Rousseau, and Locke align with sociological models of social inequality.

II Status Inequalities: Class and Poverty

All known societies are characterized by status inequalities (used in the Weberian sense of prestige or social superiority [Chan and Goldthorpe 2007]). The most privileged enjoy a preferred social status alongside a disproportionate share of wealth, power, and prestige. Those whose status is maligned as inferior, irrelevant, or threatening are out of luck. Sociologists are dedicated to describing the contours of and the justification for this status inequality. They want to explain its persistence, scope, and impact, especially in those contexts that purport to embrace egalitarian values and a commitment to inclusiveness. This interest is understandable: patterns of status inequality are neither an anomaly nor randomly distributed. Societies are stratified instead in ascending and descending order of who is important or what is valued. Status differences in accessing scarce resources are also stratified through achieved (earned) and ascribed (inherited) lines (Newman 2011). Furthermore, all forms of status inequality are underpinned by ideologies that justify patterns of exclusions within contexts of power (Pinder 2013).

The stratification of society along status inequality lines represents an enduring feature of all complex human groupings. Valued resources are distributed unequally based on social class membership as well as on status designations related to gender, race, ethnicity, and aboriginality (see Harvey and Bourhis 2013). In theory, the status markers of race, gender, ethnicity, aboriginality, and class reflect analytically distinct dimensions of inequality inasmuch as they cannot be reduced to each other. People's social location with respect to class as well as gender or race or aboriginality also shape their identities, experiences, and opportunities and outcomes; how people relate to them and they relate to others; and the choices people make in light of the options that are open to them. In reality, each of these identity markers is known to intersect with other dimensions to generate overlapping and mutually reinforcing hierarchies of social exclusion (Hankivsky 2011). Those historically disadvantaged minorities who find themselves on more than one devalued hierarchy are further penalized since these interlocking patterns of exclusion compound the chances of being left out of the loop (Walby 2009).

Status inequalities are shown to fall into two positional categories: socio-economic and identity-based. The socio-economic category is represented by *social class*, in terms of family background as it impacts market situation or, alternatively, in relation to the means of production as owners or workers. The second category consists of *identity groups* related to race (status inequality due to visibility in a racialized society); ethnicity (status inequality because of cultural differences and prejudice); gender (status inequality based on perceived sex differences in patriarchal systems), and aboriginality (status inequality because of "being indigenous" within a colonized context). The content of Part II provides a framework for analyzing social inequality and the inequalities of exclusion at the level of class and poverty. The guiding assumption throughout this part is straightforward enough: Canadians like to think of themselves as a meritocratic society, one in which social status and economic achievement are unrelated to race, class, gender, and aboriginality (Wotherspoon and Hansen 2013). However comforting this fiction might be, reality points to a series of uncomfortable truths and awkward contradictions (for the US, see also McNamee 2014; Longoria 2006). Status inequalities associated with class and poverty matter in increasing the chances of making things happen, from intensifying patterns of exploitation or exclusion to shaping people's lived realities and life chances.

Chapter 4 explores the debate over social class as a contested category of inequality in its own right as well as in its application and expression in Canada. The chapter argues that classes matter in influencing opportunities and outcomes, despite ongoing debates over their heuristic value as an explanatory framework and their ontological status as socially constructed or intrinsically objective. An analysis of media representations of class and class relations reinforces the many ambiguities and complexities that underpin this tricky domain. Chapter 5 continues the discussion on class by focusing on the poverty and homelessness of the most disadvantaged, destitute, and socially isolated (loosely referred to as the "underclass"). Special attention is paid to the politics and the politicization of poverty in Canada (and its correlates, homelessness and food scarcity) with respect to definition, measurement, and solutions. Together, these two chapters confirm what sociologists have long known: claims that Canada is "classless" and relatively equal should not be taken at face value but explored more carefully to separate reality from ideology, truth from fiction.

4 Class Matters: Causes, Controversies, Costs

Learning Objectives

1. To appreciate how classes matter by specifying how Edwardian notions of social classes influenced who lived and died on the doomed *Titanic*.

2. To determine why there is widespread resistance to the notion that class still matters as a predictor of inequality.

3. To understand why even academics cannot agree on whether classes exist or if they still matter as an explanatory framework.

4. To point out some of the key sociological debates about class and inequality, especially as they relate to Marx and Weber.

5. To describe how and why mainstream media often incorrectly portray the representation of classes and class relations.

Introduction: Class on the *Titanic*

Sociologists have long acknowledged the principle that social location matters. People's placement in society (including gender, race, ethnicity, age, etc.) will influence identity (how they see and think about the world); experiences (how others relate to them, and they relate to others); and outcomes and opportunities (based on their family background and/or their relationship to productive property [as owners or workers]). The concept of **class** as social location is no exception to this sociological principle. Debates over social class in terms of causes, controversies, and costs continue to dominate the social scene, with two questions dominating. First, are social classes real in the objective (naturally occurring) sense? Or is it more accurate to say the class concept has

evolved into a proxy term (shorthand or code) to describe socio-economic differences? Second, does reference to class analysis possess any redeeming value as an explanatory framework over a wide range of outcomes related to inequality and exclusion (Breen and Rottman 1995)? Or has the concept lost its heuristic value as explanation in light of evolving realities? Additional questions follow from these concerns. Should reference to class remain a descriptive category or should it retain its original status as a prescriptive category with predictive value? What is it that class analysis is intended to explain? Who says class matters—or doesn't matter—in influencing people's lives and life (and death) chances?

To be sure, class as social location need not be objectively (intrinsically) real to exert an impact. Even if class is not real as a naturally existing phenomenon "out there," people perceive class to be real or they tend to act as if it was real, with the result that individuals experience the effects of social class whether or not they are aware of its empowering or disempowering impacts. For example, children born into wealthy families are more likely than poor children to enjoy good health and access to good daycare; to receive more nurturing time, live longer, and perform better at better schools; to be able to afford extracurricular activities; and to stay out of jail and succeed in a career—not because they are better but because their affluence and privilege enriches, empowers, and energizes (Putnam 2015). Or consider how a person's family background with respect to wealth and power, in addition to one's socio-economic status as worker or owner, will play a key role in defining who gets what (Johnson 2015). An analysis of who lived and died in the sinking of the *Titanic* provides a useful (if somewhat macabre) illustration not only of how class counts (matters) when the chips are down but also how survival probabilities reflected the intersection of class with gender, age, and race in determining life-and-death outcomes.

The "practically unsinkable" RMS *Titanic* slowly sank nose first into the North Atlantic on the morning of 15 April 1912, after striking an iceberg that ripped a 300-foot gash into the hull and flooded five bulkheads. Two-thirds of the *Titanic*'s complement of some 2,200 passengers and crew—1501 people—lost their lives (Frey et al. 2011). But not everyone who died on the ship's maiden voyage had the same probability of dying. Marked differences in gender, age, and social class prevailed. Women and children were much more likely to survive, especially if they were from first and second class; by contrast, men from all class levels were doomed. Class differences were discernible as well: about 60 per cent of those women, men, and children holding first class tickets survived, as did 36 per cent of the second class passengers, but only 24 per cent of those in third class (or steerage, including the crew) survived. A similar pattern applied to men as well, with survival rates generally correlated with class status. The figures in Table 4.1 from Hall (1986) provide a breakdown by gender and social classes of those who died and those who were saved.

A bit of context might help in sorting through these discrepancies. European societies at the turn of the twentieth century were sharply divided into social classes based on family background and ownership of wealth (Brewster 2011). In the case of the *Titanic*—which in many ways represented a floating microcosm of Edwardian society at

Table 4.1: Survival on the *Titanic*

	Survived	Died
First class		
Men (M)	57	118 (67.4%)
Women/Children (W/C)	146	4 (2.7%)
Second class		
M	14	154 (91.7%)
W/C	104	13 (11.2%)
Third class		
M	75	387 (83.8%)
W/C	103	141 (57.8%)
Crew		
M	192	670 (77.7%)
W/C	20	3 (13.1%)

Source: Adapted from Hall, Wayne. 1986. "Social Class and Survival on the SS *Titanic*." *Social Science & Medicine*, 22(6): 687-690.

the time—first-class aristocrats enjoyed plush accommodations in addition to opulent amenities from open air decks to gymnasiums and Turkish baths. Second-class passage, with its complement of teachers, professionals, and merchants of a middle-class bearing, were accorded somewhat less lavish surroundings but shared access to the open deck with the first class, a key factor in saving lives thanks to the location of the lifeboats. The third-class passengers were those ambitious or desperate persons from Britain, Ireland, and other countries seeking their fortunes in the Americas. They endured cramped living quarters with few amenities and were physically barred from access to the first- and second-class sections.

The *Titanic* was designed and organized (as was society in general) along rigid class lines. It is doubtful if the rich or poor would ever meet or mix except under tightly scripted conditions (for example, master–servant relations as portrayed in BBC productions from *Upstairs Downstairs* to *Downton Abbey*). In that sense, the pattern of intergroup dynamics as portrayed in James Cameron's 1997 blockbuster *Titanic* is misleading. The organization of society and the ship was structured so that the affluent never made contact with social inferiors. The inaccuracies in portraying a romance between a social elite (Kate Winslet as Rose DeWitt Bukater) and third-class riff-raff (Leonardo DiCaprio as Jack Dawson) are the stuff of Hollywood's dream machine, not of Edwardian era realities. The film also emphasized class differences by depicting the rich as despicable and self-centred cads—boring, foppish, and foolish—in contrast to the working classes as authentic, lively, and insightful. Particular bile was reserved for those upper-crust males who tried to buy or bribe their way onto the lifeboats. Nowhere does the movie mention upper-class noblesse oblige (those who claim nobility have a responsibility to act nobly). For example, Walter Lord in his book *A Night to Remember* (1956:13), recounted how Benjamin Guggenheim and his valet appeared on the upper deck in their tuxedos, but without their life-vests, and announced "We've dressed up in our best and are prepared to go down like gentlemen." (Highly recommended for separating myth from fact is the commentary version of the 1952 film/DVD of Lord's book.)

What does the *Titanic* tragedy tell us about the status of social classes and class relations? Was the *Titanic* a symbol of noblesse oblige or that of rank elitism? Did the sinking expose acts of male chivalry or reflect class warfare by according privileged treatment to the rich (Phillips 2011)? Are there aspects of class dynamics on the *Titanic* that carry over into the present? The following themes provide a useful entry point for debate.

Class Matters

By today's standards, the conclusion seems inescapable: class counted in terms of who died and who lived. Paradoxically, however, the British Wreck Commissioner's inquiry (headed by high court judge Lord Mersey) into the *Titanic* disaster did not take social classes seriously as a contributing factor in explaining the different rates of survival or death. Admittedly, some accused Mersey's report of being a whitewash for largely ignoring class differences in its investigation. But the inquiry's framing of blame was simply a product of the times. As Lord points out in his book *A Night to Remember*, little thought was given to the plight of the lower classes. Social classes as systems of unquestioned privilege were so taken for granted that few lamented the carnage among third-class passengers, who were simply left to fend for themselves in clambering their way from the bowels of the boat to its deck. Besides, the tacit assumption was that the price of a first-class ticket also included an increased chance of surviving a sinking ship. Clearly then, the class differences in survival were generally regarded as a reflection of the natural order and, as collateral damage, hardly worth paying much attention to.

Gender Matters, Too

Evidence indicates that 73.3 per cent of women survived the sinking, 50.4 per cent of the children survived, and 20.7 per cent of the men (Nordstrom 2012) survived. Women and children were more likely than men to survive for several reasons. First was culture—the code of chivalry as the dominant mode of masculinity, especially upper-class masculinity, as Walter Lord points out in his book (1956). Second was policy—maritime history dictated preferential access to lifeboats for women and children. Third was a dearth of life boats: the ship carried only 20 lifeboats with a seating capacity of 1,178 to accommodate the 2,201 passengers (according to the existing British trade regulations, the number of lifeboats on large ships was tabulated on the basis of a ship's tonnage rather than on the number of passengers). In an age of gallantry, the crew were instructed and trained to prevent males from boarding lifeboats—by force if necessary (the captain of the *Titanic* threatened to shoot any male who did not yield his lifeboat seat to a woman or child [Nordstrom 2012]).[1] The relatively high rate of survival for crew members reflected standard practice of ensuring a small complement of crew to row each lifeboat (Phillips 2011). Interestingly, according to Lord Mersey's report into the disaster, only 18 of the 20 lifeboats were launched, many only partially filled to capacity, possibly because of the mayhem and disorganization, a lack of boat crew training, and a collective disbelief in thinking the unthinkable, with a corresponding unwillingness on the part of passengers to jump ship.

The Centrality of Intersectionality

As the statistics amply demonstrated, gender combined (intersected) with class to improve a woman's chance of survival. Women and children had a 65 per cent chance of survival, compared to about 20 per cent for all men. If only women and children from first and second class are considered, the figure rises to about 95 per cent. Age also intersected with class and gender to improve survival rates, including 28 of 29 children from first and second class. Finally, perceptions of race intersected with gender and class to play a key role. A commitment to the social norm of "women and children first" symbolized more than good manners or lawful behaviour. These acts of noblesse oblige reinforced the racial/civilizational superiority of the British "stiff upper lip," namely, a shorthand (proxy) for stoicism, emotional restraint, sense of duty, self-discipline, and lack of hysteria. These qualities not only distinguished the upper crust from all others, brown or white, they also justified a racialized white supremacy across the British Empire. As Colonel Archibald Grace famously opined about his "stiff sinewed genes"

in his book *The Truth about the Titanic*, (cited in Renzetti 2012:A2):

> The coolness, courage, and sense of duty that I here witnessed made me thankful to God and proud of my Anglo Saxon race that gave this perfect and superb exhibition of self-control at this hour of severest trial.

Blaming the (Racialized) Victims

Who was to blame for the disproportional patterns of deaths on the *Titanic*? The ship's captain? The prevailing social norms? The self-serving upper classes? Structural barriers? Lord Mersey's 1912 inquiry pinned the blame on the steerage class passengers for their predicament. The inquiry concluded that third-class passengers were not denied access to the lifeboats. Nor did the conditions and structure of the ship disadvantage the lower classes. Rather, steerage passengers were accused of compromising their chances for survival through their own short-sighted behaviour. Their dearth of British-style reserve prevented them from following instructions or obeying authority. Their natural inclination to hysteria (unlike the cool, calm, and collected manner of the appointed upper classes) made a bad situation even worse. It should be noted that the partial sinking of the *Costa Concordia* off the coast of Italy in January 2012, with a loss of 32 lives, also hinted at a host of unflattering national stereotypes (Renzetti 2012).

Systemic Bias

Were steerage passengers victims of systemic racism? It may be true that neither senior officials nor the crew systematically (deliberately) excluded the lower classes from manning the lifeboats, although it is likely steerage class passengers were deliberately kept back until the very end. (In the movie *Titanic*, the crew locked the steel doors preventing the third-class passengers from the deck while threatening to kill anyone who dared board the lifeboats assigned to first class passengers). But systemic (unconscious) biases and structural exclusions were at play that the inquiry ignored. Consider, for example, the positioning of the lifeboats on the first/second class deck; the architecture of the *Titanic*, including complicated passageways and stairways onto the ship's deck confusing in the calmest of time[2]; and social barriers that assumed the lives of the poor were worth less than those of the rich.

Plus ça change, plus c'est la même chose?

The class politics associated with the sinking of the *Titanic* demonstrate how class mattered because it represented a difference that influenced what happened. A person's life chances, then and now (from health and life expectancy to employment and victimization by crime), continue to be shaped by his or her parents' background related to income, occupation, parenting styles and education—in other words, class (or socio-economic status) (Gavron 2009; Sherman and Harris 2012; Johnson 2015). A deep-seated aversion to class as reality or explanatory framework notwithstanding, there is no shortage of contemporary examples that may prove as class-sensitive. For those who have endured the cramped discomforts of international flights, the partitioning of planes into first class, business class, and economy class may not differ from what might have prevailed on the *Titanic*. It would be interesting to analyze flight records of crashes to determine which class of passengers is more likely to survive a crash landing—those in the first-class cabins of 747s, those in the business class at the front of the plane, or those crammed in "cattle" class throughout. (A 2007 analysis of plane crashes since 1971 by *Popular Mechanics* concluded that survival rates increased for those toward the back of the plane, although much depends on the nature of the crash.) Moreover, as airlines try to squeeze yet more profits from every flight, those relegated to economy class will confront the threat of potentially fatal strokes because of cramped seating arrangements (Mouawad and White 2013). Or they will lash out (air rage) at the indignities of class-based seating arrangements (DeCelles and Norton 2016).

We can glean one final lesson from this case study by invoking the concept of hubris—that is, extreme presumption, overbearing arrogance, and overestimation of one's capabilities. The *Titanic*'s

demise by a chunk of ice rattled people's belief in the inevitability of Progress in moving forward and overcoming all obstacles (Geiger 2012). But just as few believed the "practically unsinkable" *Titanic* could do the unthinkable—an act of technological hubris if ever was one—so too is a similarly flawed mindset at play that is devastating the planet Earth through carbon emissions, global warming, desertification of arable lands, and deterioration of potable water supplies. For as many have commented, nature has a way of punishing those foolish enough to take it for granted.[3]

This chapter explores the concept of social class as a marker of inequality and exclusion in Canada. Canadians like to think of themselves a predominantly meritocratic society that rejects the class-obsessed rigidities of European society, with its concomitant notion of class as pivotal in shaping lives and defining life chances (Gwyn 2012). But class differences, both real and perceived, continue to permeate Canada, although Canadians are generally loathe to acknowledge their reality and importance to society (see Lareau and Conley 2010). Marxist and Weberian perspectives on social class provide competing platforms for theorizing its ontological status as inherently objective or socially constructed. The chapter makes it abundantly clear: class matters because it increases the probability that social inequality and exclusion will be generated; it provides an explanatory framework for explaining who gets what and what goes where; and its existence can prove detrimental when barriers inhibit the qualified and ambitious from advancing up the social hierarchy. A look at runaway income and wealth gaps in Canada and the United States exposes a key contradiction: class matters even in a society that prides itself on the principles of individualism and meritocracy. The chapter concludes by looking at how media frame the concepts of social classes and class relations in ways that misrepresent the meaning, scope and impact of class inequalities (Gandy Jr. 2007).

Contesting the Class Concept

Debates over social inequality initially addressed the politics of social class. The concept itself was rarely disputed as a description of reality in terms of prescribing who got what, including its implications for society and a wide range of outcomes pertaining to people's lives and life chances. Consider the primacy of class in Britain: its significance in securing a relatively stable English national identity (Englishness) stands in sharp contrast to those countries where distinctiveness is rooted in ethnicity or religion (Aughey 2012). England's population was divided into higher and lower classes based on background and upbringing and their influence on employment and occupation status (Savage et al. 2013). A kind of classism often prevailed as well, namely, a belief in the innate superiority of the rich and ruling classes, with an attendant right to do as they pleased. Controversies pivoted around how social classes originated, who belonged to what class and why, the kind of relationship between the classes, and how many existed. For some (Marx), class-based inequalities reflected people's relationship to the means of production (owner versus workers). Others (such as Weber) did not dismiss the importance of occupational status vis-à-vis the means of production, but also emphasized how family background shaped people's lives and life chances by improving their market situation (placement in the economy). The resulting lack of consensus over the nature, magnitude, and scope of class as inequality—as exemplified in the debates between Marx and Weber—did little to blunt ongoing controversy.

Interest in social classes as analysis or reality appears to have waned in recent years (Crompton 2008), although growing dismay over spiraling income inequalities points to renewed attention, thanks in part to the Occupy Wall Street movement (Savage et al. 2013; Roberts, Atkinson, and Savage 2012). Perceptions prevail that class is less valid now than in the past because of lifestyle changes, ideological shifts, and new economic realities. Class boundaries are blurring and becoming less meaningful in everyday life as class identities give way toward the identity markers of age, gender, race, ethnicity, and sexual orientation (Evans and Tilley 2015). The struggle for the recognition of difference under the banner of identity politics continues to supplant class interest as the primary medium for political mobilization, while cultural domination

displaces exploitation as the key injustice, and cultural recognition supersedes socio-economic redistribution as remedy for social injustices and the goal of collective struggles (Fraser 1997). Shifting patterns of group formation, the greater individualization of society, and new socio-political cleavages are a contributing factor as well (Reay 1998). The dynamics of an all-consuming commodity culture are no less important in fudging class lines. A person's class position could once be predicted by his or her appearances because everyone knew their place and acted accordingly. But in a world where brands such as Nike or Lululemon are available to rich and poor alike (at least in theory), these distinctions are less reliable as predictors of class. Moreover, thanks to a combination of twenty-first-century technology advances—from affluence to travel—people tend to realign themselves along lifestyle choices rather than traditional class markers (Adams 1997, 2010). In short, an individual's layered sense of identity is increasingly reflective of experience rather than ethnicity or nationality, trajectory rather than place (routes rather than roots), and shifting contexts rather than predetermined categories (Adichie 2013).

Challenging deterministic theories of class relations is one thing. The perceived moral superiority of some classes over others is contested as well. But rejecting the relevance of social classes in explaining social inequality is quite another. New forms of inequality in a globalized world of postmodern realities have not necessarily displaced older (class-based) forms (Lemel and Noll 2003). The long term consequences of this gap are real regardless of awareness, as pointed out by Diane Reay (1998:259):

> . . . regardless of whether we see ourselves in class terms, class just as much as race, gender, age, and sexuality shapes, and goes on shaping, the individuals we are and the individuals we become.

Nor do new inequality forms invalidate the salience of conventional discourses as an explanatory framework. Rather, it may be argued that the real divide in society is neither gender nor race but social class, insofar as the uber-elites represent a class unto themselves, sharing much in common with each other regardless of race or gender in terms of ambition, interests, and concerns (Kay 2015; Wolf 2013). For example, studies demonstrate the effects of social class on distinctive parenting styles informing parent–child interactions inside the home (Frenette and Chan 2015; Lareau 2002). Recent research by David Putnam (2015; Johnson 2015; Brooks 2012) confirms how parenting matters: a study by Hart and Risley (1995) found that children of professional families heard on average 2,100 words per hour, whereas working class children heard 1,200 words, and those families on welfare heard 600—or 30 million less words by the age of three than a rich child. Affluent and educated parents also invest more time and energy (both intellectual stimulation and emotional support) with their children than the less affluent (less educated, lower income, often single parent), resulting in subsequent behaviour gaps ranging from poorer test scores to greater risk of teenage pregnancy or criminal conviction (Reeves and Howard 2013). Not only is this parenting gap a key factor in the opportunity gap, conclude Reeves and Howard (2013), but those lucky enough to have involved parents inherit advantages and disadvantages (the "birthright lottery" as a path to success) in a way that undermines perception of the United States as a classless society.

The centrality of social classes and class relations conceals yet another paradox. Public aversion to the "c" word reflects a social and historical reality in Canada and the United States. The Occupy movement may have propelled class issues to the top of the public agenda (including references to class warfare or concerns over a shrinking middle class), but North American indifference and/or antipathy toward social classes (notwithstanding the popularity of *Downton Abbey* and its focus on the structure of class relations in post-Edwardian England [Pilon, 2016]) differs from, say, that of the United Kingdom (Aughey 2012). Social class in the UK has long served as a system of social organization, a framework for appropriate behaviour, a marker of social distinctions, a guide to identity, a sign of breeding and sophistication, and a device for evaluating the worth of individuals (classism). And this narrative continues to matter in positioning groups of people in relationship to each

other. A recent BBC study entitled the Great British Class Survey (see Table 4.2) defined seven distinct classes that differ in occupation, total household income and savings, home value, and age (Savage and Devine 2013; Savage et al. 2013; Waldie 2013). The study points to the growing fragmentation of the middle class because of more diverse cultural activities and social contacts, in addition to an expanded working class divided into ageing traditional workers, emergent service personnel, and precarious workers. It also demonstrates how the usual distinction between upper/middle/lower classes based on occupation, employment, and income are too simplistic in an increasingly complex, changing, and diverse world (Waldie 2013).

By contrast, references to class in Canada and the United States rarely elicit much attention except as shorthand (rich versus poor), slogan (class wars), or cliché (middle class). The class concept is dismissed as an irrelevant and feudalistic remnant of relevance to those European countries whose inherited aristocracy bordered on caste-like ascription. Canadians instead prefer to think of themselves as classless—apart from reference to a sprawling middle class, although what they really reject are old class-consciousness values; that is, a person's class placement is thought to reflect his or her value and worth as an individual (Allemang 2013; also Bottero 2009). Reference to Canada as a graded hierarchy of social classes is also rejected, with most Canadians seemingly content to be bunched into a sprawling middle class. Even more contested is the "heresy" that class placement influences people's lives and life chances, despite the prominence of class relations and conflict that informs popular films such as *The Hunger Games* or *Snowpiercer*. Reference to a class-based society contravenes North America's fierce attachment to the principles of meritocracy (people are masters of their destiny), equal opportunity, social mobility, and rugged individualism (Alvarado 2010; McNamee 2014). Nevertheless, class membership remains an integral part of a person's identity in the United States, with over 97 per cent of Americans, when prompted, identifying themselves with a particular class.

Yet another paradox persists: the United States may possess one of the world's highest standards of living as well as one of its extremes of income

Table 4.2: New Class Organization in Britain

	Occupation	Household Income/Savings (in £)	Home Value (in £)	Average Age
Elite Most privileged, with highest levels of economic, social and cultural capital. Increasingly disconnected from society	CEOs, financial managers, dentists	355,000 (approx.)	500,000	57
Established middle class (25%) Culturally engaged and socially connected	Engineers, professionals, planners	112,000	270,000	46
Technical middle class (6%) Prosperous but not socially connected; low cultural capital	Pharmacists, pilots, professors	160,000	250,000	52
New affluent workers (15%) Non-university class that are culturally engaged in pop culture	Electricians, postal workers, retail cashiers	52,000	200,000	44
Traditional working class (14%) Moderately poor but own homes and have savings	Cleaners, secretaries, home workers	35,000	195,000	66
Emergent service workers (19%) Relatively poor but high levels of social and cultural capital (but not "highbrow" stuff)	Bar staff, musicians, nursing assistants	34,000	27,000	34
Precariat or precarious proletariat (15%) Scoring low at all levels; disconnected from society; little upward mobility	Carpenters, van drivers, cleaners	13,000	41,000	50

Source: Savage et al. 2013. Copyright © 2013, © SAGE Publications.

inequality. It also possesses one of the lowest levels of social mobility, despite the tenacity of the American Dream with its promise of a payoff so that anyone (not everyone) can be a winner if they really try (Pew Charitable Trusts 2010). A constellation of powerful ideas, tacit assumptions, and cherished ideals reinforces the centrality of individualism, fear of the collective (government),

and the primacy of independent achievement and hard work as pathway to success (Markus and Fiske 2012). Such a meritocratic ideology clearly served the interest of frontier expansion and capitalist accumulation (Orlowski 2011). Yet Americans express an ambivalence about class. To one side, consider the spate of references to the shrinking middle class in the United States (where median net worth and median income in 2011 plummeted to about the same level as in 1983, based on US Census Bureau and Pew Research Center data). To the other side, and despite President Obama's references to class war and fears of an atrophied middle class, Americans continue to buy into the concept of classlessness, even though evidence (see Spotlight box below) reinforces how people's socio-economic placement in society influences their opportunities and outcomes.

Spotlight: Living it Up in Richistan

In 2007, Robert Frank published *Richistan*, a book that equated the lives of America's very wealthy to that of a distinct nation within the United States. According to Frank, the very wealthy are a relatively recent phenomenon, albeit reflecting a third wave of dramatic wealth accumulation after the Gilded Age (1865–1890) and the Roaring Twenties (1918–1929). The period after the Second World War resulted in a redistribution of wealth in part because of Keynesian economics. By 1975, the top 1 per cent could only claim 20 per cent of the nation's wealth, although the post-Reagan era saw that figure rise to 33 per cent. Currently the top one per cent control about half of the nation's wealth.

But the third wave has created many more "richistanis" than have previous eras, including a doubling of American millionaire households to 8 million between 1995 and 2003. Much of this wealth is the result not of inheritance but of liquidity assets that flow from sales of companies, shrewd investments, or fiscal wheeling and dealing (i.e., the "financialization" of capitalism [Cushen 2013]). Moreover, today's richistanis have redefined the meaning of wealth. A million bucks is chump change for a vulgar mob of 7 million households in lower Richistan where the average cost of a wristwatch is $2,100. A household in middle Richistan needs between $10 million and $100 million. The average cost of a wristwatch here is $71,000, while a typical home is valued at $810,000. The few thousand upper richistanis worth up to $1 billion are willing to pay $182,000 for a wristwatch, and have a typical home value of $3.2 million. Finally, the 400 or so who live in the "billionaireville" section of upper Richistan and whose homes are valued at $416 million, don't need to buy a wristwatch. They can hire a consulting firm to negotiate the time (Killian 2007).

The rich are different from the rest (Markus and Fiske 2012; Gwyn 2012; Linneman 2012; Freeland 2012b). Those at the top of the social ladder see, think, and act differently than those on the lower rungs, especially when it comes to money (from wealth to success), including how they see themselves, what they are entitled to, and how they relate to the world around them (Siebold 2010). America's aristocracy tend to see themselves as relatively independent of others and in control of social interactions; they regard money and selfishness as a virtue; and they actively take charge of their interests and futures. Their interests and attitudes matter a great deal when it comes to framing policy issues, whereas the preferences of the common folk rarely matter, thus reinforcing the view that the political system is driven by moneyed interests, America no longer works for ordinary citizens, and the overall system is rigged in favour of the rich (Gilens and Page 2014; Kristof 2016). These oligarchs also tend to be less connected to those citizens left behind and the society that launched their success (they have more in common with a transglobal community of high-flying peers) (Freeland 2011). Light-speed information technology and the globally connected economy reinforce their self-perception as deserving winners in a tough world of intense economic competition. Less compassion is expressed for those who didn't make it. They are, indeed, a

continued

community (or class) unto themselves. How else to explain the construction of the 525-foot yacht *Platinum* completed by the Crown Prince of Dubai? Larger than a Second World War destroyer and just as potent as a weapon of mass destruction, its amenities include an airplane hangar, sophisticated weaponry to fend off pirates or paparazzi, a health spa with a full medical staff, and the obligatory mini-submarine. The "new normal" makes it abundantly clear: boats in the 150-foot range are now dismissed as "starter yachts" (Keister and Southgate 2012).

Ironically, using *class* as a description is acceptable. The concept of class may be tolerated when referring to distribution of material rewards associated with layered rankings of people in prestigious occupations or high incomes. Surveys suggest Americans think of class structure in cake-like images, with groups of individuals stacked in layers from high to low (Perucci and Wysong 2008). The table below summarizes such a class structure in the United States (Perucci and Wysong 2008:29). It draws attention to how society is divided into classes based on people's socio-economic position in the current economy, ranging from those who own or control capital or corporations, to the highly credentialed and self-employed, to those with varying skills who have little to offer except labour power.

In short, a degree of ambiguity underpins the North American aversion to class analysis. The class concept may be employed descriptively to depict people with sophisticated tastes or jet-set lifestyles: those with privileged family backgrounds are entitled to more of everything because they deserve it or because they can have it. But there is a certain skepticism in isolating the concept of class as a key variable or explanatory framework that accounts for people's privileges, opportunities, and outcomes. Of course, few would completely dismiss the salience of class in limiting people's choice or options;

Table 4.3: Class Structure in the United States

	Class Characteristics	Percentage of Population
Privileged class/superclass	Owners and employers; investment income; seven-figure income	1–2%
Credentialed class/ managers	Mid- to upper-level managers and CEOs; up to seven-figure incomes	13–15%
Professionals	University/professional degrees; high levels of social capital; income from $100,000 up	4–5%
New working class/ comfort class	Nurses, teachers, civil servants, electricians $35k to $50k range	10%
Contingent class/wage earners	Clerical and sales, personal services, machine operators, transportation; less than $30k income	50%
Self-employed	Modest incomes	3–4%
Excluded class	Part-time, unskilled, temporary	10–15%

Source: Adapted from Perucci and Wysong 2008.

nevertheless, there is some aversion for locating class within an economic context involving the ownership and control of productive property. References to class in terms of a struggle between the haves and the have-nots is criticized as ideologically bankrupt and historically antiquated. To the extent reference to class as concept is analytically acceptable, it reflects a category of individuals based on the *effects* of their personal initiative, drive, and skills.

Academics, too, have shown a growing disdain for class as a key explanatory variable. Some argue that rapid changes in society have delegitimized class analysis to the point of irrelevance, giving way to different forms of social identification, including identity politics based on religion or culture. They argue as well that divisions based on race or gender are not reducible to class even if closely related, and that reference to class cannot possibly capture the diversity and complexities at the heart of contemporary realities. Class consciousness is rapidly fading as well: even vast disparities in income and privilege do not automatically translate into "class wars." Others disagree with moves to abolish class as an analytical tool for explaining inequality. True, classes are less visible than in the past, but reports of its demise and death as reality and explanation are greatly exaggerated (Crompton 2008). They reject the notion of reducing society to the level of atomistic actors, preferring instead, to situate people within a broader context in which they share common socio-economic interests or, alternatively, confront similar structural barriers. Furthermore, class is more than a descriptive category of people based on similar amounts of property, power, or prestige. Rather class counts (i.e., matters) because a person's socio-economic location influences his or her life chances and lived realities. Simply put, those in higher income brackets tend to be healthier, live longer, receive better medical treatment or protection from the law, and generally possess more opportunities. Those at lower levels tend to be denied, excluded, or exploited (Wilkinson and Pickett 2009; Hankivsky 2011).

Let's put this into perspective: any consensus over social class as reality or analysis is notoriously slippery as might be expected of a concept that means different things to different people (Bottero 2009). Social classes in Canada may or may not exist in the naturally occurring sense of the word but rather as socially constructed categories (aggregates) of persons who share similar socio-economic position. Yet social classes are real insofar as people act as if they were real, with corresponding consequences for themselves and others. They are real since analytical constructs need not be objectively (intrinsically) real to be real in their effects (Chan and Goldthorpe 2007:518). Class placement as social location will profoundly influence how people see themselves, how they think others see them, how others relate to them, what they want, how they can get what they want, and their chances of success (Crompton 2008; Keister and Southgate 2012; Fiske and Markus 2012). Social class location also constitutes a key determinant of a person's work, wealth, income, and education; counts as key variable that accounts for patterns of inequality, whether people are aware or not; and contributes to how individuals think, experience, and relate to others and, in turn, how others relate to them. Finally class matters even as a proxy for socio-economic status in expanding one's access to desired resources (including money, power, networks, healthcare, and educational opportunities) that, in turn, enable individuals to prosper. As Markus and Fiske (2012:1, 3) write, reminding people *that class matters*:

> Social-class differences and the inequality they reflect now organize American society more than ever. Differences in resources and in the associated status and cultural capital influence whether we fight in a war, vote, or get divorced. They matter for the music we listen to, what we eat for dinner, how we talk, how much we weigh, and how long we live. Social class also shapes social interaction in every domain of life . . . how people make decisions; how they perceive and are perceived by others; their sense of self, agency, and identity; their feelings of trust, certainty, belonging, or fit; their orientation to time; their perceptions of health, sickness, and well-being; their social responsiveness to others; their understandings of in-group and out-group and social hierarchy; their attitudes to politics, religion, and life in general; their hopes and dreams and possible selves.

Conceptualizing Class

Definitions of social class are varied. Hardly surprising, since references to class can mean everything yet nothing, or whatever people want it to mean depending on the context. In general, class may be defined as a category of persons who occupy a similar socio-economic situation (position or rank) in relation to other socio-economic placements within a stratified hierarchy. More specifically, classes are defined as groups of individuals who stand in a comparable relationship to scarce and valued resources such as wealth, power, or privilege, and are ranked accordingly in terms of ownership of productive property and/or family background (see Schutz 2011). Finally, class may be defined as the interplay of economic capital (wealth), cultural capital (education), and social capital (networks) whose combined impact influences a person's lifestyle and life chances. Those possessing the largest amount of this class capital can impose their power, privilege, and preferences over those with lesser amounts (Roberts, Atkinson, and Savage 2012).

Marxist and Weberian approaches provided the template for class analysis (see Grabb 2006 for fuller discussion). These theories differed, although both emphasized the importance of the economy in determining class and class relations. Marxists focused on the economic domain of production, whereas Weberians inclined towards the primacy of market situation as influenced by occupational status and family background (Perucci and Wysong 2008). Marx emphasized the relational aspects of class (workers versus owners), whereas Weber inspired what is now known as a gradational class scheme arranged in ascending and descending order of stratified upper-middle-lower layers (see Clement 1988:20). For Marxists, the concept of class is synonymous domination and exploitation, most notably an antagonistic struggle between exploiters and the exploited for controlling the benefits associated with the means of production (Skeggs and Wood 2011). Class exploitation is an objective phenomena, according to Marxists, featuring the extraction of surplus from producers, which invariably generates class consciousness (individuals become conscious of themselves as a class) in addition to a subjective component of a shared awareness of class placement, identity, and predicament. The resultant class structure revolves around three core strata based on people's common relationship to the means of production as a system of exploitation. The first consists of a group of individuals who own productive property (make a living through ownership of land, equity, debt, or means of production). The second consists of workers who earn a living through the sale of their labour power, yet lack autonomy or control over their labour (Ginsburgh, 2012). A third incorporates an intermediate category of professionals, small business owners, administrators, and wage-earners, all of whom possess some certifiable credentials and authoritative power to control others.

For Weber and Weberians, class analysis went beyond focusing strictly on production. Yes, class reflected economic circumstances such as ownership and relationship to the means of production, since people's occupational sets influenced their type of work and the rewards they received (Macionis and Plummer 2008). But factors that differentiated individuals based on similar family background related to market situation were equally relevant in defining social classes (Breen and Rottman 1995; Crompton 2008). Whereas Marxists focused on production and exploitation in analyzing class, Weberian class analysis put greater emphasis on the market and people's class (market) situation in shaping their life chances—as defined and determined by the kind and amount of power to profit from goods and skills in a specific economic order (Gerth and Mills, 1958). Unlike Marxists, moreover, Weberians did not necessarily see class as a major source of conflict in society, much less as a primary source of collective action. Rather, as Breen and Rottman (1995) argue, classes were of interest primarily because of their role in linking people's position in a capitalist system (i.e., their market situation) to inequalities that shaped the distribution of outcomes and life chances. For fuller discussion see Weber's posthumous publication *Economy and Society* (1922).

No less contested are debates over the onto-logical status of class as a social construct or objective reality (Lareau and Conley 2010). This is hardly surprising since class constitutes a "complicated mixture of the material, the discursive, psychological predispositions, and sociological dispositions"—not only embodied in and by objective economic conditions but also a lived reality and dynamic aspect of identity and interactions (Reay 1998). Or as Grabb and Guppy (2009) point out, the conceptual disarray associated with the class concept reflects a lack of precision and general disagreement over its positioning in reality. This in turn prompts the following questions of whether a class analysis (both Weberian and Marxist) is of any heuristic value in explaining contemporary patterns of inequality and exclusion (Breen and Rottman 1995):

1. *Real or construct?* Are classes real in the sense they exist "out there" in the world? Should they be viewed as pre-existing boxes that slot individuals into groups with a shared awareness of their "groupness"? Or should we acknowledge the possibility that classes are real, albeit not in the *naturally* occurring sense, but as a *socially* created classification in which similar units are grouped into categories for purposes of description or analysis (such as accounting for patterns of social inequality) (Porter 1965)? While this social construct may not be objectively real in the *naturally* occurring sense, it exists in the *reality* sense *because people think it's real or act as if it were real in making things happen (class matters), resulting in consequences related to identity formation, lived experiences, and access to opportunities and outcomes.* In brief, the class concept has predictive powers rather than serving just as a descriptive category to describe the effects of people's past actions and outcomes.
2. *Socio-economic aggregate or lived groups?* Are classes real (authentic) in the sense they point to a distinctive reality out there based on people's shared identities, perceptions, values and traditions, and an awareness of unity and common purpose (Porter 1965)? Do we conceive of classes as groups of persons who embrace a common membership with a shared (yet often dormant) awareness of their socio-economic situation as basis for identity or action? Or are

classes better seen as a shorthand or proxy term describing a category (aggregate) of individuals occupying a similar socio-economic status by virtue of comparable amounts of property, power, and privilege (Crompton 2008)?
3. *Fixed or fluid?* Are classes fixed groups or static categories within a predefined hierarchy? If so, how do we arrive at a consensus for locating the upper and lower boundaries of each class level (see Cross and Munir 2015)? Or are they better understood against a backdrop of a more fluid social system whose dynamics and fortunes reflect situational circumstances (Jones 2012 Markus and Fiske 2012)?
4. *Objective versus subjective?* Should criteria for defining social classes embody subjective elements such as self-definition based on public opinion polling techniques or assessments by members of the community about class position or class reputation (Porter 1965)? Or should the definition of classes reflect objective criteria such as income, occupational levels, or people's relationship to productive property either as workers or owners—even if they lack awareness of this positionality (Porter 1965)? Should classes be self-defined by categories of individuals who share a similar market situation because of their family background? Or should references to classes be restricted to economic conditions involving ownership or control over the means of production? Should classes be viewed strictly in economic terms or, alternatively, along more comprehensive lines to include the political, social, and cultural (lifestyle) factors (Linkon 2012)?
5. *Income or lifestyle?* Should income differences serve as the basis for defining class categories so that they can be measured—despite disagreement on the appropriate income levels and brackets to be included (Cross and Munir 2015)? Or are income, birth or occupation themselves no longer an appropriate measure, with emphasis instead on consumption and lifestyle (i.e., values and taste) as key variables?
6. *Ascription or achievement?* In contrast to caste systems which are ascriptive in status (based on heredity and predestination, and fixed for life), the concept of class tends towards the principles

of achievement, merit, and mobility. Or should classes acknowledge an ascriptive dimension (Johnson 2015) that, by definition, renders all playing fields un-level, given the importance of family background (inheritance), the presence of discriminatory barriers, and foundational principles of a society's constitutional order?

7. *How many?* How many classes exist? Two? Three? Nine? Are there two major classes— dominant (capitalist) and subordinate (proletariat)? Or is slightly more complex entailing at least three major components: capitalists (owners of productive property), the working class (sellers of their labour power), and a middle class consisting of professionals, managers, or workers with some certifiable credentials or money-making skills? Alternatively, should classes be defined along multiple lines by acknowledging the importance of non-economic factors such as power and prestige as grounds for class typologies? According to this line of thinking, classes consist of the upper, middle, and lower. These in turn can be further subdivided into upper-upper, middle-upper, and lower-upper, and so on.

Responses to these questions are sharply contested and resist simple answers. Markus and Fiske (2012:3) acknowledge the complexities when demonstrating that social class is neither a fixed set of inherent attributes nor simply a ranking in a hierarchy, a marker of prestige, and control over material resources. Not surprisingly, any class analysis must acknowledge an ontological ambiguity inspired by the opposition between Marxists and Weberians. For Marxists, social classes exist: they represent an objective reality consisting of actual groups who stand in a fundamentally different way relative to the means of production. For Weberians, class constitutes a social construct incorporating an aggregate of persons with shared socio-economic attributes related to their market situation. Classes represent a defined category of individuals occupying a common socio-economic position based on family background, with a corresponding set of characteristics and circumstances that influence

lives and life chances (market situations). In both cases, the concept of class is deemed to be real, albeit in ontologically different ways: one is real because it exists as a durable object in reality, the other is real as a socially constructed convention that is willed into existence. The complexities and ambiguities associated with the class concept are captured through the prism of media representations of class and class relations.

Mediatizing Inequality: Media Representations of Class and Class Relations

People's knowledge of social inequality in regards to classes and class relations is largely media driven (Fleras 2011a). What people know about the world of inequalities is rarely crafted from personal experience. Media often provide the preliminary and primary point of contact with the world out there, yet mainstream media are not necessarily an objective or reliable source of information about issues related to social inequality and the inequalities of exclusion. Nor do mainstream media exist in a political void or economic vacuum. Rather they are situated within a capitalistic framework that has intensified the rational pursuit of profit. Their (in)corporatization into larger conglomerates for control of the information/ entertainment package has proven consequential. Mainstream media have evolved into intensely competitive business ventures whose bottom line mentality prevails over national interests, common good, or social justice. The conglomeration of media industries into turbo-charged, money-making machines not only dictates media decisions with respect to what is on and who is in. It also generates a conflict of interest between private gain and public good, since revenue-obsessed media gravitate toward audiences who appeal to advertisers. Or as a retired editor of *The Philadelphia Inquirer* once quipped "You can't sell many ads when your readers [viewers] don't have credit cards, and thus some readers are worth more than others" (in Cunningham 2004).

A class bias prevails in media representations of society and social reality by virtue of who owns, controls, and distributes content (Fleras 2011a; Jones, 2011). Commercial imperatives exert a powerful if largely unarticulated influence in shaping representations of social inequalities as they pertain to class and class relations (Hackett et al. 2000; Winter 2001). Yet there remains a dearth of studies about the representational nexus of media, inequality, and class relations, even though the relationship is unmistakable, given the intertwining of corporate with class interests in sharing a common economic agenda (for United States, see Mantsios 2001; Croteau and Hoynes 2003; Benson 2005; Butsch 2005; Leistyna and Mollen 2008; Kendall 2005/2010). What little is out there tends to reinforce what many suspect: ownership and control of commercial media by the rich and powerful may indirectly influence depictions of class, classes, and class relations. Coverage and content are presented in a way that attends to the interests of shareholders and stakeholders, in large part because those who work for the moneyed interests tend to frame reality from their own point of view—as natural and normal and as desirable and acceptable—whereas other perspectives are dismissed as irrelevant, inferior, or threatening (Fleras, 2014c). Not surprisingly, media representations are slanted toward lavish depictions of the rich and professionals as deserving and inherently interesting, sometimes fatally so, whereas the working classes, labour unions and the undeserving poor are generally ignored or negativized, or mocked by being played for laughs (Kendall 2005).

Just as media institutions are biased in ways consistent with media priorities and vested interests, so too are media representations of social class an exercise in distortions (Fleras 2014c). News media are also classed when reporting on classes and class relations (Croteau and Hoynes 2003). This class bias significantly affects the framing of newsworthiness, partly because of cross-ownership or mutual interests, fears that unfavourable coverage might alienate advertising, and the routine nature of most newsgathering, with its emphasis on official sources. What appears as news and news sources is likely to reflect government interests and business representatives rather than labour officials or consumer advocates. The

"newshole" allows very few articles on the working conditions of workers or their economic problems. Articles that feature working classes are relatively short, near the back, at the bottom, or under the fold; they rarely discuss economic alternatives and generally bypass union leaders as primary sources of information for fear that politicizing the discourses would expose widespread social exclusion and economic inequality (Kollmeyer 2004). In short, mainstream media reflect, reinforce, and advance the interests and priorities of ruling elites, largely because the organizational culture and structural bias of newsmedia favour coverage of those with privilege and power. The net result? Patterns of social inequality are promoted and perpetuated by **mediacentric** representations of social classes and identity groups.

Herein lies a core contradiction of a classed media. The elite corporate media play a pivotal role in defining what stories will be told, by whom and how, and whose voices will be heard. But out of deference to their economic "masters," media discourses rarely explicitly address the topics of class or class relations (Kendall 2005). Such media antipathy means many class-based issues are not framed as such, even if most entertainment-based shows are about class in one way or another, albeit not self-consciously so (Skeggs and Wood 2012). Rather TV depictions of classes deploy themes that conflate class and classes with variations in family background, cultural tastes, and levels of sophistication. The tension and conflict that invariably inform societies organized around ownership and control of productive property is generally downplayed (Croteau, Hoynes, and Milan 2012; Jones 2011). Even less attention is devoted to the concept of class location in society and its influence on people's thought and behaviour as well as opportunities and outcomes. To the extent that class is portrayed on entertainment media, (for example, in the former hit sitcom *Frasier*), it de-emphasizes class as a differential access to means of production or control of key resources. Hierarchies of personal taste or individual preferences prevail instead (Skeggs and Wood 2012; Bullock, Wyche, and Williams 2001).

Depictions also tend to ignore the macro-level causes such as structural determinants of inequality and class positions (Kendall 2005; Jones 2011). Root (or macro-level) causes of inequality are glossed over, including the centrality of family inheritance, social and cultural values, educational opportunity, or underemployment because of moves toward downsizing, offshoring, or outsourcing. Media representations depict financial markets as catalysts that fuel broader public good without acknowledging how such processes reinforce the power and wealth of elite at the expense of working

folk who are then reduced to abstractions such as employment figures. Minimal attention is directed at the exploitative aspects and human costs at the core of capitalism. In that a classed media gaze is selective in how class and classes are depicted, the potential for misinformation is real by virtue of distracting people from the real issues (Fleras and Dixon 2011 for additional explanation). The following Spotlight box casts additional light on how mainstream media depict (represent) different classes.

Spotlight Classes through a Media Lens: Upper, Middle, Working, and Poor

Entertainment media have long flirted with the lives and antics of the super-rich. The wealthy tend to be depicted as fascinating and generally admirable, with a few bad apples thrown into the mix, although they are rarely portrayed as a class in the Marxist sense of ruling, owning, and profiteering. A pre-occupation with the power and privilege afforded by wealth prevails, even if some members of the pampered classes are shown to behave badly—lie, cheat, sleep around, or even murder. The high and mighty are so fascinating to mainstream media that they continue to be portrayed as having eminently worthwhile if somewhat flawed lives (Kendall 2005). In other words, as many have noted, if the subjects are wealthy, people will watch. Barbara Ehrenreich (2009) captures a taste of this contradiction when she writes of a media enamoured with the views, realities, or experiences of society's upper crust: "When a millionaire cuts back on his crème fraiche and caviar consumption, you have a touching human interest story. But pitch a story about a laid-off roofer who loses his trailer home and you're likely to get a big editorial yawn."

The televisual fortunes of the middle class are mixed (N. Johnson 2009). Historically they were positively framed in terms of values and as highly valued (Kendall 2005). In contrast to the negativiz-ing of working-class families, middle-class parents were defined as intelligent, sensible, and mature, calm and affable. As super-parents they served as moral compasses for guiding their children along

the right path (Butsch 2005). Admittedly, the por-trayal of middle classes has lost some of its lustre. Once positive examples are increasingly displaced by more ambiguous representations as the mid-dle class forfeits its cash and cachet. Middle-class males are no longer as perfect as they once were (for example, Jim Anderson of Fathers Knows Best or Ward Cleaver of Leave it to Beaver). But while they are sometimes cast as emotionally confused or clueless—even immature to a degree (from Seinfeld to Tim Taylor of Home Improvement) (Butsch 2005)—they continued to be framed as relatively intelligent and successful by comparison with those "beneath" them.

The poor (or, loosely, the underclass) are ren-dered largely invisible by mainstream media (Mantsios 2001). When portrayed, the poor and homeless are packaged as statistical abstrac-tions—that is, the number who are unemployed or on benefits, (Kendall 2005); as outsiders whose moral and cultural compass lacks any middle-class bearings (Bullock, Wyche, and Williams 2001); or as moral failures responsible for their predicament (Redden 2014). Negative and stereotyped depic-tions ensure their status as dependent, passive, responsible for their plight, and without initiative and morality (Bullock, Wyche, and Williams 2001)—precisely the features that drive "trash-talk" shows like The Jerry Springer Show or reality-based shows like Cops (Mantsios 2001). True, poor whites may be framed as honest, hardworking, honourable, simple, loyal, god-fearing, and patriotic folk. That was the case in the early days of television with shows such as *The Honeymooners*. But most often they are caricaturized as whisky drinkers, monster-truck-show watchers, abusive and violently red-necked, infantile, dirty, fat, insensitive, close-minded and uneducated (see video *Class Dismissed* 2005). White "trailer trash" folk, especially those on welfare, are demonized as the embodiment of racism, ignorance, violence, filth, with moronic desires and delinquent antics land them outside the bounds of society's laws and cultural norms—a theme pursued by the antics of Julian, Ricky, and Bubbles in the Canadian mockumentary *Trailer Park Boys*. In addition, both the poor and poverty stricken tend to be framed disproportionately as problem of racialized minorities (Baumann and Johnston 2008), thus reinforcing the concept of media representations as racialized as well as classed.

Not all poor are similarly depicted as welfare cheats, drug addicts, street criminals, or aggressive panhandlers (Kendall 2005). A distinction between the deserving and undeserving poor can be detected. To one side are the deserving poor such as the working poor or older folk, in addition to the once middle-class now ravaged by the recession (deMause 2009). To the other side are the so-called undeserving poor, the working-age unemployed poor or those able-bodied poor on welfare who collectively deserve societal contempt (Baumann and Johnston 2008). They are depicted as lazy, stupid, incompetent, and lacking self-control, resulting in too many babies or crippling addictions (deMause 2009). Unflattering representations of the poor often reflect their failure or refusal to embrace the principle of meritocracy (you can make it if you *really* try) (Leistyna and Mollen 2008). But mainstream media provide more sympathetic portrayals when poverty victimizes children, older adults, and the ill—namely, those worthy poor who deserve our sympathy and support (Kendall 2005). Lastly, the poor may be framed as happy with their lot or cheerfully resigned to their fate, especially when poverty is romanticized as virtuous or the poor as simple, honest folk happily coexisting with the wealthy (the equality of inequality). The end result is a normalizing of elites as ordinary folk while naturalizing the poor as spiritually rich (Baumann and Johnston 2008).

Working class portrayals on television span a wide spectrum (Mantsios 2001; Butsch 2003, 2005; Leistyna and Mollen 2008). Media perceptions of a particular image of the working class as thick, violent, and criminal is offset by frames that romanticize workers as valued, worthy, and reliable. Those in the "professional" working classes—police, nurses, and firefighters—are accorded kid glove treatment on the screen in contrast to the largely negative framing of blue-collar, assembly-line workers. A gender divide can also be discerned. The portrayal of working wives tends toward middle-class professionalism and careers rather than in menial occupations, thus exempting them from the slings of blue-collar indignities. But respectful treatment has proven elusive, despite a history of working-class television, from *Coronation Street* to *Roseanne* to *The Simpsons* filtered through the prism of disdain, patronizing and mired in cliché (Janzen 2009). The working classes may have once been portrayed as the salt of the earth whose authenticity could be milked for laughs, but a reversal of fortune could be detected by the early 1970s (Manzoor 2008). They had assumed the media status of super-patriotic hawks whose racist and reactionary political views coalesced around the bumper sticker "America, love it or leave it" (Ehrenreich 2009). The dominant image, especially of working-class males, remains that of a stock character both inept and buffoonish (Butsch 2005). Working-class males tend to be depicted as dull (even stupid), immature and irresponsible (thus requiring supervision by their betters), as deviants who must lie and cheat to compensate for personal shortcomings, and as clowns on sitcoms like *Married with Children* (Butsch 2003). They come across as "uncouth, beer bellied loudmouths, alcoholic thugs, slovenly in appearance, couch potatoes, feckless scroungers, wife beaters, racist hooligans, and supporters of right wing causes" (Jones 2011; Butsch 2005). Predictably the families of working-class males tend toward the derogatory and dysfunctional, including a host of unhealthy dependencies from drinking to gambling

continued

to philandering. Working-class youth tend to be framed as moral panics. The sharpest slings are reserved for unionized workers who are exposed as corrupt or lazy, and overwhelmingly responsible for labour unrest that costs or inconveniences (see Class Dismissed 2005). Not surprisingly, even in programs with a pro-working class slant, mainstream media remain resolutely anti-labour by emphasizing the dignity of work while demonizing the evils of unions.

Exceptions to the rule and alternative narratives exist, as might be expected in a category that runs the gamut from janitors to health care workers, from blue collar factory workers to retail clerks to service providers (Linkon 2012). Working class portrayals in advertising between 1950 and 2010 focused on nostalgic images of workers as happy and hard-working—even as blue collar jobs disappeared (Paulson and O'Guinn 2012). No less discernible is media infatuation with the dignity of blue collar jobs as the work ethic that keeps the country afloat (Working-Class Perspectives 2008). Working-class work is shown to require resilience and toughness for those physically demanding jobs that few appreciate. For example, the United States' three major sports leagues (MLB, NBA, and NFL) claim solidarity with the American workingman—especially football commentators who routinely praise members of the defensive and offensive line as a "lunch bucket brigade" for "getting down and dirty in doing the job" without complaint (Carroll 2008). Finally, a slew of documentary-style reality shows portray working-class men as anything but blunderers or shirkers. Indeed, they are depicted as heroic in pursuing dangerous occupations, from ice road truckers to deep sea crab fishers, in the process reasserting and valorizing their masculinity, autonomy, and authenticity (Fleras and Dixon 2011).

The conclusion is inescapable: media coverage of classes and class relations is neither balanced and objective nor independent and neutral. Rather, media are classed in three ways: first, by virtue of monopolistic ownership; second, by a class bias that permeates representations of the rich and accomplished; and third, in selectively defining what constitutes acceptable content in terms of who is perceived as more important or powerful (Jones 2011). Is there is a common theme that might be gleaned from analyzing the often mixed messages involving class and class relations? It would appear that, on the whole, mainstream media are complicit in advancing the American dream, with its concomitant notion of meritocracy and individualism as the path to success (Johnson 2015). Success, as defined by positive media representation, belongs to those who work hard regardless of class status. Conversely, those who fail to take advantage of equal opportunities in an allegedly fair and meritocratic society are negatively framed for "screwing up." In a meritocratic society, individuals get what they deserve, regardless of background, thereby denying the impact of class on people's lives and life chances, while entrenching the belief that individuals are responsible for their predicament (Ginsburgh 2012). Those in between—they try but fail for reasons largely beyond their control—deserve the benefit of the doubt by way of sympathetic media depictions. Clearly then, media coverage of classes reflects the principle of neo-liberal functionalism: society = good; individuals = must change. Individuals are framed primarily as responsible for the predicament (from success to failure) they find themselves in (blaming the victim). The structures and systems that create inequality and exclusion (blaming the system) get off lightly (Jones 2011).

Summary

1. Edwardian notions of social classes were central in influencing the patterns of who lived and died on the doomed *Titanic*.

2. Social class is a contested category of inequality in its own right as well as in its application to Canada.

3. Resistance is widespread in Canada and the United States to the salience of the class concept as an explanatory framework, largely because of historical, geographic, and cultural factors.
4. Classes are shown to matter in influencing opportunities and outcomes despite ongoing debates over their heuristic value in predicting success or inequality and their

ontological existence as socially constructed or intrinsic (naturally occurring).
5. Continuing sociological debates about class and inequality reflect the work of Marx and Weber.
6. Mainstream media mis-portray classes and class relations because of inherent biases associated with the politics of representation.

Review Questions

1. This chapter is premised on the assumption that class matters. Indicate how and why.
2. Explain how survival on the *Titanic* reinforces the idea that not only class matters but also gender and race.
3. Discuss why the concept class matters is not a popular sell in Canada and the United States.

4. Demonstrate some of the challenges associated with analyzing the concept of class.
5. The section on media representations and class suggest the media images of the working class tend to be ambivalent. Indicate how this is true, paying particular attention to media construction of the working class.

Endnotes

1. New research indicates the *Titanic*'s adherence to the social norm of women and children first as the "unwritten rule of the sea" may be the exception rather than rule. Using a database of 18 maritime disasters spanning three centuries, Elinder and Erixson (2012) arrive at the following conclusions:
   a. Women are about half as likely as men to survive.
   b. Children have the worst survival rate.
   c. Captains and crew are slightly more likely to survive than passengers.
   d. Only 9 of 16 captains went down with the ship.
   e. The discretion of the captain is critical in activating the "women and children first" scenario.
   The authors of the report conclude that the sinking of the *Titanic* did not conform to a more generic pattern; that when it comes to matters of life and death, it's every man for himself, a refrain literally endorsed by the captain of the grounded Italian cruise ship, *Costa Concordia*.

2. In 1972, the author sailed from Vancouver to Auckland in the steerage class compartment of the 26,000 ton P & O *Orsova* (the *Titanic* displaced about 52,000 tons). I can assure readers that in case of emergency or evacuation, the chances of escape struck me as minimal. The narrow and often intricate passageways in the hold of the boat would have sealed our fate, consigning the whole lower-class lot of us off to Davy Jones's Locker.
3. Unless indicated otherwise, material for this section is taken from Wayne Hall (1986), "Social Class and Survival on the S.S. *Titanic*," *Social Science and Medicine* 22(6):687-690; Bruno Frey, David A. Savage, and Benno Torgler (2011), "Behavior under Extreme Conditions: The *Titanic* Disaster," *Journal of Economic Perspectives* 25(1):209-222; Douglas W. Phillips (2011), "*Titanic*'s Sinking Pervades our Culture," *Toronto Star*, 9 April; "The *Titanic* Numbers Game," President of the Christian Boy's and Men's *Titanic* Society and Vision Forum Ministries, retrieved from www.titanicsociety.com.

5 The Politics of Poverty

Learning Objectives

1. To grasp the magnitude of poverty in a bountiful Canada.
2. To explain why little agreement exists over the definition, scope, and measurement of poverty.
3. To point out how poverty matters not just in material concerns but in sustaining patterns of social exclusion.
4. To apply a social class lens for analyzing poverty and homelessness in Canada.
5. To demonstrate how the framing of poverty as exclusion will influence poverty reduction strategies.

Introduction: Framing Poverty

I've been rich and I've been poor. Believe me, rich is better. — Attributed to Mae West

The year 1989 proved to be epoch-making. The dismantling of the Berlin Wall symbolized the collapse of a system whose obsession with engineered equality compromised the right of individual freedoms. No less disruptive than the Soviet Union's demise as a world superpower was the explosion of freewheeling (neo-liberal) globalization. The dismantling of Cold War borders encouraged a relatively unrestricted movement of capital and trade goods, a global system of production and division of labour, and the triumph of the market as the guide, arbiter, and regulator of all state and human activity (Dean 2009). But the benefits of unfettered market freedom over the costs of a bureaucratized economy proved illusory. The promise of the trickle-down effect whereby the rising tide would lift all ships was dashed by a sobering reality: the world's rich became substantially richer while the global poor grew relatively poorer. Put alternatively, instead of the promised trickle-down effect, many found themselves "pissed on" (as eloquently expressed by a Maori student in one of my classes at the University of Canterbury, Christchurch, NZ), with only the yachts drifting toward the surface while the dinghies and rowboats sank to the bottom.

Another event transpired in 1989 that was of somewhat less international import, yet significant to Canada. In that year, an all-party House of Commons resolution vowed to eliminate child **poverty** by the year 2000 (deBoer, Rothwell, and Lee 2013). The challenge certainly seemed doable in light of Canada's seemingly inexhaustible resources and the boundless resourcefulness of its population. Canada's success in reducing the poverty levels of older Canadians was proof of political will to orchestrate successful outcomes (Osberg 2012). But rhetoric has not matched reality. Despite an economy firing on all cylinders over the past two decades, Canada's war against child poverty elicited mixed results, in part because the necessary Canada-wide action plans never materialized (Polanyi et al. 2014; Campaign 2000 2012). Using the low income cut-off (LICO) measure, the poverty rate for Canadian children, after taxes and transfers (AT), declined to 8.5 per cent in 2011 from a peak of 18.4 per cent in 1996 and a base of 11.9 per cent in 1989 (Statistics Canada 2013d). But according to a different set of measures—the low-income measure (LIM)—rates of child poverty moved in the opposite direction, to nearly one in five (19 per cent) children, from a base of 15.8 per cent in 1989, albeit down from a peak of 22.3 per cent in 2000 (Campaign 2000 2015). Another 700,000 children would have been included in this tally if not for government transfers (from HST/GST credit to the Canada Child Tax Benefit) in reducing poverty. Children of people with disabilities (30 per cent), racialized minorities (33 per cent), lone female parents (37 per cent), Indigenous peoples (40 per cent), and recent immigrants (46 per cent) also experience exceptionally high rates of poverty (Report 2014a; Campaign 2000 2015; Macdonald and Wilson 2016). Provincial, territorial, and urban variations persist: child poverty rates range from 37.7 per cent in Nunavut to 14.8 per cent in Quebec, with Manitoba having the highest provincial rate at 29 per cent (Campaign 2000 2015). Toronto remains Canada's child poverty capital (Polanyi et al. 2014), and cities remain sites of concentrated poverty: child poverty in Toronto grew to 29 per cent of all children in 2013 (based on LIM), including rates of over 40 per cent for residents in 15 Toronto communities, with variations ranging from 5 per cent in Lawrence Park to over 50 per cent in Regent Park (Report 2014). These unflattering data would imply that Ronald Reagan's famous quip, "We fought a war on poverty and poverty won," could well apply to Canada.

To be sure, not all the news on the poverty front is bad. Depending on the measure employed, the percentage of Canadians living in poverty has declined (Lamman and Macintyre 2016). Specific demographics have also seen an improvement in fortunes. According to the Conference Board of Canada (2011b), the poverty rate among older Canadians in general stood at 5.9 per cent (after transfers) compared to 20.4 per cent in 1990. That put Canada second best out of 17 peer countries, according to the OECD, prompting Dalhousie University's economics professor Lars Osberg to claim

that this reduction is "the major success story of Canadian social policy in the twentieth century." But recently released income data from Statistics Canada indicate an increase to 11.1 per cent in 2013 (LIM-AT) in the incidents of poverty among older folk, including a disturbing low income rate of 27.1 per cent among single (often women) adults (Jackson 2016). Improving? Regressing? Stagnating? Such mixed messages are worrying. Canada's international reputation takes a hit when a UNICEF report (2013) ranks Canada seventeenth out of twenty-nine rich countries in securing the well-being of its children (based on 26 indicators across 5 dimensions), a ranking that has barely budged in the last decade (Monsebraaten 2013). Canadians are also bewildered and frustrated by these mixed messages. In contrast to the well-established transfers that provide income and assistance for older folk, Canadians appear to be baffled by the persistence of child poverty, without fully comprehending the detrimental effects of such indecisiveness. Child poverty matters—physically, mentally, emotionally—because it causes children to suffer loss of dignity, the ability to participate in their communities, and the opportunity to learn, grow, and develop (Polanyi et al. 2014). This passage from the UNICEF report (2012; Broadbent Institute 2012) reminds us that shortchanging the most vulnerable is a recipe for future social problems.

…[F]ailure to protect children from poverty is one of the most costly mistakes a society can make. The heaviest cost of all is borne by the children themselves. But their nations must also pay a very significant price—in reduced skills and productivity, in lower levels of health and educational achievement, increased likelihood of unemployment and welfare dependence, in higher costs of judicial and social protection systems, and in the loss of social cohesion.

In other words, growing up poor negatively affects children across the life cycle, with major implications for society (deBoer, Rothwell, and Lee 2013). Put more bluntly, if children are an investment in the future, a disaster of epic proportions is looming due to a neglect of poverty, and the poverty of neglect.

Many regard the polarization of affluence and poverty as one of Canada's foremost inequality problems (Campaign 2000 2013; Conference Board of Canada 2011a). A growing number of Canadians are "making a killing" because of extraordinary compensation for CEOs and financial managers (Mackenzie 2015); conversely, poverty is killing (literally and figuratively speaking) those less fortunate children who endure contaminated water, food insecurities, and inadequate shelters (Frank 2013; see also Galea et al. 2011). And while the prospect of putting people at risk by shutting them out of Canadian society is bad enough, no less menacing is the shredding of the social fabric that undersews a coherent coexistence. Studies repeatedly point to the social costs of poverty: it is an incubator for a host of poorer outcomes, including health, literacy, crime, school attainment, aborted maturity, and increased family stress (Silver 2012). Children are particularly vulnerable because of long-term effects caused by the toxicity of early childhood stress, culminating in costly adult problems, self-destructive behaviours, cognitive impairment, and expensive social services (Polanyi et al 2014; Campaign 2000 2011). In short, Canadians as a whole pay the price for poverty in Canada by way of higher public health care costs, increased policing and criminal justice involvement, and higher income supports but less tax revenues (Ivanova 2011).

The enormity of the poverty problem has not produced any agreement over its meaning, magnitude, and measurement. Questions abound: what precisely do we mean by *poverty*? Who says what it is, why, and on what grounds? How much is there? What are the causes and consequences of poverty? How should we measure it? How should societies be compared with each other and over time to evaluate the success of policies designed to reduce poverty? What does it mean to be poor in a relatively affluent society? Does poverty mean the same in sub-Saharan Africa as it does southern Ontario? Does being poor mean not having enough to eat or not eating out? Is a person poor if they do not own a smartphone or have access to high-speed Internet connections, thus depriving them of social, educational, and employment opportunities (Monsebraaten 2016)? Who is to blame for the poverty problem? Is poverty the

result of social injustice and structural exclusions? Or should individuals be blamed for their lack of resolve and resourcefulness (also Winlow and Hall 2013)? Are moral failures or societal failings to blame? Should intervention focus on Band-Aid solutions that address immediate needs? Or should the aim be to break the cycle of poverty by targeting root causes through integrated poverty reduction programs that collectively improve children's lives and future life chances (Ontario 2013)?

Finding answers to the above questions is more vital than ever. The consequences of poverty go beyond a lack of income or wealth, however painful that might be. (Keep in mind that, although related, poverty is not the same as inequality [Sarlo 2016; UN 2009]. Levels of inequality can increase even as poverty rates fall or the standard of living for the poor improves. As Marston [2003:3] notes, poverty is about not having enough, whereas inequality is about not having as much as others.) The poverty of social exclusion—lacking self-esteem, hope, opportunity, and freedom, and experiencing stress and depression—is no less debilitating to both individuals and society. Of particular salience is the issue of powerlessness: it's true that the poor and marginalized require income and opportunity, but they must also acquire a degree of power over their lives since powerlessness may well strike at the core of social exclusion and diminished life chances (Green 2012). Clearly then, any set of poverty-reduction strategies will rest on how poverty is framed as an inequality problem in need of solution. If defined in personal terms, solutions must be tailored to encourage attitude change or behavioural modification; if defined in structural terms (not just a glitch in the system but a systemic feature of society [Abramsky 2013]), the focus shifts to institutional barriers and systemic biases. To be sure, preoccupation with definitions can be controlling in its own right. Excessive theorizing could sap the spirit of activism that mobilizes people into action (paralysis by analysis). Energy dissipates into endless debate over the parameters of the problem instead of directing attention at intervention strategies. Worse still, relief may be denied to those in genuine need who get lost in the definitional shuffle.

No discussion of social inequality is complete without addressing the politics of poverty. Poverty is political for a variety of reasons but mostly because of the public nature of debates and disagreements over entitlements and allocations involving who gets what and what goes where. Even well-intentioned initiatives may be politicized. For example, to what extent are policies designed for the poor really intended to mute civil disorder, discipline the chronically unemployed, and reinforce a work ethic (see Piven and Cloward 1974)? References to poverty as social class is no less relevant as a point of departure. For in the final analysis, poverty discourses are as much about family background, market situations, and ownership of productive property as they are about deprivation—relative or otherwise. This chapter accepts this challenge by assessing and analyzing the concept of poverty through the lens of social class inequality (Fleras 2005). Attention is focused on the politics of poverty as the definitive expression of social inequality and class stratification, both as an analytical puzzle as well as a lived reality with very real consequences. Attention is also directed at the sharply contested nature of poverty with respect to what it is, how much of it there is, how it is measured, what the cause is or who is to blame, where it tends to cluster, what kind of consequences are exerted, and controversies over framing reduction plans. The correlates of poverty—namely, homelessness and food scarcity—are also discussed.

To assist in unravelling an array of paradoxes and perplexities related to poverty, this chapter reframes the politics of *poor* along the following sociological lines. Doing so provides an opportunity to debunk those misconceptions and stereotypes that undermine both political and public understanding of poverty to the detriment of the poor.

First, poverty reflects a socially constructed convention instead of anything natural in reality or inevitable about society. Poverty as inequality and exclusion is social in its origins and causes, defined as such by anti-poverty activists in Canada, and subject to correction by way of resource allocation and political will. However defined, poverty is real; nevertheless, its magnitude and scope are subject to endless controversy over *what* and *how much* and *how to find out*. Those with power can impose their definitions by controlling prevailing discourses and debates over proposed solutions. Not surprisingly, the politics of poverty often say more about the definer than the defined.

Second, neither poverty nor the poor constitute an undifferentiated or static category. References to the poor may also include those who work or those on welfare; those in a permanent state or whose situation is dictated by circumstances; and those variations related to gender, age, race, immigration status, or aboriginality. Nor does it make sense to refer to the poor as a fixed category since only a small percentage remain permanently lodged below the poverty line but rather move in and out as circumstances change over their life course (Lamman, Karabegovic, and Velduis 2012; Lamman and Macintyre 2016). It is therefore doubly important to reframe poverty accordingly: to make a distinction between the optimistic poor (new Canadians) and the embedded (chronic or downwardly spiraling) poor across generations; to distinguish between different intensity levels of poverty, from the really poor to those just below the poverty line; and to emphasize how poverty itself is much more fluid, dynamic, and situational than often implied in the literature and debates.

Third, too much reliance on the economic dimensions of poverty overlooks a key factor: for many, poverty is not only about money. More importantly, it's about social exclusion involving a gnawing sense of powerlessness and loss of self-potential; feelings of worthlessness, shame and failure—even humiliation—at not being able to provide for dependents; an inability to engage in and contribute to social and political life; and a lack of human capital to live as a free and dignified human being with full potential to achieved desired life goals (Silver 2015). For children, the best indicators of poverty are neither income nor abundance but environment and family, especially how often a child is read to or hugged (Kristof 2015; Putnam 2015). Without inclusion, the poor lose control of their lives or the ability to integrate into the community, resulting in a corresponding inability to participate fully and equally in society or to exercise their democratic and citizenship rights. Studies also indicate that poverty may impair cognitive functions. Chronic poverty imposes a burden on the mental capacity (from concentration to optimizing good decisions) of those who must struggle on a daily basis with difficult choices in just trying to eke out a living without adequate resources (Shafir and Mullainathan 2013; Mani et al. 2013).

Fourth, the social costs of poverty (and inequality) affect everyone in society (Canadian Medical Association 2013). Children who live in poverty are at increased risk of maturing into poor adults because of deprivation, lack of opportunities, exposure to anti-social behaviour, and questionable role modelling (Hyslop 2012). The adult poor tend to stay sick longer and more often because of malnutrition, higher stress, substandard accommodation, and so on. The added burden of poverty on Ontario's health care system costs the province between a staggering $32 and $38 billion a year (Fiorito 2013; Canada without Poverty 2016). In other words, poverty should not be seen just as a "poor" problem. Society at large bears the costs associated with being poor, from a loss of productivity to the high costs of emergency health care services (Rank 2011).

Fifth, poverty per se is not necessarily the cause of social problems such as violent crime. McMurtry and Curling (2008) argue that if it were, the magnitude of social problems in Canada would be truly frightening. Downward spiraling poverty is a more likely risk factor in precipitating the likelihood of anti-social behaviour. McMurtry and Curling (2008:7) make this point:

> But poverty without hope, poverty with isolation, poverty with hunger and poor living conditions, poverty with racism, and poverty with numerous daily reminders of social exclusion can lead to the immediate risk factors for violence . . . .

Sixth, far too many misconceptions about poverty continue to circulate (Rank 2011; Iceland 2012). For example, the poor are perceived as moral failures (i.e., unmotivated, lazy, shiftless, irresponsible) and lacking in appropriate skills or a proper work ethic. Yet such mistaken perceptions ignore a growing reality, namely that poverty is not a case of bad attitudes or character defects or faulty lifestyles (Ehrenreich 2014). Many of the working poor

work hard; they simply don't earn enough to make a go of it in today's pricey housing market (see Gorski 2008b). Consider how 37 per cent of children in poverty have one parent who works full-time, full-year (Campaign 2000 2015), a situation likely to worsen since nearly 75 per cent of all jobs created in recent years have been part-time, temporary or contract, self-employed, low-waged, and without essential benefits. For those on social assistance, taking a job may prove perilous: clawback of wages and benefits makes a mockery of escaping dependency on the welfare safety net. Metaphorically speaking, the current welfare system resembles a spider web that ensnares those unwary poor who want to work their way out of poverty but are penalized for doing so (Coyne 2012; also Warwick-Booth 2013). Accordingly, the challenge lies in constructing a welfare system that creates an incentive to get off the "dole" without punishing people for taking initiative.

Poverty in Canada: How Much? Who? Why?

By almost any measure, Canada is surfing the crest of a relatively buoyant economy, despite a recent economic downturn (*The Economist*, 30 March 2013). Having been spared the worst of the great recession, indicators suggest significant improvements across all dimensions of Canada's economic well-being. Yet not all Canadians are benefiting from these bullish good times. The lustre is off the conventional optimism that poverty can be diminished through the flow-through effect of neo-liberal economic growth (OECD 2014). In its place is growing disillusionment with the prevailing ideology of neo-liberalism that bolsters corporate fortunes at the expense of the common good (Piketty 2013). The poor and disenfranchised are left behind, with the result that poverty is now firmly entrenched in Canada, with no signs of retreating in the near future.

That poverty as a problem exists in Canada is beyond dispute; however, there is no consensus regarding what it means to be poor or how much poverty there is. No widely accepted methods exist for quantifying the number of poor, largely because nobody can agree on a definition of poverty or how to measure it. This consensus gap serves to remind us that social phenomena are never simple to define or assess and that measurements themselves are neither perfect nor free of normative considerations and political contamination (Noel 2012). The following figures provide a generalized overview of poverty numbers in Canada in comparison to global figures.

How Much, By Comparison

How much poverty is there in Canada? How do poverty rates in Canada compare with the rest of the world? International studies are inconsistent because of different measures and shifting time frames. A survey by the OECD (2013a) puts average income poverty at 11 per cent for all OECD countries, with Canada ranked just above average at 13 per cent and the United States near the bottom at 18 per cent. An estimated one in seven Canadians—4.8 million people—currently live under conditions of poverty and struggle to access basic goods and services. They are at higher risk of homelessness, more prone to poor physical and mental health, and experience both anxiety and emotional difficulties (Canada Without Poverty 2016). The poverty situation for children may be more acute. According to a UNICEF report (2012) that defines a household as poor if its disposable income is less than half that country's overall median income (the low-income measure, or LIM), Canada's child poverty rate ranked 24th out of 35 industrialized countries, with Finland at the low end and the United States and Romania at the high end. Macdonald and Wilson (2016) also conclude that Canada's overall child poverty rate (they put it at 18%) is among the worst in the OECD (the US rate is 22%), putting it in 27th place out of 34 countries. Generally speaking, Fennoscandia, with its tradition of income distribution, boasts the lowest child poverty rates, while the richest country in the world, the United States, often ranks among those countries with the highest rates. The official poverty measure in the United States pegs just over $23,000 as the cut-off line for a family of four, resulting in some 45–46 million Americans (15 per cent) who are defined

as poor, in effect reinforcing how this country's struggling economy and labour market, as well as its post-market institutions ("the safety net") remain in deep disrepair for many Americans (Stanford Center on Poverty & Inequality 2014). One in three black children and one of every four Latino children live in poverty, compared to one in seven white children (Lin and Harris 2012). Not unexpectedly, a 2010 UNICEF report ranked the United States twenty-third of twenty-four countries, just ahead of Slovakia, in terms of child health, education, and material well-being, based on comparing a society's poorest children with those who fall into the median range.

Other measures point to a substantially different pattern of poverty disparities. A UN study concluded that only six per cent of Canadians live in poverty—less than half the proportion in the United States, and about one-third the rate claimed by some indicators in Canada (also Sarlo 2013). This figure gives Canada the second lowest poverty level among major industrial countries, immediately behind Norway (3 per cent) and Finland, Japan, and Luxemborg at 4 per cent, and substantially ahead of the United States (14 per cent), Britain (13 per cent), Ireland (37 per cent), and Spain (21 per cent). These figures are based on the number of people who live on less than the equivalent of US$14.40 per day, adjusted to reflect the purchasing power in each country. In Canada, this figure works out to about CAD$20 per day or about $7,000 per year per person, a figure that many dismiss as embarrassingly miserly, even risible and unrealistic.

To what extent have living standards in Canada improved to the point of eradicating poverty? According to the economist Christopher Sarlo of Nipissing University in North Bay, Ontario, historically high rates of poverty have sharply declined, from one in three Canadians in 1951 to only one in twenty by the late 1970s—a figure (5 per cent) that has since remained constant (Sarlo 2013). Unlike developing world countries, Sarlo argues, Canada has virtually no poverty if measured by the presence of a destitute underclass in sprawling ghettos or squalid slums. Nobody in Canada needs to starve to death, he contends, and only a handful are forced by circumstances to live out in the open. Few are denied access to health care and welfare services, although some individuals may suffer by falling in between bureaucratic cracks. Even those defined as poor in Canada are appreciably better off than the affluent in some developing countries of the global south. What many define as *poverty* or *being poor* is dismissed by Sarlo (2016) as relative deprivation in which some are more deprived than others or less well off than average in terms of living standards. In short, inequality and poverty are not the same thing, argues Sarlo (2016): poverty is about severe deprivation (hunger); by contrast, inequality is a measure of the gaps in living standards based in indicators such as income or wealth.

National, regional and provincial differences are clearly evident yet open to interpretation due to variations in time frames and poverty measures (Hay 2009; Frank 2013 for Nova Scotia). Poverty rates in 2010 ranged from a high of 11.2 per cent in Manitoba to a low of 2.3 per cent in Prince Edward Island, with Ontario's rate of 8.0 per cent just below the national average of 8.2 (deBoer, Rothwell, and Lee 2013). But according to Poverty Free in Ontario, the percentage of poor Canadian households in 2009 was 13.3 per cent. The figure in Atlantic Canada stood at 15.6 per cent, while the Prairie figure was 10.8 per cent. Ontario occupied the midpoint at 13.1 per cent. Urban variations exist as well. Toronto residents with racialized and immigrant backgrounds were more likely to be poor in 2011 based on the LIM-AT measure, including 41 per cent of those whose origins are Southern and Eastern Africa, 38 per cent from Central and West Africa, and 34 per cent from West Central Asia and the Middle East. Those from the British Isles, at 12 per cent, had the lowest percentage of poor individuals (Report 2014; Polanyi et al. 2014).

Other factors contribute to variations in poverty rates. Time frames can be critical in making assessments about the magnitude of poverty (Selley 2012). For example, 22.8 per cent of children under six years were mired in poverty in 1989, based on Statistics Canada data and LIM-AT measures (Campaign 2000 2015). This figure increased to 25 per cent in 2000, then declined to 20.3 per cent of all children in 2013. For all children, the poverty rates were, respectively, 15.8 per cent, 22.3 per cent, and 19.0 per cent. Poverty rates also vary by levels of education and family types (Silver 2015). In 2007, those with less than high

school education but living in families experienced a poverty rate of 10 per cent; by contrast, the rate for unattached individuals without a high school diploma was 34 per cent. In terms of household arrangements, Campaign 2000 (2015) concluded that 16.3 per cent of children under 17 years in 2012 lived in low-income households, based on LIM-AT. The percentages varied from 12.9 per cent of children in two-parent families to 44.5 per cent for those living in a single-mother household. Finally, government transfers also remain a key driver in shaping poverty rates. For example, Canada allocates $40 billion to stave off poverty among old folks, resulting in poverty rates that are half of those of Canadian children. Before-tax and after-tax transfers can yield substantially different rates of poverty, depending on the measures employed. For example, reductions in child poverty as a result of government transfers in 2013 yielded the following figures (LIM): for Canada, a child poverty rate of 29.1 per cent before transfers, 19.0 per cent after transfers; for Nunavut, 53 per cent before transfers, 37.7 after transfers; for Manitoba, 37.5 per cent before transfers, 29 per cent after transfers (Campaign 2000 2015).

Who Is Poor?

Poverty is not randomly distributed among Canadians but tends to cluster around several high-risk groups, including children; female-headed, lone-parent households; families headed by a person with a disability; young adults between 18 and 24 years of age; unattached individuals; and older women on their own (Conference Board of Canada 2011a). The existence of adult poverty is bad enough. Even more distressing is the spectre of children in poverty—who deservedly have attracted most of the attention. As many studies indicate, early adversity can cause life-long impairments in physical, social, and psychological development. Far too many children face a higher than average risk of poor physical and mental health, increased deprivation and social exclusion, and higher rates of delinquency and school drop-out (Campaign 2000 2015). Children's learning ability is affected by poverty-related hunger, violence, illness, domestic problems, and deprivation. Those who live in poverty are less ready to learn when they enter school, are more likely to live in dysfunctional families, and are apt to exhibit behavioural problems pertaining to aggression, depression, and academic lapses such as failing a grade or becoming easily distracted. They also are subject to various forms of cognitive dysfunctions since those who must endure a constant state of poverty related distress and deprivation may find it difficult to focus or function when preoccupied with thoughts of survival or exclusion (Banerjee and Duflo 2011).

Despite these danger signals, numbers point to a continued crisis. Just over 8 per cent of children were defined as poor in 2010, based on LICO measures (after tax and transfers, but 13.7 per cent before transfers) (Broadbent 2009). If the LIM is employed, the number of poor children increases in absolute numbers from 1989 to 2010 (from 912,000 to 979,000) or proportionately (from 13.7 per cent to 14.5 per cent) (deBoer, Rothwell, and Lee 2013; Campaign 2000 2012; UNICEF 2012). Most recent figures (2013) peg the number of children living in poverty at 1,334,930, or 19 per cent, based on Revenue Canada tax filer data (LIM-AT) (Campaign 2000 2015). Yet references to child poverty also conceal deep variations. A study by Macdonald and Wilson (2016) concluded there were three distinct tiers of child poverty in Canada:

1. 51 per cent of status First Nations children, rising to 60 per cent of children living on reserves, including rates of 76 per cent and 69 per cent of children on reserves in Manitoba and Saskatchewan.
2. 22 per cent of racialized children; 23 per cent of Metis children; 32 per cent of immigrant children.
3. 12 per cent for all other children—a ratio similar to the average among all other OECD countries.

The racialization of poverty is also unmistakable as demonstrated in the above list (Douglas et al 2014). Toronto residents of African, Asian, Middle Eastern, Caribbean and Latin American backgrounds are much more likely to experience poverty, including 41 per cent of persons with Southern and East African ethnic origins, compared to 12 per cent for British Isles background (Polanyi et al. 2014). Data from the Toronto District School Board reinforce these disparities: fully 48 per cent of black children and 56 per cent of Middle Eastern children (but only 9 per cent of white children) lived in families with incomes less than $30 000 per year. Child poverty tends to be higher among offspring of recent immigrants who are unable to either crack the labour market or earn a sustainable living wage. Lastly, chronic levels of child poverty among Aboriginal peoples are deemed a national embarrassment and grave moral injustice. A study by the Canadian Centre for Policy Alternatives and Save the Children Canada found that 40 per cent of aboriginal children are living in poverty—two-and-a-half times the rate of non-aboriginal children (Macdonald and Wilson 2013).

The term *feminization of poverty* may be a slogan, but it is a slogan with substance, since the face of poverty in Canada is often a woman's face. An estimated 36 per cent of aboriginal women live in poverty, 35 per cent of racialized women, and 26 per cent of women with disabilities (Sekharan 2015 for the Homeless Hub). Twenty-one per cent of single mothers are raising their children in poverty, in part because women spend more time in unpaid work, confront a lack of affordable child care, and resort to employment that is precarious (part-time). Admittedly, fewer lone parents (the majority are women) now rely on social assistance since many are moving out of poverty (a 25 per cent decrease between 2000 and 2011), thanks in part to better education, better access to child support, and new child benefits. Still, as Campaign 2000 (2013) pointed out, 38.2 per cent of children in single-mother households in Ontario were poor. Paradoxically, a new gender shift may be materializing. Shifts in the economy, from male-dominated manufacturing to female-friendly services, are giving rise to the *masculinization of poverty* for single males (Stapleton 2011).

Another category of poor comprises the growing number of employed persons living in poverty (the working poor). The linking of working with poverty may appear contradictory, yet the concept of *working poor* is now part of the poverty discourse in Canada, especially in Toronto where 9.1 per cent of workers are living on poverty-level wages. Do the math: how does a household of four in Toronto cope when one wage earner earns a minimum wage of about $20,000 a year? Even two minimum-wage workers with two dependents barely earn enough to escape the poverty line of just over $37,000 in a city which has the highest cost of living in Canada and the second most expensive housing market (Stapleton, Murphy, and Xing 2012). In today's dollars (Stapleton 2015) Canada ranks fifteenth among seventeen peer countries, with a working-poor rate of about 12.2 per cent, up from 9.4 per cent in the mid-1990s (Conference Board of Canada 2011b). These figures are not surprising in a Canada where incentives to get off welfare and get a job clash with the realities that things could get worse (for example losing supplemental drug and dental coverage for children) (Hyslop 2012; Lankin and Shiekh 2012).[1] For example, a study using US Census Bureau and public benefit programs data found that 52 per cent of low-wage workers in the largest fast food restaurants (from cooks to cashiers) earned so little (less than $9 per hour) they had to rely on public assistance such as food stamps to survive (Abrahamian 2013). A similar predicament exists for Walmart employees who also rely on public assistance to offset low wages (Kasperkevic 2014). In brief, the emergence of working poor is a problem and challenge. Nevertheless, the prospect of defining the working poor is not without debate (Shillington and Stapleton 2010:9); for example, who should be included as working poor? Part-timers, seasonal workers, students, or the self-employed? Such a range of alternatives should curb any temptation for a one-size-fits-all assessment and solution.

Who or What to Blame?

What is the cause of poverty? Who is to blame? How should responsibility be framed? Two ideal-typical models have dominated responses to these questions: blame-the-victim (individualistic) models versus blame-the-system (structuralist) models (Royce 2015). Some think the scope of poverty is overstated (Sarlo 2013) and believe the poor should do more to help themselves since they are the authors of their own misfortune (Mills 2011). Others disagree and point to a host of social and structural factors that are often beyond individual control. The distinction between these models embodies a familiar ideological divide that informs many contemporary social controversies, including the debate between functionalism and radical conflict theories

of society. Individualist models reflect a functionalist theory of society as a meritocratic and level playing field that rewards hard work and determination, thanks to the magic of the market. For structuralist models of a radical conflict bent, society is theorized as a site of domination, exploitation, and control, emanating from power disparities and system biases in determining who gets what. A series of questions flow from these opposed models of society as they relate to the politics of blame: is poverty the result of a lack of effort (flawed character) or a lack of opportunity (restricted options) (Schiller 2004; Rank 2004)? Are people poor because of their personal weaknesses (defects in character) or are they poor because of weaknesses (distortions) in the economy? Is poverty reduction best addressed by reforming individuals or by transforming society?

Responses to these questions—poverty as personality versus poverty as power—tend to align themselves along individualistic or structuralist lines. Individualistic models portray poverty as a moral failure that results in faulty choices among those individuals who tend to be deficient in intelligence, competence, or ability; lack ambition and perseverance to take advantage of available opportunities; possess poor attitudes related to motivation and values; make bad decisions or engage in self-destructive lifestyles; or are insufficiently skilled or educated. The poor are poor because they drop out of school, have children out of wedlock, join criminal gangs, commit to drugs or alcohol abuse, and jump from one job to another. By contrast, structuralist models frame poverty as a by-product of various economic and political forces outside the control of the poor. Structural circumstances include a shortage of jobs that pay a living wage; corporate profit-making strategies that focus on reducing labour costs through on-demand ("just-in-time") work arrangements, outsourcing and off-shoring, and technology fixes; political leaders that cater to the rich and powerful over the needs of the poor; and the persistence of **discrimination** and residential segregation. Unlike individualistic models that attribute poverty to bad decisions by the poor, a structuralist model acknowledges the importance of decisions—albeit by those who occupy positions of power and who manipulate this power to downsize, relocate, privatize, impose austerity programs, enact tax cuts, cut trade deals that profit corporations at the expense of workers, and propagate the myth of free and fair market outcomes (Royce 2015). Yet decisions by the poor are not necessarily irrational; rather, they must make difficult decisions that appear illogical to many, albeit in difficult contexts involving constant trade-offs (food versus high speed Internet access) (Monsebraaten 2016; Banerjee and Duflo 2011).

The individualistic perspective focuses on the characteristics and deficiencies of the individual (especially as they relate to income access), whereas structural perspectives emphasize the dynamics of the larger political economy, failings of social institutions, and disparities *in power*, with a corresponding ability to influence favourable outcomes (Lukes 2005; 2007). For individualistic models, poverty is a "damaged personality" problem that must be solved at the individual level. Being poor may be unfortunate but fair in a relatively sound and open system (functionalism). For structuralists, poverty is a social problem and thus demands a political solution, with the result that no poverty reduction strategy can be taken seriously unless the politics of power are painted into the picture (Royce 2015). Table 5.1 captures the distinction in a schematic form.

Table 5.1: Models of Poverty Causation

Blame the Victim/Individualistic Model	Blame the System/Structuralist Model
Poverty as Personality	Poverty as Power
Poverty is an individual problem located in those values, attitudes, and behaviour that foster the inadequacies and failings of the poor (such as laziness or lack of education).	Poverty is a social problem located in the economic and political institutions of society that foreclose opportunities and options for those "born unlucky."
Poverty is a cultural and moral problem arising from broken family arrangements and a weak work ethic. Poverty is the outcome of the decisions of the poor.	Poverty is an economic and political problem originating with decisions by the ruling elites in allocating valued resources. Poverty is the outcome of those who call the shots in a rigged system.
Poverty derives from failure of the poor to take advantage of the relatively equal opportunities available to them on a roughly equal playing field, with everyone having a similar chance for success.	Poverty derives from inequalities in the distribution of power and resources. The poor confront an INequality of opportunity since they must compete on an UNequal playing field.
The poor are different from the middle class in terms of values, choices, and aspirations. Thus the allocation of valued resources in society reflects the distribution of ability.	The poor and rich possess similar values and aspirations but differ in available opportunity structures and the prevailing distribution of power.
Prejudice and discrimination are no longer a barrier because of a commitment to a post-racial and pro-multicultural society. The poor have no one to blame but themselves.	Power, prejudice, and discrimination remain significant barriers to achievement, despite claims of a colour-blind and inclusive society.
Government intervention ("bureaucratic bloat") is generally unhelpful in alleviating poverty compared to market outcomes which are fairer and more efficient.	Government intervention is critical since market outcomes tend to enrich those with the benefit of a head start in the competitive race to succeed.

continued

Table 5.1: *continued*

Poverty reduction can be addressed by re-socializing individuals with the skills, attitudes, and motivation necessary to compete in the market.	Poverty is best challenged by restructuring the labour market to create better job opportunities that in turn boost wages and benefits.
The best anti-poverty strategy for the poor is hard work and improvement of skill levels (i.e., human capital).	Anti-poverty strategies must entail collective political action to bring about a redistribution of valued resources.

Source: Table adapted in part from Royce (2015).

Which of these models is more correct? Neither is technically more correct than the other if evaluating poverty as a set of contested narratives (although the text embraces the structural model as the preferred approach). Much depends on whether one is inclined to endorse functionalist models of society (society is OK, individuals must change) or radical conflict models (individuals are OK, society must change) as a framework for analyzing and assessing poverty causes. Furthermore, reducing all arguments into two binary models cannot possibly capture the complexities of a problem that entails a mutual interplay of individualism and societal structures—of personality and power—in shaping outcomes. In other words, it is not a case of *either/or* but rather of *both/and*, depending in part on the specific context (a blame-the-situation approach associated with symbolic interactionism). As noted earlier, individuals must take some responsibility for their actions; to do otherwise is to rob individuals of agency and transform them into mindless robots. But while personal responsibility must be factored into the blame equation, people's actions and social status do not exist outside of a societal framework. Many may find themselves in contexts and circumstances largely beyond their immediate control in terms of options, opportunities, and outcomes. Or to rephrase a popular cliché: if people are to pull themselves up by their bootstraps, first they need boots. Finally, there are dangers in exclusively endorsing an individualistic approach. It is difficult to take poverty seriously as a social problem when politicians and the public approach it as a case of

moral failings and self-destructive behaviours; dismiss its impact on the Canadian poor since they do much better than the abject poor in the world; and see it as a personality problem in need of disciplining by austerity measures since generous government programs foster disincentives to "get off the dole" (see Royce 2015).

Framing Poverty: Absolute versus Relative

That poverty exists and excludes is certainly beyond doubt. Still, it is one thing to analyze the magnitude and scope of the problem. It may be quite another to define and implement solutions consistent with the definition of the problem. Problems must be appropriately defined (framed) in terms of causes and scale for any hope of sustainable solutions. But poverty is one of those thorny issues that eludes a commonly accepted definition. The absence of a consensus definition makes it impossible to determine the nature and scale of poverty in Canada—its incidence (how much), depth (how poor are the poor), and duration (for how long)—thus leading to puerile polemics whereby people literally miscommunicate by talking past each other. An article in Perception (2007:4) pointed out the attendant dilemmas of such a situation:

. . . Canada has no official poverty line. Different agencies measure poverty in different ways and each of the definitions makes certain assumptions. Given the complexity of the problem—the fact that poverty can vary from place to place, from decade to decade, and even from household to household—none of the definitions are exhaustive or precise.

Defining poverty for measurement purposes is not as simple as it looks (Shillington and Stapleton 2010). On what grounds is poverty framed as something absolute and measurable or, alternatively, as something relative and context-dependent and difficult to measure? Is poverty about subsistence needs (enough to eat) or about inclusion through participation? In what way do different definitions influence the calculation of the number of poor in Canada? We look to the UN for inspiration. The UN High Commissioner for Human Rights defines poverty as a human condition characterized by the sustained or chronic deprivation of resources, choices, security, power, and participation necessary for enjoyment of an adequate standard of living and rights. The key here is equating poverty with deprivation in terms of income and basic needs as well as social exclusion and access to goods and services relative to widely accepted community standards. Yet even this definition may conceal more than it reveals. Those living in poverty consist of upward and downward poor, the near-poor and "real" poor, and the temporarily poor versus the chronically poor. Not surprisingly, governments in Canada reject any reference to the term *poverty*. They prefer to depoliticize the issue by relying on references such as *straitened circumstances, low income cut-off line*, and *substantially worse off than average* (Hay 2009). This conceptual void has prompted a competition over definitions, with each having its own bias, subjective assumptions, and emotional language. Depending on which definition is employed, the results can produce wildly diverse measures of poverty at either the high end or the low end.

Absolute Poverty

Most definitions of poverty fall into one of two categories: **absolute** versus **relative**. These categories usually coincide with poverty definitions that are either needs-based (absolute) or more inclusive and relational (relative). Poverty defined along absolute lines points to a threatened physical existence because

of a chronic absence of the fundamental necessities of life ("needs") pertaining to food, shelter, and clothing (Shillington and Stapleton 2010). Poverty is a condition of serious deprivation (rather than a case of being less well off than others) for those five per cent of Canadians, resulting in a sense of real urgency and desperation that is not the case for those above the poverty line (Sarlo 2013). Absolute measures look at what it takes to survive in Canada by examining a basket of basic goods for physical well-being and survival (approximately $24,300 for a family of four) (Sarlo 2013). The basic needs measure excludes so-called non-essentials such as books, toys, haircuts, dental services, and school supplies. The food budget is restricted to basic subsistence; for example, tea and coffee are not included (Shillington and Stapleton 2010). Health items are excluded from the basket on the grounds the poor can supposedly access emergency facilities and community resources.

Public criticism of this mean-spirited approach (a position endorsed by the Fraser Institute) has prompted a less tight-fisted definition. The federal government now endorses the concept of market basket measure (MBM), which defines poverty in terms of a particular basket of goods. Broader than subsistence or income, but narrower than full inclusiveness in definition, Statistics Canada describes MBM as a measure of low income based on the cost of a specific basket of goods and services deemed to represent a basic yet modest standard of living perceived as necessary for a healthy and involved life. This measure acknowledges that children should not feel excluded from society by being denied the things that many take for granted, such as school trips and smart phones.

According to MBM, a family of four requires a basket of goods that includes food (a nutritious diet as specified in the National Nutritious Food Basket), clothing and footwear, shelter (a two- or three-bedroom rental unit including appliances and services), transportation (public transit where available or a modest vehicle where public transit is unavailable), and miscellaneous expenses. Specifically, the basket is valued at $27,343 a year, including $5,778 for food, $2,992 for clothing and footwear, $11,399 for shelter, $2,316 for transportation, and $5,558 for incidentals. A rural Ontario family would need $25,117 a year, including access to a mid-size Chevy with

Spotlight   Foodbanks as Canaries in the Coal Mine of Poverty

As recently as 1980, food banks did not exist in Canada; by March of 2014, there were some 800 food banks and some 2,000 agencies operating an emergency food distribution program for approximately 841,000 monthly users, a slight decrease (1.0 per cent) from 2013 but still 24.5 per cent higher than pre-recession 2008 (Food Banks Canada's eighteenth annual report 2014). It is estimated that 12.5 per cent of households at some point, including about 1 million children, experience food insecurity (Campaign 2000 2015; Tarasuk, Mitchell, and Dachner 2013). Youth and children may comprise only 20 per cent of Canada's population, but they constitute about one-third of food bank recipients. One in eight food bank users is employed. (Keep in mind that a minimum wage is not a living wage since it is nearly impossible to survive on minimum wage without recourse to

food banks [Porter 2013].) One in ten is aboriginal; a similar ratio applies to recent immigrants (Grant 2013): 51 per cent of those using food banks were born outside of Canada, and 28 per cent are university graduates.

The implications of this reliance are worrying. For Craig Alexander, chief economist at the TD Bank Group, it's an indictment of Canada: "Food-bank usage is one of the more tangible measures of how society is faring. It's worth paying attention to because it gives a 'true depiction' of the challenges that low-income people face." Worse still, the very existence of food banks creates the mistaken illusion that the problem of food insecurity is under control and no longer requires political attention. As a result, writes Nick Saul (2013), the very existence of food banks may compound the problem they set out to solve.

insurance and 1,500 litres of gas. A family in Montreal is entitled to a market basket totaling $22,441 because of lower housing costs.

The MBM may have the advantage of clarity and comprehensiveness, given its attentiveness to the actual cost of basic goods and services that vary across Canadian towns and cities. Yet there is some debate over its validity in defining the content of the basket (Shillington and Stapleton 2010). Moreover, how counterintuitive is the recent decision by the federal government to adjust housing costs? For example, the shelter portion of the MBM for a family of four in Vancouver dropped 40 per cent to $7,455 a year, which works out to $621 a month. Yet the monthly rental of an unheated car garage may well exceed that amount in Canada's most expensive housing market (Goldberg, Kerstetter, and Klein 2012).

Relative Poverty

Poverty in Canada is more commonly framed along relative lines. According to a relativist

approach to poverty, what constitutes being poor is relative to time, place, and level of development. Nineteenth-century poverty is unlikely to be the same experience as it is at present, any more than it could possibly mean the same thing in Canada as in Haiti. In a society in which virtually everyone has access to the necessities of life, poverty cannot focus exclusively on subsistence or survival. Poverty is better measured in terms of how people compare to commonly accepted standards of living. A checklist of items displaced by a focus on how people fare in their ability to be fully engaged in, connected to, and integrated into the life of the community. Reference to poverty as social exclusion is key here, with its attendant notion of participation and involvement (social capital), powerlessness, belonging (social citizenship), and valued contribution (Saloojee 2003).

Statistics Canada has historically used two relative measures based on income adequacy (Hay 2009). First, a low-income measure (LIM) draws the line at half (50 per cent) the median income of Canadian households adjusted for family size and location (Sarlo 2013). For example, based on Statistics Canada LIM-AT data, the poverty line for a single adult with no children is $17,371; for a lone parent with two children it is $29,531; and for a couple with two children it is $34,742 (Campaign 2000 2015). These figures were revised upward in 2013: $20,993 for an individual and $41,866 for a family of four, after taxes (Monsebraaten 2016). Defining the poor as relative to a nation's median adjusted household income makes the LIM useful for comparison with other countries (Shillington and Stapleton 2010). Second, the popular low-income cut-off line (LICO—before or after tax) compares spending on necessities between low-income families and so-called typical families. Statistics Canada defines LICO as an income threshold below which a family will devote a disproportional amount of income for basic necessities compared to an average family. A low-income threshold (poverty) is defined as implicit in any household that spends more than 63 per cent of its income on food, shelter, or clothing (or 20 per cent or more of their income than the average family on basic necessities [deBoer, Rothwell, and Lee 2013]). This admittedly arbitrary figure is based on what an average family in 1992 spent on the basic necessities of food, shelter, and clothing (43 per cent of its after tax income), plus an additional 20 per cent for good measure. This "poverty" line also takes into account seven different family sizes, distinguishes between five different community sizes, and is frequently updated (rebased) to reflect cost-of-living allowances (deBoer, Rothwell, Lee 2013). For example, in 2008, the LICO line for a family of four in an urban area with a population between 30,000 and 99,999 was $29,013. It should be noted that Statistics Canada has consistently emphasized that LICO is not a measure of poverty; it's a proxy concept that simply identifies those who are substantially worse-off (possess a lower income threshold) than the average household.

Poverty Politics

The persistence of hunger, homelessness, and hardship is transforming Canada into a land of extremes: poverty amid plenty. Those who prefer to dwell on the *plenty* point out that average family incomes have risen, most Canadians are materially better off than before, few are sleeping in the streets, fewer still are starving, and no one is denied basic health care. Success stories in poverty reduction should be acknowledged (Lamman, Karabegovic, and Veldhuis 2012; Lamman and Macintyre 2016): the percentage of single-parent families living below the LICO line after taxes has plunged by more than a half in the past 15 years, from about 50 per cent to just under 20 per cent (Hyslop 2012). Those who dote on the downside accentuate rising rates of poverty for certain demographics, a stubbornly high number of food banks and widespread food scarcity, and patterns of homelessness that show no signs of subsiding. Those in between acknowledge the possibility that both pictures of Canada are true. The poverty glass is neither half full nor half empty but both half full and half empty, depending on the optics.

The debate is clearly polarized by the metrics employed. Relative measures define people as poor if they fare worse than others in the community; by contrast, absolute measures don't take into account how anyone else is doing. Some believe poverty should be defined in relative terms that take into account levels of social inclusion. Others prefer a more absolute measure that focuses on the basic necessities of food, shelter, and clothing. Admittedly, the distinction between absolute and relative may be overstated. Reference to "basic needs" rests on a value judgment about which needs are more important relative to the commitment and capacity of society to do something about them (Pyatt 2013). Furthermore, references to framing poverty reflect values about a specific vision of society. Are we comfortable with bulging gaps between the rich and poor in society? Can we live with the idea of homelessness in a climate that punishes the roofless? Do we believe in a society where poor children are deprived of the competitive edge for success, thus perpetuating the poverty cycle? Is there a place for food banks in a society that produces an annual food surplus?

Caveats aside, absolute and relative indices of poverty differ in emphasizing a distinction between restrictiveness and expansiveness. Restrictive definitions of poverty often convey a sense of destitution, including those normally perceived as the poor such as the bedraggled in appearance, perpetually hungry, and homeless. According to this basic-level-of-subsistence scenario, poverty-stricken individuals should be given sufficient necessities to ensure they do not sicken and die, become a public nuisance or national embarrassment, or impose an unnecessary burden on society. More expansive definitions tend to reflect more inclusive entitlements. The emphasis is not simply on staving off disease or starvation; more to the point, it is about inclusion to ensure that no one is excluded from full integration and equal involvement in society. As Steve Kerstetter, director of the National Council of Welfare, writes (1999: A-19), in upholding a more generous definition of poverty:

> If they were, we could provide every poor person with a giant bag of oatmeal, a gunny sack, and a cot in the flophouses, and feel we had done our job as a compassionate and fair-minded people. In reality, poverty lines are about a minimum standard of living in one of the richest countries of the world. They should mark a standard that allows a person to participate in society, not merely to go on breathing.

Critics of a relative poverty measure continue to dispute what they see as grossly inflated figures. At the forefront of this criticism is Christopher Sarlo (2013) who refutes the notion that those who live below the poverty line are actually poor. Poverty lines are arbitrarily constructed, with income cut-offs providing much more than required for survival. Much of what passes for poverty, Sarlo contends, confuses being poor with deprivation or inequality—that some are doing less well than others in acquiring middle-class amenities. For Sarlo, true poverty is rare if measured in terms of "stomach stretching" starvation or roofless homelessness. To claim that three to five million Canadians are living in poverty is hyped as little more than a fabrication, concocted by welfare advocacy and lobby groups for self-serving purposes. Moreover, relative measures of poverty are designed to ensure a constant supply of poor, regardless of improvements in the economy. For example, consider how the LIM measure (with its focus on half the median income of Canadian households) precludes the possibility

of ever eliminating poverty; after all, even a doubling of incomes across the board would not disturb the ratio of poor to rich. This relativistic standard makes it difficult to gauge progress on the poverty front. It also reinforces the counter-intuitive notion that Canadians at present are disproportionately poorer than in the past.

The politics of these number games should be self-evident. Those whose livelihood depends on the presence of the poor may have a vested interest in inflating poverty figures. Other vested interests and a neo-liberal logic would like nothing better than to reduce the number of official poor for self-serving reasons. The current figures are so grossly inflated, they contend, that the government invariably looks bad for shirking its responsibilities. Conversely, a reduction in absolute numbers can be seen as part of a wider government strategy for putting a positive spin on their social programs. Put candidly, governments may be accused of trying to define the poor out of existence. The net result is a hardening of public attitudes towards poor folk as undeserving and a gradual demonization—even criminalization—of the poor as lazy freeloaders and a burden on Canadian taxpayers, thereby justifying cutbacks in government welfare spending. Such attitudes and government practices are not without consequences. As pointed out in Chapter 1, the underclass poor will react when poverty intersects with powerlessness to diminish prospects or diffuse social commitments.

Homelessness: Street-Level Poverty

Poverty as social inequality can be expressed in different ways. The profile on homelessness as a major poverty problem has grown rapidly in recent years, in the process revealing difficulties in defining the problem and proposing solutions. To be sure, homeless people (without a home) have always existed; nevertheless, it's only in recent years that the state of homelessness has become defined as a problem. Initially thought to afflict only a small number of single males with addictions or mental health issues, the scope of homelessness has evolved to reflect a poverty crisis affecting a diverse range of individuals and families (Hulchanski 2009; Gaetz 2010). Still, the prospect of the homeless creating shanty towns under bridges and viaducts akin to those in overseas slums seems strangely incongruous in a Canada that has so much going for it (Hulchanski 2009). Small wonder then that the concept of homelessness elicits a strong visceral response: to some, homelessness represents an affront to the work-and-save ethic of hardworking Canadians everywhere. To others, its existence is an indictment of an increasingly uncaring Canadian society. Lars Osberg (2007:25) expresses the symbolism conveyed by homelessness:

> In the same way as broken windows and graffiti are a visible indicator of the physical neglect of a neighbourhood, the homeless are a highly visible indicator of Canada's social neglect of the less fortunate.

Many Canadians would be startled to learn that homelessness is of crisis proportions in Canada (Heffernan, Todorow, and Luu 2015; Gulliver-Garcia 2016). Homelessness is not restricted simply to jobless "bums" who think nothing of gulping down a couple bottles of cheap plonk or hand sanitizer. It goes beyond a bunch of rebellious teens who prefer a life on the streets over the stifling confines of life at home under house rules. According to Bruce Rivers of Toronto's Covenant House (cited in Goar 2016), 75 per cent of the youth that come through Canada's largest youth homeless shelter are escaping physical or sexual abuse, domestic violence, or substance abuse at home; 43 per cent have no home but come out of the child welfare system; 32 per cent are diagnosed as having psychiatric disorders; and 50 per cent come from middle- to upper-income families. Even more shocking is the realization that homelessness is not always a lifestyle choice, but a response to destitution or inflicted by default. Homelessness now includes the "deserving poor"—people who find themselves in dire straits through little fault of their own (mental health problems) or in straitened circumstances beyond their control (from government austerity measures to corporate labour-shedding practices related to downsizing, outsourcing, and off-shoring). The number of homeless has increased in recent years, yet access to affordable housing has deteriorated to the point where children are now forced to live in hostels or in substandard private dwellings. Visible homelessness is only the tip of the iceberg (Gulliver-Garcia 2016): rapidly rising accommodation costs in major centres results in the emergence of the working poor (those whose minimum wage cannot possibly cover the bare essentials in large urban centres such as Vancouver or Toronto). The fact that 20 per cent of Ontario households spend 30 per cent of their income on rent or live in overcrowded and substandard homes (either too small or in decrepit condition) puts even more pressure on affordable rental housing for those on the financial edge (ONPHA/CHF Canada, Ontario Region 2013).

Homelessness is an inequality problem comparable to that of poverty. Both poverty and homelessness are social in origin, definition, impact, and treatment. They are difficult to define or measure, resulting in ongoing debates about how much and what can be done (Gaetz et al. 2013). Neither poverty nor homelessness can be regarded as good for individual health or the collective well-being of Canada. For the chronically homeless (the 20 per cent who remain homeless for more than three months), life on the streets and in shelters concocts a toxic brew of addiction, abuse, and suicide (Trypuc and Robinson 2009). Chronic homelessness is a recipe for self-destruction that results in an estimated 1,400 deaths annually, since life expectancy for a long-term homeless person in Canada is just under 40 years. Most of the homeless in an Ottawa-based survey reported physical and mental health problems, with 60 per cent having a diagnosable mental illness, mainly depression (cited in Picard 2000; Gulliver-Garcia 2016). Finally, life is lonely on the streets: two-thirds of the homeless count less than four people in their social circle, including family, with the result that their only friends are often other homeless people (Picard 2000). This collapse of a social network (or social capital) from failure to foster positive self-esteem may magnify major social problems later in life.

References to homelessness and poverty as mutually linked concepts are revealing. Just as a lack of definition precludes any reliable measure of poverty, so too is there no agreement on defining homelessness. The concept of homelessness has evolved into an "odd-job word" (Hulchanski 2009) pressed into service to cover a hodgepodge of activities and states, from social dislocation and extreme poverty to seasonal and itinerant work. Even defining who qualifies as homeless is not without its quirks. Without a home? No fixed address? No roof? The definition may include runaways, Aboriginal peoples in the streets, psychiatric patients, families on waiting lists for shelters, drug addicts, panhandlers, and those who simply like to live "on the edge." York University's Canadian Homelessness Research Centre has parsed the homeless into 12 categories, from the hardcore to the precarious (at risk of ending up on the street) (Gaetz et al. 2013). Nobody knows the overall number of homeless since reliable national statistics are nonexistent, given the challenges in counting a shifting demographic without a fixed address, often hidden from public view (Hulchanski 2009). Trypuc and Robinson (2009) estimate a total of 157,000 homeless in Canada, whereas Andre Picard (2013) points to an estimated 300,000 Canadians in 1,086 homeless shelters or on the streets, costing taxpayers $1.4 billion in health care, justice, and social services. According to Stephen Gaetz et al. of the Canadian Homeless Research Network (2013), 200,000 people use shelters in Canada annually, including 30,000 homeless on any given night. Just under 3,000 sleep outside while another 50,000 constitute what is called the "hidden homeless"—from couch surfers to those occupying derelict houses. About 15 per cent are thought to be chronically homeless. Finally, a report by the advocacy group Raising the Roof (Gulliver-Garcia 2016) points to about 35,000 homeless people across Canada on any given night, including 235,000 who used homeless shelters at least once in 2015. One in every seven users is a child—a dramatic increase in recent years despite evidence that family homelessness (and its correlates from proper nutrition to schooling to a safe environment) can have a lifelong impact on children's health and well-being. About 3.1 million Canadians are precariously housed in crowded, substandard, or unaffordable housing (based on 30 per cent of income consumed by housing costs).

As well, few concur on the causes of homelessness (Gulliver-Garcia 2016). Is it a lifestyle choice? Forced dislocation? Individual preference? The usual factors are often cited, including the following root and precipitating causes: inadequate affordable housing; greedy landlords; a not-in-my-backyard-mentality that thwarts the establishment of shelters; changes in the labour market; declining incomes; soaring rents; slashed social spending; mental illness and closure of mental health institutions; substance abuse; urban renewal; or domestic abuse (HRSDC 2011; Trypuc and Robinson 2009). To some, the homeless are largely victims of circumstances beyond their control. Their ranks have swelled with the deinstitutionalization of the mentally disabled as well as those in drug and alcohol recovery programs. To others, homelessness is the price for living in a freewheeling competitive society in which some win, others lose. For example, civic improvement projects that cater to the upwardly mobile may have the effect (if not the intent) of eliminating inexpensive housing in city cores (Turner 2000).

For still others, homeless Canadians are seen as architects of their own misfortune. The poor can only blame themselves if they refuse their medication or disregard house rules at overnight shelters. Such a blaming-the-victim mentality makes it difficult to generate sympathy for the homeless, much less to commit resources for improving their welfare. Initiatives for improvement also cuts against the grain of many Canadians who believe any "mollycoddling" induces more dependency and fosters laziness. Too often, homelessness is viewed through the distorting lens of morality or character, dismissing those living on streets as lazy, undeserving, and responsible for their lot in life (Trypuc and Robinson 2009). This Victorian mentality toward the "undeserving poor" defuses the political will and financial investment to do something for fear of rewarding the indigent. It also underscores the inconvenient fact that housing is the single largest expense for low-income families. As Campaign 2000 (2010) pointed out, one in four households spends more than 30 per cent of income on housing. To make matters worse, the Ontario Association for Food Banks 2011 Report concludes that for those who rely on food banks, 72 per cent of their income goes to housing.

Federal government initiatives to address the homelessness problem do exist. They include the 1999 National Homelessness Initiative (now the Homelessness Partnering Strategy), which has a budget allocation of just over $750 million over three years. But recent initiatives such as the Investment in Affordable Housing Program have failed to offset an acute shortage of affordable homes (Shapcott 2012). Provincial responses are no less uneven (for example, Ontario has no homelessness secretariat or a coordinated homelessness strategy). Much of the innovation and action has occurred at the municipal and community level via programs and strategies that, admittedly, are strong on compassion but slack on coordination and comprehensiveness (Gaetz 2010). The different needs of the homeless, from addiction treatment and job training to housing or mental health support, can also complicate the possibility of common solutions. Some homeless require access to simple and basic shelter, even if this accommodation comes with a set of rules. Others need to find jobs, while still others, incapable of working, require information about how to stay off the streets and collect the welfare or disability cheques they are entitled to. Those with mental health problems require a caring community agency. A progression of ongoing supports may be required as people transition from the streets to temporary or transitional housing, then to permanent housing and independence (HRSDC 2011). In theory, what is required is a holistic and integrative strategic approach involving all levels of government that focus on prevention, and emergency responses and transitions, yet acknowledges the need to address structural changes and changes in government policy related to a national housing strategy (Gaetz 2010). In reality, what passes for intervention is a series of ad hoc measures that address the symptoms rather than causes.

Put bluntly, homelessness is not a simple problem with a single cause but a complex problem with multiple causes (Fleras 2005). The post-1980s crisis in homelessness reflects a combination of structural changes to the economy (from trade liberalization to de-industrialization), with shifts toward neo-liberal government policy, including support cuts for low-income individuals,

deinstitutionalization of psychiatric facilities, dismantling of national housing strategy, and reduction in affordable housing stock (Gaetz 2010). Solutions to a complex and multidimensional problem are clearly a major challenge, neither reducible to simple slogans nor solvable through quick-fix formulas such as throwing money at the problem. For example, a study by the Mental Health Commission of Canada (Gaetz 2012) reinforced the proactive value of furnishing the homeless with affordable housing rather than a patchwork of emergency services which can range from just over $9,000 per year for a mentally ill homeless person to just under $26,000 per the chronically ill homeless in constant need of social services. The Housing First recovery-oriented approach concurs that a permanent home (no matter how tiny) enables the homeless to restart their lives in safety and security (Gratzer, 2015; Homeless Hub 2015). But others are more cautious: according to Heffernan, Todorow, and Luu of the Advocacy Centre for Tenants (2015), providing housing for the homeless does not address the root causes of the problem, tends to focus on the visible homeless (those living on the street), and overlooks the diversity of people who experience homelessness ("invisible homeless") but do not qualify for social or subsidized housing. Doing nothing is not an option: the chronic homeless incur significant economic costs amounting to just over $7 billion annually because of health care costs related to emergency hospital use or social and correctional services (Gaetz et al. 2013). Clearly, only a slew of initiatives along a broad front—at the level of families and individuals, local and municipal initiatives, and federal and provincial resources—can possibly address a problem whose complexity and intractability dismiss a one-size-fits-all, quick-fix solution. Until the structural conditions that create and sustain homelessness are addressed, homeless reduction strategies will prove a hit and miss affair. Regardless of the challenges, Canada has no choice but to acknowledge the human right for everyone to adequate housing as set out in the 1948 Universal Declaration of Human Rights and the Covenant on Social, Economic, and Cultural Rights, ratified in 1976 (Hulchanski 2009).

Rethinking Poverty, Reframing Poverty Reduction Strategies

> In a world that often lionized wealth, it is worth remembering that no-one can be rich unless others are poor.
> —Dorling (2011:13). Reprinted with permission.

Discussions of poverty tend to be obscured by the use of different measures that are neither clearly explained nor convincingly justified in terms of what is being measured, why, how, and when. This conceptual disarray results in a string of contradictory interpretations and incompatible numbers that confuse Canadians to the point of disengagement (tuning out) (Shillington and Stapleton 2010). Measures and numbers are important for poverty reduction initiatives since decision-makers often pay attention only to what is measured. Even more critical in fighting poverty are mindsets infused with popular misconceptions. The poor are poor, it is argued, because they are idle, lack a work or saving ethic, are morally bankrupt, devalue education, and prefer handouts over honest labour (Gorski 2008b). Of course, there are individuals in poverty who fit this bill. But such a blanket statement may well take the exception and make it the rule. Approaches to poverty that emphasize individual responsibility (i.e., blame the victim by attributing moral attributes to poor folk) conveniently ignore contextual factors and structural causes (Redden 2014). They are also consistent with a neo-liberal and market-oriented mindset. According to neo-liberalism, government interventions such as pay equity or employment equity interfere with the free play of market forces. Reliance on welfare assistance is accused of compromising Canada's international competitiveness while perpetuating the very conditions of dependency and addiction it sought to eradicate.

The conclusion is disheartening but inescapable. In a country with such bounty and fortune, Canada's reluctance to solve the poverty problem must come as a shock. The persistence of poverty is not an inevitability as spun by the Bible in proclaiming the poor will always be with us. Nor is it the result of market forces beyond people's control. To be sure,

not everything can be attributable to government cutbacks or to a perverse welfare system of transfer payments that tends to entrap individuals, thwart initiative, and impede social mobility (Sheikh 2015). Individuals too must take some responsibility for their choices, although options may be severely limited because of the context in which the poor find themselves. But this reference to individual responsibility hardly justifies unconscionable levels of poverty inequality in a Canada blessed with such abundance. Unacceptable levels of poverty reflect political decisions and policy choices by authorities who withhold resources or lack the political will to challenge or change. Governments may exhort the poor to work but then penalize them by clawing back benefits when the poor initiate a move from welfare to work (Laurin and Poschmann 2013; also footnote 1). Poverty may be inadvertently perpetuated by social service agencies that inflict additional humiliation by inducing patterns of dependency and powerlessness. Policy changes over the past two decades have further eroded Canada's safety net for the poor.[2] The political will to improve the position of the poor has been further aborted by an obsession with fiscal austerity and deficit reduction in the name of global competitiveness and balanced budgets (Macdonald 2015; Tiessen 2016).

The multidimensionality of poverty complicates the possibility of a silver-bullet solution. Strategies of poverty reduction are much more complex and nuanced than narrow technocratic visions that offer up the balm of economic growth (UN 2009). Debates over the causes of poverty must acknowledge cumulative effects of disadvantage, neglect, and abuse in perpetuating poverty across generations (Lin and Harris 2012). Poverty does not arise from a single source; multiple and overlapping sources create a **cascading disadvantages** effect—that is, each new disadvantage is harder to overcome, given the lingering effects of past disadvantages. Disadvantages cascade, as Lin and Harris (2012:3) argue, so that difficult but solvable problems, from food insecurity to disruptive peer groups, begin to accumulate. Eventually a tipping (boiling) point is reached, resulting in a wholesale collapse from which recovery is remote (Gladwell 2000). Moreover, when multiple disadvantages exist, even solutions can intensify problems; for example, a reliance on food stamps or food banks can reinforce demeaning stereotypes. Finding a remedy is thus doomed to failure if the proposed solutions do not address those new vulnerabilities created by the economy, enabled by policy, or institutionalized by government. By contrast, Lin and Harris concede, advantages can be insulating. The presence of enough advantages can make it easier to cushion the negative impacts of single or intermittent disadvantages. Bad choices or bad luck are unlikely to result in devastating disadvantage when problems are staggered one at a time or slowly enough to reinstate stability. The Spotlight box addresses the politics that often accompany a linking of a solution to a problem.

Even seemingly progressive solutions are suspect if they oversimplify the challenge (problem) (Clemens 2012). Framing the poverty problem as an income issue puts undue emphasis on money-oriented solutions through subsidies, cash transfers,

and tax credits. But throwing money at a problem cannot capture the multiple exclusionary aspects that constitute poverty (from powerlessness and degradation to a lack of numeracy/literacy/digital skills), whereas short-term solutions such as food banks get the government off the hook by offloading its responsibilities to local levels without addressing root causes (Winckler and Trickey 2014; Kimmett 2012; Stapleton 2011). Yes, people are poor because of inadequate income supports, minimum wages that do not provide a living wage, lack of affordable housing and access to reliable child care (Saul 2013; Tiessen 2016). Yet the human and social costs associated with the powerlessness, marginalization, and exclusion are no less critical. How long can people endure deprivation before inflicting long-term damage to their self-worth and coping ability? Poverty wears people down by making it painfully difficult to be productive or to participate (Wilkinson and Pickett 2009). Being poor can also impair cognitive

Spotlight Cultures Matter: A Culture of Poverty or a Poverty of Culture?

Are the poor, poor because of their immersion in a culture of poverty (blame the system)? Or are they poor because they suffer from a poverty of culture (blaming the victim)? Do lowered expectations and short-term gratification reflect a cause or symptom of poverty (Isserman 2012)? Does the concept itself suffer from a poverty of explanatory value?

The American anthropologist Oscar Lewis (1959) published one of the more controversial books of the twentieth century on the "culture of poverty." Based on a study of the urban poor and slum dwellers in Central America, reference to a culture of poverty reflected a design for living in which poor individuals possessed a unique culture whose values rendered them marginalized, powerless, inferior (personal unworthiness), lacking trust in others (including governments), unco-operative and non-involved, and fatalistic—that is, resigned to the primacy of luck or fate (Lewis 1964). In other words, as Charles Murray (2012) writes, poor people are trapped by distorted norms and twisted aspirations that attribute their

failure to lack of middle class values and ambitions. This impoverished lifestyle is then transmitted from generation to generation; as a result, young children not only absorb these values but also are psychologically incapable of taking advantage of changing circumstances. The Moynihan Report in 1965 racialized the concept of culture of poverty and extended it to describe the situation of urban blacks in the United States, engulfed in a cycle of single mothers, welfare dependency, moral deficiencies and anti-social activity (Cohen and Venkatesh 2010).

Following an initial burst of acceptance, the concept of a culture of poverty came under such sweeping criticism that it was eventually expelled from academic circles (Gorski 2008b). Three reasons predominated: first, it portrayed the lifestyle of the poor in pathological terms, thus implying a kind of "poverty of culture," In doing so it invokes a sense of classism, namely, some groups of people are worse than others because of inherent shortcomings pertaining to language, moral

continued

reasoning, and overall capacities (Gorski 2008b). Bluntly put, they are different from us (Redeaux 2011). Second, it assumed the poor uniformly shared a largely monolithic, consistent, and predictable set of beliefs and practices that determined their behaviour (also known as *essentialism*). Third, it tended to blame the poor for being poor by virtue of internalized values, in the process ignoring the institutional and structural basis of poverty. A refusal to acknowledge the broader context of poverty transformed the concept of culture into a rigid, homogenous, and constraining force which mechanically determines people's behaviour ("essentialism," i.e., fixing people into immutable categories and ignoring the dynamic and shifting nature of people's identities and commitments).

Despite criticism, there is much of value in the culture of poverty as an explanatory concept. But its value requires an analytical shift toward the principles of symbolic interactionism. The concept of culture in the culture of poverty should not be framed as a permanent, deterministic, and pathological lifestyle. Rather it should be seen as a shared yet situational set of rules (blueprints) about how the world works. As James Nazroo and

Saffron Karlsen (2002) have noted, references to culture should be approached as a fluid and flexible resource that is always changing and contested; open to diverse interpretation; intersecting with and structured by gender, race, or class; and modulated by previous experiences and relationships in providing guidelines for understanding and action. Reframed thusly, reference to a culture of poverty reflects and embodies a coping mechanism and a resilient response—akin to a perpetual high wire act, especially if there are children to support (Ehrenreich 2014)—to a set of unequal circumstances. For example, the much maligned Moynihan Report in 1965 argued that those patterns of thought and even destructive behaviour associated with a culture of poverty did not reflect an inherent moral deprivation. They embody a realistic reaction to the entrenched problems of racism, social segregation, and economic deprivation (Cohen 2010). Or alternatively, a culture of poverty can be seen as a pragmatic response to situational constraints. As Eliot Liebow's *Tally's Corner* argued, the poor and non-poor share similar values about success, but the poor acquire additional beliefs in responding to their perceived helplessness toward these ideals.

functioning (Mani et al. 2013; Khazan 2014). People in poverty may expend considerable mental energy coping with immediate problems such as food scarcity or paying the bills. As a result, they are often left with less cognitive capacity to cope with more complex issues such as taking steps to overcome financial woes. They are also more likely to be error prone or to make poor decisions that exacerbate their marginality or vulnerability.

Poverty reduction strategies must shift from a reactive focus to a greater emphasis on proactive interventions. For example, the Generation Squeeze campaign offers a proactive movement to reduce child poverty. According to its founder Paul Kershaw (cited in Charbonneau 2014), instead of focusing only on the poor, the campaign begins with the assumption that the needs of all young families must be addressed. The campaign points out that in 1976, poverty struck 10 per cent of families whose household heads were aged 25–34 years.

In 2013, poverty informed 12 per cent of families with a similar composition. By contrast, while senior poverty was 30 per cent in 1976, the figure had dropped to about 6 per cent in 2013, thanks to a combination of improved medical care and increased pensions and government transfers. The government spent $45,000 annually per senior, compared to only $12,000 for each person under the age of 45. And yet the 25- to 34-year-old generation experienced substantial time and financial squeeze. The solution resides in making an investment in the squeezed generation by reducing the number of hours worked while offering more generous parental leave; providing young couples with affordable day care; and securing housing credits to defray costly shelter payments. Increased government transfers to the squeezed generation would result in savings of $50,000 annually, yet cost the government only $13,000 per year per person. The lesson is fairly obvious: poverty may be reduced when focusing not just on the poor or a short-term spending approach, but on a proactive (investment) model that prevents poverty in the first place. And an investment model to poverty and homelessness is much more likely to save costs in the long run.

Any fight against poverty must also ensure the importance of securing jobs and a living wage if low-income families are to move from welfare to work. Governments must play a development role in making the transition by not dissuading the poor from seeking work (clawing back transfers and benefits [Lankin and Sheikh 2012; UN Department of Economic and Social Affairs (DESA) 2009]), while attending to the work-related costs of transportation, access to job training, tax incentives for lower paid workers, and availability of child care arrangements. In other words, a benefits (government transfers) strategy must complement a job strategy to make working financially worthwhile (Conference Board of Canada 2011a). Passive, benefits-only reduction schemes that focus largely on individuals must give way to comprehensive anti-poverty strategies that incorporate multi-pronged initiatives across governments, departments, and service providers (Conference Board of Canada 2011a). The federal government could save billions of dollars (as much as $25 billion per year), according to the National Council of Welfare (2011b), if the roots of poverty were tackled through a long term *investment* model (initially more costly and time-consuming but paying off in the long run) rather than by short-term program spending fixes (from emergency health care to prisons[3]) that do little to root out the problem. For example, a Canadian Centre for Policy Alternatives (CCPA) report (Ivanova 2011) concludes that poverty costs British Columbia anywhere from $8.1 billion to $9.2 billion per year (through higher public health costs, increased policing and crime costs [crimes of desperation including recourse

to survival sex], and lost productivity). A $4 billion investment could support a comprehensive poverty reduction plan (such as investing in new social housing, increasing welfare, improving working conditions and low wages, more accessible education or retraining programs, or implementing universal access to child care).

No less important is a national anti-poverty plan that acknowledges a collective national responsibility (Ehrenreich 2014). The Canadian National Council of Welfare ([CNCW] 2007) proposes such a national agenda with a focus on a long-term anti-poverty strategy, including measurable targets, workable timelines, identifiable indicators, and monitoring mechanisms, in addition to a plan of action for coordinating the actions of governments and stakeholders. In 2008, the board of directors of the National Anti-Poverty Organization adopted the following vision statement based on the proposals of the CNCW:

1. Poverty is a violation of a human right to security of the person;
2. Poverty must be eradicated because it constitutes an affront to the values of fairness, justice, and inclusion;
3. Elimination of poverty by 2020 will require the exercise of political will, corporate responsibility, and community involvement; and
4. Its elimination and creation of full and equal participation for all Canadians entails policies and programs that provide sufficient income and related social supports.

It remains to be seen whether these promises can translate into progressive actions. Judging by the failure to eliminate child poverty by 2000, despite an all-party agreement in the House of Commons in 1989, the prospect of substantial change on the anti-poverty front does not look promising.

Summary

1. The magnitude of poverty in a bountiful Canada was examined, as was its influence in intensifying the gap between the reality of inequalities and exclusions and the ideal of equality and inclusion.

2. A dearth of agreement over the definition, scope, and measurement of poverty reflects its tricky status as a political and politicized phenomenon in defining who gets what and what goes where.

3. The politics of poverty embody the definitive expression of social inequality and class stratification, both as an analytical puzzle as well as a lived reality with very real consequences.

4. Poverty matters in sustaining patterns of social exclusion, especially for poor children.

5. Poverty is not just about income or material comforts, but about quality-of-life factors such as power, participation, self-esteem, and contribution.

6. A social class lens is applied in analyzing poverty and homelessness in Canada, involving as it does issues related to family background, market situations, and ownership of productive property.

7. The sharply contested nature of poverty pivots around what it is, how much of it there is, how it is measured, what the causes are or who is to blame, where it tends to cluster, what kind of consequences are exerted, and what to do about it.

8. The framing of poverty as a social problem will influence the appropriate kind of poverty reduction strategies.

Review Questions

1. What is meant by the expression "the politics of poverty in Canada"?

2. Compare *absolute* versus *relative* approaches to poverty in terms of how the problem is defined and measured, and proposed solutions.

3. How does poverty matter in terms of shaping people's lives and life chances?

4. Discuss the reasons homelessness as a poverty issue is difficult to analyze and assess.

5. The chapter points out that the concept of poverty is undergoing a conceptual shift in terms of who is poor, why they are poor, and how this poverty is expressed. Explain.

Endnotes

1. Clawbacks continue to derail the prevailing belief in jobs as a poverty solution. In 1993, a lone parent with one child could keep $50 dollars in earnings each month before allowances were reduced. Now earnings are reduced from the first dollar earned (Stapleton 2013). Not surprisingly, low-income Canadians are reluctant to sacrifice subsidized drug or dental plans in addition to eligibility for social housing in scaling the "welfare wall" (Sheikh 2015). There is some merit in calls to reinstate full earning exemptions to allow the poorest to bank more of their earnings (Lankin and Sheikh 2012).

2. Ontario's single social assistance rate in 1993 was fixed at $663 a month, or 60 per cent of full-time minimum wage. If adjusted for inflation since 1993, the current rate would be $944 per month. In real dollars, the rate in December 2012 was $606 a month, or 36 per cent of minimum wage—a base income drop of 56 per cent over the past 20 years (Stapleton 2013). Once the cost of shelter, food, and clothing are factored in, there is a deficit of –$344 each month (Stapleton 2011). Disability support payments are currently fixed at $1,064 per month or $12,768 per year, while a single parent with one child receives $1,529 per month or $18,351 annually.

3. The cost per year of incarcerating a woman in a federal prison is estimated at just over $211,000 (Thibault 2014).

III Status Inequalities: Gender, Race, Aboriginality

Part III continues the discussion and debate on status inequalities from Part II. Unlike Part II, however, which focused on the socio-economic categories of class and poverty, Part III shifts the frame of reference to those status inequalities involving identity groups and the politics of recognition that challenge the inequalities of exclusion. As pointed out in Part II, socio-economic status inequalities such as class (or any group with a problematic relationship to the market) usually entail debates over *redistribution*. Emphasis is focused on socio-economic injustices (from exploitation to income gaps) and the need to restructure market relations around a more equitable pattern of production, distribution, and consumption. In contrast to the politics of redistribution, the politics of *recognition* incorporates those identity status groups that experience a loss of prestige or privilege vis-à-vis other status groups. Attention is directed at challenging those conventional patterns of cultural domination and social exclusion rooted in the misrepresentation or undervaluation of the cultural other—in the hope of affirming group differences as a basis for inclusion and equality (Levrau and Loobuyck 2013; Fraser 1997). Admittedly, while this distinction is theoretically useful, in reality, the politics of redistribution and recognition are mutually constitutive of and complement each other. In other words, the politics of redistribution and recognition constitute intertwined dimensions of social inequality with respect to gender, racialization, and aboriginality.

The chapters in Part III are predicated on the idea that identity-based statuses and group differences in esteem, honour, and respect may even supersede resources and power as interrelated drivers of inequality in complex societies. After all, as Ridgeway (2014) argues, individuals and groups not only care about their sense of being valued in the society to which they belong; they also regard public acknowledgement of their worth as intensely as money and power in motivating behaviour shaping outlooks. Yet the mainstream have long oppressed, excluded, or exploited the identities of historically disadvantaged groups such as women, racialized minorities, and Aboriginal peoples. But taking a cue from an historical precedent, the situation is changing. Just as American blacks in the post-civil rights era reclaimed their blackness as a rallying cry, so too do the politics of identity (or recognition) capitalize on people's devalued identities as a basis for resistance and change (Clifford 2000). People's politics emerge out of and are informed by the politicization of their identities for the purpose of galvanizing people around a common cause and mobilizing them into action groups. To be sure, identity politics and the politics of recognition have come under criticism by both conservatives and radicals since their very inwardness undermines the possibility of more inclusive solidarities, collective action, and co-operative coexistence (Smith 2008). Nevertheless, reference to identity groups and identity politics of recognition provides insight into how gender, race, and aboriginality and their intersection continue to serve as predictors of success as well as targets of **bias** (Gee, Kobayashi, and Prus 2007).

Chapter 6 employs a social inequality lens to examine gendered exclusions in Canada, and vice versa: to analyze social inequality via a gender lens. Patterns of social inequality are shown to be deeply structured in a patriarchal Canada that is gendered for women generally and racialized and classed for minority women more specifically. This chapter also acknowledges how a commitment to intersectional analysis focuses on the interplay of factors—race, gender, class, and ethnicity—in creating a multiplier exclusionary effect. Chapter 7 is concerned with racialized inequality in Canada. Both racialized minorities and immigrant Canadians continue to be marginalized by systemically biasing structures that deny, exclude, or exploit. Two explanatory models—ethnicity (blame the victim) and critical race theory (blame the system) are thought to account for patterns of inequality and exclusion. Chapter 8 addresses a key paradox in Canada. Aboriginal peoples may comprise Canada's *First* Peoples, yet they often occupy *second*-class status and live under conditions that would embarrass some *Third* World countries in the global south (Maaka and Fleras 2005; Coulthard 2014). The framing of the so-called "Indian" inequality problem in terms of assimilationist/autonomist/accommodationist models draws attention to the complexities of the challenge in repairing a broken relationship.

6 Gendered Inequality, Engendered Exclusions

Learning Objectives

1. To demonstrate how progress on the equality front for Canadian women is offset by continuing inequalities and exclusions.

2. To point out how gender relations are fundamentally unequal relations that must be analyzed accordingly.

3. To draw attention to how female inequalities in a gendered society remain structurally embedded in a systemic patriarchy.

4. To describe how gendered inequalities as social exclusions are differently expressed across different domains.

5. To convey how the diverse social location of minority (aboriginal, racialized, migrant) women intensifies patterns of inequality and exclusion.

6. To show how an intersectional/intrasectional analysis provides a better framework for analyzing violence and minority women.

Introduction: Living in a Man's World? Mixed Messages, Paradoxical Trends

The one hundredth anniversary of International Women's Day was a time of both celebration and consternation. Mixed messages about the status of women continue to persist in light of paradoxical trends and contradictory outcomes. The first International Women's Day in 1911 was marked by rallies across Europe for the right of women to work, vote, become lawyers or physicians, hold public or political office, live free of discrimination, possess equal property rights, control their fertility, enjoy personal autonomy, and (in Canada) to be legally defined as persons. A century later, much has changed for the better, especially for women in

the global north who have secured hard-won gains across different levels (Rosin 2012). Improvements notwithstanding, however, women continue to be underrepresented in areas that count (from federal politics to corporate boardrooms), overrepresented in areas that do not count (from part-time employment to victims of intimate partner violence), and misrepresented (such as in mainstream media) in ways that leave them out of the count.

For women in the global south, the situation is even more precarious (World Economic Forum 2012; 2013). Women around the world remain second-class citizens, little more than male property to be pushed around with impunity, excluded and exploited, and punished for acting outside the bounds of male approval. They live in a world where obstacles, hardships, and prejudicial discrimination are the rule rather than the exception, despite formal equality statutes. Blatant expressions of **patriarchy** incite patterns of abuse and violence, ranging from honour killings and disfigurement to femicide and mass rapes in war zones. Clearly there is value in commemorating the hundredth anniversary of International Women's Day, and yes, the distance travelled is impressive. Yet the distance that remains is long and formidable, and change is elusive.

Another milestone transpired in 1963, just past the fiftieth anniversary of International Women's Day. Betty Friedan published *The Feminine Mystique*, a scathing criticism of gender relations that proved as revolutionary in raising public consciousness as had Rachel Carson's *The Silent Spring* in launching the environmental movement. *The Feminine Mystique* was not the first book to articulate this "problem with no name." A groundbreaking book by Simone de Beauvoir, *The Second Sex* (1961), had already criticized the perception of women as second-class citizens whose worth and work suffered because of a male dominated world. Earlier still, Helen Mayer Hacker published an article in 1951 that framed women as a "minority" whose caste-like status pervaded all aspects of society. But it was Friedan who captured the zeitgeist of an era by equating the unhappiness and boredom of middle-class women to "comfortable concentration camps." According to Friedan, a profound sense of emptiness tormented those women who sought fulfillment and identity beyond the grocery aisle or the ironing board. Options for women had narrowed to the point of accepting male domination as natural and normal, doting over children and husbands at the expense of personal empowerment or careers, obsessing over appearances, assuming a sexually passive stance, and embracing housework as a calling. So pervasive and internalized was this presumption of women as "natural born nurturers" that few dared to step outside the gender straightjacket for fear of rebuke, ridicule, or rejection.

Women indeed have come a long way since those heady consciousness-raising days of resistance and rebellion (Rosin 2012). The emergence of feminism as a powerful social movement proved consequential in challenging conventional views about the status of women in society; contesting the rigidly defined rules, roles, and expectations associated with womanhood; and reassessing their relational status along more equitable lines (Marsden 2012). The consequences of this feminist ferment have proven extraordinary: in a relatively short period of time, the politics of gender evolved beyond the days when women and children were regarded as male property; rape within marriage was dismissed as a contradiction in terms; a woman's place was in the home or between the sheets; a working woman was pitied as irresponsible or an embarrassment; unwed mothers were stigmatized, shunned, or secluded in shame; universities were institutes for snaring husbands rather than securing credentials; and tightly scripted gender norms defined men as "kings of the castle" but diminished women to little more than "ladies of the house." By contrast, women in Canada are doing relatively well, especially in comparison to millions of women in the past and in the developing world at present. They are protected by human rights, enjoy pay equity and inclusive employment standards, and benefit from laws and organizations that advocate for the full integration of women into all domains of public and private life (Heyninck 2014). Women are increasingly striding the corridors of power at both economic and political levels, in addition to exercising greater control over their lives in terms of education, family arrangements, marriage options, and work/life balances. Many are outliving their spouses and assuming greater control of financial affairs, including over one-third of all financial assets and wealth in North America (Nelson 2014). As of this writing, women occupy leadership positions at the world's two major economic institutions—the International Monetary Fund and the United States Federal Reserve System; in addition, Angela Merkel, the leader of the world's fourth largest economy, may yet dislodge Otto von Bismarck as Germany's greatest chancellor (Olive 2013b). Even such traditional male domains as workplaces are experiencing a transformation. American women in their twenties are often out-earning men in their twenties, in addition to occupying 12 of the 15 fastest-growing professions (Brooks 2012; but see Cohen 2013; Coontz 2012), while the appointment of female CEOs—once a rarity—no longer attracts the kind of media attention it once did (Deveau 2013). Female "soft power" skills, including social intelligence, collaborative communication, and commitment to compromise and consensus, are increasingly in demand in a post-industrial world that is networked rather than hierarchical (Rosin 2012). A sea-change toward formal equality has all but banished the most egregious expressions of sexism, with the result that many young women are questioning the relevance of feminism in a seemingly post-gender society (Redfern and Aune 2010). Even the worth of men and their future in the so-called new matriarchy is under scrutiny, as demonstrated in the Spotlight box below (Rosin 2012).

Spotlight From the End of Men to the Rise of Women: Towards Matriarchy?

In the summer of 2012, Hanna Rosin published a book that put a new spin on the much maligned gender wars. Entitled *The End of Men*, Rosin's book argued that male domination and control were being whittled away by female empowerment across almost every measure of success. Rosin's argument that male supremacy no longer prevailed was supported by data and trends, namely, female parity with men in many professions, disproportionate success at post-secondary levels, women's ability to form families without relying on male support, and the disappearance of working-class and younger men from higher education levels and the job market (male work accounted for three-quarters of the 7.5 million jobs lost in the 2008 great recession). For Rosin, women's success could be attributed in part to those interpersonal and communication skills (empathy, flexibility, collaboration) more attuned to the sensibilities of the new information age. Not only were women more ambitious and adaptable, Rosin concluded, they were also astute enough to gravitate to largely recession-proof jobs in human services and support staff. This take-charge attitude contrasted sharply to the loser-mentality of "cardboard" men whose manufacturing jobs disappeared during the "mancession." Men who once dominated the old social order remained hostage to conventional ways of thinking and doing, unable to bend, adapt, or renew (Rosin 2012; Brooks 2012). Even down-on-their-luck men appeared either reluctant or incapable of making the effort to reinvent themselves (see Harris 2012; Kimmel 2013).

To be sure, reference to "the end of men" should not be taken literally, in the same way that reference to a post-racial society doesn't mean the end of racialized inequality. More accurately, the end of men refers to the end of traditional masculinity in monopolizing entitlements related to power and privilege. Nor does this reference herald the immediate disappearance of male privilege and power; after all, a transition period is inevitable before an archaic masculinity lapses into oblivion. In other words, what is coming to an end, as Chloe Angyal (2012) writes, are those "benchmarks of a particular model of masculinity" that privileged males as "natural born leaders" with a God-given right to have it all (Kimmel 2013). Men no longer enjoy what the Australian sociologist R.W. Connell (1996) calls a "patriarchal dividend," namely, those perks that rich white men took for granted in a world they claimed as theirs. Failure to adjust to a series of humbling recessions may have rendered them emasculated, humiliated and betrayed, and discarded like worthless trash, yet nothing to date has replaced the male crisis of confidence (Fleras and Dixon 2011; Faludi 1999; Eichler 2012). But instead of directing their ire at those corporate decision-makers who have shipped their jobs overseas and rendered them expendable, male anger is redirected at immigrants, women, and diversity initiatives as convenient scapegoats (Kimmel 2013).

Rosin's reference to the "end of men" may join the lexicon of other popular slogans such as "lean in" (Sandberg 2013) or "second sex" or "feminine mystique" or "beauty myth." But Rosin's optimism

continued

has come under attack, including a stinging rebuke by Stephanie Coontz (2012) who challenged the notion that women are assuming control as the new breadwinners and corporate captains while men supposedly seek "refuge in a perpetual adolescence" by hunkering down in parental basements (also Kimmel 2009). If it's the end of men, Coontz asks, why do they still control the most important industries (women constitute 16 per cent of boards of directors in the United States, 10 per cent in Canada [Eichler 2012]), monopolize the list of the top CEOs (96 per cent of *Fortune*'s top 1,000 companies), represent the richest body of people in the world, consistently earn more than women (approximately 25 per cent more), and continue to call the shots at all levels and across all domains? Women, in turn, continue to be marginalized in politics and mainstream institutions such as the media. True, Coontz concedes, women are occupying a more level playing space, thanks to the elimination of egregious institutional biases and sexist barriers, curtailment of blatant male privilege, and expansion of women's legal and economic rights. But to call this gender shift the onset of a new matriarchy is unsupported by the evidence.

For Coontz and others (Sandberg 2013) references to "the end of men" and the "ascent of women" are exaggerated. Deeply entrenched perceptions of women and men in the workplace remain notoriously resistant to change, especially in adopting family-friendly work practices (e.g., equal parental leave to reduced workloads) and social policies (affordable daycare) (Coontz 2013). In some cases, female progress has stalled; for example, stereotyped job segregation remains intact. In 1980, 75 per cent of teachers and 64 per cent of social workers were women; currently the figure is 80 per cent and 81 per cent respectively. Two interpretations follow: for some such as Coontz, women are educating themselves for occupations that pay less, in part to counteract the impact of traditional job discrimination that restricted female options in the past. For others, such as Rosin, this gender job segregation should be seen as a strength rather than a weakness. Women gravitate to so-called pink ghetto professions because they intuitively understand the kind of recession-proof jobs that will persist in the new information, service, and care economy.

Just as the supposed ascent of women overstates the evidence, so too do references to the decline of men—who remain in charge of just about everything (van der Gaag 2014; Sandberg 2013; Connell 2011). Nor is there any proof that most men are regressing into obsolescence rather than making adjustments. As a June 2015 report from Statistics Canada revealed, stay-at-home fathers/husbands now constitute 11 per cent of families in Canada, up from 2 per cent in 1976. Of course, a boorish rump of disengaged and slovenly men are confused by the new rules of manhood, can't find work, and reject commitment or meaningful relations. They continue to abide by the principles of never showing emotion, admitting weakness, or displaying any behaviour even remotely connected with "being gay," and defending their "masculine mystique" as worthwhile in its own right (Kimmel 2009). Admittedly, women no longer have to put up with this kind of cavalier behaviour in light of available resources that permit them to go it alone or to take it to court (Kimmel 2009). Nevertheless, it's too simplistic to describe this new dynamic as a case of women win–men lose (Friedman 2015). Rather what appears instead is a *convergence of female empowerment with a diminishment of male privilege* that is proving revelatory yet contradictory. For example, the widely publicized sexual assault charges and subsequent court appearances of CBC radio host Jian Ghomeshi and the increasingly beleaguered American actor Bill Cosby (in addition to increased media attention devoted to the case of nearly 1,200 murdered and missing aboriginal women in Canada) make it abundantly clear: women are not going to take it anymore. No matter how powerful a man, he can no longer commit crimes with impunity; no woman is so powerless that a crime against her doesn't matter; and the court of public opinion will not automatically side with a powerful man against victims in a world of higher sensitivity to sexual assault, its impact, and the seriousness with which it must be taken (Editorial, *Toronto Star*, 29 December 2014; Kingston 2016).

But theory is one thing, reality has proven quite another. Notwithstanding changes to Canada's

Criminal Code to remove the stigma and stereotyping around sexual violence, including the introduction of the rape shield provisions to prevent courtroom airing of an accusers' sexual history (Kingston 2016), the onus remains on the victim to establish the fact of being violated (Das Gupta 2009:9). The right to aggressively grill complainants at the preliminary inquiry to demonstrate their honesty and non-complicity has had the effect of putting the victims (rather than the accused) on trial, while proving as demoralizing as the sexual assaults in the first place (Birenbaum, Cross, and Dale 2016). Threats to "whack" those who dare come forward to press charges—in large part by challenging the credibility of the accuser through

humiliating cross-examination based on sexist and antiquated stereotypes—also reinforce how the system is rigged to secure male advantage (Tanovich 2015; Tanovich and Craig 2016). The conclusion seems inescapable: real change in sexual assault cases will come about when the male-friendly principle of "innocent until proven guilty" is balanced by a counter-principle to ensure the fair administration of justice for female victims. In other words, any transformation will require more than changing the conventions that refer to the rules. The underlying rules that inform everyday conventions will need to be challenged and overhauled in ungendering the inequalities of systemic exclusion (FAFIA 2009).

However impressive the gains at present and optimism for the future, the past persists. Substantial improvements in opportunities and choice, notwithstanding, there is still much to do before attainment of economic parity, social equality, political representation, and institutional power-sharing (Ridgeway 2011; Homans 2012; Coontz 2012; McInturff 2013a; FAFIA 2008; van der Gaag 2014). According to the fifty-ninth session of the UN's Commission on the Status of Women (2015) to mark the twentieth anniversary of the 1995 Fourth World Conference on Women held in Beijing (the Beijing Declaration and Platform for Action), parity and progress in some **gender** domains are offset by inequalities of exclusion in others. Much of this ambiguity can be attributed to a mix of tepid political commitment, a dearth of resources, rise of religious fundamentalism, and the lived realities of sexism, violence, and exploitation. Sexist assumptions have had the effect of marginalizing women; undervaluing their achievements and contributions; relegating them to lesser-paying jobs in lower-ranking institutions; ghettoizing them into less prestigious corporate domains such as staffing functions (human resources); and inhibiting their full and equal participation in society (Nelson 2010). Moves toward gender inclusion are notoriously slow despite

evidence that gender inequality reflects poorly on a progressive and democratic Canada. The 2014 Annual Report by the Canadian Board Diversity Council contended that, if Canadian corporations were left to their own devices, women would not achieve equal boardroom representation until the twenty-second century. In terms of political participation, closing the gender gap would require an additional 400 years of struggle (McInturff 2013a). The following gender inequality gaps provide a more specific picture of those exclusions that women confront:

1. Improvements have proven more symbolic than real—that is, legal equality (principles and promises) does not necessarily translate into substantive equality (practices and enforcement) (UN Women 2015; Birembaum, Cross, and Wade 2016). Institutional inequities from the family to the workplace are showing dogged resistance to change. Women are praised for their maternal domestic qualities but dismissed as too erratic and emotional for leadership material (El-Naggar 2012). Women in all fields of endeavour remain victimized by double binds (damned if they do, damned if they don't) and double standards. As a result, behaviour deemed to be normal for men (assertiveness) is

judged to be abnormal for women (aggressive-ness)—thus reinforcing Sandra Bem's (1994) prescient insight: in a male-dominated world, female differences are devalued and taken as proof of female inferiority.

2. The World Economic Forum conducts an annual measure of the world's countries in closing the gap between the participation of women and men in society (i.e., the access women and men have to the resources that are available, not the available level of resources). That might explain why low-income Mongo-lia came in first in the rankings for economic opportunity while Canada ranked twelfth. The average income for Canadian women is substantially higher than in many countries (including Mongolia), but so too is the gap between male and female income (McInturff 2013a). According to the Conference Board of Canada (2010), Canada scored a "C" on the gender income report card, with a gap of 21 per cent in 2007 (Denmark was lowest at 9 per cent and Japan highest at 32 per cent), putting it twelfth out of seventeen peer countries.

3. Women may have more freedom and choice; nevertheless, institutionalized access to power, privilege, and property remains as elusive as ever (Sandberg 2013). Initiatives from pay equity to employment equity to the contrary, women in the workplace are more likely to earn less than men, to work part-time, and to be excluded from the highest echelons of the corporate ladder (Homans 2012). Women were also more likely than men to start their careers at basic entry-level jobs; received fewer high-profile projects that bol-ster career advancement; were offered fewer international assignments and postings; and accepted lower starting salaries, the impact of which is compounded over a working career. (A Catalyst study in November 2013 concluded that high-potential women earned $8,167 less than men in their first post-MBA job [Beninger 2013].) Studies in the United States confirm the contradictions. In contrast to downward spiralling wages for men without a post-secondary education, women's real wages have increased over the past 30 years, especially for female professionals whose gains have vastly outpaced those of their male counterparts (Cohen 2014). Yet women remain dispropor-tionately clustered at the lowest income levels, in minimum wage jobs, working part-time and raising a family on their own.

4. A climate of fear and violence remains a con-stant in many women's lives (*The Lancet* 2014; RCMP 2014; True 2012; Mann 2012; Report 2014b). Women from all class groups suffer from physical, emotional, and psychological abuse at the hands of men (WHO 2013). Vulner-ability to violence is exacerbated for females during disasters and emergencies, with the likelihood of dying increased by a factor of 14 (Plan International 2013; Yang 2013). The problem of gender violence is compounded by the availability of (or awareness of) fewer options to escape abusive contexts, particu-larly for aboriginal women and racialized immigrant women.

5. Mixed media messages persist. Whereas men continue to be defined as natural-born leaders, ranging from corporate heads to heads of state, women tend to be framed as natural-born nur-turers or fashion-obsessed eye-candy (Fleras 2011a). For example, Disney films such as *Frozen* and *Tangled* portray young women as positive, plucky, and assertive. Yet these same young women in the Disney princess mer-chandising division receive the Kardashian makeover treatment that privileges appear-ances over substance (Cooper 2014). Who can be surprised by studies indicating that girls in America as young as six increasingly define themselves along sexual lines? Finally, does anyone need reminding that when it comes to measuring the value of women, their value is largely about appearance, as amply dem-onstrated by fawning media attention over women as fashionistas at award ceremonies from the Oscars to the Emmys (Murphy 2014).

6. Demeaning stereotypes persist in keeping women down and out. Women are taken less seriously, pre-judged on the basis of what they look like rather than what they do, and are thought to excel as caregivers rather than decision-makers. The effect of linking personal

success with perpetual makeovers in measuring women's worth creates unrealistic expectations about what is attainable, an obsession with physical appearance at the expense of health, and a preoccupation with weight loss and body image that borders on the pathological (Kilbourne 2010). These biases are largely subtle, often unconscious, and inconspicuously cumulative. Or in the words of Samantha Brennan of Western University, "[t]here is no one point of bias against women, but rather it happens at every step along the way. Each one is small, and not each one makes the whole story" (cited in Eisenkraft 2013:22).

7. Politics remains a no (wo)man's land because of an "old boys network" that refuses to jettison a cranky political culture at odds with contemporary realities and female sensibilities (Goodyear-Grant 2013; Homans 2012). Yes, by early 2014, five provinces and one territory, representing 85 per cent of Canada's population, were governed by female premiers (Hepburn 2013). (By mid-2014, the number had dropped to two provincial premiers, but was back up to three in mid-2015.) Yet women occupy just over one-quarter of the seats in Canada's Parliament, 4 of 25 mayoralties of Canada's largest cities, and just 28 per cent of senior leadership roles in the GTA (Omidvar and Tory 2012). Women in politics continue to be perceived as passive, emotionally soft, and inclined toward the soft power of consensus and persuasion (El-Naggar 2012). By contrast, men are defined as assertive, ambitious, competitive, and goal-oriented, and comfortable with the hard power of command (Nye 2012). To secure credibility in the rough and tumble world of politics, female politicians must work harder, know their facts better, be prepared to be defined by and compared to male standards, and endure accusations of imitating or emasculating men (Taber 2012).

8. The term "women's work" continues to resonate with a coded subtext (Miranda 2011). It stands as a proxy for describing unpaid maternal-domestic work around the home or confinement to low paying "girl ghettos" such as service, sales, or clerical jobs. Despite signs of greater partner involvement, women continue to shoulder a disproportionate share of childrearing responsibilities, unpaid caregiving, and domestic chores (Coontz 2012)—despite evidence that men have doubled their share of housework while tripling their contribution to child care (Duxbury and Higgins 2012; Lutz 2011). For example, the OECD Better Life Index (cited in McAlaster 2013) concludes that women in Canada spend 248 minutes per day on domestic unpaid labour, compared to 146 minutes for men (the OECD average is 279 minutes for women, 131 for men). (For comparable US figures, see Marche 2013.) In its annual survey of 165 countries to determine the best place to be a mother, based on factors from a mother's health and education to the nutritional status of children, a 2012 Save the Children report ranked Canada nineteenth, well behind top-ranked Norway.

9. Opportunities for women and labour market outcomes are compromised by the persistence and pervasiveness of the "second shift" (Lindsay 2008; Slaughter 2012; Mason, Wolfinger, and Goulden 2013). The nerve-wracking demands of balancing paid employment with unpaid household work yields a punishing cycle of double days without much relief in sight (Lutz 2011). Few could be surprised when the editor-in-chief of *Harvard Business Review* claimed he had never met a working mother who expressed satisfaction with her work-life balance (Ignatius 2013).

10. Hard-won gains can be chiselled away by the politics of expediency. Decisions by the federal government to roll back financial support to women's human rights groups has compromised Canada's international standing on gender issues. In 2004, Canada was ranked seventh by the World Economic Forum Gender Gap Index; by 2014 it had dropped to thirtieth of 145 countries (World Economic Forum 2015). In 2009, Canada was ranked seventy-third in a UN Gender Disparity Index owing to patterns of female poverty, violence against aboriginal women, and curtailment of programs for addressing women's needs and interests (CFAIA/CLC 2010). Other surveys are more positive: global polls such as one by

TrustLaw (a news service of Thomas Reuters Foundation), consisting of 370 gender experts from around the world, ranked Canada as the world's most woman-friendly country based on the following criteria: freedom from violence, workplace opportunities, and quality of health (Bascaramurty 2012). A US News et al (2016) survey placed Canada as the world's third best country for women, given its commitment to human rights, gender equality, income equality, safety, and progressiveness.

The verdict on the gendered inequalities of exclusion is layered with contradictions (Timson 2011). To one side, contemporary Canadian woman are cresting an unprecedented wave of entitlement and empowerment. They are no longer dismissed as inferior or submissive; gender roles are not nearly as rigidly scripted as before; rules defining masculinity and femininity are increasingly blurred and contested; female distinctiveness can be leveraged for advantage; and the female-driven principles of co-operation, communication, and consensus are touted as pivotal for doing business in the new economy (Rosin 2012). The status of women in Canada sparkles by comparison to the status of women in many developing world countries of the global south, where brutal suppression may be the norm (Plan International 2013; US News et al 2016). To the other side is a different picture: gender gaps are real and resistant to change (McInturff 2013a). Women's growing economic clout is offset by persistent wage gaps and corporate glass ceilings; impressive political gains are offset by continued underrepresentation of women at federal and municipal levels; a disproportionately high number of female postsecondary students is offset by the dearth of women as full professors, Canadian research chairs, and university presidents (Charbonneau 2013); the growing empowerment of women is offset by dismaying levels of intimate partner violence; perception of women as "movers and shakers" is offset by continued stereotyping of women's worth in terms of relationships (nurturers) and appearances; and more supportive domestic arrangements (male partners doing more cooking and child-caring than

Spotlight A Systemic Patriarchy: It's a Man's World

Prominent feminists from Carol Gilligan to Marilyn French agree: patriarchy remains the prevailing form of social and political organization in society (Carter 2014; but see Rosin 2012). In some cases patriarchal privileges are blatantly expressed; in many cases, the privileges are systemically biasing when embedded within the founding assumptions and foundational principles of a society's unwritten constitutional system. Its ubiquity as a social phenomenon is difficult to explain, although patriarchy may well have originated from a pervasive male obsession to control other men combined with a male fear of women as threats to their privilege and power (Johnson 1997). The combination of male physical strength and women's biological destiny may also have played a role.

Patriarchy can be defined as a social system designed, organized, and prioritized by, for, and about men. A society structured in patriarchy tends to reflect male realities as natural, reinforce male experiences as normal, confer privileges to men as desirable, and advance male interests as superior. Other interests, realities, and experiences are dismissed as irrelevant or inferior. Reference to patriarchy is deeply systemic: a systemic patriarchy can be visualized as a system in which the social, political, economic, and cultural are controlled by men; masculinity is more highly valued than feminine values; males have preferential access to the good things in life because they are deemed to be superior; and males or manliness constitute the norm by which others are judged (Boyd and Pikkov 2008). Manifestations of patriarchy can be differently expressed because of interrelated constituents, namely misogyny, sexism, and androcentrism. *Misogyny* refers to hatred of women. *Sexism* covers that constellation of beliefs and practices that openly assert the superiority of one gender over the other because of preconceived notions of what is normal, acceptable, and superior. *Androcentrism* in the past) are offset by punishing work-life-career choices that breed burnout or dropout. Mixed messages and double standards remain the rule: you can be anything you want but motherhood should be a priority. A woman's place may be in the workplace, but be prepared for the sniping if career choices or job commitments interfere with parental obligations (Putnam 2011; Brooks 2012). You can do anything you want but you must look good doing it. You can have it all but you will have to do it all by yourself (Timson 2011). Predictably, the second decade of the new millennium is proving a confusing mixture of progressive and regressive as traditional gender scripts persist in practice if not always in principle, while progressive principles are proving difficult to put into practice across all domains (Birembaum, Cross, and Wade 2016). True, traditional rules about gender relationships may appear increasingly passé. Nevertheless, new norms have yet to be formulated to everyone's satisfaction in a Canada that remains a systemic patriarchy.

Males too are buffeted by the gender quake that challenges the very notion of what men are "for" in a post-masculine world. Many men are experiencing a crisis of confidence in trying to figure out who they are and what is expected of them in a system that propagates rigid and toxic gender roles. Traits once negatively "essentialized" as "feminine" are now perceived as strengths; conversely, male virtues of independence, assertiveness, and control are defined increasingly as vices. Such inversion requires men to redefine their status and role in a world where their brawn is no longer in demand, their skills can be outsourced, and they are displaced as women enter into workplaces once the preserve of men. Particularly vulnerable are those men in the lower and middle classes who formerly worked in the manufacturing economy but are increasingly un/underemployed, depressed as empty shells of their former selves, and dependent on others to support them (Rosin 2012). A double standard quickly asserts itself for those men looking to reinvent themselves: No sooner do men show a "softer" side than they are precluded from female-dominated professions, discouraged from working with children, and criticized for acting "wimpy."

is the inclination to automatically and routinely interpret reality from a male vantage point; to posit this interpretation as natural and normal, while assuming that others will think so as well if given half a chance; to judge others on the basis of this masculinist standard; and to dismiss or criticize alternate interpretations.

The implications of living in a systemic patriarchy constructed by, for, and about men are consequential. Playing the male game by men's rules on male grounds may compromise female-preference ways of doing, thinking, relating to, and experiencing. The contradictions of living and working within what, systemically speaking, is a man's world compels women to co-operate with a patricentric system of rules and rewards often at odds with their interests, experiences, and realities (Slaughter 2012). Women may enjoy equal rights with men (on paper), but they must exercise these rights in a society designed and organized to reflect male experiences, reinforce men's priorities, and advance male interests. To be sure, female success stories are increasingly common; nevertheless this attainment is gained by going against the grain of what women may aspire to—metaphorically akin to walking up a down escalator. In other words, as Susan Pinker (2008) argues, women are unfairly penalized because ". . . they're expected to play by the same testosterone driven rules men do, rules that men made up decades ago while women were kept barefoot, pregnant, and even illiterate."

Time will tell if recent social changes related to the end-of-men debate will hasten the end of a systemic patriarchy and its replacement by a matriarchy (a society foundationally designed and constitutionally ordered by, for, and about women) (Rosin 2012). Glib references to matriarchy aside, the challenge in redesigning society along matriarchal lines is formidable. The rules that inform the conventions must be transformed to bring about fundamental changes. Simply changing the incumbents and conventions that refer to the rules may have the perverse effect of establishing a more female-friendly patriarchy.

But appearances are deceiving since rhetoric may not match reality, despite all the talk of a gender quake, including references to a feminized post-industrial economy with a corresponding shift of power and privilege (Mundy 2012; Cohen 2013). Canada remains systemically a (white) man's world in terms of first principles, societal priorities, hidden agendas, core values, institutional frameworks, and constitutional orders. The design, organization, and reward structure of Canadian society are neither neutral nor value free. Rather, Canadian society is gendered (**gendered society**) by virtue of being organized around a culture-specific agenda that systemically bolsters masculinist interests, norms, experiences, and aspirations. Of course, the most egregious expressions of sexism and patriarchy have been discredited and dismantled. The ready-made scripts that historically secured male power and privilege are being whittled away by demographic shifts, changes in intellectual fashion, government initiatives, and female assertiveness. But men as a group remain firmly in control of those agendas that shape political, economic, social, and cultural outcomes, with just enough exceptions to prove the rule. Women continue to be "put down" because of institutional and systemic bias, "put in their place" by way of outright violence or harassment, or "put out of sight" as inferior or irrelevant. In other words, as Laura Bates puts it in her book *Everyday Sexism*, women have become so distracted and/or complicit by apparent liberties that they cannot see the injustices inherent in both everyday interaction and social structures. The paradox in deciphering the improved relational status of women in a Canada dominated by men and male interests is clearly before us (Jackson 2010). Is it possible to analyze and assess the paradox in which women as a whole have made astonishing progress, while continuing to be largely excluded from the corridors of power and privilege because of historical inertia, patriarchal foundations, and systemic biases, while conversely, men appear to have lost their automatic entitlement to power and privilege, yet they and their agendas remain firmly in control of the political and economic domains? The juxtaposition of these seemingly intersecting yet contradictory trends—"the end of men" versus "it's still a man's world"—continue to perplex and provoke the domain of gendered inequality as a contested site of progress and stagnation.

The chapter is predicated on a recurrent premise: gender relations are ultimately unequal relations that pivot around the dynamics of power, privilege, and property. These relations are invariably unequal because a gendered social location remains relevant in defining opportunities and influencing outcomes in a world whose design, organization, and priorities neither reflect women's realities nor advance their interests (Jiwani 2006; Sheppard 2010). Neither deliberate nor conspiratorial, this **gendered inequality** reflects the logical consequences of seemingly neutral yet ultimately biased ground rules that remain firmly planted in **androcentric** assumptions about what is normal, desirable, and acceptable. *Gendered inequality* refers to those systemic exclusions (gendered exclusions) that deny or exclude individuals from activities or outcomes based on their gender. It also refers to the systemic biases inherent within the founding assumptions and foundational principles of an unwritten patriarchal constitutional order, one that is founded by men, organized to reflect their interests, revolving around their realities, and normalizing their experiences. (The systemic [or structural] basis of a gendered inequality within corporations was examined in Chapter 3.) Finally, inequality as exclusion is gendered because society is ideologically loaded and deeply embedded with values, beliefs, and norms with men in mind. Framing gendered inequalities as social in origin, definition, consequences, and treatment puts pressure on analyzing gendered exclusions in terms of how they are constructed, expressed, and maintained, as well as challenged, and transformed by way of politics, reform, and protest. A focus on inter/intrasectional analysis and its application in analyzing violence against women further reinforces the value of situating human behaviour within the context of gendered inequality and a systemic patriarchy.

This chapter takes its cue from movie history. Hollywood stars of yesteryear Ginger Rogers and Fred Astaire appeared in numerous movies as a gifted and graceful dancing team. The question of who was better a dancer was raised on occasion. Ginger was alleged to have snappily responded that she was every bit as good as Fred; however, she had to *dance backwards and do it in high heels* (an online search suggests that Bob Thaves, creator of the *Frank and Ernest* comic strip, is the true author of this response). For women the challenge of gender inequality can take its cue from this prescient notion (Jackson 2010): first, women may possess the same rights as men do; however, they must work and excel in a male-ingrained context ("in high heels") not of their making. Second, they must cope in a cultural environment created essentially by, for, and about males ("backwards") as they struggle to juggle a career, children, and social life (Slaughter 2012). Women may outperform men at school and in the early years of work, but the punishing effect of exhaustion and frustration—and the dead weight of conventional roles—reassert themselves with the onset of a family (Asher 2011). Corporate Canada continues to be structured around a military model of hierarchy and power-seeking that creates both impediments and unattractive options. To the extent they must emulate masculinity to attain success, women are labelled as pushy and aggressive. If they refuse to play along, they are dismissed as superficial or irrelevant, and ignored accordingly. The double bind is unmistakable, claims Kimmel (2000:17):

> Either way—corporate frump or sexy babe—women lose, because the workplace is, itself, gendered and standards of success, including dressing for success, are tailored for the other sex.

The fact a similar line of reasoning can be applied to society at large is testimony to the paradoxes of living in a "man's world." This paradox also points to the counterintuitive: gender differences do not create gendered inequality; rather, the reverse is true. Gendered inequalities exaggerate female differences (Kimmel and Holler 2011), in the process reinforcing Bem's (1994; also Kanter 1977) insight into how women's differences in a male-dominated world are devalued and manipulated to justify the inequality of exclusions.

Gendered Inequalities: Dimensions of Exclusion

Because it's 2015.
　—Prime Minister Justin Trudeau defends the creation of gender parity in the federal cabinet. 4 November 2015.

Assessing the global status of women is rooted in a paradox (Kristof and WuDunn 2009; UN Women 2011). The past century has witnessed immense strides in women's legal rights and lawful entitlements across the world (UN News 2015). More than a century ago (1911), only two countries allowed women to vote; at present, the right is virtually universal, in addition to the expansion of women's human rights at economic, civil, social and cultural levels. To date, 186 countries have ratified the Convention for the Elimination of all Forms of Discrimination against Women. Moves to remove discriminatory barriers to gender equality and justice have resulted in the following initiatives:

- 173 countries provide paid maternity leave;
- 139 countries have constitutionally enshrined the principle of gender equality;
- 125 countries have outlawed domestic violence;
- 117 countries have equal pay laws; and
- 115 countries guarantee women's equal property rights.

Women now hold more leadership positions than in the past; in addition, they can own and inherit property, run for public office, and get married and divorced on the same terms as men (UN Women 2015).

A commitment to gender equality may be highly valued in many parts of the world, but the promise of equality (legal rights related to access to health care, prospects of a decent job, and freedom from violence and discrimination) is not the same as its delivery (lived-rights) (UN Women 2015). No country treats its women as well as its men, according to the UN Commission on the Status of Women (2015), with wildly varying degrees of gender-based exclusions. For many women, the rights and the laws that exist on paper rarely translate into the reality of justice and equality. Their rights are undermined by extremism and regional conflicts, climate changes that make life almost inhabitable, volatile energy and food prices that endanger the lives of their children, and state austerity measures that negatively impact women's lives and life chances (UN Women 2015). All too often women are denied control of their bodies (61 countries severely restrict a woman's right to abortion), access to maternal health and basic education, a voice in decision-making, protection from intimate partner violence (127 countries do not explicitly criminalize rape within marriage) and workplace protection in precarious employment (53 per cent of women work in dirty or dangerous jobs). Women remain vulnerable to both domestic abuse and non-domestic assaults, including victimization by the brutal sexual violence increasingly a hallmark of modern sectarian conflicts, either to punish husbands suspected of collaboration or to defile and infect women (a kind of ethnic "uncleanliness"). Women who already are the most vulnerable in the best of times incur additional pain or exclusion during periods of crisis or catastrophe (Plan International 2013). Throughout the world, politics remains a misogynist terrain that routinely dissuades women from meaningful engagement (El-Naggar 2012). Women also languish near the bottom of the socio-economic ladder. The average pay gap between men and women (especially those with children, i.e., a "care penalty") hovers in the 10 to 30 per cent range because of low paid domestic work and poor quality jobs (UN Women 2015). The irony is dismaying: women may represent about half the world's population and perform nearly two-thirds of the work; nevertheless, they earn about one-tenth of the income while owning less than one one-hundredth of the property (White 2015).

Canada is not entirely exempt from this damning indictment of gender inequality. In a United Nations Development Programme survey of selected countries ranked according to the Gender Empowerment Measure, 2009, Canada scored twelfth of 109 countries. Canada's score of 0.830 means Canadian women were about four-fifths of the way to equality with men as defined by their share of Parliamentary seats; proportion of administrative, professional, and managerial jobs; and earning power. Another measure by the World Economic Forum in its 2015 Global Gender Gap Report placed Canada thirtieth of 145 countries, down from a peak of fourteenth place in 2006 but up from thirty-eighth in 2008 based on inequality indicators in four areas: economic opportunity, political participation, educational attainment, and health and survival indicators. A sense of perspective is useful: comparison to other parts of the world confirms the relatively lofty status of

Canadian women across a broad range of domains (US News et al. 2016). In relationship to Canadian men, women have also engineered astonishing strides in a remarkably short period of time. Yet this relational status is compromised when compared to Canada's normative ideals and constitutional guarantees. Put candidly, advances in some areas are marred by stagnation or regression in others. Disparities persist and are pervasive, and these inequalities of exclusion are manifest in employment status, income earnings, media communication, educational levels, political involvement, and vulnerability to intimate partner violence.

Employment Status

Women are prominent in the labour force (Status of Women Canada (SWC) 2015). They comprised 47.3 per cent of Canada's labour force in 2009, up from 37.1 per cent in 1976, representing an employment rate of 61 per cent compared to 70 per cent for men. Nearly 73 per cent of all adult women with children under the age of 16 and living at home were in paid employment in 2009, compared to only 24 per cent in the 1950s. In addition, nearly 12 per cent of working women were self-employed in 2009, up from 8.6 per cent in 1976. At a rate of 70 per cent, women remain overrepresented in part-time work (defined as fewer than 30 hours per week), a percentage that has remained steady over the past 30 years (SWC 2015). Women continue to be overrepresented in certain occupations: they are most likely to be employed in sales and service occupations (27.1 per cent); business, finance, and administration (24.6 per cent); and education, social, government, and legal services (16.8 per cent). More specifically, female work prevails in four occupations: elementary school teaching; nursing and health-related occupations; secretarial and office clerk jobs; or retail sales/service, including cashiers. By contrast, men were most likely to be in trades, transport, and equipment operations (25.5 per cent); sales and service (18.7 per cent); and management (13.9 per cent) (SWC 2015). Other occupations remain overwhelmingly male dominated. Of the 19,000 uniformed officers within the RCMP ranks, 400 are women, including only 81 women among the 700 commissioned officers, most in the lowest officer ranks, such as inspectors. Who can be shocked when such a male-dominated organization is accused of abusing authority, bullying and intimidation, crude sexual innuendos, and systemic gender bias? Not surprisingly women walk a tightrope of conflicting expectations: they are pressured to take dead-end feminine roles (for example, "office mother" who "puts men first") or they confront a backlash for displaying masculine traits such as assertiveness ("a personality problem that nobody wants to work with") (Schwartz 2015). They are also known to experience what is called "workplace shock" when joining the workforce. Participation and promotion in the corporate world increasingly resembles a cut-throat contest in which women are demeaned and threatened—when not openly exposed to misogyny. This undervaluation of women is consequential. Women find themselves working and competing in a combat zone where a pit bull mentality is critical, even if largely inconsistent with any sense of identity, happiness, or work/life balance.

Advances in the Canadian labour market have not dislodged patterns of occupational inequality (SWC 2015; McFarland 2012; Gazso 2004). Canada may have the highest percentage of women in the workforce of any G20 country, according to OECD data, but four in ten women say men have better career opportunities and 42 per cent believe men have better access to jobs. Forty-nine per cent of Canadian women cite equal pay to men as the most pressing issue, while 48 per cent point to work–life balance and 33 per cent endure harassment by co-workers (Thomson Reuters Foundation and Rockefeller Foundation 2015). A gendered division of labour (occupational segregation) persists, argues Amber Gazso (2004), including vertical segregation (status) and horizontal occupation. Yes, women are moving into professional fields; for example, they comprise 51 per cent of business and financial professionals (Rosin 2012), although they remain underrepresented in the technology field, from a low of 28 per cent of Microsoft's workforce in the United States to a high of 37 per cent for Yahoo (Sopinski 2014). Yet further progress in desegregating occupations has stalled because of the challenges that women confront, including the double shift, precarious work arrangements,

wage gaps, shortage of high quality daycare, and "motherhood penalties." According to a TD Economics Report on the "motherhood gap" in wages, women who take maternity leave experience a significant earnings gap even upon returning to the workforce. (Mothers in Canada, on average, earn about 12 per cent less in hourly wages than women without children [Fister 2014].) The wage gap is compounded across the entirety of their careers (Mazurkewich and Pett 2010)—a scenario similar for men who take paternity leave only to be tracked along a slower path to corporate success (Coontz 2012; Reid 2015). And while domestic roles and household contributions between men and women are converging, gaps remain (Parker 2013). Women spend more time than their male partners looking after children and doing drudge work (although much depends on where people are located in their life cycle [Marshall 2011]), and doing so against the backdrop of an always-on workplace that makes it difficult to balance career with a positive family presence (Slaughter 2015; Lindsay 2008; Miranda 2011). To no one's surprise, many marriages flounder because of a failure to negotiate an equitable division of household labour, especially when baby makes three.

Income Earnings

An analysis of income differences is prone to inconsistencies that border on misleading. The inconsistency often reflects failure to disaggregate the category of "women's income"—full-time versus part-time work; annual income versus hourly wage; public sector versus private sector; continuous employment versus interrupted careers; post-secondary education versus high school dropouts; conventional versus nonconventional career choices; and age and marital status. Combining full-time and part-time work for women yields a ratio of 61 per cent of what men earned. Women in full-time, full-year employment earn around 71 cents for every male-earned dollar, an improvement from the 58 cents they earned in 1967, but down from the 73 cents in the early-1990s (SWC 2015). Much of the gap can be explained by the prevalence of women in part-time work, interrupted career trajectories because of family responsibilities, and labour market segregation which concentrates women in lower-waged occupations. But a different picture appears if factoring in gender differences in industry, occupation, education, age, job tenure, province of residence, marital status: women's annual wages amounted to 92 per cent of men's in 2011 (SWC 2015). The public–private sector divide is critical (McInturff 2015): university-educated women in the public sector earned 82 cents for every dollar by a university-educated male public sector worker, whereas in the private sector, the amount dipped to 73 cents—a pattern repeated for other historically disadvantaged workers including racialized minorities (88 cents versus 80 cents) and aboriginal workers (86 cents versus 56 cents)—thanks, in part to higher unionization, family leave benefits, and a stronger commitment to pay equity (McInturff and Tulloch 2014). Marital (proxy for no children) status matters: single women earned 95.5 per cent of what single men earned, whereas married women earned only 67.5 per cent of what married men earned. Age matters, too, especially when combined with marital status: women between 45 and 54 earned only 67.2 per cent, although those in the same age bracket who were single and university-educated compared favourably with their male counterparts (OECD 2012:5). Women aged 25 to 29 with a graduate or professional degree in full-time, full-year employment in 2005 earned nearly the same amount (96 per cent) as their male cohort (Turcotte 2010). Education levels matter as well: young women with a BA earned 89 cents for every dollar by their male counterparts; by contrast, young women without a high school diploma earned 67 cents for every dollar earned by young men with similar lack of credentials. Finally, the dynamics of gender discrimination in driving the wage gap should not be discounted (Carnevale and Smith 2014). Table 6.1 provides an overview of wage differences by gender and occupation.

Admittedly, gender income differences based on annual earnings may prove inconclusive. Gaps may reflect the cumulative effect of differences in starting salaries, relative to variations in salary negotiations, income expectations, and prospects for promotion (Carnevale and Smith 2014). Or they may reflect the fact that wages increase with seniority and experience, with men working longer hours and without interruption to careers, thanks to fewer family responsibilities. A slightly different picture appears when focusing on hourly wages rather than annual income. The gap between women and men based on an hourly rate has narrowed to about 87 per cent (SWC 2015), while women's salaries in female-dominated occupations such as health care hover in the 98 per cent range (Anderssen 2012). Finally, Canadian-born racialized women of colour generally earn less than other Canadians, although exceptions exist (Woolley 2012; Pendakur and Pendakur 2011; also National Women's Law Center 2013). A Canadian-born racialized minority woman earned 3 per cent less than a non-racialized white woman, whereas a racialized minority male vis-à-vis a non-racialized white male earned 18 per cent less. This pattern does not prevail across the board (Jedwab and Satzewich 2015). Canadian-born Chinese and other Asian women earn 6 per cent more than women of British descent, whereas women who self-identify as black or African earn about 20 per cent less. For men, Canadian-born Chinese men earn 8 per cent less than British-origin men, all things being equal, while black males earn about 40 per cent less.

Corporate Boardrooms

Women continue to be blocked from access to the upper echelons of corporate power (TD Economics 2013; Rothkopf 2013; Randstad Institute 2014). According to Wendy Cukier of Ryerson's Diversity Institute, the boards of large American companies on the Fortune 100 list are dominated by white males. But the 73 per cent figure in the United States is dwarfed by the situation in Canada where white males maintain such a monopoly on board seats of large corporations that Canada ranked seventh last in a review of 22,000 firms among 91 countries (Noland et al. 2016; SWC 2015). In 2013, Catalyst Research, a workplace research and advocacy group that aims to expand opportunities for women in business, concluded that female directors occupied 15.9 per cent of the board seats of the FP (*Financial Post*) 500 organizations (40 per cent of the organizations had no women board members). Racialized minorities, peoples with

Table 6.1: Women and Men in the Three Highest and Lowest Paid Occupations in Canada

Occupation	# of Women in Occupation	# of Men in Occupation	Women's Average Earnings	Men's Average Earnings
Specialist physicians	11,255	21,800	$135,065	$202,467
Judges	695	2,085	$173,747	$179,503
Senior managers	11,745	42,155	$111,747	$168,627
Food preparers	16,680	5,550	$14,681	$17,912
Food/beverage servers	38,250	11,940	$13,861	$18,192
Babysitters/nannies	34,625	740	$12,662	$15,106

Note: Men outnumber women in all of the 10 highest-paid occupations in Canada, in some cases by ratios of 7:1. Women are paid less in every highest-paid occupation (generally around 60 per cent of what men are paid), with only judges approximating parity. By contrast, women outnumber men in all of the 10 lowest-paying occupations in Canada, with the exception of service station attendants, yet are paid less across the board. At times this income gap is deliberately designed (systematic), including occupational segregation, undervaluing of women's work, their status as the principal caregivers for children and the elderly, the restructuring of women's work because of privatization and outsourcing, or lack of access to affordable public childcare. At other times, inequities are systemic—that is, they arise from within a system designed around foundational principles that promote "pale male" interests at the expense of others (DeKeseredy 2011; FAFIA 2008, 2009).

Source: Women & the Economy. UN Platform for Action Committee. Manitoba. 2011. Data for tables on the 10 highest-paying occupations taken from the 2006 Census, whereas the 10 lowest-paying occupations are drawn from the 1996 Census.

disabilities, and Aboriginal peoples were under-represented as well, holding 4.6 per cent, 2.7 per cent, and 1.1 per cent of corporate board seats respectively, based on self-reporting. A 2014 survey by Catalyst (using a somewhat different methodology and benchmark from the previous year) indicated a marked increase, with women occupying 20.8 per cent of board seats on the Canadian Stock Index. Gender parity matters: a report by the Credit Suisse Research Institute based on 2,360 companies worldwide found that companies with female boards of directors outperformed male-only boards by a margin of 26 per cent between 2005 and 2011 (Berman 2012; Noland et al. 2016). Removing barriers to putting women in positions of corporate authority would appear to be a win–win situation (Noland and Moran 2016). And in theory, it has never been a better time for women to succeed, writes Kirstine Stewart (2015), thanks to a digital realm that is rapidly dismantling the old boys' ways of doing things and a leadership track that values traditional female traits from communication to collaboration. But as Sheryl Sandberg (2013) points out, it's a chicken and egg situation. Yes, women will crash through the glass ceiling once they achieve leadership roles. But the glass ceiling must be smashed before women can assume positions of authority.

Media Representations

Canadians live in a mediated world. Few would deny the centrality of mainstream media (media = plural of medium) as an information source with persuasive powers to move or motivate. Rather than a frivolous diversion for amusement or distraction, mainstream media representations are influential in framing who we think we are, what we think about, the nature of our experiences, whose voices will prevail, and how we relate to others and how they will relate to us. Media representations draw attention to some aspects of reality as normal and necessary by constructing public discourses about what is socially acceptable and societally desirable. The power of media representations is in their ability to frame issues and persons in ways that encourage a preferred reading of reality consistent with media priorities and dominant interests (Fleras 2011a). Other aspects of reality are framed as inferior or inconsequential, and dismissed accordingly. The underlying value assumptions inherent within media representations reinforce an inescapable truth: media representations do not represent reality per se—a kind of mirror to society. Far from passively reflecting fixed meanings in a so-called objective world, they *re-present* the world "out there" by creating a new symbolic reality consistent with media priorities and corporate interests (Hall 1997). The cumulative effects of such negative representations exact a cost. For audiences who lack meaningful firsthand contact with diversities and difference, mainstream media often constitute the preliminary and primary source of information about the social world out there. Insofar as they see no reason to believe otherwise, many take media representations at face value, despite widespread awareness of their potential to distort or inflame.

Historically, mainstream media were institutionally biased in content and structure—that is, they were designed by, for, and about men to advance male interests, experiences, and priorities (Nelson 2010). Those outside the framework of a white middle-class male demographic were either ignored as irrelevant or stigmatized as inferior (Fleras 2014c). They were portrayed as troublesome constituents or problem people who possessed problems or created problems involving costs, inconvenience, or discomfort to the dominant sector. An androcentric media gaze prevailed by virtue of framing media representations of women from a male point of view as normal and necessary (Fleras 2011a). Representations of women were generally relegated to the maternal–domestic domain, deemed as inferior or irrelevant, except in their role as *fosterers* or *fashionistas*, stereotyped by way of mis-, over-, or under-representations, objectified to the point of dehumanization, victimized by body images that linked success and desirability with sexuality and physical attractiveness, and typecast as the second sex whose worth lay in appearances, domesticity, or nurturing (Graydon 2001; Kilbourne 1990; 2010).

The relatively small number of media representations that were open to women—namely, as mother, wife, girl next door, spinster, whore, or saint, or as castrating b/witch—exposed a world of waif-like, wasp-waisted women in positions of passivity, with a corresponding restrictive code of femininity that undermined the real-world prospects and progress of women and girls (Kilbourne 2010; Kanellakis 2007).

Is this assessment true in the new millennium? Are media sexist? Do representations of women remain refracted through the prism of a male-dominated media that projects sexist fantasies or misogynist fears? Evidence suggests gender representations in terms of content, tone, and amount of coverage are much more diverse and complex than in the openly gendered past (Lawrence and Rose 2009; Jiwani 2011). An exclusive diet of openly derogatory or demeaning media frames are relinquishing ground to mediated images that are more reflective, respectful, and responsive. Images of women and their myriad relationships are continually changing and sharply contested across a wide range of media outputs—albeit subject to multiple interpretations and ambiguous readings—thanks to the emergence of women as eager consumers with hefty amounts of disposable income, spending power, and control over financial decisions (Graydon 2001). The combination of shifting demographics, growing economic clout, and viewing patterns are challenging the media's gendered agenda, with the result that women are no longer automatically banished to the outer fringes of programming or newscasting. Gynocentric tendencies are thought to prevail across some media domains because of content that caters predominantly to female audiences. Ironically, it is men who now complain of diminishment as the "new second sex" whose irrelevance or inferiority are particularly noticeable for lower-class males (Fleras and Dixon 2011; Vallis 2009). Finally, the surge in women's Internet involvement is reshaping the gender landscape, with women using online communication and social media to expand networks, skirt around old boys' networks, increase contacts, and enrich relationships.

In short, media representations of women appear to be in a state of flux and disarray (Burton

2015; Gauntlett 2008; Dent 2008). To one side are measured improvements in the quality of media representations of women and their relationship to men. Representations of gender are more complex and more diverse than in the past, with less stereotyping and objectification, as might be expected in a less scripted era of increasingly fluid and transformative identities (Gauntlett 2008). Yes, men may be calling the shots in terms of hidden agendas and operating priorities; yet there is sufficient slack in the patriarchy for oppositional messages to challenge and resist (Douglas 1994). To the other side, however, it's still a man's world when it comes to prevailing media representations of women as women or in the public domain (Goodyear-Grant 2013; Women's Media Center 2015). Moves to un-gender a gendered media agenda along re-gendered lines are fraught with perils and second guessing, in part because no one really knows whether ungendered media representations are feasible, desirable, or even recognizable. Not surprisingly, media representations continue to be gendered in ways that speak truth to the power of mediated image. Media representations continue to be gendered, inasmuch as they make a distinction between men and women, assign a set of expectations that distinguish men from women, and then devalue the roles and status of women in comparison to that of men—as pointed out below (Newsom 2011; Kilbourne 2012).

1. Gendered media representations are ideologically slanted *toward, by, around*, and *for* men and male realities. A patricentric ideology prevails whose primary purpose—or logical consequence—is the circulation of ideas and ideals for preserving male power and masculinist privilege. Male agendas, priorities, and interests are advanced, not necessarily deliberately or conspiratorially but logically as a consequence of framing the world from a male (androcentric) point of view as natural and normal. Media projections of male fears and masculinist fantasies tend to promote images of women—from mothers to murderers, from passive to manipulative, from weak to powerful—that rarely reflect female realities and experiences. Male

perceptions of what is, or projections of what is thought to be, are promoted instead as if inevitable and self-evident rather than constructed and conventional.

2. Media are gendered in representations because males are the tacitly assumed norm in defining what is normal and necessary as well as acceptable and desirable. Maleness embodies the reference point by which women as women are defined, assessed, and criticized because of double standards. For example, while male tennis players are allowed to be grating and self-centred, as Cathal Kelly (2014) points out in his article on the media flaying of Canada's tennis sensation Eugenie Bouchard, women players find themselves in a character trap. They are cast in Disneyesque roles where they are expected to be "nice"—demure, friendly, and innocently cheeky—and expected to maintain that illusion or else. According to Jennifer Siebel Newsom in *Miss Representations* (2011), the sexual objectification of women on screen (including sports coverage) fosters a trivialization and disempowerment of women in the cultural and political domain. Is it any wonder, Newsom asks, that 78 per cent of girls hate their bodies and 65 per cent admit to an eating disorder?

3. Media representations are gendered because women and men use and consume different media. There are women's and men's magazines, "chick flicks" versus "boy flicks," "chick lit" versus "lad lit," guy video games versus girl video games, and so on (Kimmel 2008). Women and men tend to have different expectations in their use of media; as a result, gender as a variable influences the production, transmission, and interpretation of media messages along the lines of his-and-her media (Kimmel 2008). A gendered media capitalizes on constructed gender differences by targeting different genders with varying messages that assume pre-existing differences. Whereas media representations of men are framed as active and controlling, women are not always cast as subjects but may be objectified as victims or survivors, with the result that issues of relevance to women are marginalized to the point of insignificance.

Do gendered media representations matter? Gendered media representations reflect, reinforce, and advance patterns of social exclusions by framing gender difference and inequalities as natural rather than constructed, in large part by concealing the media's authorship so that its "normalness" seems to flow from the nature of things (Kimmel 2008:238). These gendered ideas and ideals become so firmly wired into media's DNA (including structure, function, and processes) that media representations are routinely and automatically promoted and normalized as if they were without bias. The misrepresentation of women and girls by gendered media could not be more forcefully, if carefully, orchestrated.

Spotlight Gendered Media Representations: Damned if They Do, Damned if They Don't

Facing the press is more difficult than bathing a leper.
—Mother Teresa

Both the quantity and quality of media representations of women have improved to the point of guarded optimism. However commendable these moves toward representational inclusiveness, contradictions prevail. For example, news representations of women in politics leaves a lot to be desired because of implicit biases, regardless of the quality of the coverage (Goodyear-Grant 2013). A host of sexist double standards and double binds can be discerned that play havoc with the practice of taking women seriously in politics, including the following (Lawrence and Rose 2009; Braden 1996).

Journalists pose questions to female politicians that they would be loath to ask of men. They often hold women politicians accountable for the actions of husbands or children; by contrast, male politicians are rarely held to the same standard. For example, there is debate over whether her daughter's pregnancy will affect Hillary Clinton's decision to run for the 2016 presidential election—as if being president and a grandparent are mutually exclusive roles for women but not for men.

Journalists tend to sexualize women rather than men and do so in ways that extol traditional maternal domestic roles or conventional images of femininity.

Journalists invariably judge women politicians on the basis of appearance. If a woman looks attractive or dresses attractively, she may be trivialized as superficial or weak (Belinda Stronach or Sarah Palin come to mind). If her physical or sartorial appearance is lacking, she is deemed unfeminine ("butch") and un-electable.

Journalists expect women to be aggressive enough to do the job but not so aggressive they threaten males in general. Women should be as smart as men but not smarter than the average male politician.

Journalists may criticize women for behaviour that is acceptable for male politicians; for example, assertiveness in men is okay; in women it is seen as pushy, domineering, or un-team-like. Men may cry in public and may be framed as sensitive; women politicians who weep are seen as weak.

Journalists test the newsworthiness of women in politics against a set of traditional news values of conflict and controversy (for example, the "horse race" or "game frames" [Lawrence and Rose 2009]), even though women may be more interested in compromise and cooperation.

The evidence is irrefutable: a gendered double standard undermines the credibility and credentials of female politicians (Goodyear-Grant 2013). Women and men are judged differently for displaying similar behaviour (Bates 2015). As a result, female politicians find themselves entrapped by double binds—a no-win, damned if you do, damned if you don't position—that relentlessly scrutinizes and dissects every move. Even seemingly non-sexist and progressive coverage of female politicians and corresponding news frames may be deeply gendered when women are framed in the same way as men via masculinist language and images that apply to male politicians. Or consider what happens when ostensibly inclusive coverage assumes a male politician is the norm, with the result that women are gendered as beings who are both novel and foreign (fish-out-of-water stories) to the political domain (Goodyear-Grant 2013). Not surprisingly, female politicians tend to be ensnared in a kind of no (wo)man's land, since the boundaries between acceptable and unacceptable are often unclear, prone to inexplicable shifts, subject to second-guessing, and reflective of a lose-lose proposition, regardless of what they do or do not do. The consequences are hardly trifling: according to Goodyear-Grant (2013), this symbolic annihilation of female politicians by news media may account for the snail-pace increase in the number and proportion of women in Canada's Parliament.

Education

Women and girls are now cresting the wave of education success. Girls are outperforming boys across the board in math, writing, and reading in Ontario primary schools, prompting seemingly counter-intuitive debates over all-boys classes to offset male disadvantages. Young women make up 58 per cent of university graduates, up from 52 per cent a decade ago. And women are gradually moving into disciplines once reserved for the "lads." Even the gender income gap for academic faculty has narrowed substantially to less than 11 per cent in 2006, from 19 per cent in 1986, with virtually no gap for lecturers (99.1 per cent) and just under a 4.5 per cent gap for other ranks, possibly because of career interruptions, differences in starting salaries, and market supplements (CAUT Bulletin 2011; Boesveld 2011).

So where is the inequality problem? Less than 25 per cent of university and college presidents are women, despite recent improvement in appointments (Charbonneau 2013). Only about 25 per cent of university faculty are women, and many are situated at the lower levels of the mobility ladder. Women have been awarded a disproportionately low percentage of federal research chairs since the program was inaugurated in 2002 (Turcotte 2010), including only one of 22 Canada Excellence Research Chairs. Faculties such as computer science or engineering still remain overwhelmingly male-dominated, particularly since women tend to graduate from the "softer" disciplines in arts and social sciences. Theories continue to circulate that girls' brains are wired very differently than boys', according to this line of thinking, only a small percentage of young women can ever hope to become engineers, no matter how hard they try

(but see Davison 2012). Finally, the increasingly corporatized university remains a gendered workplace that rewards those masculinized behaviours that are competitive to the point of confrontational, ranging from the publish-or-perish syndrome to the punishing face time that is pivotal in navigating a tenure and promotion system (Baker 2012).

Political Involvement

Canada is the third best country in which to be a woman, according to a survey by the US website *Newsweek/The Daily Beast*, just behind Iceland and Sweden (also US News et al 2016). The survey gave Canada an overall score of 96.6 out of 100. But Canada's lofty status faltered at the political front where it received only a 66.9 per cent rating. Although women comprise 52 per cent of the population, they make up only 28 per cent of the MPs in the House of Commons, and only 21 per cent of all politicians from federal to local levels (Goodyear-Grant 2013). In some ways, these figures are not surprising: Parliament remains little more than a bullying pulpit in which verbal slings and shameless putdowns ensure its growing irrelevance to women—and to backbenchers in general, regardless of gender (Goodyear-Grant 2013). None of the leaders of the major federal political parties (with the exception of the Green Party) are female, although the six female provincial/territorial premiers in 2014 (Newfoundland/Labrador, Quebec, Alberta, British Columbia, Ontario, and Nunavut) encompassed 85 per cent of Canada's population (only three female premiers remained in office by mid-2015). The few women who enter Parliament find themselves in "soft" legislative committees pertaining to culture or welfare, while those in Cabinet tend to be ghettoized into pink-collar portfolios such as health or human resources—neither of which is seen as a career move toward the highest political office (MacIvor 2003).

Intimate Partner Violence

Violence against anyone in Canada is bad enough. Violence involving those in intimate relations is particularly deplorable because it entails ongoing incidents, longstanding relationships, deep emotional attachment, acts of betrayal, and negative effects on innocent victims such as children (Sinha 2012). Yet incidents of intimate partner violence are disturbingly high (McInturff 2013b). In 2007, over 40,000 incidents of spousal violence (including the legally married or the divorced) were reported to the police, thus accounting for 12 per cent of all police reported violent crime in Canada (Canadian Women's Foundation, n.d.). Police reported data indicate the risk of intimate partner violence is higher (363 incidents per 100,000 population in 2010) than stranger inflicted violence (307 per 100,000 population), while women were four times more vulnerable than men to intimate partner violence in 2010: 574 versus 147 per 100,000 population (Sinha 2012). Other data reinforce these grisly figures and trends. The WHO estimates that that one in four Canadian women will experience intimate partner violence or sexual assault in her lifetime (cited in McInturff 2013b). In the five years prior to the 2004 General Social Survey (GSS), 7 per cent of women and 6 per cent of men aged 15 years and over experienced some form of spousal violence, according to the Canadian Women's Foundation (2012), a figure that has barely budged in recent years. The fact that more than two-thirds of the victims failed to report an earlier incident points to the possibility of a larger problem (Department of Justice Canada, 2012). The 2009 GSS also indicated that aboriginal women were three times more likely than non-aboriginal women to be victims of spousal violence (with aboriginal women eight times more likely to be killed than non-aboriginal women [Report 2014b; Canadian Women's Foundation 2012; Legal Strategy Coalition 2015]). Immigrant women were more vulnerable to domestic violence because of their economic dependence, language barriers, lack of access to available social services, and reluctance to call authorities for fear of further victimization, retribution, or even deportation. Finally, both police and self-reported data indicate that younger women are at a much higher risk of violent victimization, judging by the spate of recent incidents pointing to the possibility of a "rape culture" on university campuses across Canada and the United States. According to widely circulated estimates, including the film *The Hunting Ground* by Dick and Ziering (2015; also Heller 2015), 20 per cent of women are sexually assaulted while at American colleges, although as few as 5 per cent of these assaults are ever reported to the police and even fewer are investigated or adjudicated by campus authorities for fear of attracting negative publicity.

Not everyone agrees with these figures or interpretations. Studies in the United States indicate that levels of intimate partner violence are decreasing in tandem with declining rates of violence overall (Coontz 2015). American data such as the Bureau of Justice Statistics' National Crime Victimization Survey (NCVS) points to significant declines in rape and sexual assault, although this violence continues to be undercounted and higher among women not enrolled in four-year colleges (Wheeler 2015). Others point out that intimate partner violence swings both ways. According to self-reported surveys (which the Canadian Women's Foundation [2012] argues are unreliable), both men and women are equally likely to strike out violently in reaction to the pressure cooker of domestic relations (Dutton 2006). However true, most studies indicate female victims are prone to serious injuries from domestic violence which require medical attention. Moreover, ignoring context, meaning, and motive in such violent encounters is misleading (DeKeseredy and Dragiewicz 2007; Nicoll 2016). Men rely on violence to control their partners, whereas women often rely on violence to defend themselves (Canadian Women's Foundation 2012). And while rates of spousal homicide continue to decline, from 16.5 per 1 million spouses in 1974 to 4 per 1 million spouses in 2007—the lowest ratio in 30 years—women are much more likely to be killed by a current or former spouse (Department of Justice Canada 2012), including 76 of the 89 spousal homicides reported to the police in 2011 (Canadian Women's Foundation; 2012).

The Minorities Within: Aboriginal, Racialized, and Immigrant Women

Gendered exclusions remain a major problem for minority women (Fleras 2012). Racialized women of colour, immigrant and refugee women, and aboriginal women continue to be denied or exploited because of their location within a predominantly "white man's" world (Canadian Heritage 2013). As a minoritized group (to emphasize process) (Mukherjee, Mukherjee, and Godard 2006), they confront denial and experience exclusion with respect to power, privilege, and property (income + assets). The employment status for immigrant and religious minority women continues to lag behind in labour force participation (Reitz, Phan, and Banerjee 2015). Both foreign- and Canadian-born racialized minority women in full-year, full-time employment earn disproportionately less than what racialized males earn. Onsite discrimination and prejudicial attitudes may account for the gendered income disparities within the workplace, but a more plausible factor reflects the much narrower range of occupations open to minority women, most of whom are lower paid with fewer chances for promotion, given the cumulative effect of gender stereotypes, double standards, glass ceilings, and sticky floors. Even those with credentials may default into low-paying employment because they lack Canadian experience or expertise. This situation is compounded by the marginality of class status. After all, to be poor in a society that values wealth is marginalizing. To be poor and different—and a female—intensifies the marginalization.

That racialized minorities experience exclusion because of race, ethnicity, and social class is hardly the issue (Galabuzi 2006; Henry and Tator 2010; Satzewich and Liodakis 2013). Compared to mainstream whites, they tend to earn less, experience discrimination and harassment at work, shoulder domestic responsibilities, and be largely excluded from the corridors of power (Wallis and Kwok 2009). But minority women (including women of colour, immigrant women, and aboriginal women) are additionally disadvantaged by discriminatory barriers because of their gender (Canadian Heritage 2013). Such disparities reinforce how the domain of race, ethnic, and aboriginal relations is no more gender-neutral nor gender-passive than the gendered assumptions that inform society (Abraham et al. 2010). Both are fundamentally gendered and deeply stratified by way of asymmetrical relations involving differential access to power, privilege, and resources (Boyd and Pikkov 2008). In addition, minority women experience reality differently than do white women, while the category of minority women needs to be disaggregated to reflect differences-within-differences in terms of identities, experiences, opportunities, and outcomes (Fleras 2012). More specifically:

1. *White women versus minority women.* Women as a group may share common experiences of disadvantage because of male dominance. Yet not all women are equally disadvantaged at work or in the public domain. Nor do women represent a homogeneous group whose experiences are universally filtered through a one-size-fits-all patriarchy. Minority women endure different patterns of control and domination because of race, ethnicity, class, and gender, reflecting their uniquely different status and social location as aboriginal women, racialized women of colour, and immigrant and refugee women. For example, whereas white women are increasingly striding the corridors of power, minority women continue to mop the corridor floors. White women are largely concerned with projecting private-sphere issues (such as accessible daycare for women in management positions) into the public realm; by contrast, minority women tend to focus on bread-and-butter issues related to discrimination, healthy children, and daily survival. White women may focus on issues ranging from glass ceilings, the cost of daycare facilities, job and pay equity, and workplace harassment, whereas racialized women of colour worry about basic survival skills related to employment, rather than employment equity; about getting and holding a job, rather than harassment on the job or barriers to promotion; and about access to any childcare facilities, rather than shattering the glass ceiling (Oluo

2015). To the extent that white women rarely experience race and racism, they are free to focus on sexism. To the degree that minority women must simultaneously confront the interplay of racism, ethnocentrism, and classism in addition to sexism, they cannot afford to privilege one "ism" over the other in the struggle for equality and inclusion (Smith 2003).

2. *Minority men versus minority women.* The concerns of racialized minority women and men often converge. Both are looking to forge productive and satisfying lives; to settle into Canada without forsaking their distinctiveness or dignity; to end discrimination in housing, employment, education, and delivery of social services; to protect their fundamental human rights without having to put up with excessive bureaucratic interference; and to achieve the best for their children without loss of their cultural heritage. But for many racialized minorities, aspirations are one thing—reality may be quite another (Galabuzi 2006). Both minority women and men suffer exclusion and exploitation because of factors beyond their control. For men, from fathers to husbands, adjustment to coping with cultural differences can prove a jolting experience because of role inversion, culture clashes, diminished social status and self-esteem, and challenges to authority (Gordon 2008). But unlike their menfolk, minority women are doubly jeopardized because of their membership in yet another historically devalued category—namely, gender in a patriarchal society.

3. *Racialized minority women of colour.* Racialized minority women of colour have long endured discrimination and exclusion in Canada. Numerous studies using different measures appear to confirm that racialized women of colour confront discrimination, both systematic and systemic (Backhouse 1999; Walker 1997). Black women were excluded from nursing in Canada before the 1940s and continue to experience racism and discrimination in Canadian hospitals, often at the hands of white female nurses who collaborate with management to monitor, control, and harass them (Das Gupta 2009; Hagey 2004). But they are overrepresented in federal prisons where black women consti-

tute 9.3 per cent of the inmates even though they account for less than 3 per cent of the total Canadian population (Anderson 2015). Niqab-wearing Muslim women in Quebec found that under Quebec's Bill 94 (the bill died) they would no longer receive government services, public employment, educational opportunities, and even most medical care (Orwin 2010; Perreaux 2010). Outside of Quebec, women from racialized minority groups say they have difficulty across a broad range of socio-economic domains, from landing a job and decent housing to finding a doctor, getting appointments, or accessing specialists (Ubelacker 2010). Fully veiled women were nearly excluded from participating in Canadian citizenship ceremonies on grounds their garb constituted an affront to Canadian values. And they may find themselves victims of honour killings or arranged marriages, while continuing to be stuck in media tropes of passivity, victimhood, and rescue (Hennebry and Momani 2013; Phillips and Saharso 2008). Both criticism of multiculturalism (that it is too accommodating) and a corresponding clash of values appear to be played out on the bodies of Muslim women. That is, Muslim women have evolved into a litmus test of tolerance and civilization in a Quebec and Canada that claim to be secular yet open and tolerant.

4. *Immigrant and refugee women.* Gender represents a key variable in analyzing international migration (Piper 2008; Fleras 2014b). Female immigrants confront a unique set of challenges because immigration disrupts family ties and social networks in their country of origins (Senate 2013; Gauthier 2016; Hogarth 2011). Immigration laws and policies affect women and men differently, resulting in both gendered patterns of immigration and gendered outcomes. Modes of entry into Canada are gendered (Boyd and Pikkov 2008). Women and men enter under different admission categories: women often arrive as wives or dependants of the men who sponsor them, although increasingly they enter as autonomous labour migrants, highly skilled professionals, and the undocumented (Khoo, Ho, and Voigt-Graf 2008). Settlement programs for integrating immigrants into society also

differently impact men and women with corresponding implications for livelihood, rights, and entitlements. Female migrants encounter a gender-stratified labour market that not only ignores their credentials and expertise but also typecasts them as worthy of "women's work" (Khoo, Ho, and Voigt-Graf 2008). They often find themselves restricted to the lower echelons of the Canadian labour force, including low-paying job ghettos such as in manufacturing, service industries, and domestic work. According to Debbie Douglas (2005), executive director of the Ontario Council of Agencies Serving Immigrants and winner of the Social Action and Justice Award, many immigrant women in Toronto work in modern-day equivalents of nineteenth-century sweatshops. They must survive on minimum wage in precarious jobs without recourse or access to union protection or employee benefits. In addition, racialized migrant women such as Filipina and Caribbean women, continue to be exploited as cheap domestic labour under Canada's Live-in Caregiver program.

Spotlight Live-in Caregiver Program: Pathway to Canada or Domestic Slavery?

Migrant labour has evolved into such a structural economic necessity that Canada is increasingly reliant on temporary workers as a form of cheap and subservient labour (Fleras 2014b). The exploitation of migrants as cheap labour for doing Canada's "dirty work" applies to men and women. But only women are specifically imported for gender-specific jobs pertaining to the sex trade, child-rearing, and domestic labour (Macklin 1999). Canada's Live-in Caregiver Program allows a family to hire a live-in caregiver for a minimum of 30 hours per week of care to children under 18 years of age, old folks over 65 years of age, and persons with disabilities—provided, of course, no qualified Canadian citizens or permanent residents are available (HRSDC 2012b). The terms of the arrangement obligate caregiver workers to live in their employers' homes without supervision for at least two years (or 3,900 hours) over a four-year period. As live-in nannies, they are legally classified as temporary workers and subject to deportation upon termination of their contract unless they apply for permanent-resident status. Upon completion of their residency requirement, they are entitled to sponsor children and partners (Omidvar 2014). In 2011, just over 11,000 caregivers and their dependants were granted permanent residency in Canada, the vast majority consisting of trained nurses from the Philippines (Manicom 2013), while 5,033 (6,232 in 2012) caregivers were admitted under the program (Atanackovic and Bourgeault 2013), a drop from 13,773 in 2007 (Alboim and Cohl 2012).

The vulnerable status of live-in caregivers as foreign and domestic workers is a recipe for abuse. The employee-specific work permits create an institutionalized power imbalance that puts caregivers at risk because of overwork and underpay, the possibility of sexual assault, and the threat of deportation (Tungohan et al. 2015). The combination of temporary work permits and the program's live-in requirements compromises their right to complain about punishing work schedules, unpaid wages (especially for overtime work), and unlawful confinement at the hands of their employers (Stasiulis and Bakan 1997; Diocson 2005). To be sure, labour laws are in place that protect the rights of live-in careworkers, but legal protections are of marginal value if live-in workers cannot exercise their rights or seek redress. Of course, not all domestic workers are exploited; nevertheless, as Audrey Macklin (1999) concludes, the potential for exploitation is bolstered by the combination of unregulated work environments, the constant spectre of expulsion and deportation if they complain, and a perception among employers they "own" these "indentured" workers.

For immigrant women, life in Canada may prove confining and conflicting (Gauthier 2016). A Canadian-born woman may have difficulty reconciling the conflicting demands of homemaking and motherhood with that of paid employment and personal growth. Immigrant women not only confront similar problems but also must simultaneously learn a new language while adjusting to a different culture, often while coping with the sometimes contradictory slings of rebellious teenagers, surly relatives, and resentful husbands. As well, they must endure loneliness stemming from isolation (limited language, lack of training opportunities, child-rearing and school-related problems, racial prejudice, underemployment, lack of "Canadian" experience, and limited services that cater to their unique situations). Women are also expected to know their place: actions that do not conform to conventional norms or stroke male privileges may be criticized as a betrayal, outrage, or irresponsibility. They are expected to defer to male authority, if only for the sake of appearance, even if such deference may inhibit the acquisition of skills or disrupt lived realities. For those who defy convention or authority, the consequences may prove punitive. The family, the community, and the culture are often regarded as bastions of privacy from prying eyes, so that those women who approach authorities with damning information may be socially ostracized or physically punished.

Refugee women are no less vulnerable. The dangers of flight experienced by women differ from those of men (Status of Women Canada 2007). Women's experiences of refugee persecution often take place in the "private sphere" of home and community and may extend to rape, infanticide, genital mutilation, forced abortion, compulsory sterilization, sexual slavery, trafficking in women, and domestic violence. Evidence that women use in support of their refugee claims may be more difficult to validate or quantify. To its credit, Canada in 1993 became the first country to issue guidelines on female refugee claimants fleeing gender-related persecution, including female genital mutilation. The recognition of gender-based violence

is now well-established within Canada's refugee determination system.

Finally, trafficking in women remains big business (Macklin 1999). Defined as use of coercion or deception to recruit, transport, or control a person against their will to exploit them for sexual purposes or forced labour, human trafficking is a greater problem than originally thought, despite evidence that much of this confinement and exploitation occurs within borders rather than the more common image of people smuggled across borders (Grant 2016). Admittedly, reliable statistics are difficult to access since human trafficking is, by definition, a clandestine operation with few victims and survivors willing to come forward and testify for fear of retaliation or embarrassment, or a misunderstanding of what is going on (Public Safety Canada, 2014). On the basis of mainly open-source information, the International Labour Organization (ILO) estimates that 21 million persons globally are thought to be victims of human trafficking and involuntary servitude from slavery to debt bondage. According to the United Nations Office on Drugs and Crime (2012; 2014), 58 per cent of all worldwide trafficking is for the purpose of sexual exploitation, while trafficking for forced labour accounts for 36 per cent. Women and girls are believed to account for up to 75 per cent of all trafficked victims and survivors. It is estimated that in Canada, aboriginal women constitute about one-half of all trafficked persons, in the process pointing to a strong connection between trafficking and the crisis in murdered and missing women (NWAC 2014; Grant 2016). Yet enforcement of laws related to trafficking remains erratic at best. One hundred thirty-two countries and territories have criminalized trafficking in line with UN protocols (for example, human trafficking is an offence under Canada's Criminal Code and Immigration and Refugee Protection Act [Public Safety Canada 2014]); nevertheless, the number of convictions remains low, with 16 per cent of the jurisdictions not having a single conviction between 2007 and 2010 (UNODC 2012).

5. *Aboriginal women.* It's tragic but true: violence begets violence so that the past intrudes

into the present. Indigenous peoples who have experienced colonialism and exploitation may internalize that hatred, then project this hate outward by inflicting violence and abuse on those most vulnerable (Deveaux 2006; also Black et al. 2011). This is particularly the case with aboriginal (or indigenous) women in Canada who confront extraordinarily high violence levels because of many factors—from the legacy of colonialism and loss of culture and social status to the imposition of racist laws and patriarchal protocols (Voyageur 2001; 2016; Cooper and Salomos 2009/10; Statistics Canada 2006; Valaskakis, Stout, and Guimond 2009; Report 2014b). The intersection of gender with colonialism has proved both complex and destructive (Green 2007b; Leigh 2009; Turpel-Lafond 2014). Gender relations and family organizations were upended in securing the operation of colonial power (Anderson 2000), while the imposition of colonization and settler values reproduced European gender norms along Victorian-era lines. Introduction of the residential school system also disrupted traditional family life, thereby initiating a cycle of domestic abuse that continues to haunt aboriginal communities into the present (Truth and Reconciliation Commission Report 2015; Pauktuutit 2006). Under the Indian Act of 1876 which infantilized Aboriginal peoples in general, aboriginal women were further marginalized by folding their legal status into that of their husbands. (Until recently, aboriginal women did not possess the same matrimonial property rights as women who live off reserves [Ambrose 2012].) Under colonization, Aboriginal nations were reorganized along patriarchal lines, in the process displacing aboriginal women from patterns of governance, while aligning the interests of aboriginal families with those of colonial powers (Leigh 2009). And the compulsory sterilization of aboriginal women during the 1900s must be seen within the colonial context and Indian policy that sought to divest Aboriginal peoples of their land while reducing the number of those dependent on government transfers (Stote 2015; Pegoraro 2015).

Both formal studies and personal testimonies indicate that aboriginal women rank among Canada's most severely disadvantaged people (Native Women's Association 2004; Mann 2005; RCMP 2014; Legal Strategy Coalition 2015). Aboriginal women are known to experience double oppression. As persons who happen to be women, they must endure the sexist bias associated with a capitalist and patriarchal society. As women who happen to be aboriginal, they suffer from repressive practices because of colonial structures imposed by the Indian Act. Aboriginal women who married non-aboriginal males were penalized through a loss of status and corresponding benefits (by contrast, aboriginal men who married non-aboriginal women retained their status). Even the repeal of the offending passage (section 12[1][b] of the 1985 Indian Act) by Bill C-31 did not remove all barriers. Although their status and that of their children was reinstated, resource-strapped bands have refused membership and residence for political and economic reasons (Weaver 1993). Economically, aboriginal women tend to perform poorly. Disparities in income levels and employment options mean the feminization of poverty bites deeply, especially for lone-parent aboriginal women in cities (Wallis and Kwok 2008). Admittedly, not all socio-economic indicators are negative. As Wilson and Macdonald (2010) point out, aboriginal women acquire university degrees at a higher rate than aboriginal men; they are earning median incomes closer to those of aboriginal men than is the case between non-aboriginal women relative to non-aboriginal men (this trend may reflect a depression of male wages rather than strength in female earnings [Mendelson 2006]); and aboriginal women with degrees are earning more than non-aboriginal women with equivalent education. Nevertheless, as a group, they tend to be marginalized as the poorest of the poor whose lives are blighted by violence and victimization.

Aboriginal women experience both psychological and physical violence because of colonialism and its aftermath (Monture-Angus 2002; Jackson 1999; Turpel-Lafond 2014; Stote 2015). Their vulnerability to exploitation and victimization both within and outside their communities is reinforced by several factors. Of particular salience is their socio-economic marginalization; coercive assimilation, including residential schools that disrupted gender relations and cultural identity; and perception of them as easy targets because of their over-involvement in the sex trade. Reports continually allude to abusive male family members, sexual assaults and rapes, inadequate and overcrowded housing, squalid living conditions, unhealthy child-raising environments, and alcohol and drug abuse. The safety and security of aboriginal women is compromised by the interplay of racism and discrimination with that of inequality and a generally precarious status in society (Mann 2005; Green 2007b). The internalization of these pressures results in depression and self-hatred among aboriginal women, which in turn contributes to high rates of suicide, alcohol dependency, and neglect of children. A Department of Justice report found that while Aboriginal women may constitute about 2 per cent of women in Canada, they represent 40 per cent of inmates in women's provincial and federal prisons, an increase of 97 per cent over the past decade. The Eurocentric lens of the criminal justice system and the Canadian state reinforces the circulation of derogatory stereotypes that highlights their invisibility, disposability, and susceptibility to violence (Fleras 2011a) as demonstrated in this Spotlight box.

Spotlight *Finding Dawn, Empowering Aboriginal Women*

Finding Dawn is an award-winning 2006 National Film Board documentary about the violence inflicted on aboriginal women in Canada. Produced and directed by the acclaimed Metis filmmaker Christine Welsh, the film focuses on the fate of Dawn Crey, Ramona Wilson, and Daleen Kay Bosse, 3 of some 580 aboriginal women who have been murdered or gone missing in Canada over the past 30 years (but see RCMP [2014] data which puts the figure at 1,181 cases since 1980). Welsh not only pays homage to those who have died or disappeared, but also emphasizes how the living (from survivors of sexual violence to family and community members of the murdered and missing) are taking life-affirming steps to commemorate the forgotten, communicate beyond the silence of the silenced, and construct a society that respects aboriginal women's rights to dignity and safety. Or as Welsh comments toward the end of the film, "I set out on this journey to find Dawn. But I also found Faye, I found Janice, I found people who strike, who search and hope." And if Welsh were to update her documentary, she would find Tina Fontaine in the murdered list, but also embrace the courage of Rinelle Harper—a survivor (Carlson 2015).

A bit of background: violence against aboriginal women remains a serious and pervasive social problem in terms of both incidence and severity, including disproportionately higher numbers of murdered and missing women, largely because they live in a society "that poses a risk to their safety" (Oppal 2012:7). An RCMP report (2014) found that between 1980 and 2012, 32 per cent of the 20,313 homicides in Canada were women, with aboriginal women accounting for 16 per cent of all victims (up from 8 per cent in 1984), although they comprise less than 2.1 per cent of the national population. Provincial variations are significant, including 55 per cent of all women murdered in Saskatchewan and 49 per cent in Manitoba. Moreover, while national homicide rates continue to spiral downward to 1.56 victims per 100,000 of the Canadian population in 2012, Statistics Canada reported, the homicide rate for the Inuit-based territory of Nunavut remains stuck at nearly 15 victims for every 100,000 population (a gender breakdown is not available). The RCMP has also concluded that approximately 70 per cent of solved murdered-women cases could be attributed to aboriginal males.

Are the most marginalized members of society vulnerable to a problem of systemic violence? As many indigenous groups point out, violence against aboriginal women has deep social roots in poverty, discrimination, and lack of education, resulting in a greater probability of high-risk lifestyle (Monchalin

2016). Are police officers guilty of failing to provide appropriate protection? (According to Minister of Public Safety Ralph Goodale, 84 per cent of murders in Canada are solved, but the figure drops to only 50 per cent for aboriginal women [Ivison 2013].) Are some rogue officers complicit in committing sexual assault against aboriginal women? For example, the police may perpetuate violence because their authority allows them to mistreat women with impunity (Price 2012). The Human Rights Watch Report (2013) drew attention to the neglect and unresponsiveness of the RCMP to concerns of aboriginal women, and, in some cases, abuse and physical coercion. Aboriginal women have nowhere to turn for protection; as a result they live in a constant state of insecurity and fear in the face of domestic and community violence on the one hand, and police mistreatment or indifference on the other.

Finding Dawn wanted to put a human face to this unfolding tragedy and national disgrace. The title itself alludes to Dawn Crey whose remains (numbered 23 by the authorities) were found on the property of serial killer Robert Pickton (see also Hugill 2010). In Welsh's hands, Dawn Crey becomes more than a number: she is a daughter and sister who at the time of her disappearance appeared to have renounced a life of drugs and "prostitution." The film then moves from Vancouver's skid row to British Columbia's Highway 16—the Highway of Tears—which runs from Prince Rupert to Prince George. Nine women (all but one aboriginal), including Ramona Wilson, have died or disappeared along that stretch of road since 1990. Filming in Saskatoon focuses on Daleen Kay Bosse, who disappeared in 2004 and whose disappearance or murder remains unsolved [authors note: the remains of Daleen were discovered in 2008]. Along the way, Welsh makes it clear that the tragedy of murdered and missing aboriginal women persists because of societal and institutional indifference to those who are poor and aboriginal; a belief by predators that nobody will miss the weakest and most vulnerable members of society; and historical, social, and economic factors that conspire to inflame yet conceal this epidemic of violence.

But the documentary is more than an un-scrolling of depressing vignettes about the dead or disappeared. To the contrary, the overriding theme is that of empowerment: aboriginal women and men mobilizing to challenge, resist, and transform. Rather than dwelling on the dark heart of aboriginal women's experiences in Canada, *Finding Dawn* resonates with messages of resilience and strength. There are rays of courage and outrage conveyed by aboriginal rights activists such as Janice Acoose and Fay Blaney, each of whom are survivors of abuse, violence, and the dangers of life on the streets. Hope and optimism are also demonstrated through the annual Women's Memorial March in Vancouver, community mobilization and vigils along the length of Highway 16, and local family commemorations of missing and murdered daughters and sisters. The film ends with a photo shoot of a large aboriginal family, with Welsh's voice-over posing a beguiling question, "What is it about numbers?"

Finding Dawn won a Gold Audience Award at the 2006 Amnesty International Film Festival in Vancouver. It was screened for the 2007 International Women's Day celebrations at the United Nations in New York. Such kudos are hardly surprising: *Finding Dawn* is exemplary as a striking testimony to the power of images to enlighten and motivate. The film draws attention to a culture of impunity that rarely punishes the murder of women who are poor, racialized, and work in high-risk occupations. Its usefulness as an indictment on society is further sharpened by the eloquent testimonials of bereaved parents and loving siblings as they struggle to cope with the devastation of lost daughters and sisters. Welsh relies largely on interviews with family members and relatives who movingly talk about the missing or murdered, about their own personal experiences as drug-addicted sex trade workers, and about the need to change attitudes that demean aboriginal women. In demonstrating how aboriginal women (and men) are organizing and demonstrating to combat violence, *Finding Dawn* shatters conventional media stereotypes of aboriginal women as passive or victims. Their capacity for forgiveness and resilience are profiles in courage. In the final analysis, however, as many have implored and as the film implicitly pleads, women can march and demonstrate, but it is men who must change.

Explaining Gendered Inequality: Intersectional Dynamics, Intrasectional Variations

How do we account for gendered disparities? Are they the result of innate differences or diverse lived experiences or market forces? Should the blame be laid on capitalism or patriarchy (and its correlates androcentrism, sexism, and misogyny)? Biological theories are generally discounted by sociologists; psychological theories of maturational development or evolutionary instincts are best left to psychologists. Sociological theories emphasize social factors as key explanatory variables. Women and men must assume responsibility for actions and outcomes, albeit within contexts not of their own making and often beyond their control. These social factors are not necessarily intentional or conspiratorial. Rather they reflect the logical consequences of a capitalist system designed to protect male interests and promote their privilege.

At the heart of much sociological theorizing is a simple but powerful premise: all societies are gendered (Fleras 2012). That is, society as a social system and moral order is neither neutral nor passive. More sociologically, it is biased (structured) in a way that reflects male values and interests, thereby advancing male privilege and power at the expense of women. Four dimensions account for a gendered society. First, all societies make a distinction between male and female (although some societies have more fluid notions of gender, including intersexed and transgendered persons). Second, societies tend to endorse a division of labour, with men monopolizing the public domain of politics (from diplomacy to armed conflict) and women gravitating towards the private realm of the maternal and domestic. Third, male public-domain activities are usually valued as superior whereas the private (maternal, domestic) world of women is devalued as inferior or irrelevant or even dangerous. Fourth, this devaluation eventually is sedimented into the framework of a now gendered society by way of values and agendas that legitimize notions of right, acceptable, and desirable as normal, necessary, and neutral rather than constructed, contingent,

and contested. The end result is the creation and maintenance of a systemically gendered society known as *patriarchy* (Jackson 2010).

A gendered society is an unequal one. Society reflects and reinforces gendered inequality because of the founding assumptions and foundational principles that govern a predominantly patriarchal constitutional order. A gendered society is organized in ways that privilege and prioritize male ways of thinking and doing, while female equivalents are dismissed or devalued as inferior or irrelevant. Gender also constitutes a primary axis around which social life is organized in terms of defining who gets what in society. Admittedly, both men and women compete for valued resources; however, women must do so in systems that are not of their making and that are often beyond their control. In short, the centrality of gender in determining patterns of entitlement and engagement further reinforces how women are subject to the same kinds of inequality, hierarchical distinctions, and (dis)advantages as those of social class or race and ethnicity.

Sociological theories emphasize the social and the structural as a key explanatory variable. Of those social variables most responsible for gendered inequality, the most relevant hierarchies of exclusion are the concepts of race, ethnicity, class, and gender. The cold analytical language of sociologists treats these concepts as relatively independent of each other in their impact on minority women. Of course, the concepts of race, gender, ethnicity, and class may be treated as analytically distinct dimensions of inequality insofar as none of them can be reduced to the other, despite the high level probability of overlapping membership in these status groups (see also Breen and Rottman 1995). Nevertheless, their status as interlocking and mutually intersecting categories of disadvantage informs any social analysis that challenges the presumption that race, class, gender, and ethnicity operate as discrete and independent identity strands that deny or exclude (Jiwani 2006; Hankivsky 2011). Taken alone or in addition, each of these barriers hinders; taken together and compounded, they create a multiplier effect by amplifying the exclusion or exploitation. In brief then, the concept of intersectional analysis refers to a complex matrix of interlocking and overlapping patterns that account for and accentuate patterns of domination and control (Aspinall and Song 2013). As Pragna Patel (2001 cited in UN 2010) defines *intersectionality*:

> The idea of "intersectionality" seeks to capture both the structural and dynamic consequences of the interaction between two or more forms of discrimination or systems of subordination. It specifically addresses the manner in which racism, patriarchy, economic disadvantages and other discriminatory systems contribute to create layers of inequality that structures the relative positions of women and men, races and other groups. Moreover, it addresses the way that specific acts and policies create burdens that flow along these intersecting axes contributing actively to create a dynamic of disempowerment.

Theoretical efforts to understand gendered inequality endorse the principle of intersectionality (Signs 2013; Denis 2008; Aylward 2010). An intersectional analysis as a critical analytic lens goes beyond an additive model approach that totes up race and ethnicity as fixed and static; ignores diversity within groups; glosses over the interactive elements of social location; and tries to capture the totality of oppression along a single axis of theorizing. A theoretical framework is proposed that incorporates the inseparability of race, ethnicity, class, and gender as interlocking and overlapping expressions of inequality, in the process reinforcing how people simultaneously span multiple categories with respect to experiences, identities, and opportunities (Johnson, Pauker, and Freeman 2012; Denis 2008). This notion of concurrent social locations as mutually constituted relationships is critical. Gender and race (and class) are shown to embody interdependent axes of stratification that intertwine in multiple ways to create complex patterns of stratification and inequality (Penner and Saperstein 2013; Feree 2008). An interactive intersectional analysis thus provides an alternative analysis to the reductionist tendencies that characterize Marxist/socialist thought (within its emphasis on the centrality of class relations in

shaping dynamics and outcomes); feminist thought that posits the "categorical hegemony" of gender as pivotal in explaining patterns of power and privilege over time and across space; those "essentializing identity constructs" that tend to homogenize and conflate (Anthias 2012); and anti-racist thought that uphold race and racism as the bane of minority women's existence (Stasiulis 1999).

There is much of value in promoting the multiple, interactive, and simultaneous experiences of race, class, and gender as intersecting systems of privilege or inequality rather than as discrete categories that stand in a mechanistic and additive form (United Nations 2010). The centrality of social location is unmistakable to an intersectional analysis (Rajiva and Batacharya 2010): Where minority women are socially located in society with respect to race, ethnicity, history, and class will profoundly influence their identities and experiences, opportunities and outcomes. Consider how minority women experience reality differently from white women because they are differently located as a result of the interplay of race, gender, ethnicity, and class (also age and sexual orientation) that generates interlocking and overlapping hierarchies of inequality. Similarly, minority women experience reality differently from minority men because of how gender intersects with race, ethnicity, and class to create overlapping and interlocking hierarchies of inequality that intensify exploitation and marginalization (Marfelt 2016). A focus on violence against racialized and immigrant women, refracted through the prism of an intersectional lens, reinforces the value of an intersectional analysis.

Violence and Visibility: Intersectionality at Work

Violence against women remains a health problem of epidemic proportions in Canada and abroad (True 2012; Statistics Canada 2006; McInturff 2013b; United Nations 2010; Black et al. 2011; Turpel-Lafond 2014; RCMP 2014). Gender violence is now a human rights violation of such magnitude that the term *femicide* is currently in vogue (Rothkopf 2013). Women worldwide between the ages of 15 to 44 are more likely to die or be maimed by male violence than succumb to cancer, malaria, war, and traffic accidents combined (Kristof 2013). About 35 per cent of women worldwide have been physically or sexually assaulted at some point in their lives by a current or former partner, according to the World Health Organization (2013). Rates of assault range from 23 per cent of women in North America to 37 per cent in Africa, the Middle East, and Southeast Asia. A survey by the European Union Agency for Fundamental Rights (2014) found that one-third of Europe's women were subjected to physical or sexual violence from the age of 15 on, with the highest incidents in those Scandinavian countries with a history of gender equality, including Denmark at 51 per cent, Finland at 47 per cent, and Sweden at 46 per cent. Another World Health Organization study (2012) concluded domestic and sexual violence afflicts up to 70 per cent of women aged 15 to 49, with most countries falling into the 29 to 62 per cent range (see also UN News 2015). The situation In Canada is worrisome as well. Police data indicate that 173,600 women aged 15 and older were victims of violent crime—that is, 1,207 per 100,000 women in the Canadian population, slightly higher than the rate of violent crime against men (Sinha 2013). This violence towards women inflicts devastating consequences. Its persistence and pervasiveness curtails the liberty of women and girls, exploits their unequal status in society, and renders them susceptible to costly and long-lasting physical disfigurement, emotional pain, and psychological stress.

Minority women in Canada (including aboriginal, immigrant and refugee, and racialized) are particularly vulnerable to violence in their lives (Jiwani 2006; Department of Justice 2009; RCMP 2014). They are violated and abused for many reasons, including a devalued status that legitimizes personalized violence within the community (including exposure to rape and domestic abuse); institutionalized state violence (such as policing) directed at communities; and racism within society at large that interlocks with others systems of exclusion to engender a form of violence in its own right (Jiwani 2010, 2001; INCITE 2006). In the case of aboriginal women, the path to becoming a missing or murdered female most often includes persistent abuse and neglect (for example, aboriginal children constitute about 8 per cent of the children in British Columbia, yet more than 50 per cent of children in care are aboriginal [Turpel-Lafond 2014; Report 2014b]). Statistics Canada data from 2011 (Landertinger 2016) reveals a nearly similar situation across Canada. As well, racialized and immigrant women continually confront racial stereotypes that routinely diminish their status to less than human and undeserving of respect. In addition to concerns shared by all victimized women, immigrant and refugee women must endure the prospect of violence because of their newcomer (and often precarious) status in Canada. The threat of violence is intensified by a lethal combination of exclusions related to the financial, legal, language, and cultural (Smith 2004).

Is there a pattern to the indiscriminate killing of aboriginal, racialized, and immigrant women? Can its prevalence and pervasiveness be explained by misogyny (hatred of women [Sheehy 2010]), or sexism (belief in the inferiority of women), or androcentrism (a tendency to see the world from a male normative standard), or patriarchy (a system designed by, prioritized for, and organized around male interests)? Is the source of the problem rooted in a misguided multicultural commitment to tolerate sexist cultural practices because of an uncritical relativism that subordinates the universality of women's human and equality rights to the specifics of a singular culture and its practices (Papp 2010; UN 2010)? Or should a political economy model prevail in which violence is rooted in structural exclusions related to material production and ideological reproduction (True 2012)? Is the violence a spontaneous and arbitrary outburst of male rage? Or is it better framed as a strategic component of a broader social framework for collectively controlling women? Is the murder of women an extreme manifestation of more banal violence women confront on a daily basis in a patriarchal system (Rebick 2014)? Do women suffer abuse because of gender (sexism) or poverty and powerlessness (class) or race (racism) or cultural values (ethnicity) within those ethnocultural communities who commit to honour as a core cultural value (Dogan 2011; Korteweg and Yurdakul 2010; Schliesman 2012)?

Or should emphasis focus on how these seemingly independent variables intersect in interlocking ways to exponentially intensify the vulnerability of minority women to violence and victimization? Rajiva and Batacharya (2010:10) frame the murder of Reena Virk along the lines of a multiplier effect:

> As a young South Asian woman, Reena was on the losing end of many of the binaries that secure social hierarchies. She was not just "different" but, rather, inferiorized according to hierarchies that privilege white skin and hairless thin bodies that are unequivocally middle class, heterosexual, and able-bodied; bodies that, in short, conform to the hegemonic definitions of gender and respectability.

In short, the interplay of discriminations based on gender, race, class, and aboriginality generates a continuum of forms and gradations of violence (Central American Women's Network 2010).

The politics of control come into play. Societal messages routinely convey the impression that men are more important than women and more deserving of power and privilege. Such an inequality narrative makes it easier for men to believe they have the right to be in charge and in control over women, even if violence is required to exert domination (Canadian Women's Foundation n.d.). Ambitious and upwardly mobile immigrant women may become targets of domestic violence by tradition-bound males who expect servitude, deference, and submissiveness. This violence would appear to reflect cultural traditions that normalize male abuse of women without necessarily condoning it; naturalize abuse as a male entitlement to dominate; discourage public disclosure for fear of airing "dirty laundry"; and so uphold the primacy and tradition of family honour believing only death can remove the defilement and restore patriarchal pride.

To be sure, references to *tradition* or *culture* to explain violence against immigrant and racialized women is problematic (United Nations 2010). Too often this pattern of violence is blamed on some cultural defect in need of an enlightened Western intervention. By contrast, the problem of violence against mainstream women is attributed

to disturbed and/or controlling individuals rather than being structurally embedded or culturally endorsed (Deckha 2010). As a result, according to Maneesha Deckha of the University of Victoria, there is a mainstream tendency to criticize minority cultures as patriarchal and their practices as violent—and yet conveniently exempt itself from these labels. For example, consider the overheated media hype over the dozen or so honour killings in Canada from 2002 to 2010 (three between 1954 and 1983, none between 1984 and 2001 [Singh 2012]), compared to the lukewarm coverage of over 212 spousal deaths in Ontario alone between 2002 and 2007 (Caplan 2010). Police reported 82 intimate partner homicides across Canada in 2012, according to Statistics Canada, with 83 per cent involving a female victim. Mainstream media may frame these killings as domestic homicides, yet this homicidal violence may be motivated by the same twisted logic as honour killings: namely, to dominate and control women perceived as chattel (property) by aggrieved men with a pathologically inflated sense of entitlement and importance (Khan 2013). The double standard is unmistakable: non-western cultures are framed in deterministic and essentialized terms, thereby reducing the problem of domestic violence to a simplistic and singular explanation (patriarchal culture) (United Nations 2010). By contrast, a focus on individual actions exempts cultures of the global north from scrutiny and criticism.

Immigrant and racialized women remain the "hushed-over" victims of violence. Many may not know that spousal abuse is a crime in Canada, or where they can go for help (if you can't speak English, how can you dial 911?), or they may fear deportation if they complain (United Nations 2010). The experience of domestic abuse is painfully intensified because of loneliness, dependency, homesickness, lack of knowledge of English or access to services, and the threat of social ostracism. As Ekuwa Smith (2004) writes:

> These women can be incredibly isolated in an unfamiliar environment where there seems to be no safe place, not even at home. The loss of traditional supports of extended family, friends, advisors from their home country of

origin weighs heavily on some of these women and compounds their isolation. Some wives have never experienced abuse until they come here, when the trauma of adjusting economically and socially to the new country disrupts family life.

However useful as a stop-gap measure for victims of domestic violence, many shelters are neither equipped nor prepared to provide culturally sensitive services. No less daunting in looking for help is a victim's wariness toward a criminal justice system that may prove as traumatizing as what triggered the response in the first place. Women may then be re-victimized (and re-traumatized) by the very system they turn to for help. Finally, even escaping from abusive relations may not prove a panacea. The dearth of job prospects because of prejudicial attitudes and institutional barriers, not to mention the loneliness and estrangement, further intensifies the prospect of yet more poverty and isolation.

No one is suggesting that domestic violence is more prevalent in immigrant communities. Abuse and violence are about power, and the abuse of power is displayed across all cultures and groups regardless of ethnicity, race, or class. But domestic abuse impacts immigrant women differently because of the unique social location they occupy in what must seem like a foreign country (United Nations 2010). Without access to knowledge or resources, few options for escape exist; moreover, alternatives often lead to more shame, physical retaliation, and isolation. The cumulative effect of such a patricentric bias is punitive. It becomes even more stressful to leave an abusive relationship when friends, relatives, priests/ministers, and others exert additional pressure to stay put. Foreign-born women are told to "learn to deal with it and make sacrifices." Mindful of less-than-viable alternatives, immigrant women and their children stay in abusive relationships for protracted periods of time, resulting in more mental health and physical injury issues (Alaggia, Regehr, Rishchynski 2009).

Class matters, too: immigrant and racialized minority women often occupy a socio-economic/ class status below that of white women. Lower class status is not necessarily indicative of greater

victimization. Nevertheless, minority women confront a doubly articulated class hierarchy, one based on their subordinate status within their communities in addition to their subdominant status in society at large (see Jiwani 2006). Thus, violence against minority women reflects their unequal status in society, together with the abuse of power within a context of inequality. Their ghettoization in dangerous and low-paying jobs—including prostitution and other sex trade activity—may expose them to greater danger in the workplace. Certain occupations are also more vulnerable to violence, including foreign domestic work secluded in private homes, without recourse or relief, and threatened with deportation if they complain of abuse (Statistics Canada 2006).

Paradoxically, what is most striking may be the class status of those who perpetuate the violence. Foreign-born males are victims as well. Those males who migrate to Canada may come from global regions where abuse of women may be formally forbidden but often tolerated in practice. The possible persistence of such practices in Canada should not be casually dismissed. In addition, the stress of making a go of it in Canada may intensify conditions that incite yet more violence. Males who once wielded economic power and political clout now find themselves marginalized and ignored. Making matters worse are those humiliations and disappointments resulting from under/unemployment or loss of domestic authority. That makes it imperative to understand how the eradication of violence must begin by understanding logic behind the deeply felt beliefs and constraints of perpetrators (see African Canadian Legal Clinic 2006).

The gender-based violence experienced by immigrant and racialized minority women within their communities is compounded by the institutionalized racism and sexism they encounter on a daily basis (Jiwani 2006). But just as none of the variables in isolation (gender, race, class, age, or ethnicity) can explain what happened to Aqsa Parvez or Reena Virk or Helen Betty Osborne, so too is it impossible to isolate a single factor to account for the pervasiveness of violence toward minority women. Violence against minority women involves multiple oppressions sustained by gendered power relations along varying axes of social difference (United Nations 2010). Gender intersects with the variables of class, ethnicity, and race to create complex and interlocking systems of vulnerability that render women more susceptible to harm (Piper 2008). With race, women of colour and aboriginal women are targets of violence by virtue of their visibility. The often impoverished and disempowered class status of racialized and minority women draws them as pawns into high-risk occupations. Their status as minority women exposes them to danger because of cultural values that complicate their lives and life chances. The realities, rights, and experiences of immigrant and racialized minority women may be further compromised by a multiculturally inspired commitment to culturalism: a (mistaken) belief that the integrity of cultural communities and their attendant beliefs and values must be protected and promoted at all costs, regardless of the harm or exclusion (Phillips 2007; UN 2010).

The interplay of these factors reinforces the necessity to contextualize violence in structural and situational terms rather than as individual pathologies. Reference to the concept of cascading disadvantages is helpful in drawing attention to how those already vulnerable along several fronts and without much margin for error tend to experience yet more disadvantages (see also Shkilnyk 1985). Emphasis must focus on those factors (variables) that expose the vulnerability of minority women to different forms of violence (because of gender, race, ethnicity, class). The interplay of these dimensions also underscores the explanatory value of both an intersectional and intrasectional analysis in exposing violence and oppression toward racialized and immigrant minority women. A commitment to intrasectionality acknowledges the multiplicity of differences-within-differences. Aboriginal women, immigrant and refugee women, and racialized women of colour tend to experience reality differently because each is differently located with respect to how identity markers (race, ethnicity, and class) intersect with gender to create a multiplier effect. For Aboriginal women, gender intersects race, class, and colonization to intensify exposure to violence and abuse (Jackson 1999). For racialized women of colour, gender intersects differently with race, ethnicity, and class to generate different patterns of violence (Rajiva and Batacharya 2010). For immigrants and refugees, gender intersects still differently with race, ethnicity, and class to amplify patterns and potencies of violence. To ignore these differences-within-difference and the need for different ways of accommodating these diverse differences is to invisibilize and normalize the violence implicit in racism and sexism (Jiwani 2006). If Canada and Canadians are serious about reaching the goal of gendered equality, nothing less will do in addressing the violence of gendered exclusions. At a two-day symposium held 30–31 January 2016 in Ottawa, entitled "Murders and Disappearances of Indigenous Women and Girls: Planning for Change—Towards a National Inquiry and an Effective National Action Plan," Dawn Lavell-Harvard, president of the Native Women's Association of Canada, and Angela Cameron, Faculty of Law at the University of Ottawa, expressed the issue quite starkly:

> The Symposium identified the crux of this issue . . . that equality will never be achieved until gendered, racialized and sexualized violence against Indigenous women and girls as perpetuated by both Indigenous men and non-Indigenous men, and by representatives of the state, is stopped. That requires action by all levels of government in Canada.

Summary

1. Progress on equality for Canadian women as well as women worldwide is offset by continuing inequalities and exclusions.

2. A social inequality lens is necessary to examine gendered inequalities/exclusions in Canada, and a gendered lens is necessary to analyze patterns of social inequalities.

3. Gender relations as fundamentally unequal relations must be analyzed in terms of how inequities of exclusion are constructed and maintained as well as challenged and changed.
4. Despite claims of "the end of men," female inequalities in a gendered society remain structurally embedded in a systemic patriarchy.
5. Patterns of gendered inequalities as social exclusions are differently expressed across different domains such as employment, education, income, media, and violence.

6. The diverse social location of minority (aboriginal, racialized, migrant) women intensifies patterns of inequality and exclusion.
7. An intersectional analysis as a holistic framework is necessary for analyzing the interplay of gendered social locations (race, class, aboriginality, and ethnicity) in intensifying patterns of exclusion.
8. Examining patterns of violence directed at minority, migrant, and Aboriginal women can be achieved by way of an intersectional/intrasectional analysis.

Review Questions

1. The chapter strongly suggests that we still live in a man's world, despite references to the possibility that we are also seeing "the end of men." Do you agree or disagree with this seemingly contradictory assessment? On what basis would you justify your response?
2. Indicate how a gendered society is deeply patriarchal in structure and why this patriarchy generates inequalities of exclusions along gender lines.

3. In analyzing violence and gender, the chapter suggests the importance of an intersectional/intrasectional approach. Explain how and why this approach is important.
4. Compare the unique inequalities of exclusion that confront aboriginal women, racialized women of colour, and immigrant and refugee women.
5. Indicate why this chapter employs the expression *gendered inequality* instead of *gender inequality*.

7 Racialized Inequalities, Immigrant Exclusions

Learning Objectives

1. To show how Canada's lofty status in managing diversity is compromised by the persistent exclusion of immigrants and minorities.
2. To expose the magnitude of racialized inequality and immigrant exclusion at the level of income, poverty, and (un)employment.
3. To illustrate how and why new Canadians are experiencing difficulties in making an adjustment to Canada.
4. To demonstrate how and why the licensing and accreditation process is stacked against skilled newcomers.
5. To compare two explanatory models of social inequality—*ethnicity* versus *critical race theory*—with respect to migrant and minority exclusion.

Introduction: Racialized Inequality: The Inequalities of Racialization

Canada is a land of paradoxes. From afar, Canada looks like a paragon of virtue in managing its race, ethnic, and aboriginal relations (Fleras 2016). Flagrant forms of discrimination are no longer tolerated or condoned in a post-racial and pro-multicultural Canada that commits to equality. A commitment to the principles of multiculturalism and inclusiveness secures a basis for living together without the differences interrupting a co-operative coexistence. Canada's dedication to engaging diversity is touted as a strength rather than a liability in light of its vast potential to improve this country's competitive edge in a global economy. **Racialized minorities** rarely endure the kind of blatant bias that once prevailed in the not too distant past; in turn, new Canadians are making their mark

in transforming Canada along more cosmopolitan lines (Bricker and Ibbitson 2013). For example, new and racialized Canadians now constitute 72 per cent of the population of Markham, Ontario, which has a median household income of $86,000 that outperforms income at the national level ($61,000) (Gee 2013). Even Aboriginal peoples in Canada are making significant political and economic strides in overcoming the structures and strictures of colonialism, while securing the rights to indigenous models of self-determining autonomy over land, identity, and political voice (Maaka and Fleras 2005; Coates and Crowley 2013; Coulthard 2014).

But a closer inspection of this canvas yields a somewhat different interpretation (Fleras 2014a). Canada is plagued by unnerving levels of inequality that reward certain groups yet penalize others because of who they are or what they look like (Block and Galabuzi 2011). Patterns of racialized bias are deeply entrenched in the founding assumptions and foundational principles of

Canada's Eurocentric and colonial constitutional order. Their expressions as racialized inequality are neither distributed evenly nor randomly allocated. They're concentrated instead among clusters of immigrants and minorities who are aligned in ascending/descending order of inclusion and exclusion along a "mosaic" of raised (dominant) and lowered (subordinate) tiles (Tepper 1988; also Porter 1965; Clement and Helmes-Hayes 2015). By contrast, non-racialized whites[1] tend to perform better in terms of income and wealth, including a disproportionate level of power and privilege that perpetuates patterns of control and domination (Saloojee 2003; Reitz and Banerjee 2007; Pendakur and Pendakur 2011). For immigrants, the cost of settlement and integration into Canada may prove excessive and exhausting for reasons largely beyond their control (Simmons 2010). A double standard prevails: those migrants and minorities who excel in Canada ("model minorities") may be criticized as "rate busters" (see, for example, the article originally entitled "Too Asian?" in *Maclean's* magazine, November 2010 [Gilmour et al. 2012]). Yet those who do poorly in Canada are castigated as "troublesome constituents" or "problem people" in need of prodding or punishment (Fleras 2014b).

A cursory inspection of Canada's historical record for managing immigrants and minorities is hardly exemplary (Fleras 2016). What is revealed instead is a chronicle of Eurocentric domination, white supremacy and control, racist exclusions, and capitalist exploitation (Henry and Tator 2010; Satzewich and Liodakis 2013). Individuals were routinely imported as a source of cheap menial labour, either to assist in the process of society-building (for example, Chinese immigrants for the construction of the dangerous British Columbia portion of the TransCanada railway) or to toil in labour-starved industries such as the garment trade or resource extraction (Bolaria and Li 1988). Once in Canada, many became convenient targets for abuse or exploitation, in addition to doing Canada's dirty work. Then and now, racialized minorities and immigrant Canadians were shunted into marginal employment ghettos with few possibilities for recognition, reward, or advancement. Their political and civil rights were routinely trampled on without much in the way of recourse for redress (Walker

1997; Backhouse 1999). Labourers from countries in the global south (especially the Caribbean and Latin America) continue to be "farmed in" on a temporary basis for seasonal employment for the dirty, dull, and dangerous agricultural jobs spurned by Canadians at existing wages and work conditions (Hennebry 2010; Fleras 2014b). Working conditions there are reported to be among the worst of any occupation, with many denied fundamental worker's rights because of language barriers, lack of familiarity with the law, and unscrupulous employers. Domestic workers (live-in caregivers) from the Philippines may be exploited by those professional class families who should know better (Atanackovic and Bourgeault 2014). Finally, Muslim Canadians and those of Middle Eastern origin remain targets of post-9/11 racial profiling, caught in the middle of a squeeze that pits the West's so-called secular superiority against the religious-rationalized fanaticism of Islamist extremists (Kazemipur 2014; Hennebry and Momani 2013).

The overall situation has improved somewhat, thanks to the passage of **employment equity** legislation, nearly 45 years of official multiculturalism, a series of institutional accommodations, a national commitment to an inclusive Canada, and de-legitimation of racism and racial discrimination from the public domain (Fleras 2016). But no amount of polite fiction can mask over some profoundly uncomfortable realities. Moves towards a more inclusive Canada may have dislodged the most egregious expressions of exploitation and exclusions. But Canadians are not on equal footing when it comes to sorting out who gets what and what goes where (F.A.C.E.S. of Peel Collaborative 2015; Reitz and Banerjee 2007). Inequality remains a fact of life in a racialized Canadian society informed by race-based disparities in power, privilege, and property (Block and Galabuzi 2011; Livingston and Weinfeld 2015). Canada's labour force may be increasingly diverse; nevertheless, visible (racialized) minorities and newcomers to Canada continue to encounter hurdles in securing employment (let alone attaining promotions) consistent with their educational qualifications or acquired credentials (Public Service Alliance of Canada 2010). Racialized minorities may account for nearly half of the GTA population; nevertheless, they represent only 4.2 per cent of the city's corporate senior leadership (Omidvar and Tory 2012). Inexplicably, the percentage of racialized minorities on corporate boards of Canada's 500 largest companies dropped from 5.3 per cent of all directors in 2010 to 3.4 per cent in 2012 (the percentage of persons with disabilities has also declined to 2.1 per cent, whereas the percentage of women and Aboriginal peoples increased to 15.6 per cent and 1.3 percent respectively (Canadian Board Diversity Council 2014).

For all the talk of inclusiveness, Canadian institutions remain sites of inequality, albeit in a more nuanced way than before. Media representations of immigrants and minorities continue to be refracted through the prism of Euro-white frames (Fleras 2014c). A commitment to community-based policing does not appear to have generated a level of trust that legitimizes the presence of police in minority communities (Cryderman, O'Toole, and Fleras 1996). Even the justice system remains colour-coded in terms of an overrepresentation in charges, convictions, and incarcerations. Aboriginal peoples may represent about 4.5 per cent of Canada's population, yet they comprise around 25 per cent of inmates in federal prisons (Sapers 2016). Provincial and territorial variations show substantially higher rates. In contrast to their proportion in the criminal justice system, racialized minorities are underrepresented at the judicial level (only 2.3 per cent of 221 federal judges), with whites accounting for 98 of Ottawa's past 100 appointees in recent years (Makin 2012). The political sector has also proven an exercise in futility. Racialized minorities are largely excluded from Canada's political corridors at federal, provincial and local levels, despite some notable exceptions (for example, Canada's first Muslim mayor in Calgary) (Tolley 2016). Yes, the GTA may proclaim, "Diversity, our strength"; nevertheless, the slogan speaks louder than action or results. Those with racialized minority status are underrepresented relative to their share of the population, both as political candidates and as elected officials at all three levels of government. Racialized Torontonians account for just 7 per cent of all 253 municipal council members across the 25 municipalities comprising the GTA, although they make up nearly 50 per cent of the population. Four large racialized groups—Arabs, Filipinos, Latinos, and Southeast Asians—lack any representation whatsoever (Siemiatycki 2012).

In short, all the deeply ingrained myths (comforting fictions) cannot disguise the obvious realities (inconvenient truths): Canada remains a *racially stratified* society where racialized differences matter because perceptions of race or newcomer status continue to make a difference in influencing outcomes (Jedwab and Satzewich 2015). **Racialized inequality** remains an entrenched and defining characteristic of a so-called post-racial Canada, notwithstanding a concerted campaign at whitewashing those inconvenient truths behind the polite fictions of multiculturalism (O'Connor and O'Neil 2010). The end result is uneven. Some "minority-ized" Canadians do well despite their race or immigrant status; others suffer and may never recover; and still others do not appear adversely affected one way or the other. Racialized and newcomer minorities may be chided for expecting too much but giving back too little, in the process exposing them to criticism for weakening social cohesion, eroding national identity, and compromising prosperity (Amin 2012). These observations activate a number of questions for discussion and debate: what causes racialized inequality and immigrant exclusions? Why are migrants and minorities excluded in a Canada that abides by inclusiveness principles? Who is responsible—the victims or the system or an interplay of victims and system? Can racialized disparities be attributed to **racism** and racial discrimination, a lack of human capital (from education to work experience to language competence), the play of market forces that limits economic opportunities, or a permanently un-level field that systemically hides behind a façade of equal opportunity (O'Neill 2012)? Is the problem attributable to minority cultures or immigrant values that discourage coping and success? Or should the finger be pointed at mainstream structures that compromise minority life chances to the detriment of Canada and Canadians (Heath and Cheung 2007; Yu and Heath 2007)? Answers to these questions prompt a vigorous debate whose varied and contradictory responses complicate Canada's status as either a pacesetter or a pariah in accommodating diversity.

A racialized distribution of valued resources makes it abundantly clear: inequality in Canada is stratified hierarchically along the line of race, ethnicity, and aboriginality (see also Porter 1965). The resultant disparities in redistribution, recognition, and representation are not simply the result of negative mindsets amenable to quick-fix solutions. Racialized inequalities and immigrant exclusions reflect biases impervious even to detection because of their entrenchment within Canada's founding principles and foundational structures (Galabuzi 2006). This chapter is also predicated on the assumption that **racialized stratification** of migrant exclusions and minority inequities is neither natural nor healthy. To the contrary, the **racialization** of inequality and exclusion can be consequential in fraying the social fabric of Canadian society (Wilkinson and Pickett 2009). The toxicity of put-downs because of a diminished social status, restricted opportunities, dominance hierarchies, and dysfunctional communities can prove dangerous, with impacts ranging from poorer health and shorter life expectancies to the erosion of social trust. Such a macro-perspective puts the onus on analyzing how racialized inequities and immigrant exclusions are created, expressed, and sustained as well as challenged and transformed by way of government initiative, institutional reform, and minority assertiveness (also Fleras 2012).

This chapter draws on these themes by exploring the patterns and politics of racialized inequality and immigrant exclusions in Canada. It is predicated on a core sociological assumption: empirical indicators of inequality such as income distribution provide insight into those social structures that trigger exclusion and injustice, the social dynamics that reinforce patterns of power and privilege, and the social fields that distribute life chances in an unequal manner (Scheurkens 2010; Hier and Walby 2006). The chapter begins by looking at the magnitude and scope of racialized inequality in Canada with respect to income, un/employment, and poverty. It explores those structural exclusions experienced by racialized newcomers to Canada throughout the adjustment cycle in terms of settling down, fitting in, and moving up. A look at the politics of accreditation exposes the challenges that confront skilled newcomers in making a go of it in

Canada. The chapter concludes by analyzing the concept of racialized inequality along competing models—ethnicity versus critical race—of inequality and exclusions.

Racialized ("Colour-Coded") Inequalities

A brief overview of racialized inequality in Canada does not inspire (Block 2013; Picot and Hou 2014; Green, Riddell, and St. Hilaire 2015; Block and Galabuzi 2011; Galabuzi, Casipullai, and Go 2012; F.A.C.E.S. of Peel Collaborative 2015). Canada purports to be a colour-blind, post-racial society where people are rewarded on the basis of what they do (merit) instead of who they are (race). But data from the 2011 National Household Survey indicates that racial status remains a significant factor in shaping disadvantage and discrimination in the Canadian labour marker and overall levels of poverty and income inequality (Jackson 2014a). A brief overview for Canada, based on Jackson (2014a), and for Ontario, based on Block, Galabuzi, and Weiss (2014), provides a basis for an expanded discussion:

- In 2011, 19.1 per cent of all Canadians self-identified as members of a racialized group.
- In 2010, median income for racialized groups in Canada was $20,153 compared to $29,649 for whites (a 32 per cent difference). For Ontario, the earning gap between racialized minorities and whites was 16.7 per cent.
- Nearly 15 per cent, or 4.8 million Canadians, lived in poverty; 41 per cent of those living in low-income neighbourhoods belonged to a racialized minority group.
- Poverty levels for racialized minorities in 2010 was 21.5 per cent, based on LIM-AT, compared to 13.3 per cent for whites. The incidence of low income for blacks was 26.2 per cent.
- In Ontario, 20 per cent of racialized minorities lived in poverty compared to 11.6 per cent of whites.
- The unemployment rate in 2011 was 7.8 per cent. It was 9.9 per cent for racialized

minorities compared to 7.3 per cent for whites. Rates between racialized women and white women were 10.6 per cent versus 6.7 per cent, and 9.3 per cent for racialized males versus 7.8 per cent for white males.

- For Ontario, the unemployment rate for racialized minorities stood at 10.5 per cent compared to 7.5 per cent for whites.
- For those with a university degree, the unemployment rate between racialized workers and white workers was 7.9 per cent versus 4.1 per cent.
- Racialized minorities born in Canada had a higher unemployment rate (11.8 per cent) compared to Canadian born whites (7.4 per cent). For young adults age 20–24, Canadian-born and educated racialized minorities had an unemployment rate of 17.2 per cent compared to 14.1 per cent for Canadian-born white workers in the same age bracket.

Income Differences

Income differentials continue to reveal marked disparities, with significant earning differences between whites and racialized; Canadian-born and foreign-born; recent versus established immigrants; women and men; and Aboriginal peoples and non-aboriginal populations (Pendakur and Pendakur 2008, 2011; Block and Galabuzi 2011; Jedwab 2012). Earning disparities also vary with

the nature of employment—namely, piecework or output-based earnings (the latter is better); employment in private versus public sectors (the latter is better); size of firms (larger is better); generational level (children of parents do better, grandchildren do better still); and pattern of compensation (better if rule-bound) (Pendakur and Pendakur 2011). These disparities remain in effect, albeit to a lesser degree, even when controlling for individual characteristics such as age, education level, ethnic background, language knowledge, employment status, household type, and occupation (Jedwab and Satzewich 2015). Consider an important study by Jean Lock Kunz and Associates (2001) for the Canadian Race Relations Foundation that exposed gaps between whites (or so-called non-racialized groups) and visible minorities (racialized groups) with regard to income, gender, and place of birth.

Table 7.1 demonstrates how labour market disadvantages exist for racialized immigrants (also Block 2013; Nakhaie and Kazemipur 2013; Jackson 2014a). Both racialized and non-racialized Canadian-born men outperform foreign-born racialized males—but not foreign-born whites. Men across all categories earn more than women regardless of visibility and place of birth, whereas Aboriginal peoples occupy the bottom of the income ladder for both genders. In other words, with few exceptions, foreign-born racialized minorities and Aboriginal peoples are underperforming in relationship to the other categories, in the process reinforcing perceptions of Canada as a

Table 7.1: Earnings* by Gender, Racialization, and Place of Birth (in $)

	Male	Female	Average
Racialized minority**	$42,433	$33,519	$38,582
Racialized minority***	$35,329	$27,075	$31,829
Whites**	$43,456	$31,150	$38,529
Whites***	$46,457	$31,627	$40,854
Aboriginal peoples	$32,369	$26,361	$29,290

*Full-time, full-year earnings for those aged 25 to 64. **Canadian-born. ***Foreign-born.
Adapted from Kunz, Milan, and Schetagne 2001.

Source: 1996 Census, Public Use Microdata File.

vertically racialized mosaic (Clement and Helmes-Hayes 2015). Other studies take exception to the specifics of these findings, given differences in timeframes and work status, but generally concur with overall patterns (Jedwab and Satzewich 2015). According to Pendakur and Pendakur (2010; also Woolley 2012), Canadian-born racialized males earned 18 per cent less than non-racialized whites, whereas Canadian-born racialized women earned about the same as non-racialized white women. Paradoxically, higher education levels may not be reflected in outcomes. Although racialized immigrants generally possess higher levels of education than whites or Aboriginal peoples (although a larger percentage of foreign-born also possess less than a Grade 8 education), they tend to lag behind Canadian-born whites with regard to employment, income, and access to professional/managerial jobs (Kunz, Milan, and Schetagne 2001; Picot, Hou, and Coulombe 2007; Block and Galabuzi 2011).

To be sure, measuring income differences across broad analytical categories such as immigrant or racialized groups can be misleading (Jedwab and Satzewich 2015). Such crude measures blur important differences related to class, race, gender, and ethnic differences within each category (Satzewich and Liodakis 2013). Table 7.2 demonstrates how certain ethnic and racialized groups out-earn others; for example Japanese Canadians are among the highest earners whereas Koreans in Canada are among the lowest. Lumping both groups into a single category as racialized (visible) minorities mistakenly implies that both Japanese Canadians and Korean Canadians are equally disadvantaged in the Canadian labour market. In addition, conceptualizing the category of racialized minorities in monolithic terms for statistical purposes underplays the complexities of people's real-life circumstances (Jedwab and Satzewich 2015). Note the table does not take into account immigrant status (foreign-born versus Canadian-born; recent or established).

Differences can be discerned when men and women are considered separately. Racialized women of colour on average earn less than non-racialized white women, whereas women of Chinese and Japanese origins are an exception, as demonstrated in Table 7.3. Moreover, some

Table 7.2: Mean Income for Canadians in 2011 by Ethnic Origin, Aged 45–54 years, with University Degree or Diploma-based

Ethnic Origins	Mean Income $
Total	64,070
Jewish	87,261
Japanese	76,215
Italian	73,323
Hungarian	72,493
British	70,641
Filipino	36,804
East African	34,071
Pakistani	34,008
Iranian	33,914
Korean	28,182

Source: Adapted from Statistics Canada, National Household Survey 2011; also Jedwab and Satzewich 2015.

second-generation Canadian-born racialized women earn more than first-generation racialized immigrant women or white Canadian-born women (Hum and Simpson 2007; Jedwab and Satzewich 2015).

Clearly, then, a different picture of income inequality emerges when focusing on differences within ethnic and racialized groups rather than simply differences between groups (Jedwab and Satzewich 2015).

Unemployment

Racialized minorities and new Canadians continue to underperform in the labour markets (Reitz, Phan, and Banerjee 2015; Teelucksingh and Galabuzi 2005; Cheung 2006; Canadian Labour Congress 2006). Both labour market participation rates and rates of unemployment expose a persistent and discriminatory gap between racialized minorities and non-racialized Canadians. For example, labour market participation rates for all Canadians in 2001 were 80.3 per cent but only 66 per cent for racialized individuals. The unemployment rate

Table 7.3: Average Employment Income in 2010 Based on Visible Minority Status, Age Cohort, 35–44, and by Gender

	Total $	Male $	Female $
Total population	61,996	69,692	52,178
Not racialized	63,404	71,427	53,109
Racialized	56,209	62,466	48,409
Japanese	70,397	86,269	54,020
Chinese	61,979	67,967	55,018
Korean	61,346	70,315	49,528
Southeast Asian	51,675	59,089	42,858
Black	50,909	54,436	46,935
Filipino	47,693	54,682	42,540

Source: Adapted from Statistics Canada, National Household Survey 2011; also Jedwab and Satzewich 2015.

for racialized groups in 2001 was almost double that of the total population (12.6 per cent versus 6.7 per cent). The 2006 Census data show slightly higher levels of labour market participation for racialized workers but also higher levels of unemployment (Block and Galabuzi 2006). With the exception of those who identify as Japanese and Filipino, racialized Canadian males were 24 per cent more likely to be unemployed than non-racialized males in 2006, whereas racialized women were 48 per cent more likely to be unemployed than non-racialized males. In 2011, the unemployment rate was 7.3 per cent for non-racialized workers compared to 9.9 per cent for racialized workers, including 14.2 per cent for Arab workers and 12.9 per cent for black workers (Jackson 2014a). Unemployment rates for racialized youth vis-à-vis non-racialized youth were much higher: 26.7 per cent versus 17.7 per cent. Finally, rates of unemployment for racialized workers born (and presumably educated) in Canada was higher (11.8 per cent) than for non-racialized Canadian-born, suggesting the unmistakable smear of discrimination, despite laws against such discriminatory behaviour, as demonstrated below (Jackson 2013).

Spotlight What's in a Name? Name Discrimination in Canada

It is widely acknowledged that prejudice and discrimination continue to mar immigrant entry into the labour market. Recent immigrants to Canada struggle in the labour market, with unemployment rates about twice as high and median wages about half as much compared to similarly aged Canadian-born (Oreopoulos 2011; Dechief and Oreopoulos 2012).

Prejudicial attitudes and discriminatory practices are much more subtle than in the past. Awareness is growing about subliminal stereotypes and implicit biases that impact people's judgment of disfavoured social groups, especially in employment contexts, and how these unconscious preferences and decisions influence subsequent interaction

continued

with others (Ansell and McDonald 2015; Beattie 2013; Levinson, Cai, and Young 2010). In short, these biases are real and exert an exclusionary impact, regardless of intent or awareness.

Consider this field experiment by Philip Oreopoulos (2009), a University of Toronto labour economist. Oreopoulos sent out 6,000 fictitious CVs for online job vacancies in the Toronto area during the economic boom. The first set of credentials described a Canadian-born individual with Canadian education and experience, in addition to a Canadian sounding name. Another set of credentials differed slightly: some used more common Chinese, Indian, and Pakistani names; others had name change plus only foreign work experiences; and still others had name change plus foreign work experiences plus foreign education credentials. The number of call-backs for interviews was then recorded and sorted accordingly. Two conclusions prevailed:

1. Interview request rates for English-named applicants with Canadian credentials were three times higher (16 per cent versus 5 per cent) than for applicants with foreign sounding names and foreign credentials.

2. Applicants with English-sounding names received 45 per cent more interview requests than those with similar credentials but foreign sounding names (16 per cent versus 11 per cent).

The evidence is inescapable: employer discrimination, based on foreign-sounding names and overseas work experience, persists against those applicants whose metrics do not fit into a conventional Canadian mould (also Skaggs and Bridges 2013; Sakamoto et al. 2013). The conclusions of a follow-up study to fathom the reasons behind this type of discrimination—prejudice or genuine concerns; conscious or unconscious—reflected those of an earlier study. That is, resumés

with English-sounding names were 35 per cent more likely to receive call backs than resumés with foreign-sounding names (Dechief and Oreopoulos 2012). When asked to justify this name discrimination, recruiters explained that employers often treat names as a proxy (or a first impression) for assessing an applicant's critical language or social skills for the job, despite offsetting positive attributes the candidate could bring to the position. Recruiters also acknowledged that pressure to avoid bad hires exacerbates the discrimination, while the bias against applicants with foreign-sounding names was amplified by the need to review the resumés quickly and without the opportunity to test language competence (Dechief and Oreopoulos 2012; Oreopoulos 2011). Finally, in-group favouritism may be at play. Whites in favour of other whites may prove as much a factor in reproducing unequal outcomes as prejudicial attitudes or racial discrimination against minorities (DiTomaso 2013).

The interplay of these implicit and subliminal biases in contributing to employment disparities makes it abundantly clear: any public policy to improve employment outcomes must move beyond improving the human capital of immigrants. This focus instead should be on changing the mindsets and behaviour patterns of those whose decisions impact employment prospects. No less important is isolating those systemic barriers that deny and exclude without really seeming to. Changes cannot come too soon. In a multicultural Canada, racial discrimination represents an affront to the principle and practice of equality and inclusion. It also constitutes an inefficient way of allocating human resources that imposes an economic cost on both racialized minorities and Canadian society (Teelucksingh and Galabuzi 2005).

Racialized minorities are also overrepresented in many low paying occupations such as textiles, light manufacturing, and sales/service industry (from call centres to security services to janitorial services [Block and Galabuzi 2011; Canadian Labour Congress 2006]). They are also underrepresented in better paying and more secure jobs such as senior management, professionals, and firefighters. The labour market is further segmented so that racialized minorities fare better in the information and

Table 7.4: Diversity in ICT Sector by Race and Ethnicity, United States

Company	Ethnicity			
	White %	Asian %	Black %	Latino/a %
Apple	55	15	11	7
eBay	61	24	7	5
Google	61	30	2	3
Microsoft	61	29	5	1
Twitter	59	29	3	3
Yahoo!	50	39	2	2

Source: Adapted from Sopinski (2014). The companies. Other/Not Disclosed/two or more races not included in this table. According to 2010, whites comprised 65 per cent of the United States population, Asians 5 per cent, blacks 13 per cent, and Hispanic (Latino/a) 16 per cent (Iceland and Sharp 2013).

communications technology (ICT) sector, including software and computer engineers and programmers (Teelucksingh and Galabuzi 2005). But as shown in Table 7.4 employee diversity statistics by major technology companies in the USA expose a predominantly white labour force, with Asian Americans comprising the major source of diversity.

Racialized Poverty

Poverty in Canada is now deeply racialized (Wallis and Kwok 2008; National Council of Welfare 2012 Jackson 2014a; Block, Galabuzi, and Weiss 2014; Macdonald and Wilson 2016). Patterns of poverty are neither colour-blind nor randomly distributed across all Canadians; rather they cluster around certain historically disadvantaged minorities (Picot, Hou, and Coulombe 2007; Galabuzi 2006). According to the National Council of Welfare (2012), the overall poverty rate in Canada was 11 per cent, based on 2006 Census data. For racialized persons it was 22 per cent (or 32 per cent of all persons living in poverty), compared to 9 per cent for non-racialized white Canadians. Another study based on the 2011 National Household Survey data indicated that the incidence of poverty for racialized minorities in 2010 was 21.5 per cent (median

income $20,153) using the LIM-AT, but only 13.3 per cent for whites (median income $29,649) (Jackson 2014a). In 2006, more than half of all poor persons living in two of Canada's largest cities were from racialized groups, including 62 per cent in Toronto and 58 per cent in Vancouver (Employment and Social Development Canada 2013). Toronto was home to 41 per cent of all racialized persons living in poverty, followed by Vancouver at 18 per cent. Within racialized communities, poverty rates varied, with a high of 40 per cent of those who identified as Korean to 11 per cent for those who identified as Filipino (National Welfare Council 2012). Of those racialized persons living in poverty, the National Council of Welfare 2012 concluded, 24 per cent identified as Chinese, 20 per cent as South Asian, and 18 per cent as black. A study by Michael Ornstein (2006) based on diversity in Toronto found that the 20 poorest groups were non-Europeans, with Somali, Afghan, and Ethiopian groups displaying poverty rates of over 50 per cent. Racialized women living in poverty outnumbered men (52 per cent to 48 per cent), while 27 per cent of those racialized persons living in poverty were less than 15 years old and 46 per cent under 25 years (National Council of Welfare 2012).

For immigrants, especially new newcomers, the situation is catastrophic. The majority of racialized persons (66 per cent) living in poverty were immigrants, including 61 per cent of racialized immigrants arriving in Canada in the previous ten years, with seven out of ten racialized poor arriving in the last five years. Overall, 90 per cent of racialized persons living in poverty are first-generation immigrants (National Council of Welfare 2012). A 2007 Statistics Canada data set concluded that poverty rates for immigrants during their first year in Canada were 3.2 times higher than for Canadian-born persons, in spite of increased levels of education attainment among increasingly skilled migrants (Picot, Hou, and Coulombe 2007). More recent studies indicate that 36 per cent of immigrants who have been in Canada for less than five years live in poverty, most notably immigrant men and those over 50 years of age (Dungan, Fang, and Gunderson 2012; also Dodd 2013). Almost three-quarters of racialized persons living in poverty have a mother tongue other than English or French (National Council of Welfare 2012). Not surprisingly, concludes the Ontario Hunger Report by the Ontario Association of Food Banks, new Canadians account for nearly one-third of the 320,000 Ontario residents who depend on food banks every month—an increase of 14 per cent since 2001—many of whom cannot find affordable housing or access to well-paying jobs. The situation is particularly grave in Toronto: recent evidence indicates 51 per cent of food bank users in the GTA are new Canadians, up from 44 per cent in 2007 (Grant 2012b). These poverty outcomes are dismaying in their own right, especially if one persists in commending Canada as an egalitarian, inclusive, and multicultural society.

Immigrant Exclusion in an Inclusive Immigration Society

Canada can be described as a society of **immigrants** (Fleras 2014b). Immigrants constitute just over 20 per cent of Canada's population, thanks to this country's robust immigration program. This percentage is expected to persist into the foreseeable future, in part to offset a declining birth rate, in part to take advantage of what immigrants have to offer. Canada is also one of the few countries in the world that qualifies as an *immigration society*. Admittedly, many societies may qualify as a society of immigrants if defined along descriptive lines; however, few can legitimately claim the normative status of an immigration society based on the following four principles (or prescriptive ideals) (see also Reitz 2012; Ucarer 1997):

1. A principled framework regulates admissions (who gets in).
2. Programs are in place to assist in the integration and settlement of immigrants.
3. Immigrants are entitled to all rights, including permanent residency and citizenship.
4. Immigrants are seen as assets for society-building, key economic players, and central to national identity.

Each immigration society establishes its own set of criteria and protocols for admission—either by choice or displacement, to settle permanently or work temporarily (Gogia and Slade 2011). A fair and democratic immigration policy provides a principled admission framework both transparent and colour-blind (see also Cavanaugh and Mulley 2013). Programs to integrate newcomers rarely elicit resentment or disapproval except, perhaps, in detail (Bauder 2011). Membership by the foreign-born reflects a commitment to principles rather than ancestry; an inclusive pluralism (**multiculturalism**) that respects differences while removing discriminatory barriers; a fluid and accommodative national identity; and a relatively easy path to naturalization, including the right to multiple citizenships (Jupp 2003; Jacobs 2010; Nussbaum 2012). Finally, immigration societies endorse the idea that economies thrive on a continuous source of newcomers as valued permanent residents rather than as rotated temporary workers (Weinstock 2010).

Canada clearly subscribes to each of these attributes, at least in principle if not always in practice. As an immigration/settler society, Canada consists primarily of immigrants and their descendants whose presence is deeply ingrained in the national consciousness. Their value to Canada-building was captured in this statement by then–prime minister Stephen Harper:

> Canada's diversity, properly nurtured, is our greatest strength. Our tolerant and welcoming immigration policy represents Canada's great competitive advantage over most of the rest of the world. (Stephen Harper, *The Globe and Mail*, 20 June 2006)

Not surprisingly, Canada remains a destination of choice for international immigrants (Fleras 2014b). The immigration public opinion survey by Washington-based Transatlantic Trends 2010 concluded that Canada may be the world's most welcoming society for newcomers. The Social Progress Index (which is composed of representatives from Harvard Business School, Oxford University, and *The Economist*) in its 2015 annual report ranked Canada first among 133 countries in the opportunities (personal rights, access to advanced education, personal freedom and choice, and [especially] tolerance and inclusion) it afforded to residents and citizens. No less effusive in praise was an international survey commissioned by the Historica-Dominion Institute, in partnership with the Munk School of Global Affairs and Aurea Foundation. Entitled "What the World Thinks of Canada: Canada and the World in 2010. Immigration & Diversity," the survey pointed out that, of the 18,600 adult respondents from the 24 leading economies, more than 53 per cent said they would abandon their homes and move to Canada if they could, including 77 per cent of Chinese respondents and 71 per cent of Mexicans. Respondents also expressed positive attitudes towards Canada's immigration welcome mat: 86 per cent believe rights and freedoms are respected in Canada; 79 per cent believe Canadians are tolerant of those from different backgrounds; 79 per cent believe that Canada has one of the best quality-of-life standards; and 71 per cent believe Canadians are welcoming toward newcomers. Other surveys are also positive, albeit more guarded in their assessments. The International Migration Integration Policy Index, based on 148 policy indicators, ranked Canada third in integrating migrants—just behind Sweden and Portugal—among 31 North

American and European societies. The OECD (2012b) proclaimed Canada to be one of the world's top immigrant integration countries for immigrants and children, based on a series of measures related to income, health, education, and civic engagement, including the highest percentage who become citizens and those who arrive with post-secondary degrees. Clearly then, Canada's success in integrating newcomers is sufficiently robust to consolidate its claim to a "Canadian exceptionalism" (Jeffrey Reitz in Ho and Natt 2012; Winter 2015).

Most immigrants appear to be relatively satisfied with their decision to come to Canada. Even the spectre of uneven economic prospects and the bigotry of sometimes unwelcoming sectors have not dulled the satisfaction (Adams 2007). Newcomers believe Canada provides them with the space where they can fit in, feel comfortable, and get on with making a new life. They appreciate the opportunities and services available to them and their children; access to quality education; safe neighbourhoods; guaranteed rights to personal freedoms; and the presence of market transparency to facilitate economic success (see also Raleigh and Kao 2010; Lewin et al. 2011). This passage is instructive:

> For young and well educated Chinese like Emily Gao, the lure of immigration to Canada is obvious: Clean air, public health care, and a strong education system are all draws compared to living in a country without them. Add the large Chinese communities that already exist in places such as Vancouver and Toronto, plus relatively cheap real estate (compared with prices in some Chinese cities), and you have something close to a dream destination. (MacKinnon 2012)

According to the Longitudinal Survey of Immigrants to Canada (Jedwab 2012), four years after admission into Canada, 84 per cent of immigrants said they would make the same decision to immigrate. (The total breaks down into the following admission categories: 80 per cent from the economy class, 88 per cent from the family class, and 93 per cent from the refugee class). A similar study by Statistics Canada in 2005 (Jedwab 2012) revealed that three-quarters of recently arrived immigrants were satisfied with life in Canada; four years later, two-thirds of the study participants said their expectations were met or exceeded. A more recent study confirmed these findings: newcomers to Canada are generally happy with their lives here, with most immigrant groups display higher levels of life satisfaction than their source-country populations, and comparable levels to the Canadian-born population (Frank, Hou, and Schellenberg 2014). It should be noted that age at immigration plays a key role in shaping success, including better labour market outcomes for those arriving before the age of 18 (Boulet and Bourdarbat 2010).

How do positive assessments stack up to reality (Kazemipur 2014; Ibbitson 2014; Root et al. 2014)? Are Canadians as receptive to immigration as they claim or should more attention be paid to an EKOS survey which pointed out that nearly half of all respondents believe there are too many racialized immigrants (Graves 2015)? Is Canada as integrative of immigrants as surveys suggest (Reitz 2012:535-536; Andrew et al. 2013)? Are immigrant experiences consistent with Canada's reputation as a progressive and principled immigration society? Sadly, realities do not always match ideals. Canada may have emerged as a go-to destination for attracting the brightest and the best in the global talent wars (Biles and Frideres 2012), but slippages in the Canadian model reinforce a gap between policy rhetoric and the reality of outcomes (Biles et al. 2012; Bauder and Shields 2015; McDonald et al. 2010). Racialized immigrants of colour continue to be judged by their origins or prevailing stereotypes; as a result, their pleas for exemptions from the general rules are not always taken seriously (Gilmour et al. 2012). A conformity model and a monocultural framework prevail that embrace tolerance in principle, yet dismiss the realities of immigrant diversities when they stray outside mainstream norms or entail adjustments that cost or inconvenience (Li 2003). For example, for the Pierre Elliott Trudeau Foundation conference the Environics Research Group (2011) concluded that immigrants are welcome and positively received (as more of a solution than a problem), but only if they adopt Canadian values, obey its laws, and do not "rock the boat" (also Canadian Race Relations Foundation [CRRF] 2014). Newcomers to Canada also find a labour market system that may penalize them for reasons largely beyond their control, especially when overseas credentials and international experiences are discounted (Foster 2011). Chronic labour shortages across Canada are compounded by the irony of immigrants who cannot find work in their fields, thus reinforcing a major twenty-first-century paradox: workers without jobs, jobs without workers. A Catch-22 prevails that many perceive as a proxy for hidden biases (Sakamoto et al. 2013): a newcomer needs Canadian experience to get a job, but she can't get Canadian experience without a job.

In short, Canada may be perceived as a postracial (colour-blind) and pro-multicultural society. This image is bolstered by the removal of discriminatory barriers, banishment of racism into the socially taboo category, and inception of positive inclusion measures. But these polite fictions conceal some inconvenient truths (Mudde 2012; Collett 2012). Immigrants are doomed to playing on an *unlevel* playing field, to the detriment of opportunities and outcomes. Yes, they may possess the same rights as all Canadians, but they must exercise these rights in a Canada neither constructed to advance their interests nor designed to be reflective of their realities. A paradox is unmistakable: Canada may be one of the world's premier immigration societies based on select measures. Nevertheless, concern is mounting over the growing gap between what Canada says (polite fictions) and what it does (uncomfortable truths) in advancing a warm welcome (Sakamoto et al. 2013). Recent immigrants whose mother tongue is neither French nor English are among the most economically disadvantaged in Canada, although results vary depending on age, gender, and source country (Gee, Kobayashi, and Prus 2007). Both settlement and integration are proving more elusive than many would have imagined for skilled and highly educated newcomers who encounter diminished work prospects (Kazemipur 2014; Nakhaie and Kazemipur 2013). This disconnect between admission criteria and employment qualifications is proving both a conundrum and a contradiction, and the following section addresses a range of immigrant exclusions by demonstrating the challenges and complexities of settlement and integration. Let's begin by analyzing immigrant experiences as an ongoing yet uneven process involving three general phases in putting down roots: settling down, fitting in, and moving up.

Pathways to Inclusion, Pitfalls of Exclusion: 1: Settling Down

> Every act of immigration is like suffering a brain stroke: One has to learn to walk again, to talk again, to move around the world again, and, probably most difficult of all, one has to learn how to re-establish a sense of community.
> —Vivian Rako, cited in Fulford 2003

Canada's immigration program emphasizes the settlement and integration of new Canadians (Fleras 2012; 2014b). It also acknowledges a three-stage process of adjustment: Immediate needs for survival assistance (settling down); intermediate needs for accessing the labour market, housing, health services, and so on (fitting in); and long-term needs for full integration into Canadian society and the economy (moving up) (Teelucksingh and Galabuzi 2010; Wayland 2006). For some immigrants, the settlement process is filled with hope and opportunity; for others it is fraught with danger and disappointment; still others cope as best they can under difficult circumstances and limited resources (Fleras 2012). Life for newcomers may prove a disappointment, resulting in feelings of hopelessness that may induce violence turned inwards (suicide) or outwards. As expressed by Debbie Douglas, executive director of the Ontario Council of Agencies Serving Immigrants:

> The acculturation process is very difficult, whether you come by choice or not. It's about developing a sense of belonging and being able to integrate economically, socially, and politically into society (cited in Nicholas Keung [2009]).

Racism toward migrant groups remains a problem (Graves 2015). A survey of 1,522 Canadians, commissioned by the Association for Canadian Studies and the Canadian Race Relations Foundation (and released ahead of 21 March 2012, International Day for the Elimination of Racial Discrimination), found that over half of all Canadians distrust Muslims. Nearly as many believe that discrimination against Muslims is mainly the fault of Muslims (see also Saunders 2012). Or consider how the growth and diversification of Brampton, Ontario, represents a mixed success story. Brampton's population might have more than doubled between 1991 and 2011 (from 234,445 to 521,315, with racialized minorities now constituting nearly 70 per cent of the population), yet the percentage of white Canadians in Brampton declined by 12 per cent in the decade between 2001 and 2011, implying (among other reasons) the possibility of a "white flight" (Grewal 2013). So much for living together with differences (also Forum Research Poll 2013). Even Canada's much ballyhooed multiculturalism may confuse new Canadians. Maharaj's book, *The Amazing Absorbing Boy* (Knopf, 2010), points out how exposure to diversity may prove both comforting yet perplexing. Newcomers must learn to navigate the social patterns of Canadian society while negotiating its diverse cultural norms, yet they must also learn to embrace the fragments of various ethnic communities without an explicit monoculture to provide a frame of reference (see also Soto 2012). The words of Constance Inju Tendoh (2009) strike a resonant note in capturing the dilemmas of settling down:

> Foreign policies of the West on immigration require total integration of immigrants in their host countries. In the eyes of the capitalist society, the immigrants are threats and need to either cooperate with their host societies or return to their countries of origin. From the immigrants' perspective, the host community talks of integration yet they make integration impossible. They have drawn lines of divide separating the included from the excluded. Despite the fact that immigrants work for the welfare of their host societies, they have been identified as the excluded and the undesired others. The word immigrant in capitalist societies is connected to marginality, inferiority, illegality, poverty, rejection, etc. Most immigrants do not feel at home in their host countries as they have become subject to discrimination, yet they cannot return because of

life uncertainty in their homeland and many blame the West for this . . . . "Government's policies insist on the return of immigrants with the logic that immigrants are dangerous. It is their nation-state and they have the right to decide who enters or leaves within the territorial boundary of their nation-state. Yet they should not forget history . . . ."

Immigrants invariably want to improve their economic lot. Surveys repeatedly indicate that securing employment (preferably in their field of experience or expertise) is the foremost settlement desire for new Canadians (Wayland 2006). But many encounter barriers to integration based on negative mainstream attitudes and discrimination, in addition to cultural differences and language competencies (Constant et al. 2009). According to an internal federal government document obtained by Richard Kurland (O'Neil 2012), immigrants who speak neither French nor English may retreat into ethnic enclaves where they experience an earning-deficit because of difficulties in adjusting to the economy. Immigrants must also internalize a "secret code" that informs a "Canadian way of doing things" on the path to success and acceptance (Derwing and Waugh 2012). In other words, newcomers and racialized minorities must work twice as hard to get half as far to make a go of it in a Canada that neither reflects their realities nor advances their interests (James 2012).

Glitches mar the integration process. The 2002 Ethnic Diversity Survey, based on 40,000 interviews, concluded that racialized immigrants are less integrated than white newcomers. The conclusion was based on questions referring to "sense of belonging," "trust in others," "feeling Canadian," "becoming a citizen," "participating in voluntary activities," "voting in Canadian elections," and "life satisfaction" (Reitz 2012b). Moreover, the gap persisted and sometimes increased over time as it did for highly successful Canadian-born children of immigrant parents. Burton and Phipps (2010) argue that, compared to their Canadian-born peers, both immigrant parents and children report lower life satisfaction, including a weaker sense of belonging to their local communities. Others, including Wu et al. (2012; also Banerjee 2012),

disagree with this blanket assessment. They contend the level of newcomer integration—based on a sense of belonging and feelings of discomfort about the host society—depends on situational factors including age, gender, level of education, city of settlement, and neighbourhood characteristics. National origins matter: the sense of belonging is higher for South Asians compared to Canadians of British origin, but lower for Chinese, and similar for African Canadians. Notions of belonging often change across immigrant generations. Feelings of discomfort are higher for first-generation racialized persons and whites, concludes Wu et al. (2012), but these discomfort levels decrease over time and across generations.

Those in Canada who seek asylum confront additional challenges (Bauder 2012; Sirin and Rogers-Sirin 2015). Traumatized en route to Canada by emotional, physical, and psychological abuses, asylum seekers and refugees understandably have complex needs, reflecting widely varying educational and literacy levels, with much to learn in a relatively short period of time. Of particular note is an awareness of community support agencies as they pertain to issues of abortion, contraception, same-sex relations, domestic violence, child supervision, divorce, and child custody (Goodwin 2010). The transitional stresses that accompany refugee claimants and asylum seekers are compounded by language difficulties, shame at their inability to work and provide, and low self-esteem due to loss of control over authority or destiny. As expressed by one refugee from Central America who fell into an abusive relationship, "I was from a country where I was the daughter of a middle-class professional. Here, I was no one. *Refugee* is such a negative word. People saw me as garbage" (cited in White 1999).

2: Fitting In

The challenges of fitting in are closely linked to settling down (Toten 2011), yet the concept of *fitting in* goes beyond the goal of simple survival. Fitting in involves a combination of social capital (connections) and human capital (skill sets) for making a go of it in Canada without necessarily relinquishing cultural preferences and religious distinctiveness. Maintaining a strong immigrant identity provides immigrants with the confidence and self-respect to move forward (Bunting 2007). Diverse immigrant groups encounter different challenges. Immigrant minorities such as Muslims are seeking ways of engaging with the secular world of Canada, albeit on their own terms. Multiple identities are the result—namely, as citizens of Canada belonging to the global Muslim community and being members of a specific Islamic sect (Karim 2009). The challenge for followers of Islam is formidable: how to remain Muslim while becoming Canadian without sacrificing the principles of faith-based differences as a precondition for successful adjustment (Adams 2014).

Fitting in along gender lines is a particularly acute challenge (Andrew 2009). Men may have a hard time adjusting to the new environment, including finding work, working at survival jobs that reflect less prestige and lower income than employment in the homeland, and a loss of status both in society at large and in their households. But the position of immigrant women is equally complex and contradictory. Many are literally caught between the old world of male-dominated submissiveness and a new world of independence, assertiveness, and opportunities. Yet they often lack the resources, skills, or support to navigate the tricky shoals of transitioning between "coming here" from "over there." Not surprisingly, thousands of new Canadians are mired in desperation and depression, suffering in silence behind walls of social alienation, financial pressure, family turmoil, and cultural values that foreclose avenues of help (Reinhart and Rusk 2006). And while no one disputes the hurdles immigrant women confront pertaining to employment status, such as precarious jobs, part-time work, and credential recognition, nevertheless opportunities do exist, including openings in employment in a Canada that commits to the principle of gender equality, increased status in households and the community at large, and greater involvement in mobilizing communities to provide services for immigrant women (see Chapter 6 on gendered inequality).

Immigrant and refugee youth are subject to a host of conflicting demands and pressures. For immigrant youth, pressures to adapt are formidable (Handa 2003). They must adjust to a new country, cope with the pressures of prejudice and racism during their formative years of identity construction, become involved with routines and friendships, and learn a new language quickly enough to finish high school and compete with the Canadian-born for places in post-secondary education (it generally takes five to seven years to develop English language proficiency). Immigrant students also confront a host of barriers that range from to curricula and textbooks at odds with minority experiences, to lack of positive role models among school staff and low teacher expectations. Others have an opposite problem: inflated teacher expectation about brainy (model) immigrant children means crushing disappointment for anything less than perfection (Hammer and Friesen 2011; also Gilmore et al. 2012). Finally, immigrant youth must navigate the byzantine demands of mainstream peer culture whose values conflict with the cultural norms of family and community (Handa 2003; Aniseff and Kilbride 2003). Young women, as the moral guardians of the culture and nation, are particularly vulnerable to restrictions, as Rajiva (2005:27) says:

> Girls are expected to maintain cultural practices that are sometimes no longer relevant in their homeland countries, and are certainly not widely accepted in Canadian society. This includes concerns with dress and behaviour; peer socializing (at night, at parties, and school dancing); growing independence at adolescence (which is often not part of immigrant community understandings of adolescence); and perhaps most importantly, interacting with members of the opposite sex and having romantic relationships with boys who are not part of the community.

Intergenerational family tensions are inevitable as parents and offspring manoeuvre to find a working balance between Canada's permissive culture and more conservative traditions (Handa 2003). Two broad narratives can be discerned in framing the intergenerational crisis: to one side are the adult immigrants who self-destruct in making the transition from there to here; to the other side are their offspring, who tend to quickly adjust and adapt (Sykes 2008). Immigrant parents may feel alienated from a language and culture that confuses or diminishes; by contrast, immigrant children assimilate rapidly, in the process assuming an assertiveness and independence that inverts conventional status/roles between parents and children. Parents are trapped in a cultural crossfire: they insist on a better future for their children, although such success may prove too much of a good thing when undermining parental authority, cultural tradition, moral standards, and family cohesion.

3: Moving Up

Equally demanding are the challenges in "moving up" (Fleras 2012). In contrast to settling down and fitting in, moving up entails the process of fuller incorporation and participation in Canadian society (Landolt et al. 2011). Yet what should be a relatively simple and straightforward move toward integration may prove complex and confusing. On arrival, immigrants may well keep to themselves, not necessarily because they are inherently tribalistic or want to recreate transplanted homelands (although the path of least resistance points to staying with "one's own kind"). More often, perhaps, the interplay of mainstream prejudice and discrimination bullies them into an ethnic corner (Scheffer 2010). Newcomers continue to experience barriers that deny or exclude not because they are second-class citizens under the law but because they must survive and succeed in a society that is systemically organized along Eurocentric lines (Valverde 2012). Canada may not be overtly prejudiced or discriminatory; nevertheless, it may practise a gentler version of benevolent racism that combines passive tolerance with politely coded biases (Henry and Tator 2009). For example, achieving success in a post-industrial, knowledge-based economy depends on intangibles such as social networks and subtle cultural codes that often elude newcomers. Such mixed messages of denial and exclusion reflect badly on Canada's much-vaunted reputation as an immigration society *par excellence* (Fleras 2014b).

No less controversial are economic prospects related to income and employment levels (Jedwab

2012; Pendakur and Pendakur 2011). Immigrants in general earn less than the Canadian-born, have lower employment rates, and are not compensated for foreign education or credentials (Javdani, Jacks, and Pendakur 2012). Immigrants once spent several years earning less than the average Canadian; over time, however, they would achieve or surpass the average (Ley and Hiebert 2001). For example, according to a special report by TD Economics (2012), immigrants who arrived in the 1970s earned 80 per cent of what a Canadian earned within five years of arrival. The gap was virtually closed after 20 years (Tal 2012). But those who arrived between 2000 and 2004 earned just 61 cents on the dollar relative to a Canadian-born; as a result, new immigrants face the prospect of working an entire lifetime before they begin to match Canadian-born incomes. As well, a distinction between recent and long term immigrants yields different results. An RBC Economics Report (2011a) concludes all immigrants in full-time employment in 2005 earned about $45,000 per year, or about $700 less than the wage for Canadian-born. But more recent immigrants (less than five years in Canada) earned only $28,700 annually, although the gap closes over time due to increased experience and improved language skills. Table 7.5 indicates gaps in economic status between recent immigrants and the Canadian-born.

Even among recent immigrants, variations in income distribution can be discerned (Lemieux and Boudarbat 2010; Kaur 2011). Some are performing better than the Canadian-born, especially those who are younger, proficient in English or French, and in possession of workplace contacts, high levels of education, and work experience (Derwing and Waugh 2012). By contrast, more recent immigrants who are older, with poor language skills and without education, are struggling just to stay afloat.

In short, immigrants are experiencing a marked decline in economic fortunes as corporate Canada continues to fumble the challenge of integrating immigrant talent into the workforce (McDonald et al. 2010; Noorani 2011; Bonikowska, Hou, and Picot 2011; Picot and Sweetman 2012; Frank 2013). The most common cited barriers to accessing skill-appropriate jobs include a dearth of Canadian work

Table 7.5: Economic Indicators: Recent Immigrants (>5 years) and Canadian-Born (Ages 25–54), 2010

	Recent Immigrants	Canadian-born
Percentage of unemployed	14.7	6.1
Employment rate (%)	63.5	82.4
Average hourly earnings	$18.74	$25.04
Percentage of those with average hourly earnings under $20 an hour	67.1	37.9

Source: Adapted from Jackson 2011, based on data provided to Canadian Labour Congress by Statistics Canada.

experience; devaluation of foreign credentials, education degrees, and work experience; lack of insight into the Canadian economy and the unwritten labour market codes that take time to learn (Derwing and Waugh 2012; George and Chaze 2014); a deficit of "soft social skills" related to official language proficiency; and increased competition with a growing educated Canadian labour force (Alboim and McIsaac 2007; Sweetman 2011b). In a risk-aversive corporate Canada, immigrant qualifications continue to be dismissed as next to worthless. Foreign experience possesses little market value in Canada (one year overseas equals one-third of a year equivalent in Canada), while foreign education counts for about half of the value of Canadian schooling in terms of earning power, as demonstrated in Table 7.6.

Refusal to recognize the credentials of new Canadians costs Canada billions in lost productivity and revenue (RBC Financial Group 2011b; Conference Board of Canada 2004). Paying immigrants comparably to the Canadian-born would add $30.7 billion (or 2.1 per cent) to Canada's GDP, in addition to translating into about 42,000 new jobs. The paradox does not sit well with newcomers: they may be selected for their skills, credentials, and work experiences, yet their economic marginalization is based on rejecting those factors that presumably got them into Canada in the first place. Not surprisingly, as labour sociologist Jeffrey Reitz (2005) puts it, the continued success of Canada's immigration policy will hinge on initiatives and institutions that link workers to jobs by facilitating an international transferability of skills, credentials, and experience. Better still, consider the pithy insight of Randall Hansen, who noted in his plenary comments at a 2009 conference at the University of Augsburg in Germany that "[i]mmigration works when immigrants work."

Table 7.6: Earnings by Place of Birth, Education

	1980	2005
Recent immigrant males with university degrees	$48,581	$30,332
Canadian-born males with university degrees	$63,040	$62,556
Recent immigrant females with university degrees	$24,317	$18,969
Canadian-born females with university degrees	$41,241	$44,545

Source: Statistics Canada. Median Earnings, using 2005 constant dollars for full-time wage earners (self-employed individuals excluded).

No less harrowing for professionally trained immigrants is the closed-shop mentality of those licensed occupations that impose restrictions and deny accreditation. Accrediting foreign certificates and establishing equivalences in qualifications is a complex and time-consuming process (Deloitte 2011). This holds true for more than 440 regulatory bodies governing 55 industries (about 20 per cent of jobs in Canada require licensing by a professional regulatory body [Keung 2011c]). The resulting bottleneck that prevents professionals from gainful employment also reflects a fundamental disconnect between admission criteria and employment qualifications. The federal government controls immigration admission, but the provinces control the licensing of professional bodies who, in turn, determine who gets licensed (i.e., qualified). Nowhere is the crisis more acute than in the (re) licensing of foreign-born doctors. The spotlight box exposes the paradox between the shortage of working physicians and the glut of foreign-trained doctors who are looking for work.

But the "moving up" picture is more complex than generally imagined. What disadvantages and inequality gaps do immigrant parents transmit to their children? Overall, compared to the adult children of Canadian-born parents, children of immigrants in Canada (as well as in the United States and Australia) register positive educational outcomes (especially for those whose parents are from developing nations such as China or India) and labour market outcomes (especially for those whose parents are from developed countries such as the United States or Australia) (Picot and Hou 2011). But mixed assessments attend to second-generation racialized minorities (born in Canada of immigrant parents). A study by Patrick Grady (2011) concluded that second-generation "immigrants" between the ages of 25 and 44 earned less ($39,814) than either non-immigrants ($40,358) or white immigrants ($45,352) for any given level of education. Except for those of Chinese and Japanese origins, this pattern holds true for all groups, especially second-generation blacks (Jedwab and Satzewich 2015). Other studies disagree: for example, according to Statistics Canada (Black 2011), children of immigrants in Canada are power performing in terms of employment

prospects and income levels compared to offspring of Canadian-born parents. But children of racialized immigrants such as black males do experience a wage gap (up to 20 per cent) compared to those of white Canadian-born parents (Picot and Sweetman 2012). Interestingly, a 2007 Statistics Canada study found Canadian-born daughters of racialized immigrant parents earned more than daughters of Canadian-born parents, in contrast to their brothers who earned substantially less in their first working years than Canadian-born males.

Entry through admission categories makes a difference in shaping outcomes. Those who arrive as economic immigrants (both male and female) consistently demonstrate the highest median annual income per admission categories, although this success has not dampened calls to reduce their numbers during economic downturns and high unemployment (Abbott and Beach 2011). Those from federal skilled-worker programs who are proficient in one of the official languages are 50 per cent more likely to find a job (and earn 40 per cent more) than someone without an official language skill (Tal 2012). Evidence indicates that minorities with at least one degree from Canada and another from abroad boast an income premium even when compared to white immigrants with an identical mix of credentials. Immigrants of colour with only a foreign degree do poorly in comparison with similarly educated white immigrants, who earn substantial returns on their schooling. There is little difference in the returns to a Canadian university degree when comparing whites with non-whites either as immigrants or as Canadian-born (Alboim, Finnie, and Ming 2005; Foster 2011). Not surprisingly, the strongest predictors of economic success are neither credentials nor degrees. Yes, foreign credentials matter, but employers are more interested in those competencies for which qualifications often serve as a proxy—namely, relative youth and competencies in one of Canada's two official languages (Derwing and Waugh 2012; CIC 2012). And not just basic French or English skills in reading and writing are sought: a level of sophistication and nuance is expected for solving problems, working in teams, and deciphering coded workplace messages (Banting, Courchene, Seidle 2007).

Spotlight Rolling the Accreditation Dice: Heads, Canada Wins; Tails, Immigrants Lose

Comedy lines making the rounds in Toronto:

Q. Where is the best place to have a baby in Toronto?
A. In a taxi: there is a good chance the driver is a foreign-trained doctor.

"I saw the funniest thing last week: a white guy driving a taxi."

"Canada has the best educated pizza delivery guys in the world." (A comment posted on Adar Aihil's Canada Immigrants' blog.)

—Cited in "Oh Canada," December 2010 issue of *The Walrus*.

How many times have we heard this before: new Canadians with professional degrees are driving taxis instead of designing buildings or delivering pizzas instead of delivering babies? But the proverbial taxi driver with a doctorate from a developing country is no laughing matter. It reflects a key contradiction in Canada's immigration paradox: the discrepancy between admission criteria (*foreign* education and work experience) and employment criteria (*Canadian* education and *Canadian* work experience) (Somerville and Walsworth 2010). Immigrants may be increasingly skilled and highly educated, yet many can't get a break because they can't utilize the very qualifications that facilitated their entry in the first place. Despite this untapped potential of underutilized labour, Canada is experiencing a skills shortage that borders on the scandalous. For example, thousands of foreign-trained doctors cannot gain accreditation to practise in Canada—some 6,500 in Ontario alone according to 2011 Statistics Canada figures (Brennan 2014b). Admittedly, even graduates of Canadian medical schools are experiencing difficulties in accessing residency or full-time jobs: a study by Michael Brandt (cited in Blackwell 2015) found that 78 per cent of ENT (ear, nose, throat) specialists who graduated in 2014 could not find a position, with

another 30 about to come on the market. Yet hundreds of thousands of Canadians must endure gaps in health-care delivery, including many Canadians who cannot find a family doctor but must rely on emergency services or walk-in clinics.[2]

An increasing number of foreign-trained medical graduates are being licensed in Ontario. Compared to 1,646 certificates for Ontario students in 2013, the Ontario College of Physicians and Surgeons of Ontario (2014) issued 1,793 certificates of registration to International Medical Graduates (a more detailed breakdown revealed the following: 707 internationally trained medical graduates were issued a certificate to practise, while 1,086 were issued post-graduate certificates allowing them to move to on-the-job training/residency). With the addition of 5,000 doctors since 2003, it is estimated that 93 per cent of Ontarians now have access to a family physician (Brennan 2014a). Yet appearances are deceiving: as Ontario Fairness Commissioner Jean Augustine points out, only 200 government-funded residency positions exist, most of which are not allocated to foreign-trained applicants but rather to Canadians who have trained abroad and want to return to Ontario (Brennan 2014b). Moreover, a licensing bottleneck persists because accrediting institutions such as the Ontario College of Physicians and Surgeons say they lack the resources to properly assess overseas credentials (Urbanski 2004). Foreign-trained doctors encounter frustrating roadblocks on the road to accreditation, ranging from costly retraining programs to a restricted number of residencies (from two to seven years of training in hospitals upon graduation). And despite a near doubling of residency positions in Ontario for foreign-trained doctors, hurdles seem almost insurmountable. Consider the process involved in becoming licensed for International Medical Graduates, according to the Association of International Physicians and Surgeons of Ontario:

Step 1   An acceptable medical degree from a list of Canadian and international schools

continued

Step 2   Equivalency exams. Must pass the Medical Council of Canada Evaluating Exam

Step 3   Post Graduate Training. Entry into one of the 200 residency training spots (internship)

Step 4   Licentiate of Medical Council of Canada. Must pass qualifying exams 1 and 2, and an evaluation exam

Step 5   Specialty certification. Upon completion of residency, must pass certification

Step 6   Ontario registration. Must be registered/certified by the College of Family Physicians or by the Royal College of Physicians and Surgeons of Canada

Not all foreign-trained medical graduates must jump the hoops to practise in Canada. For example, foreign-trained doctors from the so-called Category 1 countries (New Zealand, Australia, South Africa, England, and the United States) can bypass the internship requirement and practise medicine immediately after an evaluating exam. By contrast, non-category 1 "foreign-trained doctors" must pass equivalence and evaluating exams before applying for a limited number of internship positions. Even Canadian-born students who have trained abroad in non-category countries are defined as foreign-trained by Ontario's medical authorities. They too must compete with the foreign-born for those coveted residency spots at university teaching hospitals. To add insult to injury, a large number of foreign (re)trained doctors cannot practise in Ontario, even after passing all required exams, but are assigned teaching-only placements (Mahoney 2007).

Foreign-born and -trained doctors are not the only ones who must undergo a battery of tests designed to evaluate and upgrade clinical skills. The situation is equally onerous for foreign-trained dentists in search of a certificate to practise in a particular province. They must pass a taxing certification exam before attending a two-year qualifying program at one of five Canadian dental schools that accept foreign-trained dentists. Similarly, foreign-trained lawyers must return to school for up to two years, article with

a law firm, then enter a provincial bar admission program. Engineers of "non-accredited" universities must demonstrate a fixed period of satisfactory practical experience and completion of exam requirements before accreditation. The licensing of professional and regulatory bodies exists ostensibly to ensure competency and protect the public. But the recertification process seems unduly harsh and punitive, especially when rules for qualifications and standards of practice vary from province to province (Cheng, Spaling, and Song 2012; Perkel 2008). Foreign-trained professionals are poorly informed about accreditation procedures prior to entry into Canada, with each province setting a different standard for certification. Many professionals must repeat the educational requirements and undergo costly and time-consuming retraining. Yet accreditation is no guarantee of a job. Canadian employers may be reluctant to hire them because of perceived gaps in their professional knowledge or lack of language skills. Not surprisingly, many are trapped inside a vicious Catch-22 cycle of systemic bias, or as John Samuel (2004) contends:

Employers do not hire foreign-trained people unless they have attained membership in appropriate professional associations while professional associations do not grant membership unless the individual applicant has some proven amount of Canadian work experience.

Or put somewhat differently,

"You can't get a job in your field without Canadian experience, and you can't get that experience without a job." (Naomi Alboim, School of Policy Studies, Queen's University. Cited in Taylor 2005:34).

The federal government has unveiled a series of initiatives to expedite the entry of new Canadians into the job market. In 2007, it established the Canadian Immigrant Integration Program to prepare immigrants for Canada while still in their country of origin. Four years later, 62 per cent of participants found employment within six months of arrival, up from 44 per cent previously (Keung 2011). In the 2007 budget, the federal government established a Foreign Credentials Referral Office to provide prospective immigrants and newcomers with information about the Canadian labour market while helping those trained abroad get their credentials more quickly processed and aligned with the standards for Canadian workers (Alboim and McIsaac 2007). In 2010, the creation of the Pan-Canadian Framework for the Assessment and Recognition of Foreign Qualifications established a set of protocols for assessing foreign credentials in co-operation with the provinces and territories. Under this Economic Action Plan framework, applications in eight priority occupations, including engineering and architecture, will be fast-tracked to ensure recognition within a year, or be advised accordingly. As well, business leaders have vowed to hire more immigrant recruits because, as put by the CEO of the Royal Bank of Canada, "governments can attract skilled immigrants to Canada but, once they arrive, businesses have to pick up the ball. And to date we have not. In fact, we are dropping it" (cited in Abraham 2005).

The situation has not appreciably improved despite promises by the Ontario government to push regulatory bodies toward more "transparent, objective, impartial, and fair" licensing practices. Immigrant professionals are still finding it nearly impossible to penetrate the regulatory barriers to access jobs in fields for which they were trained. According to the study by the Office of the Fairness Commissioner, skilled (professional) immigrants earn about one-half, on average, what their Canadian educated counterparts earn; only 25 per cent have obtained a license to practise in one of Ontario's 37 regulated professions, compared to 60 per cent of Canadian-trained; and 1 in 10 have given up trying to get a professional recertification (Keung 2011). It's worth noting that even Canadian medical graduates have difficulty finding jobs, according to a report by the Royal College of Physicians and Surgeons, with one in six specialized doctors unemployed and 40 per cent unhappy with employment options [Zlomislic 2013]).

The contradiction is palpable: much is made of Canada's loss of highly trained talent (brain drain) into the United States. But Canadians are less likely to acknowledge how Canada is a recipient of a brain gain, thanks to an immigration policy that poaches the best from those countries that can scarcely afford to lose their brightest. For example, many would be shocked to know the percentage of skilled nationals from developing countries who reside in the global north includes 27 per cent of graduates from Western Africa and 41 per cent from the Caribbean regions (for example, the island of Grenada apparently must train 22 physicians to retain the services of one). Researchers who studied nine sub-Saharan countries found those countries spent nearly $2.2 billion training doctors who left for Canada, the United States, Britain, and Australia, thus saving these rich countries billions in training costs (Mills et al. 2011). The net effect of this brain drain dooms these countries to perpetual poverty and poor health (Kapur 2005).

Put bluntly, Canada practises its own version of a great brain robbery. It poaches medical talent from those countries who can least afford the loss of these lifesaving skills (Mills et al. 2011). Worse still, these medical skills may be wasted once the skilled are in Canada (Conference Board of Canada 2004). Criticism is mounting over Canada's inability to effectively integrate professionally trained immigrants into the regulated-professions labour market (PROMPT 2004). After all, to encourage the highly skilled to Canada, then deny them access to good jobs, is an inexcusable waste of human talent. Soon the word will get out that Canada's welcome mat is not what it seems to be. Canada may excel in leveraging immigrants into Canada, but falter in putting them to work in their chosen fields. In the end, the inevitable is inescapable: Canada's underutilized *brain gain* will yield yet another *brain drain* (Kapur 2005).

Putting it into Perspective: Inclusionary Hopes, Exclusionary Realties

The primary concerns of new Canadians are practical and survival related. This pragmatism stands in contrast to the more politicized demands of Canada's founding (Indigenous or Aboriginal) peoples who claim a right to self-determining autonomy over land, identity, and political voice (Maaka and Fleras 2005). Sociologically speaking, immigrants constitute "voluntary people" who are looking for ways of "getting in" and "settling down," unlike forcibly incorporated Aboriginal peoples who want to '"get out" of political arrangements and social structures neither of their making nor of benefit to them (Fleras 2012). Immigrants insist on integration into Canada, albeit through their ethnicity and on their terms, even if this means opting for residence in their own immigrant communities because of convenience or comfort; exerting pressure on institutions to accommodate their difference-based needs and religious identities; insisting on mainstream acceptance of faith and spirituality as a positive dimension of difference; and putting down roots without necessarily severing ties with their cultural tradition and ancestral homelands. More specifically, immigrant needs can be itemized as follows:

1. Meaningful employment in a workplace with opportunity but without discrimination.
2. The expansion of opportunities in the labour and education markets as well as access to housing, government institutions, and social services.
3. Conferral of full citizenship rights, including the right to move, participate, and criticize.
4. Access to the best that Canadian society has to offer without diminishing their children's sense of cultural distinctiveness.
5. The capacity to express their identity without paying a penalty in the process.
6. Respect for their differences as a legitimate and valued part of society.

It goes without saying: immigrants and their descendants want the best both worlds have to offer (Fleras 2012). They want to be treated as individuals and be accepted for their accomplishments instead of being lumped into an amorphous and inchoate mass because of who they are perceived to be. Conversely, they also want respect and appreciation for who they are, culturally speaking, without sacrificing meaningful involvement in society, in effect prompting the plea "Don't judge me by my background but never forget where I came from" (Scheffer 2010:17). Full citizenship rights are important, yet so too is recognition of their cultural worth as humans with a meaningful past and a dynamic present. Successful immigrant integration is contingent on managing change on their own terms and at a pace that takes into account their unique circumstances. Maintaining a strong immigrant identity is critical in making the move from there to here. It provides a buffer of confidence and self-respect for facilitating the settling down process.

But what new Canadians aspire to is not necessarily what they attain (Ng et al. 2013; Chan 2012; McMahon 2013). Their centrality to Canada-building and for growing the economy notwithstanding, racialized immigrants continue to bear the brunt of unequal outcomes, prompting fears of an emergent underclass at odds with Canada's self-image (Black 2013). The resultant exclusion from full and equal participation detracts from Canada's lofty reputation as an immigration society of immigrants. The resulting gap between the much-hyped reference to Canada as a land of opportunity (comforting fiction) versus the inconvenient truth that thousands of immigrants can't find meaningful work is both counterproductive and counter intuitive (Deloitte 2011). Immigrants are robbed of what they can offer to Canada while Canadians are shortchanged in terms of the immigrants' talents, optimism, creativity, and connections (McDonald et al. 2010).

Explaining the Inequality of Exclusions: Ethnicity versus Critical Race Models

How to account for these migrant and minority disparities? How indeed, especially when evidence from the United States suggests less income disparities between newcomers and the American-born, while foreign-born college graduates out-earn their American counterparts?[3] Two theoretical perspectives provide an explanatory framework that accounts for racialized inequality and newcomer exclusion. Functionalists tend to blame inequality on ethnicity and individual shortcomings (the ethnicity paradigm). Conflict theories see the problem as more deeply embedded within institutional structures and opportunity outcomes inherent within a foundationally unequal system (the *critical race paradigm*). The ethnicity paradigm is most closely linked with a blaming-the-individual model; by contrast, the critical race paradigm reflects a blaming-the-system model. How then do the blaming models stack up against each other?

1. Some argue newcomers are largely responsible for the predicament in which they find themselves. Studies suggest labour market conditions may account for 40 per cent of decline in newcomer earnings since the 1980s (from local labour market supply and demand to declining returns on educational qualifications and overseas work experience to a mismatch of immigrant skills with the needs of a changing economy). Contributing to this malaise are changes in the labour market because of economic globalization, the interplay of outsourcing and downsizing, and knowledge-based economies. But the remaining 60 per cent reflect variations in the human capital of immigrants (such as the lack of Canadian experience) (Jedwab 2012). Of particular salience is proficiency in one of Canada's two official languages (Tal 2012). Most studies conclude that the strongest predictor of economic and labour market success is neither credentials nor degrees, but competencies in one of Canada's two official languages. Yet many immigrants from the non-economic admission class have neither French nor English as a first language (nearly 27 per cent in 2010 [CIC 2011; Simmons 2010]).
2. Others prefer an alternative narrative. If immigrants are doing badly, the fault must be structural and systemic, and Canada is to blame because of changes to immigrants and their mother tongue with the shift in source countries since the 1960s; declining returns to foreign work experiences and educational levels among non-European immigrants; and a general decline in labour market outcomes for labour entrants where immigrants are treated as new entries in competition with a growing pool of highly educated Canadian graduates (Aydemir and Skuterud 2004; Statistics Canada 2006). Newcomers are held back by a host of structural factors, including subtle discriminatory hiring practices (Oreopoulos 2009); the changing composition of immigrants and the attendant racism toward newcomers (Fleras 2014a); a reluctance or resistance on the part of employers to evaluate foreign credentials and educational degrees (credential devaluation); a corresponding discounting of foreign skills (skills discounting) because of biased assessments; unrealistic and unnecessary job requirements (Sakamoto et al. 2013); a vicious cycle of lowered expectations leading to lower achievement; and a poisoned or hostile work environment (Saloojee 2003; Biles and Burstein 2003; Foster 2011).

Ethnicity (Blame the Individual) Model

Not long ago, references to racial(ized) stratification were couched within the discursive framework of an ethnicity paradigm (Porter 1965; Fleras 2012). Canadian society was envisaged as an open and competitive marketplace in which individuals competed as equals and were rewarded because of their skills or production. Individual success or failure reflected a person's level of human capital: those with training, skills, and education succeeded; those without, did not. Ethnic differences were pivotal. To one side, immigrant minorities had to discard the debilitating aspects of their ethnicity that precluded participation. To the other side, those in charge also had to discard those prejudgments that precluded inclusiveness. Inception of a multiculturalism policy in 1971 sought to remove prejudice from the workplace by ensuring people's differences did not get in the way of success, acceptance, or participation. It also sought to depoliticize ethnicity by neutralizing its salience as a basis for public recognition and reward (Fleras 2009).

According to functionalist perspectives, a lack of expertise (or credentials) or adjustments accounts for the failure of migrants and minorities to penetrate the market. Efforts to boost their "human capital" would focus on improving minority "skills" consistent with labour market demands. Ethnocultural deficits are no less a deterrent to minority success. As John Porter argued in his landmark book, *The Vertical Mosaic*, ethnicity matters. It represents a key variable in predicting who will get what, with non-British and non-French ethnic groups at the bottom of a vertical ranking (also Helmes-Hayes and Curtis 1998; Clement and Helmes-Hayes 2015). Of particular relevance for Porter were those cultural values—from a lack of work ethic to kinship obligations—at odds with upward mobility and occupational performance. Clearly, becoming modern was key. To secure success, migrants and minorities had to discard their unmodern attachments and assimilate by embracing modernist values, even if doing so could risk alienation from a supportive community of like-minded kin (Porter called this dilemma the *ethnic mobility trap*). To be sure, the specifics of this explanatory framework are no longer applicable. Nevertheless, differences continue to matter in defining who gets what except that now Canada's ethnic vertical mosaic is racialized (i.e., colour-coded) (Teelucksingh and Galabuzi 2005).

The Critical Race (Blaming the System) Model

The concept of inequality underwent a paradigm shift from the 1980s onward. Attainment of **formal equality** rights failed to generate the increased equality of outcome that many had anticipated. Hardly surprising: after all, racialized minorities may have possessed the same formal rights as all Canadians, but they had to exercise these equality rights in deeply Eurocentric contexts that neither reflected nor advanced their interests or experiences. As a result, treating unequals as equals was deemed a form of inequality in its own right for failure to take into account specific needs in a society where no one begins from the same starting point and the playing field is infrastructurally unlevel. In applying the metaphor of a competitive footrace

with staggered starting blocks, not all contestants are equally positioned to compete in the labour market. The race is rigged because of ascribed characteristics that handicap some because of skin colour or gender differences, while advantaging others for precisely the same reasons. This notion is aptly captured in the words of Lyndon B. Johnson, former president of the United States, in a speech justifying the legitimacy of affirmative action:

> You do not wipe away the scars of centuries by saying, "now you are free to go where you want, do as you desire, and choose the leaders you please." You do not take a man who for years has been hobbled by chains , liberate him, bring him to the start of the race saying, "You are free to compete with others," and still justly believe you have been completely fair. (Lyndon B. Johnson, 4 June 1965, Howard University)

A conceptual shift in rethinking inequality reflected a corresponding "influx" of racialized immigrants from developing countries. Individual attributes such as prejudice and ethnicity as the source of the inequality problem gave way to an emphasis on discriminatory barriers and racism at both individual and institutional levels. Multicultural commitments that focused on ethnicity no longer resonated with relevance in a Canada of "deeper diversities." Proposed instead were new racialized discourses carried along by the principle of institutional inclusion, removal of racism and discriminatory barriers at structural levels, and eradication of a normative whiteness that underpins a **systemic white supremacy** (Fleras 2014a). The rooting of the problem within the institutional *structures* of society was pivotal (Skaggs and Bridges 2013). Inequality and barriers to advancement reflected structural constraints that were largely systemic in advancing pale male interests. That is, while the system pretends to be value-neutral under the guise of universality and colour-blindness, a foundationally unlevel playing field puts racialized minorities at a structural disadvantage. References to inequality shifted accordingly, from a focus on individuals to a focus on structure, from ethnicity to race, from equality

Table 7.7: Explaining Migrant/Minority Inequality: Ethnicity versus Critical Race Models

	Ethnicity Model	Critical Race Model
Problem	Individuals "blaming the victim"	Institutional structures "blaming the system"
Root cause	Personal deficiencies	Discriminatory barriers
Focus of solution	Increase human capital	Improve institutional inclusiveness
Means of solution	Market forces	Government intervention
Sociological perspective	Functionalism	Conflict perspectives
Animating logic	"Change the conventions that refer to the rules."	"Change the rules that inform the conventions."
Intended goal	Equality/inclusion	Equity/inclusivity

of opportunity to equal outcomes, from inclusion to inclusivity, and from a commitment to formal (abstract) equality to that of substantive equality (**equity**)—as detailed in Table 7.7.

A blame-the-system approach to the inequalities of exclusion is consistent with the dynamics of a racialized model. This **critical race model** of inequality begins with the assumption there is no such thing as a neutral/colour-blind society. Human societies are socially created yet carefully concealed constructions whose founding principles, deliberately or inadvertently (systemically), reflect, reinforce, and advance the realities, experiences, and interests of the dominant sector. The values, ideals, and priorities of those who created or control society are deeply embedded in the governance, institutions, and founding assumptions. The premises and principles of a society's constitutional order are designed, organized, and operated in ways that

promote mainstream priorities without people's awareness of the systemic bias at play. Dominant interpretations of reality are defined as normal and necessary as well as desirable and acceptable, while those of the non-dominant sectors are dismissed as irrelevant or are demonized as inferior or threatening. The result is a racialized society: ideas and ideals of what is acceptable or desirable promote mainstream **Eurocentric**/white interests over those of other racialized groups. Equal rights may remove the legal barriers to individual achievement, but such a formality conveniently ignores that in a racialized society there is no such thing as a level playing field and no one starts from the same starting place (also Burke 2012). Clearly then, *colour-blind society* is a contradiction in terms, at least in the foundational sense of the term, since a Euro-systemic bias will continue to matter in defining who gets what, why they get it, and how.

Summary

1. The chapter surveyed the patterns and politics of racialized inequality and immigrant exclusions as they apply to migrants and minorities in Canada.
2. Canada's lofty status in progressively managing diversity is compromised by the persistent exclusion of migrants and minorities.
3. Just as inequalities for women tend to be gendered (rather than just gender inequality), so too are inequalities racialized as a reflection of systemically biasing structures that deny, exclude, or exploit (i.e., are structurally embedded).
4. The magnitude of racialized inequality and immigrant exclusion was examined

at the level of income, poverty, and (un)employment.

5. Structural exclusions are experienced by newcomers to Canada throughout the adjustment cycle in terms of settling down, fitting in, and moving up.

6. The accreditation process in licensed occupations such as medicine or engineering is stacked against skilled newcomers.

7. Two explanatory models of social inequality—ethnicity versus critical race theory—account for migrant and minority exclusions.

Review Questions

1. Why does the chapter use the expression *racialized inequality* instead of the more popular expression *racial inequality*?
2. Discuss patterns of racialized inequality in terms of income, employment, and poverty levels.
3. Indicate why new Canadians are experiencing difficulty in making an economic adjustment to Canada. Also indicate in your answer why newcomers with professional degrees and skills are experiencing difficulties in having their skills and degrees recognized (accredited).
4. Discuss the challenges that confront new Canadians as they attempt to settle down, fit in, and move up.
5. Compare the ethnicity versus the critical race models in accounting for the inequalities of exclusions experienced by migrants and minorities.

Endnotes

1. The term *non-racialized white* is used to avoid confusion. Technically speaking, however, whites are racialized as well (i.e., assigned a racial category), suggesting the expression *racialized whites* (or *racialized majority*) as more appropriate but also more cumbersome. Excluding whites from a racialized discourse is tantamount to excluding males from reference to gender even though it's obvious that it takes (at least) two to gender.
2. The video *The Big Wait* is highly recommended for exposing a very Canadian paradox: foreign-trained physicians who want to work while many parts of rural Canada are desperate for medical staff.
3. Keep in mind the comparison may be invalid. Unlike Canada, the United States possesses a very restrictive approach to the admission of skilled workers. Employer-sponsored visas for skilled workers (i.e., an immigrant needs a job offer to qualify for immigration) ensures a high level of employment and remuneration in contrast to Canada's open ended (sink or swim) approach.

8 Aboriginal Peoples: Canada's First Inequality

Learning Objectives

1. To understand how and why Aboriginal peoples as a group rank at the bottom of Canada's socio-economic ladder.

2. To survey the range of social inequality problems within aboriginal communities without neglecting a slew of success stories.

3. To show how three explanatory frameworks provide contrasting models that account for aboriginal inequality and exclusion.

4. To explain why addressing Canada's first inequality hinges on repairing a broken relationship.

5. To point out how the principles of constructive engagement may secure a post-colonial governance model for relations repair.

Introduction: First Nations, Second Class Citizens, Third World Conditions

Let's situate the status of Canada's **Aboriginal peoples** against a global backdrop. Canada may be perennially ranked by UN measures as one of the world's best places to live. But if Canada's on-reserve peoples are disaggregated from the population and assessed independently, according to a human development index, Canada's global ranking plummets into the 70s–80s range. That Aboriginal peoples live shorter lives in often substandard conditions puts aboriginal communities on par with medium-developing countries such as Mexico and Thailand. No less jarring are patterns of poverty and powerlessness shockingly inconsistent with Canadian values and overall standards of living (Palmeter 2015). Factor in deplorable levels

of violence turned inwards (suicide) and outwards (homicide)—nine of Canada's ten most violent communities are aboriginal according to Statistics Canada's violent crime index—and what emerges is a toxic cocktail of depression, disarray, and destruction (McMahon 2014). These and other data are a blistering indictment of Canada's inability to address the so-called "Indian problem" (or perhaps, more accurately, the *Indians' Canada problem*). To add insult to injury, various human rights committees such as the UN Special Rapporteur on the rights of indigenous peoples have roundly criticized Canada's mistreatment of Aboriginal peoples as a hidden shame; contrary to international law; and its most egregious human rights violation (Anaya 2014; Fontaine and Farber 2013; Olson 2013). Despite this condemnation at international levels, a general commitment for improving the standard of living for Aboriginal peoples remains mired near the bottom of a national to-do list (Nanos 2012).

No matter how they are evaluated or assessed, Aboriginal peoples as a group cluster near the bottom of the socio-economic heap (Frideres and Gadacz 2012; Cooke and McWhirter 2010; Douglas and Lenon 2014; Manuel and Derrickson 2015). Aboriginal communities comprise 92 of Canada's poorest 100 communities, based on a community well-being index (income, housing, employment, and education). (Note: Aboriginal is capitalized when referring to Aboriginal peoples as a nation, otherwise the lower case is employed). Child poverty is punitively high, including 40 per cent of indigenous children in Canada according to a report by the Canadian Centre for Policy Alternatives based on 2011 data (Macdonald and Wilson 2016). Just over one-half of status Indian children live in poverty (using an after-tax LIM measure), a figure that increases to 60 per cent for on reserve status Indian children, rising to 76 per cent in Manitoba and 69 per cent in Saskatchewan. The figures for non-status First Nation children are 30 per cent, for Inuit children, 25 per cent, and Metis children, 23 per cent. Compounding the poverty problem is the housing situation on many reserves, which fails to provide basic amenities such as sewer outlets and clean water connections. For example, in what must amount to a contradiction of baffling proportions, aboriginal communities across Canada confront a host of water-related problems, despite Canada's status as one of the world's premier fresh water sources (Beaton 2013). In July 2015, Health Canada issued 133 drinking water advisories in 126 First Nations communities, with 93 of these advisories having been in place for two years or more (editorial, *The Globe and Mail* 2015). Remote reserves such as Marten Falls First Nations, 500 km north of Thunder Bay, continue to rely on flown-in bottled water since Health Canada imposed a boil-water advisory a decade ago (Angus 2014). Almost 80 per cent of homes on the Six Nations Reserve near Brantford, Ontario, have no access to water lines but rely on wells or cisterns, although 86 per cent of these sources are contaminated, mostly from agricultural field runoff or buried contaminated waste (Pecoskie 2013). The potable water crisis is not exclusive to this locale. About half of Ontario's aboriginal communities remain on water boil alert, while the federal government confirmed in 2011 that about 75 per cent of water systems on aboriginal reserves posed high or medium risk to human health (Health Canada 2013).

Good health and access to health care services pose a problem (Wilk and Cooke 2015; Allan and Smylie 2015; Wynne and Currie 2011). On-reserve peoples are exposed to an array of serious health problems more reminiscent of depressed communities in the global south (McMahon 2014; Statistics Canada 2013b). Compared to non-aboriginal Canadians, they are more likely to suffer chronic ailments, addiction and substance abuse, higher obesity and diabetes rates, and chronic food shortages. A study of Inuit families in Arctic Quebec found that hunger and food insecurity was so severe that half the children scored below average in height (Trovato and Romaniuk 2014; Pirkle 2014). Despite these adverse conditions, many residents are reluctant to abandon reserves for fear of losing band entitlements, resulting in what critics call "subsidies-to-stay" programs whose perverse effects are thought to foster an unhealthy dependence (Flanagan 2001; Fiss 2004)—including a third of the aboriginal population who rely on social assistance (McMahon 2014). The lives and life chances of those living off-reserve are also under pressure. Urban aboriginal folk encounter patterns of discrimination in accessing housing, employment, education, and social services that, frankly, pose an embarrassment to a country that touts its tolerance (Reputation Institute 2015).

Equally worrying is the ticking demographic time bomb in many aboriginal communities. The combination of a relatively high (albeit declining) birth rate with a youthful population puts pressure on divvying up limited reserve resources such as housing and jobs. (This shortage of space and employment [in addition to the preservation of cultural tradition] is thought to justify the Kahnawake Mohawk decision to expel from the community those Mohawk who marry non-Mohawk—the "marry out, get out" ruling.) The aboriginal population is much younger (average age, 28 years) than the non-aboriginal population (41 years average). Just under 400,000 children are aged 14 and under (or 28 per cent of the total aboriginal population), with fewer than half (49.6 per cent) living in a domestic arrangement that includes both parents (biological or adoptive). Aboriginal children represent nearly one-half of the 30,000 children in Canadian foster care (Statistics Canada 2013b; Metis Nation of Ontario 2013; Johnson, Faille, and Barr 2013). Economic projections do not bode well: the fact that the aboriginal population is relatively younger and has fewer educational qualifications and less labour market experience exposes the vulnerability of this demographic to economic slumps and job layoffs (Delic and Abele 2010). The awkward location of many reserves combined with their limited resources constrains the prospect of employment or development. Other locations are more fortunate, thanks to Supreme Court rulings and comprehensive land settlements, and should be able to cash in on Canada's natural resource boom through joint ventures (Coates and Crowley 2013; Poelzer and Coates 2015). With rates over double the national average, unemployment is a major cause of poverty and powerlessness. The jobless rate for non-aboriginal Canadians was 6 per cent in 2011, whereas the aboriginal unemployment rate stood at 13 per cent and 22 per cent for those living on reserves (DePratto 2015; also National Aboriginal Economic Development Board 2015). In 2011, according to the National Household Survey, the employment rate for non-aboriginal Canadians was 76 per cent, whereas the figure for aboriginal populations was 63 per cent, but 55 per cent for those on reserves (DePratto 2015; also National Aboriginal Economic Development Board 2015 which pegged on-reserve employment at 35.4 per cent). Even these figures are misleading: on some reserves, up to 95 per cent of the population are so un/underemployed that government transfers are primary income sources.

Income inequality poses a problem for those persons disproportionately ranked among the poorest in Canada (Wilson and Macdonald 2010; Pendakur and Pendakur 2011; AANDC 2013). According to the 2015 National Aboriginal Economic Development Board Report, the *median* income for Aboriginal peoples in 2010 was $20,701 or 30 per cent less than the median income for non-aboriginal Canadians ($30,195). *Average* incomes in 2010 were no less glaring: on-reserve income—$18,586; off-reserve—$30,226; and non-aboriginal—$41,052

(see Friesen 2015 for comparable data in Alberta). Those who live off reserve tend to do better than those on reserves (National Aboriginal Economic Development Board 2015): in a study that looked at wage growth between 2007 and 2014 (DePratto 2015), aboriginal males who lived off-reserve earned a weekly wage of $973 in 2014, compared to $1,024 for non-aboriginal males, whereas off-reserve aboriginal women earned $697 per week compared to $773 for non-aboriginal women. Gender differences are notable: data from Pendakur and Pendakur (2011) concluded that income and earning gaps for aboriginal women from 1995 to 2005 were 10 to 20 per cent lower than for non-aboriginal women of British origin, controlling for age and education. (Registered Indian women fared worst, followed by non-status Indian women and Metis women, with Inuit women the exception.) For aboriginal men, the income and earning gap was about 20 to 50 per cent below the figure for non-aboriginal males of British origins with similar age and education characteristics, but the gap for non-status Indians and Metis men was significantly less (10 to 20 per cent bracket) (Pendakur and Pendakur 2011). Higher education levels matter, although even highly educated aboriginal persons confront an income gap relative to the mainstream population (Wilson and Macdonald 2010; AANDC 2013). Moreover, far fewer aboriginal individuals possess degrees; according to Delic and Abele (2010), 43.6 per cent of the total aboriginal identity population had less than high school education in 2006. By 2011, 48.4 per cent possessed post-secondary qualification, including 9.8 per cent with a university degree. By contrast, the comparable figures for the non-aboriginal population stood at 67.4 per cent and 26.5 per cent respectively (Statistics Canada 2013e). A Catch-22 is at play: attainment of higher education may secure an escape from dire straits (Richards and Scott 2009; Widdowson and Albert 2013), but it is precisely the straitened circumstances of those with low socio-economic status that makes them least likely to possess the resources or resourcefulness to capitalize on educational opportunities (Mendelson 2006).

The interplay of powerlessness and poverty spurs inner- and outer-directed violence. Domestic abuse is endemic in aboriginal communities according to Dawn Harvard, president of Ontario Native Women's Association, with many aboriginal women victims of extreme violence (LSC 2015; Hill 2012; also Samuelson 2012). Nearly 21 per cent of the population experienced spousal violence compared to 6 per cent for the non-aboriginal population; not surprisingly, few aboriginal children grow into adulthood without first-hand experience of interpersonal violence (Drost et al. 1995; Government of Canada 2010 [see also Chapter 6]). Aboriginal peoples not only suffer trauma-induced injuries and violent deaths at four times the rate in Canada (Picard 2012), they also represent one of the most self-destructive groups in the world at present, with a suicide rate of six to eight times the national average for age-specific groups, including 126 per 100,000 for aboriginal males compared to 24 per 100,000 for non-aboriginal males; and 35 per 100,000 for aboriginal women compared to 5 per 100,000 for non-aboriginal women. Remote communities are particularly vulnerable to deprivations that speak volumes of lives that are nasty, brutish, and short (Taylor 2015). In Davis Inlet, Labrador, the Innu suicide rate is the equivalent of 178 per 100,000 of an admittedly small population base, in contrast to the Canadian average of about 11 per 100,000 of population. (The tiny Baltic country of Lithuania has the dubious distinction of ranking first in the world in suicide, at 35 per 100,000.) Nunavut's suicide rate is 15 times the Canadian average (with most suicides involving single, unemployed, and poorly educated men), even though suicides were rare prior to the 1980s (Alexander 2014). Or consider Pikangikum, a small reserve with just over 2,000 residents about 300 kilometres northeast of Winnipeg. A suicide rate of 250 per 100,000 in 2011 (note, a small sample can grossly inflate ratios) has led the British suicide expert Colin Sampson to label Pikangikum Canada's (or even the world's) suicide capital (Patriquin 2012).

The devastation of suicide goes beyond immediate family. The entire community is ripped apart by the ripple effect of trauma that can destroy closely knit groups (Patriquin 2012). The absence of protective factors amplifies the feasibility of suicidal tendencies in dysfunctional communities that often serve as incubators for youth

suicides (Chandler and Lalonde 1998). Studies in Canada and abroad indicate the importance of good **governance** (including both rule of law and property rights) in creating positive conditions for economic development (Cornell and Kalt 2003; Flanagan and Beauregard 2013; MacDonald, J. 2014). Communities with some form of self-government arrangement displayed the lowest suicide rates, followed by communities with settled land claims and educational services. The lack of effective parenting has also contributed to this breakdown in community life. But dysfunctional parenting itself may reflect earlier negative experiences, ranging from intergenerational poverty cycles to the painful legacy of residential schools. The situation is exacerbated when combined with feasibility factors related to a lack of opportunity, boredom and despair, confused identities, and a dearth of positive role models to assist in meeting life's challenges. A void in which emptiness and ennui induces anti-social behaviour (Richard Wagamese [2013] defines ennui as a kind of life-long tiredness and disinterest, a relentless feeling of nothingness, and a pattern of giving up because nothing is possible and nobody cares) remains the lot of those aboriginal youth who are excluded from mainstream society yet alienated from an idealized version of traditional life—that is, strung between two cultures yet psychologically in neither (Royal Commission on Aboriginal Peoples 1996). The conclusion is inescapable: communities that fail to provide boundaries and coping skills are ticking time bombs.

Violent crime victimization is of pandemic proportions (Monture 2011). Aboriginal peoples are victimized at a rate of 319 per 1,000 population, including 461 per 1,000 for those in the 15 to 34 age bracket, compared to 101 per 1,000 for non-aboriginal Canadians (Government of Canada 2010). Almost one-quarter (23 per cent) of Canada's 516 homicide victims in 2014 were reported by police as aboriginal—six times the rate for the non-aboriginal population. Aboriginal males were at greatest risk (10.86 per 100,000 versus 1.61 per 100,000 for non-aboriginal males and 3.64 for aboriginal women [Statistics Canada 2015]). Nearly one-third (32 per cent) of the 431 persons accused of homicide in 2014 were aboriginal. Of particular concern are shockingly high imprisonment rates: although aboriginals make up just over 4 per cent of Canada's population, aboriginal offenders account for 25.4 per cent of federal penitentiary admission, including 48 per cent of federal inmates in the Prairie provinces (Sapers 2016). Among female offenders, 36 per cent of federally sentenced offenders are aboriginal. By contrast, according to Correctional Investigator of Canada Howard Sapers (2016), the country's prison ombudsperson, only 10 per cent of federal inmates were of aboriginal ancestry 30 years ago. Provincial incarceration rates for aboriginal women are even more alarming, making up 80 per cent of admissions in Saskatchewan, despite comprising a small percentage of that province's population (Samuelson 2012; Roberts and Melchers 2003). Young aboriginal men aged 12 to 17 represent about 3 per cent of the young males in Ontario; yet they account for 15 per cent of the male admissions to the youth facilities (Sapers 2013). Worse still, those with prison records may be doubly penalized in the search for legitimate post-prison employment (also Alexander 2012). That on-reserve aboriginal youth are more likely to do jail time than to graduate from high school is a scathing indictment of the exclusions at play. And yet the federal government appears reluctant to invest in programs to rehabilitate federal aboriginal offenders (for example, Correctional Services employs 19,000 workers, yet only 12 are assigned to work with aboriginal inmates [Sapers 2013]).

To be sure, these incarceration figures have prompted a response on the judicial front. The Gladue Supreme Court decision of 1999 ruled the courts had to take **aboriginality** into account when sentencing aboriginal offenders, including disadvantaging factors such as colonialism, domestic abuse, dislocation, unemployment, and racism. The federal government's Aboriginal Justice Strategy is also contingent on "doing it differently" by using alternative sentencing strategies informed by the holistic and healing principles of restorative **justice**. But principles and promises aside, incarceration remains the response of first resort in dealing with social problems (Sapers 2013; see also Davis 1998). These inequalities of exclusions—including unemployment, poverty,

mental illness, substance abuse, and endemic violence—are often concealed from (or disappear from) public view when conveniently lumped together under the default category of *crime*, the automatic linking of criminal behaviour to a marginalized peoples, and the warehousing of "criminals" in prisons. The criminalization of Aboriginal peoples is further intensified when civil actions to protect lands, water, resources, and rights from clearcutting, hydro-fracking, or pipelines are blocked by RCMP intervention and enforcement (Palmeter 2015). But as Angela Davis (and others such as Alexander 2012) conclude in response to skyrocketing rates of black imprisonment in the United States (nearly 2 million people are locked in America's private-for-profit prison system, eight times the number from as recently as 30 years ago, with 70 per cent consisting of people of colour, mainly blacks and Native Americans): "*prisons do not disappear problems, they disappear humans.*"

Demoralizing data on the socio-economic front should not distract from more hopeful narratives (Long and Dickason 2011; Saul 2014). Not all indicators on the aboriginal front are distress signals: aboriginal communities increasingly play the role of economic drivers who are cashing in on developments in energy, forestry, and mining resources, and earnings as landlords of on-reserve condos and high-end golf resorts (Coates and Crowley 2013; Poelzer and Coates 2015). Few developments have shown as much potential in advancing aboriginal empowerment as the Tsilhqot'in decision in late June 2014, which marked the first time a Canadian court legally recognized aboriginal land title based on tribal traditional use and control of the lands (IWGIA 2015). Things look more promising at the educational level (Statistics Canada 2013e; Parkin 2015). Aboriginal education outcomes based on 2011 Census data (Richards 2014) indicate that those aged 20–24 who identified as Metis and off-reserve peoples attained higher rates of secondary school graduation than they did in 2005. Nevertheless, the non-completion rate for this demographic is still three times higher than for non-aboriginal youth. For on-reserve aboriginal youth, the non-completion rate is 58 per cent higher (with provincial variations)—with little improvement since

2006. Nor should all communities be tarred as dysfunctional, despite media coverage to this effect (also Newhouse et al. 2012). For example, although many communities experience punishing rates of suicide, other communities, such as those with a solid governance structure in place, appear relatively immune to the scourge of violence turned inward (Chandler and Lalonde 1998; Alcantara and Whitfield 2010). Finally, not all Aboriginal peoples are destined to fail, even when measured by Eurocentric standards. Nor should success be evaluated exclusively along mainstream lines. There is no shortage of aboriginal individuals who possess secure and satisfying prospects and enriched lives without rejecting one or both cultures—as demonstrated in the Spotlight box below.

Spotlight Robust Economic Growth in "Indian" Country: Osoyoos Indian Band

Aboriginal communities are not unaccustomed to success stories. Aboriginal economic growth is impressive and critical to Canada's future prosperity (the National Aboriginal Economic Development Board 2015; also Newhouse et al. 2012). Aboriginal land base has grown to 3.2 million ha, a 25 per cent increase since 1990, thanks to the infusion of revenue from successful land claim settlements (Alcantara 2013). As pointed out by Bill Gallagher (2012), lawyer and author, aboriginal claimants have won over 150 court case victories involving control or ownership of resources and projects vital to Canada's economic future (also Ivison 2012). The surge in aboriginal enterprises and entrepreneurs is unmistakable: from airline companies and construction firms to wineries and technology consulting firms, aboriginal entrepreneurship is thriving like never before, according to Roberta Jamieson, CEO of the National Aboriginal Achievement Foundation (Freeland 2010). This includes 37,000 aboriginal owned and operated businesses (First Nations, Metis, and Inuit), according to the 2006 Census, in addition to 50 financial institutions, and an aboriginal trust company and bank (Grant 2013). Clearly, then, Aboriginal peoples have arrived as a natural resource superpower in Canada. That kind of clout exerts pressure to establish an equal economic partnership involving power-sharing and meaningful participation in which aboriginal communities benefit from the value created by their ownership, involvement, and expertise (Coates and Crowley 2013).

The list of success stories includes the Membertou First Nation, which employed a strategic approach to economic development and self-government (NCFNG 2010). But few have achieved the level of accomplishment as the Osoyoos Indian Band. Situated on 32,000 acres of prime real estate in the Okanagan region with a population of about 400, the Osoyoos Indian Band is one of seven bands that comprise the Okanagan Nation of British Columbia. Under the leadership of Chief Clarence Louie, a commitment to create community-based economic self-sufficiency has paid dividends through a series of profitable economic projects in agriculture, eco-tourism, and commercial, industrial, and residential enterprises (Louie and Matahbee 2015). The annual net benefits of $26 million in business revenue and $2.5 million in profits have proven beneficial in eliminating unemployment for the 520 band members (MacDonald 2014). Successful business ventures include a multimillion dollar expansion of a resort golf course, a partnership with Vincor (Canada's largest wine producer), and joint ventures with the timber industry. In addition to financial independence as a basis for preserving tradition and culture, the band operates its own business, health, social, educational, and municipal services. The conclusion seems convincing: the combination of tools, vision, and commitment, coupled with good governance (from removing mismanagement to instituting sound corporate structures) can translate into sustained economic development and cultural renewal (MacDonald 2014; NCFNG 2010).

The conclusion is inescapable: the impoverishment that confronts Aboriginal peoples is a blistering indictment of an unequal status quo. An unacceptable number endure punitive conditions that evoke gut-wrenching images of grinding developing-world poverty and the powerlessness of the underclass. Aboriginal peoples tend to score poorly on those indicators that positively count, yet monopolize those indicators that do negatively count, with only intermittent flashes of improvement to disrupt the tally. The aftermath of **colonialism** continues to infuse and distort the lives of Aboriginal peoples who also remain victimized by racism and racial discrimination (Truth and Reconciliation Commission Report 2015; Paul 2012). To be sure, there are risks in framing Aboriginal peoples only as "problem people" who have or create problems of inequality. Framing aboriginality as comprising "troublesome constituents" tends to gloss over the broader context of colonization, its ongoing legacy, and pervasiveness at present (Simpson 2013; Warry 2009; Coulthard 2014). References to Aboriginal peoples as "problem people" may also reinforce stereotypes that do little to improve public empathy (Harding 2010). But a number of questions about the origins, causes, and persistence of aboriginal inequalities follow, especially when the socio-economic status of Canada's Aboriginal peoples (as well as of the Maori tribes of Aotearoa/New Zealand and the First Australians) showed negligible improvement between 1981 and 2006 in employment, education, and income (Cooke et al. 2014). It also speaks volumes about the need for new approaches to recast the relationship.

1. What is the root cause of inequality problems within aboriginal communities? Individuals (blaming the victim) or society (blaming the system)? Insiders or outsiders? Too much external pressure from **assimilation** or not enough? An excessive amount of autonomy or not enough? If the source of the problem is a broken relationship between Canada and Aboriginal peoples, what must be done to repair the relation?
2. Who ultimately is responsible for solving the inequality problem of social exclusion? If it is a so-called Indian problem, should responsibility rest with aboriginal persons and communities? If it is a white problem, surely Canada is responsible for taking charge. If the problem is a mutual one—a "white–Indian" problem—a two-way process of negotiated compromises and mutual adjustment offers possibilities.
3. Politics of redistribution or politics of recognition? Should solutions focus on modernizing aboriginal communities (to become more mainstream-like) through economic development, even if traditional practices are compromised in the process? Should economic development be postponed to make room for political solutions that focus on indigenous-controlled levels of self-determining autonomy over land, identity, and political choice (to be *less* mainstream-like)? Will a business model of development (with its focus on jobs, income, and start-ups) prove more sustainable than a political model based on nation-building (Graham and Levesque 2010; Cornell and Kalt 2003)?
4. Should solutions to inequalities of poverty, ill health, educational failure, and family violence proceed on an incremental (piecemeal) basis? Or should solutions recognize how these problems mutually reinforce each other so that they must be tackled together to disrupt the cycle of cascading disadvantages, where family violence leads to educational failures leads to poverty leads to ill health and back again (Centre for Social Justice 2010)?
5. Should change focus on the conventions that refer to the rules or focus on changing the rules that inform the conventions? Is it best to work within the system and through conventional channels in addressing aboriginal inequality and exclusion? Or are these inequalities and exclusions so deeply woven into the founding assumptions and foundational principles of Canada's colonial constitutional order that any escape from this inequality gridlock is profoundly transformational?

These questions represent a powerful indictment of the challenges in store. Contradictions and gridlocks abound: James Anaya (2014), the UN special rapporteur on Indigenous people rights, commends Canada for making significant progress on aboriginal issues, including constitutional recognition of aboriginal rights, processes in place to resolve land claims, and steps to repair the legacy of historical injustices. Yet this country faces a deeply entrenched crisis when it comes to the depressed socio-economic situation of Aboriginal peoples, despite increased wealth and prosperity in Canada; unresolved treaty and land claims and human rights violations despite laws and protections; and persistent levels of aboriginal distrust toward federal and provincial governments despite initiatives to repair the relationship. Or as John Ralston Saul (2014) argues in his book *The Comeback*, the growing power and prosperity of Canada's Aboriginal peoples was offset by the Harper government's Victorian-era mentality to aboriginal affairs and the appropriation of indigenous lands. And yet, however formidable the challenges that confront and confound aboriginal communities, there is so little agreement over a crisis so formidable in its reach and depth that nobody knows where to begin (McMahon 2014). For some, Aboriginal peoples are widely thought to have brought inequality on themselves by choosing to live in regions of little employment on remote and barren reserves whose traditional economies cannot possibly thrive and new economic opportunities cannot take root. Others rightly believe the legacy and impact of colonialism (from legislated segregation to systemic violence) is driving an exclusionary wedge (Wilson and Macdonald 2010). Actions easily defined as crimes against humanity (or even genocide), such as starving Aboriginal peoples into submission, played a key role in Canada-building (Daschuk 2013; MacDonald, Dan, and Farber 2015). The lasting trauma of the residential school system (see the Spotlight box in Chapter 10) has scarred generations of aboriginal adults and parents, with a corresponding impact on children at present (Truth and Reconciliation Commission Report 2015). The erosion of aboriginal land, identity and culture, and political voice under (neo-)colonialism has made it abundantly clear: the dispossession of Indigenous peoples and the perpetuation of colonial power continues to be masked by the conferral of entitlements and accommodation of demands within the framework of the Canadian state (Coulthard 2014).

Finally, over a century of patronizing submission and paternalistic servitude has instilled a host of psychological barriers and social impediments that amplify patterns of helplessness, powerlessness, and hopelessness (Adams 1999; Alfred 2005; Cannon and Sunseri 2011).

This chapter addresses and explains the nature and scope of inequality and exclusions that inform the lives and life chances of Canada's Aboriginal peoples. The chapter argues that a broken relationship anchors the root of aboriginal inequality; accordingly, this relationship requires a major overhaul ("relations repair") if there is any hope of a co-operative and equitable coexistence. Two themes prevail. First, in theory, Canada may possess a well-developed legal framework and positive policy moves that are protective of Aboriginal peoples' rights; in reality, however, the numerous initiatives have failed to address socio-economic problems and have generated increasing levels of distrust toward federal and provincial governments (Anaya 2014; Manuel and Derrickson 2015). Second, the directly coercive rule of the past 150 years has given way to more indirect (neo-colonial) governance whose political, economic, and psychological structures—despite appearances to the contrary—continue to co-opt, appropriate, and marginalize (Coulthard 2014). The chapter begins by examining three competing governance models (assimilationism, autonomism, and accommodationism) that purport to explain why aboriginal inequalities exist; how a malfunctioning relationship between Aboriginal peoples and Canada generated and continues to generate the inequities of exclusion; and what must be done to repair this relationship. The preconditions for relations repair are explored next. The principles of constructive engagement demonstrate the possibility of a new **post-colonial** governance model as a framework for living differently together as a power sharing partnership (Maaka and Fleras 2005). Or as Zeid Ra'ad Al-Hussein, the UN High Commissioner for Human Rights, opined in praising Canada for its renewed efforts in advancing aboriginal rights (cited in McCarthy 2016: A-3):

Not many countries have the strength to really take an unalloyed view of the past, reflect on it sincerely and embroider it into their national curriculum so the country can move on, having gone through this rather painful but needed exercise. Hopefully Canada can be encouraged to continue along this path and then be an example for other countries who are wrestling with these sorts of issues.

Framing Aboriginal Inequality: Assimilationism, Autonomism, Accommodationism

Aboriginal people's realities are layered in contradictions. They constitute what George Manuel called Fourth World peoples (original inhabitants) who now live as second class citizens, often under Third World conditions in what many see as a first class country. Their lives are immersed in and marred by a barrage of challenges (problems) ranging from the socio-economic and the cultural to those dealing with health issues or environmental toxicities. To be sure, variations in socio-economic status, gender, age, proximity to major centres, and location (off-reserve or reserve) make it abundantly clear: some individuals and communities experience inequalities and exclusions more intensely than those who lead productive lives within supportive contexts. This variation across aboriginal communities prompts a number of questions about inequality and exclusions: What are the causes? Who is responsible? Why? Who gets blamed? How can we achieve solutions consistent with the problem definition?

To date, three ideal-typical governance models are proposed for analyzing the inequalities of exclusion that confront aboriginal communities: **assimilationism** (too much autonomy, not enough modernization); **autonomism** (too much modernization, not enough autonomy) or **accommodationism** (too much of both, not enough of either). For the assimilationists (also called "integrationists" [Widdowson and Albert 2013]), both special treatment and tribalism create the inequality problem that only a commitment to modernization can fix. For the autonomists (or "parallelists" [Widdowson and Albert 2013]), assimilation and

modernization are the problem that can only be fixed by a commitment to aboriginal models of self-determining autonomy. For accommodationists, too much of the wrong kind of assimilation/autonomy and too little of the right kind account for inequalities, so that any solution resides in balancing assimilation with autonomy. However much they diverge in their underlying assumptions, problem definitions, and proposed solutions, each of these models is predicated on one overriding assumption: the relationship between Canada and Aboriginal peoples is broken and requires wholesale repair to abort the cycle of inequality and exclusions. But each governance model differs in how and why the relationship is broken, what must be done to foster a relations repair, and what kind of governance outcome is anticipated (Fleras and Maaka 2009a).

Assimilationist Governance Model: Living Together Similarly

At one end of the debate continuum is the assimilationism model (Flanagan 1999; Fiss 2004; Gibson 2009). This model is predicated on the assumption that Aboriginal peoples must modernize (assimilate) if they hope to achieve equality. It's also based on the functionalist premise that the existing political/economic/social/cultural system is sound and worthwhile, so that refusal by Aboriginal peoples to join and participate in Canadian society is both counterintuitive and counterproductive. According to this line of thinking ("blame the individual/victim"), Aboriginal peoples are themselves the architects of their misfortune because they insist on continuing to distance themselves— geographically, legally, socially, economically, and culturally—from Canadian society. They must take responsibility for solutions by becoming more modern through exposure and involvement in the mainstream, while discarding those social patterns and cultural values at odds with the demands of Canadian realities.

The special status enjoyed by Aboriginal peoples is a deterrent to equality attainment (see Widdowson and Howard 2008). According to assimilationists, true equality arises from treating everyone the same, regardless of their race or ethnicity or aboriginality. The fact that all Canadians are fundamentally alike and equal before the law condemns any preferential treatment based on race (or aboriginality in this case) as morally wrong, bad policy, and socially divisive (Fiss 2004; Gibson 2005). Assimilationists believe the racist and paternalistic edifice of laws, status, and programs for Aboriginal peoples (from reserves to the Department of Aboriginal Affairs and Northern Development Canada) must be abolished in favour of normal citizenship. The Indian Act is a particularly noxious stumbling block. Its imposition of outdated property rights hobble reserve residents from leveraging as collateral the ownership of their land and houses in economically productive (to invest or borrow) ways (Flanagan, Alcantara, and Le Dressay 2009; Flanagan and Beauregard 2013). Moreover, the critics argue, the Canadian government spends up to $9 billion per year shoring up aboriginal communities, with little to show for the expenditure except precarious living standards, a glaring lack of accountability and transparency in the spending, constant criticism for not doing enough, and aboriginal demands for more and more (Fiss 2005). Worse still is the resultant culture of dependency. As Calvin Helin (2006) argues, the federal government has manufactured a situation where transfer payments or welfare constitute the bulk of local wealth, thus reinforcing a dependency mindset at the expense of self-reliance as a community value. For assimilationists then, the solution to the aboriginal inequality problem involves their incorporation (absorption) into Canadian society. The strategies for modernization are fourfold:

1. First, to eliminate the collectivist mindset that underpins these special provisions and preferential status, while exposing Aboriginal peoples to the balm of modernist values pertaining to individualism, competition, and private property rights (Flanagan 2001; Fiss 2004).

2. Second, to wean Aboriginal peoples away from those "artificially preserved" cultural values and residential patterns that no longer resonate with relevance in a twenty-first-century society but compromise their ability to participate in a modern economy (Widdowson and Howard 2009; 2013).

3. Third, to expose Aboriginal peoples to the discipline of the market—most notably, conversion to the municipal level of elected government that generates income from taxing individualized property rights instead of relying on federal transfers for wealth creation (Fiss 2005).

4. Fourth and finally, to foster Aboriginal self-sufficiency by incorporating Aboriginal peoples into the economy (Graham and Levesque 2010). Towards that end, the federal government has endorsed the establishment of well-capitalized and partnership-oriented programs whose objective is to foster economic development by encouraging a robust Aboriginal business sector while bringing Aboriginal workers into the labour market (Delic and Abele 2010).

The above-listed points may sound good on paper, especially for those who subscribe to a functionalist model of society and inequality, with its emphasis on modernizing (or assimilating into the mainstream) both individuals and the community. But the Spotlight box on the following page provides an example of how assimilation as governance model (either deliberately or by consequences) continues to generate a series of cascading disadvantages that accumulate over time until a tipping point is reached that can nearly destroy a community.

Autonomist Governance Model: Living Separately Together

The history of indigenous peoples in the modern era is, fundamentally, a story of struggle to overcome the effects of colonization.
—Taiaiake Alfred and Lana Lowe (2006:4). Reprinted with permission.

At the other end of the aboriginal inequality debate are proponents of the autonomy model (see Alfred 2005; Blaser et al. 2011). The autonomy model is premised on a core principle: Canada remains colonialist in terms of the founding assumptions and foundational principles (structure, values, and ideology) that inform its constitutional order (Kulchyski 2013; Barker 2015; Kino-nda-niimi Collective 2014). Moves to

Spotlight The Cascading Devastation of Assimilation

Grassy Narrows (or Asubpeeschoseewagong Netum Anishinabek, its Ojibway name) First Nations consists of about 1,000 Anishinabek band members who occupy a reserve of 14 square miles near Kenora, Ontario, with access to an additional 2,500 square miles of traditional land use area, as promised in Treaty 3. Like many other aboriginal communities across Canada over the past century, the Grassy Narrows peoples have experienced numerous dislocations and appropriations. A toxic brew of historical mistakes and ecological miscues, alongside a series of industrial misdeeds and misguided government policies, brought about their near destruction (Shkilnyk 1985). The Grassy Narrows peoples were pushed to the brink by the cumulative effect of a series of cascading devastations—from residential school traumas and influenza epidemics to the flooding of sacred lands for hydroelectric development. Another set of events in the 1960s—namely, forced relocation to their current reserve, coupled with mercury contamination of their waterways—proved a tipping point for an already beleaguered community. A closer look at the factors that precipitated the collapse of Grassy Narrows peoples exposes an uncomfortable truth that no amount of comforting fictions can gloss over.

1. Government aboriginal policy and its implementation by the Department of Indian Affairs pursued an aggressive policy of assimilation in hopes of modernizing the community (also Hedican 2013). Early government initiatives focused on transforming the Grassy Narrows peoples into something altogether different through exposure to the assimilationist pressures of missionization and the residential school system. The Grassy Narrows nation was forcibly relocated to a site near Kenora in 1963, in part to facilitate their absorption into mainstream society by improving access to education, housing, and services; in part to pave the way for dam and road construction; in part to facilitate the travel of the local Indian Agent (Harada et al. 2011).

This exercise in forced relocation proved to be profoundly unsettling: the transition from a relatively nomadic life to a more sedentary community life eventually threw the Grassy Narrows peoples into social turmoil, cultural confusion, physical deterioration, and psychological breakdowns (Shkilnyk 1985).

2. The introduction of the clear-cut logging industry proved unsettling in two ways. First, it diminished the community's subsistence base by depleting the habitat that had sustained traditional patterns of livelihood. Second, the actions of both government and multinational corporations such as Weyerhaeuser and Abitibi Consolidated violated Treaty 3 promises of unimpeded access to traditional hunting, gathering, fishing, and trapping grounds. Their actions also usurped Grassy Narrows' control over their lives and life chances, in the process eroding any sense of community-based self-determining autonomy across their traditional environments (Vecsey 1987). Reaction to this infringement of aboriginal title and treaty rights culminated in a 10-year blockade from 2002 to 2012 (the longest running aboriginal blockade in Canadian history) to curb those rapacious logging practices that many likened to the massive resource exploitation and cultural genocide in the Amazon Basin during the 1980s (Fobister 2003).

3. The final straw (tipping point) involved the dumping of 9,000 kilograms of mercury into the English-Wabigoon river system by local pulp and paper industries, with the permission of the Ontario government. The mercury contamination of the fish and water (as well as soil and game) eroded the subsistence economy of the Grassy Narrows (and White Dog) First Nations; in turn, closure of the commercial fishery crippled tourist related businesses (Kraus 2013). The problem of mercury poisoning was identified in 1969; shortly thereafter, the Ontario government ordered Reed Paper to discontinue releasing mercury into the water. By the mid-1980s, both government and industry implicitly acknowledged their

continued

culpability in the debacle. They offered a $17 million compensation package for social and economic improvement, including individual compensation based on a point system related to the severity of symptoms. Unfortunately, there was no provision for inflation adjusted payments; as a result, 60-year-old Steve Frobisher, who suffers severe disabilities because of the poisoning, continues to receive only $250 per month in payment. By contrast, mercury-poisoned victims in Japan received $800,000 as compensation in 1973 and continue to receive between $2,000 and $8,000 per month based on severity indicators (Harada et al. 2011; also CBC News 2012). To add insult to yet more injury, the long-term effects of mercury pollution (including airborne emissions of mercury not initially identified as toxic) continue to pose a grave health threat more than 40 years after closure of the fishing industry. Grassy Narrows residents tested in 2010 displayed symptoms of mercury poisoning; as well, just over one-third of the tested target group were diagnosed as potential Minamata disease patients (Harada et al. 2011).

To be sure, the near destruction of Grassy Narrows was not necessarily the result of deliberate government conspiracy or bureaucratic bungling. Rather the negative impacts of policy and programs reflected the logical if deadly consequences of well-intentioned motives, albeit based on faulty assumptions (they want to be like us) and misplaced concerns (they can be more like us through assimilation and modernization) (Shkilnyk 1985; Hedican 2013). But the unintended impact of these systemic biases proved devastating. Members of the Grassy Narrows community drifted from a position of relative self-sufficiency to an unhealthy reliance on federal government subsidies and welfare and unemployment cheques. Any sense of community and family life disintegrated because of these changes, resulting in a sharp spike in alcohol-induced anti-social behaviour, from domestic abuse to general violence and suicide. Kai Erikson, in his foreword to Shkilnyk's book (1985: xv), described

the inhabitants of Grassy Narrows as a "broken people" who live a life of "sullen pain" resulting in the "neglect and abuse [of] themselves and their children." Their mindsets and dispositions became increasingly passive, resigned, and listless as they slept-walked through the motions of pretending to live (Shkilnyk 1985). In short, Grassy Narrows' peoples suffered from what is now called ennui—a lifelong malaise of tiredness or disinterest, an unrelenting sense of nothingness, and a refusal to try because nothing is possible and nobody really cares (Wagamese 2013).

What lessons can we glean from this sorry story of relations between Aboriginal peoples and Canada (also Hedican 2013)? First, the situation at Grassy Narrows is tragic but not unique in Canada. For example, the environmental impact from tar sands development in northern Alberta has curtailed the ability of Treaty 8 aboriginal communities to hunt and trap, while people are increasingly fearful to drink water or eat fish from polluted waterways because of toxins. Aboriginal leaders refer to this development as a case of "industrial genocide" (Huseman and Short 2012). Second, too often aboriginal communities are portrayed as hapless and helpless victims of genocidal forces and colonial legacies largely beyond their control. But there is another narrative that mainstream discourses ignore, one in which aboriginal communities and individuals are actively taking control of their destinies through measures that resist, challenge, and change (Willow 2012). The Grassy Narrows First Nations are but one example of communities and individuals who bend but don't break. Their struggles to survive against seemingly all odds, despite the long-term ravages of both mercury poisoning and ruthless clear-cut logging on their tradition land, is testament to human resilience under the most intimidating circumstances. This resilience also reinforces a twenty-first-century model of aboriginal protest and indigenous resistance against state domination, called "indigenism," that is anchored in the rootedness and cultural connections to land yet also linked to recent innovations in communication technology and globalization (Willow 2012).

But their struggles are far from over (Kraus 2016). In the summer of 2012, Ontario Premier Kathleen Wynne promised to rebuild Ontario's relationship with Grassy Narrows. Fine words, indeed, although recent actions point to a continuation of the colonial mindset that historically informed this relationship, including plans to further clear-cut forest while infringing on aboriginal title and treaty rights without appropriate levels of consultation, consent, and adequate compensation (Fobister 2013). Members of the Grassy Narrows First Nations challenged an Ontario Court of Appeal decision in March of 2013 that conferred provincial right to mine and log on treaty land (Vincent 2013). They are also rejecting Ontario's Forestry Management Plan 2012–2022 to issue (clear-cut) logging permits that would further denude their already depleted land. This willingness by the Grassy Narrows community to resume a temporarily suspended ten-year blockade of illegal logging practices on their ancestral territory makes it abundantly clear: when it comes to Aboriginal peoples–government relations, the more things change . . .

modernize and incorporate Aboriginal peoples into this colonialist project known as Canada-building cuts to the core of the inequality problem. Then as now, Aboriginal peoples continue to suffer the consequences of being framed as impediments to Canada-building who had to be forcibly incorporated into Canada's project as little more than "hewers of wood and drawers of water" (Neeganawedgin 2012; Hedican 2013; Carter 1990). Many Canadians would be shocked to learn that government officials treated reserve populations as guinea pigs, conducting experiments on aboriginal children and adults during the 1930s and 1940s to determine if a tuberculosis vaccine was a cheaper alternative than goods and services in improving their socio-economic conditions; and to see if the use of vitamin supplements could ward off starvation and nutritional deficiencies among children (Mosby 2013; Weber 2013a, b). No less shocking is the MacDonald government's lack of compunction about starving Aboriginal peoples into submission to ensure their compliance in facilitating railway construction and prairie settlement (Daschuk 2013). Current settler regimes may be less callous in the mistreatment of Aboriginal peoples. In light of these misguided moves to assimilate, autonomists argue, the so-called "Indian problem" is really "the Indian's Canada problem" (Newhouse and Belanger 2011; Warry 2009). Hence, any solution to the inequalities of exclusions must begin by challenging (neo) colonialist arrangements that created the problem in the first place, including those constitutional provisions that box in aboriginal communities while indoctrinating individual mindsets to think like the colonizers (Alfred 2005). Autonomists not only challenge Canada's unilateral assertion of sovereign jurisdiction over its vast territory and original inhabitants, they also endorse Aboriginal peoples' claims as sovereign political nations with inherent and collective rights to aboriginal models of self-determining autonomy over land, identity, and political voice (see Asch 2014). Government policy must play its part in securing the inherent and treaty rights of Aboriginal peoples, in effect pressuring the federal government into honouring its fiduciary responsibilities, protecting the legitimacy of **Aboriginal difference** as a basis for recognition, reward, and relationship, and upholding aboriginal sovereignty by way of self-determining autonomy models of governance. In short, Aboriginal peoples are not a minority with problems in need of solution. More to the point, autonomists argued, they have rights in addition to the powers, sovereignty, and resources that flow from this recognition.

The logic behind the autonomist claim reflects the principles of dependency theories. Dependency theorists argue that sustained contact with the West, with its capitalist pressures to assimilate and modernize, creates more harm than good (see also Helin 2006). Poverty and powerlessness will not disappear with better opportunities or increased expenditures. Throwing money at a problem may be effective in the short run, but recourse to such short-sightedness downplays the structural (and more costly) roots of aboriginal inequality—namely, the lack of power and resource control. Even formal powers and authority delegated to aboriginal communities through various comprehensive land claims agreements and self-government arrangements (such as the Nisga'a; see Spotlight box at the end of this section) consolidate state power and make it increasingly difficult to curb certain forms of development and extraction on Indigenous peoples' lands (Coulthard 2014). Significant improvements will materialize only when Aboriginal peoples secure a degree of autonomy, including access to power-sharing, an equitable share of revenue from reserve resources, and Aboriginal title to land (Cornell and Kalt 2003). Two aboriginal models of self-determining autonomy can be discerned: ideological/traditional and radical/sovereign.

1. An ideological/neo-traditional model of self-determining autonomy rejects any assimilationism—or even co-operation with current governments—as a basis for governance, renewal, and relations repair. For activist scholars such as Taiaiake Alfred (2005; also Coulthard 2014) of BC's Victoria University, a non-violent, spiritual (or ideological) revolution entitled Wasáse (see below) is the key whose ideology is rooted in sacred wisdom and motivated by aboriginal teachings and traditional ethics. Resistance must begin by delegitimizing the exercise of state power and corporate control, continue by reclaiming land and resources rightfully belonging to Indigenous peoples, and culminate in eliminating colonialist beliefs and values internalized by Aboriginal peoples and replacing them with authentic indigenous identities under tribal authority (Alfred and Lowe 2006). Taiaiake Alfred and Jeff Corntassel (2005:297–298) write of the need to move beyond neocolonialism as a basis for renewal and resurgence:

   . . . the struggle to survive as distinct peoples on foundations constituted in their unique heritages, attachment to their homelands, and natural ways of life is what is shared by all Indigenous peoples, as well as the fact that

their existence is in large part lived as determined acts of survival against colonizing state's efforts to eradicate them culturally, politically, and physically. The challenge of "being Indigenous" in a psychic and cultural sense, forms the critical question facing Indigenous peoples today in the era of contemporary colonialism—a form of post-modern imperialism in which domination is still the Settler imperative, but where colonizers have designed and practice more subtle means . . . of accomplishing their objectives.

With Wasáse, the path to autonomy lies in transcending colonialism in a personal and collective sense. Co-optation into mainstream society is rejected by refusing to play by settler-defined rules for political concessions or economic development. The position is principled; after all, why should First Nations, whose governments, laws, and communities predated settlement and colonization, co-operate with an occupying governance built on lands and resources stolen from them (Noisecat 2015)? Moves to decolonize a Canada constructed on colonialist principles requires a corresponding decolonization of aboriginal mindsets through the rejuvenation of tradition and culture ("heeding the voices of the ancestors") and restoration of their authenticity, autonomy, and authority over unsurrendered land (Onkwehonwe) (Alfred 2005). The principles of Wasáse are set out below:

Wasáse is the Mohawk (Kanien'keha) word for "ancient war dance of unity, strength, and call for action."

About the movement: Wasáse is an intellectual and political movement whose ideology is rooted in sacred wisdom. It is motivated and guided by indigenous spiritual and ethical teachings and dedicated to the transformation of indigenous people in the midst of the severe decline of our nations and the crisis threatening our existence. It exists to enable indigenous people to live authentic, free, and healthy lives in our homelands.

Aim: Wasáse promotes the learning and respecting of every aspect of our indigenous heritage, working together to govern ourselves using indigenous knowledge, and unifying to fight for our freedom and the return of our lands. It seeks to liberate indigenous people from euroamerican thoughts, laws, and systems.

Approach: Wasáse is a resurgence of diverse actions. It works by awakening and reculturing individuals so that indigenous thoughts are restored to their proper place in the people's minds and their attachment to false identities is broken . . . . Wasáse challenges indigenous people to reject the authority and legitimacy of the colonial system and to rebel against its institutions . . . . [T]he movement does not use violence to advance its aims. Its political struggle is conducted through intellectual confrontation and mass communication; revealing the corruptions, frauds and abuses of colonizers and collaborators; and supporting direct action in defense of indigenous communities, their rights, and their land. Statement retrieved from www.wasase.org.

2. The territorial sovereignty autonomy model is endorsed by the Mohawk Nation of the 150,000-strong Iroquois (Haudenosaunee) Confederacy, whose community at Akwesasne/ St Regis is partitioned by the Canadian and American border. Mohawk peoples argue that they are neither Canadian nor American citizens since the Mohawk Nation never relinquished its independence (sovereignty) nor its jurisdiction over territory or peoples. Their status as sovereign, both collective and inherent, has never been usurped by treaty or declaration between Iroquois and Europeans. What they propose instead is a distinct relationship based on the Two Row Wampum Treaty with the Dutch in 1613, which affirmed the partnership of two distinct peoples coexisting on one land while securing a framework for living together separately (Briarpatch 2010). Several consequences follow from this politicized claim. First, Mohawk prefer to travel on a Haudenosaunee passport issued by their confederacy as a symbol of their identity and citizenship as a sovereign peoples (and have done so since 1923; it was first officially recognized by Switzerland in 1977), although these passports are now rejected by the United Kingdom, United States, and Canada

because their travel documents no longer meet post-9/11 security requirements (Friday and Cohen 2010). Second, as an extension of Mohawk territorial sovereignty, Canadian authorities rarely interfere in businesses considered illegal by the Canadian state (from online gaming operations to cigarette smuggling) if practised on Mohawk land (Horn 2010). Third, a band council decision to evict non-Mohawk married to Mohawk was deemed regrettable by the government, albeit legal (or at least understandable), given the Mohawk constitutional right to define membership and secure their cultural integrity (Hamilton 2010).

Accommodationist Model: Living Together With Differences

In between these admittedly ideal-typical positions are accommodationist models for addressing aboriginal inequality. An accommodationist model represents a compromise that strives to balance the strengths of both autonomy and assimilation models while repudiating the weaknesses of each. Or to phrase it differently, inequalities are inevitable when aboriginal communities suffer from a surfeit of "bad" assimilation but a dearth of "good" assimilation. Conversely, exclusions follow if there is too much destructive autonomy but not enough progressive autonomy. An accommodationist model differently frames the causes of aboriginal inequality problems and proposed solutions. Although aboriginal communities are the site of social inequalities and exclusions, it's neither an "Indian" problem nor a white problem: more to the point, it's an Indian–white problem. According to this mutual-blaming frame, Aboriginal peoples must assume responsibility for the choices they make and the predicament in which they find themselves. But as sociologists rightfully point out, people's options and choices do not originate in a political, historical, or economic vacuum. No less important is the broader context of restrictions, oppressions, and impositions, including the legacy of colonialism and genocide. A degree of relative autonomy is critical in breaking the bonds of dependency and constructing self-reliance through interdependence with other community members, other aboriginal communities, and society at large (Helin 2006). Aboriginal cultural differences are not necessarily an obstacle to socio-economic success, but may prove helpful in facilitating an integration into the mainstream on aboriginal terms (also Widdowson and Albert 2013). In other words, for accommodationists, it is the mutual adjustment process and the relationship within that is broken and in need of realignment. The words of Ovide Mercredi, former National Chief of the Assembly of First Nations, seem apropos in advancing an accommodationist position:

> The greatest ambitions of aboriginal peoples are to restore and reclaim their assaulted cultures and languages, to own land and resources, to rebuild their economy, and to re-establish governments based on indigenous concepts of consensual democracy that will provide their people with the legacy of good government Canada has failed to offer. Our vision includes respect for civil and human rights, and the freedom of individuals to participate in Canada's national life, free from discrimination, racism, or poverty. It is a vision that would allow our people to be themselves, to advance as distinct peoples, and yet remain active and contributing citizens of a country that has finally stopped hurting them. (cited in Long 2011)

Two models of accommodationism can be discerned: political and economic. The first is a political accommodation solution proposed by Alan Cairns (2000) in his book *Citizens Plus: Aboriginal Peoples and the Canadian State*. The term **citizens plus** was first used in the Hawthorn Report of 1966 (Cairns participated in the commission that produced the report). The report emphasized how Aboriginal peoples have the same rights as all Canadians; they also possess additional rights because of their historical and treaty status. The principle of coexistence (a compromise involving aboriginal autonomy within the wider framework of Canadian society [Cairns 2005]) provides the framework for solving complex aboriginal problems without destroying Canada or undermining its legitimacy in the process. Rejecting a nation-to-nation paradigm is thought to secure a middle ground that recognizes both Aboriginal

difference and rights (thus rejecting assimilation), yet embraces a commitment to belonging and citizenship in Canada (thus rejecting autonomy) (Cairns 2000:86). In doing so, a citizens plus model provides a vehicle for ameliorating the conditions imposed by colonialism without Aboriginal peoples having to relinquish the benefits of citizenship in a modern state.

The second model of accommodationism is an economic development model built on the premise that any escape from debilitating patterns of dependency and underdevelopment must begin with self-sufficiency at individual and community levels (Helin 2006; 2010). Aboriginal leaders and communities alike have endorsed the cause of self-sufficiency through sustainable economic development. A "constructive partnership" (Helin 2006:16) with governments and businesses is proposed, including the 2009 Federal Framework for Aboriginal Economic Development, which emphasized the following priorities: supporting skills and training; leveraging investments and promoting partnerships; and removing barriers to aboriginal entrepreneurship, including improving access to capital for aboriginal businesses. As Helin (2006:39) writes, advancing wealth creation is the way to solve problems and sever the cycle of dependency and entitlement mentality, including the $18 billion spent on services and transfers to aboriginal communities.

> To exploit these opportunities will require a fundamental change in the dependency mindset of Aboriginal people. For lasting solutions, decisions have to come from within Aboriginal people themselves . . . . Aboriginal citizens must take ownership of these problems and assert control over their destinies . . . . It's time to re-take control of our lives from government departments, bureaucrats and the Indian Industry. To do this, we must create our own wealth, develop a focussed strategy to educate youth and control our own purse strings . . . . The object is to ensure that larger numbers of Aboriginal people are leading enriched, rewarding lives . . . . [T]his process in turn should pay huge economic and social dividends for Canada as a country.

To date, government initiatives to break the bonds of economic dependency appear to have faltered. Much of the problem reflects the federal government's insistence that it knows best instead of partnering with the communities in question to do what is workable, necessary, just, and fair. But the developmental model to nation-building proposed by Cornell and Kalt (2003) and Graham and Levesque (2010) points to the possibility of putting accommodationist principles into practices that sidestep government stonewalling. A degree of de facto political sovereignty is proposed in which aboriginal communities take charge of what happens on reserves to create sustainable growth. The nation-building model of economic development endorsed by aboriginal communities such as the Osoyoos Indian Band relies on the accommodationism of "practical sovereignty"—not as an end in itself but as a means to foster business growth. In brief, the principle of accommodationism is about incorporation not separation—about "getting on" rather than "getting out"—in hopes of completing the "circle of confederation" (cited in Hawkes 2000:142). The next Spotlight box looks at the principles and practices of Nisga'a self-governance and demonstrates how framing *inequality* and *relationship renewal* may be differently interpreted by each of these governance models.

Spotlight Nisga'a Self-Governance: Assimilationism? Accommodationism? Autonomism?

The finalization of the Nisga'a settlement in 2000 predictably drew criticism from diverse quarters. Some accused the government of impeding the transformation (i.e., assimilation) of Aboriginal peoples into becoming "more like us" by conceding too much to Aboriginal difference. The end result of discouraging modernization is more of the same: poverty and powerlessness. Others believe the opposite is true: the government provides the illusion of self-determining autonomy by situating the settlement within the restrictions and rules of the Canadian state. The end result: even less control over aboriginal lives and life chances. For still others, Nisga'a represents a compromise agreement that acknowledges the mutually reciprocating realities and obligations of Aboriginal peoples as citizens-plus. In other words, is the government taking Aboriginal peoples (nationhood) too seriously by promoting yet more divisiveness and deprivation? Or alternatively, not seriously enough, by insisting on ever-more-clever ways of fostering self-sufficient assimilation to solve the inequality problem? Or does any assessment of the Nisga'a settlement—assimilationism or autonomism—lie somewhere in between these polar positions (accommodationism) in striking a new working relationship?

The politics of "relations repair" was played out with the ratification of the Nisga'a Final Ratification/ Agreement in May 2000—the first modern treaty settlement in British Columbia since 1859 and the first of 50 outstanding land claims encompassing the entire province. The Final Agreement did not materialize overnight. Since 1885, the Nisga'a First Nations of central British Columbia have looked to Ottawa for compensation for the Crown's unilateral confiscation of their land (Godlewska and Webber 2007). They petitioned the British Privy Council in 1913, and in 1968 took their case to court where the Supreme Court ruled against the Nisga'a in 1973 (on a technicality rather than on substance). Nonetheless, the Calder decision (as it came to be known) conceded the possibility of something called aboriginal title to unsurrendered land, culminating in the historic agreement. The conclusion is inescapable: the Nisga'a have come a long way since the days when Pierre Elliott Trudeau denied the existence of aboriginal rights by declaring that no country could be built on "historical might-have-beens."

The actual terms of the agreement are clearly articulated but subject to diverse interpretations. The Nisga'a Final Agreement provides 5,500 members of bands who live 800 kilometres north of Vancouver

continued

with a land base of 1,900 km (a fraction of the amount originally proposed). They have control over forest and fishery resources; $200 million in cash; release from Indian Act provisions without loss of Indian status; a supra-municipal level of self-government (not simply self-administration or self-management [Quesnel 2012]), including control over citizenship, land and assets, policing, education, community and health care services, harvesting rights, and direct taxation (Quesnel and Winn 2011). To help pay for this infrastructure, the Nisga'a will receive forest and timber cutting rights, oil and mineral resources, and a fishery conservation trust, as well as 26 per cent of the salmon fishery, plus $21.5 million to purchase boats and equipment. This transfer in wealth and jurisdiction is expected to alleviate community dysfunctions, including high levels of unemployment, criminal activity, and crowded homes.

In 2010, the Nisga'a celebrated 10 years of self-governance, with some advances in material prosperity from new construction to new rules for business engagement offset by the losses due to the collapse of the forestry sector (Hunter 2010; BC News 2014). The 2009 Nisga'a Landholding Transition Act allows members of the community to assume full property rights over small residential lots, since Nisga'a lands are no longer governed by the regulatory hurdles imposed by the Indian Act (Quesnel 2012). As well, Nisga'a citizens profess to have more trust in Nisga'a authorities, think they're more honest, and provide better service delivery. But concerns remain over poor governance habits such nepotism, less consultation, less accountability, and less transparency (Quesnel and Winn 2011).

A wave of reaction greeted the settlement of British Columbia's first land claims test (see Scott 2012). According to critics, an "extraordinary agreement" with the Nisga'a Nations has "raised the spectre of racially autonomous development across Canada" because of provisions that provide the Nisga'a with more autonomy and self-government than they constitutionally deserve; empower the Nisga'a to pass laws on any matter other than defence, currency, and foreign affairs; allow specific aboriginal rights to challenge Canadian citizenship rights; confer benefits unavailable to other Canadians based solely on culture or colour; and

prohibit non-Nisga'a from voting for the region's administration, thus disenfranchising local residents who continue to pay taxes but lack representation. Critics charge that the agreement has entrenched a racially based order of government (Nisga'a Lisims government) with constitutionally protected powers to create laws that will trump federal and provincial legislation while greasing the slippery slide towards a patchwork of semi-sovereign states—a de facto third order of government—where citizens live by different rules than do other Canadians (Flanagan 1999; Widdowson 2003; Fiss 2004).

For others, however, the Nisga'a settlement is neither autonomy nor accommodation: it's an assimilationist sell-out that generates the illusion of self-determining autonomy. The settlement constitutes a cleverly disguised instrument of assimilation in which the Nisga'a peoples are co-opted into the very Canadian system that created the problems in the first place. As proof, critics contend, Nisga'a received only about 10 per cent of the land they claimed as part of the settlement, while voluntarily extinguishing their rights as Indigenous peoples (Tully 2000). And with the elimination of on-reserve tax exemptions, there are fears that Nisga'a peoples will have to sell their land and resource rights just to fund self-government and community services (Corntassel 2008). In other words, the principle of recognition and a few symbols of autonomy tossed in the direction of the Nisga'a do little to undermine this exercise in neo-colonial subjugation (Alfred 2005; also Coulthard 2014).

How do these accusations stand up to scrutiny? Business as usual or postcolonial sovereignty (Scott 2012)? Is the Nisga'a Final Agreement another form of racial apartheid, or is it about the collective and inherent rights of the Nisga'a for self-rule? Is it about racial entitlements or about aboriginal rights for self-determining autonomy? Is it about living apart in segregated enclaves or about living together separately yet equitably? Critics tend to overestimate the aura attributed to the Nisga'a. True, Nisga'a self-governing powers may be constitutionally protected under section 35 of the Constitution, a status that no municipality can claim at present. Nor are Nisga'a laws subject to override except by mutual agreement with federal and provincial authorities. The Nisga'a government will have exclusive jurisdiction in matters related to language and culture in addition to citizenship and property, even when these conflict with federal/provincial laws. Nevertheless, the federal government can infringe (even extinguish) these constitutionally protected rights, provided there is a compelling and substantial objective for the interference and its actions are consistent with the special trust relationship between Aboriginal peoples and the Crown (Harris-Short 2007).

In other words, Nisga'a powers are not unlimited. They are circumscribed and consistent with those articulated by federal recognition in 1995 of Aboriginal peoples' "inherent right to self-government." Nisga'a powers are restricted to those of a super-municipality, including authority over policing (but not the federal Criminal Code), education, taxes, and community services, with a few provincial bits thrown in for good measure. The Canadian Charter of Rights and Freedoms still applies; so do federal and provincial laws, although any conflicts or inconsistency must be reconciled with the principle of Nisga'a autonomy. As well, health, education, and child welfare services must meet provincial standards. In short, Nisga'a governance will reflect a "concurrent jurisdiction"—that is, shared and overlapping jurisdictions rather than watertight compartments—as both Nisga'a laws and federal and provincial jurisdiction will continue to apply to communities, citizens, and lands (Quesnel and Winn 2011).

It is true that voting in Nisga'a will be restricted to Nisga'a citizens. According to critics, a government based on race is wrong and contrary to Canada's territorially based federal system where individual voting rights are acquired by residence—that is, if you live in Toronto, you can vote in Toronto even if born in Bissett, Manitoba (Fiss 2004). In contrast, rights in the Nisga'a nation are based on the principle of aboriginality, with the result that only the Nisga'a can claim rights of citizenship or vote for government. But Nisga'a are not the only jurisdiction in Canada to restrict voting rights. The proposed Tlicho Land Claims and Self-Government Act also restricts who can hold office (Ivison 2004). And nearly 2,600 reserves across Canada also restrict voting to membership in one of 633 bands. Besides, what is the point of self-government if "others" can vote, thereby undermining the very point of self-rule (Peach 2005)?

Even more disconcerting is critics' penchant for "racializing" the Nisga'a pact. Nisga'a is not about racially separate development or race-based governments along the lines of apartheid (Fiss 2004). Apartheid was forcibly imposed on South African blacks to exclude, deny, and exploit them. By contrast Nisga'a is about advancing *aboriginal rights* rather than entitlements by race, including the right of Aboriginal peoples to construct self-governing models as constitutionally stipulated (Fontaine 2005). It is about the rights of six generations of Nisga'a who prevailed over time to establish Aboriginal title to ancestral land that had never been surrendered to European powers (Dufraiment 2002).

Put into a broader context: Canada is widely renowned as a country constructed around compromises. The Nisga'a settlement, as a distinct third tier of governance, is yet another compromise in crafting an innovative political order in which each level of government—federal, provincial, and aboriginal—is sovereign in its own right yet shares in the sovereignty of Canada as a whole by way of multiple and interlocking jurisdictions. To date, the Nisga'a model of aboriginal governance continues to be supported and trusted by its citizens, while economic progress is likely with the adoption of limited property rights under Nisga'a Landholding Transition Act in 2009 (Quesnel and Winn 2011). The challenge is formidable: how can aboriginal rights to self-determining autonomy be reconciled with the Crown's right to govern and regulate? Or as the Supreme Court put in response Section 35(1) of the Constitution Act (which recognizes and affirms existing aboriginal and treaty rights), the assertion of Crown sovereignty over Canadian territory must be reconciled with the prior occupation of North America by distinct aboriginal societies (*R. v. Van der Peet* [1996] 2 S.C.R. 507, paragraphs 49–50). How can these seemingly valid but mutually exclusive claims be balanced without spiralling into chaos? Is it possible to construct future Nisga'a-like arrangements that are safe for Canada yet safe from Canada? Answers to these post-colonial conundrums rarely elicit agreement. But then nobody said that living together separately would be easy.

To Sum Up: Dueling Discourses or Different Dimensions?

Three ideal-typical models of governance provide competing explanatory frameworks for framing the aboriginal inequality problem. Each of the models concurs the relationship is broken and needs to be reset in the march toward justice and equality. Where they differ is in defining the nature of the broken relationship, how it got to be that way, and how to repair it to maximize benefits for both Canadians and Aboriginal peoples. Assimilationist models argue that the most workable solution involves normalizing the status of Aboriginal peoples as citizens and taxpayers through absorption into mainstream society. For autonomist models, Aboriginal peoples' inequities are thought to arise from *too much coerced absorption* into a colonial system that doesn't work for them, resulting in dependency, underdevelopment, and loss of autonomy and authenticity (Coulthard 2014). For autonomists, any restructuring of Aboriginal peoples–society relations as part of a new post-colonial governance must acknowledge their status as a sovereign political community, with a corresponding right to aboriginal models of self-determining autonomy (Maaka and Fleras 2005; Hoehn 2012). The accommodationism model seeks a compromise between these two options. A dual commitment is proposed—treatment as Canadian citizens as a rule, but incorporation of Aboriginal peoples' rights and difference when necessary, albeit within the broader framework of Canadian society.

In short, all three models concur that equality problems plague aboriginal communities. But they disagree in framing the issue of equality: are Aboriginal peoples a *minority* with needs? A *peoples* with rights? Or *citizens* with rights and responsibilities? For assimilationists, inequality problems are seen as *needs* that require modern solutions; for autonomists, the inequalities of exclusion reflect violation of their self-determining rights that must be restored and the relationship repaired for any sustainable renewal; and for accommodationists, solving the problems is all about a finding a working balance between competing governance models. Clearly, the assimilationist model is consistent with the blaming-the-victim approach endorsed by a functionalist perspective. A blaming-the-system approach in defining the problem/solution nexus is commensurate with a radical conflict perspective and autonomist governance models. And the blame-the-situation approach implicit with an accommodationist model capitalizes on a symbolic interactionist perspective. Table 8.1 compares these three ideal-typical models of governance for repairing a broken relationship. These models for solving the problem of aboriginal inequality and exclusion are shown to differ in terms of their underlying assumptions, proposed solutions, preferred means, and anticipated outcomes.

Constructive Engagement, Constructing Equality

Aboriginal peoples do not self-identify as a social inequality problem (Fleras 2012). They contend material poverty is not entirely responsible for their deprivation, alienation, and marginalization—without necessarily denying the many inequality challenges that confront aboriginal communities. Powerlessness associated with (neo)colonialization and denial of aboriginal rights is just as problematic (Adams 1999). Patterns of poverty and inequality are symptoms of more fundamental causes related to a relationship that simply doesn't work (Truth and Reconciliation Commission Report 2015). Not surprisingly, those political and social frameworks that once colonized and controlled are rejected in favour of post-colonial arrangements that not only challenge those founding assumptions and foundational principles of Canada's constitutional order, but also reinforce their status as *peoples* (i.e., "nations within") with corresponding rights, powers, and privileges (Maaka and Fleras 2005). In other words, it is not a case of solving the aboriginal inequality problem because they are minorities with needs. The core issue is fixing the relationship because Aboriginal peoples constitute *peoples with rights* (Fleras and Maaka 2009b).

Three key planks secure the foundation for renewing the relation along post-colonial lines

Table 8.1: Framing the "Indian" Inequality Problem: Assimilationism, Autonomism, Accommodationism

Model	Assimilationism	Autonomism	Accommodationism
Nature of the inequality problem: "Who is to blame?"	"Indian" problem: blame the victims	White problem: blame the system	"Indian"–white problem: blame the situation
Source of inequality problem	Broken relations because of not enough assimilation	Broken relations because of too much assimilation	Broken relations because of too much of the wrong kind of assimilation/autonomy, too little of the right kind of assimilation/autonomy
Solving the inequality problem	Repair the relationship by modernizing (becoming more like us as basis for getting in)	Repair the relationship by indigenizing (becoming less like you as basis for getting out)	Repair the relationship through mutual adjustment (becoming both more like me YET less like you as basis for getting on and getting along)
Means	Primacy of inclusion (fit into the system)	Primacy of inclusivity (adjust the system)	Primacy of inclusiveness (adjust the system + modify aboriginal mindsets)
	Address needs by eliminating special status (Indian Act) and preferential treatment	Recognize aboriginal rights to self-determining autonomy at cultural, political, economic levels	Acknowledge mutual interdependence: Aboriginal peoples as citizens but with distinct rights
Results	Common citizenship (same)	Coexistence as Nations within	Citizens plus
Outcomes	Living together similarly	Living separately together	Living together with differences

of partnership and power-sharing, in addition to meaningful participation and property return. They include taking aboriginality seriously (Aboriginal difference) as the basis for differential status, rights, and treatment; promoting **self-determining autonomy** over land, identity, and political voice through aboriginal models of self-governance; and acknowledging aboriginal title and treaty rights by way of land claims both specific and comprehensive (see Fleras 2012 for extended discussion). As put by Shawn Atleo, former National Chief of the Assembly of First Nations (in Coates 2013b), Canadians must rediscover the spirit of the **treaties** with their promise of partnership and sharing. After all, without the legitimacy conferred by the treaties, writes Tobold Rollo (2013), Canada is little more than an illegitimate colonial encampment, and Canadians are essentially squatters on Turtle Island (also Saul 2014). Two lines of argument are pursued: first, contemporary patterns of inequality and exclusion are largely the result of failure to recognize the principles of Aboriginal difference, aboriginal title and treaties, and self-governance. Second, a commitment to these principles provides the precondition for removing the inequalities of exclusions, renewing the vitality of aboriginality, and repairing the relationship between Canada and Aboriginal peoples.

As might be expected under these conditions, pressure is mounting to transcend confrontational models as a blueprint for reframing Canada's relationship with Aboriginal peoples. A more co-operative governance model is proposed that emphasizes engagement over sharp-dealing, negotiation over litigation, relationships over legalism, interdependence over opposition, co-operation over competition, rights over needs, entitlements over grievances, reconciliation over restitution, and power-sharing over paternalism (Maaka and Fleras 2005). Advocated too is a principled approach that acknowledges the importance of working together by standing apart as grounds for belonging separately. A **constructive engagement** model provides a respite from the interminable bickering over "who owns what" while brokering a post-colonial governance contract for co-operative and equitable coexistence. The following foundational first principles of constructive engagement establish the *preconditions* that must be observed if Canada is

to secure a new governance framework for living together separately:

1. *De facto sovereignty/sovereignty as a relationship.* The right to sovereignty is the fundamental right upon which all other aboriginal rights rest (Tomsons and Mayer 2013: xxxii). Aboriginal peoples do not aspire to sovereignty per se. Strictly speaking, they never surrendered their sovereignty by explicit agreement, so that *they already possess it* by virtue of original occupancy and common law. The fact that Aboriginal peoples are sovereign for purposes of entitlement or engagement (a de facto sovereignty) would imply only the creation of the appropriate framework for putting these principles into practical expression. In proposing to repair the relationship along fundamentally different lines, Canada's Aboriginal peoples are not looking to sever all relations with the Canadian state or to declare independence. Except for a few ideologues, appeals to sovereignty as governance are largely about establishing relationships of *relative yet relational* autonomy (Blaser et al. 2011; Young 2005; Scott 1996). To the extent that Aboriginal peoples are sovereign in their own right, yet sharing in the sovereignty of society at large, they also possess the right to meaningfully participate in the political and legal process of the state, including a veto-like power over unfavourable laws and input into a new constitutional order (Wilmer 1993; Fleras and Maaka 2009a, b). Canada's decision in May 2016 to fully adopt the provisions of the UN Declaration of Indigenous Peoples' Rights is a step in this direction (CBC News 2016).

2. *Relations repair.* Indigenous peoples around the world are defined as much by their relationship to the state as they are by any intrinsic characters they possess (David Mayberry-Lewis 1997:54). Repairing the relationship goes beyond a few cosmetic changes. What is required to restore the relational status of Aboriginal peoples is a transformation of the rules upon which governance is based, rather than simple changes to the conventions that refer to rules (Maaka and Fleras 2008). Such a transformational agenda in establishing a new relationship would incorporate a commitment to a power-sharing partnership,

acknowledgement of Aboriginal peoples as the "nations within," the primacy of rights over needs, and establishment of a nations-to-nations, government-to-government relationship.

3. *Peoples with rights.* Aboriginal peoples are neither a problem to be solved nor a need to be met. To the contrary, they are peoples (or nations) with collective and inherent rights to aboriginal models of self-determining autonomy (Tomsons and Mayer 2014). These collective and inherent rights flow from their indigenous status as descendants of the original occupants; the law of nations upon which government-to-government relations are based; and international legal norms that uphold human rights in general; and are based on protecting activities that not only have continuity to pre-traditional activities but also are integral to social and cultural distinctiveness of pre-contact society.

4. *The nations within.* Acceptance of Aboriginal peoples as fundamentally autonomous political communities is critical in crafting a new post-colonial governance contract for separately living together. Unlike ethnic and immigrant minorities who are looking to settle down, fit in, and move up within the existing social and political framework, Aboriginal peoples constitute the "nations within" who want to "get out" (symbolically speaking) of a political arrangement that doesn't work for them. Proposed is a relationship based on the principle of government-to-government, nation-to-nation, and peoples-to-peoples.

5. *Power-sharing.* Power sharing is pivotal if co-operative engagement and collaborative coexistence are to be advanced. Deeply divided societies that have attained some degree of stability endorse a level of governance involving a sharing of power that is constitutionally or statutorily entrenched (Linden 1994). Precise arrangements for rearranging power distributions must be predicated on the principle of giving, co-operating, and sharing, rather than taking, competing, and monopolizing.

6. *Sorting out jurisdictions* Concerns over jurisdiction cannot be taken lightly since all successful relations are based on a relatively clear division of what is mine, what is yours, and what is ours. In allocating a division of jurisdictions along

the lines of mine, yours, and ours, parties must enter into negotiations not on the basis of jurisprudence but on the grounds of justice, not by cutting deals but by formulating a clear vision, not by litigating but by listening (Cassidy 1994).

7. *Self-determining models versus state-determination models.* The principle of advancing Aboriginal models of self-determining autonomy over jurisdictions related to unceded land, identity, and political voice is key. These rights to *aboriginal models* of self-determining autonomy must be recognized as inherent not "granted," and they must be rooted in rights not needs. By contrast, government-imposed models of self-determination for self-sufficiency and development may reinforce—however inadvertently—the very inequalities of exclusion under question (Coulthard 2014; Maaka and Fleras 2009).

8. *Rethinking citizenship.* Innovative patterns of belonging, such as dual citizenship, are critical when two peoples share the same political and territorial space but neither is willing to be dominated by the other without losing face in the process (Oberschall 2000). Aboriginal proposals for belonging to society are anchored in primary affiliation with the group rather than as individual citizens, without necessarily revoking Canadian citizenship or rejecting loyalty to Canada. In other words, Aboriginal peoples can belong indirectly and differently to Canada through group ("tribal") membership rather than as individual citizens.

9. *Partnership.* Reframing Aboriginal peoples *not* as competitors to be jousted and defeated puts the onus on governments to see Aboriginal peoples as partners to work with through differences, in a spirit of mutual accommodation (RCAP 1996). Placing partnership at the centre of a relationship entails a fundamental rethinking of living together separately—not just in the narrow sense of offloading or delegating as might be the case between a senior partner and a junior partner. A true partnership is informed by two senior peoples sharing the land as co-equals without intruding on the other's sphere of jurisdiction. In acknowledging that "we are all here to stay," as former Chief Justice

Antonio Lamer once observed, is there any other option except to nurture a partnership?

10. *Reconciliation*. An apology and expression of regret for the deplorable acts of a colonial past is not meant to humiliate, embarrass, or extract reparations. A commitment to reconciliation intends to exorcise the anger, depression, and humiliation endured by the aggrieved party. The atonement is intended to create the basis for healing and restoration on an ongoing basis, rather than to be an exercise in closure (Truth and Reconciliation Commission Report 2015; Maaka and Fleras 2005).

The principles of constructive engagement make it abundantly clear: neither colonialism nor **neo-colonialism** as governance models possess any legitimacy in advancing aboriginal interests or addressing the inequalities of exclusions. A post-colonial governance model is proposed whose contractual obligations extol the principles of a power-sharing partnership as a basis for engaging constructively. A commitment to constructive engagement transcends the legalistic (abstract rights) or restitutional (reparations)—however important these concerns are for identity construction, nation-building, economic developments, and political representation. A reliance on jurisdictional squabbles over ownership may have elevated litigation to a preferred level in resolving differences (Spoonley 1997); however, this focus on the legalities of rights and reparations tends to fixate on the past at the expense of the current, the situational, and the evolving (Mulgan 1989). By contrast, a new governance contract based on the constitutional first principles of constructive engagement goes beyond restitution or cutting deals. Emphasis is focused on advancing a relationship on a principled basis by taking into account shifting social realities in sorting out who controls what in a spirit of give and take. Policy outcomes based on a post-colonial governance contract cannot be viewed as final or authoritative any more than they can be preoccupied with "taking" or "finalizing," instead of "sharing" and "extending." In short, wisdom and justice must precede power, rather than vice versa (Cassidy 1994).

A rethinking of the relationship cannot come too soon. Canada's economic growth strategy is predicated on the principle of massively expanding its highly profitable natural resources sector

(Coates and Crowley 2013). Ottawa is projecting $650 billion worth of resource-extraction projects in the next decade (McCarthy 2013a, b), but most of these projects involve incursions into and across traditional aboriginal territory. Who will get what from the proceeds of Canada's natural resources (especially mining and petroleum) that generate $30 billion annually in federal and provincial taxes and royalties (Whittington 2013)? Is it possible to balance booming resource development across Canada with aboriginal rights, without diminishing their distinctiveness and identity or compromising environmental protection (Coates 2015a)? Both companies and the government will need to consult and compensate Aboriginal peoples not just as stakeholders but as partners in advancing development or securing social peace. But conflicts of interest are looming: in Canada, the federal government retains jurisdiction over status Indians on reserves, whereas the provinces own the resources. Aboriginal peoples want the federal government to push provinces in revenue-sharing deals, but the provinces may dismiss this intrusion as little more than poaching on jurisdictional turf (McCarthy 2013). The federal government in turn is often reluctant to even negotiate, much less commit to the principles of free, prior, and informed consent in advancing meaningful accommodation and rightful compensation.

The widening rifts between Canada/Canadian governments and Aboriginal peoples should come as no surprise. Stephen Harper's agenda focused on unlocking land and resources for multinational exploitation. To accomplish this without causing undue damage to investment prospects and international reputation, Aboriginal peoples would need to be integrated into existing orders of federal and provincial government—a project that could extinguish inherent, aboriginal, title, and treaty rights [Diablo 2014]) (Palmater 2015). This approach to aboriginal affairs is best described as pragmatic not ideological, incremental not transformative, reactive not proactive. It reflects a commitment to the principle of practical and immediate changes fixating on the art of the possible within the bounds of political and economic reality (for example, tinkering with the Indian Act rather than overhauling it [Curry 2013]). For the government, reference to a new relationship and ways of working together points to initiatives in building opportunities (capacity-building) within the existing system rather than increased transfers of power and authority (Crowley and Coates 2012). Upholding treaties involves addressing the specific obligations without inconvenient disruptions to the status quo. Federal authorities generally eschew references to Aboriginal peoples as sovereign nations with full entitlement to land, governance, and resources they claim to be theirs (Ibbitson 2013). For Aboriginal peoples, a new way of working together involves a package of demands related to aboriginal and treaty rights, sovereignty and self-governance, enforcement of a duty to consult and accommodate, sustainable fiscal arrangements, a spiritual responsibility to the earth and its preservation for future generations,

and a restoration of a nation-to-nation relationship (Monture 2014). They expect nothing less after decades of political, legal, and constitutional activism in which unprecedented power and authority were acquired, especially in the natural resources domain (Crowley and Coates 2015). In short, both government officials and Aboriginal peoples often use similar words yet speak a different language involving fundamentally different meanings. This breakdown in communication —talking past each other—does not bode well for closing the gaps by repairing the relationship. It remains to be seen whether Prime Minister Justin Trudeau's commitment to "make Canada Canadian again" will pay dividends in repairing the relationship between Canada and Aboriginal peoples by recasting it along the lines of the "nations within."

Summary

1. Aboriginal peoples may comprise Canada's First Peoples, yet, paradoxically, they often occupy a second-class socio-economic status and live under dystopian conditions that would embarrass some Third World countries in the global south.
2. The nature, scale, and scope of inequality and exclusions distort the lives and life chances of Canada's Aboriginal peoples.
3. Aboriginal peoples as a group rank at the bottom of Canada's socio-economic ladder with respect to employment, education, housing, health, income levels, and power.
4. The range of social inequality problems within aboriginal communities is partly offset by a growth of both economic clout and individual/community success stories.

5. Three explanatory frameworks (assimilationism, autonomism, and accommodationism) provide contrasting, albeit ideal-typical, models that account for aboriginal inequality of exclusions yet also draw attention to the complexities of the so called Indian problem.
6. Addressing Canada's first inequality hinges on repairing a broken relationship if there is any hope of a post-colonial coexistence.
7. The directly coercive rule of the past 150 years has given way to more indirect (neo-colonial) rule whose political, economic, and psychological structures continue to co-opt, appropriate, and marginalize.
8. The principles of constructive engagement may secure a post-colonial governance model for living differently together and equitably in a power sharing partnership.

Review Questions

1. Based on chapter material, discuss how both colonialism and neo-colonialism continue to create or reinforce patterns of inequality and exclusions in many aboriginal communities.

2. Compare the assimilationist, autonomist, and accommodationist models in terms of how they frame the aboriginal social inequality problem. Focus on underlying assumptions and proposed solutions.

3. Indicate how and why the concept of "relations repair" as it pertains to Aboriginal difference, aboriginal title and treaty rights, and aboriginal models of self-determining autonomy is at the heart of improving Aboriginal peoples–Canada relations.

4. Explain how the principles of constructive engagement are consistent with the principles of a post-colonial governance model.

5. Is the Nisga'a settlement an exercise in assimilationism, autonomism, or accommodationism? Defend your answer on principled grounds.

IV Institutional Exclusions

Many take it as axiomatic that discrimination-based inequalities permeate the domain and dynamics of Canadian institutions (Henry and Tator 2010; Das Gupta et al. 2007; Hier et al. 2009). Racialized minorities, Aboriginal peoples, newcomers to Canada, women, older folk, and gays and lesbians continue to be vilified and victimized by barriers both open and deliberate as well as deeply embedded and inadvertently conveyed by consequences (systemic) rather than intentionally (systematic). Debates over causes, characteristics, and consequences of institutional exclusions may have evolved over time in response to ideological shifts and grounded realities. But the politics of institutional inequality remain as volatile and divisive as ever. Institutions from media and policing to schooling and education are under pressure to create workplaces that are reflective, respectful, and responsive in offering community-based services that are readily available, easily accessible, and culturally appropriate. Considerable energy and expense have gone into the design and implementation of inclusive initiatives and equity interventions, but results have proven uneven—as might be expected in those institutional contexts largely impervious to reform, bewildered by new demands, oblivious to alternatives, or resentful of criticism. The tilt toward inclusiveness and equality notwithstanding, institutions can never attain the status of a level playing field. More accurately, they represent deeply uneven and foundationally biased terrains of competing interests, power dynamics, hidden agendas,

shifting priorities, calculated trade-offs, and competition for scarce resources (Chesler, Lewis, and Crowfoot 2005).

Reference to institutional bias and institutionalized exclusion opens yet another window into the domain of social inequalities. Institutions are sites of inequality in their own right in addition to their complicity in reproducing patterns of social exclusion in society at large. They give rise to inequalities of exclusion by reflecting, reinforcing, and reproducing those social patterns and belief systems that advantage some, disadvantage others (Albiston 2010). To be sure, institutions only rarely openly discriminate against those once perceived as inferior or irrelevant. Both law and the court of public opinion have put an end to such odious practices. But institutions are not neutral sites without hidden agendas. They are socially constructed and ideologically loaded conventions infused with values, ideals, and priorities that reflect, reinforce, and advance vested interests. The implications are deeply sociological: first, institutions are inherently unequal in terms of those founding assumptions and foundational principles that define who gets what, why, and how; what is acceptable and desirable, normal and necessary; and what counts as differences and what differences count as basis for reward or recognition. Yes, the historically disadvantaged (from workers to the recipients of services) may possess the same Charter rights and equal opportunities as all Canadians. Yet in a world ostensibly created by, for, and about powerful males, both women and minorities must work within an institutional framework neither designed to reflect their realities nor formulated to further their interests. Second, institutions also contribute to patterns of social inequality in society. They deliver services, such as educational outcomes or media outputs, that may reinforce existing patterns of societal exclusion, often in ways that are systemic (consequential) rather than systematic (deliberate).

Part IV addresses the topic of institutional inequalities by analyzing the institutions of work, as well as schooling and education, as two core workplaces at the forefront of progressive change yet chronic inequalities. Each of these institutions constitutes sites of inequality in their own right because of exclusionary structures (systematic bias) and structural exclusions (systemic bias). They also create outputs and services that reflect, reinforce, and advance broader patterns of social exclusion. The two chapters in this part are predicated on a key contradiction: institutions are undergoing unprecedented change and challenge in response to neo-liberal demands and the freewheeling dynamics of the new economy. Yet institutions are also under pressure to disrupt market dynamics through interventions that improve the inclusion of historically disadvantaged groups. The interplay of competing logics—the unfettered market versus social engineering—generates those mixed messages that can confuse or provoke, especially when the rules of the game undergo change without a road map to point the way into uncharted territory. Not surprisingly, institutions and institutional workplaces in the twenty-first century are experiencing what might be called an identity crisis of confidence as they try to figure out who they are and what they

should be doing during times of change, diversity, and uncertainty.

Chapter 9 looks at the rapidly changing and increasingly uncertain world of work (jobs or paid employment) working (the action of doing work), the workforce, and the workplace against the backdrop of the new economy. The interplay of globalized production, digital and automation technologies, and neo-liberal ideologies is transforming what work means today and how it's being performed. The emergence of a three-tiered workforce of privileged, perfunctory, and precarious workers is shown to engender new patterns of inequalities that pose some serious questions about work-related exclusions. Chapter 10 demonstrates how schooling and education, especially at post-secondary levels, are no less prone to ambiguity in responding to new expectations and shifting realities. To one side they are touted as paths to enlightenment and equality (the great equalizer); to the other, they remain sites of inequality that reinforce societal patterns of power and privilege (the great fortifier) (Foley and Green 2015). In short, the workplaces of work/working and education/schooling represent institutional sites of inequality due to indifference, domination, exclusion, or conformity. To be sure, these institutions are not the only organizations embroiled in uprooting the inequalities of exclusion, albeit with varying degrees of success. As the book has demonstrated throughout, most notably in chapters 4 and 6, media representations of social classes and women still leave much to be desired. But as key instruments of achievement and success in a diverse and changing society, both workplaces and schooling possess an additional obligation to become more inclusive to ensure no one is denied, damaged, or excluded.

9 The New Economy, New Exclusions: Work, Working, Workplaces

Learning Objectives

1. To deconstruct how the principles of the new economy provide a new business model for creating wealth by improving productivity.

2. To better appreciate how the rules of the new economy are intensifying patterns of workplace inequality.

3. To demonstrate how the new economy promotes a three-tiered workforce of winners, losers, and survivors.

4. To point out how the inequities of the old economy remain a reality for many Canadian workers.

5. To describe how exclusionary patterns persist in the new workplace (ageism), including a growing reliance on educated precarious workers.

6. To analyze two models of workplace governance—**inclusion** and **inclusivity**—as competing templates for creating a more inclusive workforce.

Introduction: The Best of Times, the Worst of Times

> There has never been a better time to be a highly skilled worker. Conversely, it is not a good time to be unskilled. This is deepening inequalities.
> —Selim Jahan, UN Human Development Report 2015

Work in the Canadian workplace is experiencing a crisis of epic proportions (Jackson 2010; Pupo, Glenday, and Duffy 2011). The interplay of macroeconomic trends and demographic shifts, alongside institutional reforms and government directives, has altered the workplace landscape in ways unimaginable a generation ago (Drummond and Fong 2010). Not too long ago, general prosperity prevailed, according to Robert Reich in his film *Inequality for All* (2013). A post-war pact between big capital and big labour (labour unions) mediated by an activist state ensured an abundance of jobs (paid work), rising wages, corporate expansion, and affordable post-secondary education (Brennan 2015). Those were the days when students chose a traditional discipline and transitioned their degree into a long and singular career (Baulcomb 2014). Even a high school diploma could be leveraged into a "real" (read: well-paying, full-time) job with life-long security and pension benefits—in contrast to the "gigs" of aspiring artists with high school dreams of rock stardom (Sundarajajan 2015). The labour market was bursting at the seams with the arrival of baby boomers whose optimism was as boundless as their sense of entitlement. Many applauded the emancipatory potential of automation for not only shedding dull and repetitive manufacturing jobs but also for freeing up both leisure time and creativity. Interestingly, computers were perceived as little more than novelties outside universities or the American defence department, with no discernible future in the workplace because of costs and inconvenience.

How times have changed. Canada's economic prosperity was once propelled by workers in relatively low-skilled but often unionized jobs which offered both security and wages in sectors such as construction, manufacturing, mining, and forestry. But many of these jobs have disappeared, while new positions in digital technology, creative content, finance, and advanced manufacturing require skill sets that are often unmet, resulting in significant levels of unemployment (Canadian Labour Congress 2014; Coates 2015b). A staggering loss of manufacturing jobs in Ontario (nearly 300,000 jobs between 2000 and 2013) has been offset by dramatic increases in both service-related jobs (an increase of one million jobs from 2000 to 2013 or 79 per cent of the Ontario labour market) and precarious work (for example, 41 per cent of jobs in Ontario now lie outside the framework of a standard full-time permanent employment contract with a single employer [Workers' Action Centre 2015; Tiessen 2014]). Full-time work (paid employment) and the perks accompanying life-long loyalty and traditional career paths are going the way of the bricks-and-mortar establishments such as travel agencies and video shops (but see Christensen and Schneider 2011). To the extent they still exist or matter, the ideals of corporate loyalty—once cherished as a sign of strength—are increasingly caricatured as a sign of weakness, lack of ambition, or a stalled career. Credential creep prevails: a post-secondary degree is defended as the minimum prerequisite for meaningful employment, even though it's hardly a job guarantee in a graduate's chosen field (TD Economics 2011; Hopper 2014). The proliferation of **precarious worker** jobs(temporary, casual, and contract) in an emerging gig economy (or a sharing peer-to-peer platform—a digitally powered hybrid that organizes economic activity by linking customers to independent traders of goods

or services through an online intermediary such as Uber or Airbnb [Sundarajajan 2015; Gardiner 2015; Matthews 2016]) means fewer benefits and less security for the unlucky ones—and possibly a lack of income to purchase the goods of a consumer economy (Ehrenreich 2014; Steinmetz 2016). And while women now constitute nearly 50 per cent of the labour market, in addition to being the primary wage-earner in about 40 per cent of households (Anderssen 2013), they continue to confront the corporate reality of "sticky floors," "glass ceilings," "revolving doors," and "double shifts" (Duxbury and Higgins 2012). Finally, the current generation sees itself falling backwards—from skyrocketing tuition fees to the prospect of precarious jobs and stagnant wages—with even steeper declines in the future in an economy that simply does not offer the same prospect of shared progress and optimism enjoyed by their boomer parents (Conference Board of Canada 2014; Graves 2014a).

Technology is also transforming the nature of work, workers, and workplaces in ways both emancipating and progressive yet regressive and exclusionary (Manyika et al. 2012). It is no secret that automation is displacing workers who toiled at assembly-line (repetitive) work in a mass-producing workplace. But instead of just shedding dull and repetitive jobs, the accelerating pace of digital technology and robotic automation may eventually dislodge (outsource) highly skilled interactive workers such as accountants and lawyers, thereby plunging them into a lifetime of un(der) employment and marginality (Frey and Osborne 2013; Saunders 2015). The fundamental shift in the relationship between machines and workers—from machines as tools to increase worker productivity to machines as workers displacing workers (Ford 2015; Carr 2015) is a cruel reminder: humans have made themselves so clever that they have become irrelevant because of machines that can do what we do and more (Harari 2014). As the founder of Momentum Machines (robots who assemble and grill gourmet burgers to order without human intervention) bluntly observes: "Our device isn't meant to make employees more efficient. It's meant to completely obviate them" (cited in Saunders 2015:F-2). Traditional job-creating machines such as manufacturing are going "south," with most industrial jobs unlikely to return, in effect pushing even more workers into precarious jobs with a corresponding loss of entitlements such as overtime pay or even minimum wage (Ng et al. 2013; McDonald 2013; Tiessen 2014; Workers' Action Centre 2015). A still-thriving **old economy** and service-based industries are increasingly staffed by immigrants, temporary foreign workers, and older workers who provide relatively cheap yet reliable labour. Youth unemployment in the post-great recession era is stalled in the 12 to 15 per cent range, with many young graduates forced into survival jobs below their qualifications and outside their field of study—a classic case of underemployment due to a mismatch between worker skills and employer needs (Sorrenson and Gillis 2013; Flavelle 2013b). This intergenerational conflict may well exert a scarring effect on today's youth by instilling a growing distrust in the political and economic system (Yakabuski 2013b).

A paradox of menacing proportions is looming: A **new economy** is evolving in which the business model for wealth creation is as different from the Industrial Revolution as that transformation was from the agricultural era. The freewheeling fluidity and dynamics of a new neo-liberal and just-in-time economy are now the unquestioned prototype for improving productivity and generating wealth. This **post-Fordist** commitment to neo-liberal principles is transforming the very nature of work and working within the new workplace, without dislodging the pervasiveness of **Fordist** principles in those old economy jobs such as quick-service industries. Or consider how the combination of automation, outsourcing, trade agreements, financialization of the global economy, and decline of manufacturing and digital technologies creates a system of almost limitless productive capacity yet also the spectre of structural unemployment and a jobless economy (Janoski, Luke, and Oliver 2014). Unemployment is not a problem of worker supply or skills mismatch but a structural problem since full employment is neither a feature nor a goal of neo-liberal capitalism (Klees 2014). Canadian employers remain reluctant to hire workers, preferring instead, to keep costs down by depleting permanent payrolls in an uncertain economic climate compounded by

currency and commodity price volatility (Grant 2015). The double whammy of corporations that hoard surpluses alongside austerity-driven governments that spurn job stimulation has yielded the quintessential twenty-first-century paradox (Dobbin 2015): a world of workers without work, of work without workers (McKenna 2012). The prospect of a jobless economic recovery and permanent (not cyclical) unemployment will invariably inflict a crippling effect on individuals (including rage, despair, domestic violence, and substance abuse), while imposing a warping impact on societies (from mistrust and divisiveness to increased criminality) (Peck 2010; Davey 2012; Coates 2015b). Or as Michael Valpy (2013) asks, what happens to society when its members are stripped of anchors and identities and forced to confront the "fearsome cave of economic insecurity"? The contradiction of chronic joblessness in an economy increasingly starved of meaningful work is also conveyed by Don Peck (2010):

> There is unemployment, a brief and relatively routine transitional state that results from the rise and fall of companies in any economy, and there is *unemployment*—chronic, all consuming. The former is a necessary lubricant in any engine of economic growth. The latter is a pestilence that slowly eats away at people, families, and, if it spreads widely enough, the fabric of society. Indeed history suggests that it is perhaps society's most noxious ill.

The magnitude of the crisis generated by the new economy should not be underestimated. The triple juggernauts of globalization, neo-liberalism, and technology expose the world of working, workers, and the workplace to upheavals as unsettling and unpredictable as any in human history (McDonald 2013; Harari 2014). Anything that can be off-shored, outsourced, downsized, and automated has been moved or expunged—or soon will be—in the headlong rush to improve the bottom line by pruning production costs, writes David McDonald (2013; also Frey and Osborne 2013; Friedman 2011c). Or as the chief economist at Decision Economics put it, ". . . business is about maximizing shareholder values. You basically don't want workers. You hire less and you try to find capital equipment to replace them" (cited in Tracy 2011). No wonder evidence points to a dramatic decline in the quality of good Canadian jobs based on an index that tracks part-time versus full-time work, paid work versus self-employment, and compensation trends for full-time workers (Tal 2015a). The consequences of this global and technological upheaval is a pyramid-shaped workforce of three tiers—a phalanx of highly sought after and well-paid creative workers (privileged) at the top; a residue of generally poorly paid contract workers (precarious) at the bottom; and an intermediate layer of workers (perfunctory) in full-time employment with decent pay and benefits, but minus the "wow" factor (Warren 2013).

Yet another paradox prevails: a global survey by Monster-GfK (2013) found the world's most satisfied workforce in Canada, with 64 per cent of Canadian workers loving/liking their jobs (in fact, 24 per cent say they would do their job for free), followed by the Netherlands at 57 per cent and Germany near the bottom at 34 per cent. But the good news is offset by a rash of labour-shedding factory closures in southern Ontario, including the Heinz plant in Leamington (with loss of 740 jobs); Schneiders of Kitchener (job loss at 1,400), in addition to US Steel in Hamilton, Kellogg's in London, Bick's Pickles in Dunnville, and Redpath Sugar in Niagara Falls (Ferguson 2013). How can one justify the reality of 1.3 million unemployed Canadians in 2012 yet the presence of 338,000 temporary foreign workers (ostensibly to offset a skills shortage and/or mismatch—skills employers want versus the skills job seekers offer) (Flavelle 2013b)? For those without work, the situation is grim. A world of work and working goes beyond the paycheque. A job represents a fundamental human need for purposeful activity, whereas the workplace constitutes the crucible that imparts meaning, dignity, and self-worth. Studs Terkel nailed it nicely:

> Work is about daily meaning as well as daily bread. For recognition as well as cash; for astonishment rather than torpor; in short, for a sort of life rather than a Monday through Friday sort of dying . . . . (*Utne Reader*, May/June, 1995)

In other words, working is so integral to many people's lives that a world without work is unthinkable. Work not only generates a livelihood and economic security, but it also allows people to fully participate in society, affords them a sense of dignity and worth, and unleashes human potential, creativity and spirit (Jahan 2015). Happiness researchers conclude that six months of unemployment is tantamount to the psychological impact of losing a spouse (Peck 2011). The human wreckage that follows from the ennui of joblessness is conveyed by a conservative American commentator (cited in Olive 2012 B1):

> Short of death or debilitating terminal disease, long term unemployment is about the worst thing that can happen to you in the modern world. It's economically awful, socially terrible and a horrifying blow to your self-esteem and happiness. It cuts you off from the mass of your peers and puts stress on your family, making it likely that further awful things like divorce or suicide will be in your near future.

For workers, then, the world of working and the workplace is a paradoxical place: to one side, a modern landscape of friendship, self-growth, and creativity; to the other side, a source of frustration, violence, numbing routine, and exclusion (Gratton 2010; Yemma 2012). Talk of worker empowerment and improving work–life balance notwithstanding, a hard-driving corporate culture remains the rule—as revealed in an exposé of Amazon.com's intensely competitive work environment (one in which the always-on obligations to the company override all other employer concerns) (Kantor and Streitfeld 2015). Organizations such as Amazon.com are pushing their teams to do more for less, continuously measuring individual performances, insisting on a come-and-go relationship between employer and employee, and making the modern office more nimble and productive yet also more harsh and unforgiving. Worse still, the inequalities and exclusions that pervade the domain of work in the workplace are unlikely to subside in the foreseeable future as the work-rich outpace the work-poor to further fortify a workforce gap. It is precisely this tension between the workplace as a linchpin for equality *and* an incubator of work inequality and worker exclusion that provides the rationale for this chapter.

This chapter explores those emergent patterns of inequality that inform the world of work, working, and workplace against the backdrop of the new economy (also Pupo and Thomas 2009). Workplace organizations in the neo-liberal-driven and the globalization-themed new economy are no longer seen as smoothly functioning "sites" but as "confluences of contestation"—that is, an ideological battleground of competitively different groups over control of the agenda within contexts informed by the politics of diversity, uncertainty, and change. Exclusionary patterns can range from increasingly alienated workers in search of employee empowerment, to a diversifying workforce in pursuit of inclusion through removal of discriminatory barriers. Paradoxes prevail: institutions and workplaces may be under neo-liberal pressure to be more market-oriented in design, process, rewards, and outputs. Yet they are constantly reminded (and prodded) by governments to be more inclusive of diversities (from gender to racialized minorities) through intervention strategies that disrupt market realities. As a result of this interplay of neo-liberalism with inclusiveness, the realities of the workplace fall somewhere in between the poles of chaos and regulation, of structure and agency, of continuity and change, and of resistance and control. Such an interpretation

neither yields elegant models of organization nor reflects the precision of simulated spreadsheets. But it does capture the dynamics and dilemmas in that "fearsome cave" of workplace inequalities where the only certainty is uncertainty.

The chapter begins by exploring how the rules of the new economy are generating new patterns of inequality in workplaces as they relate to work, working, and the workforce. The new economy, with its freewheeling and neo-liberal model of wealth creation, is contrasted to the protectionism (interventions) of the old nationalist economy. The evolving and contested nature of work, workforces, and workplaces is then examined against the backdrop of the old economy versus the new economy (also Krahn, Lowe, and Hughes 2010; McMullin and Marshall 2010). The argument is relatively straightforward: work is not disappearing per se; rather work as conventionally defined is being superseded by new forms because of broader changes to the economy. The combination of ideological shifts (neo-liberalism) and structural readjustments (globalization) in the new economy has given rise to three-tiered workforces, namely, privileged, perfunctory, and precarious. The chapter concludes by analyzing two models of institutional governance—inclusion and inclusivity—both of which in their own way propose a more inclusive workforce. Before beginning, however, a brief overview of the job market in Canada:

Overview of Work and Workers in Canada: The National Household Survey, 26 June 2013

- The Canadian labour force numbered 18 million in 2011, with 16.6 million, or a rate of 61 per cent of the total population, employed. Calgary's employment rate of 70 per cent is highest in Canada, while Windsor's is lowest at 53.3 per cent. Employment rates in Yukon (69.7 per cent) and Alberta (69 per cent) are highest in the country; Newfoundland and Labrador is

lowest at 50.7 per cent (Statistics Canada 2013c).

- The retail sector accounted for 11.5 per cent of the country's workforce, followed by health care and social assistance at 11.4 per cent, and manufacturing at 9.2 per cent (down from 11.8 per cent in 2006). Earnings in the retail sector amounted to $524 on average per week, compared

continued

to over $800 a week for those in health services. On average, Canadians earned just under $900 per work week, based on 2012 data (Mackenzie 2014).

- The most common occupations for women—retail sales, administrative assistant, registered nurse, cashier, and school teacher—reflect a historical pattern.
- The most common occupations for men were also conventional: retail sales, truck driver, retail and wholesale manager, carpenter, janitor, caretaker, and building superintendent.
- Eleven point eight million Canadians aged 25 to 64 had post-secondary qualifications: 26.9 percent had a university degree, 21.3 percent had a college diploma, and 12.1 per cent had a trades certificate. Twelve point seven per cent of adults had no certificate, degree, or diploma. Only 9.8 per cent of aboriginal adults possess a university degree.

Labour Force Survey

- The unemployment rate in October 2013 stood at 6.9 per cent—its lowest rate since the onset of the great recession of 2008, where it peaked at just under 9 per cent (in March 2016, it was 7.1 per cent). Saskatchewan has the lowest jobless rate at 3.6 per cent; by contrast, the highest rate of unemployment is in Newfoundland and Labrador at 9.4 per cent. The employment rate increased as well by 1.2 per cent compared to October 2012, with gains in both full-time and part-time jobs. Jobs continue to be created, especially in health care and construction, but this growth comes with strings attached (Statistics Canada 2013c):
  - The number of well-paying factory and manufacturing jobs continues to decline (82,500 jobs lost over the past year).
  - Public sector employment rose by 47,300 jobs, but private sector shed 22,100 jobs, while self-employment shrank by 12,000.

- The jobless rate for women 25 and older dropped to 5.2 per cent but increased to 6.3 per cent for older men.
- The youth unemployment rate rose by 1.6 per cent from the previous October and stood at 13.4 per cent.
- Workers over the age of 55 now comprise 18.7 per cent of the workforce, up from 15.5 per cent in 2006.

Patterns of Employment: Part-time versus Full-time

- Between January and August 2014, 95,000 new jobs were added to the Canadian economy. Sixty percent of the new jobs were part-time positions; nevertheless full-time jobs still account for 80 per cent of total employment. Women account for the 70 per cent of part-time employment (TD Economics 2014).
- According to TD Economics report (2014), about 1 million Canadians who constitute so-called involuntary part-time workers would prefer a full-time job.

Income Patterns

- The highest paying job sector in Canada belongs to specialist physicians, whose annual income of $350,000 topped the list in 2014. Next on the list of best paid are judges at $260,000, and senior managers of financial, communications, and other business services at $225,000 (Statistics Canada 2015). The lowest paying job sectors are babysitters, nannies, and parent helpers who earn $12,662. Next on the list are female-dominated sectors including food and beverage servers at $13,861, and food preparers/service counter attendants at $14,681. The lowest paid male-dominated jobs were parking-lot attendants, who pocketed around $21,000 per year.
- Wages and salaries for most Canadians have flat-lined since the 1980s (Broadbent Institute 2014; Mackenzie 2015; Tal 2015b).

The *median* household income in 2012 was $74,400, according to Statistics Canada (2014), based on income tax returns filed that year. The *average* worker income was about $49,000. Those in the mining/quarrying/oil and gas extraction industries averaged the highest earnings at about $110,000, whereas those in accommodation and food services earned on average just under $20,000 (Statistics Canada 2015).

- The average compensation in 2013 for Canada's 100 highest paid CEOs was about 195 times the pay of the average worker (Mackenzie 2015). In Britain in 2011, the ratio stood at 162 times (Dorling 2012); in Germany about 12 times (in 1999), and in Japan, about 17 times.
- The top 1 percent in Canada earn about 11 per cent of all national income; the figure for the United States is 22 per cent.

The New Economy, Newer Inequalities

Popularity aside, references to the new economy are imprecise and subject to diverse interpretations. Generally however, the new economy refers to those ideological shifts, structural readjustments, and technological changes involving innovative patterns of production and wealth creation. Wealth creation in the new economy reflects post-industrial employment patterns rooted in knowledge and services instead of manufacturing (Pupo and Omas 2009). Take Canada: although the Canadian economy is often associated with resources and industry, Canada is first and foremost a services economy (from ICT and financial services to hospitality and health services) at the level of employment, economic productivity, and international business (tradeable services geared toward the global market [Schwanen 2014]). These account for over 70 per cent of Canada's GDP and 80 per cent of employment growth over the past three decades, including many highly skilled and well-paying jobs (Goldfarb and Palladini 2015). Related to this transformational shift is the distinction between the old and new economies, which is often framed as a contrast between Fordist and post-Fordist models of production and wealth creation (Adelaja 2008). Fordist (or industrial) models under the old economy emphasized mass and standardized production, Taylorist management techniques, vertical integration, economies of scale, de-skilled labour, and nationalized economies buffered by protectionist tariffs. By contrast, post-Fordist (post-industrial) models for growing the economy embrace new economy principles, namely, a novel set of rules and priorities consistent with the flexibility afforded by a freewheeling neo-liberalism at national and international levels; a just-in-time agenda for production; the production of goods and services geared primarily for export rather than domestic consumption; and the financialization of the economy (wealth and profitability through money-dealings such as investments, futures, hedge funds, etc.) (Bello 2013). The following structural features are uppermost:

1. The new economy is driven by the primacy of a *neo-liberal ideology* with its corresponding commitment to more market, less government, and more individual responsibility. Neo-liberal agendas for growing the new economy uphold the private sector as innovative and efficient in contrast to the sluggishness and bureaucracy of the public sector. They tend to emphasize aggressive market competitiveness, a flexible workforce to address the demands of just-in-time productivity, regulations that work to the advantage of employers as the path to prosperity and growth, and a belief that the discipline of the market (i.e., inequality) improves productivity (Warwick-Booth 2013). Under neo-liberalism, the concept of a free market is defined as a solution to both economic and social problems. By contrast, blame for economic inequality is pinned on either big government or personal flaws. Free market principles of neo-liberalism are applied to society as well as the economy, on the assumption that societies work best when

resource allocation reflects a neo-liberal logic rather than government intervention or social engineering (Vallas 2011).

2. The principles of *production* have undergone a transformational shift towards new patterns of wealth creation. The old industrial-manufacturing economy has lost its hold in a world where digital and transportation technologies make it easy to off-shore, downsize, and outsource. The following post-Fordist initiatives have taken its place: delivery of parts as needed (just-in-time); availability of disposable labour; reliance on outsourcing (contracting out); small batch production to meet demand; and elimination of any operations (such as storage) that do not directly contribute to corporate value. Reliable suppliers and predictable markets are virtually a thing of the past. Pattern and prediction in the economy have been displaced by highly competitive and unpredictable environments that are difficult to control or that resist regulation. For example, the ride-sharing app Uber consists of drivers who, as freelancers, earn their income in a so-called gig (on-demand) economy that bypasses the traditional employee-employer relationship in ways that befuddle (and infuriate) regulators such as the taxi industry (Yakabuski 2015). Uber may be the fastest growing start-up in history—now valued at $60 billion in just five years—yet it has accomplished this without hiring a single driver, instead simply providing software that allows willing parties to connect (Steinmetz 2016). New ways of organizing work and working typify a post-Fordist economy, with its reduction of management tiers, emergence of an on-demand workforce, and more flattened approaches to management-worker relations, with layers of management pared away to create a more democratic (horizontal) pattern of decision-making and power-sharing.

3. The *global mobility of productivity* is situated within an intensely competitive global market economy. Whereas wealth creation in the old economy consisted of a series of local industries locked into closed national economies and buttressed by protectionist tariffs, the new economy promotes the globalization of production within a global division of labour. Both the production

and distribution process are partitioned into components, from research to final assembly, then (out)sourced or off-shored throughout the world (Breznitz and Zysman 2013). By facilitating communication and coordination on a global basis, the ICT revolution allows businesses to seamlessly coordinate activities anywhere in the world (Alexander and Fong 2014). The net result is a dynamic system of integrated and cost-effective sites of production and wealth creation that transcend national borders and realign patterns of global inequality by improving the economies of developing countries in the global south at the expense of inequalities for low- and middle-income workers in advanced economies.

4. Information (creativity) and communication (digital) technology (ICT) is central as a *source* of wealth production rather than simply a *means* to growing the old economy. New technologies have transformed how people work, the skills they need, the demands imposed on them, their relationship to changing demographics, and the kind of career plans for navigating a topsy-turvy world. But continued reliance *on technology* as a cost-effective source of wealth creation is proving double-edged. Labour-saving devices may reduce much of the drudgery associated with traditional tasks, allowing the lucky few to pursue more creative pursuits. Advanced technology may also help firms become more productive, efficient, and profitable (Arshad 2012). Yet wholesale restructuring due to job-stripping automation tends to displace workers in the constant quest to do more with less and do it cheaply (Carr 2015; Ford 2015). Investments in machinery and equipment have eliminated both low- and middle-income work (or deeply eroded the bargaining power of workers). The opposite is true for high-skill workers since technological advancements create a substantial premium for those with the talent to unlock the full potential of new technology (Alexander and Fong 2014; Jahan 2015). Such a scenario points to an unsettling conclusion: contemporary inequalities not only reflect the unequal availability of opportunity, but also the unequal ability to exploit opportunity (Muller 2013).

5. Workers are redistributed across a three-tiered pyramidal model. Companies are looking for ways to prune costs by shedding those personnel whose salaries and benefits compromise the bottom line. CEOs prefer a workforce that can be adjusted to meet fluctuations in the business cycle: just-in-time workers can be hired quickly during business upturns, then swiftly dismissed when demand drops or profits shrink. A sharper division of workers and a greater flexibility of work practices prevails: a cadre of well-paid knowledge workers (including professionals and senior management) and privileged creative workers is superimposed on a swelling mass of low wage service and contract-type workers at the bottom (precarious) who can be rotated in and out as the situation demands. Sandwiched in between is a solid mass of service workers—from hospitality and retail (personal services) to human, health, education and information sectors (specialized services)—engaged in largely repetitive and relatively mundane work (perfunctory).

6. *The employer–employee social contract is being re-thought.* The old social contract promised a lifelong career to anyone who applied him or herself and demonstrated loyalty to the company. By contrast, the new freelance (gig) economy contract envisions a flexible workplace, including a just-in-time template applied to work and workers so that the workforce can be upsized or downsized to match boom-bust cycles (Sorenson 2012). The new social contract puts the onus on individual adaptability (namely, a freelance mentality and a free agency mindset) as dreams of an upwardly mobile career path go up in smoke (Hoffman, Casnocha, and Yeh 2013; McDonald 2013). Employers are looking for workers whose creative and critical thinking skills not only add more value to jobs than either a robot or an operator in India; they also want workers who can reinvent their jobs and increase productivity on a daily basis to take advantage of global opportunities (Friedman 2011c). The shift from lifetime employment and career aspirations to temporary employment puts the focus on personal "re-skilling" and lifetime learning.

Rethinking Work and Working in the New Workplace

Work has been around since the beginning of human history. It remains an inextricable component of contemporary human existence across the life course. Students engage in work when going to school; upon graduation many will begin to work at jobs or pursue careers. Some will continue to work at home by looking after children, albeit without a formal wage. Others will work out of their homes by exchanging goods and services for payment. Still others will be paid for working outside the house, often in large corporate settings with a corresponding risk of losing creativity, control, and individuality. A few see work as the crowning glory of a meaningful existence; others prefer to shirk jobs that are a source of aggravation or humiliation. Still others simply go through the motions—as robotic in their actions as the moving conveyor belt that enslaves as it degrades. Others still wonder about the meaning of work in the twenty-first century, given the withering away of manufacturing jobs, the hollowing out of labour unions, the spread of digital technology, just-in-time models of wealth production, global mobility of the production process, and the demise of full-time employment and stable careers (Vallas 2011).

Work: From Jobs to McJobs to Joblessness

Work as a socially constructed activity has undergone changes (Vallas 2011). Until the nineteenth century, people did work instead of having jobs per se (Keegan 1996). Work was not factory drudgery in exchange for pay; rather, it was an activity for doing something at a certain time and place, according to personal and seasonal rhythms. But organized work (paid employment in the labour market [Vallas 2011]) emerged with the Industrial Revolution and the mechanization of the production process. Work was abstracted and divorced from the rhythms of daily life. It was reincarnated, instead, as a factor of production that could be measured to create products with market value (Baldry et al. 2007). Even so, barely 50 per cent of the workers in the industrialized world a century ago worked for a company. Workplaces were small, family-owned, and rudimentary in organization. It was not until the early 1970s that labour-intensive industrialization raised the figure to nearly the entirety of the workforce.

The concept of work as jobs has continued to evolve (Vallas 2011). Just as the Industrial Revolution ushered in a major reorientation of the workplace—with its promise of a full-time job for life, well-defined career paths, and corporate loyalty in exchange for job security—so too are countervailing forces of the new economy dismantling the very nature of work in creating wealth, the composition of the workforce, and the organization of the workplace (Pupo, Glenday, and Duffy 2011). Technology has rendered obsolete nineteenth-century notions of work, with its connotation of passive workers tethered to a spot for a specified period of time in exchange for pay. Emerging instead are "flex-time" models in which workers are entrusted with greater autonomy and control over where, when, and how they work (Maitland and Thomson 2011). The youthful cohort of Generation Y take for granted the greater flexibility afforded by technology to connect with their peers anytime without sacrificing work outputs. They also expect to work in workplaces that encourage a life–work balance rather than one that enslaves workers to their jobs (Maitland and Thomson 2011). Work in the new workplace is no longer a linear wage-by-age activity (i.e., earning in the $20,000s in one's twenties, the $30,000s in one's thirties, etc.) from nine to five each day every day. It is more of a zig-zag of holding patterns, career trajectories, and blocked opportunities in an on-demand work world that must be negotiated and customized through choices and risks (Sorenson 2012).

Jobs may become an endangered species with the onset of a new economy. Computers may be creating more jobs than they rendered redundant; however, technology is undermining the viability not only of unskilled workers in repetitive jobs but also of white collar jobs that involve patterned interaction and decision-making. The advent of digital technology has expanded the volume of work done by robots and machines, none of which require costly dental plans or spark labour disputes. Admittedly, not all jobs will disappear because of the new economy. A knowledge-based economy will safeguard jobs for scientists, engineers, software analysts, and biotechnology researchers—namely those privileged few who can extract value from modern technology (also Coates and Morrison 2012). Those in the specialized service sector (from teachers to eldercare providers) should prosper as well, despite the often perfunctory nature of their jobs. But there is little hope for those on the job margins with ordinary skills and abilities (Jahan 2015). Part-time and temporary jobs will predominate in an economy that prospers from the precariousness of underemployment. No amount of retooling or upgrading will help the millions discarded because of planned obsolescence, especially if there is no meaningful work out there regardless of people's credentials or skills. The gradual decline of smokestack industries raises another slew of inequality issues as profit-hungry companies seek off-shore locations to prune production costs.

However impressive this shift in rethinking wealth creation in the new economy, the cliché "nothing changes except change" is strangely apropos when applied to the world of work and working. The new economy does not dispense with the old economy of work; more accurately, it superimposes itself on the old economy to forge a mixed (hybrid) model of productivity and wealth. The Taylorist principles of scientific management (managers manage, workers work) continue to dominate the organization of production in those old economy workplaces that rely on the assembly-line dogma of efficiency, calculability, predictability, and control ("McDonaldization") to enhance productivity and outputs (Ritzer 2012). The Spotlight box on the following page demonstrates the relevance of this model to the quick service industry.

Despite the dehumanizing activity described in the Spotlight box, the centrality of work in defining the human condition cannot be denied (Valpy 2013). Historically, people's lives and identities revolved around work and their relationship to workplaces. But the concept of conventional work is gradually being redefined or discarded because of computer-mediated automation, a neo-liberal mentality that elevates markets/profits over all other considerations, and a corporate reorganization that treats workers as

Spotlight Making Assembly-Line Burgers: Old Fordist Work in a New Post-Fordist Economy

Any trained monkey could do the job.
—Reiter 1992, 167

Mass production for most of the twentieth century was the dominant organizational framework, influencing both corporate strategy and the design of jobs. Fordist means of production dovetailed with Taylorist principles of scientific management—namely, mass production, standardized products, strict division of labour, and labour de-skilling. Taylorism (named after Frederick Taylor) sought to make complex organizations more efficient by applying the principles of rationality for controlling both the work process and the workforce. The drive for cost efficiency transformed the workplace into a glorified machine with mechanistic precision and control to maximize productivity and wealth creation along the following lines:

1. A simple division of labour, best summarized in the aphorism, "managers think and command, workers do and obey."
2. The use of carefully calibrated methods to determine the most efficient work routine. Through precise measurement and reliance on time-and-motion studies, an optimum level of performance could be devised.
3. Division of the production process into its smallest constituent units for assignment to trained workers. Train the best person for each particular job and no other.
4. Encouragement of productivity by increasing monetary rewards as the key incentive.
5. Routinizing work by eliminating the human element (i.e., uncertainty, risk, or choice) in the production while improving control over the entire process.

The traditional workplace was authoritarian by nature. Most workers exerted little control over the production process; the work itself was often alienating or exploitative, if not openly dangerous;

stress factors contributed to high rates of staff turnover and absenteeism; and mind-numbing routines could induce thoughtless complacency or open sabotage. Managerial interests took top priority at the expense of workers who were relegated to the bottom or the background. But that was then—what about now? Talk of workplace revolution notwithstanding, the fast-food (quick-service) industry continues to rely on the principles of scientific management (a conveyor belt mentality) for dealing with production, customers, and employees (Ritzer 2015). The embodiment of fast food principles reflects the rationalities of efficiency (optimum method for getting from point A to point B), calculability (exacting measurement to ensure speed and reduce costs), predictability (assurance of product control no matter where), and control (limit options to ensure customer flow-through). This portrayal of work experiences at a Toronto-based Burger King restaurant demonstrates how the preoccupation with standardization applies not only to food preparation but also to customer relations and workplace dynamics. The fact that everyone and everything is reduced to a cog in the fast-food machine confirms the attractiveness of Taylorism (or "McDonaldization") as a principle of organization and wealth creation.

Central to scientific management principles is a commitment to regulate the workplace by de-humanizing it. Rigid operational procedures and standardization are adopted not to improve food quality, but to eliminate the uncertainty—the human element—from the production process. Or, as one of the original McDonald brothers once said about his golden arches: "If we gave people a choice, there would be chaos" (Love 1995: 15). This dehumanization process is organized around the pursuit of quantity (the ideal of standardization and predictability in the preparation of food), service (speed in the delivery of food to each customer), and cleanliness (associated with "order" and consumer "appeal" rather than healthfulness) (see also Ritzer

continued

2012). Each outlet combines unskilled machine operators and auxiliary staff with sophisticated technology to produce a highly polished product through painstaking attention to design and presentation (Reiter 1992: 75). To the extent that these goals are achieved, each fast-food outlet conforms to the ideals of scientific management. Many of the examples below are taken from Ester Reiter's (1992/1996) book on a Burger King franchise in Toronto, *Making Fast Food: From the Frying Pan into the Fryer*.

The operations of a Burger King franchise are regulated to the minutest detail. Pots and pans, as well as chefs and dishwashers, have been replaced by automated routine and a crew of undifferentiated machine-tenders. With the aid of computer technology, Burger King can slot almost any crew member into any food-processing function by simply cross-training workers to conduct a number of simplified tasks. Both movements and emotions are controlled by the franchise. Those who work at counters and take customer orders are expected to display a ready smile, a cheerful yet energetic disposition, and clichéd lines in promoting the sale of meals. Kitchen workers are no less programmed in terms of appearance and lines of interaction. Jobs are divided and arranged in ways easy to master and measure for the sake of efficiency. Workers are treated as commodities: they are expected to place their responsibility to the franchise above family or friends. Each worker is asked to work as hard as possible, to come to work at short notice, or to comply with irregular hours. The authority over workers in the back region contrasts sharply with the controlled-indulgence offered to customers at the counter.

Consider the preparation of a conveyor belt burger. All food enters the store in its final pre-cooking stages: hamburgers arrive as frozen precooked patties, while buns are precooked and caramelized to ensure an appealing image. French fries, chicken, and fish are precooked to ensure a standardized product. Condiments such as onions or pickles (with the exception of tomatoes) are pre-sliced or pre-shredded. The in-store preparation of these foods is essentially that of machine-tending—the incorporation of assembly-line technology in the quick service industry. For example, hamburgers are placed on a conveyor belt that "cooks" the frozen meat patties in 94 seconds. A worker at the other end of the broiler transfers the cooked patty to the bottom half of the bun. The ungarnished hamburger is then placed in a steamer where it can remain for up to 10 minutes before being discarded. Workers at the burger board "assemble" the burger by adding the condiments (cheese slices, pickles, onions, mayonnaise, lettuce, tomatoes, ketchup, and mustard). Pickle slices are spread evenly over the meat or cheese (no overlapping is allowed). Ketchup is spread in a circular motion over the pickles. Mayonnaise is then applied to the top of the bun in a single stroke, while three-quarters of an ounce of shredded lettuce is sprinkled over the mayonnaise. Two slices of tomato (three is permissible, but only with management's permission) are placed on top of the lettuce. The assembly process for a Whopper itself should take no longer than 23 seconds. The finished burger is placed in a box or wrapper, reheated in a microwave for 14 seconds, then placed in a chute.

The fast-food industry relies on deeply managed work processes and authoritarian labour-management relations that reduce labour and work to its simplest components. The principle of formal rationality (McDonaldization) strikes at the core of this process and relationship (Ritzer 2012). Applied to the fast food industry, a commitment to rationality ensures the following dimensions: the operation is predictable (consistent when it comes to taste, appearance, and speed of delivery) and calculable, since quantity is emphasized over quality (the bottom line is about the number of customers processed, the speed with which they are processed, and the profits produced); workers are expected to act in robot-like fashion (people are trained to work in an automatic, unthinking way, whether preparing food or serving customers); and control over the product is secured by disciplining the workforce. Customers are thus shielded from the exploitative work situation that confronts Burger King workers (see also Kantor 2014); they see only the benign image of benevolence and wholesomeness. This gap between illusion and reality may prove to be the biggest whopper of them all.

"profit busting liabilities" (Hatton 2011:3; Rifkin 1995). The rules of the new economy have altered the nature of work, how work is organized, and the relationship of work to wealth production. A globally based, profit-driven economy cannot possibly provide work for everyone. By the same token, the resiliency of a free-enterprise system should never be underestimated. Admittedly, the demise of work may be greatly exaggerated. Even the much touted skills shortage and mismatch may be overblown by employers who inflate the crisis as an excuse to keep a lid on wages and training costs (Flavelle 2013b). Each new technological advance has the potential to create new products, redefine workplace routines, invent new needs, and alter existing employment patterns. In other words, what is happening in the new economy is not so much the end of work but the end of work (or jobs) as we know it.

Workers and Working: The Privileged, the Perfunctory, the Precarious

> [Companies] used to think that their most important asset was skilled workers. Now by contrast, it looks as though firms think that their workers are much more disposable— that it's their brands or their machines or their procedures or their organizations that are the key assets. They still want to keep their workers happy in general, they just don't care as much about these particular workers.
> —Berkeley Economist Brad DeLong, cited in Hatton 2011:X

What is good for the business component in growing the economy does not necessarily benefit the workforce. Changes in the new economy are generating opportunity and success for some, but social inequality and exclusion for others as wages stagnate, work disappears, and people's sense of self-worth plummets (Fanelli et al. 2011; Valpy 2013). Tensions are palpable as individuals must manage their portfolios at the same time companies are struggling to survive and compete in the global marketplace (McMullin and Marshall 2010). The demand for contingent workers and a highly flexible labour supply may bolster the bottom line of a just-in-time workplace. Yet many workers pay the price of this structural readjustment because they lack the benefits of steady employment, including overtime pay, employment compensation, health care coverage, or retirement packages (Gonick 2011; Hatton 2012). For the unlucky ones, work is a necessary and burdensome chore for making money rather than a path to self-fulfillment (Armstrong 2012). Not surprisingly, a Gallup poll (cited by Lopez 2013) indicated that 70 per cent of American workers are disengaged from their jobs, including 50 million who are simply going through the motions and another 20 million who loathe what they do. Still others are simply cast aside as little more than expendable fodder in a labour-shedding, just-in-time economy. Access to adequately waged jobs is further jeopardized by a combination of people-displacing technologies and a globalizing economy that outsources jobs to lower-paid offshore workers. Let's put it into context: paid work remains the most essential of human activities in securing personal identity and informing social experiences (Pupo, Glenday, and Duffy 2011; Krahn and Lowe 1994). Yet worker disposability may be the reigning orthodoxy in the new economy.

Much of the inequality and exclusion can be attributed to rule changes that formerly governed "how work was done around here." Work is rapidly disappearing in certain quarters, as workplace automation kicks in and workers are kicked out. More sophisticated assembly line robots are warehousing workers as management obsesses over reducing costs to stay competitive in global markets (Markoff 2012; Harari 2014). Even the prospect of job permanence and career security is vanishing because of restructuring, managerial de-layering, and workforce downsizing. With risk-averse companies increasingly reluctant to offer full-time jobs with benefits except to the exceptionally skilled, precarious employment is becoming the new norm, a shift that imposes financial strain and emotional stress on households (Lewchuk et al. 2013). Career patterns may entail a combination of contract work for a variety of companies, interspersed with periods of unemployment or underemployment. To be sure, for those with skills and connections, work is not necessarily a penalty for pay as much as an opportunity for empowerment. They possess meaningful and significant jobs involving high levels of autonomy, opportunity to use skills, opportunity to see the whole product, and positive feedback (McDonald 2013). For others, work will remain a dreary cycle of dead-end McJobs, from fast-food floors to white-collar factory workers (for example, call centres), with few rewards and fewer opportunities. Some have so much work on a 24/7 basis that personal and family life suffer because of the always-on communication technologies. Others have so little work that they too suffer personal and social marginality in a world where individual worth is often measured by a person's relationship to work. For still others, as Studs Terkel writes, there is no life after work, only a Monday-to-Friday kind of dying.

A globalizing new economy has exerted bewildering pressure on the nature and dynamics of the workplace. The combination of intense global competition with automation and digital innovations has proven both dismaying and disruptive. Both the private and public sector have embarked on labour-shedding processes that eliminate the most costly element in the production process: workers. Jobs are disappearing as decisions to downsize, outsource, or off-shore reflect and reinforce a model of doing business that reduces labour costs (Saunders 2015). As Michael Dunkerley writes in his book, *The Jobless Economy*, "People are now the most expensive optional component of the production process. . . . People are now targeted for replacement as soon as the relevant technology is developed to replace them." Whereas workers in the old economy were organized around mass labour and material outputs, in the new economy they reflect a polarized division of labour: on the one hand are the knowledge workers, with high-paying and prestigious jobs whose creative skills are deployed to generate wealth (privileged). On the other hand are the poorly paid and underemploying jobs in personal care, food services, and retail sales—McJobs that have been de-skilled by automation or eliminated by the shift of manufacturing to low cost countries, that lack decent wages or benefits or any long-term security, that often expose individuals to stress and danger and are casualized to the point of underemployment (precarious) (Florida and Mellander

2012). Employers take advantage of lax employment laws for precarious work to bypass basic worker entitlements (e.g., overtime pay) by outsourcing, hiring through temp agencies, and misclassifying workers as independent consultants (Workers' Action Centre 2015). In between are those with relatively secure and benefits-based job—if not exactly inspiring routines that provide a specific service (perfunctory).

In short, workers in the new economy are trifurcating into three analytically separate streams. The "work-rich" have secure jobs with value-added employment as a function of their privileged status. If anything they have too much work because of an expectation to be always on, always connected. So much for John Maynard Keynes's rosy, Depression-era prediction that a surplus of wealth from economic growth and automation would lead to a world of prosperity and increased leisure (Skidelsky and Skidelsky 2012). To the other side is a wobbly perimeter of part-time or contract workers often without benefits, livable wages, or job security, with little opportunity for advancement or success. The "work-poor" are relegated to precarious status, including dull and dirty jobs that pose a danger to workers. Adding insult to injury is an untapped pool of hundreds of thousands of workers on the margins of society (*precariat*, an amalgam of *proletariat* and *precarious*) with no work and little chance of snaring a job with a decent wage, sense of career or security, or expectation of entitlements, occupational identity, and benefits (Standing 2012). In the middle are those stuck in McJobs that may offer little in the way of intrinsic rewards, but generally provide decent pay, benefits, permanent work, and the possibility of a career path.

Table 9.1 provides a comparison of the three-tiered stream of workers, based on select criteria in the left hand column. The classification is based not on the level of job satisfaction or occupational prestige, but on the kind of work that workers do, their employment status, and the degree of control they exercise over working conditions and employment prospects. Keep in mind the inevitability of overlap and inconsistencies between and within categories, as might be expected of an ideal-typical arrangement. Any given institution may also incorporate

Table 9.1: Three-Tiered Workforce in the New Economy: Privileged, Perfunctory, Precarious

	Privileged	Perfunctory	Precarious
Context for wealth creation	a. New economy b. ICT revolution c. Global in scope d. Networked	a. Old economy b. Industrial Revolution c. Local/regional	a. Old economy b. Industrial Revolution c. Local/regional
Status of workers	a. Valued core + b. Flexible contract	a. Job secure b. Specialized service c. Blue collar factory d. White collar office	a. Expendable b. Quick service status c. Flexibility = new norm
Nature of work	a. Always-on skills b. Knowledge work c. Creative d. Risk-taking/innovative e. Catalyst f. Career changes	a. Just-in-place skills b. "McJob" c. Manufacturing d. Service industry (personal care) e. Life-long career	a. Just-in-time skills b. "Work poor" c. Dull, dirty, dangerous d. Casual/part-time/ self-employed e. Expendable
Patterns of working	a. Creative skills b. Collaborative c. Teamwork d. Work–life balance	a. Skilled b. Social contract = loyalty and productivity for wage, job security, benefits	a. Un/De/skilled b. Dehumanizing c. Alienation
Workplace as site	a. Post-Fordist b. Flattened hierarchy c. Decentralized d. Participatory	a. Fordist (Taylorism) b. Pyramidal hierarchy c. Centralized d. Authoritarian	a. Fordist b. Exploitative c. Dangerous d. Authoritarian

all three models of workers as part of their workforce (see Spotlight box on precarious professors on the next page).

The contractual basis of work is transitioning into a new normal (Nazareth 2012). The standard form of employment contract/relationship based on full-time continuous employment with worker access to good wages and benefits is giving way to employment patterns increasingly defined as precarious. Precarious work can be differently defined but normally includes the following characteristics (Law Commission of Ontario 2012):

1. Little job security, few benefits, low wages, no pension, no union protection, and minimal control over working conditions;
2. Includes work that is contract, part-time, self-employment, and temporary as well as service industry job and food services and accommodation jobs;

3. Part-time workers, in addition to women, recent immigrants, and temporary foreign workers, are most likely to be in precarious jobs;
4. Greater susceptibility to injury and stress because of dangerous jobs or lack of training and experience, but less access to medical care;
5. Standard Employment Act practices are not always enforced; for example, according to the Law Commission of Ontario (2012), about 1.7 million workers (or about 20 per cent of Ontario's workforce) work for less than minimum wage, work on statutory holidays without overtime pay, and work under duress because they are not allowed time off for illness or family emergency. Employers expect full-time availability from their part-time workers (but pay part-time wages), yet insist on imposing a flexible work schedule with no fixed hours or time slots, making it difficult to organize household activities or to hold down a second job.

Contrary to popular perception, precarious jobs and vulnerable workers are not restricted to fast food joints or dingy sweatshop arrangements. Even highly educated Canadians are increasingly vulnerable to the precariousness of the just-in-time-workplace—as exposed in the Spotlight box.

The consequences of this brave new world without work are dismaying. Those employees clever (or lucky) enough to seize the opportunity will prosper at the expense of the less fortunate, in the process rupturing the sense of community at the core of a sustainable society. As Benjamin Tal (2012) points out, those in demand fields (mining, engineering, health care) have a low unemployment rate (1 per cent) and growing wages (4 per cent, or twice the economy as a whole). By contrast, those in labour surplus fields account for 16 per cent of the nationally unemployed while experiencing nil wage growth. A large reservoir of underemployed (or never-employed) will intensify the gap between rich (skilled) and poor (unskilled). Young Canadians have been hit especially hard by this rupture, with unemployment rates for those under age 25 at twice the national rate, even without taking into account those drop-outs who have stopped looking for jobs or have returned to school for up-skilling and no longer count as part of the unemployed. A recipe for social disaster is looming: the disenfranchised may see few options except crime and violence, for no other reason than having nothing to lose when little is at stake. Yet there is little consensus in dealing with the

Spotlight The New University Normal: Precarious Professors

Universities are normally regarded as bastions of enlightenment and excellence because of a commitment to **fairness** and justice. The reality (an inconvenient truth) differs from the constructed image (a polite fiction): post-secondary institutions are increasingly sites of exploitation because of a growing reliance on contingent/part-time/ contract labour to complement full-time and tenured faculty (Brownlee 2015; Rajagopal 2002; Canadian Federation of Students 2011). Studies show that around 65 per cent of faculty in American universities are not permanent (Farran 2007; Charbonneau 2012). A study by the American Federation of Teachers found 73 per cent of instructional staff were non-tenured, with most working as part-time or full-time adjuncts, in the process reinforcing deep structural changes that are transforming the academy (Mullings 2013). In Canada, the number of non-permanent faculty is difficult to determine because of gaps in research (Field et al. 2014). Magnusson (2011) cites the possibility that contingent faculty teach 80 per cent of Ontario college courses. But no precise figures exist for university part-time faculty at present, partly because university administrators may be reluctant to divulge their complicity in perpetuating these inequalities of exclusion (but see Brownlee 2015). Recent strikes at York University and University of Toronto suggest that contract faculty and teaching assistants carry between 60 and 65 per cent of the teaching loads. Data compiled from Statistics Canada, the Canadian Association of University Teachers, and Common University Data Ontario (cited March 7, 2015, in *The Globe and Mail*) indicate that the number of part-time professors at York University almost equals that of full-time professors (1,382 versus 1,475). Another study at Wilfrid Laurier University found the teaching load of part-time instructors represents 52 per cent of student enrolments when factoring in all classes, tutorials, and labs. Yet their remuneration accounts for only 3.4 per cent of the total expenses (Monteiro 2013a).

To be sure, sessionals are not a homogenous group. They include those who teach part-time but have careers outside the university, and those who teach part-time but aspire to a full-time university employment (Field et al. 2014). In the past, contingent academics addressed short-term gaps created by faculty on leave or by need for specialized expertise thousands of workers who have been cut adrift from the rhythms of the world, unsure of how to make their contribution in a society that defines personal worth by the work people do. Wallace Clement in his foreword to Jackson's book (2010) pitches it succinctly:

> Work life is fundamental to how we experience life in general. Most of us work to live but many of us also live to work. We gain our quality of life, identities, and much of our sense of meaning from our work lives. And, the link between work life and family life and/or leisure and education is also shaped by the quality of our work lives—our hours of work, its rewards, self-esteem and social interactions.

It is important to have a holistic view of work—that it is embedded in a series of economic, political, social, and cultural forces.... How we understand work in terms of how we frame it as a value for individuals and societies matters. Work does not just happen. It is created, conditioned, and destroyed by the political economy in which it is embedded.

The New Workplace: A "Fearsome Cave" of Anxiety

The certainties of the old workplace environment are being abandoned under the new economy (Weil 2014). Workplaces were once socially constructed and designed by, for, and about a working

(Smallman n.d). But university administrators are hiring more contingent faculty for a simpler reason: they are cheap, eager to please, and readily disposable. A tenured faculty who is paid in six figures may teach four three-credit courses each year (in addition to administration work and related responsibilities such as graduate supervision). By contrast, a part-timer with the same teaching workload might earn between $24,000 and $40,000, depending on the university's pay scale. Unlike tenured faculty, contingent academics have little job security, sketchy benefits, marginal status, and no meaningful academic freedom because they can be un-hired at will (Charbonneau 2012a; Pankin and Weiss 2011; MacDonald 2013). They are also excluded from the perks of tenure: for example, contingent workers of all stripes are exempt from sabbaticals that entitle each tenured member to paid annual leave for research purposes every seven years.

Needless to say, contingent faculty provide an attractive alternative to universities who must do more with less to stay financially afloat, although there is no shortage of revenue dollars for non-academic streams, including new buildings, administrative bloat, and endless form-filling (Vose 2015). The increasing reliance on and justification for these precarious workers in a knowledge economy reinforces the growing corporatization (neo-liberal restructuring) of higher education

(Pankin and Weiss 2011). The university has also produced a trifurcated workforce: a core of creative knowledge workers (including professors and senior management) supported by a large number of administrative staff and a growing number of contract and part-time workers who are shuffled around as the situation arises. Increasingly, universities resemble a corporation contracting with a temp agency to hire just-in-time workers who are paid less and receive fewer (or no) benefits for the same jobs as permanent staff (Pimlott 2014). This casualization of faculty is not without consequences: an academic underclass is created that appears to have flunked out of the tenure jackpot for reasons largely beyond their control, despite often possessing the same credentials as their luckier counterparts. As Jamie Brownlee (2015) points out, in no other occupation is there such a pay-and-benefit disparity between groups of individuals with similar training and jobs. And while there is no evidence that contract faculty are poorer teachers, the precarious nature of their part-time status reinforces stereotypes. But with Canada producing 6,393 PhD graduates in 2012, compared to only 3,030 new full-time faculty positions between 2009 and 2011, the continuation of this academic merry-go-round may further imperil the quality of education that fee-paying students expect and demand.

population that was white, male, Christian, and able-bodied, supported by a full-time, unpaid housewife, and slotted in a relatively permanent career trajectory (Agocs and Jain 2001; Agocs 2004). But the moorings that once secured "how things are done around here" are increasingly contested and cast adrift by vast uncertainties and conflicting expectations. Old ways of doing business are waning in the new economy because of advances in automation and digital technologies, the border-busting dynamics of globalization, and new business models of wealth creation (Peck 2010; 2011a, b). Of particular note is the reluctance of downsized firms to rehire laid off workers as they did in the past (much less to hire new employees), thus reducing overhead while compelling the retinue of retained workers to do more with less. The

end result is a dramatic shift toward a freelance economy of contract, contingent, and temporary labour as work is farmed out on a piecemeal basis when needed or convenient (Sorenson 2012). The very notion of a workplace as a physical place is losing its lustre as corporate offices are being replaced by virtual offices/virtual corporations that exist only in name, in effect severing workplaces from the constraints of time or space.

Appeals to the virtues of empowerment, workers as assets, partnership, participatory (bottom-up) management, and life–work balance sound good on paper. In reality, these shibboleths are little more than window-dressing. The new workplace claims to be ostensibly less hierarchical—without the rigid pecking order that relegated the lowly worker to the bottom and a byzantine maze of management on

Spotlight Discrimination in the Workplace: Ageism in the New Economy

If you thought racism or sexism were the most common forms of discrimination in the workforce, guess again. **Ageism** (stereotyping and discrimination based on age) represents one of the last bastions of workplace "ism" (Tarkan 2012); it also remains the workplace's most prevalent form of discrimination (Revera Report 2013). Of those singled out for displacement, older workers are often age-stereotyped as inflexible, technology-challenged, bad for the corporate image, and too expensive (pensions, health benefits, wages) to justify their benefits (Roscigno 2010). Worse still, evidence suggests age discrimination may be increasing in both federal civil service and federally regulated industries because of a legislative loophole that whisks age-of-retirement workers out the door against their wishes (Whitten 2012). And yet few seem to care: while ageism as a belief system may be analogous to racism and sexism in its impact and effects, it rarely evokes the same volume of moral outrage and social condemnation (Law Commission 2009).

Ageism consists of those beliefs that prejudge people on the basis of age. Specific and

deterministic qualities are attributed to persons because of their age, thus rendering them less worthy of respect while discounting their value in making a contribution to society (Law Commission 2009). Ageism appears to be rife in Canada. According to the Revera Report on Ageism (in conjunction with the International Federation on Ageing), based on an online sample of 1,501 Canadians (2012; 2013), 51 per cent of respondents believe age discrimination is tolerated in Canada, compared to 20 per cent for gender discrimination and 14 per cent for racial discrimination. Sixty per cent of older folk over 66 years say they have been treated differently or unfairly because of their age, with the main culprits being younger people, governments (not taking elderly needs into account in decision-making), and health care professionals (who do not take their complaints seriously). The most common expressions of age discrimination consist of the following putdowns: being ignored or rendered invisible; being seen as unimportant with nothing to contribute; and being deemed incompetent. Twenty-one per cent of top, but more democratic and inclusive. A flattened hierarchy would provide a platform for a decentralized and participatory decision-making. Yet many workplaces remain as autocratic as ever because of competitive pressures. The illusion of inclusion is conveyed without relinquishing any levers of power, while decisions regarding relocation or hiring or hours remain a management priority or a software application (Kay 2014). Emphasis *may be* directed at being more inclusive, flexible (less rigid, more participatory and discretionary), and worker-friendly (less harassment); nevertheless, structural barriers continue to obstruct a workplace democratization. Employees *may be* touted as a company's greatest asset, although bottom-line calculations are not averse to slashing labour costs to bolster shareholder returns. Instead workers are increasingly vulnerable to slash-and-burn management priorities whose bottom line mantra is more profit with less cost, prompting management guru Peter Drucker to ruefully note "Employers no longer chant the old mantra 'People are our greatest asset.' They are more likely to complain that 'People are our greatest liability.'" The irony is inescapable: that thousands of workers are losing their jobs in the midst of an economic boom makes a mockery of the concept of worker empowerment. The Spotlight box on ageism captures a pattern of disempowerment that intensifies exclusion through discriminatory biases.

The workplace is undergoing transformative change not only in the relationship between employer and worker but also in how businesses define and organize work (Weil 2014). The reality of

the respondents also viewed older adults as a burden on society.

Inconsistencies are prevalent: employers often praise older workers as loyal, experienced, hardworking, and uncomplaining. In some cases, employers have taken steps to reasonably accommodate the needs and realities of older workers, says Susan Eng of the advocacy group CARP (cited in Rogers 2012), if only to ensure retention of those workers who provide mentoring value and a wealth of experience. But ageism is increasingly an issue as older workers are stigmatized as inconsistent with a company's image or detrimental to the bottom line (Roscigno 2010; Tarkan 2012). Employers are under pressure to reduce costs, embrace new technologies, and cater to the demands of younger workers for promotions (Whitten 2012). A grab bag of stereotypes is retrieved to justify the removal of older workers, including the belief that they are rigid and stuck in their ways; that they have health issues that impede performance, productivity, and attendance; they are luddites with a phobia toward new technology; they are slow to learn, change, and accommodate, they are risk-averse; and they are energy depleted (Edwards 2011). These broad stereotypes do not apply to all older workers (as well, younger folk can exhibit similar symptoms), especially since today's older folk are healthier and display more vitality than their parents (Tarkan 2012), according to the Revera Report (2012), and insist on a different ageing experience. An active, take-charge, and successful boomer generation possesses a different set of expectations about what *old* means. Ironically, unlike the perceptions of the younger generation, the majority of older folk are optimistic about ageing.

As others have noted, judging a person solely on the basis of age is as unfair and unreasonable as basing a decision on race or gender. Neither race nor gender—or age in this case—are themselves deterministic of behaviour or reflective of a person's character. Nor should ageism be tolerated in a Canada whose foundational principles endorse a commitment to individual rights, equal opportunity, and non-discriminatory treatment. Moves to remedy the situation must begin by acknowledging that ageism is not a demographic problem but a societal problem involving collective responsibility. A mindset shift is required, one that acknowledges the legitimacy and value of age as another element of diversity similar to that of gender and race—and just as valuable (Tarkan 2012).

the workplace is more *work* and less *place* because of new technologies, an uncertain economy, and demands on a new generation of employees who may encourage more flexibility through non-office based work (from cloud services to online collaborative tools) in exchange for greater expectations and always-on availability (Henderson 2016). The combination of competitive globalization pressures and new information technologies of the late 1980s and early 1990s put pressure on companies to rethink their business model. Large companies with recognized brands that are confronting intense competition are increasingly inclined to jettison activities they deemed peripheral to their core business model—outsourcing the work of janitors, security guards, delivery services, front desk clerks, and so on, to small companies in fierce competition with each other—to focus instead on core competencies that produce value for investors and build a devoted customer base. For example, Apple may be one of the world's most highly valued companies, with more than 750,000 global workers, yet it only directly employs 63,000 core workers (Weil 2014:7–8). (The Spotlight box on the Rana Plaza disaster in Chapter 1 is another example of outsourcing/off-shoring by major clothing companies to devolve responsibility for products and workers to a complex network of global supply chains and franchisees.) Corporations are able to profit from the core activities that create value and maintain brand loyalty—even as they shed the production of goods and services—by insisting on maintaining rigorous goals, standards, and detailed work practices to protect the brand (as Weil notes, a classic case of having their cake and eating it too).

Contracting out employment formerly done inside the corporation to other companies has proven a successful business strategy (Weil 2014). It reduces costs, streamlines operations, and eliminates responsibilities such as wage setting and supervision, and transforms the employer–worker relationship into an arms-length contractual decision and market transaction without tarnishing the carefully cultivated reputations of their brand (goods and services), yet reaping the price benefits from their loyal customer base. However much shareholders and managers benefit from this new wealth creation arrangement,

workers bear the brunt of cutting labour costs by way of downward pressure on pay, security, and working conditions (Kantor 2014). In contrast to large firms—which are more likely to be unionized, tend to set wages above market levels, establish human resources departments, comply with health and safety rules, and enforce mandated social security benefits—subcontractors and franchisees do it differently. To stay competitive without sacrificing razor thin margins, they often scrimp on wages, benefits, and security when they assume subcontractor status. The net results are low paying entry level jobs that entrap workers without much chance of escape (Ehrenreich 2014); stagnation in real wages and loss of benefits for many of the jobs once done inside; wages so low that it becomes impossible to accumulate enough money to transition over to a better paying job; little control over the work schedule and sporadic hours making it difficult to arrange child care or take a second job; more precariousness as responsibility for the liability, oversight, and supervision of workers is invested in outsourced companies who themselves confront fierce competitive pressures; greater exposure to health and safety risks as responsibility for conditions is blurred; and a growing unlikelihood that they will comply with standards set out in law (Weil 2014; Ehrenreich 2014). And in some cases, as the Spotlight on the following page explains, a toxic workplace environment can render workers as disposable.

Towards an Inclusive Workforce: Inclusion and Inclusivity

The barrage of intrusive disruptions to institutional workplaces makes it abundantly clear: workplaces must address the proliferation of demands from diverse constituents both internally (workforce) and externally (customers or clients) if they are to remain relevant and responsive (Smith and Lindsay 2014; Herring and Henderson 2015). Nearly every workplace must now hire a diversity of genders, abilities, and races, if only to remain financially afloat or to stay one step ahead of the law. The movement of women and minorities into the labour force

Spotlight Workplace Dangers: Is Today the Day You Die at Work?

On 6 February 2012, ten migrant workers, most of them from Peru, were killed when their 15-passenger cube van slammed into a truck (the truck driver also died) at an intersection in the tiny hamlet of Hampstead (near Stratford), Ontario. The probable cause of the accident was cited as driver error related to an inappropriate driver's licence for this type of vehicle, lack of training to drive a passenger van that many regard as potentially dangerous, and fatigue from overtime and exposure to dull and dangerous work. However horrifying, such fatalities are not uncommon. An additional three migrants workers in Ontario were killed in job related incidents by September 2012, according to the Agricultural Workers Alliance, (Canadian Press 11 September 2012).

Many Canadians would be startled and shocked to learn that accidents (from negligence to attacks) and occupational diseases kill over a thousand Canadian workers each year—five killed per working day, or 6.8 per 100,000 workers.[1] The number of people dying each year because of unsafe workplaces has increased over the past 15 years (in contrast to the declining rates in most OECD countries, including 24 of 29 countries with significantly lower death rates than Canada [Human Resources and Skills Development Canada 2012a]). This transatlantic discrepancy may be attributed to cutbacks in Canada's monitoring of labour and safety standards. Despite Canada's commitment to comprehensive health and safety

laws, a reluctance to lay charges against employers who knowingly create or tolerate dangerous (even criminal) conditions may also prove a contributing factor (Canadian Labour Congress 2012; also Snider 2015; Ryan 2015).

Who are the victims of workplace fatalities? Among those who died in 2010, the following patterns prevail (Deane 2012): men are overwhelmingly susceptible to workplace deaths; older men die more often than younger men (although young men and new hires are at greater risk of injury [Deane 2012]); more deaths occur in mining and construction per 1,000 employed workers (that dubious honour in the United States goes to fishers and loggers [Jiang 2013]); Northwest Territories had the highest fatality rate; and cause of death divided nearly equally between accidents and occupational-induced disease in 2005 (Sharpe and Hardt 2006). As well, 1 out of every 65 employed workers in 2009 received worker's compensation because of job-related injuries. According to Human Resources and Skills Development Canada (2012a), the total cost of occupational injuries to the Canadian economy amounted to $19 billion annually.

1. Worldwide, more than 6,000 workers die each day (about 2.5 million per year) from workplace accidents. The most dangerous jobs? Ship-breaking in Pakistan and Bangladesh (Case and Freifelder 2013; Gwin 2014).

is perhaps the quintessential expression of this move toward inclusiveness. Workplace accommodation of people with disabilities and Aboriginal peoples has further diversified an increasingly complex organizational mosaic. Another sign of the times is the expanding presence of racialized (visible) minorities. Racialized people of colour now constitute nearly 20 per cent of Canada's population, according to 2011 Census data, with the majority concentrated in the largest urban areas. Racialized

minorities are no longer content to linger as tokens along the institutional sidelines. They want a rightful measure of recognition, reward, and participation—even if institutional workplaces are not necessarily inclined toward that direction. Institutions have responded by redesigning the workplace to better integrate the once historically excluded, in part through the removal of discriminatory barriers related to recruitment, retention, and promotion, in part by introducing proactive measures that aim to create a more level playing field (see employment equity debate in Chapter 11).

Nevertheless, the ideal of integration doesn't always match the inequalities of institutional workplaces. Consider, for example, the representational biases at the corporate boardroom level. According to the 2014 annual report by the Canadian Board Diversity Council, Canada's demographic diversity is underrepresented at the boardroom table. Women occupy 17.1 per cent of board seats of Canada's 500 largest companies (up from 14.4 per cent of all board seats in 2012). But of deep concern is the decline in the number of seats held by racialized minorities (2 per cent, despite accounting for nearly 20 per cent of the population); aboriginal individuals (0.8 per cent, but 4.3 per cent of the population); and persons with disabilities (1.4 per cent). Admittedly corporations are increasingly aware of the benefits and importance of demographically diverse boards. A highly diverse workforce (especially at the corporate decision-making level) delivers a better financial dividend, argues Pamela Jeffrey, founder of the Diversity Council (cited in Yew 2012). It also offers a different problem-solving perspective that overcomes the blinkers of groupthink (but see Cohen 2013 for a different perspective). Not surprisingly, rules for entitlement (who gets what, and why) are changing in response to minority demands for a bigger slice of the corporate pie. But the transitioning of principle into practice has proven trickier than many anticipated.

Institutional workplaces in both the private and public sector are under pressure to integrate increasingly diverse, discerning, and demanding demographics (Smith and Lindsay 2014; Herring and Henderson 2015). Awareness is growing that institutional workplaces do not work like they used to in light of a looming identity crisis ("who are we" and "what should we be doing?"). Environments can no longer be controlled because of confusions and uncertainties; individuals cannot be pre-programmed to think and act in a predictable way; and ground rules cannot be formulated to everyone's satisfaction. The focus on diversity goes beyond a simple "celebration" of workplace differences. Racialized minority women and men want to be valued as productive members of the workforce with full and equal participation, opportunities, and rewards. Yet facilitating workplace reforms and achieving institutional goals may prove elusive, given the magnitude of the challenges in diversifying workplace dynamics and institutional design. Tension and conflict associated with an accommodative workplace loom large when newcomers are growing the new Canada while the Canadian-born watch and worry (Bricker and Ibbitson 2013; Ibbitson 2012). Migrants and minorities may bring different values, ethics, expectations, and communication styles, leading others (the Canadian-born) to fear the loss of entitlements related to privilege and power in having to move over and make space. The end result is a breakdown of social trust that fosters misunderstanding or conflict (Graves 2013; Tatia 2010).

Five criteria define an inclusive workplace: workforce representation, organizational rules and operations, workplace climate, service delivery, and community relations (Fleras 2012). First, the workforce should be representative—that is, the composition and distribution of its workers should be relatively proportional to that of the regional labour force, taking into account both social and cultural factors as extenuating circumstances. Such numerical representation applies not only to entry-level jobs but to all levels of management, access to training, and entitlement to rewards. Second, workplace rules and operations cannot deny or exclude anyone from the process of job recruitment, selection, training, and promotion. This commitment to root out all types of discriminatory barriers demands careful scrutiny of company policy and protocols. Third, an inclusive workplace must foster a working climate conducive to the health and productivity of all workers. At minimum, such a climate cannot tolerate harassment of any form; at best, differences are embraced as normal and necessary for co-operative functioning and creative growth. Fourth, an inclusive workplace ensures that delivery of its services is community-based and culturally sensitive. Such a commitment requires both a varied workforce and a sense of partnership with the community at large. Fifth and finally, workplaces do not operate in social isolation or a political vacuum. They are part of a community and cannot hope to remain outside of it in terms of accountability and responsibility if success is anticipated. Institutions and their workplaces must establish meaningful relations with all community members to ensure productive lines of communication and community involvement in the decision-making process.

Inclusiveness: Inclusivity versus Inclusion

Its emergence as a popular buzzword poses a tricky question: what does workforce *inclusiveness* mean? Is it about assimilation or integration; about integration or accommodation; about diversity or disadvantage; about culture-blind or culture-conscious initiatives; about changing attitudes or modifying behaviour; about individual predispositions or institutional structures; about cumulative reform or radical change? Does it extend to replacing white personnel with minority hires; accelerating the promotion of minorities along the corporate ladder; or celebrating differences to enliven a dull corporate culture?

Inclusiveness as a workplace governance yields two analytically distinct models: inclusion and inclusivity (see Roy 1995 for analysis of these terms). *Inclusion* as inclusiveness is predicated on the principle of removing discriminatory barriers to ensure integration into the existing system. It is based on the belief that no one should be excluded because of their differences since everyone deserves similar treatment within the existing arrangements. The principle of *inclusivity* differs: a commitment to inclusivity insists that everyone should be included precisely because of their differences-based needs, entitlements, and rights, thus necessitating interventions that enhance the concepts of belonging, participation, recognition, and contribution (see also Senate 2013; Richmond and Saloojee 2005). Inclusivity can be broadly defined as a process and framework for modifying institutions in terms of design, organization, assumptions, operations, outputs, opportunity and reward structures along accommodative lines (within limits and without undue hardship) for those formerly excluded. This is done in part by creating a workplace that is *reflective of, respectful of,* and *responsive to* diversity and difference, and in part through the delivery of community services that are *available, accessible, accountable, and appropriate* (Fleras 2012).

In short, the principles of inclusion and inclusivity articulate fundamentally different models of institutional/workplace inclusiveness. Consider the contrasts: inclusion is associated with principles of equal treatment—that is, true equality arises from treating everyone the same (*equally*) because everyone is equal before the law, regardless of their differences. However, exemptions to rules are acceptable in extenuating circumstances since exceptions do not alter the general rule. For inclusivity, the principle of treatment *as equals* acknowledges that, *at times*, people's difference-based disadvantages must be recognized to ensure genuine equality. A commitment to inclusivity/equity (as equals) invariably draws attention to the principle of differential accommodation for successful outcomes, namely, instituting different ways of accommodating a diversity of differences. Inclusion tends to frame diversity as a problem to solve or obstacle to surmount (that is, how to integrate differences so they no longer constitute a problem [Modood 2011]). A commitment to inclusion creates a climate that recognizes, respects, and values a diversity of diversities (including the unique differences of each person) (Wilson 2009) as neither a problem to solve nor a challenge to surmount, but as an asset for improving workplace climate and the delivery of social services (Fleras and Spoonley 1999). Finally, a commitment to inclusivity as governance logic entails changing the rules that inform the conventions; by contrast, inclusion as principle is focused on changing the conventions that refer to the rules. In other words, inclusivity is transformative in bringing about major change, whereas inclusion is more reform-oriented in modifying the existing status quo. Or to phrase it a bit differently: inclusion is about fitting individuals into the existing system even if exemptions are tolerated; inclusivity is about re-fitting the system to accommodate diverse individuals.

In theory and as ideal-typical constructs, the principles of inclusivity and inclusion embody competing models of accommodation. Inclusion models of inclusiveness begin with the largely functionalist assumption that the existing system is essentially sound and equitable, although a few tweaks might be required to level the playing field. Any inequalities or exclusions are largely the fault of individuals who must be fixed to fit into the existing system (Harmon, n.d.). To the extent differences are recognized, they tend to be framed around a commitment to pretend pluralism (differences = superficial and irrelevant) and liberal universalism (our commonalities as individuals outweigh our group differences). By contrast, inclusivity models entail a fundamentally different principle consistent with a radical conflict perspective: the workplace must be restructured to accommodate the needs of or to ensure a better fit for an extremely diverse demographic. According to this line of thinking, commitment to inclusivity must go beyond developing skills or modifying mindsets for advancing fundamental change. The focus instead is on structural changes to shape how service institutions view their role in addressing diversity and the action they take (Council of Europe 2011). Cosmetic changes to institutional conventions—minority hires or sensitivity sessions—are a good start. Nevertheless, according to inclusivity principles, they are unlikely to dislodge those foundational rules that reinforce power structures and institutional culture. Little of value or permanence prevails in advancing a more equitable workplace without a corresponding removal of discriminatory barriers and systemic biases (Wilson 2009).

Few would dispute the value of modifying workplaces to make them more inclusive of a diverse and changing Canada. But putting inclusiveness principles into workplace practice is quite another prospect. Institutional workplaces are complex and baffling sites of domination, power, and control, often pervaded by prejudice, nepotism, patronage, bureaucratic managerialism, and the "old white boys" network. An array of personal and social barriers interferes with the process of workplace inclusiveness (Fleras 2012). Stumbling blocks include people, hierarchy, bureaucracy, corporate culture, and occupational subcultures. People themselves are a prime obstruction. Dismantling these barriers is not without its politics and problems. Mainstream institutions are neither neutral in design nor value free in process or outputs. Rather they are ideologically loaded with ideas and ideals about normalcy, acceptability, and desirability that are deeply entrenched within the founding assumptions and foundational principles of the constitutional order (from institutional design and organization to operations and outcomes). A conflict of interest ensues: to one side, conventional views remain firmly entrenched as vested interests balk at discarding the tried and true. To the other side, newer visions are compelling yet lack the critical mass to scuttle the past. The interplay of these oppositional tensions can prove disruptive as workplaces evolve into a "contested site" involving competing world views and opposing agendas with no road map to navigate the labyrinth of puzzles and pitfalls of paradoxes. Under the circumstances, who can be surprised at the enormity of the challenge of constructing inclusive institutions and workplaces—both universal and particular as well as market-sensitive and diversity-responsive?

Summary

1. The world of work, working, workforce, and the workplace is rapidly changing and increasingly uncertain against the backdrop of the new economy as a business model for creating wealth by improving productivity.

2. The principles and rules of the new economy exacerbate patterns of workplace inequality due to an interplay of globalized production, digital and automation technologies, and neo-liberal ideologies.

3. The new economy, with its freewheeling and neo-liberal model of wealth creation, stands in contrast to the protectionism (interventions) of the old nationalist economy.

4. Ideological shifts (neo-liberalism) and structural readjustments (globalization) have converged to construct a three-tiered

workforce of winners (privileged), losers (precarious), and survivors (perfunctory).

5. Despite the displacement of conventional forms of work, work is not disappearing per se, because of broader changes to the new economy.

6. The inequities of the old economy were a reality for many Canadian workers such as quick-service employees or those employed in high-risk occupations.

7. Persistence of exclusionary patterns persist in the new workplace (ageism), in addition to a growing reliance on precarious workers, both low-skilled (temporary foreign workers) and highly educated (contract faculty).

8. Two competing models of workplace governance—inclusion and inclusivity—aim to bolster a more inclusive workforce.

Review Questions

1. Compare the following: neo-liberal principles of the new economy as a system for creating wealth and improving productivity versus the interventionist principles of the old economy.

2. Demonstrate how the new economy is creating new patterns of inequality with respect to work and the workplace.

3. Indicate how the trifurcating of the workforce into the privileged, the perfunctory, and the precariat is consistent with and yet reinforces the dynamics of the new economy.

4. What is meant by *ageism* in the workplace? Why does it exist? How is it expressed? What can be done about it?

5. Explain what is meant by an *inclusive workforce* with respect to an inclusion model versus an inclusivity model.

10 Schooling and Post-secondary Education: "Enlightened" Exclusions

Learning Objectives

1. To appreciate Canada's leadership in advancing positive education indicators, while acknowledging how schooling remains a site of inequalities.

2. To grasp how schooling and education[1] can stimulate social mobility (the great equalizer) yet fortify the status quo (the great fortifier).

3. To demonstrate how residential schools as instruments of aggressive (genocidal?) assimilation continue to negatively impact aboriginal individuals and communities.

4. To expose how a systemic whiteness at the post-secondary level excludes non-conventional ways of knowing and knowledge.

5. To become critically aware of how universities are experiencing an identity crisis and crisis of confidence in terms of who they are and what they should be doing.

Introduction: The Great Equalizer or the Great Fortifier?[2]

All societies must socialize their children for participation in adult life. The means for achieving this goal may be diverse, yet invariably include both formal and informal patterns that vary with time and place. Tribal societies survived without formal arrangements for socialization, relying instead on informal procedures such as parental or peer instruction. By contrast, the formalization of schooling and education in urban-industrial systems reflects a demand for a literate population as a precondition for progress, democracy, and prosperity. Three major functions of schooling and education feed into this line of thought: to impart knowledge and skills; to prepare individuals for citizenship and the work world; and to foster self-actualization through intellectual cultivation.

Education and schooling embody a powerful instrument for challenging both the social structures and individual attitudes that underpin the inequalities of exclusion (Ghosh 2011). But there is a flipside: schools as instruments of social control also constitute sites of inequality whose outcomes perpetuate patterns of social exclusion for the historically disadvantaged (Foley and Green 2015). They prepare people for adult work by socializing ("indoctrinating") workers to function compliantly in mainstream society (Keister and Southgate 2011; Davies and Guppy 2010; Bowles and Gintis 1976). They also appear to be designed for conformity rather than change, for rigidity rather than flexibility, for consensus rather than disagreement, for social reproduction of the status quo rather than the reconstruction of social reality, for credentials over creativity, and for working in an industrial age instead of an information-driven global economy. That **schooling** and **education** constitute agents of socialization whose ostensible mission to enlighten and empower is betrayed by an assimilationist and controlling logic should lay to rest any romanticized notions (Dei and Kempf 2013).

Canada is no slouch when it comes to funding education and schooling (Parkin 2015; OECD 2014a). It invests more in schooling and education than almost any other society, according to a report by the Council of Education Ministers (Education Indicators in Canada) (Morrow 2010). At 2.6 per cent of the GDP allocated to colleges and universities, Canada's post-secondary spending ranks second only to the United States'. Another ranking of post-secondary institutions across 48 countries by Universitas 21 (an international research network of 24 universities and colleges) puts Canada third on the list behind the United States and Sweden, based on resources, output, connectivity (collaboration) and environment (government policy) (Williams 2012). Canadians remain one of the most educated populations in the world if measured by credential attainment, with well over 50 per cent of the adult population aged 25 to 64 possessing a tertiary qualification (OECD 2014)—although Canada's ranking drops if considering only young adults (25–34 years), suggesting other countries are catching up and overtaking Canada as they make gains at a faster pace (Parkin 2015; Hopper 2014). Canada's main advantage is reflected at the community college level, which accounts for a large portion of the post-secondary population, compared to the average among the OECD countries (Morrow 2010). The Conference Board of Canada Education and Skills Report Card (2012) confers an "A" on Canada (and Finland) for increasing the number of students graduating in math and sciences as well as engineering and computer science. In addition to favourable global comparisons, developments over time are no less impressive. Twenty-five per cent of young Canadians at present are enrolled in university, according to the Association of Universities and Colleges of Canada, compared to only 10 per cent in 1980. Even the number of Canadians without a high school diploma dropped from 21 per cent to 13 per cent between 1998 and 2008, while 92 per cent of adults between the ages of 25 and 34 had completed high school (Morrow 2010). Lastly,

barriers no longer apply as they once did. Women post better academic achievements than men at all levels, with female graduation from high school at 8 per cent higher, 11 per cent higher from college, and 18 per cent higher from university. And higher education matters: the 2011 National Household Survey shows that median income was higher for aboriginal women aged 25 to 64 with higher education than for aboriginal women with no degree or diploma ($49,947 versus $15,208) or non-aboriginal women with the same level of education ($47,742). However, First Nations, Métis, and Inuit women are less likely to have a post-secondary degree than other Canadian women (Arriagada 2016).

These largely positive figures conceal a downside. Negative indicators abound that sully many of the gains in the schooling and educational field (Ravitch 2009). Education is often touted as the path to personal growth, social progress, and national prosperity; unfortunately, the opposite appears equally true (Marsh 2011). Systems of education are themselves marked by patterns of inequality in terms of access to quality education, in its treatment of stakeholders, in benefits and outcomes that are unevenly distributed, and through metrics of underachievement as both a cause and a consequence of powerlessness and exclusion (Dale 2010). Fixation with behaviour management and social control reinforces ideologies of punishment and discipline that, perversely, facilitate the transitioning of aboriginal youth and racialized students into prisons (Gebhard 2012). Canada, among OECD countries, may possess the highest percentage of adults with degrees or diplomas (51 per cent). But Canada also tops all OECD rankings for the largest share of graduates who make less than the national median income; for having fewer than half (between 60 and 70 per cent) of all aboriginal students complete high school; and for barely reducing the proportion of university students from lower income families over the past two decades (Davies, Maldonado and Zarifa 2014). Equality of access continues to be elusive: those from the wealthiest quarter of the population were more likely than the poorest quarter to attend university (CAUT 2014/15; Foley and Green 2015). Patterns of exclusion are thus reinforced, especially for those outside a major urban centre or unable to afford escalating tuition and living expenses. In terms of literacy or numeracy, Canada no longer ranks among the best. A recent survey by the OECD (2013b) ranking 24 industrial countries put Canada's literacy score at eleventh, whereas its numeracy proficiency score for 16- to 65-year-olds placed it below the global average—a drop in both scores since the initial survey in 2003.

Worse still, higher education does not always translate into hefty incomes. A study that followed both men and women over two decades (1991–2010) indicated high variation in cumulative earnings (Ostrovsky and Frenette 2014). The study grouped individuals between the ages of 26 and 35 years in 1991 and those between the ages of 45 to 54 in 2010 on the basis of their highest level of completed education and the major field of study reported in 1991. Labour market outcomes of BAs and college diplomas were then compared across and within fields of study. The median cumulative earnings for male bachelor degree graduates ranged from $840,000 among those in fine and applied arts, to $1.8 million for male engineering graduates (but see Finnie et al. 2014). Those in the top 90 percentile of the engineering category (i.e., earning more than what 90 per cent of this group earned) accumulated over $4 million in earnings during this period. For women the median figures were $650,000 in fine and applied arts and $1.2 million in business administration. (Another study had indicated that women with a post-secondary education earned just 63 per cent of what similarly educated men earned in 2008, albeit up slightly from 61 per cent in 1998 [Morrow 2010]). Similar relative patterns were evident among college certificate holders. Finally, male high school graduates earned $882,000 during this period, compared to male college graduates who earned $1,137,000 (for females the figure was $643,000) and male bachelor graduates who earned $1,517,000 (for women, the figure was $972,000 or twice as much as female high school graduates) (Ostrovsky and Frenette 2014).

Issues of quality are no less pressing. For many, neither education nor schooling are creative or progressive (Marsh 2011). They are proving both inflexible and bureaucratic, at odds with the fast-paced demands of a hyper-technological era (Spender 1997). Lip service to the creative and the

critical is betrayed by the harsh realities of authority, dogma, routine, rote learning and regurgitation, conformity, cost-cutting, and credential inflation. Credentialism appears to have replaced education (i.e., thinking and learning) as the core component of schooling (Hopper 2014). Robertson (1987:383) captures a sense of this paradox when he writes, "Not all schooling is educational. Much of it is mere qualification earning . . . ritualistic, tedious, suffused with anxieties, destructive of curiosities, and imagination; in short, anti-educational." For critics, aspects of Canada's education and schooling seem stuck in the past. Instead of a twenty-first-century model of schooling and education, what seemingly prevails is a nineteenth century factory–industrial model employing twentieth-century tools of communication (Wente 2012). Critics like to pounce on universities for being out of touch with twenty-first-century economic realities (Coates and Morrison 2016). Schooling and education should be undergoing transformational change from a print-based knowledge economy to a digitally driven system, with a corresponding shift in educational aims, conventional divisions of knowledge and disciplines, methods of teaching and learning, the role of teachers, and the nature of the student-teacher relations (Spender 1997). The fact that educational authorities are aware of these incongruities, yet appear unwilling or incapable of addressing these challenges, attests to the power of inertia in defence of the status quo (Coates and Morrison 2012).

Others disagree with this assessment although for different reasons. The system of education and schooling is changing too quickly and often in the wrong direction. Schools were once expected to forge a coherent, stable, and unified amalgam out of diversity. But contemporary education is geared toward economic utility and career prospects, consumerism as ultimate lifestyle statement, reliance on technological gadgetry rather than critical judgment, and information instead of knowledge and wisdom (Postman 1995). Not surprisingly, schooling and post-secondary systems are experiencing an identity crisis in terms of who they are, what they should be doing, and how they should do it. To be sure, a sense of perspective is useful in contextualizing this predicament. Universities didn't necessarily create this crisis of mismatch between the economy and education. More accurately, it was the government who condoned the principles and practices of a neo-liberal economy, then insisted universities assume a training function inconsistent with their historical mission of educating (enlightening) citizens (Salutin 2012). Business elites used the cover of globalization to ship jobs to low-wage overseas destinations, then blamed the universities for flubbing a chance to replace depleted ranks with just-in-time graduates. Unsure of their roles and responsibilities in contemporary society, yet resigned to plod along as best they can under the circumstances, all levels of schooling find themselves under pressure to do more with less.

No level of education is exempt from scrutiny (Wotherspoon 2009; Davies and Guppy 2010). At the primary level, parental concern is growing over declining educational standards, demoralized teachers and exasperated principals, deteriorating pupil performance levels, laxity in discipline, and learning without the "basics" (Leithwood et al. 2002). Public schools in remote and isolated parts of Canada, but especially on-reserve schools, continue to underperform because of depleted resources, dwindling population and tax base, and funding formulas that tend to favour the urban and affluent boards (Wotherspoon and Schissel 2003). Even well-intentioned initiatives are known to backfire because of misinformed assumptions and unanticipated consequences. The Eurocentrism of residential schooling and provincial schools enforced a pattern of cultural extinguishment that bordered on the genocidal. All aspects of schooling—from teachers and textbooks to policy and curriculum, from daily routines to decision-making at the top—were aligned to facilitate cultural indoctrination and societal assimilation. Admittedly, the explicit assimilationist model that once informed educational circles is rarely articulated or openly endorsed. Nevertheless, the logic of assimilation remains an unspoken but powerful ethos that infuses all schooling levels, not in the openly racist sense of deliberate (systematic) indoctrination but through the logical consequences of a systemic (or institutionalized) bias that is raced, gendered, and classed (Henry and Tator 2010).

Compounding the confusion are those educational philosophies that continue to flip-flop between the "progressives" and "traditionalists." To one side of the debate is an outcome-oriented, curriculum-driven ("back to basics") schooling model with a focus on competition for high grades through standardized testing and measurable performance indicators. This model is consistent with the principles of accommodation through inclusion. To the other side, an inclusivity-oriented, "child-centred" model aims to bolster individual self-esteem through customized learning and cultural sensitivities. A movement entitled 21st Century Learning rejects an emphasis on rote learning and an industrial model of education with its focus on facts, conformity, hierarchy, and deference to authority. Proposed instead is a commitment to broad concepts and big ideas involving creativity, innovation and digital literacy (C21 Canada, n.d.). This shift toward rethinking curriculums and pedagogical styles may well improve educational outcomes. However, parents worry that students will be untutored in basic literacy/numeracy skills, but awash in pedagogical mumbo-jumbo about self-esteem and personal creativity. Stroking "kiddy" egos is fine to a point, they might concede, but how does it prepare children for the rigours of a knowledge-based, global economy?

The secondary school level is no less prone to finger-pointing and second-guessing. High schools are portrayed as ticking time bombs because of alcohol and substance abuse, teenage pregnancy, sexual activity and disease dissemination, racism and right-wing recruitment, and overt sexism. Violence remains a major problem, from the banalities of everyday (cyber)bullying to the sickening ritual of killing sprees for revenge or recognition—including 168 school shootings in the United States from 2013 to (October) 2015. Yet school efforts to improve student safety may be criticized as "paranoia correctness"—little more than blanket solutions that border on the extreme as reputation-conscious boards overreact to allay parental concern and pre-empt potential lawsuits (Boesveld 2011). Students are accused of suffering from a terminal overdose of media exposure, resulting in boredom, stress, and unhappiness; diminishing attention spans; discomfort with the written word; acceptance of discontinuity and superficiality as normal conditions of existence;

disrespect for the past as a source of inspiration or wisdom; and defiance of authority (S. Watson 2015). Most young adults are so attuned to peer group pressure, yet so seemingly indifferent to adults, that parental involvement in youth issues is quietly dismissed or openly scorned (Keith 1997). Conflicting pressures compound the situation. Just as young people are expected to excel academically, so too must they adjust to bodily changes, wean themselves psychologically from parents, develop a working network of friends and allies, work part-time, and commit to education or vocational goals.

Post-secondary institutions are subject to spirited criticism (Cote and Allahar 2007; Coates and Morrison 2012, 2016). Canadians may be the world's most educated people (with 1.2 million university students and 700,000 community college students) but not necessarily the *best* educated in preparing students with the background, skills, and flexibility to soar in the global knowledge economy (Anderssen 2012c; Hopper 2014; Coates 2015b). Universities are depicted as imperious ivory towers, impervious to the demands for diversity and change and inoculated from business realities and globalizing forces. According to Harvey Weingarten, president of Ontario's higher education think tank (HEQCO), executives in 20 recent employer surveys blamed universities for the dearth of employable students with the "soft" skills such as communication, problem-solving, critical thinking, and teamwork (cited in Brown 2016). The university enterprise is confronting relentless yet conflicting pressures to be everything to everybody, yet it lacks both the resources and resourcefulness to do it all without a national body to oversee standards and outcomes. (Canada's system of education is in fact 13 relatively distinct systems [10 provinces and 3 territories], making Canada one of the few countries in the world without a national department of education or a federal education policy [Parkin 2015].) Universities continue to be buffeted about by both internal and external pressures, namely, a debilitating brew of government funding cuts, tuition increases, grade inflation, dumbed down curricula, political correctness, and labour market glut. Rationalization and routinization have had the effect of "McDonaldizing" the university system along the business lines of efficiency,

calculability, predictability, and control (Readings 1997; Rolfe 2014; Ritzer 2015; also Coates 2012).

The dominant university model (broad-based teaching and research institutions supported by a large asset base and a body of bureaucrats) is increasingly under pressure to transition into one more aligned to a corporate business model, while incorporating new learning systems based on the democratization of online knowledge and digitalization of delivery technologies (Charbonneau 2012b). Even the foundations of a bricks-and-mortar institution may be imperiled. A broadcast model of pedagogy is increasingly contested by online offerings that tap into the learning styles of today's wired students involving interaction with classmates, collaboration outside the classroom, and digital experiences (Tapscott 2012; Community Foundations Canada 2012). Still others fear that corporate interests are calling the shots, thus upsetting the balance that historically mediated the relationship between the practical and the contemplative (Vose 2015b; Rolfe 2014; Readings 1997). Talk of a fiscal crisis and corporate links camouflages a deeper malaise revolving around the question "what is the university for?" A crisis of identity is pending as elitist assumptions (educating critically informed citizens) and populist mindsets (progressive social change) jostle with corporate demands (training job-ready workers) and student expectations (a ticket to rewarding careers). Nevertheless, a corresponding crisis of confidence looms menacingly as well, as universities try to figure out who they are and what they should be doing in a changing and diverse society.

Within this context of turmoil and second-guessing a sense of perspective is critical. Nothing is wrong with Canada's public education system, according to Michael Fullan, former dean of the Ontario Institute for Studies in Education (OISE)—if it were addressing the educational needs of the *nineteenth century*. But a radical revamping of the system is inescapable if it is to play a twenty-first-century role in advancing social equality and societal prosperity. Educational models that worked well when advanced knowledge was irrelevant to most and priorities focused on teaching children to read and write so they could become factory workers or domestic help no longer apply in a significantly transformed world. Charges of irrelevance are compounded by concerns over yet more exclusion. Critics point to a combination of chronic underfunding, dwindling resources, increased commercialization, mounting workloads, inadequately prepared students, impossible teaching conditions, and concerns over access and equity as persistent sources of inequality (Eggins 2011). A near universal belief in the importance of increasing human capital and advancing societal progress through education is offset by the countervailing reality that returns to education and a more educated work force are unevenly distributed, with disastrous consequences for already disadvantaged individuals and groups (from early school leavers to aboriginal students) (Dale 2010; Foley and Green 2015). Even the traditional credential is losing its cachet: where once viewed as a commonly agreed upon shorthand to convey critical information about a person's skills and maturity, there is now less agreement of its status as a proxy for competence and status (Staton 2014). Four inequality issues are uppermost in an institution many believe to be pivotal in moderating the inequalities of exclusion by improving the lives and life chances of those less fortunate (Keister and Southgate 2011; but see Marsh 2011):

1. *Education and schooling as sites of inequality.* Education has long been endorsed as an instrument for attaining social equality (the great equalizer). Yet the educational system has proven to be a site of inequality because of differences in class, family expectations, cultural background, language competence, teacher attitudes, and peer group influences (the great fortifier) (Bowles and Gintis 1976; Giroux 1996; Foley and Green 2015). Studies indicate that children of richer parents perform better on average than children of poorer parents, with gaps ranging from better grades and higher standardized test scores to higher rates of participation in leadership and extracurricular activities (Reardon 2013; Mullen 2013). Parenting matters: as a result, middle-class kids are raised in a way that equips them with the resources and resourcefulness to excel in a system designed to reflect, reinforce, and reward

these skills and aptitudes (Lareau 2002; Putnam 2015). Gender inequities continue to persist, except now it is young women who have overcome the gender gap in science and math at school. Not only are boys widely outdistanced by girls on standardized literacy tests, but boys also have higher suspension and expulsion rates as well as higher dropout rates. Their struggles over reading and writing raises concerns about lifelong deficits unless schools customize instruction to capitalize on different ways of learning in an era of mass testing and standardized curricula.

2. *The challenges of accommodating diversity (-of-diversities).* Schools have become demographically diverse as a result of robust immigration patterns. Changing demographics and increased demands are putting pressure on school and education to adjust accordingly. A growing number of students in public, elementary, and secondary schools are of visible (racialized) minority or immigrant status, with projections of a numerical majority by 2017 (Areepattamannil 2005). The figures for Toronto are even more impressive where racialized minorities comprise nearly 50 per cent of secondary students. In turn, schools are staggering under the weight of schooling the unschooled while fanning fears that they are failing to provide a positive learning environment that values cultural diversity without sacrificing educational credentials. Or consider how Canada continues to aggressively seek high tuition-paying foreign students (221,000 students attended Canadian universities and community colleges in 2011, or about 8 per cent of total enrolment [Charbonneau 2014]). Yet there is little in the way of accommodation in terms of pedagogy, content, and evaluation. Criticism is also directed at universities when they value and legitimize a limited range of knowledge and ways of knowing (Kuokkanen 2007). Such a cacophony of criticism puts the system under alert. Schooling and education must become more representative of, reflective of, and responsive to differences, if they are to retain legitimacy in a changing and diverse Canada (Areepattamannil 2005).

3. *The crisis of confidence in post-secondary education.* This mismatch reflects a conflict of interest between the old and the new, with the result that educational institutions are experiencing a crisis of confidence in terms of who they are and what they should be doing (Wotherspoon 2009). Should universities focus on advancing commercial goals (starting a career), cognitive skills (instilling information and critical thinking), moral standards (building character or an integrated self), or social change (Brooks 2014)? There is a danger that, in trying to be everything to everybody, universities end up creating gaps between ideals and reality, principles and practice. Contributing to the crisis are proposed moves to overhaul all schooling and education along free market lines, including merit pay for those teachers who improve student test scores, standardized testing for students, longitudinal data collection to track performance, data-based decision-making, and improving choice, competition, deregulation, and accountability (Barkan 2011). As institutes of higher learning, will universities continue to lean on a neo-liberal business model informed by a growing number of part-time and contract faculty (Clift 2016; Brownlee 2016)? Such a proposal raises the question of whether neo-liberal market principles that apply to the economy should be applied to society and its social institutions. Such turmoil and pressure has prompted this response from Antonia Maioni (2015), a McGill professor and past-president of the Federation for the Humanities and Social Sciences:

> There is no more ivory tower. Modern universities are at the crossroads of evolving social, economic, and scholarly environments. . . . As institutions, Canadian universities are struggling to keep pace with this complex environment, while responding to the budgetary, technological and demographic demands brought about by the (welcome) influx of millennials.

4. *Education and schooling in perpetuating inequality and exclusion.* Schooling and education may be complicit in reinforcing patterns of inequality/exclusion in society at large (Wotherspoon 2009; Foley and Green 2015; Marginson 2016). Many factors that have little to do with education influence whether students go to university and graduate, including parental income, maternal health care, and neighbourhood quality. Consequently, higher education takes the inequalities given to it and magnifies them (Fischer 2016). Those students with middle-class values, resources, and skills will perform well and leverage this success into well-paying jobs in the knowledge economy (Putnam 2015). By comparison, aboriginal children, children of economically deprived immigrants, and some racialized minority groups (young males of Caribbean origin) are not performing well in school, experiencing lower achievement in test scores, grades, graduation rates, and college applications. This is particularly true for those refugee children who possess interrupted (or non-existent) education trajectories. Such underachievement comes with a hefty price tag: those students of colour who leave school without the basic tools for job success or learning skills suffer from underachievement that affects everything from the quality of life to self-esteem.

Such a dismaying assessment makes it doubly important to explore schooling and education along the lines of institutional inequality. Schooling and education are themselves sites of inequality with respect to access, participation, and success rates. They also are accomplices in creating and/or reproducing patterns of inequality within society. To be sure, it may be simplistic to label education and schooling as a failure or a social inequality problem. Who says schools are failing, why do people make this assertion, and on what grounds do they make these accusations? The "let's-solve-it-through-schools" mentality tends to inflate the importance of schooling and education as change agents, yet underestimate the significance of the media and peer pressure as catalysts for change or conformity. The school system must increasingly cope with the results of poor parenting, a tendency to dump all social problems into teachers' laps, and intense competition for student attention in a world of digital gratification. Such a mindset also allows primary caregivers to wriggle out of responsibilities while scapegoating schools for shortcomings that rightfully belong to parents, institutions, or society. Insult is heaped on injury when schooling and education are blamed for the miscalculations of those Canadian businesses that fumble opportunities to compete globally. In brief, the impossibly high standards expected of schooling and education by a demanding and diverse public may subject them to more criticism than deserved.

The conclusion cannot be lightly dismissed. A world convulsed by the dizzying pace of social change and assertive diversities puts pressure on schools to be all things to all people—parent, guardian, moral compass, social worker, and babysitter. Not surprisingly, they constitute sites of contradiction—safe havens that nurture, empower, and protect, yet hell holes where students must perform, reform, and conform (Reist

2012). The fact that schools are simultaneously all of these things—places of love and acceptance as well as spaces of criticism and rejection—reinforces their status as sites of inclusion and exclusion. This paradox may explain why many of the mass shootings in the United States and Canada are school-related. Michael Reist (2012) writes to this effect in response to the horrific incident in Connecticut where 20 children and 6 teachers were gunned down on 14 December 2012. School shooters may themselves be trauma victims, entrapped in a desperate attempt to resolve inner conflicts related to disengagement, humiliation and alienation—a reaction to the pressures of complying to the three fundamental rules of school—sit still, be quiet, and do as told (Reist 2011). But the violence engendered by the school system is neither restricted to the present nor isolated in mainstream institutions. The intended and unintended effects of the residential school system in Canada (and the United States) reinforce the hoary cliché "violence begets violence"—as captured in this Spotlight box.

Spotlight Residential Schools: Aggressive Assimilation or Schooling as Genocide?

The burden of this experience has been on your shoulders for far too long. The burden is properly ours as a government and as a country. There is no place in Canada for the attitudes that inspired the Indian residential-school system to ever again prevail. You have worked on recovering from this experience for a very long time and in a very real sense, we are now joining you on the journey. (Stephen Harper, cited in Rolfsen 2008)

On 11 June 2008, then–prime minister Stephen Harper stood in the House of Commons and apologized for the failings of the residential school system. The apology covered the treatment and deprivation of aboriginal students in terms of its lasting impact on aboriginal families, culture, and

language (Rolfsen 2008). His apology was the latest salvo in a string of atonements, including a formal apology in 1998 for decades of coercive assimilation, theft of aboriginal lands, suppression of cultures, and the physical and sexual abuse of aboriginal children in an atmosphere of neglect, disease, and death. "To those who suffered the tragedy of residential schools," then–minister of Indian Affairs Jane Stewart once proclaimed, "we are deeply sorry." According to the statement of reconciliation, the government apologized for enforcing policies that forcibly removed children from their families and warehoused them at residential school sites often hundreds of kilometres from their community, leaving behind a legacy of emotional and physical scars. To be sure, central authorities were initially reluctant to apologize

continued

for past misdeeds since admitting liability would solicit lawsuits. Nevertheless, they saw little choice except to "plea bargain" in hopes of limiting damages to manageable proportions. As a token of atonement, the government pledged $350 million for counselling programs and treatment centres for school victims (Regan 2010).

For many Aboriginal peoples, the violence, mismanagement, and perversion of the residential school system is the defining moment in a 500-year history of oppression, appropriation, and assimilation (Truth and Reconciliation Commission Report 2015; Niezen 2013; Paul 2012; Rolfsen 2008; Castellano, Archibald, and Degagne 2008). The federal government and Canada's major churches institutionalized the concept of a residential school system in the hopes of "taking the Indian out of the child," according to then–Indian Affairs deputy superintendent Duncan Campbell Scott, in effect resolving the so-called "Indian" problem for once and for all. The boarding school system in the United States also embodied a similar sentiment by Capt. Richard Pratt who designed the first school: "Kill the Indian in him, and save the man" (Gustafsen 2007:2).[3] The residential school system as a **total institution** proved to be a thinly disguised pogrom of coercive assimilation that was genocidal in its consequences if not by intent, partly because of its commitment to remove and isolate children from their homes and communities; eradicate all aspects of aboriginal culture on the assumption Aboriginal peoples were inferior or dangerous; and disrupt cultural transmission from one generation to the next in ensuring "no more Indians" (Indigenous Foundations 2009; Niezen 2013). The deaths of between 3,000 and 6,000 aboriginal children of the 150,000 or so who attended residential schools—most from disease—are a scathing enough indictment (Perkel 2013). Admittedly, not everyone equated the schools with an exercise in forced assimilation and cultural genocide. To demonize all residential schools as instruments of oppression emphasizes the negative to the exclusion of any positives, while failing to contextualize the system or to compare what

aboriginal children experienced in provincial or on reserve schools (Clifton and Rubenstein 2015). Still, it is difficult to avoid the conclusion that the schools were designed to strip aboriginal children of all that was indigenous in terms of language, culture, traditions, and values (Petoukhov 2013).

Which interpretation is correct, keeping in mind that, historically, Canada's aboriginal policy sought to eliminate culture, ignore rights, acquire land and resources, terminate treaties, and assimilate Aboriginal peoples by stripping them of their legal status as a lived and distinct reality (Truth and Reconciliation Commission Report 2015)? Is the residential school system an act of systemic (or cultural) genocide intended to destroy Canada's First Peoples (Truth and Reconciliation Commission Report 2015; Thielen-Wilson 2014)? Or should it be framed as a generalized act of aggressive assimilation whose intentions aimed at transforming aboriginal youth along Eurocentric lines? Should the system be judged on its misguided intent or on the basis of unintended yet negative consequences of good intentions? Should the system be assessed on the grounds of hindsight based on the twenty-first-century standards? Or should the evaluation reflect the historical context that informed its origins and development?

Context

Residential schools were founded and operated by Protestant and Roman Catholic missionaries, although they were funded primarily by the federal government under the auspices of the Department of Indian Affairs (Niezen 2013). An idea borrowed from the United States, where industrial boarding schools formed the principal feature of President Grant's "aggressive civilization" policy of 1869 (Davin 1879), residential schools (or industrial schools, as they were called initially in Canada because of their emphasis on vocational skills acquisition) were established in every province and territory except Prince Edward Island, Nova Scotia, and Newfoundland and Labrador (which did not become a province until 1949). The vast majority were concentrated in the

Prairie provinces. From two residential schools at the time of Confederation, the number expanded to 80 by 1931, of which 44 were Roman Catholic, 21 Anglican, 13 United Church, and 2 Presbyterian (Miller 1996). By the time the system wound down in the mid-1990s, a stocktaking revealed the following figures: a total of 70 Roman Catholic schools with 68,250 students (or 65 per cent of the total residential school population), followed by 37 Anglican schools with 23,100 students (22 per cent), 14 United Church schools with 10,500 students (10 per cent), 4 Presbyterian schools with 1,050 students (1 per cent), and 7 government-run schools with 2,100 students (2 per cent). About 100,000–150,000 aboriginal children attended the schools before they were mothballed in the 1970s, although four residential schools operated until 1996, albeit under aboriginal jurisdiction (Miller 1996).[4]

Rationale

From the mid-nineteenth century onward, the Crown engaged in a variety of measures to assimilate and "civilize" Canada's Indigenous peoples. The Indian Act of 1876 proved the quintessential instrument for control and containment through the micromanagement of aboriginal lives, realities, and opportunities. The Act codified a series of laws and regulations that embraced the notions of European cultural and moral superiority to justify the domination and dispossession of Aboriginal peoples. The Act also provided a rationale for paternalistic initiatives to aggressively civilize Aboriginal peoples by stripping them of their culture and society, then absorbing them into a dominant white culture as self-supporting members. The mandatory placement of aboriginal children in off-reserve residential schools fed into the racist and supremacist assumptions implicit in the Indian Act. The government insisted on taking aboriginal children away from their parents (who were seen as unfit) and putting them in total institutions, under the control of religious orders (on the assumption that European culture and religion were superior) (Truth and Reconciliation

Commission Report 2015). The rationale for the residential school system was captured in an 1889 annual report by the Department of Indian Affairs:

> The boarding-school dissociated the Indian child from the deleterious home influence to which he would otherwise be subjected. It reclaims him from the uncivilized state in which he has been brought up. It brings him into contact from day to day with all that tends to effect a change in his views and habits. (quoted in Roberts 1996:A7)

To be sure, residential schools were but one part of an archipelago of colonial institutional complexes in Canada (Dooley 2013). From the 1940s to the 1970s, the federal government operated a separate system of 22 segregated Indian hospitals, mostly in western Canada, that institutionalized aboriginal individuals with TB or measles (Drees 2013).

The school's guiding philosophy embraced the adage "how a twig is bent, the tree will grow." Federal officials believed in the need to capture the entire child (adults were dismissed as beyond hope [Davin 1879]) through immersion in segregated facilities and indoctrination into Western ways. Day schools didn't work, according to the Davin Report of 1879 because ". . . the influence of the wigwam was stronger than the influence of the school." Over time, the adoption of English, Christianity, and Canadian customs would be transmitted to their children, resulting in the eventual disappearance of aboriginality. But the residential school system had a more basic motive than simple education: the removal of children from home and parents was aimed at their absorption into Canadian society through the creation of a distinct underclass of labourers, farmers, and domestics (Rotman 1996). This program sought to destroy aboriginal language and culture, while supplanting aboriginal spirituality with Christianity in the hopes of "killing the Indian in the child" (Royal Commission on Aboriginal Peoples 1996). Sadly, this exercise in anglo-conformity ended up nearly killing both the child and the "Indian."

continued

Reality

This experiment in forced assimilation through indoctrination proved destructive (Truth and Reconciliation Commission Report 2015). Many of the schools were poorly built and maintained, living conditions were deplorable, nutrition portions barely met subsistence levels, and the crowding and unsanitary conditions transformed them into incubators of disease. Many children succumbed to tuberculosis, along with other contagious diseases. A report in 1907 on 15 schools found that 24 per cent of the 1,537 children in the survey had died while in the care of the school, prompting the magazine *Saturday Night* to claim: "Even war seldom shows as large a percentage of fatalities as does the education system we have imposed upon our Indian wards" (quoted in Matas 1997). Or as Duncan Campbell Scott ruefully noted, "...50 percent of the children who passed through these schools did not live to benefit from the education which they have received therein" (cited in Rolfsen 2008). Other reports, including the Royal Commission on Aboriginal Peoples (1996), highlighted the pervasiveness of disciplinary terror through physical violence or sexual abuse. As one former residential school student told the Manitoba Aboriginal Justice Inquiry:

> My father, who attended Alberni Indian Residential School for four years in the twenties, was physically tortured by his teachers for speaking Tseshalt: they pushed sewing needles through his tongue, a routine punishment for language offenders. . . . The needle tortures suffered by my father affected all my family. My Dad's attitude became "why teach my children Indian if they are going to be punished for speaking it?". . . I never learned how to speak my own language. I am now, therefore, truly a "dumb Indian." (quoted in Rotman 1996:57)

Reports of abuse appeared in anecdotal form by the 1940s, went public during the 1960s and 1970s, but did not incite the public indignation until Phil Fontaine, the National Chief of the Assembly of First Nations, disclosed his personal experiences in 1990. Admittedly, some aboriginal children profited from the knowledge and skills they acquired in the residential school system (Indigenous Foundation 2012). But many suffered horribly in the long run: children grew up hostile or confused, caught between two clashing worlds but accepted in neither. Young and impressionable children returned without a sense of self-worth because of verbal abuse and physical violence. Confused and inferiorized, many lost fluency in their own language or any sense of identity or belonging to traditional ways (Rotman 1996). Adults often turned to prostitution, sexual and incestuous violence, and drunkenness to cope with the emotional scarring. Worse still, the legacy of residential schools continues to negatively influence relations across and within generations (Mohammed 2010). As Jennifer Llewellyn (2002) writes:

> The painful legacy of residential schools continues to affect the survivors of residential schools. The effect of the abuses are not however limited to these individuals, but extend to their families, communities, culture, and reach across generational lines. The harms caused by residential schools thus are not limited to the physical and emotional scars from sexual and physical abuse. Rather, fully comprehending the harms of residential schools requires one to understand the relational nature of these harms. The harms of residential schools are at their most fundamental and enduring level harms to the relationships between Aboriginals and non-Aboriginals and within the Aboriginal community itself. The harm, and the legacy of the residential schools, is the perpetuation of relationships of oppression and inequality.

Implications

This inhumane experiment in social engineering is unconscionable when judged by contemporary standards of human rights, multicultural inclusiveness, and the politics of aboriginal sovereignty. In an interview with the Truth and Reconciliation Commission chair (Kennedy 2015), Murray Sinclair criticized a residential school system that not only scarred thousands of aboriginal children but also symbolized wider Canadian attitude that inferiorized Indigenous peoples as incapable of managing their own affairs (also Truth and Reconciliation Commission Report 2015). Of course, it's easy to judge and condemn actions in hindsight, especially when implemented by people who were convinced of Christianity's moral superiority and the inevitability of European progress (Clifton and Rubenstein 2015). Many believed they acted in good faith as devout Christians in improving the spiritual status and material progress of the First Peoples. Government initiatives were condoned as enlightened, given the alternative—namely, eventual extinction without conversion to Christianity and civilization to blunt the ruthless pressures of evolutionary progress (i.e., adapt or die) (Indigenous Foundations 2012). Nor should the role of aboriginal parents be ignored: according to Miller (1996), many insisted on a European-style education for their children, although no one would have condoned such austere living conditions or extreme punishment, despite being in an era when corporal punishment was rationalized as part of the "spare the rod, spoil the child" mentality. Still, the Royal Commission concluded that the residential school system was an "act of profound cruelty" rooted in racism and indifference and pointed the blame at Canadian society, Christian evangelism, and policies of the churches and government.

The 2008 apology, a Truth and Reconciliation Commission Report (2015), and proposed reparations may prove a useful starting point in acknowledging those past injustices that denied recognition of Aboriginal peoples as complete citizens and human beings (see Niezen 2013; also Gustafsen 2007). It remains to be seen whether psychologically scarred survivors, broken families, and dysfunctional aboriginal communities will respond to the balm of compensation packages, counselling

centres, and healing programs. Yet danger signals abound. Aboriginal peoples and mainstream whites tend to differently frame the apology and reconciliation (Denis 2012). The dominant white frame is both individualistic and ahistorical; by contrast, Aboriginal frames tend to be holistic, fluid, and processual. For whites, the apology represents closure; for Aboriginal peoples, it's but one step in an ongoing healing process. Whites insist it is time to stop dwelling in the past because the past has no bearing in the present and complicates any effort to move forward. Such an ahistorical response reflects a Canadian style laissez faire racism that justifies racial inequality, avoids responsibilities, and defends dominant interests without sounding racist. For Aboriginal peoples, however (to borrow a phrase from William Faulkner), the past is not dead, it's not even the past. History is alive and resonates with the present because of its damaging effect on both residential school children and their descendants (Indigenous Foundations 2012). Less than half of the population finished high school, with the result that a relatively small percentage of the aboriginal population have a university degree—in part because of a deep distrust of education as a tool for aggressive assimilation. In the words of Laura Arndt, strategic director for the Ontario office of the Provincial Advocate for Children and Youth:

In my house, it is not a proud thing to be a university graduate. It means you're less Indian because you're educated. Why would children want to get a good education when they feel they lose themselves in the process? (cited in McMahon 2014:20)

If one takes seriously that residential school injustices are genocidal—in consequences if not by intent—a commitment to justice demands a fundamental restitution based on aboriginal understanding and experiences. As Denis (2012) points out, the proof in any reconciliation is in an apology that is more than atonement but leads to actions.

Universities in Crisis: Ivory Tower Inequalities, Exclusions, Disruptions

Everyone has the right to education . . . higher education shall be equally accessible to all on the basis of merit.
— Article 26(1): United Nations Universal Declaration of Human Rights

Many regard post-secondary school as a fundamental right. This was not always the case. The notion of post-secondary schooling for the "masses" originated in the post-war period and blossomed during the 1960s. Until then, higher education was just that: education for the higher-ups (Coates and Morrison 2012). Universities were once the most pampered and privileged of all institutions, and a university degree was a mark of distinction rather than proof of a credential. They represented communities distinct in both mission and values in shaping law, diplomacy, policy, politics, and civil bureaucracy at the vanguard of a progressive society. Universities also served as finishing schools for the well-heeled and upwardly mobile. As a socializing, civilizing, and even moralizing agent, university education was aimed at creating a trained professional class, a cadre of endowed elites to staff the public bureaucracies of an expanding dominion, while preserving the cultural assumptions of Christian civilization through knowledge and research. Or as Susan Mann, former president of York University notes, universities educated elites to service those in powers, from the church and the monarchy to the bureaucracy and the state.

But gone are the days when universities were truly ivory towers remote in time and place and beyond the reach of the masses. The massification (or democratization) of post-secondary education proved transformational in redefining the status and role of universities. This institutional transformation dovetailed with the growing liberalization of society, with a corresponding commitment to equal opportunity for everybody, not just the elites. Consider the numbers: less than two per cent of the population aged 15 and over in 1951 possessed a university degree; by 2007, the figure

for those of working age had risen to 25 per cent, according to the Conference Board of Canada. If all levels of tertiary education are taken into account (namely community college and university), the figure for 2012 stood at just under 60 per cent of Canadians between 25 and 64 years of age with some post-secondary credentials (34 per cent had a community college diploma, 17.5 per cent indicated a BA, and 8.3 per cent reported a graduate degree), in effect making Canada the leader among OECD countries in the proportion of adults with a post-secondary degree (CAUT 2014-2015; Statistics Canada 2012; Hopper 2014).

More specifically, nearly 1.2 million students attended university in 2010 (AUCC 2011). Students in degree programs included 755,000 full-time undergraduates, 143,400 full-time graduates, and 275,800 in part-time study. The participation rate for youths aged 18–24 in university programs was 24 per cent in 2011–12, up from 17 per cent in 1992–1993 and a doubling since 1980, with 60 per cent of undergraduate enrolments in the humanities and social sciences (CAUT 2014–2015). The gender balance has shifted as well: women accounted for the majority of full-time students (57 per cent) enrolled at the bachelor and other undergraduate degree programs in 2011–12, 55 per cent in MA programs, and 48 per cent at the PhD level). They also accounted for the majority of community college enrolments (CAUT 2014–15). About 8 per cent of enrolments are international students, while among first year undergraduate students in 2012–2013, 36 per cent identified as members of a racialized minority group, 8 per cent as persons with disabilities, and 3 per cent as aboriginal (CAUT 2014–2015). The number of aboriginal individuals aged 25 to 64 with university degrees has increased from 2 per cent of the population in 1980 to 9.8 per cent in 2011 (48.4 per cent of adult aboriginals possessed post-secondary credentials, including trades certificates and college diplomas; by contrast, 64.7 per cent of the adult non-aboriginal population had a post-secondary credential, including 26.5 per cent with a university degree) (Statistics Canada 2014b). Race and class continue to matter in terms of admission and attendance in both Canada and the United States, with class the strongest predictor of who will attend and graduate (Mullen 2012). In

2006, youth aged 18–24 whose parents earned at least $100,000 in annual pre-tax income were more likely (49 per cent) to be enrolled in university as those with parents who had annual incomes less than $25,000 (28 per cent) (CAUT 2014–15).

The massed-growth process has profoundly upended the dynamics and logic behind post-secondary schooling and education (Cote and Allahar 2007; Coates and Morrison 2012). Universities have become more inclusive by accommodating the historically disadvantaged, including members of the working class, women, and people of colour. Yet success has unleashed many of the inequalities associated with underfunding (a 50 per cent increase in full-time enrollment over the past 12 years, yet per-student funding has dropped to historic lows [Davidson 2013]). As a result, universities are under pressure to accomplish more with less, while doing what they were never designed to do: cater to the masses or staff corporate Canada. The levelling trends associated with this massification are contrary to the elitist principle that historically informed post-secondary education (Kubes 2014). The "pragmatization" of post-secondary education has perplexed a once pampered university enterprise, stretched to the limit by rising enrolment yet undercut by a dwindling financial base and rudderless because of an identity crisis. The demise of exclusivity, with its concomitant belief in education as a privilege rather than right, has had a powerful impact on post-secondary education, resulting in unintended consequences that pose a challenge at present (Cote and Allahar 2007). Or as Coates and Morrison (2012:36) write,

> . . . since World War Two, Canadian universities have shifted from being preserves of the rich, the gifted, and the intensely ambitious into the academic equivalent of intramural sports, where the premium rests on mass participation rather than on high achievement.

Conflicting options prevail. To one side, an egalitarian and democratized university is accused of sabotaging the principles of deference to authority, esteem for hard-earned accomplishments, reverence for heritage and knowledge of the past, a commitment to rationality and science, and a willingness to assert the superiority of one idea or standard over another. To the other side is the charge of elitist irrelevance. Too much of what passes for schooling and education remains anchored in nineteenth-century pedagogy (some would say more akin to the fourteenth century regimes), in effect sabotaging students for the realities of the digitally driven, knowledge-based, post-industrial economy. Critics argue universities are woefully out of touch with the economic realities of Canada, yet institutions of higher learning are not necessarily comfortable with their imposed mandate as job training institutions. They also are accused of pandering to people's passions by promoting the idea that a student's personal choice of study should trump all other considerations (Coates and Morrison 2012; but see Finnie et al. 2014). However important the pursuit of self-actualization, the mantra of pursuing a degree of choice may well contribute to a surplus of graduates at odds with what the economy demands, in effect reinforcing the paradox of an economy consisting of jobs without workers and workers without jobs (Coates 2015b).

The post-secondary bubble has burst, at least in the arts and humanities, in effect prompting the ivory towers to shift into rethink-redo-rebrand mode (but see Finnie et al. 2014). Universities are increasingly misunderstood by governments that see them as an expensive luxury in a no-frill economy; lampooned by politicians for perceived excesses in political correctness and minority pandering; ignored by decision-makers as irrelevant to intellectual life in a world of think tanks and information technologies; criticized by the private sector for mismatching education with the needs of the national economy (Coates and Morrison 2012); and taken to task for trying to be all things to everybody. Canadian parents and youth remain committed to university education as the key to success, although the development of the workforce through post-secondary education has evolved in a manner insensitive to the job market and the changing economy (Coates 2015b). Universities no longer possess the moral authority as critic or as conscience of society; rather they appear more obsessed with an impulse for power, revenue, and growth for growth's sake. Martin Loney (1999) skewers the misuse of universities: "Funded by taxpayers and student fees, they are run in the manner of a medieval guild for the benefit of tenured academic staff whose jobs-for-life guarantee requires no commensurate commitment." It is impossible, he writes, to think of another occupation that offers such generous rewards for such minimal output (Robson 2015).

Quality continues to be compromised: overcrowded classes and inaccessible professors have resulted in a diminished capacity to foster excellence—replaced by tedious ritual that requires memorized input and scheduled regurgitation, an exercise not dissimilar in consequences to intellectual bulimia. Even the much-touted MOOC initiatives (massive open online courses) are proving unsuccessful. Moves by MOOC to deinstitutionalize the traditional pedagogical model for a more open-ended and collaborative model have rarely worked out as planned. Instead MOOCs tend to be co-opted by cash-strapped administrators to do what universities have always done—transfer course content from expert to student—but more cheaply and on a grander scale (Bady 2013). New faculty are not being hired; sessionals and contract workers are replacing full-time faculty in hopes of balancing budgets (Berger and Ricci 2011), and students are shouldering an increased burden of operating costs by way of spiraling tuition fees (CAUT 2014–2015; Rajagopal 2002). The ratio of full-time faculty to university students has declined accordingly, especially in Ontario, from about one professor for every 17 students in 1992–3 to around one professor for every 25 students in 2009–10 (CAUT 2012/13)—a trend that surely diminishes the quality of a university experience. Five additional concerns intensify the identity crisis, while fostering the inequalities of exclusion.

Escalating Tuition: Inequality or Investment?

The post-secondary system relies on four primary sources of funding: government grants, endowments and donations from private sources, internal revenue such as sale of patents, and individual user fees (i.e., tuition). Universities in the past relied primarily on governments to defray operational costs; at present, however, they are experiencing a financial

crisis as a result of government cutbacks (Canadian Association of University Teachers 2010; Canadian Federation of Students 2011). This was not always the case: financing concerns rarely entered the equation during the 1960s and 1970s. Post-secondary institutions were recipients of limitless dollars by governments who revered them as future cash cows and catalysts for economic growth, social equality, cultural sophistication, scientific advancement, and political democracy. Intellectuals flocked to them as oases of enlightenment and research. Taxpayers did not mind the extra burden since universal access to post-secondary education opened avenues of social mobility for their daughters and sons.

Revenues from all levels of government declined substantially from the 1990s to the mid-2000s. As recently as 1984, government funds accounted for about 80 per cent of a university budget, while federal transfers for post-secondary education constituted about 0.5 percent of the GDP. By 2004, government funds represented about 50 per cent of a university's operating revenue, while federal cash transfers for post-secondary education as a percentage of the GDP shrunk to 0.15 per cent, albeit inching up to about 0.20 per cent from 2008 onwards (CAUT 2014–2015), in effect making Canada one of the OECD's laggards in publicly funding post-secondary education (CAUT 2013/14).[5] The reduction of public funding (government funding) as a share of a university's operating costs (from 83 per cent in 1982 to 55 per cent in 2012) has reinforced a reliance on private income. Sources such as increased tuition fees accounted for 38 per cent of a university's operating fees in 2012 compared to 14 per cent in 1982 (Shaker and Macdonald 2014; CAUT 2014–2015). In addition to fewer professors and larger classes, post-secondary institutions have turned to contingent faculty (sessional, part-time, and contract instructors) in an effort to do more with less.

Tuition fees have escalated to offset this loss of revenue (CAUT 2014–2015). Canada's undergraduate students paid an average of $6,885 in tuition and other fees in the 2014–15 year (Shaker and Macdonald 2014), although students rarely pay the "sticker price," thanks to a range of government grants and loans (Usher 2015, 2016a, b). (In 2011–12, the average Canadian student loan for full time university students was $5,406 [CAUT 2014–15]). Undergrads in Ontario paid the highest fees at $8,474 (including compulsory and tuition costs) in 2014-15, while students in Newfoundland and Labrador paid the lowest fees at $2,871. (There was a 3.2 per cent on average increase in 2015–16 for tuition fees alone, according to a CAUT Bulletin 15 October 2015, putting the national average at $6,191, with Ontario undergraduate students paying the most fees.) Graduate students paid an average tuition fee of $5,599 in 2011–2. Ontario graduate students paid the highest fee at $7,578. International undergraduate students paid an average tuition fee of $17,571 in 2011–2, while the figure for full-time foreign grad students was $12,802. Tuition hikes in non-regulated programs are substantial. Undergrad students in dentistry paid the highest annual fee ($16,024), followed by medicine ($11,345), and pharmacy ($9,806). At the graduate level, the most expensive programs were the executive MBA with tuition fees of $37,501, compared to the regular MBA program at $21,528. Additional compulsory fees for Canadian undergraduate students increased to an average of $820 nationally, ranging from $212 in Newfoundland and Labrador to $1,399 in Alberta. The combination of annual costs for tuition, books, rent, and transport reinforces the obvious. The average debt burden of each student at graduation ranges between $25,000 and $30,000 (Carrick 2015; Macdonald and Shaker 2011; Community Foundations 2012), despite relatively generous government grants and tax credits of which a substantial portion is non-repayable (Usher 2016a, b). And while English-speaking Canadian students appear resigned to the costs and increases, Quebec students have proven much more adamant about who pays, in effect keeping tuition fees at a fraction of the cost across Canada (Levy 2012; Lyder 2012).

Two key questions underpin the debate over rising tuition fees. First, are high tuition fees justified? The answer depends on who is seen as prime beneficiary of a post-secondary degree. For some, a university degree is a private gain rather than a public good, and as such, users should defray operational costs through tuitions at levels determined by whatever the market will bear. Post-secondary education should not be framed as an investment for society at large, according to this line of thinking, but rather a highly subsidized service to students who should pay more up front. Others disagree, arguing that an educated workforce is a public good not just a private gain. If a university degree is prerequisite for meaningful employment, Kent Kuran (2012) argues, post-secondary education should be virtually free as is the case in many European countries. Still others might argue corporate Canada should shoulder the cost of post-secondary education since university graduates are a prime source of increased productivity and wealth creation.

Second, are high tuition fees worth it? With tuition fees and auxiliary costs rising rapidly, the risk of acquiring a university degree has never been higher, with the possibility of little or no payoff for arts and humanities graduates (Carrick 2013). As if to reinforce this dilemma, a recent study by the OECD (2012; also Taylor 2012) pointed out a baffling paradox: Canada allocates one of the highest amounts for post-secondary education (colleges and universities) of any country, in the process creating proportionally the largest number of best educated adults in the world. Yet 17 per cent of the highly educated (including 6 per cent in the prime earning ages 35–55) earned less than half the national median employment income in 2009 (mostly in arts and humanities, whereas those in maths, engineering, and sciences doubled the median income [Kubes 2014]). Another report by CIBC World Markets using Statistics Canada data concluded that about one-half of all recent graduates in psychology, social sciences, education, and humanities earn less than half the median income in Canada (Tal and Enenajor 2013). To be sure, obtaining a university degree is still the best route to a well-paying quality job in Canada (admittedly, a necessary but no longer sufficient condition) (Frenette 2014). In January 2014, the unemployment rate for the overall population was 6.3 per cent; by contrast, it was 4.2 per cent for those with an undergraduate degree, 5.2 per cent for those with a graduate degree, and 5.9 per cent for those with a post-secondary diploma or certificate (CAUT 2014–15). But the premium is declining because too few students are graduating from programs in high demand growth areas or in financially advantageous fields (medicine, law, and engineering) (also Coates 2015b; Coates and Morrison 2016). It should be pointed out that in a Workopolis study (Harris 2014) based on a large number of resumés, the following degrees were most likely to lead to a job in their field: nursing (97 per cent), pharmacy (94 per cent), computer science (91 per cent), engineering (90 per cent), and human resources (88 per cent). The areas of study that produced the highest starting salaries were engineering ($76,000), health care ($69,600), computer science ($68,000), law ($67,600), and math ($67,600).

A cruel hoax is now in play: a university degree no longer guarantees a decent job. Yet landing a (decent) job is getting more difficult without a post-secondary degree, despite a credential creep that transforms universities into the new secondary schools (Kuran 2012). Furthermore, the income premium of a university degree is generally substantial (Davidson 2012), as demonstrated by the annual income breakdowns for the year 2011 (TD Economics 2011):

- Average income in Canada, both full-time and part-time was $31,757
- Average full-time earnings in Canada, regardless of education, was $43,231

- Canadians with a high school diploma earned $36,278
- Canadians with a college degree earned $41,825
- Canadians with a university degree earned $61,823
- Men with a university degree in full-time employment earned $72,000

These differential earnings multiply exponentially over a person's lifetime, especially when higher earnings can translate into investment income compounded annually (TD Economics 2011). Indirect advantages prevail as well since those with higher education levels tend to engage in healthier lifestyles and a better standard of living. In short, the immediate cost of a post-secondary education can be daunting, while the resulting debt poses a seemingly insurmountable burden. Nonetheless, a degree or diploma remains the best investment a person can make, especially if one chooses an applied degree or specialized discipline (Coates and Morrison 2012). But this Spotlight box suggests a different spin:

Spotlight Earnings of University Graduates: The Bigger the Picture, the Better the Picture

It is commonly assumed that BAs can yield substantially different returns on income and earning potential, depending on the faculty source. Graduates from the so-called hard sciences (business, math, engineering, natural sciences, computer science, and health) are thought to do extremely well compared to those with the misfortune of a degree in the humanities or social sciences. But a study by Ross Finnie et al. (2014) and his associates arrived at a different conclusion. Using a dataset of 82,000 students who graduated from the University of Ottawa from 1999 to 2011 and who filed at least one tax return, he concluded that the situation is more complex and nuanced—and much more hopeful—for those clutching an arts degree. The major findings included:

1. One year after graduating, earnings for all graduate students varied between $41,000 and $47,000 over the entire 1998–2011 period. Those in engineering, computer science, and business performed best in the labour market, although this was driven almost entirely by the top earners in these disciplines. Earnings for all cohorts increased substantially in the years following graduation. The lowest group (humanity grads) is now making $70,000, on average, 13 years after graduation—and keep in mind they are still in their mid-30s (Finnie in Tamburri 2015).

2. Graduates from different faculties experienced substantially different starting incomes, but increases over time varied. For example, health

graduates perform better than most other disciplines in the first few years after graduation (first year earnings are about $50,000, but graduates in humanities and (especially) the social sciences eventually surpass them.

3. Those in hard sciences (except for health) may have had higher earnings all around, but they also experienced more volatile earning patterns over time than arts graduates whose earnings remained stable across all 13 cohorts—in part because of the general nature of their skills and wide range of employment. Such variability in earnings suggests that graduates from the harder sciences experience more vulnerability to changes in the business cycle.

4. Significant differences in earnings persist between women and men. This was especially true among engineering, math, and the natural

sciences graduates. By contrast, there was no initial gap in the social sciences, humanities, and health; however, the gap grew over time (Finnie in Tamburri 2015).

What lessons can be gleaned from Finnie et al. (2014; also Frenette 2014)? First, if we want to understand post-graduate earning patterns, a longitudinal (long-term) perspective is critical, given the importance of the timing of graduation (Is the economy tanking? Is your discipline hitting the skids?) and cumulative years of experience. Second, students making choices about what to pursue should continue to follow what they are passionate about—even in the much maligned humanities and social sciences (Finnie in Tamburri 2015; but see Coates 2015b)—because in the long run, it doesn't seem to matter that much.

Academic Freedom under Siege

A growing commitment to institutional inclusiveness has further sharpened the crisis in post-secondary education. Universities and colleges are now confronted by the paradox of preserving academic freedom within a bias-free environment without trampling on gender or minority rights for inclusion. Both are under pressure to foster environments in which all individuals can enjoy the freedom to study, teach, and conduct research. Yet a commitment to inclusiveness may compromise the historic role of higher education. Critics have argued that universities are losing their status as bastions of higher learning by curbing free expression, abdicating an attendant "right to offend" if necessary, or caving in to unproven allegations of racism and sexism without due process (Fekete 1994; Furedy 1995). According to the 2012 Campus Freedom Index by the Justice Centre for Constitutional Freedoms (2012), the status of free speech is in a perilous place, with most universities and student unions receiving a failing grade for stifling a campus-wide right to speak. Others contend that a commitment to an inclusive environment implies free speech restrictions to ensure no one is excluded because of fear, intimidation, or

threats. Efforts to reconcile these mutually exclusive yet seemingly valid perspectives—the right to free expression versus a minority right to be free of malicious hatred or "chilly climate"—casts an uncomfortable spotlight on an institution that prefers a low profile.

The corporatization of universities is also imposing restraints on the hallowed principle of academic freedom of expression (Westheimer 2010; Marklein 2015). Universities now model themselves after corporations or businesses in seeking to maximize revenue, growth, and marketability, thus impeding their democratic vision of academic freedom and intellectual independence. But the displacement of critical thinking and a culture of criticism by a creeping entrepreneurialism cannot be taken lightly (Westheimer 2010). The principle of academic freedom and the right to provocatively challenge conventional wisdom about society is central to the very mission of a post-secondary enterprise. Other values pale by comparison, as confirmed by the CAUT upon adoption of its Policy Statement on Academic Freedom in 1977:

> The common good of society depends upon the search for knowledge and its free exposition. Academic freedom in universities

is essential to both these purposes in the teaching function of the university as well as in its scholarship and research. . . . Academic members of the community are entitled, regardless of prescribed doctrine, to freedom in carrying out research and in publishing the results thereof, freedom of teaching and of discussion . . . in a manner consistent with the scholarly obligation to base research and teaching on an honest search for knowledge. (cited in McGill, 1994:12–13)

For many, a capacity to pursue impartial truth and value-free knowledge without fear of reprisals is seriously compromised without guarantees of non-interference. Support for free expression presupposes that one's adversaries have something useful to say, with every right to articulate it provided, of course, a similar right is extended to others. The principle of "agreeing to disagree" is not simply an idle luxury or post-secondary perk. This principle is critical in sorting out competing truth claims as a precondition for intellectual discoveries. Impartiality and objectivity are seriously compromised without guarantees of non-interference by vested interests. Moves to "muzzle" through outside interference are openly resisted as fundamental infringements to academic freedom and institutional autonomy (de Toro, 1994:15). Without academic freedom, in other words, what is the university for?

Corporatizing the Ivory Towers

The design and structure of the university are changing in response to internal and external pressures. Without a firm centre to hold their focus in place, universities are losing the sense of historical mission that once exalted their status in society. Initially, universities were historically focused on the grand narratives of reason and, later, the pursuit of truth, while promoting the ideal of a national culture and informed citizenship (Readings 1997; Rolfe 2014). But with nation-states declining as prime creators of wealth or sources of identity, the protection and promotion of national culture is less urgent than in the past, thus reinforcing the increasingly

tenuous relationship between higher learning and nation-state status in a globalizing and post-national era. As a result, teaching and reflection as core activities appear to be taking a back seat to revenue-generating research priorities as universities evolve into bureaucratic corporations with a corporatist focus that extol a market-driven focus on research, deliverables, and social payoffs that can be measured for outcomes (Brownlee 2015). The corporatization of universities includes commodification and commercialization of knowledge; increased presence of corporations on campus; transfer of university know-how to the corporate sector, including industry-driven research aimed at skills training and workforce preparation; production of market oriented outputs such as degrees as "purchasable commodities"; inroads on academic freedom; the self-proliferation of a managerial class [6]; and their operation along corporate lines, from CEO-like salaries for university presidents to the casualization of academic work (Vose 2015; Polster and Newson 2015; Marklein 2015; Westheimer 2010). Neo-liberal capitalist narratives prevail as well in opening the university to the dominant logic of marketization and its organization as a major business player in the increasingly lucrative knowledge economy (Rolfe 2014; Readings 1997; Coleman and Kamboureli 2011; Baker 2012; Bok 2004). This passage by Ronald Barnett (2013:1) captures the evolutionary trajectory of universities from the metaphysical to the monetary:

> For some hundreds of years, the idea of the university was . . . that of a metaphysical university, reflective of an inquiry that enhanced humanity's connections with God, or the Universe, or Truth or Spirit or even the State. That conception gave way to the research university which is now giving way to the entrepreneurial [innovation oriented-] university, which in turn is closely aligned to the emergence of a tacit idea of the corporate university.

The chummy links between business and education are controversial (Brownlee 2015; Pocklington and Tupper 2002). In an era of dwindling resources and intense competition, universities are increasingly corporatizing the three Rs: restructuring, refocusing, and retrenchment (Lewington 1997). Yet this zeal to enter into research and program collaborations with industry and donor foundations may compromise academic integrity and principles (CAUT 2013). When governments trim post-secondary funding, cash-strapped universities have little choice but to increasingly rely on corporate dollars to defray operational costs. A pipeline between the boardroom and the classroom provides a refuge from chronic government underfunding. Businesses, in turn, look to universities for connections, personnel transfers, and contract work arrangements. Commercialization continues to infiltrate universities, ranging from ads in washrooms to corporate donations to foreign buyouts of campus bookstores. The dilemma is palpable: if universities are too closely identified with established powers and measurable outcomes, they sacrifice their independence and creative scholarship. If too divorced from the outside world, they risk losing students, relevance, and respect. To be sure, a university disconnected from the real world is hardly an option that Canadians can afford. Nevertheless, many balk at the corporatization of universities that casualizes academic labour, redefining students as consumers; promotes corporate job training instead of liberal education and profit-making instead of public service; implements managerial models of governance; and commercializes academic research (Brownlee 2015).

Universities increasingly engage in money-grubbing activities to generate external funding (from education, research, and service) in a fiercely competitive environment (Hoffman 2012). The defining mission of reflective inquiry, independent thought, and free dissemination of knowledge is increasingly subservient to the primacy of the market. The corporatist motto of "academic capitalism" (Hoffman 2012:12) boasts of achieving new efficiencies, servicing the new knowledge economy, and viewing faculty as human resources and students as customers (Vedder 2012:19; also Rolfe 2014). Universities are closing down departments and programs in hopes of saving money by mimicking the for-profit efficiencies of business, while

acknowledging they can't do everything with current funding and human resource levels. The "bean counters" of the world have managed to convince universities that everything must be quantifiable so that failure to measure something is tantamount to being "worthless." Such a shift may explain the popularity of *Maclean's* annual "measurement of excellence" ranking of Canadian universities to help prospective customers (read: students) make a more informed choice of where to study. In its annual review of excellence in university education, *Maclean's* bases its rankings on measurable indicators such as library holdings, entrance standards, and alumni support. Yet educational "outputs" related to the creation, quality, and dissemination of knowledge are excluded on grounds they are notoriously difficult to operationalize for measurement. But post-secondary education and schooling are not a commodity for consumption or comparison shopping. Nor can they be reduced to an itemized list of measurable properties. They instead embody unique personalities in their own right as they go about shaping people's lives, challenging minds and imaginations, nurturing a sense of self-worth, and transforming individuals into engaged and critically informed citizens. Moreover, post-secondary education and schooling are more like governments than private corporations, and are better served by collegial governance models than by corporate governance models (Epperson 2014).

The Pale Male Towers?

That a gender bias existed in post-secondary schooling is beyond doubt. The systemic biases embedded in the academy were gendered as well as racialized, inasmuch as maleness and the power and privileges associated with masculinity prevailed in the past (Monture 2009). For the most part, women did not attend universities or, if they did, it was presumably for ulterior reasons unrelated to academic excellence. Those who attended rarely were taken seriously, in part because of personal bias by indifferent teachers and bullying males, in part because of structural factors related to curriculum and assessment protocols. But times have changed: women continue to excel as a percentage of university enrolment, having accounted for over three-quarters of all university enrolment growth in the past 20 years. Consider the following shifts (Turcotte 2010):

1. In 1990, 14 per cent of women aged 25 to 54 had a university degree. In 2009, that figure had doubled to 28 per cent.
2. In 2009, 34 per cent of women aged 25 to 34 had at least a bachelor's degree, compared to 26 per cent of men.
3. In 2008, women comprised 62 per cent of all university undergraduates, 54 per cent of all master's graduates, and 44 per cent of all PhDs (up from 32 per cent in 1992). According to the AUCC report (2012), the percentage of women in university declined slightly to 58 per cent in 2011.

However impressive the figures, conflicting messages and mixed patterns remain (Mullen 2012). Women continue to be overrepresented in some areas but underrepresented in others. They are generally paid less than their male counterparts, largely because engineering graduates (mostly male) out-earn graduates who major in humanities or social sciences (Council of Canadian Academies 2012; Mullen 2012).

1. In 2008, women accounted for three-quarters of all graduates in education and health sciences. Women comprised approximately two-thirds of those graduating from social and behavioural sciences, law, and visual and performing arts and communication technologies.
2. By contrast, women represented 22 per cent of graduates in architecture and engineering (up from 18 per cent in 1990). They accounted for 30 per cent of graduates in mathematics and computer and information sciences, down from 35 per cent in 1990.
3. In 2011, women comprised 36.8 per cent of university academic staff across all levels, up from 28.7 per cent in 2001. Women represented 22 per cent of full professors, up from 15.1 per cent in 2001 (CAUT 2013/14). A pattern is inescapable: the higher the rank, the lower the percentage of female faculty in comparison to men (Council of Canadian Academies 2012).

4. There are 11,064 women with PhDs employed full-time in degree-granting institutions compared to 22,875 men in this category (Council of Canadian Academies 2012).
5. Female university teachers earn less than their male counterparts. Female full professors earn an average of 95.1 per cent of male full professors; associate professors earn 97.2 per cent, and assistant professors earn 98 per cent (CAUT 2013/14).
6. According to the CAUT (2013/14), women filled 44.2 per cent of new faculty hires in 2011. Women now occupy 32.9 per cent of tenure positions (a doubling between 2001 and 2011), while 43.3 per cent of female university teachers were slotted into tenure track positions. However, many promotion and tenure processes continue to lack non-punitive exit and re-entry procedures for women who take time off work to raise children (Schwartz 2015).
7. Women occupy an increasing per cent of federal research chairs as of October 2014 (Samson 2014), including 38 per cent in the humanities and social sciences, but considerably less in the natural sciences and engineering (Grant and Drakich 2011). More specifically, in 2014, women held 16.3 per cent of tier 1 chairs and 35.8 per cent of tier 2 chairs (CAUT 2014–15).
8. Of the 22 Canada Excellence Research Chairs, 21 are occupied by men (Schwartz 2015).

The Ivory-White Towers: Zones of Eurocentrism, Nodes of Whiteness, Sites of Racialized Bias

Not long ago the ivory-white towers were precisely that: sites of whiteness oblivious to criticism and shielded from control. Now however, they are prone to criticism as institutionalized bastions of bias, from racism to sexism (Chesler, Lewis, and Crowfoot 2005; Henry and Tator 2009; Stewart 2009; Stockdill and Danico 2012; Ramos 2012; Cote-Meek 2014). Charges include the following criticisms: underrepresentation of racialized faculty; excessive demands on faculty of colour as mentors and (token) representation on university committees; undermining of their legitimacy and authority by white students; the dominance of Eurocentric curricula and pedagogy; the de-legitimization of alternative knowledge and ways of knowing as too subjective or too political (or ideological); undervaluation of topics and research utilized by minority faculty; patterned avoidance by white faculty; a culture of whiteness in fostering a chilly climate that excludes or denies; concerns over equitable hiring, promotion, and tenure; and seemingly progressive administrators who appear more adept at "talking the talk" instead of "walking the walk" (Henry 2004; *Canadian Ethnic Studies Journal* 2012; Conference Notes 2015).

Systemic biases are known to flourish in the ivory white towers (Fleras 1996). The structure, function, and processes that inform the academy continue to be racialized in ways that invariably produce and reproduce patterns of racisms and racial discrimination—not always as something out of the ordinary but as integral to the foundational principles, founding assumptions, and everyday practices of a predominantly Euro-systemic academic enterprise. The interlocking nature of institutionalized racism intersects with that of sexism, classism, and homophobia to heighten the difficulty of transforming the white Eurocentrism of the academy (Stockdill and Danico 2012). More specifically, the following points of contention provide a snapshot of those racialized hotspots under scrutiny and criticism (Fleras 2014a; see also Chesler, Lewis, and Crowfoot 2005):

1. *Curriculum and pedagogy.* Curriculum content remains overwhelmingly biased toward Eurocentrism. Improvements and some notable exceptions have hardly dissuaded the humanities and social sciences from focusing largely on developments in the global north while neglecting advances and accomplishments in the so called developing world countries of the global south. The perceived superiority of "Western culture" as solely deserving of study is thus reinforced (Engler 2004). The bias that informs Eurocentric domination of the ivory white towers for framing intellectual debates and academic research is deeply racialized. It reflects and reinforces perceptions of the Western canon as universal rather than culturally specific. For example, textbooks in Canada (as well as in Australia and New Zealand) reposition history from a white perspective, whereas the viewpoint of Indigenous peoples is diminished or dismissed (Guo and Jamal 2007). Textbooks are also accused of stereotyping racialized minorities, thereby reinforcing a commitment to Eurocentric whiteness as a central reference point.

2. *Student body.* Students of colour indicate they are victims of racism because of discriminatory interaction with other students, faculty members, and administration (Samuel and Burney 2003). For example, on 21 March 2007, the Canadian Federation of Students released the final report of the Task Force on the Needs of Muslim Students that highlighted 11 major concerns, ranging from food facilities and availability of prayer space to Islamophobia and Muslim-bashing. For racialized minority students, the learning process can be undermined by faculty member bias, ideology, and lack of knowledge of the culture of others. Students report being stereotyped and stigmatized, resulting in what Claude Steele of Stanford University calls "stereotype threat"—that is, doing poorly academically because their intellectual abilities are devalued or dismissed. Racialized minority students are overlooked for their contributions or, alternatively, they are singled out as spokespersons for their race and ethnicity—even as their heritage and concerns are Disneyfied, demonized, or discarded. Patterns of marginalization are further complicated by the intersection of multiple identities (including race, gender, ethnicity, class, age, sexuality) in contexts that are predominantly white, male, and Eurocentric (Spafford et al. 2006). Such a paradox yields the awkward question of what it means to be "visibilized" (to imagine oneself being "racialized") in an institutional context where normative whiteness prevails (Hernandez-Ramdwar 2009). The end result is captured by the concept of tall poppy syndrome: some minority subcultures may impose a burden on individual excellence because academic success is despised as a

sell-out while who those who excel are ridiculed, ostracized, or chopped down to size (Webb 2013).

3. *International students.* Racialized international students encounter additional problems related to their "foreignness." About 8 per cent of Canada's university enrolment consists of fee-paying foreign students (many from Asian countries) because universities increasingly rely on private funding (Saltmarsh 2005; Rhoads and Torres 2006; CAUT 2014–15). But this reliance on internationalization as a revenue source has not translated into action to accommodate the distinct needs and untapped talents of international students, much less to bring about changes in the curriculum, evaluation procedures, and pedagogical techniques (Fleras 2005). Instructional strategies and classroom environments that condone competitiveness and individual achievement may prove awkward for those foreign students more familiar with group work—and vice versa (Guo and Jamal 2007). As well, foreign students often must bear the brunt of suspicion as conniving and thieving opportunists who are thought to routinely rely on plagiarism to compensate for shortcomings, in effect reflecting and reinforcing racialized notions of ability, deviance, and moral deficit (Saltmarsh 2005).

4. *Faculty.* Universities benefit from the presence of racialized faculty members who improve the scholarship of the institutions through innovative pedagogies, distinct epistemological orientations, and student recruitment and engagement (James 2011). Nevertheless, faculty of colour confront a host of racism-related challenges as they navigate their way through those racialized spaces within the academy (Spafford et al. 2006; James 2009). Visible (racialized) minority faculty may comprise 14.9 per cent of university teachers in 2006, up from 11.5 per cent in 1996, with those of Chinese and South Asian background accounting for nearly one-half of the total (CAUT 2012/13), but racialized and gendered minority faculty are generally underrepresented outside of the hard sciences, routinely undermined by being excluded from communication loops, subject to racist slurs/taunts both inside and outside the classroom, and prone to having their concerns dismissed or trivialized by white colleagues who perceive themselves enlightened and beyond criticism (Back 2007). Their scholarly credentials, status, and authority may be questioned (i.e., not taken seriously) or challenged by students, colleagues, or administrators—especially in domains that are unconventional, contest notions of white privilege, or aggressively advance the principle of social justice (Monture 2009). They may be labelled as biased or politicized when delivering content on diversity, yet criticized as dilettantes when offering courses outside their racialized field (Spafford et al. 2006). Publishing careers may be compromised because many are swamped with requests to mentor students of colour, in addition to sitting on committees as the token minority voice. In short, the multitude of experiences and barriers that reinforce a sense of otherness and marginality may expose minority faculty to mental stress and physical exhaustion, thus negatively affecting their ability to teach, publish, research, and excel (Chesler, Lewis, and Crowfoot 2005).

5. *Administration.* The few racialized administrators that make it to the top may confront the same challenges as minority faculty. Being cast as different and treated differently may prove career-inhibiting. Yet a commitment to treating everyone exactly the same may inadvertently reinforce institutional barriers that deter racialized minorities from the upper echelons of success. In either case, the absence of differences at senior levels is counterproductive. Without any incentive for thinking outside the box, a business-as-usual mentality prevails. Such a mindset not only restricts the circle of creativity; it also reflects and reinforces the monoculturality of an era when universities were literally finishing schools (or playing grounds) for affluent white males pursuing careers as diplomats, clergy, or lawyers.

6. *Boards of governors.* These highly influential decision-making bodies continue to be overwhelmingly white and male. This demographic is not necessarily brighter or more skilled; however, it may be better connected corporate wheeler-dealers, with a known capacity

to generate revenue for the university (Engler 2004). Paradoxically, those in positions of institutional authority are often oblivious to the privileges and power associated with a systemic whiteness as the preferred normative standard in defining normalcy, desirability, and acceptability (McIntosh 1988). Not surprisingly, they vary in their willingness and capacity to address inequities, bridge the many gulfs of misunderstanding, and respect the many experiences and realities in the ivory-white towers (Dua 2009). The absence of a diversity of voices at the governance level makes it easy to underestimate the gravity of the problem (Dua 2009). Moves towards inclusivity—to the extent they exist—may be motivated *not* by minority grievance resolution or a commitment to justice. Motives may be animated by a face-saving preference for damage control (to ensure continued alumni support), public relations (avoiding unflattering publicity), and impression management (running a smooth enterprise) (Chesler, Lewis, and Crowfoot 2005).

The conclusion appears inescapable if somewhat uncomfortable. Rather than being above the fray, as commonly assumed, universities are no less susceptible than other institutions to charges of racial bias (see *Canadian Ethnic Studies Journal*, 2014, Vol. 44, No. 2). To their (dis)credit, they appear to have done a better job of denying the existence of

bias by cloaking their most egregious expressions behind the hallowed ivy walls of the ivory white towers. In reality, however, ivory tower biases constitute a widespread if somewhat under-theorized aspect of university life, embedded in the culture of academia, reflected in curriculum and pedagogy, and reinforced by practices related to hiring, retention, and promotion (Fleras 1995; Henry and Tator 2009). Put bluntly, the problem of bias in the ivory white towers is not what many think it is or manifest the way they think it is. First, ivory tower biases tend to be institutional rather than personal—that is, racialized bias that is systemically embedded in the founding assumptions and foundational principles of a university's unwritten way of doing things. Reference to the racialization of the academy along the monocultural lines of a Euro-systemic whiteness is consequential. In a system designed by, for, and about affluent white males, minority and foreign students must perform, compete, and excel in a context neither of their making nor reflective of their realities or interests. Second, ivory tower biases often reflect patterns of omission rather than acts of commission. Indifference or resistance toward transformative change may be just as biasing as active measures in reinforcing a Eurocentric culture of whiteness (Henry and Tator 2009). Nowhere is this more disconcerting than in the troubled relationship between aboriginality and the academy, as this Spotlight box explains.

Spotlight Aboriginality in the Academy: Sanctioned Ignorance, Systemic Indifference, Scholarly Arrogance

The centrality of a culture of Euro-systemic whiteness ensures the ivory white towers are deserving of their name (Henry 2004; Battiste 2013). Universities are not value-neutral and impartial places; they are ideologically loaded and socially constructed (yet concealed) conventions that operate under the sheer weight of a cultural of whiteness (Back 2007; Srivastava 2008; Gunstone 2009; Tuhiwai Smith 2012). Linda Tuhiwai Smith (1998) acknowledged

as much in her landmark publication *Decolonizing Methodologies: Research and Indigenous Peoples*:

The form that racism takes inside a university is related to the ways in which academic knowledge is structured, as well as to the organizational structures which govern a university. The insulation of disciplines, the culture of the institution which supports disciplines, and the systems of

continued

management and governance all work in ways to protect the privileges already in place.

They are known to support and reproduce certain patterns of knowledge and ways of knowing that rarely reflect aboriginal philosophies and world views (Fleras 2014a). In doing so they are silencing aboriginality and rendering it invisible, while visibilizing the normative tyranny of whiteness (Kuokkanen 2007; also Belanger 2014: Chapter 1). The more holistic frameworks of aboriginal students may clash with the generally fragmented and compartmentalized-into-disciplines nature of university knowledge (Battiste 2013). Of particular relevance in the university's intellectual traditions is a commitment to rationalism, with its premise that truth resides independently of human perception of it and is amenable to discovery through reason—notwithstanding challenges to the contrary by postmodernism and its espousal of a mind-dependent world. But such a commitment reflects a very narrow reading of a world that excludes aboriginal philosophies and indigenous world views. For example, as Joyce Green (2004) notes, students may study John Locke's ideas on private property and state sovereignty, yet they are rarely exposed to the impact of these ideas in advancing capitalist property relations in a context of colonization—in the process investing Locke with pre-emptive authority at the expense of indigenous approaches to property and political legitimacy.

Reference to one legitimate intellectual tradition dismisses other perspectives as irrelevant or inferior (Voyageur, Brearley, and Calliou 2015; Kuokkanen 2007). Or alternatively, other perspectives are offered only superficial and token acknowledgement, in the process creating a pattern of ignorance, indifference, and arrogance that propels racism by consequence rather than malevolent intent (Kovach 2009). Aboriginal students are expected to park their cultural knowledge at the entrance to the academy by assuming the trappings of a fundamentally different reality. The establishment of intellectual spaces for aboriginal students, together with programs from counselling to support/access services, are justified on grounds they require special assistance for bridging the cultural/intellectual gulf toward success.

What remains under-theorized and unattended to are those barriers such as structures, discourses, practices, expectations, values, and assumptions that underscore the academy's sanctioned ignorance, systemic indifference, and scholarly arrogance.

Predictably then, aboriginal students find themselves the focus of change. They are expected to fit into the academic culture and environment (inclusion model) rather than the system being refitted to address their lived-experiences (inclusivity model). But few seriously consider the possibility of aboriginality as an opportunity to enhance the parameters of learning by capitalizing on Aboriginal peoples' perspective and experiences. Prevailing instead is a *difference as deficit* mindset that frames aboriginality as inherently problematic or as a hurdle to surmount. A race neutral (colour-blind) perspective dismisses aboriginality as an anomaly in an allegedly colour-blind academy; operates on the mistaken belief that racism and inclusion are no longer a major problem in a post-racial academy; and promotes the idea that issues of inequality and injustice will disappear if all students are treated the same (Guo and Jamal 2007). Such a blinkered perspective could only prevail among those whose privilege and power blind them from seeing the relations of dominance that persist within the academy.

This inability or unwillingness to acknowledge alternative forms of knowledge and ways of knowing reflect what is known as *epistemological racism*—that is, an inclination to perceive reality from Eurocentric patterns of knowledge and ways of knowing (research) as normal, desirable, and superior, while assuming that others are doing so, should do so, or would do so if they could. Alternative knowledge and knowing are excluded or marginalized as inferior to the conventional Western stream of acceptability (Kuokkanen 2007:179). Yet indigenous forms of traditional knowledge represent a distinct knowledge system with its own epistemological concepts of truth and wisdom in addition to its own logical and scientific validity (Battiste 2013). Compounding the insult, aboriginal scholars must become accomplished in epistemologies that arise from history and context that historically proved hostile to them—yet, paradoxically, was viewed by the dominant sector as free of any specific history and culture (also Scheurich and Young 2002). Epistemological racism enables the privileged to occupy positions of universality and objectivity while caricaturizing other ways of knowing as partial and particular positions. The intent of such an epistemology may not be racist, to be sure, but the consequences certainly are in benefiting some at the expense of others, while preserving the Eurocentric foundational principles of the ivory white towers.

Institutions in general and the academy in particular are neither neutral nor value-free. Rather they are systemically biased/racialized along monocultural lines, including design, values, and practices that reinforce a Eurocentric way of seeing and doing. The academy's reputation as remote (ivory white) and removed (towers) is reinforced by this refusal to acknowledge how the founding assumptions and foundational principles of its Eurocentric constitutional order continue to deny or distort. In that sense, aboriginal students attending post-secondary institutions confront what to them is tantamount to assimilation by another name— inadvertently completing the job of absorption initiated by the residential school system (McPherson and Rabb 2013). Changes are in store; still, references to the concept of ivory white towers— either in the traditional sense of sanctity (purity) or, alternatively, in the more common and current sense of disconnect from reality (isolation)—will be

dislodged only when a counter hegemony unsettles those founding assumptions that undergird these bastions of whiteness. Any fundamental tilt toward an inclusivity model must embrace both the legitimacy of aboriginal knowledge and knowing by acknowledging the monoculturality of the academy's intellectual model.

Time will tell if the ivory white towers are able or willing to confront their ignorance, arrogance, and indifference toward other intellectual traditions. Overhauling the Eurocentric notion of whiteness as the normative and normalizing will prove a tough slog and a difficult goal. A culture of white normativity prevails that falls outside the realm of overt discrimination or deliberate marginalization of minority contribution. The problem resides in a widespread lack of awareness and an attitude of denial in acknowledging how the primacy of white privilege and a culture of whiteness influence the university enterprise, from everyday discourses to institutional practices (Henry 2004; Smith 1998). No less problematic are those systemic biases and structural barriers that deny and exclude by reinforcing the legitimacy of the academic status quo. The prognosis for change is not particularly promising. Universities at their very core were largely imperialistic/colonialistic transplants with a civilizing mission (Cote-Meek 2014). Their intellectual traditions remain anchored in colonialist (and racist and patriarchal) paradigms that continue to reflect, reinforce, and advance Eurocentrism in the global north (Henry and Tator 2009).

Remodelling the Academic Enterprise

> . . . white privilege and power continues to be reflected in the Eurocentric curricula, traditional pedagogical approaches, hiring, promotion and tenure practices, and opportunities for research. . . .
> —Frances Henry, 2004: Appendix

The prospect of intervention strategies to improve inclusiveness have proven contentious. There is

little agreement as to whether a problem of exclusion exists, what the nature and scope of the problem is, what the proposed solutions must do, and what the anticipated outcomes are. Proposals for challenging the inequalities of exclusion range from accommodating diversities to promoting equity, from changing individual mindsets to revamping institutional structures, from incremental reform to transformational change, and from inclusion models to models of inclusivity. The entrenchment of ivory tower biases will not disappear in the foreseeable future, given universities' astonishing capacity to thwart change or deflect criticism. Despite all the rhetoric and a spate of reports in promoting inclusiveness, the concepts of justice and equity are rarely applied in the everyday life of the university (Back 2004). The removal of bias in hiring, promotion, curriculum, leadership, and governance have rarely materialized, reinforcing how universities resist change as much as any other institution (Smith 2016; Henry and Tator 2009).These institutional biases that often go beyond the individual and the incidental (sporadic and random) are intrinsic to the very structure, values, and operation of academe. Seemingly neutral ideas and ideals such as academic freedom, objectivity, universalism, or meritocracy are not value-free, but value-laden concepts that bolster an ideological framework in defending yet camouflaging racialized patterns behind good intentions and lofty principles (Back 2004). Nor are they simply attitudinal mental quirks involving conscious acts with an intent to hurt or degrade. Ivory tower biases tend to be institutionalized in ways that reflect and reinforce the normative functioning of a Eurocentric system in defining what is acceptable, desirable, and normal in knowledge creation and distribution. Nevertheless, universities continue to react to charges of bias and racial discrimination as if such accusations disrupted the norm of an otherwise healthy enterprise. To the extent they exist, any flaws in the system are thought to reflect individual aberrations, while improvements are readily solvable by expelling students, counselling sessions, equity committees, and sensitivity training (Chesler, Lewis, and Crowfoot 2005). The Eurocentric whiteness of the academic towers as systemic bias is rarely problematized as the probable source of exclusion.

A fundamental shift is required in challenging ivory tower bias. Systemic biases predominate within the ivory white towers because they are built into (intrinsic to) the academy; are reflective of its normal functioning, despite a lack of awareness or intent to do harm; incorporated into designs, rewards, policies, and operations as normative and necessary; expressed through the logical consequences of rules and expectations that when evenly applied exert a discriminatory effect; and sustained through ideologies that rationalize discrimination and prejudice as deviations from a seemingly fair and just academy (Fleras 2014a; Chesler, Lewis, and Crowfoot 2005). Ivory tower biases may be produced and reproduced systemically by this business-as-usual format that purportedly treats everyone the same regardless of their differences—even though people's differences must be taken into account (for example, through exemptions) to ensure a more level playing field. Nevertheless, it's the cultural attitudes and ideological assumptions of individuals that perpetuate prejudice and discrimination (Kobayashi 2009). This institutional culture of denial and resistance is likely to prevail as long as the Eurocentric whiteness of the ivory tower culture remains largely invisible to those who remain convinced of and committed to its neutrality, universalism, openness, fairness, objectivity, racelessness and colour-blindness (Henry and Tator 2009; James 2009). As long as those with power and privilege resist critically reflecting upon the seemingly neutral yet value-laden ideals that undergird the inevitability of an unlevel playing field, exclusion by omission could not be more forcibly articulated and imperceptibly imposed.

Summary

1. Schooling and education, especially at post-secondary levels, are prone to ambiguity in responding to new expectations and shifting realities.
2. Canada's leadership in advancing positive education indicators is marred by indicators that reinforce the status of schooling as a site of inequalities and exclusions.
3. Schooling and education can stimulate social mobility (the great equalizer) yet fortify the status quo (the great fortifier).

4. Residential schools as instruments of aggressive (genocidal?) assimilation continue to negatively impact aboriginal individuals and communities.
5. A systemic culture of whiteness at the post-secondary level tends to exclude non-conventional ways of knowing and knowledge.

6. Universities are experiencing an identity crisis in terms of who they are and what they should be doing.
7. Both workplaces and schooling possess an additional obligation to become more inclusive to ensure no one is denied, damaged, or excluded.

Review Questions

1. What is meant by the idea that schooling and education constitute both the great equalizer and the great fortifier?
2. Indicate how and why universities as ivory white towers are undergoing identity crisis in terms of who they are and what they should be doing.
3. Explain how this identity crisis at the post-secondary level is transforming universities into sites of inequality and exclusion.

4. Discuss the rationale behind the introduction of residential schools in Canada. Based on chapter content, did the residential school system attempt to transform (assimilate) aboriginal students or to destroy (eliminate) them?
5. How and why are universities racialized as a Eurocentric culture of whiteness?

Endnotes

1. A distinction between education and schooling is important. *Schooling* refers to the entire program of formal socialization, including governance issues related to values and norms, teachers and teaching, students and learning, and decision-making and power relations. *Education* is one component of schooling and is concerned primarily with a corpus of knowledge, knowing, curriculum, and classroom that schooling encompasses.
2. From Jason DeParle's review of Robert Putnam's book *Our Kids, New York Times*, 15 March 2015.
3. To be sure, Canada was not the only country to compulsorily (after 1920) remove children from their parents for resocialization in schools or foster families. From the 1910s to the 1970s, about 100,000 part aboriginal children in Australia were placed in government or church care, a practice that was deemed tantamount to cultural genocide by Australia's Human Rights Commission. (The movie *Rabbit-Proof Fence* is very highly recommended.) The film *Oranges and Sunshine* (2014) estimates that about 130,000 children-in-

care from the UK were shipped off to colonies such as Australia, without their mother's consent and with promises of a bountiful childhood in a land of milk and honey.
4. According to the First Nations Child and Family Caring Society of Canada, three times more First Nations children are in childcare than there were at the height of the residential school system. First Nations children are also up to eight times more likely than non-aboriginal children to go into custody arrangements.
5. The federal government provides a block of funds to the provinces who then decide how much of the block will be allocated to post-secondary education. In 2008, the BC government cut funding to universities by $50 million, despite receiving $110 million in new post-secondary funding from the federal government. By contrast, Quebec's government continues to prop up post-secondary education, with the result that students pay some of the lowest tuition fees in Canada (Canadian Federation of Students 2011).

6. For critics, universities too are bureaucratized (hierarchical) and insular (siloed), and so over-administered that, like many oversized corporations, they simply encourage the alpha drones to produce future drones (Pocklington and Tupper 2002). For example, according to Herbert Pimlott (2015), communications professor at Wilfrid Laurier University, student enrolment at WLU increased by 36 per cent between 2005 and 2012–13, while the complement of full-time faculty increased by only 24 per cent (as a result, the faculty-to-student ratio grew by 10 per cent, up to 34 students for every professor). By contrast, management staffing expanded by 114 per cent, with the result that management-to-student ratio went from 166 students per senior manager to 105 students.

V The Big Picture: Global Inequality, Social Equality

We live in an era of unprecedented challenges and perplexing changes. An interplay of interlocking trends points to growing complexities and proliferating crises that threaten to upend planetary life as we know it (Petersen 2009). Of particular concern are global trends whose potential to create or exacerbate existing patterns of inequality needs no introduction, including, massive urbanization, explosive population growth in the developing countries of the global south, persistent patterns of poverty around the world, climate change and natural disasters, a run on the global financial system resulting in collapse, and appalling incidents of human rights abuse (Goldstone 2010; Burgis 2015). Each of these potentially disruptive trends is worrying in its own right. The convergence of these dynamics could unleash a cascading sequence of catastrophes whose cumulative impact may derail or destroy (Petersen 2009; 2012). These convergent trends also have the potential to generate global inequality problems beyond the scope of any government to address. And while many have endorsed the principle of international co-operation for coping with the challenges of global inequality, the danger of isolation and protectionism is all too real as each country hunkers down to optimize its interests, regardless of broader implications (Petersen 2012).

Part V steps back from the fray in Canada to examine global inequalities of exclusion against the backdrop of globalization as logic and dynamic. Chapter 11 addresses the concepts of global inequalities and globalization, including a look at their causal relationship, on the assumption that the persistence of worldwide inequities is reason enough for addressing globalization as principle and practice. Globalization is shown to represent a dynamic process of cleavages and connections that generates massive contradictions (Korzeniewicz and Moran 2009). To one side, a confluence of globalization trends has promised an internet-enabled global playing field of co-operation and exchange in real time and across space (Friedman 2005). A general improvement in global living standards is reflective of this transformation. To the other side, globalization has intensified the pace of global inequality gaps related to the environment, relative poverty, urbanization, human rights, and population growth. The continuation of corporate-based globalization over people-oriented alternatives reinforces the prospect of yet more polarized inequities between the haves in the global north and the have-nots in the global south. Canada's dual status as both a problem and a solution to global inequalities provides a fitting if ironic theme to the chapter.

The last substantive chapter (Chapter 12) turns social inequality on its head by asking the question, What do we mean by **social equality**? The chapter makes it abundantly clear: just as there is no consensus in defining social inequality, so also is the concept of equality plagued by a lack of agreement in terms of what it is or what it looks like, whether it is a realistic goal (why or why not), what needs to be done and on what scale, how attainable a socially equal society is, and what are the benefits—that is, does equality matter? A closer inspection of the logic behind neo-liberal capitalism exposes its role in creating and sustaining patterns of inequality. By contrast, the way forward is contingent on rehabilitating capitalism along more responsible lines by balancing a commitment to people and the planet with that of profits. The chapter concludes by discussing the feasibility of constructing a more equitable society by situating it within the realm of the possible. The concluding chapter in Part V provides an overview and summary of *Inequality Matters*. The chapter examines how social inequalities in Canada are misinformed by a series of polite fictions that paper over painful truths; reviews the major themes that inform the book; and posits a reminder that more equality is preferred over more inequality if Canadians aspire to live together equitably with their differences.

11 Global Inequalities, Exclusionary Globalizations

Learning Objectives

1. To survey the nature and scope of global inequalities related to the environment, urbanization, overpopulation, income disparities and poverty, and human rights.

2. To appreciate how global inequalities matter on various grounds from the moral to the material.

3. To explore how the developed countries in the global north (including Canada) must assume some responsibility for inequalities in the global south.

4. To better understand how globalization can be framed simultaneously as inequality and equality depending on the context, criteria, and consequences.

5. To propose a humanistic globalization as a corrective to the neo-liberal version.

Introduction: A World in Social Disarray

The world at present is inundated with waves of deepening crises and worrying contradictions. Progressive developments such as enlightened human rights ideologies and improved living standards are offset by the depravities of conflict, cleansing, and injustices. A globalizing world that purports to be on the precipice of unprecedented peace and universal prosperity is contrasted with images of emaciated refugees, drowned migrants, or mangled corpses—routinized and repeated to the point of losing all shock value. Lip service to democratic ideals is routinely dashed by the authoritarianism of despots, military juntas, terrorism, tribal cleansings, sectarian violence, and religion-based fanaticism. Massive reductions in overall global poverty (especially in China) are juxtaposed by growing inequality gaps both within and between countries (*The Economist*, 1 June 2013). To the extent global incomes are converging, they reflect a closing of the income gaps between countries rather than the reduction of the distribution within countries (R. Clark 2011) as described below:

> The triumph of globalization and market capitalism has improved living standards for billions while concentrating billions among the few. It has lowered inequality worldwide but raised inequality in most countries. (Richard Freeman, professor of economics, Harvard, Keynote address to an OECD Policy Forum, cited in Conference Board of Canada 2011b)

Of these so-called hot-button issues, severe global inequality ranks uppermost in its capacity to destroy, exclude, oppress, or distort (also OECD

2014b; Todd 2012; Piketty 2014; WEF 2015; Oxfam 2013; 2015). Nearly 30 million people worldwide remain subjected to modern day versions of slavery (not sold in chains in public auctions but coerced into slave-like practices such as human trafficking, forced/bonded/indentured labour, the sex trade (young adults), and child marriage (Kristof 2013; Upadhayaya 2012; Urbina 2015). The freedom of this twenty-first-century chattel is curtailed since they are controlled, perpetually indebted, or exploited for profit, sex, or the sheer thrill of domination. (According to the Global Slavery Index 2014, 4,600 individuals live in slave-like conditions in Canada, placing it at 136 in world rankings, well behind the 14.3 million in India.) Children, in particular, continue to be victimized by global inequalities. For example, in its 2012 report entitled *A Life Free From Hunger*, Save the Children estimated 2.6 million children die each year because of food scarcity, accounting for about one-third of all child deaths annually, albeit down from a recent high of 12 million deaths in 1990. Those who survive suffer irreversible and disfiguring damage from the scarring effect of chronic malnutrition. Their lives as adults are compromised because of this stunted growth, as are the life chances of their offspring who remain the unwitting victims of a ceaseless cycle of poverty. The optics are not looking good. For perhaps the first time in generations, the World Economic Forum (WEF) Report concluded, many believe the next generation will be poorer because of diminished opportunities and reduced services (also Canadian Index of Wellbeing 2012). Even this prognosis is based on the iffy assumption of a viable terrestrial home in the first place. The global drive for profit and market penetration is destroying a rapidly resource-depleted planet that cannot possibly sustain a consumer-driven lifestyle without imploding in the process.

No one should underestimate the cumulative impact of these unruly forces. Developing countries in the global south appear to be hopelessly mired in an endless cycle of crisis, conflict, and catastrophe (Nutt 2011). The social fabric of any society is further frayed when juxtaposing a scarcity of resources with an abundance of poverty, crime, disease, pollution, and overpopulation. Countries in the global north are no less conflicted and confused by the

spectre of tanking economies, spiralling wealth and income gaps, and a despondent uncertainty over what is going on. Contradictions prevail, and they are expressed in a division of the world into three stratified layers: those that spend vast sums of money to keep their weight down, those who possess sufficient food resources to feel full, and those who wonder if they will eat again (Kawachi and Kennedy 2002). Countries in the developing global south crave the material trappings of a modern society, with a comparable standard of living and quality of life. Yet they appear incapable of paying the price for economic progress. Instead of pulling together for national unity and the common good, the prognosis points to more tribalism, xenophobia, and intergroup conflicts.

The enormity of the challenge outstrips current capacities. Many developing countries in the global south are recipients of foreign aid development, favourable trade arrangements, or significant foreign remittances (Saunders 2015). Yet developmental opportunities are squandered because of corruption, expediency, miscalculation, or gross incompetence on both sides of the give-and-take ledger (Nutt 2011). The politics of blame and debates over causes are proving deceptive. Centuries of exploitation under colonialism have entrenched cycles of impoverishment and powerlessness that are difficult to break. Poor but resource-rich countries have been ruthlessly stripped by ruling elites and multinational corporations of the very resources they require for recovery (Burgis 2015). Yet they are forced to compete as best they can in an open global market slanted toward the interests of the rich and powerful. Admittedly, patterns of exploitation are shifting: direct colonial rule has given way to indirect patterns of governance and less egregious forms of co-optation (i.e., neo-colonialism). Nevertheless, the logic of global capitalism in its most recent incarnation—namely, globalization—is no less exploitative in defining who gets what and what goes where. Finally, mobile platforms and social media may offer economic benefits and personal freedoms for the media savvy. But the same technologies yield a dark side that fosters online crime, cyberbullying and trolling, intrusions on privacy, stealth surveillance, and terrorism of magnitudes yet to be imagined (WEF Report 2012).

Globalization and global inequality are currently a politically charged battleground (Korzeniewicz and Moran 2009). Questions and disputes invariably arise: how does exclusionary globalization create and sustain patterns of inequality within and between nation-states (M. Spence 2011; OECD 2011)? How do current global crises such as rising economic inequality reflect and reinforce those globalization driven market dynamics (Smith and Wiest 2012)? Admittedly, responses to these questions and reactions to globalization vary: for some, it is a catalyst for universal progress, including cross-border flow of capital and ideas in reshaping domestic governance and economic performance. For others, globalization is tantamount to a race to the bottom. Overall incomes may improve under globalization; however, not everyone benefits from its trickle-down effects, with losers and winners clearly demarcated as the global gap broadens and intensifies (Oxfam 2015; Walby 2009; Nel 2008). Ecologically destructive practices accompany global governance that extols commercialism, consumerism, and disenchantment to the detriment of any sustainable future and a green society (Klein 2014). For still others, globalization heralds a free market penetration of both benefits and costs as side effects. The triumph of globalization has crafted an integrated worldwide grid (M. Spence 2011) that differentially incorporates societies and capital into a vast, productive loop of cost-effective links. The creation of selectively free markets and free trade arrangements provides cheaper-priced goods. But Western consumers pay a price for this convenience, including the outsourcing of low- to medium-value manufacturing work to developing countries in the global south, with a corresponding shift to precarious employment for workers in the global north.

Such a bleak scenario does not bode well for the creation and maintenance of a sustainable world order. This chapter addresses the dilemma and danger of a world in disarray by exploring social inequality from a global perspective and within the context of globalization as a promise and a peril. Skeptics aside, most believe globalized inequality matters to the extent that it generates a raft of social problems and exclusionary structures at worldwide levels (Moellendorf 2009; Miller 2011). First, it is immoral and unjust since massive inequalities violate the inherent dignity of all persons as espoused by the Preamble to the Universal Declaration of Human Rights as well as other UN-based international covenants. Second, global inequalities are major contributors to poverty-based injustices and abuses associated with extreme income gaps. Third, the persistence of global inequality ensures the domination of the global north over the global south at the expense of co-operative actions across borders. Fourth, the political imbalance associated with global inequality may prove a catalyst for social unrest, ethnic conflict, and intergroup violence, up to and including world conflagrations. With these frightening scenarios in mind, the chapter begins by looking at a host of global inequality problems at present, namely: poverty and income inequality; overpopulation; urbanization; the looming ecological catastrophe; and human rights violations. The focus then shifts to the concept of globalization as a powerful dynamic with a double-edged capacity to enrich or impoverish, to include or exclude. The chapter emphasizes the relationship between an exclusionary globalization and global inequalities in terms of root causes and causal relations. Proposed solutions to the problem of globalized inequality focus on rethinking neo-liberal globalization along more humanistic lines.

A word of caution in playing the blame game. Who should take the blame for the social inequities of the global south? Should the inhabitants of the global south take responsibility (blame the victim) for the poverty and disempowerment that infuse their daily lives? Or should blame be pinned on external factors related to the predatory actions and structural adjustments of the global north (blame the system) (Engler 2016)? Reference to global inequalities in this chapter is not intended to pin the entire blame on the developing world. The countries of the global south are no more the sole architects of their own misfortunes than poor Canadians are wholly responsible for their plight. Just as poverty in Canada often stems from exclusionary structures and structural exclusions, so too must the policies and priorities of the global north shoulder the load for perpetuating patterns of dependency and underdevelopment. To do otherwise—by holding the victims entirely accountable for developments or arrangements largely beyond their control—is too simplistic and judgmental in a world where choices and options reflect broader contexts and situational circumstances. The Nigerian novelist and poet Ben Okri (2015:20) writes to this effect:

> . . . the terms of African independence were flawed at birth; Africa stepped on to the world stage with its hands tied. . . . It was joining a game in which all the contestants had been in training for centuries, had set the rules, and had all the best facilities and the biases of the ages; and it was joining this game with broken arms and legs, confidence and spirit scattered.

Nor should developing world countries be expected to make disproportionate sacrifices toward solutions. On the contrary, global inequalities are arguably a "Western" problem; as a result, the responsibility for solutions must be framed accordingly. In other words, the global north must re-position itself as a solution to those global inequalities created through invasions, investments, or interventions. Yet even seemingly progressive initiatives can backfire in unexpected ways, as demonstrated below.

Spotlight Distorting Development: Canadian Tourist Dollars in Cuba's Peso Economy

What comes to mind when you think of Cuba? If you are like many Canadians, two images will prevail: first, Cuba is a socialist country that aspires to the principles of egalitarianism so that everyone is relatively equal in terms of access to basic necessities (such as basic health care or access to education). Second, Cuba is a site of winter getaways in which relatively cheap flights and accommodations are bundled into all-inclusive packages of sun, sand, and safety (in travel industry parlance, "authentic" Cuba is renowned as a value destination for the budget traveller). The injection of tourist dollars provides a much needed boost for an economy that has seen better days. Unfortunately, the two images clash when played out in a Canadian winter. In theory, our vacation needs create new opportunities for Cubans, which is good; in reality, we need to ask if our choices are improving their lives. However inadvertently, Canadian vacationers are creating a new class divide that threatens to erode an egalitarian ethos where even the poorest Cuban is educated to believe that everyone is equal (Amuchastegui 2008). Peter Sanchez and Kathleen Adams (2007:27) capture the two-edged dynamics of a capitalist infusion into a socialist country:

> The average Cuban lives in hardship, as the basic requirements of life are scarce.

At the same time, Cuba is under siege by foreigners, many of whom stay in opulent government-owned hotels and dine at restaurants where food is abundant and varied. This duality of existence has created a serious strain on Cubans who have already experienced long term deprivations. Although tourism is increasingly important to the Cuban economy, observers cannot help but wonder if the island can survive this capitalist abundance amidst socialist scarcity.

Canadians comprised 36 per cent of the some 2.2 million (McNally 2016) visitors to Cuba, the largest national group. These numbers are surprising in their own right; after all, a primary aim of the Cuban revolution in 1959 was to abolish tourism as a bourgeoisie luxury at odds with the ideals of a socialist country. Tourism dropped drastically from 272,000 (mainly American) visitors in 1957 to about 15,000 in 1974 (consisting mostly of exemplary Soviet citizens as a reward for service or productivity). But a turn toward mass tourism was necessitated by the implosion of the Soviet Union in 1991, which deprived Cuba of its primary source of export income (sugar to Moscow). To compensate for the loss of revenue that underwrote much of universal health and education programs, the Cuban state incorporated the principles of big tourism in hope of escaping its economic doldrums. The courting of hotel chains with investor-friendly laws appears to have paid dividends (Winson 2006; Zuckerman 2010). Mass tourism has evolved into Cuba's primary source of hard currency ($2.1 billion annually). But its expansion has not only unsettled the very notion of what Cuban society is for, it has also transformed entire parts of the island, such as Varadero, into segregated tourist zones generally off limits to Cubans except for resort workers.

The 300,000 Cubans who work in the tourism industry possess a job that really pays. The average Cuban makes about 300 pesos (CAD$10–12) a month to spend on necessities; a medical practitioner earns about US $20 a month (Sanchez and Adams 2007:32). By contrast, a tourism worker can earn that amount from *a single day's tips*, which can then be converted into dollars (convertible pesos) for purchase of non-essential items only at "dollar stores" or on the black market. Not surprisingly, as Amuchastegui (2008) writes in pointing out the inequality between those who have dollars and those who do not, "Cubans with access to the dollar economy are vastly wealthier than Cubans who are stuck in the peso economy. The way to survive economically in Cuba is to get a piece of the dollar economy." As a result, even communist party members or those with advanced degrees gravitate toward employment in tourism —demeaning yes, but financially lucrative—a curious inversion of the pay scale where the social value of their work was inextricably linked to advancing the cause. This obsessive quest for dollars has also spawned the usual suspects in a commodity economy, including hustlers and scam artists, beggars, and sex industry workers.

The economic benefits of tourism for Cuba as a whole and for the lucky few are mixed. Foreign dollars (including remittances from the American mainland) are creating a two-tier economy (Zuckerman 2010): those with access to the lucrative tourist industry (the "dollar economy") versus those professional, industrial, and agricultural workers working in the peso economy. A new class of middle class Cubans with access to tourism hard currency are becoming conspicuous consumers with lifestyles far more comfortable than those without, especially now that the government no longer subsidizes the cost of basic needs or promotes the notion of full employment. The result is patterns of poverty comparable to those in capitalist developing world countries of the global south (Sanchez and Adams 2007). The fact that tourism worker earnings easily outstrip those of most Cubans must be deeply unsettling to a country whose credo of egalitarianism clashes with the principles of foreign domination and middle class pursuits (Amuchastegui 2008). Perhaps more damaging still is the emergence of a more materialistic and consumerist population as Cubans begin to crave the things they don't have—a situation likely to be exacerbated with the normalization of relations with the United States. That Canadian tourist dollars are undermining the relatively egalitarian nature of Cuban society should make us think more critically about our next winter escape.

Disclosure: the author attended a conference at the University of Matanzas, Cuba, in February 2011, yet encamped at an all-inclusive resort in Varadero, thus proving part of the problem (however unwittingly) rather than solution. Much of the above analysis was verified through conversations or observation.

Global Inequality Problems

The world we inhabit is convulsed by a slew of conflicts, contradictions, and dilemmas. Too many people exist, too many live in the wrong places with too many problems and not enough resources to meet exponential demands. Even slavery, long thought to have been abolished from human history, continues to persist, with an estimated 30 million people enslaved in different degrees—more than at any time in human history (Power 2012). Admittedly, it would be disingenuous to ignore equality advances: 50 years ago, up to 60 per cent of the world's population lived on less than one

American dollar a day, countries such as South Korea and Singapore were among the world's poorest, the concept of middle class in emerging economies was unheard of, and India was in a constant state of famine (Raymond and Martin 2012).

Nevertheless, major inequalities and exclusions persist, despite improvements on the global equality front. There is also no consensus regarding which inequality problems to select for analysis. But certain patterns, expressions, and conditions of inequality are of such gravity and scope that they leap into prominence. Foremost are the issues of income, poverty, overpopulation, urbanization, ecological trauma, and human rights violations. Each of these inequalities of exclusion is worrying in its own right. The cumulative impact of their convergence has the potential to terminate planetary existence as we know it.

Poverty and Income Inequality

Income
Global inequality gaps continue to expand (Milanovic 2011). In the OECD countries (OECD 2011), the average income of the richest 10 per cent is about nine times that of the poorest 10 percent—a ratio of 9 to 1. The ratio is lower than average in Fennoscandia and some European countries, but

higher elsewhere, including a 14 to 1 ratio in the United States and Israel and 27 to 1 ratio in Mexico and Chile. According to a report by the Conference Board of Canada (2011b), countries with the highest inequality are clustered in South America and Southern Africa. The lowest inequality gaps (based on the Gini coefficient, a standard measure of income inequality) are in Fennoscandia and Western Europe, whereas Canada and the United States have intermediate to high levels of inequality (Rajotte 2013). The extent of income inequality varies by country: the lowest Gini index is in Slovenia at 0.24, the highest in Namibia at 0.4, with Canada ranking thirty-second on a Gini index of 0.32 (the United States is in sixty-second place with a Gini reading of 0.38). To be sure, development in the poorer parts of the world has been impressive. Between 1820 and 1950, per capita income in China and India was basically flat. The 68 per cent increase between 1950 and 1973 was impressive but dwarfed by the 245 per cent jump from 1973 to 2002. Not surprisingly, decreases in world income inequality reflect the phenomenal economic growth in China and India. Exclude China and (to a lesser extent) India from the equation, and world income inequality flatlines (*The Economist*, 1 June 2013). The persistence of massive global inequalities is captured in the following Spotlight box.

Spotlight Lucky Fido: It's a Pooch's Life in Dogland

The magnitude of global disparities really hits home when contrasting a dog's life in the United States with the lives of less fortunate humans (Korzeniewicz and Moran 2009). According to the American Pet Products Manufacturing Association, owning a dog in 2007–8 cost Americans on average $1,425 yearly ($749 in health care, $217 in food, and $459 in grooming, boarding, toys, and treats). If these 75.8 million (in 2015) pampered pooches were allowed to create their own nation (Dogland), with average maintenance costs representing the average income of a nation gone to the dogs, their collective income would position Dogland as

a middle-income nation, just ahead of Egypt and Paraguay and above more than 40 per cent of the world's population (or 60 per cent above, if China's high growth rates were excluded). If the focus is just on health care expenditures, the canines of Dogland would exceed that of 80 per cent of the world's population. Moreover, if the amount the world spends (US $49 billion) on pet food every year were channelled into maternal and child health, according to the vice-president, public affairs, of World Vision Canada, it could eliminate deaths of 8.8 million children who die each year before the age of five (Riseboro 2010).

No less an inconvenient truth is the ecological imprint of having a pooch as a pet. The environmental paw print of a medium-size dog is apparently twice the equivalent of building a big SUV (Toyota Land Cruiser) and driving it for year (10,000 km in New Zealand); for a cat, the environmental impact is about equivalent to a VW Golf (Vale and Vale 2009). Dogs and cats not only consume about $1.5 billion worth of protein-rich food each year, they also produce a significant amount of waste (up to 620,000 tons of "doggy-doo" annually) (Mitchell 2013). With the population of dogs and cats approaching the one billion mark, we may need to rethink our relation to the canine/feline world.

This global gulf between rich and poor is coalescing into a twenty-first-century equivalent of apartheid. Extremes of income and wealth are compressed into geographically segregated zones to create pockets of inequality every bit as punishing as those in the colonial past. For example, the gap in per capita income level between high-income countries and low-income countries increased from $18,500 in 1980 to $32,100 in 2010, bottoming out at $185 per capita in Zimbabwe (Conference Board of Canada 2011b). Individual wealth and income gaps are no less stark. The 2008 UN University-WIDER report revealed that the richest 1 per cent owned 40 per cent of all global assets (by 2014, the figure had grown to 48 per cent [Oxfam 2015]); by contrast, the poorest 50 per cent owned just 1 per cent. Two-thirds of the world's population of 7 billion had net assets of under $10,000, whereas 24 million millionaires (or less than one per cent of the population) owned over one-third of the world's household wealth (Pomfret 2012). Even the aftershocks of the 2008 recession have not derailed the enrichment of the wealthy (MacKenzie 2015). According to the 15th Annual World Wealth Report by Merrill Lynch Global Wealth Management and consultancy firm Capgemini (2011), the world's "high net worth individuals" quickly surpassed the 2007 pre-crisis levels. By 2016, the world's richest 1 per cent will own 50 per cent of the world's wealth (up from 48 per cent in 2014) or more than the combined total of the other 99 per cent of the world's population (Oxfam 2015). The world's 80 richest people own as much wealth as the bottom 3.5 billion. The net worth of Warren Buffet ($62 billion) is estimated to be greater than the combined annual GDP of 129 countries, while Bill Gates remains the world's richest person with a net worth of US $87.6 billion (Newcomb and Sazonov 2014).

Poverty
The scope of global poverty is staggering (OECD 2008; 2011; Ilcan and Lacey 2011). Nearly a billion people are thought to be illiterate; another billion go hungry; and about one-third of the developing world population will die before middle age. According to the World Health Organization, a child born in Sierra Leone in 2004 had a life expectancy of 39 years, less than half the average lifespan in Canada. True, the scope of global poverty is shrinking, according to the multidimensional scale devised by an Oxford University consortium based on ten weighted indicators such as nutrition and education. Still, 1.6 billion continue to live in MPI (Multidimensional Poverty Index) poverty, including 440 million in the poorest eight major states in India (OPHI 2015). The new poverty line is elsewhere defined as surviving on the equivalent of US $1.25 per day (raised to $1.90 in 2015). Based on a $1.25 cut-off point, 836 million people, or 14 per cent of the world's population, live below this line, compared to 1.9 billion, or 47 per cent in 1990, using the old measure of $1 a day (adjusted for inflation). Regional variations persist: thanks to its booming economy, China's poverty rate fell from 85 per cent of the population to just over 11 per cent in 2010 based on the $1.90 measure, thus accounting for three-quarters of all global poverty reduction (Stuart 2015; *The Economist*, 1 June 2013). By contrast, the poverty rate fell by only 8 per cent in sub-Sahara Africa (Dharssi 2015).

To live a life free of poverty is a fundamental human right enshrined in the UN Declaration of Human Rights (1948) and reaffirmed in several Covenants (UN Department of Economics and Social Affairs 2009). And yet in 2007, the UN General Assembly proclaimed the Second United Nations Decade for the Eradication of Poverty (2008–2017).

The pervasiveness of poverty throughout much of the world, including 1 in 2 in sub-Saharan Africa who survive on less than $1.25, in effect poses the foremost global challenge in advancing sustainable development. Poverty kills more children and young adults than all modern wars combined, according to the Concept Notes for the UN International Day for the Eradication of Poverty 2012. Children who experience chronic poverty "die quietly" because of food insecurity (hunger, undernourishment, and malnutrition), precarious work conditions, and degraded environments, and are at higher risk for health problems, developmental delays, and behaviour disorders. Moreover, women and girls are estimated to account for up to 70 per cent of the world's poor despite recognition that improving their status enhances local development and prosperity (Chant 2010). According to the UN inspired International Day of the Girl, an investment in girls (from education to health and safety) is the best option for empowering communities and changing the world. Finally, the poor are poor not necessarily because of bad habits or poor choices. Rather poverty is often the result of government policies that bolster the interests of local elites or transnational corporations in addition to those structural adjustment programs (with corresponding cutbacks in health and education services) imposed by the IMF (International Monetary Fund) and World Bank as conditions for loans and investment.

Overpopulation

Sociologists used to have an iconic saying: "The rich get richer, the poor get children." Despite its mocking tone, the expression latches onto a popular perception of the developing world as teeming with people with neither the resources nor the space to support the "masses." There is some truth to this perception (Weisman 2013). The world is experiencing a population explosion unprecedented in human history. From 1804, when the world population reached the 1 billion mark, it took 123 years to reach 2 billion, but only 12 years to go from 5 billion in 1987 to 7 billion in late October 2011—in effect doubling in less than 40 years. Projections point to as many as 10 billion earthlings by 2050, based on estimated growth patterns (Angus and Butler 2011; Thornett 2012). Much of the surge in growth is concentrated among

the poorest of developing countries, despite initiatives aimed at improving family health and family planning (Leisinger, Schmitt, Pandya-Lorch 2002). Sixty per cent of the world's population increase is concentrated in 10 countries, with India and China leading the way. Not surprisingly, many people are alarmed—and for good reason—in light of the planet's limited carrying capacity (Moyo 2012; Cohen 1996).

Why this demographic explosion? Why indeed, given that half of the world's married women rely on family-planning techniques, so that women's fertility rates dropped in over 60 countries below the replacement level of 2.1 children per woman. Skyrocketing rates reflect the arrival of one billion teenagers who are entering their reproductive years, including 45 per cent of the sub-Saharan population (Leisinger, Schmitt, Pandya-Lorch 2002). Longer lifespan is another obvious answer. Life expectancy is expanding substantially, thanks to plummeting infant mortality rates because of improved medical care, the eradication of certain fatal diseases, and advances in technology. For example, in 2009, worldwide, the infant mortality rate was 42 deaths for every 1,000 born. Cuba's infant mortality rate stood at 4 per 1,000 (despite being one of the world's poorer countries), in contrast to the 7 per 1,000 in the more wealthy United States. In India the rate was 50 deaths per 1,000 births, whereas the rate in China was 17 per 1,000 (Dorling 2011). Poverty is deemed to be a contributing factor. Larger families provide a margin of safety and survival in those economies without any state-based safety net to cushion the blows of being old, disabled, or unemployed. In other words, what is often defined as a global problem (that is, large families) represents a survival solution in the absence of alternatives such as rudimentary social programs and safety nets.

The politics of population is proving vexing. Yes, life expectancy in the developing world now stands at 63 years (compared with an average of 75 in the industrialized world. In 1900 the world average was 31 years, albeit higher in Western Europe and North America [Pomfret 2012]). Much of this increase can be attributed to better survival rates among infants due to improved immunization programs. Yet the downside is inescapable. Increases in life expectancy in many developing countries may compound the problem of overpopulation, resulting in upwardly spiralling demands on dwindling resources and sprawling urbanization (McMahon 2015). Control of diseases and death rates is a positive goal, yet these life-affirming benefits are offset by additional pressure on existing social services and food supplies. Local environments are especially vulnerable to escalating expectations. The depletion of basic necessities, coupled with the proliferation of waste, is worrying in its own right. According to the 19 July issue of *The Economist* (2014c), one billion people worldwide have no toilet, including 600 million in India who defecate in the open, with all that implies for public health. Satisfying the food needs of 80 million additional people each year will intensify competition in regions of scarcity. A famine in Somalia between 2010 and 2012, triggered by war, extremism, and government indifference, claimed 260,000 lives, half of them children (York 2013). But questions remain: is overpopulation at the root of social inequality (a kind of blaming the victim) (Thornett 2012)? Or should blame be directed at global capitalism and neo-liberal globalization for forging patterns of consumerism, greed, and waste (Angus and Butler 2011; Suzuki 2011; Graham-Leigh 2012)?

Advances in agricultural biotechnology have expanded the limits of the earth's carrying capacity (a limit to the number of people that can be sustainably supported without irreversible damage to the planet), despite dire predictions of a catastrophic depletion of natural resources (see Diamandis and Kotler 2012). But improvements in food production have not translated into a world free of hunger or malnutrition. Spectacular changes in food yields, including a doubling of grain harvests and tripling of livestock production since the early 1960s provide the potential for adequate nutrition if equitably distributed to meet global needs (Angus and Butler 2011). Yet nearly one billion individuals remain food deprived—that is, cannot produce or procure enough food at all times to lead healthy and productive lives (Leisinger, Schmitt, Pandya-Lorch 2002). And those most affected by food insecurity are children whose nutritional deficiencies may doom them to permanent deformities. Up to 165 million children worldwide are stunted—physically, emotionally, and psychologically—because

of food scarcity and nutritional gaps (Pogatchnik 2013). Even more worrying are future projections. The intense and short-lived emergencies in the past because of bad weather and solved through humanitarian efforts are increasingly a thing of the past. A slow-burning humanitarian crisis is looming instead, including chronic (persistent and pervasive) patterns of hunger and malnutrition in the poorest countries of the world.

Urbanization

Slightly over half (54 per cent) of the world's population of 7 billion-plus people now live in cities (UN 2014). Regional variations are significant: in the global south, about 23 per cent of the population is urbanized, up from 13 per cent in 1950. Africa and East Asia have the lowest rates of urbanization, while 71 per cent of the Latin American population is urban (including 86 per cent in Argentina). The rates in Canada and the United States are currently in the 80 per cent range. Singapore and Hong Kong are almost entirely urban. Yet even in areas with low urban-to-rural ratios, the presence of sprawling urban agglomerations prevails, from Sao Paulo at 20.8 million and Shanghai at 23 million down to Manila at 12.8 million and Lagos at 12.6 million. A UN report (2014) provides a list of rapidly growing super cities (megacities) preceded by figures for the largest cities in 1900 and 2001.

World's Largest Urban Areas in 1900 by Millions of Population	World's Largest Urban Areas in 2001 by Millions of Population
London 6.5	Tokyo 26.5
New York 4.2	Sao Paulo 18.3
Paris 3.3	Mexico City 18.3
Berlin 2.7	New York 16.8
Chicago 1.7	Mumbai (Bombay) 16.5
Vienna 1.7	Los Angeles 13.3
Tokyo 1.5	Calcutta 13.3
St Petersburg 1.4	Daka 13.2
Manchester 1.4	Delhi 13.0
Philadelphia 1.4	Shanghai 12.8

Source: Adapted from Sheehan 2003.

World's Largest Urban Areas in 2014 by Millions of Population

Tokyo 37.8

Delhi 25.0

Shanghai 23.0

Mexico City 20.8

Sao Paulo 20.8

Mumbai 19.2

Osaka 20.1

Beijing 19.5

New York-Newark 18.8

Cairo 18.4

Source: UN 2014.

Cities are seen as the drivers of globalization (Khanna 2010). They may well dislodge nation-states in dominating patterns of governance in the foreseeable global future. The emergence of global institutions built around dense communities of individuals who embrace their new proximities as drivers of production and creativity—rather than nations and their armies—could spur the onset of a new city-dominated global governance (Dey 2012; Khanna 2010). But the drawbacks of massive urbanization in the developing world needs little elaboration. The inequalities of power, wealth, opportunity, and survival that hobble humanity have a way of crystallizing in cities. Shortcomings in transportation, accommodation, and avail-ability of services provide a reminder that most "instant" cities were never envisaged as massed population sites. Even more daunting is the pros-pect of rapid growth in "infrastructureless" cities whose inhabitants must survive without garbage collection and waste-water treatment. The only constant is the ever-present threat of diseases such as bubonic plague or malarial fever. Dangers and drawbacks aside, however, many are attracted to the city because of "push and pull" factors. Migrants are pushed out of rural communities because of unemployment, limited land resources, lack of opportunity and employment, boredom, and dis-like of social dynamics such as factionalism. They

are pulled into cities for precisely opposite reasons. For some, sheer survival for themselves and their children is a compelling reason; for others, the lure is one of glamour, excitement, and sophisti-cation. The decision to uproot is not always pro-ductive. Livelihood from rural fields is exchanged for low-paying urban jobs, often supplemented by proceeds from scavenging and participation in the invisible economy.

In theory, many developing countries pro-fess to discourage urban migration (Fleras 2005). Problems abound, related to employment, sani-tation, limited transportation and traffic snarls, pollution, access to services, and crime. In reality, public policy is geared towards urban residents in hopes of keeping them contented, distracted, and subservient. Only lip service is paid to solidifying rural economies. Resources are diverted to sus-tain the activities and appetites of those urban-ites whose lifestyle habits now include consumer goods and conspicuous consumption. National pride is often at stake as well. For elites, even the prevalence of poverty, homelessness, and slums does not detract from cities as symbols of progress in advancing industry, wealth, and prestige. Slums themselves elicit conflicting assessments. For some, they are sinkholes of misery and despair; for others, they illustrate the ingenuity of people in desperate circumstances, while exposing gov-ernment failure to capitalize on human resources. The informality of slums provides urban dwellers with a tenuous toehold on the employment front, yet obstructs them from securing long-lasting economic improvements. What makes living in slums so inexpensive is the dearth of govern-ment services. Nevertheless, slum residents may end up paying more for essential services from private sources, whereas the more affluent and stable neighbourhoods may receive government-subsidized services.

Reactions to the extraordinary expansion of megacities remain mixed (Tibaijuka 2009/10). Cities are sites of concentrated advantages, from opportunities and employment to services and excitement to higher levels of literacy, education, health care, and political participation (UN 2014). They also represent sites of inequality; accordingly, opportunity eludes many of their inhabitants.

Opportunities associated with the so-called urban advantage are often closed to women and young people, to the detriment of livelihood and health. Lastly, the prosperity that thrives on global linkages also lures the rural poor to cities in hopes of making it (big). But a lack of credentials, skills, and education confine most to a slum-based informal economy whose outputs complement the conventions of the formal economy. In short, developing world urbanism represents a bona fide social inequality problem. Paradoxically, however, inhabitants of these cities may not see urban life as a cost or problem. Even the inconveniences and dangers of city life are perceived as a trade-off for the opportunities lacking in resource-depleted rural environments

Our Fragile Planet

The natural environment is critical in shaping each country's global agenda. Environmental politics can easily influence government policy or public reactions in responding to a shortage of raw materials, drought and crop failure, depletion of ocean life, deforestation in the tropics, and pollution ranging from waste mismanagement and noxious emissions, to global warming and ozone depletion. The worst case scenario assumes a direct link between environmental scarcity and intergroup violence (Taras and Ganguly 2009). Others reject such a causal link. Scarcity per se is not the problem; more accurately, blame should be affixed to those powerful enough to determine patterns of distribution and consumption (Suzuki 2011). Put bluntly, the world produces enough food to provide every man, woman, and child with about 3,600 calories per day. But the greed and excesses of the affluent countries in the global north create large pockets of hunger for countries in the global south. The trap of hyper-consumerism and conspicuous consumption that animates the reality of the world's rich countries is killing the planet. For example, according the Boeing Web Site, fuel consumption of a Boeing 747 in the course of a 10,000 km trip is 36,000 gallons (or about 150,000 litres) of highly polluting jet fuel. The International Civil Aviation Organizations points out that a tourist who flies from Britain to Kenya and back (about 13,500 kms) generates nearly a ton of carbon emissions (*Economist* 2015). Or consider how discarded electronics from TVs to computers pose major environmental challenges and health hazards when dismantled by hand for parts recycling. Rich countries such as Canada produce voluminous amounts of municipal waste—including 777 kilograms of city garbage per capita in 2008, in part owing to overconsumption—putting Canada last among 17 peer countries (Conference Board 2013; Aulakh 2013). Not surprisingly, as Vale and Vale (2009) like to remind us, if the rest of the world consumed at the same rate as North Americans, five earths would be required to handle the capacity. In brief, shortages do not trigger conflicts over environmental scarcity. More accurately, it's the politics of abundance, and efforts to do something about this pending ecological crisis are often lost in a haze of platitudes and finger-pointing, rarely leading to concerted action or coordinated co-operation.

This beautiful but beleaguered planet now confronts a global eco-crisis of catastrophic proportions (Klein 2014). Many believe the outer limit of the earth's carrying capacity to support its inhabitants is edging toward a saturation (or tipping) point. Population, pollution, and production have been accelerating at exponential rates to amplify social inequalities and ecological disasters—from climate change to global warming because of heat trapping carbon dioxide gas (Intergovernmental Panel on Climate Change 2014; World Meteorological Organization 2014). The increasing integration of the developing world into a consumption-based global economy puts unprecedented pressure on exploiting natural resources such as fossil fuels to generate economic growth and satisfy consumer demand (Bland 2013). Profits from exploration, extraction, and transportation of fossil fuels are just too important to dwell on climate change or a green economy (Engler 2013). Yet it is often the poor countries that pay the price of Western greed and rampant consumerism. According to Germanwatch, a think tank funded in part by the German government, the developing countries of the global south suffer the most from escalating greenhouse gases in the atmosphere, including the possibility of extreme weather patterns that over the past two decades have killed 500,000 people and caused property damage in the vicinity of $2.5 trillion (Reuters 2013b). Disruptions that portend an apocalyptic catastrophe include the dangers of pollution that disrupts global cycles and ecosystems: for example, the possible disappearance of coral reefs (which would represent the first whole ecosystem destroyed by human activity [Sale 2012]) can be envisaged as the canary in the coal mine of human existence. As well, the risks associated with toxic chemicals include nitrogen fertilizers that fuel productivity but also contaminate groundwater and suffocate fish life (Charles 2013). Ecological decline in which diversity diminishes has caused species to disappear (for example, explosive development coupled with decades of pollution have endangered thousands of wildlife species in Florida, resulting in the deaths of rare marine mammals [Wines 2013]). The perils of biotic mixing have the potential to unleash a SARS-like scenario of microorganisms that migrate or proliferate (Bright 2003). And fossil fuel companies think nothing of polluting the planet to keep profits afloat (Klein 2014).

The prevailing economic model is the main driving force behind this planetary destruction. An economic model that pivots around the principles of "more," "bigger," and "newer" distorts people's priorities at the expense of a sustainable environment. Of particular note is neo-liberal-driven globalization based on unbridled growth, wanton greed, international trade, accelerating energy needs, increasing levels of consumption and consumerism, and reckless extraction of natural resources (Steffen et al. 2015). Yet solution advocates tend to cleave along "class" lines. The rich countries believe environmental degradation such as global warming is a global problem; hence, all countries must do their part to combat it. Failure to extract concessions from poor countries will torpedo moves to ratify any deals. Poor countries find it both ironic and hypocritical that they are expected to proportionately contribute to solving the global environment problem created by the profligate consumer habits of the rich (see Spotlight box on "growing bananas"). For example, the world's wealthiest 10 per cent are estimated

to consume 60 per cent of the world's resources, whereas 40 per cent of the world's poorest use less than 5 per cent. The wealthiest also contribute to 60 per cent of global pollution, according to the World Bank 2008 World Development Indicators (cited in Magdoff 2012). Or consider how the average electricity consumption in the United States, based on kilowatt hours per capita per year in 2011, was 13,250 (16,453 in Canada); in Haiti the figure was 30 (World Bank 2015). In short, countries in the global north should be at the forefront of fixing rather than those in the global south who can least afford to do so without aborting local economic development or damning millions to yet more poverty.

Admittedly, chronic environmental degradation threatens the lives and life chances of the rich and poor alike. Moreover, as Paul Watson, founder of the Sea Shepherd Conservation Society observes, it's not despoliation per se that's the problem, since the earth will continue to survive in some form or another regardless of our recklessness; rather the issue is whether humans—rich or poor—can adapt quickly enough to ecological changes. Nevertheless, a sense of perspective is useful: the poor of the world have little choice except to extract from the environment if they want to survive. Contrast this with the consumption patterns of the affluent who plunder the environment without much remorse. Blaming the developing world for ecological woes is common and convenient. Yet many of the world's environmental problems emanate from Western patterns of conspicuous consumption, obscene levels of waste and wastefulness, and an obsession with the cult of more or bigger (Fleras 2005). Food preferences in the global north play havoc with the lives and livelihoods of those in the global south. For example, the export of prawns and shrimp to the richest countries has evolved into a major industry (US $9.5 billion in prawns alone) (Barnett and Wasley 2003). But establishing the crustacean farms for prawning and shrimping disrupts massive swathes of coastal mangrove forests (Goldsmith 1999; Shanahan 2003). Environmental violence—ranging from human rights abuses, rampant corruption, illegal land appropriation, and intimidation leading to violence and death—often accompanies the loss of sustainable resources (Stonick and Vandergeest 2001). Cash-cropping is also creating a host of global problems, from land grabs by hired thugs to incidents of displacement, destitution, and starvation (Monbiot 2012b). Even moves to become "greener" are fraught with pitfalls. For example, a growing reliance on greener biofuels (creating fuel from crops such as corn) may sound environmentally sound in theory, yet is offset by our fixation with coffee. Modern plantation-grown

coffee (unlike coffee that naturally grows in shade) requires huge amounts of chemicals that can lead to deforestation, impoverished soils, and reduced habitat for natural species of birds and animals (Mittelstaedt 1999). In both cases, local farmers lose their self-sufficiency, as arable lands are converted into cash-crop holdings, thus intensifying peasant dependence on wage labour. The following Spotlight box captures the politics and perils of catering to the whims of the global north.

Spotlight Growing Bananas in the Global Economy: Pleasing Palates in the Global North, Wreaking Havoc in the Global South

It's commonly known that catering to the food tastes of the global north imposes hardship on countries in the global south. People's hunger for shrimp, for example, devastates mangrove environments throughout the world (Fleras 2005). Our taste for beef is also transforming parts of the world into huge cost-inefficient pastures whose yields deliver more harm than benefits. High on the list of items that symbolize imperialism, injustice, and globalization of the agricultural economy is yet another foodstuff—the lowly banana (Shah 2010). The consumption of bananas was virtually unknown to the western world prior to 1870. But bananas are now the staple fruit in Europe and North America, thanks to their innocuous taste, pleasant appearance, nutritional value, and relative low cost. In 2006, bananas generated US $20 billion in revenue, based on sales from 15 million tons, making bananas the world's fourth most important staple crop after wheat, rice and corn, and citrus fruits (Gillard 2011). Bananas are grown in developing world countries because of ideal tropical climates. Ten countries produce 75 per cent of the banana crop, with India, Ecuador, Brazil, and China accounting for about half of the total production. Interestingly, although bananas are cheap for consumers, they are a grocery store's most profitable item, according to Spring Gillard 2011; Shah 2010). Yet only 12 cents on every dollar spent on bananas in the countries of the global north stays in the producing country.

It's been argued that bananas are the ultimate low-carbon footprint food (Berners-Lee and Clark 2010). Others disagree, and point out the perils of perfecting bananas as a food industry:

- Blemish-free bananas are a chemical nightmare. According to Gillard, the banana industry uses 10 times more pesticides, herbicides, and fertilizer than conventional agriculture in the developing countries of the global south (also McCracken 1998). Fungicides (many of which are carcinogenic) are sprayed by air up to 60 times a year to ensure high yields of blemish-free fruit. Field workers are routinely exposed to dangerous agro-chemicals resulting in corresponding health problems, from sterility to cancer. To add insult to injury, the fruit is washed in disinfectants (formaldehyde), then packaged in plastic bags and tags coated in insecticides.
- Heavy chemical use devastates the environment. Chemicals and industrial waste (two tons for every ton of bananas) are leached into the earth and waterways, to the detriment of local ecological viability. Massive deforestation and clear-cutting of lowland (marsh) environments contaminates the delicate ecological balance of the former rainforest.
- Thousands of acres of rich and diverse tropical ecosystems and biodiversity have been destroyed to make way for banana

continued

agri-businesses (McCracken 1998). Depletion of forest cover intensifies both exposure to sun and rainfall erosion, resulting in soils that are quickly exhausted and abandoned. (It is generally known that single-crop monoculture quickly compromises soil quality by making it more susceptible to erosion or leaching.)

- The conversion to banana plantations displaces patterns of local self-sufficiency since farming for export disrupts domestic food production and generates food import dependency (Grossman 1998). Even fair-trade bananas, with their promise to respect land and workers, are hardly a solution; after all, farmers must be displaced to replace resource-depleted old plantations.

- Political fallout is no less evident. The coup in Guatemala in 1954 planted the seeds of a 36-year civil war over the extreme social and economic deprivation encountered by Guatemalans on banana farms. Evidence reconfirms the continued exploitation of banana workers who toil long hours for minimal pay (Fridell 2010) in physically demanding labour (McCracken 1998). Workers tend to live in cramped conditions such as barracks with modest amenities.

- Three large fruit companies control 65 per cent of the world's banana trade. Those Central American countries that depend on Dole, Chiquita, and Del Monte for revenue and employment have little choice except to defer to corporate social, political, and economic priorities (McCracken 1998). Not surprisingly, labour exploitation is rife, and includes children who work 12-hour days for less than US $2 under dangerous conditions and with little job security (Furstenau 2010).

Many solutions have been proposed to soften the banana trade crisis. They range in scope from reintroducing polyculture to rotating crops and using less chemicals. Perhaps the focus is on the wrong culprits. Unsustainable processes will remain as long as the demand for unblemished bananas continues (Furstenau 2010). Only a change in consumer demand for more sustainable practices will push the industry to end environmental destruction and worker exploitation (McCracken 1998).

Even Canada's once squeaky-clean image dims under scrutiny. If anything Canada has evolved into an outlier among developed countries (akin to a rogue state) for its antediluvian stance on a number of environmental issues (Killian 2015; Center for Global Development 2013). Canada's environmental ledger has deteriorated dramatically because of air and water pollution, extraction of "dirty oil," the fracking of shale rocks, loss of wetlands, clear-cutting and deforestation, noxious waste and nuclear waste disposal, and chemical poisons in soil and the food chain. Environmentalists have criticized Ottawa for reneging on a promise made in 1995 to reduce noxious emissions to a pre-1990 level. Greenhouse gases have risen by 13 per cent since then, prompting the Montreal-based Commission for Environmental Cooperation to single out Ontario as the continent's third worst jurisdiction for hazardous emissions and industrial pollutants, just ahead of Texas and Ohio (Mittelstaedt 2003). Canada's refusal to address climate change at international conferences has earned it global scorn as the "fossil of the year." A Washington-based group, the Center for Global Development (2013), ranked Canada's climate policy as the worst in the developed world, placing it last out of 27 countries. Another European report by Climate Action Network Europe and Germanwatch (2013) put Canada at 55 out of 58 countries for tackling greenhouse gases (including emissions per capita, renewable energy development, and international climate policy); only Iran, Kazakhstan, and Saudi Arabia did worse (Cheadle 2013). Finally, treatment of waste is proving a national disgrace, says the Sierra Legal Defence Fund (Mittelstaedt 1999). Major Canadian cities such as Montreal and Victoria continue to abuse the environment by using rivers, lakes, and oceans as a dumping ground for untreated sewage and excrement, on the grounds of emergency, expediency, or lack of less polluting alternatives (Perreaux 2015; Hutchinson 2016). The virtual collapse of the cod fishing industry in the Atlantic Provinces, coupled with widespread layoffs in BC fishing, attest to the damage that can be inflicted by short-sightedness, carelessness, or indifference.

In theory, Canadians put a premium on protecting the environment without abandoning a commitment to economic growth. In reality, most vote with their wallets, since "thinking green" may entail inconvenience or costs. Politicians in Canada continue to prattle on about economic growth and energy exports as though a resource-depleted world can readily yield endless profit and productivity (Suzuki 1998). The end result is a natural environment under siege—not because Canada lacks resources to defuse the crisis but because it lacks political will to do something about air pollution, water quality, wetlands protection, forest cover, greenhouse gases, and biodiversity. Time will tell whether the profit-motivated private sector can possibly protect the "ecological capital" that sustains all planetary life. Evidence would suggest the troika of capitalism, global free trade, and neo-liberal globalization is unlikely to embrace environmental concerns (Klein 2014).

A mindset shift is required as well to abort this frantic and senseless growth that loots and pollutes the planet (Smith 2013). We are all in this together and together we have to make changes if there is any hope of life, let alone any possibility of living together. First, a wakeup call: the very idea of an environmental crisis or shortage of any kind is perceived by many Canadians as counterintuitive. But Canada is not a sprawling swath of unlimited landscape and untapped resources, although it remains a site of astonishing environmental abundance, including 20 per cent of the world's undeveloped areas, 25 per cent of remaining wetlands, 20 per cent of freshwater holdings, and 10 per cent of the outstanding forests (Hawaleshka 2003). However bountiful this abundance, these resources are finite and under stress, and are gradually being whittled away by greed or need. The combination of industrial scale agriculture, road and dam construction, aquaculture and excessive fishing, urbanization, forestry and mining, and gas and oil exploration should further disabuse Canadians of any complacency or smugness.

Second, the natural world does not exist in isolation from human communities. One billion people live in unprecedented prosperity; another billion live in abject destitution. Both rich and poor engage in consumption patterns (one from greed, the other from need) that exert pressure on existing resources such as water, land, forests, and atmospheres. Proposals to address environmental issues must be couched within the inequalities of the neo-liberal capitalist framework. Capitalism (especially corporate capitalism and market globalization) is the main driver towards planetary ecological collapse (Smith 2013; Klein 2014). Much of the world is increasingly locked into an economic system in which corporations expand exponentially to compete, reward shareholders, and accelerate growth (especially in resource extraction), which logically and routinely takes priority over ecological concerns. Yet human needs and a healthy environment are not mutually exclusive, writes Jared Diamond (2003), but inexorably linked since there is no such thing as human survival without a functioning environment. The challenge lies in recreating patterns of human activity that combine a high standard of living, with a sustainable environment that is biologically diverse and ecologically resilient in its capacity to absorb stress without either permanent damage or collapse—from which there is a point of no return (Sale 2012). That is the theory: transforming talk into action will prove to be the quintessential twenty-first-century challenge.

Human Rights: The All-Encompassing Global Inequality

In 1948, the Universal Declaration of Human Rights established the principle of civil, political, economic, and cultural rights of all individuals. The concept of creating a global safety net, applicable to everyone regardless of race, ethnicity, origin, or creed, put focus on protecting the inherent dignity, freedom, and equal worth of individuals (Larking 2014;Blau 2007). Different dimensions of rights and freedoms eventually came into play as the birthright of all humans, including freedom *to right to life*, freedom *of speech*, and freedom *from fear and want*. Also included in this package were legal rights, political rights, economic rights, and rights of national minorities to self-determination (Beitz 2001). Conceptual shifts took place as well: no longer were human rights seen as a magnanimous gesture bestowed by benevolent authorities.

To the contrary, these rights and freedoms were inextricably linked to the realities of human existence, and no one could be exempted or denied (Hafner-Burton 2013; Tharoor 1999/2000). In the words of Romeo Dallaire, who acknowledged the inalienability of human rights (cited in the *Report of the Task Force on Human Rights*), "All humans are human. There are no humans more human than others. That's it."

What seemed like a relatively straightforward agenda at mid-century has proven complex and contested (Sjoberg et al. 2001). The first human rights codes were aimed at redressing specific instances of open and deliberate discrimination. Current human rights codes tend to be more diffuse and expansive by virtue of focusing on discrimination both systemic and institutionalized rather than open and personal. Human rights abuses are no longer defined by blatant hatred. Rather, rights violations may reflect the consequences of even well-intentioned actions or interventions that, when evenly and equally applied, may inadvertently inflict a disadvantaging impact on vulnerable minorities. Human rights are no longer framed exclusively in terms of what is done to deny or exclude; just as relevant is what is *not* done to improve the quality of living conditions for those marginalized and oppressed. In other words, the principle of equal outcomes is just as important as abstract appeals to equal opportunity. Finally, human rights discourses are moving from an exclusive focus on individual rights to a greater emphasis on minority rights, including the legitimacy of indigenous peoples' collective (group) rights (Maaka and Fleras 2008). This in turn has spawned debate over the balancing of individual human rights with the common good, state sovereignty, and national security (Etzioni 2014).

The inception and acceptance of human rights discourses has proven revolutionary in its impact and implications. References to human rights have catapulted to the forefront of national and international affairs—even to the point of what's called "rights inflation," in watering down its transformative power to the level of an empty cliché (Clement 2016). The internationalization of human rights now supersedes once sacrosanct claims such as the inviolability of state sovereignty to do as it pleases.

The UN bombing of Serbia in 1999 to avert genocide in the province of Kosovo articulated a powerful message, especially when followed by Kosovo's unilateral declaration of independence in early 2008. The universal status of personhood and human rights now trumps the principle of state sovereignty as final authority to run roughshod over its citizens (see Levy and Sznaider 2006). Nevertheless, the supremacy of the nation-state remains a jealously guarded and fiercely defended remnant of bygone days (Castles 2011), albeit in reconfigured form, status, and role (Karim 2010; Castells 2010). Political systems and the global order are increasingly informed by the once unthinkable principle of broadly shared human rights: that is, each person possesses the inalienable right to belong, to participate, to be recognized, to speak, and to be heard (Ignatieff 2001a; Forsythe 2006). The doctrine of human rights has also emerged as a moral touchstone that offers a standard of assessment, criticism, and reform when evaluating prevailing laws, institutions, and practices as they relate to individuals and groups (Beitz 2001). It also secures a tool of empowerment for the disadvantaged and marginalized, resulting in ongoing tension between the universalism of human rights and the sovereignty of modern nation-states (Larking 2014).

However progressive it seems, a commitment to the principle and practice of human rights remains more ideal than reality. Sixty years of good intentions and international criticism of violators have not disappeared human rights abuses (Hafner-Burton 2015). Consider only the slaughters in Sudan and Congo Republic; sectarian violence in Syria and Iraq that has killed hundreds of thousands of civilians and combatants while displacing millions from their homes; violent repression in Zimbabwe; and Burma's military crackdown of dissidents. Compounding the gravity of the situation is the persistence of torture or extrajudicial killings in 81 countries, unfair trials in 54 countries, and curtailment of freedom of speech in 77 countries (Ward 2008). Nearly a billion people are malnourished around the world, according to Amnesty International (2013), another billion live in slums, and a woman dies from complications of pregnancy or childbirth every 90 seconds. Finally, the legally binding guarantees of equality and non-discrimination, especially among the marginalized of the world, remains a glaring human rights issue (Human Rights Watch 2012). Not surprisingly, although universal human rights may exist in theory as an international norm, they have yet to be practised or enforced. David Rieff (2002:70) writes of this gap: "The twentieth century may have had the best norms, but it also had the worst realities." The next Spotlight box addresses the gap between ideals and reality.

Spotlight Living Homosexually in a Heteronormative World: Social Exclusion as Human Rights Violation

One of the more pressing human rights issues at present is the continuing violation of sexuality rights of members of the LGBTQQIAAP (lesbian, gay, bisexual, transgender, queer, questioning, intersex, asexual, allies, and pansexual) community (herein shortened to LGBT). On paper, all people, regardless of sexuality or sexual orientation, are entitled to the protections promulgated by international human rights laws, including right to life, freedom of expression and association, and freedom from torture, hate-motivated violence, or arbitrary arrest and detention (EUAFFR 2014a). In reality, many within the LGBT community (of all ages and across all regions of the world) continue to experience subtle—and not so subtle—violations of their human rights because of deeply ingrained homophobic and transphobic attitudes. The lives and life chances of members of the LGBT community may be severely compromised by a dearth of legal protection against discrimination in the labour market, schools, and hospitals, as well as exposure to verbal slurs, demeaning stereotypes, and physical assaults. According to the OHCHR (2013), discriminatory laws in 77 countries criminalize same-sex relationships between consenting adults in private, in the process subjecting individuals to the threat of arrest, prosecution, imprisonment, and death in at least five countries. For example, until recently, individuals in many American states who engaged in consensual same sex relations could be arrested for violating sodomy laws.

Canadians continue to label, devalue, and discriminate against on the basis of race, gender, social class, and ethnicity. Those whose sexual orientation does not comply with the heterosexual norm (or heteronormativity) also are victimized through exclusion, harassment, and abuse. The fact that sexual orientation serves as grounds for social inequality and exclusion may come as a surprise to some; after all, Canada has laws in place that provide legal protection from discrimination based on sexuality or marriage (same-sex) preference. Federal antidiscrimination protection for sexual minorities was introduced in 1996, followed by a Supreme Court ruling in 2004 that upheld an earlier provincial rule legalizing same-sex marriages (Carpenter 2008). The introduction of Bill C-16 in Ottawa in May 2016 proposes to amend the Human Rights Act to ban discrimination against individuals based on gender identity or expression (Coren 2016). The number and popularity of pride events in Canada and globally attests to the social distance travelled by the LGBT community (Walters 2014).

However impressive these gains, homosexuality continues to be stigmatized in Canada and globally (in the latter case, often institutionalized in formal law as sinful, criminal or immoral). For example, natural catastrophes such as the Hurricane Katrina disaster were framed by some as God's punishment for the growing acceptance of homosexuality and same-sex marriage (Ferguson 2014). Homophobia (an irrational fear of and intolerance towards homosexuality) is reflected in various ways, including unfair and socially devalued treatment in the workplace ranging from pejorative name calling to harassment related to jokes or inappropriate questions about sexual practices (Walters 2014). LGBT members are routinely exposed to stereotyping and abuse in the digital domain of cyberbullying, often leading to ruined

continued

reputations—and lives—as the price for coming out without a safety net. Finally, income disparities exist as well, with self-identified gay men earning 12 per cent less than similarly situated heterosexual men (ironically, lesbians have higher incomes compared to heterosexual women) (Carpenter 2008; also Walters 2014 in the United States).

Clearly then, the human rights revolution applied to sexual orientation remains a work in progress. Members of the LGBT community are subject to the inequalities of exclusion through discriminatory practices, sometimes openly, other times systemically. Moreover, the exclusion is further amplified when a negatively defined sexual orientation overlaps and intersects with other devalued identity markers related to gender, race and ethnicity, and social classes (Veenstra 2011). Even the law is no protection at times. Members of the LGBT community may possess formal rights to equality; nevertheless, they must exercise these rights in a context neither designed to reflect their interests nor constructed to advance their interests—akin in part to the perils of living left-handed in a right-handed world. As long as homophobia is deeply entrenched in social structures and societal values that exclude and marginalize the LGBT community, the force of law to bring about substantial transformation will be sharply compromised.

Globalization as Inequality

The world is full of contradictions, conflict, and change. Whether we approve or disapprove, broad historical forces are rearranging the contours of the familiar in ways both disruptive and destructive. For some, the greatest danger comes from religiously inspired insurgents or state-sponsored terrorist groups who brazenly deploy a culture of hate against civilian targets. For others, the major threat is the systemic "terrorism" of global market forces, including transnational corporations and WTO/IMF–driven structural adjustments. For still others, disruptions to the global economy are transformational. Just as the Industrial Revolution signified a radical break from its feudal predecessors, so too has an information-rich, post-industrialism established a profoundly different way of creating, defining, and distributing wealth that may prove just as revolutionary as its predecessor in transforming society along unequal lines.

It's hard to imagine two more politically charged yet interlinked concepts than **globalization** and inequality (Milanovic 2012). Yet the term *globalization* is one of those nebulous turns of phrase with a fathomless capacity to infuriate or enlighten. An inexact term for a wild assortment of activities and processes, globalization is often hailed as the defining historical moment of our times, despite suffering from overuse as the prevailing mantra of business, politics, and culture (Fleras 2005). People read different meanings into globalization over and above its common connotation of "beyond the local." Some focus on the rapid and unfettered flow of capital under a fundamentally redesigned set of political and economic arrangements. Others emphasize access to relatively cheap overseas labour that displaces low- to middle-value jobs in high-wage countries. Still others concentrate on the information and communication technologies that link our lives with those of globally dispersed others (Legrain 2003). And yet others point to the proliferation of non-state actors such as transnational corporations who are establishing a new global order. If restricted to economic globalization, different aspects can be discerned, including free trade agreements, financial integration, incorporation of poorer countries into a world economy, information and technology transfers, production relocation, and international migration (OECD 2011).

A globalized economic order is not simply a reorganization of widgets around a digitally driven economy. A revolutionary shift in "doing business" is now taking place, in effect offering an opportunity for some, marginalization for others, but confusion for still others. With globalization, the ground rules are changing. In contrast to days when economic activities were contained within the framework of a protectionist nation-state, globalization consists of a world economy that transcends the nation-state as the unit of production and wealth creation, with a corresponding capacity to operate on a global scale in real time and across an increasingly borderless world (Beck 2005; Castells 2010). Those local industries, once locked behind the protective barriers of closed national economies, are being displaced by a dynamic system of integrated and cost-effective sites whose productive loops transcend national borders. The economic game is changing as players and strategies realign themselves within the broader framework of a just-in-time global division of labour. Significant consequences follow: the patterned predictability of rules, roles, and relationships that once prevailed no longer applies in a world of complexity, change, and connectivity (Goldin 2013). In their place is a globalization game board with few boundaries; the rules of the game are up for grabs; exponential increases in the number of players make it a buyer's market; owners and industries relocate when the financial tap dries up; and every so often an already tilted playing field gyrates wildly out of control.

The end result of such tumult is a cacophony of contradictions (Goldin 2013). Globalization may represent one of history's most progressive forces, yet the most severe crises of the twenty-first century reflect the very success of globalization—in effect giving birth to its own potential demise (Goldin 2013). Globalization has the capacity to foster universal harmony through a single global economy, yet fears persist of anarchic global forces that propel vested interests into more dangerous rivalries. Many believe globalization erodes national sovereignty to the point of paralysis, yet others take comfort in a process that exposes human rights violations while taming the lawlessness that hides behind the cloak of national sovereignty. The primary objectives of modern globalization—namely, scale, access, speed, efficiency, predictability, and control—may enhance people's ability to control their lives, yet increased interconnectedness leaves humankind more vulnerable to unforeseen risks, especially when instantaneous communication strips away the insulating effects of a delayed response. Globalization and global capitalism may possess the potential to deliver billions from poverty, create opportunities for choice and

personal development, and prop up the legitimacy of democracies around the world (see Diamandis and Kotler 2012), yet globalization and global markets also embody dis-equalizing tendencies, making rising inequality a reality around the world (Birdsall 2006). A globalized free market provides cheaper prices for goods, yet the free flow of labour and capital off-shore has also diminished employment opportunities in the lower and middle layers of the "tradable" sector, while the interplay of downsizing, outsourcing, and off-shoring has the potency to oppress or exploit workers in both the global north and south (Spence and Hlatshwayo 2011; Shantz 2012; Davey 2012). This two-edged character of globalization—connectedness as controlling or out of control—generates much of the concern, criticism, and controversy.

Even the ontological status of *globalization* is up for grabs. On the one hand, some acknowledge globalization as a real and profoundly transformative force, despite an underside that rankles and provokes. They also endorse globalization as a business model that fortifies the progressive integration of the global economy in enhancing the prosperity of developed countries (from reducing the cost of consumer goods to creating new markets for goods) while lifting millions around the world out of poverty, thanks to sustainable global growth and increased opportunities (Straw and Glennie 2012). On the other hand are those skeptics who regard this diagnosis as highly exaggerated and distracting from the real forces at play—namely, corporate capitalism (Held and McGrew 2002; Atasoy 2003). Corporate globalization may provide benefits that trickle down to the "masses"; however, the major beneficiaries remain the wealthy few, especially with the realignment of the state from a welfare provider to a market booster (Sivanandan 2010). Even financial transactions under globalization can be a recipe for chaos or crisis: the vast sums traded daily on the financial markets do little to enhance national economic performance because any wheeling and dealing is divorced from trade, production, or people's lived realities (Plender 2012). Corporate mergers rarely generate productive gain since rising stock prices simply provide corporations with more cash to swallow up competitors. Free trade agreements and trade liberalization are now exporting ("outsourcing") formerly tariff-protected and thriving manufacturing sectors to lower wage and union-averse countries, resulting in benefits for some, costs for others (Walkom 2013b). As ruefully noted by Yalnizyan (2012), "If memory serves, globalization was sold as an opportunity to export the First World economy and conditions, not import a Third World standard for workers." Moreover, in contrast to the narrowing of poverty and inequality levels between countries, the inequalities of exclusion within countries has intensified as the rewards of globalization become increasingly concentrated (Straw and Glennie 2012). The interplay of positive and negative is captured by Ian Goldin (2013:1) who talks of the paradoxes at play:

> Globalization increasingly presents a paradox: It has been the most progressive force in history, but the most severe crises of the 21st century will arise due to the very success of globalization. . . . [G]lobalization will have given birth to its own downfall. A succession of crises that result from increased integration will lead to a backlash. Citizens will see increased integration as too risky. They will become increasingly xenophobic, protectionist, and nationalist. Our integrated financial and trade systems, and other networks such as energy systems and the internet, could become fragmented into silos.

Also open for debate is whether the status of globalization is unique and recent or a resumption of the freewheeling trade dynamic that predated the World War I era (Straw and Glennie 2012). Although some would argue there is nothing radically new about globalization as a powerful force that integrates societies into a worldwide web of trade and investments, many disagree (Fleras 2005). Globalization is not distinguished by the volume of international trade in a post-protectionist world that only now is approaching the exceptionally high levels of pre-1914 worldwide trade (Atasoy 2003). What is new is the striking speed, intensity, and magnitude of these interconnections. Globalization is innovative in organizing neo-liberal market principles into an

ideological framework that extols the virtues of unregulated free market dynamics, free trade as a catalyst for growth, elimination of import substitution economies and protective tariffs, privatization of public enterprises, new information and technology transfers, and a global frame of reference for doing business and creating wealth (M. Spence 2011). Borders that regulate the flow of capital from commerce to investment have become increasingly porous with the advent of microchip technologies and free trade arrangements, although the growing militarization of borders against the movement of unwanted migrants points to ramped-up patterns of surveillance and security (Fleras 2014b). Worldwide market integration and a global division of labour promotes the production, distribution, and consumption of goods and services along global lines whose linkages *transcend* national boundaries rather than simply *crossing* them. The conflating of time with space because of advanced technologies transforms the global economy into a single domestic market, with export trade as primary rather than residual.

Globalization may be defined along descriptive or prescriptive lines. As description, globalization entails a process involving the worldwide integration of countries and economies into a global division of labour (M. Spence 2011). This closer integration of countries and economies reflects reduced costs of communication and transportation that, in turn, facilitate the flow of goods, capital, and knowledge (Straw and Glennie 2012; Stiglitz 2012). Conceptualizing globalization in this way points to transformations in spatiality and temporality, including time–space compression, increased density and frequency of interactions relative to local and national levels, expanded flows of people and products around the world, a rethinking of society in terms of boundedness and relative autonomy, and relationships between social systems in the world (Walby 2009). As prescription, globalization can be defined in hegemonic terms, namely, the geographic penetration of capitalist principles into new domains in the relentless quest for profits, markets, and shares. Globalization represents an extension of colonial/corporate/neo-liberal capitalism that exploits cheap labour through international agencies and transnational corporations (Nagra 2003). In this sense, globalized neo-liberalism represents a twenty-first-century version of the capitalist world system based on an international division of labour in which core regions dominated and exploited the peripheries—except now technology and communication transcend (de-territorialize) particular regions or nations-states (Harvey 2005). Reactions vary to framing globalization as capitalism gone wild. Some associate globalization with a "soft hegemony"—that is, a tool rich societies use for securing disproportionate advantage (Chan and Scarritt 2002). Others are less sanguine: in a strongly worded critique, William Robinson (1996) couches globalization in apocalyptic terms—as a clash between the global rich and the global poor, the human and environmental impact of which is comparable in predatory scale to nineteenth-century colonialism.

The dynamics of globalization are supplanting the old world order (Davey 2012; Fleras 2005). These dynamics operate at a global level rather than at national or local levels; consequently the old world order of discrete bounded units (known as nation-states) is challenged by transformative patterns of human organization, wealth creation, and social action. The creation of a favourable investment climate for large corporations under globalization is known to displace workers and set migration in motion by uprooting people (Bacon 2008). Yet the labour of these migrant workers is then criminalized, as is the case in the United States with undocumented Mexican migrants (Fleras 2014b). With globalization, national economies are reorganized around an integrated system of production that may transcend national borders. Increasingly irrelevant are Fordist models of production, with their emphasis on mass and standardized production, vertical integration, economies of scale, and de-skilled labour. A post-Fordist model of wealth creation is activated instead, based on more flexible systems for producing varied and specialized goods and services geared primarily to export rather than domestic consumption. Inefficient industries are abandoned while foreign investment and onshore jobs are vigorously pursued through discovery of "business-friendly" environments. This reorganization of production into global loops of cost-effective sites compels economies to specialize or perish in the competition for markets, investments, and jobs. Yet this globalization shift in wealth production is not without impact and costs for workers (Milanovic 2012). Canada is no exception to this paradox as described in following Spotlight box.

Spotlight Jobs Going South: Sound Business Sense or Irresponsible Globalization?

How natural or unnatural is inequality? For sociologists of a functionalist bent, inequality is a natural and necessary component of a complex and functioning system. Without inequality to stimulate risk, creativity, and entrepreneurship, a complex and prosperous society could not possibly survive. Others, such as radical conflict theorists, disagree and argue that high levels of inequality reflect distortions in a system designed around profits rather than people. For example, Derek Bok, a former Harvard University president, has argued that CEOs are paid huge sums largely because they must make decisions and produce results that often clash with their better judgment as managers and sensibilities as humans. That is, their focus is directed at short-term returns (share price) instead of the company's long-term interests, their employees, and the local community (see Dobbin 2011). The consequences are unsettling: the economics of inequality can compel even good people to act short-sightedly, in the process demonstrating how a society's governance contract for living together is more fragile than many realize.

continued

The relentless push by the CEOs of global corporations to slash operating costs is wreaking economic havoc. The closure of Caterpillar's Electro-Motive Diesel plant in London, Ontario—with a corresponding loss of over 450 jobs and perhaps 1,700 additional spin-off jobs—is just one of many moves by foreign companies to shutter Canadian plants off to cheaper cost sites. Kellogg's decision in late 2013 to curtail its operations in London put another 500 out of work. The combination of competition from low-cost countries (from China to Mexico and even non-unionized sectors in the United States) and the disadvantages of doing business in Canada has struck a crippling blow to Canada's already beleaguered manufacturing sector. As David Olive (2012) says, "We pay a stiff price as the world's biggest branch-plant economy." The anatomy of the demise of Caterpillar's Electro-Motive is plotted below.

Timeline

2005: Berkshire Partners LLC and Greenbriar Equity Group LLC—two private equity firms—buy the locomotive division Electro-Motive from General Motors.

2010: Heavy equipment maker Caterpillar buys Electro-Motive for US $820 million from Berkshire Partners LLC and Greenbriar Equity Group LLC. The federal government approves the sale.

2011: Caterpillar's Electro-Motive allegedly receives a CAD $5 million federal subsidy (tax benefit) personally delivered by Stephen Harper during a factory visit. References to a 2008 tax benefit are also in the news, but both allegations are disputed (Moffatt 2012).

January 1, 2012: Caterpillar locks out workers at the Electro-Motive plant who went on strike after rejecting the company's offer of pay cuts of up to 50 per cent in many job categories (from about $32 per hour to $16 per hour); elimination of a definite benefit pension plan; reduction in dental and other benefits; and the end of a cost-of-living allowance. Such a take-

it-or-leave-it offer prompts some to ask whether Caterpillar was negotiating in good faith or deliberately provoking a crisis as a cover to justify the closure.

February 3, 2012: Caterpillar shuts down the 90-year-old plant, arguing in a news release, "The cost structure of the operation was not sustainable and efforts to negotiate a new competitive collective agreement were not successful." Caterpillar subsidiary Progress Rail Services argued the cost structure in the London plant was unsustainable (i.e., wages were too high) even though Caterpillar reported a 58 per cent increase in its quarterly earnings with a record profit of nearly US $5 billion. The company planned to move the work to a plant in Muncie, Indiana, where wages range in the $12 to $16 bracket and a right to work prevailed (no compulsory unions), in the process transferring Electro-Motive's specialized, made-in-Canada technology and intellectual property developed in London to a low-wage, non-unionized jurisdiction.

2012: In 2009 Caterpillar laid off 20,000 workers (which may be something of a record for mass pink slips). Since then, corporate revenues have doubled, profits quadrupled ($5.7 billion in 2012 [Kimes 2013]), stock prices have soared by 270 per cent, and the CEO earned a hefty $10.5 million annual paycheque.

2013: In April 2013, Caterpillar announced the closure of its tunnel boring machine facility in Toronto, which it purchased five years earlier. Three hundred thirty jobs were lost (Spears 2013). In the same month, Caterpillar announced a $22 million pay packet for the company's CEO, while the corporation's executive officers enjoyed pay raises of 56 per cent over the past six years, catapulting their annual salaries into the $10 million strato-bracket (Kimes 2013).

The closure of the Electro-Motive plant raised some disturbing questions about the cost of doing business in a world of globalization. Put bluntly, globalization provides cover for Caterpillar and other corporate behemoths to bolster profits by squeezing workers through coordinated attacks on unions with relatively high paying jobs in favour of union-free workplaces. Yes, Caterpillar's actions may be unfortunate and disruptive, yet they reflect the cost of doing business in an increasingly integrated and ruthlessly competitive global economy—one that is driven by profit at any cost; reshaped by technology and economic and demographic shifts; buffeted by the rise of economic powerhouses such as China, India, Brazil, and other emerging markets on the world stage; and the structural rearrangements grounded in globalization (from off-shoring to outsourcing), with the worldwide integration of markets profoundly affecting (eliminating) traditional job patterns, incomes, and opportunities (M. Spence 2011).

Welcome to the complex, unforgiving, and intensely competitive world of international business. Like it or not, approve or disapprove, these are the new rules of the game, rules that work well for the shareholders of the world. For the rest of us, not so good (Yalnizyan 2012). The economics of wages are key: manufacturing workers in Canada are more highly paid and more likely to be unionized than their counterparts in the United States. For example, the average hourly wage for machine operators in Canada is $4.53 higher than for American machine operators, and 42.2 per cent of Canadian machine operators belong to a union compared to only 14.1 per cent in the United States (McMahon 2012). Why would the auto industry want to remain in Canada when assembly plant workers in Mexico earn the equivalent of just under US $3 per hour, or about 10 per cent of what is earned by Canadian and American workers with full seniority (Keenan 2015)? As might be expected in light of such wage differentials, about 20 per cent of the jobs in vehicle assembly and auto parts in Canada have disappeared since 2001. The imperative to remain competitive and slash production costs in a global market economy puts pressure on shedding labour and mothballing operations regardless of the human costs. In the words of the CEO of Progress Rail in a letter to all employees:

All facilities within EMC, EMD, and Progress Rail Services must achieve competitive costs, quality, and operating flexibility to compete and win in the global marketplace, and expectations at the London plant were no different. (cited in Polushin 2012)

Caterpillar might not have done anything wrong or illegal in mothballing the Electro-Motive plant—they were playing the game by the new rules, including the need to be cost-efficient and operationally flexible in a mercilessly competitive global market (Grant 2012; also Ng et al. 2013). But in the clash between profits/astronomical CEO salaries and worker wages, how ethical is it to scuttle over 450 jobs to satisfy a commercial imperative, especially when the parent company is generating record profits (Olive 2012; Kimes 2013)? Should foreign companies be allowed to take over Canadian factories and accept government/taxpayer subsidies, only to shut the factories down, while stripping and shipping their technology and know-how? (Keep in mind, however, Electro-Motive was previously owned by another US-based multinational, General Motors; as for patents, apparently, 47 of the 48 patents associated with Electro-Motive list their inventors as American [Moffatt 2012b].) What should the federal and provincial governments do (if anything) to prevent more of these calamities from ravaging an already beleaguered manufacturing sector (1.5 million Canadians work in manufacturing, the third largest sector after health care and retail [Grant 2012])? How does Canada equip itself to cope with the new power alignments of the global economy, such as the amorality of job-slashing corporations, regardless of the impact on workers and their families (Lewenza 2012), yet ensuring both jobs and a decent living wage for Canadian workers? Responses to these questions are not readily forthcoming in a topsy-turvy world where workers are no longer human capital but rather treated as a cost-cutting measure. As long as profit only remains the name of the game, the free market dynamics of neo-liberal globalization will continue to act irresponsibly, even to the detriment of people and the planet.

But Canada is not a passive player in the globalized economy. Canada is often framed as a branch-plant economy in which foreign investment plays a disproportionate role in shaping this country's economic affairs. Yet its overseas foreign investment portfolio may be larger dollar-wise than investment in Canada, while its foreign policy agenda emphasizes economic interests, including the sale of Canadian military equipment to countries with spotty human rights records (Blanchfield 2013). Of particular note is Canada's strong presence in the global mining industry, with about 1,500 projects currently on the go (Sandborn 2014). For example, the world's largest gold mining company is Barrick Gold Corporation, which operates some two dozen mines and projects on five continents employing 20,000 workers. But Barrick and its founder and chair Peter Munk continue to attract criticism as the face of corporate and globalizing evil for what some see as exploitative and/or unethical behaviour toward the downtrodden of the world (McQuaig 2011). Barrick's operations may have contributed $9.7 billion in economic benefits to the countries in which it operates, including operations in Tanzania (no longer listed on the company's website, www.barrick.com) that generated export income, created thousands of jobs, and provided workers with access to health care, education, and electricity (York 2011). But critics point to the downside: Tanzania may have sat on $40 billion worth of gold reserves, although it collected a pittance in taxes and royalties, thus reinforcing its global status as one of the world's ten poorest countries (McQuaig 2011). To add injury to insult, conflicts are ongoing between the locals and security forces/police (York 2011). In May 2011, Barrick security forces shot and killed seven villagers scavenging for gold-laced rocks, an act of violence that drew worldwide outrage over the plight of those who rely on scrounging for a living because many have abandoned farming, yet despair of wage employment (York 2011; 2014).

The implications must be addressed: Canadian companies are among the biggest players in the mining sector of the global south (Engler 2016). They are often on the receiving end of privileged treatment by host governments, argues Jean Symes of Inter Pares (2013), because of their wealth and the political and financial support provided by the Canadian government. Not surprisingly, mining profits are soaring because of tax exemptions and deregulation of the industry (York 2011). There are growing fears that Canada is lax in ensuring that mining firms with Canadian head offices take responsibility when human rights abuses are perpetuated (Sandborn 2014). True, mining companies are increasingly held accountable for environmental crimes, violence by local personnel, tax avoidance, and influence peddling with local governments. But nothing will bring about local enrichment and community empowerment until the mining sector adopts a more environmentally friendly stance, becomes more inclusive in terms of sharing benefits and providing compensation, and assumes socially responsible commitment and accountability to local communities (Graham 2012). Until then, African countries will continue to confront what Burgis (2015) calls a "resource curse": Africa's mineral abundance dooms it, paradoxically, to exploitation and underdevelopment by multinationals and corporate investors in cahoots with coup leaders and national elites (Engler 2016).

Towards a Humanistic Re-globalization?

There is little doubt that corporate globalization has redefined the business of doing business. Advances in telecommunications and transportation have compressed the world into a globally integrated production loop of cost-effective sites. On paper, the economic benefits of globalization are too tempting to dismiss. Taken as a whole, global market integration is a desirable process for improving living standards through local employment and cheaper goods. There is much to commend in the logic that correlates national wealth with the removal of pesky tariffs for international trade, improving productivity through competition, enhancing the climate for jobs and investment, and reducing unwarranted government intervention and social spending. Freeing up global economies through the discipline of the market is thought to increase choice, reward risk, unleash creativity, and eliminate waste. Business elites have welcomed the prospects of fostering a global market economy. They want the right to invest and divest with minimal restriction, to establish their businesses without unnecessary encumbrances, and to apply universal standards to ensure harmonization between countries. In short, a fundamental restructuring in the relationship between society and the economy is taking place under globalization (Atasoy 2003). Those with the resources and resourcefulness to take advantage of this transformation have been amply rewarded. Others are not so fortunate.

The promises associated with globalization have not panned out as many had hoped. Compelling statistical evidence points to a growing gap in the economies between countries in the global north and those in the south that often mirrors the divide between the privileged and disadvantaged classes within any given country (Global Policy Forum 2006; Braeuninger 2008; Chan and Scarritt 2002). Critics like to point out how market-motivated philosophies can throw people out of work and reduce social service access, in effect foreclosing choices, widening disparities, diminishing capacity, and creating austerity in all the wrong places (see Held and McGrew 2002). Transfer of economic control from an interventionist state to the unfettered market may inflict collateral costs, most notably the realization that what is good for the economy in terms of the GDP (gross domestic product) is not necessarily good for either society or workers—or the planet. Trade liberalization has been a boon to some workplaces but a bust for those whose goods and services incur a "value-added tax" because of higher environmental, social, and labour costs (Bacon 2008). A more competitive money market has enriched a few, yet the pressure for profit amplification has dampened employment prospects for those without the resources to take advantage of a freewheeling global economy. Globalization driven patterns or global warming and the extinction of species stride alongside worries over the onset of a global monoculture, ethnic conflicts, and intensifying levels of poverty.

Critics of globalization like to remind us that a "different world is possible" because the "world is not a commodity" (Sarkar 2011:5). Such an optimistic outlook provides insight into the major challenge for the twenty-first-century: to create an open and democratic society in which market freedom is balanced with the principle of social justice. Central to this challenge is a working balance between markets (globalization) and society (state intervention), between an ethical/human rights approach and an elitist/neo-liberal approach—that is, how to unleash the creative syn/energies of globalization without eroding the co-operative basis of human social existence, including the promotion of democracy, human rights, community development, and a sustainable environment (Chan and Scarritt 2002). A humanistic orientation situates human needs and concerns within the framework of differently managed globalization. Humanistic-driven globalization puts a premium on the well-being of people and the planet by adopting a "limits to growth" paradigm, providing children with a sustainable future, renewing relationships with the natural world, establishing free trade agreements that meet people's needs rather than bolster corporate profits, employing resources that are locally available, and encouraging a diversity of diversities beyond the clutches of a conformist global monoculture and the Americanization of culture. The UN Development Report (1999) captures a sense of the challenge:

> The challenge of globalization in the new century is not to stop the expansion of global markets. The challenge is to find the rules and institutions for stronger governance—local, national, regional, and global—to preserve the advantages of global markets and competition, but also to provide enough space for human community and environmental resources to ensure that globalization works for people, not just for profits.

The forces of global capitalism and realities of globalization are neither immutable nor irreversible, with no alternatives to consumerism, free trade, or economic growth (Chan and Scarritt 2002). Instead of something natural or normal, these global dynamics are socially constructed conventions for doing business and creating wealth. They consist of conventions created by vested interests that put profit before people and the planet. The challenge is to undo the exploitative and exclusionary by creating a more humane and inclusive globalization. In other words, it is not a case of either/or—of globalization or no globalization. The question instead is what kind of globalization works best? Do Canadians want globalization that is driven by transnational corporations primarily for the benefit of corporate elites? Or do they prefer more humanistic globalization that ensures benefits are equitably distributed, is protective of Canada's political autonomy, ensures some degree of progress and prosperity, and promotes a vibrant market economy without reducing Canada to a

market society, one that mistakenly believes economies operate most effectively when resources are allocated along market lines rather than through government intervention or public input (Vallas 2011)? Globalization need not be a zero-sum game. A properly regulated globalization has the potential to raise living standards around the world, but only when framed as a means for achieving sustainable growth and enhanced living standards for everyone, not just the lucky elites (Glennie 2012; Straw and Glennie 2012).

Summary

1. The dilemma and danger of global inequality and globalization can be examined by exploring social inequality from a global perspective and within the context of globalization as a promise and a peril.
2. The nature and scope of global inequalities are related to the environment, urbanization, overpopulation, income disparities and poverty, and human rights.
3. Global inequalities matter for various reasons, including being a catalyst for social unrest, ethnic conflict, and intergroup violence, up to and including world conflagrations.
4. Developed countries in the global north (including Canada) must assume a degree of responsibility for inequalities in the global south.
5. Globalization can be framed simultaneously as inequality and equality, and regression and progress, and as having benefits and costs, depending on the context, criteria, and consequences.
6. A relationship exists between a neo-liberal globalization and global inequalities in terms of root causes and causal relations.
7. The possibility exists of humanistic globalization as a more humane corrective to the neo-liberal version.

Review Questions

1. How does globalization represent a catalyst for improving social equality while also reinforcing more inequalities of exclusions?
2. How does humanistic globalization differ from neo-liberal globalization?
3. Explain who or what is responsible for the slew of global inequality problems discussed in the text. Refer to the blame-the-victim versus the blame-the-system debate.
4. Indicate how consumerism, greed, and lifestyle choices in the global north contribute to continuing patterns of inequality in the global south.
5. Indicate how and why the concept of human rights is the all-encompassing global inequality.

12 Social Equality Matters Too

Learning Objectives

1. To see how a commitment to social equality may prove an ideal to strive for rather than an attainable goal.

2. To unpack the highly contested and complex concept of social equality.

3. To draw attention to two major models of equality—namely, equal (formal) versus equitable (substantive).

4. To demonstrate how the logic of capitalism does not bode well for social equality.

5. To show how rehabilitated capitalism may point to a more egalitarian society.

Introduction: Equality: A Riddle Wrapped in a Mystery inside an Enigma

> We cannot solve our problems with the same thinking we used when we created them.
> —Albert Einstein (cited in Suzuki and Hanington 2012:2)

Imagine a society of perfect equality. What would a more equitable society look like if it was designed with people and planet (rather than profits and consumption) at the centre? Picture a social setting in which individuals are exempt from extremes of privilege, wealth, or power. Valued resources and necessary services would be distributed in an equitable fashion so that no one would suffer from a lack of material necessities that compromises their full potential. Not the superficial brand name prosperity of Trump or Gucci in this egalitarian model of social equality—

but a world of abundance with clean water, nutritious food, an end to poverty, affordable housing, first-class education and health care, and sustainable energy sources (Hertz 2012; Diamandis and Kotler 2012). From each according to their ability, yet to each according to their need, as Karl Marx once proclaimed in defending his communist utopia. Individuals, of course, would not be clones of one another as satirically portrayed in Kurt Vonnegut's "Harrison Bergeron" (1961), a future dystopia of masks and weights to impose a dumbed-down conformity. To the contrary, freely chosen differences would flourish and contribute, as pointed out years ago:

> So to criticize and to desire equality is not, as sometimes suggested, to cherish the romantic notion that men are equal in character and intelligence. It is to hold that, while their natural endowments differ profoundly, it is the work of a civilised society to aim at eliminating such inequalities as have their source, not in individual differences, but in

its own organization, and that individual differences, which are a source of social energy, are more likely to ripen and find expression if social inequalities are, as far as practicable, diminished. (R.H. Tawney 1964:57)

Instead of problems for disposal, people's differences would be respected and accepted as incubators and catalysts for personal growth and society-building innovation (Herring and Henderson 2015). Difference-based needs would be taken into account when necessary in leveraging the more level playing field of an ideal society. Individual creativity and success would be strongly encouraged, although the bulk of the benefits from personal achievement would be shared with the community at large. Equal rights across the board would ensure a commitment to both equal opportunity and equitable economic outcomes in addition to universal access to education and health. Exclusion and exploitation would become things of the past, thanks to the removal of discriminatory barriers based on race, gender, religion, nationality, or sexual orientation. The interplay of the inclusion principle (no one is excluded because of their differences) with the principle of inclusivity (everybody is included precisely because of their valued differences) would herald the onset of an egalitarian society. This egalitarian ethos would apply as well to disadvantaged groups on grounds that social exclusions are inexcusable in a civilized society that abides by human rights principles and the principles of justice (Walker and Walker 2011). Finally, intergroup conflict would diminish over time with the elimination of crass competition over scarce resources and false wants.

Does this scenario sound too good to be true? The prospect of constructing a perfect society in an imperfect world is remote at best—at least outside of some utopian fantasy world of science fiction where societal ideals are unencumbered with pesky realities (but see Levitas 2005). There is no historical evidence of a perfectly equal society. All known societies are characterized by some degree of inequality among their members, with the most privileged enjoying a disproportionate share of

valued resources (Tepperman 2012; Turner 2000). Even the simplest hunting and foraging communities allocated power and privilege unevenly. A commitment to egalitarian principles may have ensured relatively open access to the basic necessities for individual survival (Pennisi 2014), but such access did little to improve the status of those on the wrong side of the status ledger, including women and younger community members. Also falling short of utopian ideals are those contemporary versions of equal societies, including the kibbutzim in Israel or the Amish/Hutterite communities in North America, despite being more egalitarian in principle and practice than surrounding communities. Lastly, there is little evidence to suggest that a perfectly equal society (however that might be defined, operationalized, or implemented) would be to everybody's liking. For many, it is not the principle of inequality that rankles or rubs. Resentment arises instead when the *degree* of inequality becomes grotesquely disproportional, institutionalized, and embedded within the structure of society; is illegally acquired through rigged rules or hijacked agendas; inflicts harm or excludes others from full participation and equal opportunities through no fault of their own; and resists timely interventions. The challenge is twofold: first, to eliminate those inequalities based on foul play, structural barriers, elite collusion, and accidents of birth; second, to safeguard the outcomes that reflect individual variation in effort and risk-taking.

That most Canadians aspire to more social and economic **equality** is widely assumed (Beach 2007; Broadbent 2012; EKOS Politics 2013b; CRRF 2014). For example, when asked by an EKOS (2013c) poll to select Canada's greatest achievement from a menu of four choices, Canadians overwhelmingly chose equality over diversity, prosperity, and safety. The principle of equality is embraced as an ideal in modern society that underscores the fundamental dignity of persons and groups to be free from discrimination and exclusion (Sheppard 2010)—not necessarily perfect (i.e., the same) equality, since some degree of differentiation is thought to solidify incentives to work, invest, and get ahead by doing better than the previous generation. Polls consistently indicate that Canadians believe income inequality is a serious problem, given its negative long-term consequence (Brison 2012). Massive inequalities produce social costs: according to Wilkinson and Pickett (2009; Dorling 2013), more equal societies in the (post) industrialized world perform better than less equal societies at the levels of health, well-being, crime, and social cohesion. Even markets and capitalism work best under conditions of relative equality; after all, workers of the world require enough earnings to purchase the produced goods. To be sure, capitalism may be the primary source of inequality (Piketty 2014), but using the market to meet human needs might prove advantageous—at least in the short-term—without abandoning a long-term commitment to curbing excess concentrations of wealth and power. This strategy would put pressure on governments to intervene and tackle inequality through more intensive human capital investment, aggressive employment promotion, more social assistance and less austerity, and tax/transfer redistribution policies (Sernau 2011).

However ennobling and aspirational, the concept of equality is subject to diverse interpretations. Mutually opposed definitions may be differently endorsed depending on an individual's location on the political spectrum. Those on the left believe equality is about equal outcomes, whereas those on the right are convinced that equal opportunity defines equality. The so-called middle might equate equality with numerical proportionality. What is the proper pathway toward equality? Should intervention focus on dampening growth at the top? Shoring up the middle? Or boosting transfers to the socially marginalized bottom (Carney 2012)? Perception of "human nature" plays a role in framing equality (Leadbeater 2012): do competition and self-interest define humanity? Are co-operation and altruism our lot as a species? Are humans inclined towards being both competitive and co-operative, depending on the context? Finger-pointing clouds the picture as well: is it possible to coax a consensus about in/equality when members of the same society often live in vastly different worlds (both perceptually and experientially) so that phrases such as "bad choices," "moral failure," or "personal responsibility" clash with references to "structural inequity," "systemic bias," and "culture of oppression" (Blow 2014)? Does a commitment to equality mean treating everyone exactly the same regardless of the context or their differences (inclusion)? Or does it entail treating people differently to ensure inclusiveness precisely because their differences (from needs to rights) are disadvantaging and in need of accommodation through institutional adjustment (inclusivity)? Or should people be treated the same as a matter of course, but receive differential treatment (i.e., exemptions from general rules or expectations) when the situation arises (inclusiveness)? This multidimensionality makes it more difficult to operationalize the concept of social equality along more tangible (objective) lines for measurement. The implementation of this principle is also rendered more remote.

The concept of social equality is not nearly as straightforward as intuitively implied or glibly articulated. What constitutes equality for some is dismissed by others as inequality (albeit under a different name), and vice versa (Saunders 2011). The ensuing debates generate more heat than light, in effect reinforcing a belief that attaining the inclusiveness of social equality will remain a lofty but elusive (and perhaps an unattainable or even undesirable) goal—a direction rather than a destination (Dorling 2013). Perhaps the attainment of equality is less important than the creation of an **egalitarian society**, one in which no one is denied access to those physical and social necessities for full community participation and equal democratic citizenship. An egalitarian commitment points to a society that strives for inclusion (no one should be excluded because of their differences or disadvantages) and inclusivity (everyone should be included precisely because they are different or disadvantaged). Still, the question remains: what would an egalitarian and inclusive society look like in practice (see also Buckmaster and Thomas 2009)? If equality is central to a democratic and inclusive Canada (Broadbent 2011; EKOS Politics 2013b), some degree of consensus is necessary to put principle into practice. But as the Spotlight box demonstrates, agreement is far from secure.

Spotlight What Kind of Canada Do Canadians Want?

The politics of social in/equality raises a key question. What kind of society do Canadians want (Canada2020, 2011; Whittington 2013b)? One in which all decisions are filtered through a materialistic lens that emphasizes "having" and "consuming" over "sharing" or "self-fulfillment" or "participating"? That measures the worth of people on the basis of wealth or appearances rather than on their contribution to community or society? That allocates valued resources along free-market principles, regardless of the social costs imposed on the most vulnerable (Vallis 2011)? That treats other people as commodities to be rotated in and out of jobs whichever way the economic winds are blowing? That reinforces a creed of personal gain without a corresponding sense of social responsibility? Or is it one that endorses civil and respectful ways of living together differently in a context of co-operative coexistence, with a corresponding commitment to the public good and general prosperity (CRRF 2014)? Do Canadians aspire to an inclusive and more equal Canada that challenges those ruthless (neo-liberal) economic policies hell-bent on resource extraction and energy exports despite costs to the environment or Aboriginal peoples' rights (McQuaig in Gonick and Levy 2013)?

Responses to the question of what kind of Canada Canadians want is complicated by an inconvenient reality: when it comes to in/equality, Canada is a contradiction. To one side, Canadians appear to be proud of a Canada that extols an equality agenda (EKOS Politics 2013a). A survey of 2,000 adult Canadians by the Canadian Race Relations Foundation (2014) asked respondents to select Canada's most important values. Respondents chose from a list of 10 values. Respect for human rights and freedoms came first, followed by equality (equal access to health care and education) and loyalty to Canada (civility [politeness, respectful of queues, etc.] was also high on the list). Canadians may be more attached to their country than the citizens of any other advanced democratic country, including even the jingoistic United States (Valpy 2013b). Eighty-six percent say they have a moderate or strong attachment to Canada (albeit down from 90 per cent in 1998). (It's worth mentioning that 94 per cent have a very/moderately strong sense of belonging and attachment to their families, while only 66 per cent say they are moderately or very strongly attached to their ethnicities, compared to 81 per cent in 1998. Foreign-born Canadians display a slightly stronger attachment to Canada than the Canadian-born (77 per cent to 75 per cent), although fewer than 40 per cent of Quebecers do. As further proof that Canada is working, an EKOS poll (2013; also Environics 2016) found both foreign and Canadian born endorsed similar values, while a Canadian Policy Research Network report based on a dialogue with 400 citizens specified the following common values: shared community, equality and justice, respect for diversity, mutual responsibility, accountability, and engaged democracy (MacKinnon 2004; also CRRF 2014).

To the other side is a downside. The bonds that bind Canadians are unravelling, in the process exposing an increasingly polarized Canada along the fault lines of age (youth disconnected from politics), education, income, and the workplace. An age divide is noticeable: younger Canadians are more

This chapter is predicated on the principle that equality matters. That is, humans thrive in societies where they are treated as equals in their abilities; they work, think, and behave best when they are free of the assumption that some are more deserving because of birth; and people are least creative and co-operative when they must live under conditions of massive yet unwarranted inequalities (Dorling 2011). Or as put by Danny Dorling (2013:39), "[g]reater equality matters because under it more people are treated as being fully human." References to equality provide a normative ideal that underpins public policy, in addition to advancing the justice principles of redistribution likely to endorse a commitment to a sustainable environment, vital communities, educated population, balanced time use, democratic engagement, activist government, availability of social services and a safety net, health and health care, and participation in leisure and culture (McGrane 2015). Canada is also thought to be less cohesive than in the past because of growing loss of trust, engendered in part by the pervasiveness of a self-serving individualism (Graves 2013; Valpy 2013b); those wedge politics that needlessly polarize; and the market fundamentalism of neo-liberal politics (see Hulchanski 2010). For example, according to an EKOS poll that tracked trust in the federal government, only 28 per cent said they trust Ottawa most or all of the time, down from just under 60 per cent who agreed in 1968. (Nurses and doctors rate high levels of trust, while politicians and social media have abysmally low levels [Graves 2013].) Moreover, too much of what passes for government policy and decision-making is refracted through the prism of neo-liberal economic growth instead of relying on the moral compass of societal well-being and general quality of life (Romanow 2012). The liberal-capitalist contract that propelled the meritocratic dream of striking it rich is unravelling because of a sluggish economy that overwhelmingly panders to the affluent few (McNamee 2014). What future is there for Canada if many Canadians believe they are worse off than their parents, and that the next generation will do even worse (EKOS Politics 2013b)?

In between the good and bad is a raft of mixed messages. Consider the following contradictions: as Canada has become more socially inclusive, it has become increasingly unequal. Race and gender in an inclusive Canada are no longer stigmas that exclude or exploit. But patterns of social inequality

pertaining to these identity markers remain steadfast in a Canada driven by a growth-at-all-costs mentality (Mandle 2011; Rajotte 2013). Canada now has one of the healthiest economies in the advanced industrialized world owing to an array of business-friendly (but not citizen-friendly) policies including deregulation, reduced corporate taxes, and a host of austerity programs. But no matter what the government would have us believe (Rajotte 2013), robust productivity and national economic growth do not automatically improve the overall quality of life. Measuring economic activity by way of a growing GDP is not necessarily the sign of a thriving society (Romanow 2012). Economic growth is laudable but not if it comes at the expense of more stress, lower personal satisfaction, thwarted personal growth, fewer social connections, and less free time (Canadian Index of Wellbeing 2012). To their credit, Canadians are not oblivious to these contradictions whose painful truths are masked by polite fictions. A poll by EKOS Research in 2013 indicated that 49 per cent of the respondents thought Canada was moving in the wrong direction, up from less than 30 per cent in 2008. Thirty-seven percent said Canada was moving in the right direction, down from 65 per cent in 2008 (*Toronto Star* Graphic 2013). Concern is mounting over this chasm between the political and public—between citizen values and government actions, between what people believe in and their lived experiences (Romanow 2012). A government that is unresponsive to people's values and perceptions is doing a disservice to the Canadian public (Canadian Index of Wellbeing 2012). It also sows the seeds of its own electoral demise.

(material), recognition (cultural and symbolic), and representation (political) (Fraser 2008). More equal societies possess higher levels of collaboration and trust, with less status competition and reduced consumerism since there is less emphasis on judging people by their possessions or appearances (Wilkinson and Pickett 2010). This chapter

deconstructs (i.e., examines, analyzes, and assesses) the concept of social equality and explores its centrality to Canada. The chapter casts additional light on this tricky subject by demonstrating how different models of social equality can yield diverse responses and analytical frameworks. Of particular relevance is an examination of the relationship between social equality and capitalism. Many regard the current iteration of capitalism as the primary source of social inequality and exclusion; after all, social inequality is intrinsic (rather than collateral damage) in global/corporate capitalism that is geared toward the principle of worker exploitation, value surplus, and the rational pursuit of profit (Piketty 2014). Moves to rehabilitate capitalism pivot around creating a more **responsible capitalism** that is accountable to both workers and communities as well as society and the environment. The chapter concludes by reaffirming that *equality matters*: just as *inequality* matters in terms of increasing the probability of creating social exclusions, making (often bad) things happen, so too does equality have the capacity to positively shape the lives and life chances of Canadians. The stakes are too high to ignore. Without equality, our lives will prove to be a terrifying mix of Rousseau's observation of "man everywhere in chains" and a Hobbesian fear of human existence as "nasty, brutish, and short."

Conceptualizing Equality: Equal, Equivalent, or Equitable?

Equality in Canada may represent a fundamental social value involving concurrent notions of equity, justice, or fairness (Beach 2007). But for all its importance to both Canada and Canadians, the concept is not easy to define. Much of the difficulty is rooted in the different ways of employing equality: the same (equal), proportional (equivalent), or substantive (equitable) (Saunders 2011; Fleras 2012).

First, *equality* is used synonymously with *sameness* (Blackburn 2008:251), and is based on the principle of ensuring that everyone is treated exactly the same regardless of their background or circumstances. No one is accorded special privileges in a system informed by the principles of equal opportunity and universal merit. After all, if everybody is equal before the law, the law must apply equally to everyone. Any measure that rewards individuals on grounds other than merit or competition is criticized as contrary to the natural sorting-out process. This type of "formal" equality focuses on due process, abstract principles, and

legal equivalence to ensure inclusion. It also tends to treat individuals as abstractions—that is, asexual, deracialized, classless, and lacking a history or context (McIntyre 1994). This emphasis on formal equality, with its commitment to equality of opportunity and equal (same) treatment, regardless of race or gender (inclusion), puts this perspective at odds with more substantive versions of equality known as equity (inclusivity).

Second, equality can be defined in the sense of numerical or proportional equivalence. Under systems of proportional hiring and promotion, each group is allocated positions and resources according to their numbers in society or the workforce. This equality model is popular in political and institutional circles since the concept of equality can be operationalized through measurements that determine any progress. Both affirmative action in the United States and Canada's **employment equity** program are predicated on the principle of proportionality in the hopes of matching organizational numbers with general population ratios or labour market availabilities.

Third, the concept of equality can be animated by the substantive principle of "different but equal." This emphasis on an equity of outcomes or equitable conditions acknowledges the importance of situational circumstances and people's lived realities (rather than the formal abstractions of equal opportunity) as grounds for defining who gets what. Substantive equality attends to unequal outcomes and systemic consequences reproduced through apparently neutral rules, standards, policies, and rewards that differentially impact some, not others. A substantive equity approach acknowledges the centrality of multiple identities and social locations in defining who gets what and what goes where. To do otherwise—apply identical treatment to unequal contexts without regard to structural barriers and intersectional dynamic—may further deepen the inequalities of exclusion. According to the substantive equality lens, people require different but equitable treatment because they have special difference-based needs, unique experiences that require exemption from the rules, constitutionally entrenched rights, or UN-backed minority and Indigenous peoples' rights (Blackburn 2008; also Mahoney, Thomas, and Payens 2013). Their differences must not only be taken seriously when necessary to ensure inclusiveness; these rights, needs, and entitlements must also be taken into account when formulating policies, making decisions, and allocating valued resources (Sheppard 2010). Consider, for example, the different-but-equal treatment that applies to individuals with disabilities. Modification such as wheelchair ramps, closed-caption TV, and designated parking spots can hardly be thought of as special or preferential. To the contrary, removing disability barriers ensures equality of opportunity by providing reasonable accommodation. Likewise, historically disadvantaged minorities with racially prescribed characteristics will encounter barriers as real and as debilitating as physical impediments. But just as building ramps for the wheelchair-bound create a more level playing field, so too does removing racially discriminatory barriers (which are just as real in their consequences if not in objective reality) reflect a similar logic. In both cases, those with socially defined disabilities require different treatment if only to ensure their right to equality of opportunity.

Each of these perspectives on equality (same, proportional, and substantive) differs in terms of assumptions, objectives and means (Fleras 2005). They also correspond with three equality models: equal (same), equivalent (proportion), and equitable (substantive). Their differences are compared in Table 12.1.

Any debate over equality also hinges on the distinction between equal opportunity (formal equality) and equity of outcomes (substantive equality). Equal opportunity focuses on the rights of individuals to be free from discrimination when competing for the good things in life. It operates on the principle that true equality arises when everyone is treated equally (the same) regardless of gender or race. The focus is on removing discriminatory

Table 12.1: Equality Models: Equal, Equivalent, Equitable

	Equal (Same)	Equivalent (Proportional)	Equitable (Substantive)
Problem	Individual shortcomings	Closed mindsets	Institutional structures
Root cause of inequality	Lacking human capital	"Old white boys network"	Discriminatory barriers
Focus of solution	Improve individual competencies	Rethink the business-as-usual format	Create accommodative institutions
Means toward solution	Market discipline	Institutional adjustment	Government intervention
Definition of equality	Formal equality	Mathematical equality	Substantive equality (context, lived reality)
Nature of equality	Fairness (treat the same)	Fairness (proportional treatment)	Justice (customize treatment—people treated as equals)
Underlying logic	Equal opportunity	Equivalent outcomes	Equity of outcomes
Anticipated outcome	Inclusion	Inclusion	Inclusivity
Status of diversity	Pretend pluralism/ liberal universalism	Pretend pluralism/ liberal universalism	Taking differences seriously and into account/ethnic particularism

barriers to achieve the inclusion goal of fitting people into the existing system regardless of their needs or differences. The principles of a relatively unfettered market would appear to be consistent with an equal opportunity framework. By contrast, an equality-of-outcomes approach concentrates on the rights of individuals for a just and equitable share of society's pie. True equality (equity) arises when contexts and outcomes are taken into account as a basis for divvying up the goods or constructing healthy environments. This perspective privileges the principle of inclusivity by acknowledging how institutions themselves must adjust to accommodate individuals when the situation demands it. It also endorses the principle of state intervention on the grounds that equitable outcomes are unlikely to materialize from freewheeling market competition. In other words, whereas a commitment to equal opportunity openly advocates the concept of competition, free market, and hierarchy as natural and inevitable, an equity perspective is concerned with controlled distribution, government intervention, and equitable outcomes (Sivanandan 2013).

In advancing a more equitable Canada, which version of equality should prevail—formal equality (equal opportunity) or substantive equity (equitable outcomes)? Is one more important than the other, or does one serve as a necessary if insufficient precondition for the other (Fleras 2012)? An equal opportunity paradigm is considered inadequate for overcoming the debilitating effects of systemic discrimination and institutional racism. Preferential treatment is required over and above that available to the general population for equality to take root; after all, the application of equal standards to unequal situations may well have the perverse effect of freezing the status quo. Context and consequences are as important as abstract principles in righting wrongs. Taking context into account may require preferential treatment to achieve equality of outcome. To be sure, outcome-oriented equity is not opposed to the principle of equal opportunities and treatment. On the contrary, a commitment to the principle of equal opportunity/treatment constitutes a necessary first step in overcoming entrenched racism and discrimination. Ultimately, however, such a commitment cannot achieve true equality when

the playing field is tilted, the competition is fixed, the starting blocks are staggered, and the rules are rigged. Only a dual commitment to equity outcomes and equal opportunities can free up the playing field for a progressive and prosperous inclusiveness, as demonstrated below.

1. Social equality entailing a twin commitment: treating everyone the same (equal) as a matter of routine yet taking their differences-based needs into account when necessary. Formal equality is insufficient since treating everyone the same in an unequal context tends to perpetuate the inequalities. To ensure no one is excluded for reasons beyond their control, institutions must reflect both inclusion (fit into existing system by removing discriminatory barriers) and inclusivity (adjust system to ensure a fit).

2. Protection and promotion of individual rights (as set out in the UN Declaration of Human Rights, with its focus on freedoms to and freedoms from). No less important is the recognition of collective rights for those nations or peoples whose group survival is paramount and a precondition for exercising individual rights.

3. Removal of both direct discrimination (predominantly an individual problem of attitudes and behaviour) and structural discrimination that acknowledges how the embeddedness of systemic biases creates adverse effects. That is, seemingly neutral rules when evenly and equally applied will generate differential effects for those whose realities, experiences, and interests diverge from the mainstream (Sheppard 2010). A decision to remove barriers must be balanced with the commitment to introduce positive measures to neutralize the effects of past discrimination.

4. A dual commitment to both market competition (to ensure productivity and creativity) and to government interventions (to keep inequities under control for the sake of social harmony). A spirit of egalitarianism must prevail: competition should be encouraged to foster the brightest and best, yet this excellence must be shared with others to ensure mutual benefits. Alternatively, the fruits of material competition must be tempered by channelling them for the public good in addition to personal self-aggrandizement.

5. Attainment of social equality may entail a trade-off (balancing act) involving the market (its fluidity, creativity, and transformative properties); an activist government (active interventions to protect the weakest members of society by creating a more level playing field); and civil society (active and engaged citizenship to re-establish political engagement) (Giddens 1999). The challenge lies in reinforcing the centrality of individual agency without forsaking the realities of structural exclusions and systemic constraints (Sheppard 2010).

What would a socially equal society look like? For some it is one based on a formally equal model reflecting neo-liberal market principles; others insist on a substantive equity model committed to the principles of equitable outcomes, structural adjustments, and government interventions (see Sivanandan 2013); for still others, the principle of proportional equivalence is a good start so that societal demographics align with institutional representation. Or consider the means towards attainment of an equal society. Does an equal society define what is good, then adjust the needs and differences of the historically disadvantaged accordingly (inclusion)? Or is an equitable society inclined to prioritize the difference-based needs and rights of the excluded in constructing the good society (inclusivity) (Sandercock 2004)? Responses to these questions rekindle the age-old question, What is society for? Is society just an excuse for the rich to get richer, regardless of consequences (Rousseau)? Or is society a community of protection in advancing the public good (Hobbes)? The Spotlight box below on taxation as a proposed solution to the equality challenge demonstrates how what sounds good on paper does not always deliver the good.

Spotlight Taxation towards Equality?

Taxes are the price we pay for a civilized society.
—Oliver Wendell Holmes Jr.

It is often said that the only two certainties in life are death and taxes. No one disputes the inevitability of the former; the latter is subject to negotiation. Debates over taxes and taxation at both individual and corporate levels have been catapulted to the forefront of social inequality issues. For some, taxes hold a partial solution to the inequality problem (Banting and Myles 2013; Piketty 2014; Heisz and Murphy 2015); for others, tax evasion and tax havens that shelter trillions of dollars are a major source of inequality (Crooks 2014); for still others, the challenge lies in getting the rich and companies to pay a fair share (Doctors for Fair Taxation 2012). For all Canadians, taxation is a reality (Milke 2013): the average Canadian household must work till June 10 (Tax Freedom Day) each year to pay off their total tax bill of $45,167 or 42.9 per cent of their annual earnings (Lamman and Palacios 2016). The ratio between taxes and household income has evolved over the years. In 2013, the average family earned $77,400 and paid $32,400 in taxes, or 41.8 per cent, whereas food, shelter, and clothing consumed 36.1 per cent. In 1961, taxes siphoned off 33.5 per cent of a household's income, while 56.5 per cent was spent on food, shelter, and clothing (Hough 2014).

Canada has a reputation as a high tax country that many thought once deterred the wealthy and businesses from setting up shop. But Canada has quietly emerged as a go-to tax destination, not only for the super-rich looking to evade hefty taxation but also for opportunistic corporations (including the hefty $12.5 billion takeover in 2014 of Tim Hortons by Burger King) and opportunistic investors, including nearly 12,000 admissions under the Immigrant Investor Program, up from just under 5,000 a decade ago (Kirby 2011). The combined federal/provincial top tax rate is 46.4 per cent in Ontario (39 per cent in Alberta, the same as the average federal/state level in the United States) (Kirby 2011). In 1948, the top marginal income tax rate of 80 per cent applied

continued

to incomes over $2.37 million in today's dollars (Jones 2012). Currently, the top federal tax bracket of 29 per cent kicks in at $136,275 (compared to $373,650 in the United States) and applies to everyone, including Gerry Schwartz, CEO of Onyx who earned $88 million in 2014 (Mackenzie 2015; Goar 2015).

The corporate income tax rate has also declined significantly in recent years. The current (2012) federal corporate tax rate of 15 per cent has dropped from 21 per cent in 2008. According to the department of finance, this reduction provides Canadian corporations with the lowest tax rate for new business investment and the lowest statutory tax rate of all G7 countries. Provincial and territorial income tax rates vary as well, ranging from a low of 4 per cent up to 16 per cent (Business Tax Canada 2012). Canadian corporations argue that money saved from tax cuts will be invested in machinery, equipment, and jobs. Statistics Canada analysis questions this claim, pointing out that businesses are hoarding cash (including $83 billion to their reserves since 2008) instead of investing in jobs or technology (Symes 2012; Yalnizyan 2012). The consequences of a diminished tax base make it difficult for cash-strapped governments to fund new or existing social programs.

To be sure, the rich are paying the bulk of income taxes (see also Johnson 2013). The top 1 per cent of earners in Canada paid 20.8 per cent of the total federal, provincial, and territorial income taxes in 2011, albeit down from 23.3 per cent five years earlier (Grant 2013). Moreover there are those who argue the rich are also paying their way. According to William Watson (2011), in 2009, the top 20 per cent of income earners paid 62.1 per cent of all income taxes, up 57.8 per cent in 2000. But despite claims of Canada's progressive taxation system, not all is fair. A study by the Canadian Centre for Policy Alternatives (Lee, Ivanova, and Klein 2011; also Ivanova 2014) concluded that when all taxes are included (sales, excise, property, income), those Canadians with earnings less than $13,500 per year paid 30.7 per cent of their income in taxes, whereas those who earned $300,000 paid a slightly smaller burden of 30.5 per cent (McQuaig 2011b). In that these taxes charge both rich and poor at the same rate, they disproportionately affect the income of poorer families (hence the expression *regressive tax*). In other words, the less well-off are increasingly shouldering a greater burden of taxes (Lee, Ivanova, and Klein 2011), although most Canadians believe everyone should pay their fair share (i.e., the higher one's income, the higher the tax rate should be).

The issue is not whether the rich are paying a larger proportion of total tax in Canada (Cross 2014). Rather, the debate hinges on whether they are paying their *fair* share of taxes—a concern raised by one of the world's richest men, Warren Buffet, in an article entitled "Stop Coddling the Super Rich," (*New York Times*, Op-Ed., 15 August 2011)[1].

Our leaders have asked for "shared sacrifice." But when they did the asking, they spared me. I checked with my mega-rich friends to learn what pain they were expecting. They, too, were left untouched. . . .

. . . [W]hile most Americans struggle to make ends meet, we mega-rich continue to get extraordinary tax breaks. Some of us are investment managers who earn billions from our daily labours, but are allowed to classify our income as "carried interest," thereby getting a bargain 15% tax rate. Others own stock index futures for 10 minutes and have 60% of their gains taxed at 15%, as if they'd have been long-term investors. . . .

. . . Last year my federal tax bill—the income tax I paid, as well as payroll taxes paid by me and on my behalf—was $ 6,938,744. That sounds like a lot of money. But what I paid was only 17.4 % of my taxable income—and that's actually a lower percentage than was paid by any of the other 20 people in our office. Their tax burden ranged from 33% to 41% and averaged 36%. . .

[In a 2007 interview on NBC, [Buffet] offered to bet $1 million with any of his billionaire peers that they were paying on average lower tax rates than their secretaries. No one took up the challenge (Gordon 2011)].

. . . The mega-rich pay income taxes at a rate of 15% on most of their earnings but pay practically nothing in payroll taxes.

Why should Canadians be concerned? Adding new tax brackets for incomes between $250,000 to $750,000 and another for those over $750,000 could generate an additional $12 billion in new tax revenue in just three years—enough for a national child care program or national pharmacare program (Gordon 2011). But creating a more progressive tax system is not without potential drawbacks: profitable firms may threaten factory closures, outsource production to cheaper locales, or insource temporary foreign workers to offset added costs of doing business in Canada (McQuaig 2012). Another study by Peter Diamond and Emmanuel Saez (2011) concluded that an optimal top marginal tax rate of 70 per cent is plausible. Such a percentage would maximize revenue intake without reducing work incentives or increasing tax evasion. To conclude, taxation reform is hardly the magic bullet to solve Canada's inequality problem. Some believe that initiatives to spur economic growth and the discipline of the market should take precedence over taxes and transfers (Cross 2015). Still, hiking the rates for the extremely rich could go a long way in forging a more equitable Canada.

Rehabilitating the Free Market: Towards Responsible Capitalism

Capitalism may be the worst economic system except for any of the others.
　　—Adrian Monck, Statement at the 42nd World Economic Forum Annual Meeting, 2012

US Steel is in business to make profits, not to make steel.
　　—Former CEO of US Steel, cited in McNally 2012:129

This culture of winning means that few people win, and many lose . . . a terrible rift is created between the rich and poor, between the so-called normal and so-called abnormal, between the rich and poor . . . the winners must look after, in every way and in particular financially, all the losers.
　　—Jean Vanier, in a prepared statement upon being awarded the 2015 Templeton Prize in recognition of his advocacy work cited in *The Globe and Mail*, 18 March 2015

More than 165 years after Marx's scathing critique in the Communist Manifesto (1848), **capitalism** is back in the news (Piketty 2014). Of particular salience is Marx's vision of capitalism as a historically specific mode of economy that is ever expanding, self-transforming, inherently exploitative and alienating, and prone to cyclical crises (Hobsbawn 2011). Its controversial status never ceases to amaze or infuriate: for some, capitalism symbolizes a pathway to prosperity through wealth creation and "creative destruction"; for others, it is an exploitative tool that privileges profits over people and the planet (Coulthard 2014). For yet others it is a workable system in need of rehabilitation to make it more accountable to various stakeholders. Not unexpectedly, the spectre of legitimacy is haunting capitalism. How else to frame a system that condones the staggering excesses of a financial elite whose unbridled greed and recklessness brought the global economy to a near collapse (McChesney 2014)? The catastrophic economic collapse in 2008 reflected a market crisis attributed in part to the shift in wealth creation from production to financial speculation (Foster and Magdoff 2009). Response to the crisis was no less revealing. Those very elites who had long agitated for less government now clamoured for taxpayer assistance via bailouts (Schweickart 2011). Bailed-out corporations quickly racked up record profits, and bank officials and financial managers hoarded multimillion dollar bonuses and income tax bonanzas. For millions, however, the recession is anything but over (Hedges and Sacco 2012).

Clearly something is out of whack (Wolff 2012): corporate profits and overpaid executives coexist alongside anemic growth, a jobless economy/recovery, imposed austerity on those who can least afford it, and stubbornly high unemployment (Plender 2012). References to capitalism no longer resonate with competitiveness, freedom, meritocracy, trust in markets, and faith in mobility. More often, it's about deepening depressions, rampant consumerism, systemic economic inequalities, and environmental plunder (Wolff 2013). Or in the words of Pope Francis, capitalism represents a "a subtle dictatorship" that "condemns and enslaves women and men" and whose excesses resemble the "dung of the devil" (cited in Yardley and Applebaum 2015). Capitalism appears to have discarded any commitment to those implicit social contracts that secured its legitimacy in the post-Depression era—namely, the continuation of a market economy in exchange for a welfare state, with its provision of employment, availability of social services, security in disability and old age, and universal education (Smith 2012). The accumulation of wealth and power under crony capitalism (convergence of business elites with political interests) portends the making of an economic and environmental disaster (Parks 2011; Zingales 2012; Samli 2008). Not surprisingly, a 2012 Bloomberg Global Poll of Business Leaders found that 70 per cent believe capitalism is in trouble because of growing income and wealth disparities (the top 1 per cent in the United States monopolize about 22 per cent of all annual income; in Canada the figure is closer to 11 per cent); persistently high levels of un/under/employment; shift in power from democratic governances to multinational corporations (over half of the world's largest 100 economies are companies); unsustainable economic growth on a finite planet; and excessive reliance on GDP to measure economic growth at the expense of income distribution and resource depletion (Warren 2013; Canadian Index of Wellbeing 2012). These trends and realities raise uncomfortable questions:

1. How sustainable is "vulture" capitalism, whose mantra of perpetual growth devours whatever stands in the way of profit, progress, and technological advancement (Jackson 2009; Lasn 2012; McMurtry 2013)?

2. Is capitalism that fetishizes profit doomed to self-destruct since an unrestrained market erodes those social values (from co-operation to collective goods) critical to society and planetary survival (Ponniah 2012; Hertz 2012)?

3. What are the costs and consequences of a two-track capitalist economy, a fast one for the über rich but a stalled one for everyone else (TD Report 2014; Langsley 2011)?

4. How much longer can consumers of the global north continue to enjoy a standard of living based on unsustainable patterns of exploitation and environment despoliation (Suzuki and Hanington 2012)? What will happen when citizens in the global south demand a comparable right to consume?

5. Can capitalism be transformed into something more inclusive, humane, and egalitarian instead of a fundamentally exploitative and an inhumane force that amorally pursues perpetual economic expansion and shareholder return, regardless of human suffering and environmental costs (Klein 2014; Winlow and Hall 2013; Leech 2012)?

6. Is there an inherent contradiction in the concept of kinder capitalism (or "creative capitalism" in the words of Bill Gates [2008]) that balances the viability of an advanced industrial economy with the ideals of a more equitable society (Yunus 2008; Lebowitz 2008; Schweickart 2011)?

7. Can a more responsible capitalism be invented that serves society and prosperity for all the people rather than worshipping on the altar of short term profit for the few (Dullien, Herr, and Kellerman 2011; Hamilton 2013; McChesney 2014)?

Capitalism is differently defined and variously expressed. Consider the descriptive modifiers attached to capitalism: Gucci capitalism (Hertz 2012), free market/neo-liberal capitalism, aristocratic capitalism, finance capitalism, corporate capitalism, crony capitalism, state capitalism, and social democratic capitalism, among others. In general, capitalism as an economic system trends toward these ideal-typical attributes: private ownership of the means of production; production of goods and services for exchange on the market, reflecting prices based on supply and demand; the class-based accumulation of capital; competitive markets and openness to new commercial ideas; wage labour; utility and profit maximization for reinvestment to generate yet more capital; and a corresponding set of institutions and ideologies to support the principles of a free market enterprise (Backhouse and Bateman 2009; Phelps 2006). A more prescriptive (or evaluative) set of definitions draws attention to systemic exploitation and structural violence inherent in freewheeling capitalism (Mainwaring 2011:10; McChesney 2014):

1. A system in which a small elite amass most of the wealth, which is used to dominate the economic and political sectors;
2. A system prone to boom and bust cycles whose collateral damage is extensive (however nasty in the short run, apologists argue, these periodic crises should be seen as market corrections within a general business cycle of free market binges and neo-liberal purges);
3. A system that promotes the worst in human nature such as greed and selfishness;
4. A system that combines impulsive investors and single-minded dedication to profits, taking a toll on everything from global markets to working families;
5. A system obsessed with short-term profits at the expense of people and the environment. The current neo-liberal style of capitalism believes governments should butt out of the economy except to provide security, safeguard people's lives and property, uphold the right of capital to do as it pleases, and maintain law and order.

As Chapter 3 made clear, class differences in terms of power, privilege, and income/wealth are spinning out of control. Neither capitalism nor the free market are entirely responsible for the outlandish pay premiums of the über-wealthy. The problem reflects the entrenchment of aristocratic (crony) capitalism at the expense of a democratic vision of capitalism (a system of responsible capitalism that ensures benefits for everyone rather than just shareholders, hedge fund managers, and CEOs). Capitalism's aristocratic form of corporate plutocracy designs corporations along the lines of a market-based feudal estate, including:

1. Paying stockholders as much as possible while offering only the minimum to employees;
2. Endorsing stockholders' claim to a disproportionate amount of wealth despite the fact they, like their predecessors, do little to earn the bulk of the proceeds;
3. Defining the corporation as private property (like a feudal estate) that can be bought and sold by the propertied class;
4. Establishing a governance structure that restricts power and privileges only to the wealthy elite—to the exclusion of workers and the community; and
5. Insisting that corporations are autonomous within a self-regulating free market, much as feudal barons asserted a version of sovereignty largely independent of the Crown.

An obsession with maximizing shareholder and stock values has hijacked the business of capitalism, in the process creating distortions and upheavals by privileging short-term gains over long-term sustainability (Chang 2010; Nocera 2012). As Kelly (2002) concludes, few would tolerate these elitist corporate principles if applied to the political sector of a modern democratic society. Yet these principles are accepted when applied to the economy, as if they somehow reflect the workings of the free market as natural law (hence, the expression, "the divine right of capital").

What is the possibility of constructing a new economic order beyond the iron grip of a neo-liberal syndrome that degrades human well-being, uproots social justice, undermines society, and destroys the planet (Lasn 2012; Jackson 2009; Coulthard 2014; see Chang 2010 for insightful debunking of capitalism in general)? Can capitalism be rehabilitated, given its strength as a highly adaptable economic system with a proven track record of cleverly mutating when confronted by major crises or public resentment (Winlow and Hall 2013)? Occupy Movements may have excelled at protesting what is wrong (a global and neo-liberal capitalistic system and the governments of the 1 per cent that prop it up); yet, they have faltered in establishing a workable alternative (Smith 2013). Proposed alternatives require an appropriate reading of the problem. Public outrage must go beyond the excess in CEO gains and focus on the seemingly

Spotlight Capitalism and Social Inequality: Doing What Comes Naturally

Every once in a while a book comes out that proves both profound and popular. In capturing the zeitgeist of the times, Thomas Piketty's *Capital in the Twenty-first Century* (Belknap Press 2014) is one of these book, a 700-page tome on economics that many compare to Darwin's *Origin of Species* or Rachel Carson's *Silent Spring* as "game changers" (Corcoran 2014). Already catapulted to the top of best seller lists around the world, the English translation of this French book provides a critique of capitalism that critics lavish with praise, comparable in stature and importance to Marx's magisterial work, *Das Kapital*. Piketty traces the economic history of Europe and North America over the past two centuries, and arrives at these Marxian conclusions:

1. Massive inequalities are not an aberration of free-market capitalism but rather an inevitable and intrinsic by-product of a system that enriches the rich and disempowers the poor. Capitalism is, by nature, prone to the plutocracy of the 0.01 per cent. The relative equality that characterized the post–Second World War era,

until about the mid-1970s, included rising wages, extensive social programs, and a robust middle class. This period also represented an exception from the longer sweep of history—one brought about by and in reaction to the Depression and the two world wars and their aftermath—that incorporated an insurgent labour movement, nationalization of industries, Keynesian-style government intervention and social welfare networks, and appropriation of property in decolonizing countries. Displacing these halcyon days is a new gilded era that is proving every bit as unequal and polarizing as the first gilded age of robber barons prior to World War I, one in which private wealth dwarfed national income, largely because it was concentrated in a few rich families who lorded over a relatively rigid class structure.

2. The global economy is reverting to a natural state of slow growth, resulting in widening disparities between the super-rich and the rest. Significant patterns of income inequality emerge when wealth (the returns on capital) on average exceed economic growth (generally

sacrosanct principle of maximizing shareholder gains to the exclusion of other concerns (Pupo and Thomas 2009). The challenge lies in constructing a scenario in which corporate boards of directors are not simply beholden to shareholder profits. They must also be accountable to all stakeholders, including those who work there and to the community that houses the corporation. But if transformative change is to materialize, certain self-serving myths must be demolished (Nocera 2012; also Chang 2010). The divine right of aristocratic capital is neither more natural and inevitable nor more divinely sanctioned than any other human creation. It is a socially constructed convention whose constructedness is concealed and conveyed as natural and normal so as to convey the illusion

of inevitability—a polite fiction to gloss over inconvenient truths.

Perhaps it's not capitalism per se that is the inequality problem. The culprit may be a freewheeling (neo-liberal) market that dominates government regulation and public interest (Change 2010; Hertz 2012). The European social market model of capitalism once came closer than most in balancing individual initiative and economic growth with public good and national interests (or did so until recently [Unger 2013; Hill 2010]). Europe's social democratic model was predicated on the assumption that an unfettered market based on private ownership of property neither results in optimal outcomes nor generates just distribution of valued resources (Curtice 2012). Yes, it may be important people's incomes). As Piketty puts it, virtually all income for the 0.01 per cent is derived from capital (dividends, investment) or financial speculation (from derivatives to corporate takeovers (also Bello 2013).

3. The commanding heights of the economy under patrimonial capitalism are largely controlled by family dynasties and the accidents of birth ("the lucky sperm club"). Piketty's conclusions challenge libertarian (free-market or neo-liberal) notions that frame inequality as desirable and unavoidable because people get rewarded for their brains and brawn. Rather, great disparities in income and wealth are increasingly entrenched and transferred across generations. Furthermore, the fruits of economic progress rarely trickle downwards to all persons. For Piketty then, growing inequality through accumulation is neither an historical accident nor incidental to the logic of capitalism—especially under the current neo-liberal format—but rather intrinsic to its operating logic.

4. Rule by the rich can only be disrupted by global calamities (including wars) or government intervention such as the introduction of progressive taxes on a global scale (i.e., a global tax in wealth to be applied everywhere to make it effective). If governments do not act soon to curb accelerating inequalities through taxation, he warns, democracy is deeply threatened.

5. Capitalism should not be discarded and replaced with socialism. In this sense, Piketty disagrees with Marx who believed the concentrated accumulation of the means of production in fewer hands under capitalism would lead to a crisis of profitability and usher in a working class socialist revolution (Robinson and Barrera 2012; Jackson 2014b). Private property, financial rewards, and the market are critical in promoting risk-taking and creativity as well as promoting innovation, entrepreneurship, and growth. They are also crucial in enhancing personal freedom, equal opportunity, and a robust democracy. Nor is there any problem with inequality under a capitalist system as long as it embraces the common interests—that is, it incorporates a moral foundation that spurs individual initiative, generates wealth that is shared by way of progressive tax measures, and promotes democratic values of justice, freedom, and fairness. Proposed instead is a responsible capitalism that assigns priority to people and the planet alongside that of profit.

to stimulate the economy since capitalism drives the engine of growth (Rifkin 2004). Yet the combination of robust trade unions, progressive political parties, and a strong civil society provides a buffer to ensure fair distribution, social balance, and fair partnership. State intervention and a state redistributive policy are key in advancing reasonably just outcomes according to the following principles: tax and transfers from rich to poorer members of society to ensure approximate equality in opportunities and benefits; provision of health and education services as a right; a guaranteed annual income that provides a living wage; and housing of acceptable quality to all members of society (Barry 2005). In that a European social market model represents more socially responsible capitalism, there is much to like about it. Nevertheless, the balance needs to be rethought, since what critics see as a cradle-to-grave welfare state appears to be fraying at the edges, as demonstrated by the ongoing Euro-crisis (Goldberg 2012).

Is it possible to construct a hybrid model that blends the best features of capitalism (good at production but not at distribution [*The Economist*, 1 June 2013; Myles 2007]) with those of socialism (better suited to creating solidarity, equality, and protection [Giddens 1998])? "Unfettered" capitalism excels at innovation and creativity, but it stumbles in the equitable distribution of goods against the backdrop of rampant competition, greed and selfishness, and an amorality that abandons people during periodic economic crises. Socialism as a system in which workers own and control the means of production sounds good in theory, yet it has never been put into practice. (With their command economies, intrusive bureaucracies and economic/political structures geared toward the state of permanent war, regimes in China, Russia, and North Korea are grossly distorted versions of socialism, best labelled as "state capitalism" [Hobsbawn 2011]). Socialism's strength resides in its solidarity and collective responsibility, albeit perhaps at the expense of personal initiative (Rifkin 2004). Both capitalism and socialism (even in its distorted form) possess strengths and weaknesses that can be reinforced or offset by way of creative synthesis. Jeremy Rifkin (2005) captures the complexity of constructing a hybridic model that balances personal accountability/individual self-interest with social solidarity/collective responsibility when he writes "You can't be so dependent on the state that you no longer have any initiative. And you can't be so abandoned by society that you're all on your own and there's no helping each other."

The challenge is clearly before us: to rehabilitate capitalism by making it accountable to and responsible for the interests of workers, local communities, society, human values, and planet earth (Meltzer 2010; Zingales 2012; Monck 2012; also Chang 2010; Breznitz and Zysman 2013; Engler 2014). A responsible capitalism does things differently to better serve society, the community, workers, and the environment. Transforming the rules of a business-as-usual model will pivot around initiatives that ensure economic rights for employers (a say in governance, voting for boards of directors, and a claim to the wealth they create) and the community in which they reside; redistribute wealth from shareholders to those who create it; insist on corporate responsibility to the public good, including democratic governance; reframe corporations as a human community rather than a private contract or private property; and acknowledge responsibility to the long-term survival and sustainability of the planet. The challenge also commits to the principle of keeping capitalism's core strengths intact while minimizing its inherently destructive tendencies (Dullien, Herr, and Kellerman 2011; Barry 2005; Zingales 2012). Put bluntly, capitalism and corporations must view

themselves as integral to the societies in which they operate, with corresponding responsibility for worker welfare, community well-being, national interests, and the sustainability of the environment (Workman 2011). This triple-line commitment to profits, people, and the planet promotes a broader local-national-international sustainability matrix than does adherence to the financial crisis-inducing pursuit of short-term profits (Tsaparis 2013; Freeland 2013). Several themes prevail:

1. First and foremost, responsible capitalism balances a commitment to profits with global social transformation, prosperity for the greater good, and sustainable development (Mainwaring 2011). In addition to providing for essential needs and constructing the building blocks for individual and community well-being, the centrality of human development is critical for advancing the creative potential of each person and the full exercise of their personality and contribution to society (Report 2014a; Lebowitz 2008).

2. Responsible capitalism encourages people to create and produce a *material* basis for wealth creation rather than financial transactions that benefit the speculators but do little for society (Bello 2013). The benefits of this creativity and productivity must contribute to social utility rather than promote private gain exclusively—that is, ensure that the benefits of capitalism are broadly distributed.

3. It is important to use market forces to address the needs of the most vulnerable, for example, by rewarding companies that produce goods and services for the poor (Gates 2008; Yunus 2008).

4. A shift in focus toward environmentally sustainable practices represents a major plank of responsible capitalism. Consumerism as a lifestyle must be challenged, in part by reducing reliance on fossil fuels, taking seriously the fragility of the planet, and reorienting economies from production for export to production for local market.

5. Some form of income distribution is inevitable, including progressive taxation (from the rich paying a fair share of taxes to closing tax havens

to implementing a financial transaction tax); greater worker control of the means of production; subjecting the private sector to civil society monitoring (including improving laws and regulations); and more bottom-up management of public affairs and decision-making in the workplace and community (Lebowitz 2008), thus reflecting the principle of "parity of participation" in which people interact with each other as equals (Fraser and Honneth 2003).

6. Government intervention is indispensable in avoiding the major contradiction of our times: increased production with declining household incomes and consumer inability to purchase products plus the continued government obsession with deficit reduction and austerity measures (McKenna 2014; Curtice 2012). National economies require sector-specific intervention that plays to their strengths and unique circumstances—in Canada, these include a vast geography with a relatively small population base within the orbit of the world's largest economy (Ciuriak and Curtis 2013).

However progressive the call for inclusive, sustainable, and responsible capitalism, time will tell if sufficient people-power can be mustered to bring about change that is workable, necessary, fair, and just (see Mainwaring 2011). Pockets of moral outrage against injustices exist to be sure, including social movements ranging from the Arab Spring revolutions, the Occupy Wall Street movement, the protracted strike of Quebec students in the spring of 2012 against planned tuition increases by the provincial government, and the Idle No More movement, which attracted national and international attention. And yet there is a sense of massive indifference to the inequities and injustices that persist, from overpaid athletes and high-flying CEOs, to abysmal living conditions in Attawapiskat and the scandal of missing and murdered aboriginal women across Canada.

A sense of perspective is critical in getting people involved. No one is saying that the struggle for justice has to change the entire world for the better. Nonetheless, everybody possesses the capacity to change their little corner of the world if only by following the Gandhian principle of being the change they want to see in the world (for example, if you believe consumerism leads to inequality issues, stop unnecessary buying). Perhaps the challenge lies in changing people's mindsets regarding the value and worth of accumulation, greed, and conspicuous consumption. Just as wearing fur, drinking and driving, smoking in public, and perhaps even carnivore diets have become socially unacceptable, so too would harmful patterns of social inequality and structural exclusion endure a similar taboo. Yes, the challenge is daunting to say the least, but as many have said (Davey 2012:9), unless our reach outstretches our grasp, what is the point in being human. Clearly then, moves toward more responsible capitalism are not about people in power, but about the power in people to challenge and resist. Even a small number of individuals who mobilize, march, and protest have the potency to effect transformative change to avert the environmental crisis, the equity crisis, and the crisis of global distribution. The words of Margaret Mead, the legendary American anthropologist, strike a cautiously optimistic yet empowering note: "Never underestimate the power of a small group of committed people to change the world. In fact, it is the only thing that ever has."

Summary

1. Just as social inequality matters, so too does social equality in enhancing the probability of making positive things happen in the lives and life chances of Canadians.

2. The concept of social inequality can be deconstructed with respect to different levels of meaning—namely, as equal, proportional, or equitable (analyzing and assessing).

3. A commitment to social equality is an ideal to strive for, rather than an attainable or desired goal.

4. The concept of social equality is highly contested and complex in terms of what it is, whether or not it is attainable, and how to get there.

5. Two major models of equality can be posed—namely, equal (formal) versus equitable (substantive).

6. Neo-liberal capitalism is seemingly incompatible with the attainment of social equality since social inequality is intrinsic (rather than collateral damage) in free-wheeling global/corporate capitalism geared that is towards the rational and ruthless pursuit of profit.

7. Rehabilitated capitalism may point to a more egalitarian society by balancing a commitment to people and the planet with that of profits.

Review Questions

1. What are some of the conceptual difficulties associated with defining and analyzing social equality?

2. Compare the three models of equality discussed in this chapter in terms of how each defines the problem of inequality and their corresponding solutions.

3. It has been said that capitalism is the worst economic system—except for all the others. Discuss the strengths and weaknesses of contemporary capitalism in terms of advancing equality or reinforcing inequality.

4. How does the concept of "responsible capitalism" represent a more viable solution to the inequality problem than neo-liberal capitalism?

5. What might a society look like that was redesigned with people and the planet at the forefront?

Note

13 Summary and Conclusion: Comforting Fictions, Inconvenient Truths

Sociology is becoming a field dominated by those who cast a critical eye on social inequality.
—Michael Kimmel. 2008. From pages 62–64.

Social inequality has evolved into one of the defining issues of our times (Piketty 2014; Oxfam 2015). The topic is less likely than ever to be defaulted into the too-hard or too-embarrassing basket, to be conveniently ignored as was once the case. Its existence and accompanying social costs are no longer tolerated as a regrettable—if necessary—price to pay for living in a consumer world of material abundance. Nor should the now massive attention to its persistence and pervasiveness be blithely dismissed as little more than an intellectual fad or a cause *du jour*. To the contrary: just as no one should underestimate the power of an idea whose time has come, so too would it be foolhardy to underestimate how the concept of social inequality has infiltrated into people's collective conscience as a spur to social activism. The data bear this out: when EKOS Politics (2013c) asked 4,568 respondents to nominate Canada's greatest achievement over the past 20 years, the creation of an equal society topped the list at 33 per cent of the responses, followed by a diverse society at 23 per cent and a prosperous Canada at 22 per cent. As additional evidence, both social and mainstream media (from newspapers to television) devote reams of space to criticizing inequality gaps, while a handful of documentaries (for example, Robert Reich in *Inequality for All*) painstakingly analyze how, why, and where we went wrong in shifting from a seemingly more equitable *then* into a more unequal *now*.

Much of the impetus for inequality's high-profile status is self-imposed. There is a mounting sense of fury and dismay as well as an air of despair and helplessness over the ravages of the great recession of 2008. The consciousness-raising work of the 2011 Occupy Movement exposed people's vulnerability to a rigged political system and a deeply flawed economic model. A disquieting dynamic has taken root in Canada as well in reaction to the interplay of globalization and global capitalism with job-shedding technologies and the imposition of austerity agendas (TD Economics 2014). Public attention is growing over how gaping patterns of social inequality have negatively impacted individual lives and life chances, fraying society's social fabric—from loss of good-paying factory jobs and a squeezed middle class to the ebbing of social mobility and the chipping away at the great equalizers of pensions, employment insurance, social assistance transfers, and a progressive tax system (Banting and Tuohy 2013). The result is a greater awareness of a fundamental truism at the heart of this book: social inequality matters because it increases the probability of making something happen—namely, the creation and reinforcement of social exclusions that inflict harm or hardship on those on the unlucky side of the inequality divide. For individuals, the consequences of exclusions related to poverty, racism, sexism, and classism are multiple, overlapping, and chronic—including powerlessness, voicelessness, vulnerability, diminished life chances, and an inability to participate as valued, respected, and contributing members of society. The inequality of exclusions at a societal level poses an additional threat to social cohesion by fomenting anti-social behaviour (Saloojee 2003).

This book draws its inspiration from situating the politics of social inequality into a social-problem framework that speaks to the inequalities of exclusion in a Canada that professes to do better. *Inequality Matters* is predicated on the assumption that Canada remains a foundationally unequal society in terms of how power, privilege, and property (wealth and income) are distributed at individual, institutional, and national levels. The persistence and pervasiveness of social inequality render critically important the analysis and assessment of how these inequalities of exclusion are created, expressed, and sustained as well as how they are challenged and transformed by government policies, institutional reform, ideological shifts, and minority resistance. A lot of ground has been covered addressing the dynamics and domain of social inequality with respect to what it is; why it's happening; how, where, and when it's expressed; what its impact and effects are; and what can be done in shrinking it to manageable proportions. In speaking truth to power, the book demonstrates how any honest appraisal of social inequality is marred by a slew of comforting fictions (myths) that paper over inconvenient truths (reality). Canadians like to see themselves as a post-racial and pro-multicultural society, with a corresponding commitment to the colour-blind principles of democracy, equality and inclusiveness, meritocracy, universal rights, and guaranteed freedoms. To some extent these socially conceived fabrications are valid, insofar as they reflect what many Canadians aspire to. They are also true in the sense that many of these polite fictions buttress Canada's lofty international reputation (Reputation Institute 2015).

But these comforting (polite) fictions paper over painful facts that shatter a smug and sanctimonious belief in Canada as a caring, kind, and just society. They politely conceal those awkward paradoxes of a "leaner" and "meaner" Canada that is democratic on paper only; constitutes a site of growing inequality and exclusion; endorses a multiculturalism that creates the illusion of inclusion; tolerates prejudices and racisms beneath a veneer of political correctness; and appears willing to suspend rights and freedoms when in its best interest to do so. Those in the vanguard of promoting an equitable Canada are generally thought of as intelligent and

reasonable, although the mask often slips to reveal a mean streak of narrow-mindedness and self-interest (Hussain 2013). For example, Canadians believe they live in a democratic society, thanks to the power of voting and Parliamentary representation. But with powers increasingly concentrated in the Prime Minister's Office and in unelected staff members, Canada more clearly resembles a "dictatorship punctuated by elections" (Elizabeth May of the Green Party, cited in Delacourt 2014). Inconvenient truths also smear Canada's international standing. At the global level, Canada seems to have abandoned its "soft" power reputation for bridging factional divides. What exists instead, argues former prime minister Joe Clark (2013), is a "lecture and leave" approach that angers and alienates both friends and adversaries. Many are also perplexed by Canada's rogue-state status in refusing to curb its share of carbon emissions.

The tensions between fiction and fact generate a reality gap that informs the content and argument of *Inequality Matters*. If nothing else, this book has repeatedly demonstrated Canadians' ambivalence about the status and worth of inequality, with often conflicting beliefs about how income and wealth should be distributed (see also McNamee 2014). To one side, Canadians appear to be genuinely concerned about the inequalities of exclusions that damage people's lives; to the other side, Canadians also endorse the idea that individuals are largely responsible for the predicaments they find themselves in, although there is continuing support for government intervention in smoothing out socio-economic injustices for the deserving poor. Not surprisingly, *Inequality Matters* contends that inequalities of exclusion persist and proliferate in a bountiful Canada precisely because of the power of polite fictions to mask uncomfortable truths and inconvenient realities. Table 13.1 provides a brief overview of the comforting fictions that gloss over the inconvenient facts at odds with Canada's projected image.

Clearly then, there is a mismatch between the ideals implicit in comforting fictions versus the harsh realities conveyed by troubling—even painful—truths. What Canada and Canadians aspire to on the strength of national myths is not necessarily reflected in everyday realities. Admittedly, it is easy

Table 13.1 Unmasking Canada: Comforting Fictions versus Inconvenient Truths

Comforting Fictions	Inconvenient Truths
Canada is the best country in the world in which to live. As proof, The Economist Intelligence Unit (2014) looked at 140 cities around the world in terms of their livability (from health care to infrastructure) and placed three Canadian cities in the top five: Vancouver (3), Toronto (4), and Calgary (tied for 5).	The much touted Human Development Index no longer ranks Canada as the world's best country to live in. Canada's ranking now hovers closer to 10, in contrast to its position at 1 for most of the 1990s. If only Aboriginal peoples are included in the current listings, Canada's position plunges into the 70–80 range. Canada is positioned at or near the bottom of the scale among OECD countries on certain measures of social inequality, from early childhood education provisions to child poverty to gender empowerment.
Canada is a relatively equal society without the extremes that polarize the United States.	Canada not only exhibits extremes of inequality related to income, wealth, power, and privilege. Evidence also suggests Canada's inequality gaps are expanding at a faster pace than those in the United States.
Canada is a classless society, with the vast majority of Canadians bunched in a vague middle.	Regardless of what people think, social classes exist in Canada. Canadians are classed in two ways: first, in terms of their relationship as owners or workers to the means of production; second as categories of people sharing similar family backgrounds and socioeconomic statuses with respect to power, privilege, and wealth. And even if classes are not real in the sense of class consciousness as naturally occurring phenomena, people act *as if* they were real, with corresponding consequences.
To the extent poverty and homelessness exist in Canada, they are the result of poor choices by morally deficient individuals who are responsible for their own predicaments and must act accordingly to solve and improve.	In some cases, poverty and homelessness reflect the cascading effects of poor individual choices. In many instances, poverty and homelessness are best attributed to structural and systemic factors, including neo-liberal ideologies that put profit before people; workplace readjustment programs related to technology and automation that toss people out of work; globalization as a system of wealth creation that profits from the principle of off-shoring, downsizing, and outsourcing; lack of access to affordable housing, livable wages, and accessible daycare; and the legacy of colonialism and genocide and its impact on Aboriginal peoples. A sense of perspective is helpful. Yes, those in poverty must bear some responsibility for their actions and choices; yet these actions and choices occur in a broader social, political, and economic context often beyond their control. Blaming individuals for being poor not only draws attention away from the rich and powerful but also undermines efforts to challenge the social determinants of poverty (Dorling 2012; Warwick-Booth 2013).

continued

Canada is a tolerant and open society whose commitment to a muscular multiculturalism program promotes an inclusive society that respects differences and fosters inclusion.	Canada's commitment to multiculturalism is often skin deep and aspirational, inasmuch as good intentions related to tolerance and openness are not always implemented and enforced. Similarly a multicultural commitment to institutional inclusiveness through removal of discriminatory and prejudicial barriers does not always translate into practices or reality. Not surprisingly, official multiculturalism is often criticized as an empty gesture ("the illusion of inclusion") that does little to improve the the socio-economic status of racialized minorities and newcomers to Canada but instead quietly papers over the prevalence of persistent problems of racism and discrimination.
Canada commits to the principles of a colour-blind and post-racial society, with the result that neither race nor ethnicity is a factor in pre-determining people's lives and life chances. Instead Canada is a meritocratic society whose commitment to the principle of a level playing field ensures people are judged and rewarded on the basis of skills, credentials, and hard work.	Canada is neither a colour-blind society nor a race neutral (post-racial) society. Nor is Canada the site of a level playing field where the principle of meritocracy prevails. Canadian society is raced, gendered, and classed in terms of founding assumptions, fundamental principles, and foundational structures. The implications are deeply sociological. Racialized minorities, newcomers to Canada, and Aboriginal peoples may possess formal equality rights, but they must exercise these rights and achieve success in a socially constructed and ideologically loaded (and decidedly unlevel) society designed to reflect white realities and advance Eurocentric interests. Predictably, people's social location in terms of race, Aboriginality, gender, and class continue to matter in terms of shaping their identities, experiences, opportunities, or outcomes.
Canada is a kinder, more gentle society (compared to the United States) at the international level, and is known for its willingness to promote the development and progress of those less fortunate countries in the global south.	Canada's international commitments once secured its lofty global position, but recent government moves at the international level openly advance Canada's national and vested interests at the expense of its moral-beacon status. Its foreign aid program tends to enrich Canadian interests rather than foster development in poor countries. Aggressive foreign investments have also put Canada at loggerheads with activists, environmentalists, and local inhabitants. And yet public opinion surveys such as GlobeScan acknowledge that Canada continues to be favourably viewed overseas, thanks to its reputation as a prosperous and stable multicultural society (Westhead 2013).
The settlement of Canada proceeded in a relatively orderly fashion (unlike the lawlessness of the American frontier), consistent with Canada's commitment to peace, order, and good government.	In contrast to the belief Canada has no history of colonialism (for example, Prime Minister Harper, 2009, G20 Conference, Pittsburgh), Canadian society was forged in the alloy of settler colonialism and white supremacist doctrines that ruthlessly removed all barriers to expansion and settlement. Aboriginal peoples were imperiously pushed aside and away through a made-in-Canada style of ethnic cleansing, through food deprivation (Daschuk 2013);

	delivered into residential schools that proved genocidal in consequence (systemic) if not in intent (Fontaine and Farber 2013; Truth and Reconciliation Commission Report 2015); misused as guinea pigs (without their consent) for nutritional experiments after the Second World War (Mosby 2013); and victimized by forced sterilization of aboriginal women in the name of eugenics (Stote 2015).
No one can match Canada's commitment to diversity and the progressive management of race, ethnic, and aboriginal relations.	True, Canada's commitment to inclusiveness is vastly more progressive than those jurisdictions that routinely violate the human rights of minorities. However true in the relative sense, Canada's record in this area cannot be divorced from the realities that informed Canada-building, including white supremacist doctrines, genocide, settler colonialism, apartheid-like colour bars, flagrant expressions of racism, and crimes against humanity, such as the internment of Japanese Canadians during World War Two.

to overstate this argument. Comforting fictions are not without some truth and value, and heavy-handed references to inconvenient truths tend to underestimate those progressive initiatives that make Canada the envy of many. Nevertheless, there is a gap between fact and fiction, and *Inequality Matters* capitalizes on this paradox between the ideal and the real, between aspirations and reality, in large part by explaining the what, why, and how behind these persistent and pervasive social inequality gaps. Eleven major themes can be discerned that summarize the book's content, argument, and organization.

1. *Inequality matters—for everyone.* This book is predicated on the assumption that inequality matters in enhancing the possibility of making generally bad things happen. But rather than simply restricting negative effects to the "usual" victims such as the poor, marginalized, or racialized, the book underscores how social inequalities impact everyone. Out-of-control social inequities threaten the foundations of liberal democratic societies by undermining the shared sense of living together. Spiralling inequalities induce polarities in society that disconnect the haves from the have-nots to the detriment of a democratic citizenry, economic prosperity, social stability, and co-operative coexistence (MacKenzie 2012). Day-to-day life in a continuous state of relative deprivation can lead to chronic stress and social pathologies, with corresponding negative health consequences that cost everyone, while eroding the social fabric and interpersonal trust at the basis of society (Brennan and Stanford 2012).

2. *Centrality of a sociological perspective.* This book has made it clear: a commitment to sociology as a discipline and a perspective provides a grounded, explanatory framework for better understanding the inequalities of exclusion in terms of patterns, politics, and paradoxes. Sociology not only cultivates a bigger-picture mentality (by siphoning attention away from excessively individualistic mindsets), it also focuses attention on the importance of data as a basis for delving into recurrent patterns and deeper (root) causes. Unlike other disciplinary approaches to social inequality (such as philosophy, with its emphasis on the ethics or morality of social equality), a sociological model emphasizes the social dimensions of social inequality along exclusionary lines. Emphasis is aimed at the impact of social inequality on society and, conversely, the impact of societal changes on social inequality.

3. *Reframing social inequality.* Responses to the question, What is social inequality? are not as

simple as appearances might suggest. References to social inequality as differential access and differential distribution provide an excellent starting point, but the issue of interest to sociologists and the focus of this book is not social inequality per se. Emphasis is directed instead at excessive or unacceptable levels of social inequality—however that may be defined or measured—in terms of social costs to both society and its more vulnerable members. Income differences are a good place to start in studying social inequality but constitute only part of the story. More important still are the income-based social exclusions that deprive individuals of access to necessary material needs and social services; deny people a standard of living and quality of life commensurate with the population at large; and deter people from achieving their full potential as valued and contributing members of society. In other words, the inequality of exclusions related to power and privilege is pivotal in shaping people's sense of belonging and participation, and recognition and self-actualization (Saloojee 2003).

4. *Accounting for social inequalities.* Sociological models of society—functionalism, conflict, and symbolic interactionism—each offer a different lens for understanding the realities of social inequality. *Inequality Matters* acknowledges the value of a multi-perspectival approach. The interplay of social circumstances (blame the situation), structural opportunities (blame the system), and individual responsibility (blame the victim) are shown to account for specific patterns of social inequality and structural exclusions. Middle-level theories—from a culture of poverty to the deregulation of the money market in recent years—may secure insight into spiraling inequalities and entrenched exclusions.

5. *Social inequality: agency × structure × context.* There is some truth in admitting individuals may be the architects of their own misfortune; as a result, they must take responsibility for their choices and actions. To do otherwise—to portray them as hapless robots and helpless victims—robs them of their agency. But this book makes it clear that individual choices occur within a broader context that is often beyond the individual's control or not of their making. A commitment to sociology draws attention to those structures and systems that preclude individual access to valued resources. In some cases these structures openly deny or exclude; in other cases, they are systemically embedded yet no less powerful as barriers in foreclosing opportunities and outcomes.

6. *The myth of a level playing field.* Time and again this book refutes reference to society as a relatively neutral domain. Societies and their constituents, such as institutions and values, are socially constructed conventions whose constructedness is carefully concealed yet ideologically loaded along racial, gender, and class lines. Two implications follow. First, the goal of creating a level playing field in systems that are gendered, classed, and racialized is more complicated than many had thought or hoped. Reforms that modify the conventions that refer to the rules are unlikely to bring about a fundamental levelling. What is required are transformative changes that dislodge the taken-for-granted framework of rules that inform the conventions (see McMurtry 2013). Second, minorities may possess equal rights; however, in a spikey and uneven playing field, they must exercise these rights in contexts neither designed to reflect their experiences and realities nor designed to advance their interests and priorities. Such a reading helps to explain the paradox of women and minorities who are moving into key positions yet continue to experience sticky floors, glass ceilings, brick walls, revolving doors—whose barriers are akin to the equivalent of walking up a down escalator.

7. *The multiplicity of inequality.* Not all inequalities are created equal since different groups occupy diverse lived-in universes. Aboriginal peoples experience a fundamentally different pattern of inequality than racialized minorities or newcomers to Canada. Much of the distinction reflects their constitutional status as descendants of the original inhabitants, with a corresponding set of rights, entitlements, and powers. As forcibly incorporated "nations

within" someone else's system, Aboriginal peoples are looking to get out of existing (neo-colonial) arrangements by challenging the rules that refer to the conventions. By contrast, both immigrants and racialized minorities are looking to get into the existing system by modifying the conventions (for example, removing discriminatory barriers) that refer to the rules. In short, a one-size-fits-all governance model will not work as a proposed solution to the complexities of minority inequality.

8. *The intersectionality of status inequalities.* Detailed attention is devoted to the social inequalities associated with status identities, including gender, race, and Aboriginality. Each of these status groups continues to confront barriers—both deliberate (systematic) or unconscious and by consequences (systemic)—that impede the attainment of social equality. But these status and identity markers do not exist in isolation from each other. The fact that they intersect with each other not only amplifies patterns of exclusion because of concurrent devaluations (a multiplier effect), but the complexity and importance of people's social location in defining who gets what and why are also reinforced.

9. *Canada in the world: foe or friend?* This book is predominantly about social inequality in Canada. It also explores how the placement of Canada in a global context has proven paradoxical. To one side, Canada is profoundly influenced by the dynamics of globalization, including trade agreements that benefit yet penalize Canadians. To the other side, Canada is a net contributor to global inequality because of its sometimes exploitative investment portfolios in the developing countries of the global south (Engler 2016). Canada's rogue-nation environmental status (from extracting "dirty" oil to reneging on greenhouse gas emissions) further sullies its global reputation (Yakabuski 2013c). Nevertheless, various global surveys reflect continuing admiration for Canada because of its openness and tolerance, democratic principles, and competitive economy (US News 2016). Paradoxes of such nature make it abundantly clear: Canada is as much a problem as it is a solution to global inequality.

10. *Challenging the inequalities of exclusion.* A new activism aims to dislodge economic and political injustices related to social inequality and undemocratic decision-making (Basok and Ilcan 2013). New social movements are emerging to challenge glaring patterns of social inequality and exclusion, including the Idle No More movement, Quebec Students' Maple Spring, and Occupy Wall Street. They may differ in origin and composition; nevertheless, they are seemingly united in establishing a broader vision that challenges the status quo (Wotherspoon and Hansen 2013). They also appear to be moving away from hero-driven protests of the past (think: Bono or Geldof) to ones that embody a more decentralized and co-operative approach around the principle of grassroots democracy and collaborative power-sharing (Stock 2012).

11. *The enigma of social equality.* This book is premised on a progressive assumption: most Canadians aspire to greater social equality instead of more social inequality, especially if income and wealth are illegally acquired, harmful to society's members, and detrimental to society. But just as there is no unanimity over what constitutes unacceptable levels of social inequality, so too is there a lack of consensus as to what social equality would look like, even if an equal society were humanly attainable to everyone's satisfaction. Perhaps the issue is not so much about social equality per se, but rather establishing an egalitarian society in which no one is precluded from access to basic subsistence necessities, equal democratic citizenship rights, and full and equal participation in society. An egalitarian society commits to the dual principle of *inclusion* (treating everybody exactly the same regardless of their differences so that nobody is excluded because everyone is equal before the law) and *inclusivity* (everyone should be included precisely because of their differences and the system restructured to incorporate differences-based experiences, interests, and realities). The fact that no society has yet attained this ideal provides a sobering reminder. What sounds good on paper may not necessarily translate into reality—at least not until

the prevailing economic system (capitalism) is rehabilitated along more humanistic lines by balancing the pursuit of profit with empowerment of people and protection of the planet.

One final word: a book that addresses social inequality is, by definition, an exercise in extolling the negative and problematic. Canada comes across as a country infiltrated by glaring patterns of social inequality at interpersonal, institutional, and national levels. Prejudicial and discriminatory barriers related to colonialism, classism, racism, and sexism continue to blight the lives of the historically disadvantaged, including women, working classes, Aboriginal peoples, racialized minorities, and newcomers to Canada. Adding insult to injury is the awareness that these social inequities and structural exclusions are persistent and seemingly inhospitable to reforms. Even ostensibly progressive measures that challenge inequality, such as official multiculturalism, may end up reinforcing or advancing social exclusions by virtue of masking inconvenient truths with polite fictions (Ahmed 2012).

However accurate these accusations, in whole or in part, there is another narrative that deserves recognition. Canada's commitment to creating a more equitable and inclusive society cannot be casually dismissed. Canada as a society commits to improving the lot of those historically disadvantaged through an array of measures, including official multiculturalism, employment equity legislation, anti-racism initiatives, gender-based analysis frameworks, and tax-and-transfer redistribution. These ideals and commitments do not necessarily spring from a sense of justice, compassion, or humanitarianism. They may well reflect political acts of containment to preserve the constitutional goals of "peace, order, and good government" in ways that paper over uncomfortable truths with comforting fictions. Still, Canada's bona fides as a relatively open and progressive society should never be underestimated. Its lofty status as a beacon of enlightenment is further consolidated in a world convulsed by spasms of terror, violence, exploitation, poverty, misogyny, xenophobia, racism, and human rights abuses. But in comparison to its lofty aspirations and projected ideals, Canada falls short of its own self-defined mark, in the process exerting even more pressure on polite fictions to hide increasingly precarious realities.

This interplay of the good and the bad with the compromised puts Canada in a league of its own. Canada is not a perfect society by any stretch of the imagination. Too many imperfections due to persistent and pervasive patterns of social inequality and structural exclusions will attest to that. And while Canadians have come a long way in dismantling barriers and improving attitudes, the last stretches of any journey are always the hardest and most elusive (Saunders 2014). Nevertheless, Canada may well be one of the world's least imperfect societies in that it is willing to acknowledge that inequalities matter and that something needs doing in ways that are workable, necessary, and fair. The prospect of living together with our differences, in dignity and equitably, begins with such recognition and commitment. An inclusive and equal Canada deserves—and demands—nothing less in making the move toward an egalitarian society. As Lao Tzu reminded us 2,500 years ago, and as many have noted since then, a journey of a thousand miles begins with the first step. So too can Canadians bask in the knowledge that they have travelled a great distance—yet also acknowledge the distance that remains to be covered in closing the inequality gap. Boots, start walking.

Glossary

Aboriginal difference The principle that Aboriginal peoples differ from other Canadians because they are the descendants of the original inhabitants and have a special relationship to the State from which flows recognition, power, and entitlements. Also *aboriginality*.

Aboriginal peoples Aboriginal peoples are the descendants of the original (Indigenous peoples) occupants of Canada who have been colonized and forcibly incorporated into Canadian society, but now want to "get out" of this arrangement by redefining their relational status in society. See also *aboriginality*.

Aboriginality The notion of "being aboriginal" as a political basis for recognition, reward, and relationship, as well as a springboard for challenge and change.

Absolute poverty Poverty defined along absolute lines acknowledges endangered physical existence because people lack fundamental necessities of life (needs) pertaining to food, shelter, and clothing. Absolute poverty tends to focus on income levels as the source and solution to the poor problem.

Accommodationism A belief that aboriginal socio-economic woes can be traced to under-recognition of Aboriginal peoples as peoples with special rights, albeit within the broader framework of Canadian society and corresponding obligations. Neither assimilation nor autonomy as patterns of governance will work as well as a two-way process of accommodation (you adjust, we adapt; we adjust, you adapt).

Ageism A set of beliefs that prejudge people on the basis of age. Specific and deterministic qualities are attributed to individuals because of their age and render them less worthy of respect while discounting their value in making a contribution to society.

Androcentrism Reflects a tendency to see (interpret and evaluate) reality from a male point of view as natural and normal, while dismissing other perspectives as irrelevant or inferior.

Assimilation A complex and dynamic process in which minorities begin to lose their distinctiveness through absorption into dominant society. As policy or political framework assimilation can refer to those formal government initiatives for absorbing minority populations into the mainstream.

Assimilationism A belief that Aboriginal peoples are unequal because they continue to receive special status and differential treatment that has the effect of preserving cultural values at odds with a modern society, isolating individuals from the balm of modern society, and encouraging residence in areas that are economically unfeasible. The solution lies in absorbing Aboriginal peoples into the mainstream by treating them as normal citizens, fostering values of private property and individualism, and relocating them into urban centres.

Autonomism A belief that the inequalities of exclusion that confront aboriginal communities are derived from too much assimilation and not enough autonomy. The solution to this problem resides in a commitment to aboriginal models of self-determining autonomy over land, identity, and political voices.

Bias Bias may be used in the sense of blatantly distorting or falsifying reality (distortion bias) in order to produce consciously biased content (decision-making bias). It may also refer to those deeply embedded distortions that inadvertently or unconsciously reflect the negative yet logical consequences flowing from the seemingly normal and neutral ways in which institutions are structured, workplaces are organized, rewards are allocated, and products/services are designed and delivered.

Capitalism An economic (and social) system organized around the rational pursuit of profit. In a capitalist system, the means of production are owned and controlled by private or corporate sectors rather than the state, while patterns of distribution and exchange are subject to competition in a predominantly free market ruled by the principle of supply and demand.

Cascading disadvantages The concept of cascading disadvantages refers to the cumulative effects of intersecting and overlapping sources that amplify negative outcomes. Each new disadvantage piles up on top of the other, with the result the lingering effects of previous disadvantages make it difficult to escape the impasse. Eventually a tipping point is reached, resulting in a near collapse from which recovery is difficult.

Citizens plus A term employed by accommodationists who believe appropriate governance is based on acknowledging Aboriginal peoples as citizens of Canada, albeit with special rights as the original inhabitants.

Class A category of persons who occupy a similar socio-economic status (position or rank) in relation to other socio-economic placements. Definitions of class vary: Marxist approaches emphasize class as groups of individuals who stand in comparable relationship (as owners or workers) to the mode of production. By contrast, Weberian notions of class tend to focus on groups of individuals who share a similar market situation because of their family background and socio-economic status.

Colonialism The term is used in two ways: first to convey the idea of annexing overseas territories; second, to describe the concept of subjugating Indigenous or tribal peoples. In both cases, colonialism is not simply an act of settlement or annexation, but a violent and invasive process that demeans and destroys the peoples within.

Conflict theory Based on the idea that societies are sites of inequality, with the result that confrontation, competition, and change are inevitable, in part because diverse groups compete for scarce resources in contexts that privilege some groups but not others.

Constitutional order A relatively stable and deeply entrenched set of founding assumptions and foundational principles that govern a society's largely unwritten political, economic, cultural, and moral order. The expression of these assumptions and principles at the level of institutional priorities, hidden agendas, tacitly accepted rules, and core values provides a guideline for decision-making over a period of time; defines what is acceptable, normal, and desirable in society; and secures the basis for identity and belonging (who is in, who is out).

Constructive engagement In contrast to the confrontational/competitive model that has long marred Canada's relationship with Aboriginal peoples, a constructive engagement model proposes a more co-operative governance arrangement emphasizing negotiation over litigation, engagement over entitlement, relationships over rights, interdependence over opposition, co-operation over competition, reconciliation over restitution, and power-sharing over power conflict.

Critical race model The concept of human societies as socially created yet carefully concealed constructions whose founding principles deliberately or inadvertently (systemically) reflect, reinforce, and advance the racialized realities, experiences, and interests of the dominant sector. The values, ideals, and priorities of those who created or control society are deeply embedded in the governance, institutions, and operating assumptions in ways that promote mainstream priorities without people's awareness of the bias at play.

Discrimination Often viewed as the behavioural counterpart of prejudice (attitudes), discrimination consists of actions that have an adverse effect (whether deliberate or not) of denying or excluding someone because of who they are. Discrimination can be expressed at different levels, ranging from the personal, intentional, and direct to the impersonal, inadvertent, and systemic. See also *Racism*.

Diversity/diversities A descriptive term that denotes variation in the human population along physical, cultural, social, moral, and psychological lines.

Education One component of schooling, concerned primarily with the transmission of knowledge and preferred ways of knowing.

Egalitarian society An egalitarian society is one in which no one is denied access to the physical and social necessities for full participation, belonging and recognition, and equal democratic citizenship. Although the focus is on equitable outcomes, a commitment to egalitarianism does not mean that everyone is the same, only that disparities in power, privilege, and property are within reasonable limits; are employed to advance the public good; ensure environmental sustainability; and do not preclude others from inclusion into society.

Employment equity Represents official government policy with a corresponding set of programs for improving institutional accommodation of targeted minorities through proportional representation.

Equality There is no single definition of equality since the concept may be employed in three fundamentally different ways: same (equal), proportional (equivalence), and substantive (equity). Both the "same" and "proportional" versions of equality correspond to the principle of inclusion (fit individuals into the existing system), whereas "substantive" dimensions fall into the inclusivity category (adjust the system to make it fit individuals).

Equity The belief that true equality rests on recognizing the relevance of context, the importance of taking differences into account, and balancing individual rights with collective rights. A commitment to equity acknowledges the primacy of equal results (not just equal opportunity) to ensure that members of a group have a fair share of valued resources.

Eurocentrism The tendency to see and evaluate a Western/Euro-American (proxy for *white*) way of looking at the world as normal and necessary—*and superior*—compared to other worldviews which are dismissed as irrelevant or inferior or dangerous.

Exclusion *Exclusion* can be defined in many ways but generally refers to denial of equal access to full participation in society; equal citizenship rights; and the rights, goods, and services associated with labour market and employment opportunities. For example, racism may be defined as a form of exclusion that utilizes assumptions of normativity and superiority to impose domination and control by one group over another.

Exclusionary structures Refers to those open, discriminatory barriers that deny or exclude (also *systematic bias*).

Fair/fairness Concerned with treating everyone the same regardless of their differences (inclusion).

Feminism A widely varied ideology and social movement that espouses the equality and worth of women. Feminisms range from those who reject the existing system as patriarchal, racist, or classist to those who are willing to work within the system by removing discriminatory barriers to equality. Feminisms also vary, depending on whether the differences between men and women are perceived as absolute or relative, substantial or minimal.

Fordist (or industrial) Models of wealth creation under the old economy that emphasized mass and standardized production, vertical integration, economies of scale, de-skilled labour, and nationalized economies buffered by protectionist tariffs.

Formal equality Equality based on strict mathematical equivalence—that is, because everyone is equal before the law everyone should be treated the same, regardless of their differences. Often associated with the principle of equal opportunity. See also *Equity*.

Framing A socially constructed process for organizing information into packages (frames) that draws attention to some aspects of reality as normal and desirable, but away from others as irrelevant or inferior, in the hopes of quietly encouraging a preferred reading consistent with a prevailing interests, agendas and biases. The constructedness (arbitrariness) of the framing process is carefully concealed to ensure audiences internalize these representations as if they were natural, unproblematic, or without bias. See also *Hegemony*.

Functionalism A sociological perspective (or theory) that sees society as a complex and integrated totality composed of interrelated parts that individually and collectively contribute to the stability and survival of society.

Gender Not simply a descriptive label assigned to men and women that varies from one culture to another. Its centrality as a primary point of contact with social reality is pivotal in defining who we are, the nature of our experiences, the construction of relations to others, and the availability of opportunities. Gender as a socially constructed convention also constitutes a form of social control and an exercise of power by virtue of boxing individuals into predetermined expectations.

Gendered inequality Gendered inequality points to those patterns of exclusion along gender lines within the structures and the normal functioning of society. It reflects and reinforces those founding assumptions and foundational principles that govern a predominantly patriarchal constitutional order. Males' ways of thinking and doing are privileged and prioritized, while female equivalents are dismissed or devalued.

Gendered society All societies are gendered insofar as they constitute a moral order that is neither neutral nor passive. Gendered societies are structured (biased) in a way that reflects male values and interests, thereby advancing male privilege and power at the expense of women. This devaluation is ingrained within the framework of society by way of values and agendas that rigidify male notions of right, acceptable, and desirable as normal, necessary and neutral rather than constructed, contingent, and contested.

Gini coefficient A measure of inequality in which a ranking of zero (0) corresponds to everyone receiving the same income, whereas reference to one (1) means the richest person owns all the income and everyone else has none.

Globalization As description, globalization is a process involving the worldwide integration of countries and interdependent economies into a global division of labour that *transcends* borders, not just crosses them. This "transcendent" integration of countries and economies reflects reduced costs of communication and transportation that in turn hasten reduced barriers to the flow of goods, capital, and knowledge.

Alternatively, globalization can be defined as the geographic penetration of capitalist market relations and outcomes into new sites of production and distribution in the relentless quest of profits, markets, and shares.

Governance Refers to a set of rules and protocols that govern the relationship between the governed and the governing in terms of how power is shared, decisions are made, resources are allocated, and outcomes are justified.

Hegemony The process by which the powerful secure consensus, co-operation and control through consent rather than physical coercion, with the result that people's attitudes undergo change without awareness that their attitudes are changing.

Ideology Defined in its broadest sense, ideology refers to a complex set of ideas and ideals that attempts to explain, justify, and perpetuate a specific set of circumstances. Employed in a critical sense, ideology consists of beliefs that rationalize the prevailing distribution of power, privilege, and resources in society by bolstering the cultural patterns of the dominant sector as natural or normal, while dismissing or demeaning subdominant patterns.

Immigrant Persons born overseas but voluntarily residing in a new country, with a right to permanent residency on the grounds of labour market contribution or family reunification. With the exception of Aboriginal peoples, all Canadians are immigrants or descendants of immigrants.

Inclusion A subset of inclusiveness, the concept of inclusion is predicated on the principle of removing discriminatory barriers to ensure integration (or "fit") into the existing system. It is based on the belief that no one should be excluded from full and equal participation because of their differences, since everyone deserves similar treatment in colour-blind equality. A commitment to inclusion also acknowledges that everyone is equal before the law so that true equality arises from applying the law equally and without favouritism regardless of race, ethnicity, or gender, although exemptions may be allowed in extenuating circumstances.

Inclusivity Inclusivity can be broadly defined as a process and framework for transforming ("refitting") institutions along more accommodative lines to reasonably accommodate (within limits and without undue hardship) those formerly excluded. As a subset of inclusiveness, a commitment to inclusivity insists that everyone should be included precisely because of their needs, entitlements, and rights, thus necessitating interventions that enhance the concepts of belonging, participation, recognition and contribution.

Inequality Inequality consists of differences in entitlements. Two dimensions prevail: differential access (who gets what) and differential distribution (what goes where). The two dimensions are not mutually exclusive since differential access to valued resources generates differential distribution of power, privilege, and property—and vice versa.

Intersectionality Intersectionality is a theoretical and research approach that emphasizes how differences move and work through one another (mutually influence) to produce something distinct from any single difference standing alone. Identity markers that are often devalued (e.g., gender) intersect with other devalued social categories (such as race or class) to amplify (the multiplier effect) the exclusion or exploitation.

Just/Justice The concept of justice acknowledges the necessity to treat people differently and adjust the system by taking differences into account when the situation demands (inclusivity). See *Fair/fairness*.

Marxism A philosophy or ideology based on interpreting the work of Karl Marx. According to Marxism, both the dynamics of history and the organization of society can be understood as an ongoing and evolving clash between the ruling (capitalist) class and the working class in the competition for scarce resources.

Mediacentrism (or media-centred) refers to the tendency for media presentations to frame (or see) the world from a media point of view that is considered normal and necessary, desirable and acceptable, while other perspectives are devalued or dismissed as irrelevant, inferior or threatening.

Meritocracy A society in which individuals are thought to succeed in direct proportion to individual effort and talent. It can be defined as a system or arrangement in which power, status, and wealth are distributed solely on the basis of a person's ability to work hard to get ahead. In a meritocracy, people are not responsible for where they start; it is about where they end up in a system that is deemed to be fair and open (a level playing field).

Multiculturalism A belief that a society of many cultures is possible as a basis for "living together with differences"—as long as certain rules are in place that reject differences (culture-blindness), or tolerate differences (culture-tolerant), or take differences seriously (culture-conscious).

Neo-colonialism A political arrangement that moves beyond the egregious domination of colonialism not in the sense of dislodging the system but rather in propping up the existing arrangement through cosmetic reforms and personnel replacements. A neo-colonial social contract rejects the explicit colonization of Aboriginal peoples, although it too continues to frame aboriginality as a problem to solve, defines Aboriginal peoples as a minority with needs, and endorses the paramountcy of the state to define what counts as aboriginality and what aboriginality counts. In contrast to post-colonialism that challenges the rules of society that create conventions, neo-colonialism tends to tinker with the conventions that refer to the rules.

Neo-liberalism An umbrella term that reflects a set of principles (structural adjustments) about improving productivity through wealth creation and societal organization; a commitment to neo-liberalism is based on commitment to more (unfettered) markets; less (small) government; hyper-individualism ("responsibilized" and competitive self); and an inequality-is-good mantra.

New economy The new economy refers to those ideological shifts, structural readjustments, and technological changes associated with new patterns of production and wealth creation as they impact notions of work, workers, and working within the new workplace. The distinction between the old and new economy as wealth creators is often framed as a contrast between Fordist and post-Fordist models of production.

Old economy See *Fordist*.

Patriarchy A social system that is designed, organized, and prioritized by, for, and about men. This system tends to reflect male realities, prioritize male experiences, confer privileges to men, and advance male interests as superior, while dismissing others as irrelevant or inferior.

Post-colonialism A term with admittedly multiple meanings, post-colonialism points to a new social contract and governance model for renegotiating Aboriginal peoples—Canada beyond a (neo)colonial social contract. Post-colonialism does not herald the end of colonialism; rather, it refers to engagement with and dis-engagement from colonialism in bringing about transformational changes to society. Aboriginal peoples are framed accordingly under a post-colonial contract (or governance) as peoples with rights with a corresponding right to aboriginal models of self-determining autonomy over land, identity, and political voice.

Post-Fordist (post-industrial) Models of wealth production that entail a shift towards new economy principles—namely, a new set of rules and priorities consistent with the flexibility afforded by a freewheeling neo-liberalism; a just-in-time agenda for production; on-demand labour supply; the removal of tariffs that impede trade and investment; and the production of goods and services geared primarily for export rather than domestic consumption.

Poverty There is no agreement on a definition of poverty. The UN High Commissioner for Human Rights defines poverty as a human condition characterized by sustained or chronic deprivation of the resources, choices, security, power, and participation that are necessary to enjoy an adequate standard of living and rights. See also *Absolute poverty*; *Relative poverty*.

Power In everyday language, the ability to make others do what they normally would not want to do. In more systemic terms, power is defined as a process inherent to relationships. The relational nature of power shifts from context to context, suggesting that minorities can wield power in certain situations, although they lack access to institutionalized power (power backed by the coercive authority of the state).

Precarious workers Part-time, casual, contingent, or contract workers who struggle to make a go of it in a neo-liberal (just-in-time) economy, often without benefits, livable wages, job security, or advancement prospects. The term can also refer to the "work-poor" (such as low-skilled temporary foreign workers) who are consigned to dull and dirty jobs that pose a health danger.

Problematize To render as problematic (i.e., to question) what on the surface seems straightforward.

Racialization A socially constructed process by which those in positions of power impose negative, biogenetic (race)-based characteristics on targeted groups (or their activities) and subject them to differential treatment because of this labelling. Reference to racialization as a definitional process by which individuals and groups are racially coded (**racialized**), distinguishes it from conventional notions that posit races as objective and existing entities with specific characteristics thought to determine belief and behaviour. The concept of *racialized* reinforces how race is not a naturally occurring fact but a social construct (a stigma) that exposes people to disadvantages, exploitation, and exclusion.

Racialized The concept of race as a (de)valued category is deeply embedded in the structures of society, institutions, core values, and people's mindsets. The concept of *racialized* begins with the assumption that neither society nor institutions are neutral or level playing grounds. Rather, both are socially constructed and ideologically loaded conventions whose founding assumptions and foundational principles privilege the interests, agendas, values, and priorities of those racialized groups (in this case whites) who create, own, or control are subsequently reinforced.

Racialized inequality The embeddedness of race-based (dis)advantages within the institutional structures of society on grounds that society is designed and organized in a way that reflects, reinforces, and advances as normal and necessary the interests and agendas of those racialized groups with the power to define or control it.

Racialized minorities This term is increasingly preferred over "visible minorities" or "people of colour" because it acknowledges how attaching a race label to minorities reflects a socially constructed process rather than a biologically-based description of reality. Racialization also acknowledges that there is no such thing as race but only individuals who are labelled as such by those with the power to make such labels stick.

Racialized stratification A hierarchical ranking of racial and ethnic minorities in ascending/descending order based on the criteria of income, education, or social class. Think of Canada as "layered" into "strata" in terms of how different minorities fare in the competition for valued resources, with whites on top and groups such as Indigenous peoples and racialized minorities near the bottom.

Racism Racism refers to a relatively organized set of ideas and ideals (ideology) that assert or imply natural superiority of one group over another in terms of entitlements and privileges, together with the institutionalized power to put these beliefs into practice in a way that denies, exploits, or excludes those who belong to a devalued category.

Radical conflict theory See *Conflict theory.*

Relative poverty According to the relativist approach to poverty, what constitutes being poor is relative to time, place, and level of development. In a rich society in which virtually everyone has access to the necessities of life, poverty cannot focus on subsistence or survival. Poverty is better measured in terms of how people compare to commonly accepted standards of living. See *Egalitarian society.*

Representations Mediated images of particular groups of people situated within an ideological framework. These representations (including visual images and verbal texts/narratives) do not reflect (mirror) reality per se; to the contrary, as others have noted, they *re*-present socially constructed versions of reality that are cloaked in the language of normalcy to impart a sheen of universality and normativeness.

Responsible capitalism The idea of rehabilitating neo-liberal capitalism by making it accountable to and responsible for the interests of workers, local communities, society, human values, and planet Earth.

Schooling The entire program of formal socialization, including governance patterns related to values and norms, teachers and teaching, students and learning, and decision-making and power relations.

Self-determining autonomy As fundamentally autonomous political communities who are sovereign in their own right, Aboriginal peoples claim to have inherent and collective rights to aboriginal models that control jurisdictions (or domains) of immediate concern related to land, identity, and political voice. Recourse to self-determining autonomy is not the same as independence or absolute sovereignty; rather it involves a commitment to restructure the foundational principles of a colonial constitutional order along the lines of a new (post-colonial) social contract.

Social As a noun, *social* refers to those spaces in society that go beyond market principles but entail notions of community, co-operation, social bonds and trust, and levels of government intervention and regulation. Used as an adjective, *social* tends to emphasize the constructed character of a phenomenon with a corresponding reference to root causes as a preferred explanatory framework.

Social equality See *Equality.*

Social exclusion See *Exclusion.*

Social inequality See *Inequality.*

Social location A core sociological principle, social location argues that where individuals and groups are positioned in society with respect to gender, race, ethnicity, class, sexuality, age, and so on, profoundly influences how they relate to others and how others relate to them in terms of experiences, identities, opportunities, and outcomes.

Social structures See *Structures*.

Social movements A collective effort by aggrieved individuals who initiate (or resist) social change through actions that fall outside institutional frameworks or conventional political channels.

Stratification Division of society into unequal vertical layers known as strata. It entails an arrangement by which categories of persons are ranked into layers of unequal worth and arranged in ascending and descending orders of recognition, reward, or significance. This division is based on criteria such as class or gender or race and results in the hierarchical arrangement of groups who stand in a relationship of advantage and superiority (or disadvantage and subordination) to each other.

Structural exclusion A bias that is inherent in (built into) the system itself (systemic bias).

Structures Patterned regularities that are external to individual behaviour, often outside people's awareness, and not reducible to the sum of individual meanings or actions. These regularities (for example, the concepts of "status" and "roles") may be seen as structural in their own right or, alternatively, as manifestations of deeper structures that regulate behaviour.

Systemic bias Systemic bias reflects a biasing process in which the one-size-fits-all rules or business-as-usual practices of an institution, when evenly and equally applied, may exert an inadvertent negative effect or consequence on certain minorities who are excluded or penalized through no fault of their own. This bias arises when members of historically disadvantaged groups whose realities, interests, and experiences differ from the mainstream are treated the same (one size fits all) yet need differential treatment since similar treatment across the board exerts a negative impact on them. The concept is based on the principle that bias and barriers may be built-in (inherent) and deeply embedded within the normal functioning of an institutional system, without people's awareness of what's going on.

Systemic white supremacist society See *White supremacist society*; *Systemic whiteness*.

Systemic whiteness In contrast to the view that white privilege/supremacy is a state of mind (a racist mindset), *systemic whiteness* refers to its status and role as an unwritten and organizing principle of society and its institutions and values. More specifically, systemic whiteness can be viewed as an ideology imbued with power that normalizes relations of white power and privilege; upholds a normative and universal standard that judges others and criticizes accordingly;

endorses a lens through which whites see themselves and others, without an awareness of the optics at play; and an implicit Eurocentrism with a corresponding tendency to see, think, and evaluate reality from the perspective of white realities, interests, and experiences as universal and superior—others not so much.

Total institution Organizations such as the prison system that seek to resocialize or rehabilitate individuals by isolating them from the mainstream for purposes of indoctrination and behaviour modification.

Treaties Transactions between the Crown and Aboriginal peoples involving an exchange of rights, duties, and obligations. Treaties of alliance and friendship exist; nevertheless, most treaties involve a transaction in which Aboriginal peoples surrender large tracts of land in exchange for goods and services in perpetuity, and rights of use of unoccupied or underutilized Crown land.

Violence Harm that incorporates physical, sexual, and psychological dimensions within the family, the community, at work or in institutions, and in the context of the state. Violence reflects abuses of power and is structured in relations of dominance both pervasive and endemic.

Wealth Whereas income refers to a flow of money over time, wealth is a portfolio of assets. Income is what people earn from work or receive as government transfers, whereas wealth is what people own (from stocks and bonds to homes) and what they use to earn more income. Wealth signifies command over those financial assets or resources a household has accumulated over a lifetime to secure a desired status or to pass status onto children. The possession of wealth or assets is a more reliable measurement of inequalities.

White supremacist society The term *white supremacist society* is not used in the sense of a caste-like or apartheid system overrun by neo-Nazi skinheads. The expression is employed in the systemic sense—that is, acknowledging Canada as *structured* around the principles and practices of a socially constructed and ideologically loaded society in which founding assumptions and foundational principles embody a commitment to a Euro-white constitutional order; the system is designed, organized, and controlled by, for, and about whites; white interests are reflected, reinforced, and advanced as normal, desirable, and acceptable in both overt (systematic) and covert (systemic) ways; and white activities, perspectives and characteristics are valued as the norm or superior, while other realities are dismissed as inferior, irrelevant, or threatening. See also *Systemic whiteness*.

White supremacy The belief, doctrine, or theory that whites are inherently superior to other races and, therefore, deserving of power, privilege, and control.

References

Abraham, M., E.S. Chow, L. Maratou-Alipranti, and E. Tastsoglou. 2010. *Contours of Citizenship: Women, Diversity, and the Practices of Citizenship.* Burlington VT: Ashgate Publishing.

Abrahamian, A.A. 2013. Majority of Fast Food Workers Need Public Assistance: Study. Reuters, 15 October.

Abramson, Corey. 2015. *The End Game: How Inequality Shapes Our Final Years.* Cambridge: Harvard University Press.

ACS (Association for Canadian Studies): History. 2015. Is Canada a Land of Equal Opportunity for All? Leger Marketing. June.

Adams, Howard. 1999. *Tortured People: The Politics of Colonization.* Penticton, BC: Theytus Books.

Adams, Michael. 1997. *Sex in the Snow: The Surprising Revolution in Canadian Social Values.* Toronto: Penguin.

Adams, Michael. 2007. *Unlikely Utopia. The Surprising Triumph of Canadian Pluralism.* Toronto: Viking.

Adams, Michael. 2010. *Staying Alive.* Toronto: Penguin.

Adams, Michael. 2015. "More Opportunist than Great Persuader." *The Globe and Mail.* 7 February.

Addichie, C.N. 2013. *Americanah.* New York: Knopf.

Adelson, Naomi. 2005. "The Embodiment of Inequality: Health Disparities in Aboriginal Communities." *Canadian Journal of Public Health.* March-April.

Alaggia, Ramona, Cheryl Regehr, and Giselle Rishchynski. 2009. "Intimate Partner Violence and Immigration Laws in Canada: How Far Have We Come?" *International Journal of Law and Psychiatry* 32 (6):335–341.

Albiston, Catherine. 2010. *Institutional Inequality and the Mobilization of the Family and Medical Leave Act: Rights on Leave.* Cambridge University Press.

Alboim, Naomi, and Elizabeth McIsaac. 2007. "Making the Connections: Ottawa's Role in Immigrant Employment." IRPP *Choices* 13 (3). Available at http://irpp.org/research-studies/choices-vol13-no3/.

Alboim, Naomi, and Karen Cohl. 2012. Shaping the Future: Canada's Rapidly Changing Immigration Policy. October. Maytree Foundation.

Alcantara, Christopher. 2013. *Negotiating the Deal. Comprehensive Land Claims Agreements in Canada.* University of Toronto Press.

Aleman, S M. 2014. "Locating Whiteness in Journalism Pedagogy." *Critical Studies in Media Communication* 31:72–88.

Alexander, Colin. 2014. "A Suicide in Canada's North: A Suicide Epidemic." *National Post.* 10 September.

Alexander, Michelle. 2012. *The New Jim Crow: Mass Incarceration in the Age of Colorblindness.* New York: New Press.

Alexander, Craig, and Francis Fong. 2014. The Case for Leaning against Income Inequality in Canada. Special Report, TD Economics. 24 November.

Alfred, Taiaiake. 2005. *Wasase: Indigenous Pathways of Action and Freedom.* Peterborough: Broadview Press.

Alfred, Taiaiake and Jeff Corntassel. 2005. "Being Indigenous: Resurgences against Contemporary Colonialism" *Government and Opposition,* 40(4):597-598.

Alfred, Taiaiake, and Lana Lowe. 2006. "What are Warrior Societies?" *New Socialist* 58:4–7.

Allan, B., and J. Smylie. 2015. *First Peoples, Second Class Treatment: The Role of Racism in the Health and Well-Being of Indigenous Peoples in Canada.* Toronto: The Wellesley Institute.

Allemang, John, 2013. "The Classless Society? Only in Canada, eh? Pity." *The Globe and Mail.* 3 April.

Alsultany, Evelyn. 2012. *Arabs and Muslims in the Media: Race and Representation after 9/11.* New York: New York University Press.

Alvarado, Lorriz Anne. 2010. "Dispelling the Meritocracy Myth: Lessons for Higher Education and Student Affairs Educators." *The Vermont Connection,* Vol. 31:10–23.

Alvarez, Alvin N. and Linda P. Juang. 2010. "Filipino Americans and Racism: A Multi Mediation Model of Coping." *Journal of Counseling Psychology* 57 (2): 167–178.

Amin, Ash. 2012. *Land of Strangers.* Polity.

Amnesty International. 2013. Human Rights for Human Dignity. Retrieved from www.amnestyusa.org .

Amuchastegui, Maria. 2008. "Last Resorts." *THIS Magazine,* January–February.

Anaya, James. 2014. The Situation of Indigenous Peoples in Canada. Report of the Special Rapporteur on the Rights of Indigenous Peoples. Human Rights Council, United Nations, May.

Anderson, Andrea. 2015. The Changing Face of Canadian Prisons: Can We Talk About Black Women? Justice Report (Canadian Criminal Justice Association) 30 (4):27–31.

Andrew, Caroline, John Biles, Meyer Burnstein, Victoria M. Esses, and Erin Tolley (eds.). 2013. *Immigration, Integration, and Inclusion in Ontario Cities.* Montreal and Kingston: McGill-Queen's University Press.

Angus, Ian, and Simon Butler. 2011. *Too Many People? Population, Immigration, and the Environmental Crisis.* Chicago: Haymarket Books.

Angus, Charlie. 2014. Letter to Bernard Valcourt, Minister for Aboriginal Affairs. 2 June.

Angyal, Chloe. 2012. "Why 'The End of Men' is More Complicated than it Seems." *The Atlantic.* September. Retrieved from www.theatlantic.com/entertainment/archive/2012/09/why-the-end-of-men-is-more-complicated-than-it-seems/261144/ .

Ansell, David A., and Edwin K. McDonald. 2015. "Bias, Black Lives, and Academic Medicine." *New England Journal of Medicine* 372:1087–1089.

Anthias, Floya. 2012. "Intersectional What? Social Divisions, Intersectionality, and Levels of Analysis." *Ethnicities.* 1–17.

Antony, Wayne, and Les Samuelson. 2012. "Social Problems and Social Power," in *Power and Resistance. Critical Thinking about Canadian Social Issues.* L. Samuelson and W. Antony (eds.), 5th ed. Halifax: Fernwood, 1-18.

Armstrong, Chris. 2012. *Global Distributive Justice. An Introduction.* New York: Cambridge University Press.

Armstrong, Pat. 2012. "Privatization is Not a Cure: Health Care Reform in Canada." In *Power and Resistance. Critical Thinking about Canadian Social Issues.* L. Samuelson and W. Antony (eds.), 5th ed. Halifax: Fernwood, 320–346.

Arriagada, Paula. 2016. First Nations, Metis and Inuit Women. Publication 89-503-x. Statistics Canada.

Arshad, Imran. 2012. People and Machines: Competitors or Collaborators in the Emerging World of Work? *Policy Horizons Canada.* Policy Brief. June.

Asch, Michael. 2014. *On Being Here to Stay: Treaties and Aboriginal Rights in Canada.* (Paperback) University of Toronto Press.

Asher, Rebecca. 2011. *Shattered: Modern Motherhood and the Illusion of Equality.* London: Harvill Secker Publishers.

Aspinall, Peter, and Miri Song. 2013. *Mixed Race Identities.* Basingstoke: Palgrave Macmillan.

Atanackovic, Jelena, and Ivy Lyn Bourgeault. 2014. The Economic and Social Integration of Immigrant Live-In Caregivers in Canada. IRPP Study No 46. April.

Aughey, Arthur. 2012. "Englishness as Class: A Re-Examination." *Ethnicities* 12(4): 394–408.

Aulakh, Raveena 2013. "Garbage Blots Canada's Record, Says New Report." *Toronto Star.* 17 January.

Axford, Barrie. 2013. *Theories of Globalization.* New York: John Wiley & Sons.

Axworthy, Thomas. 2015. "A Referendum on a Meaner Canada." *Toronto Star.* 6 August.

Aydemir, A. and M. Skuterud. 2004. "Explaining the Deteriorating Entry Earnings of Canada's Immigrant Cohorts: 1996–2000." Family and Labour Studies Division, Statistics Canada. 11F0019MIE. No 225.

Aylward, Carol A. 2010. "Intersectionality: Crossing the Theoretical and Praxis Divide." *Journal of Critical Race Inquiry* 1 (1): 1–22.

Back, Les. 2007. "Ivory Towers? The Academy and Racism," in *Institutional Racism in Higher Education.* I. Law et al. (eds.), Sterling, VA: Trentham Books, 1–6.

Backhouse, Constance. 1999. *Colour-Coded: A Legal History of Racism in Canada: 1900–1950.* Toronto: University of Toronto Press.

Backhouse, Roger, and Bradley Bateman. 2009. "Keynes and Capitalism." *History of Political Economy* 41 (4):645–671.

Bacon, David. 2008. *Illegal People: How Globalization Creates Migration and Criminalizes Migrants.* Beacon Publishers.

Bady, Aaron. 2013. "The MOOC Bubble and the Attack on Public Education." *Academic Matters.* May. 17–20.

Baker, Maureen. 2012. "The Rise of the 'Research University': Gendered Outcomes," in *Reading Sociology. Canadian Perspectives.* L. Tepperman and A. Kalyta (eds.), Toronto: Oxford University Press, 117–121.

Banerjee, A., and E. Duflo. 2011. "Poor Economics: A Radical Rethinking of the Way to Fight Global Poverty." *Public Affairs.*

Banerjee, Rupa. 2012. "Perceptions of Workplace Discrimination among Canadian Visible Minorities." *Canadian Diversity,* 29–33.

Banting, Keith, Thomas J. Courchene, and Leslie Seidle (eds.). 2007. *Belonging? Diversity, Recognition, and Shared Citizenship in Canada.* Montreal: Institute for Research on Public Policy (IRPP).

Banting, Keith, and John Myles. 2013. "Introduction," in *Inequality and the Fading of Redistributive Politics.* K. Banting and J. Myles (eds.). Vancouver: UBC Press.

Banting, Keith, and John Myles. 2015. "Framing the New Inequality. The Politics of Income Redistribution in Canada." Institute for Research on Public Policy. 21 May.

Banting, Keith, and Carolyn Hughes Tuohy. 2013. "To Reduce Inequality, We Must Focus on Our Politics." *The Globe and Mail.* 18 October.

Barkan, Joanne. 2011. "Got Dough? How Billionaires Rule Our Schools." *Dissent.* Winter.

Barker, Adam, J. 2012. "Already Occupied: Indigenous Peoples, Settler Colonialism, and the Occupy Movements in North America." *Social Movement Studies* 11 (3–4): 327–334.

Barker, Adam, J., 2015. "A Direct Act of Resurgence, A Direct Act of Sovereignty: Reflections on Idle No More, Indigenous Activism, and Canadian Settler Colonialism." *Globalizations* 12 (1):43–65.

Barnett, Ronald. 2013. *Imagining the University.* New York: Routledge.

Barreto, M., M.K. Ryan, and M.T. Schmitt. 2009. *The Glass Ceiling in the 21st Century: Understanding Barriers to Gender Inequality.* Washington, DC: APA Books.

Barry, Brian. 2005. *Why Social Justice Matters.* Cambridge, MA: Polity.

Bascaramurty, Dakshana. 2012. "Canada Ranked Best in the G20 for Women." *The Globe and Mail.* 13 June.

Bastia, Tanja. 2013. *Migration and Inequality.* New York: Routledge.

Bates, Laura. 2014. *Everyday Sexism.* New York: Simon & Schuster.

Bates, Laura. 2015. "Female Academics Face Huge Sexist Bias— No Wonder There Are So Few of Them." *The Guardian,* 13 February.

Battiste, Marie. 2009. "Eurocentrism, Racism, and Resilience among Aboriginal Peoples." Lecture to STARS. University of Saskatchewan. 19 November.

Battiste, Marie. 2013. *Decolonizing Education: Nourishing the Learning Spirit.* Saskatoon SA: Purich Publishing.

Bauder, Harald. 2008. "Immigration Debate in Canada: How Newspapers Reported, 1996–2004." *International Migration and Integration,* 9:289–310.

Bauder, Harald, and John Shields. 2015. *Immigrant Experiences in North America: Understanding Settlement and Integration.* Toronto: Canadian Scholars Press.

Baumann, Shyon, and Josee Johnston. 2008. Who Cares about Class Inequality? The Framing of a Social Non-problem in Gourmet Food Writing. Available at www.allacademic.com.

Beach, Charles. 2007. "Why Does Inequality Matter? Why Inequality Matters in 1000 Words or Less: Growing Gap." CCPA, December 13–15.

Beaton, Danny. 2013. "Mohawk Community Advised to Boil Water for over Five Years by Canadian Government." *First Nations Drum.* September.

Beattie, Geoffrey. 2013. *Our Racist Heart? An Exploration of Unconscious Prejudice in Everyday Life.* East Sussex, UK: Routledge.

Beck, Ulrich. 2005. "The World Horizon Opens Up: On the Sociology of Globalization," in *What is Globalization?* Polity Press, 17–30.

Beck, Ulrich. 2007. "Beyond Class and Nation: Reframing Social Inequalities in a Globalising World." *The British Journal of Sociology*, 58(4).

Belanger, Yale. 2014. *Ways of Knowing: An Introduction to Native Studies in Canada*, 2nd ed. Toronto: Nelson.

Bello, Walden. 2013. *Capitalism's Last Stand: Deglobalization in the Age of Austerity*. New York: Zed Books.

Bem, Sandra Lipsitz. 1994. "In a Male-Centered World, Female Differences Are Transformed into Female Disadvantages." *The Chronicle of Higher Education*, 17 August, B1–2.

Beninger, Anna. 2013. "High-Potential Employees in the Pipeline: Maximizing the Talent Pool in Canadian Organizations." Catalyst Publication Code D 123. November.

Benson, Rodney. 2005. "American Journalism and the Politics of Diversity." *Media, Culture, and Society* 27 (1):5–20.

Berners-Lee, Mike and Duncan Clark. 2010. "What's the Carbon Footprint of ... a Banana?" *The Guardian*, 1 July.

Birdsall, Nancy. 2006. Rising Inequality in the New Global Economy. Annual Lecture of the World Institute for Development Economics Research, United Nations University. Helsinki.

Birembaum, Joanna, Pamela Cross, and Amanda Dale. 2016. "No Right to Having a Discriminatory Defence." *Toronto Star*, 8 February.

Black, Errol. 2011. Fast Facts: "Mean Streets" Society Coming. Canadian Centre for Policy Alternatives. 19 May.

Black, Mary, K. Basile, M.J. Breiding, S.G. Smith, M.L. Walters, M.T. Merrick, J. Chen, and M.R. Stevens. 2011. National Intimate Partner and Sexual Violence Survey: Summary Report. Atlanta: National Center for Injury Prevention and Control, Centers for Disease Control and Prevention.

Blackburn, Robert M. 2008. "What is Social Inequality?" *International Journal of Sociology and Social Policy* 28(7/8):250–259.

Blackwell, Tom. 2015. "Untrained and Unemployed: Medical Schools Churning Out Doctors Who Can't Find Residencies or Full-Time Positions." *National Post*. 12 June.

Blanchfield, Mike. 2013. "Canada Exporting Arms to Countries with Dicey Human Rights Records." *The Globe and Mail*, 8 December.

Bland, Douglas L. 2009. *Uprising: A Novel*. Toronto: Blue Butterfly Books.

Bland, Douglas L. 2013. "Canada and the First Nations. Cooperation or Conflict?" MacDonald Laurier Institute Publication.

Bland, Douglas L. 2014. "Time Bomb. Canada and the First Nations. Point of View Series." Toronto: Dundurn.

Blaser, Mario, Ravi de Costa, Deborah McGregor, and William D. Coleman (eds.). 2011. *Indigenous Peoples and Autonomy: Insights for a Global Age*. Vancouver: UBC Press.

Blatchford, Christie. 2013. "'Uprising' Both Fact and Fiction." *National Post*, 4 January.

Block, Sheila. 2013. *Rising Inequality, Declining Health: New Report*. Wellesley Institute. Toronto.

Block, Sheila, and Grace-Edward Galabuzi. 2011. Canada's Colour Coded Labour Market. Canadian Centre for Policy Alternatives/Wellesley Institute. Toronto.

Block Sheila, Grace-Edward Galabuzi, and Alexandra Weiss. 2014. the Colour Coded Labour Market by the Numbers. A National Household Survey Analysis. Wellesley Institute. Toronto.

Blow, Charles M. 2014. "Crime and Punishment." *The New York Times*, 6–7 December.

Boesveld, Sarah. 2011. "The Risks of Overprotective School Policies." *National Post*, 28 December.

Bok, Derek. 2004. *Universities in the Marketplace: The Commercialization of Higher Education*. Princeton, NJ: Princeton University Press.

Bottero, Wendy. 2009. "Class in the 21st Century," in *Who Cares About the White Working Class?* K.P. Sveinson (ed.). London: Runneymede Perspectives. January.

Bourdieu, Pierre. 1991. *Language and Symbolic Power*. Cambridge, MA: Harvard University Press.

Boyd, Monica, and Deanna Pikkov. 2008. "Finding a Place in Stratified Structures: Migrant Women in North America," in *New Perspectives on Gender and Migration*. N. Piper (ed.), New York: Routledge, 19–58.

Boyer, Yvonne. 2014. *Moving Aboriginal Health Forward: Discarding Canada's Legal Barriers*. Saskatoon, SK: Purich Publishing.

Breen, Richard, and David B. Rottman. 1995. *Class Stratification: A Comparative Perspective*. Harvester Wheatsheaf Publishers.

Brennan, Jordan. 2012. "A Shrinking Universe. How Concentrated Corporate Power is Shaping Income Inequality in Canada." Ottawa: Canadian Centre for Policy Alternatives. November.

Brennan, Jordan. 2015. "The Creation of a Shared Prosperity in Canada: Unions, Corporations, and Countervailing Power." Ottawa: Canadian Centre for Policy Alternatives. April.

Breznitz Dan, and John Zysman. 2013. "Introduction: Facing the Double Bind; Maintaining a Healthy and Wealthy Economy in the Twenty-First Century," in *The Third Globalization*. D. Breznitz and J. Zysman (eds.). Toronto: Oxford University Press.

Brewster, Hugh. 2011. *Gilded Lives, Fatal Voyage. The Titanic, Her Passengers, and Their World*. New York: HarperCollins.

Bricker, Darryl, and John Ibbitson. 2013. *The Big Shift*. Toronto: HarperCollins.

Bridge, William. 1995. *Job Shift. How to Prosper in a Workplace without Jobs*. Jackson, TN: Da Capo Press.

Brison, Scott. 2015. "Harper's Hate for the Charter." *National Post*, 1 April.

Broadbent, Ed. 2009. "How to End Child Poverty: Tax the Rich." *The Globe and Mail*, 23 November.

Broadbent, Ed. 2011. Equality is the Core Value of Democracy. Canadian Centre for Policy Alternatives. Available at www.policyalternatives.ca/publications/monitor/equality-core-value-democracy .

Broadbent Institute. 2012. Towards a More Equal Canada: A Report on Canada's Economic and Social Inequality. October. Retrieved from www.broadbentinstitute.ca/towards_a_more_equal_canada .

Broadbent Institute. 2014. Haves and Have Nots: Deep and Persistent Wealth Inequality in Canada September.

Retrieved from www.broadbentinstitute.ca/haves_and_have_nots .

Brock, Deborah, Rebecca Raby, and Mark P Thomas. 2012. "Unpacking the Centre," in *Power and Everyday Practices*. D. Brock, R. Raby, and M.P. Thomas (eds.). Toronto: Nelson, 2–10.

Brooks, David, 2012. "Why Men Fail." *The New York Times*, 10 September.

Brown, Louise. 2016. "Young Grads Must Brush Up on Skills, Schools Told." *Toronto Star*, 22 February.

Brown Wendy. 2015. *Undoing the Demos: Neoliberalism's Stealth Revolution*. New York: Zone Books.

Brownlee, Jamie. 2015. *Academia Inc.: How Corporatization is Transforming Canadian Universities*. Halifax: Fernwood.

Brownlee, Jamie. 2016. "The Role of Governments in Corporatizing Canadian Universities." *Academic Matters*, January, 17–19.

Brunon-Ernst, Anne (ed.). 2012 *Beyond Foucault. New Perspectives on Bentham's Panopticon*. Farnham Surrey: Ashgate.

Bryant, Michael. 2015. "George's Death Dishonoured, 20 Years Later." *Toronto Star*. 23 January.

Buckmaster, Luke, and Matthew Thomas. 2009. "Social Inclusion and Social Citizenship: Towards a Truly Inclusive Society." Research Paper No. 08 2009-10. Social Policy Section of Parliament of Australia, Canberra, 23 October.

Buist, Stephen. 2010. "Code Red: Spec Report Finds Health, Wealth Worlds Apart in Hamilton." *The Hamilton Spectator*.

Bullock, Heather E., K.R. Wyche, and W.R. Williams. 2001. "Media Images of the Poor." *Journal of Social Issues* 57(2), 229-246.

Burgis, Tom. 2015. *The Looting Machine: Warlords, Tycoons, Smugglers, and the Systemic Theft of Africa's Wealth*. London: William Collins Publishers.

Burke, Meghan A. 2012. *Racial Ambivalence in Diverse Communities. Whiteness and the Power of Color-Blind Ideologies*. Lanham, MD: Lexington Books.

Burton, Julie 2015. "Foreword," in *The Status of Women in the U.S. Media 2015*. Women's Media Center.

Business Tax Canada. 2012. Corporate Income Tax Rates. Retrieved from www.canadabusinesstax.com .

Butsch, Richard. 2003. "Ralph, Fred, Archie, and Homer: Why Television keeps Recreating the White Male Working Class Buffoon," in *Gender, Race, and Class in Media: A text-reader*. 2nd ed., G. Dines and J. Humez (eds.). (pp. 575–585). Sage.

Butsch, Richard. 2005. "Five Decades and Three Hundred Sitcoms about Class and Gender," in *Thinking outside the Box: A Contemporary Genre Television Reader*. Gary Edgerton and Brian Rose (eds.). (pp. 111-135). Kentucky: University Press of Kentucky.

CAHS [Canadian Academy of Health Sciences]. 2014. Improving Access to Oral Health Care for Vulnerable People Living in Canada. Retrieved from www.cahs.acss.ca .

Cairns, Alan C. 2000. *Citizens Plus: Aboriginal Peoples and the Canadian State*. Vancouver: UBC Press.

Cairns, Alan C. 2005. *First Nations and the Canadian State: In Search of Coexistence*. Kingston: Queen's University Institute of Intergovernmental Relations.

Cameron, Mark. 2011. "Why Canadians Should Care about Income Inequality," in *Reducing Income Disparities and Polarization: The Canada We Want in 2020*, 1–6. Retrieved from www.canada2020.ca .

Campaign 2000. 2010. Reduced Poverty=Better for All: 2010 Report Card on Child and Family Poverty in Canada. Family Service Toronto.

Campaign 2000. 2011. Revisiting Family Security in Times of Insecurity: Report Card on Child and Family Poverty in Canada. Family Service Toronto.

Campaign 2000. 2012. Needed: A Federal Action Plan to Eradicate Child and Family Poverty in Canada. 2012 Report Card. Family Service Toronto.

Campaign 2000. 2013. Annual Report Card on Child and Family Poverty in Canada. Family Service Toronto.

Campaign 2000. 2015. Let's Do This: Let's End Child Poverty for Good. Campaign 2000 Report Card on Child and Family Poverty in Canada 2015. Hosted by Family Service Toronto.

Campbell, Ken, and Jim Parcels. 2013. *Selling the Dream: How Hockey Parents and Their Kids Are Paying the Price for our National Obsession*. Toronto: Viking.

Canada 2020. 2011. Reducing Income Disparities and Polarization: The Canada We Want in 2020. Retrieved from http://canada2020backup.see-design.com/canada-we-want/wp-content/themes/canada2020/assets/pdf/en/Canada2020_E_Income-5.pdf .

Canada without Poverty. 2016. The Cost of Poverty. Retrieved from www.cwp-csp.ca .

Canadian Board Diversity Council. 2012. Annual Report. Conference Board of Canada. In association with KPMG and the Conference Board of Canada.

Canadian Board Diversity Council. 2014. Annual Report. Conference Board of Canada. In association with KPMG and the Conference Board of Canada.

Canadian Ethnic Studies Journal. 2012. Race, Racialization, and the University. Special Issue. Vol 44 (2).

Canadian Federation of Students. 2011. Funding for Post-Secondary Education. Retrieved from www.cfs-fcee.ca .

Canadian Heritage. 2013. Women in Vulnerable Situations: Minority, Immigrant, and Refugee Women. Retrieved from www.pch.gc.ca .

Canadian Index of Wellbeing. 2012. How are Canadians Really Doing? The 2012 CIW Report. Waterloo, ON. October.

Canadian Institute for Health Information. 2015. How Canada Compares: Results from the Commonwealth Fund. 2014. International Health Policy Survey of Older Adults. Ottawa. CIHI, January.

Canadian Labour Congress. 2006. Racial Status and Employment Outcomes. Research Paper #34. Author, Leslie Cheung. January.

Canadian Labour Congress. 2012. Day of Mourning. Retrieved from www.canadianlabour.ca .

Canadian Labour Congress. 2014. Underemployment is Canada's Real Labour Market Challenge. 6 March.

Canadian Medical Association. 2013. Health Care in Canada. What Makes Us Sick? July.

Canadian National Council of Welfare. 2007. Solving Poverty: Four Cornerstones of a Workable National Strategy for Canada.

Canadian Race Relations Foundation (CRRF). 2014. Report on Canadian Values. 19 November.

Canadian Women's Foundation. 2012. The Facts about Violence against Women. Retrieved from www.canadianwomen.org .

Cancian, Francesca. 1995. "Truth and Goodness: Does the Sociology of Inequality Promote Social Betterment?" *Sociological Perspectives* 38:339–356.

Cannon, Martin J., and Lina Sunseri (eds.). 2011. *Racism, Colonialism, and Indigeneity in Canada.* Toronto: Oxford University Press.

Caplan, Paul J., and Jordan C. Ford. 2014. "The Voices of Diversity: What Students of Diverse Races/Ethnicities and Both Sexes Tell Us about Their College Experiences and Their Perceptions About Their Institutions' Progress Toward Diversity." *Aporia* 6(3).

Carnavale, Anthony, and Nicole Smith. 2014. "Gender Discrimination is the Heart of the Wage Gap." *Time.* 19 May.

Carney, Diana. 2012. "Inequality: Defining the Defining Issue of our Time." *iPolitics.* 19 November.

Carpenter, Christopher S. 2008. "Sexual Orientation, Work, and Income in Canada." *Canadian Journal of Economics* 41:1239–1261.

Carr, Nicholas. 2015. *The Glass Cage: How our Computers are Changing Us.* New York: W.W. Norton.

Carrick, Rob. 2013. "When University Doesn't Pay." *The Globe and Mail.* 29 August.

Carrick, Rob. 2015. "Canadians Shouldn't Be Complacent about our Student Debt." *The Globe and Mail.* 1 November.

Carroll, Hamilton. 2008. "Men's Soaps: Automotive Television Programming and Contemporary Working-Class Masculinities." *Television & New Media* 9 (4):263–283.

Carroll, William K. 1997. *Contemporary Social Movements in Theory and Practice.* Toronto: University of Toronto Press.

Carter, Jimmy. 2014. Patriarchy and Violence against Women and Girls. *The Lancet.* Published online, 20 November.

Carter, Sarah. 1990. *Lost Harvests.* Montreal and Kingston: McGill-Queen's University Press.

Castellano M., L. Archibald, and M. Degagne (eds.). 2008. From Truth to Reconciliation: Transforming the Legacy of Residential Schools. pp 183–203. Ottawa: Aboriginal Healing Foundation.

Castells, Manuel. 2010. "The New Public Sphere: Global Civil Society, Communication Networks, and Global Governance." In *International Communication: A Reader.* D.K. Thussu (ed.). pp. 36–47. New York: Routledge.

Castles, Stephen. 2011. "Migration and Citizenship in the Making of a Global Labour Market," in *Nationalism and Globalisation.* D. Halikiopoulou and S. Vasilopoulou (eds.). pp. 137–156. New York: Routledge.

Catalyst. 2012. Women on Boards. August. Retrieved from www.communitybusiness.org .

Catalyst. 2015a. Women in S & P 500 Companies by Race/Ethnicity. New York: March.

Catalyst, 2015b. Women CEOs of the S&P 500. New York: April.

CAUT [Canadian Association of University Teachers]. 2010. 2010/11: Almanac of Post-Secondary Education in Canada. September.

CAUT Bulletin. 2011. CAUT Report: Gender Pay Gap Narrows. March.

CAUT. 2013. Open for Business—On What Terms? An Analysis of 12 Collaborations between Canadian Universities and Corporations, Donors and Governments. November.

CAUT Almanac. 2013/14. Post-secondary Education in Canada. Ottawa.

CAUT 2014–2015. CAUT Almanac of Post-Secondary Education in Canada. Ottawa: Canadian Association of University Teachers.

CAUT Bulletin. 2015. Tuition Fees on the Rise. October.

CBC News. 2012. Mercury Poisoning Effects Continues at Grassy Narrows. 4 June.

CBC News. 2016. Canada Officially Adopts the UN Declaration on the Rights of Indigenous Peoples. 10 May.

CFAIA/CLC [Canadian Feminist Alliance for International Action/Canadian Labour Congress]. 2010. Reality Check: Women in Canada and the Beijing Declaration and the Platform for Action Fifteen Years On: A Canadian Civil Society Response. 22 February.

Chakma, Amit. 2013. "Rooting Through the Causes of a Garment Factory Tragedy." *The Globe and Mail.* 7 May.

Chalmers, John. 2013. "How Garment Bosses Rule Bangladesh." *The Globe and Mail.* 4 May.

Chan, Wendy. 2012. "Keeping Canada White: Immigration Enforcement in Canada," in *Power and Resistance: Critical Thinking about Canadian Social Issues.* L. Samuelson and W. Antony (eds.). pp. 167–193. 5th ed., Halifax: Fernwood.

Chan, Wendy. 2014. News Media Representations of Immigrants in the Canadian Criminal Justice System. Working Paper Series. Metropolis British Columbia, Vancouver.

Chan, Tak Wing, and John H. Goldthorpe. 2007. "Class and Status: The Conceptual Distinction and Its Empirical Relevance." *American Sociological Review* 72: August, 512–532.

Chang, Ha-Joon. 2010. *23 Things They Didn't Tell You about Capitalism.* New York: Bloomsbury Press.

Chant, Sylvia. 2010. "Gendered Poverty across Time and Space: Introduction and Overview," in *The International Handbook of Gender and Poverty.* S. Chant (ed.). pp. 1–15. Northampton, MA: Edward Elgar.

Charbonneau, Leo. 2012a. "The 'New Majority' of Contingent Faculty Try to Get Heard." *University Affairs.* 14 February.

Charbonneau, Leo. 2012b. "The Future of Universities is all Doom and Gloom." *University Affairs.* 6 November.

Charbonneau, Leo. 2013. "Progress is Slow for Women in Senior Roles at Canada's Universities." *University Affairs.* 16 October.

Charbonneau, Leo. 2014. "Professor Leads Campaign to Improve Lives of 'Generation Squeezed.'" *University Affairs.* 16 December.

Charles, Dan. 2013. "Our Fertilized World." *National Geographic.* May. pp. 94–111.

Cheadle, Bruce. 2013. "Climate Policy in Canada Worst in Developed World: Report." Canadian Press. Reprinted in the *Waterloo Region Record.* 19 November.

Cheng, L., M. Spaling, and X. Song. 2012. "Barriers and Facilitators to Professional Licensure and Certification

Testing in Canada: Perspectives of Internationally Educated Professionals." *International Migration and Integration.* Published online 5 December.

Cherti, Myriam, and Clare McNeil. 2012. Rethinking Integration. Institute for Research in Public Policy. October.

Chesler, Mark, Amanda E. Lewis, and James E. Crowfoot. 2005. *Challenging Racism in Higher Education: Promoting Justice.* Lanham, MD: Rowman and Littlefield.

Christensen, Kathleen, and Barbara Schneider. 2011. "Making a Case for Workplace Flexibility." *The Annals,* AAPPSS 638, November, pp. 6–17.

Churchill, Ward. 2004. *A Little Matter of Genocide.* San Francisco: City Lights Publisher.

Citizens for Public Justice. 2013. Poverty Trends Highlights: Canada 2013. Ottawa. October.

Ciuriak, Dan, and John M. Curtis. 2013. The Resurgence of Industrial Policy and What this Means for Canada. IRPP. 18 June.

Clark, Joe. 2013. *How We Lead: Canada in a Century of Change.* Random House Canada.

Clark, Brad. 2014. "'Walking Up a Down-Escalator': The Interplay between Newsroom Norms and Media Coverage of Minority Groups." inMedia. Retrieved from http://inmedia.revues.org/749 .

Clark, Rob. 2011. "World Income Inequality in the Global Era: New Estimates, 1990–2008." *Social Problems* 58 (4):565–592.

Clarkson, Adrienne. 2014. *Belonging: The Paradox of Citizenship.* Anansi.

Class Dismissed (video). 2005. *Class Dismissed: How TV Frames the Working Class.* Co-written and co-produced by Pepi Leistyna and Loretta Alper. Media Education Foundation.

Clemens, Jason. 2012. Income Inequality: Oversimplifying a Complicated Issues. iPolitics Insight. 1 May. Retrieved from www.ipolitics.ca .

Clement, Dominque. 2009. *Canada's Rights Revolution.* Vancouver: UBC Press Council of Europe.

Clement, Dominque. 2016. *Rights Inflation and the Crisis of Canadian Rights Culture.* Waterloo, ON: Wilfrid Laurier Press.

Clement, Wallace. 1988. *The Challenge of Class Analysis.* Ottawa: Carleton University Press.

Clement, Wallace, and Rick Helmes-Hayes. 2015. "Foreword," in *The Vertical Mosaic: An Analysis of Social Class and Power in Canada.* by John Porter. 50th Anniversary Edition, Toronto: University of Toronto Press.

Clifford, James. 2000. "Taking Identity Politics Seriously: 'The Contradictory Stoney Ground . . .'" in *Essays in Honour of Stuart Hall.* P. Gilroy, L. Grossman, and A. McRobie (eds.). pp. 94-112. London: Verso.

Clift, Robert F. 2016. "A Cautionary Tale of Marketization of Postsecondary Education." *Academic Matters,* 13-16. January.

Clifton, Rodney E., and Hymie Rubenstein. 2015. "No Truth, No Reconciliation." *National Post.* 3 June.

Climate Action Network Europe/Germanwatch. 2013. Climate Change Performance Index. 18 November. Author.

Coates, Ken. 2012. "The Quiet Campus: the Anatomy of Dissent at Canadian Universities." *Academic Matters,* 23–26. November.

Coates, Ken. 2013a. "Chief Atleo's New Model of Aboriginal Politics." *The Globe and Mail.* 17 January.

Coates, Ken. 2013b. Canada Needs More Non-Aboriginal Engagement with First Nations People. The MacDonald-Laurier Institute. Retrieved from www.macdonaldlaurier .ca/canada-needs-more-non-aboriginal-engagement-with-first-nations-people/ . 17 January.

Coates, Ken. 2015a. *#Idle No More and the Remaking of Canada.* Regina SA: University of Regina Press.

Coates, Ken. 2015b. Career Ready: Towards a National Strategy for the Mobilization of Canadian Potential. Report Commissioned by the Canadian Council of Chief Executives. March.

Coates, Ken, and Bill Morrison. 2012. "The Uses and Abuses of University." *The Walrus.* October. pp. 34–39.

Coates, Ken and Bill Morrison. 2016. Dream Factories: Why Universities Won't Solve the Youth Jobs Crisis. TAP Books/Dundurn.

Coates, Ken, and Brian Lee Crowley. 2013. *New Beginnings.* McDonald Laurier Institute. May.

Cohen, Joel. 1996. *How Many People Can the Earth Support?* New York: W.W. Norton & Company.

Cohen, Madeleine. 2014. Women Professionals Advance in Masculine Societies: Gender Inequality is a Global Issue. Retrieved from https://prezi.com .

Cohen, Patricia. 2010. "'Culture of Poverty' Making a Comeback." *The New York Times.* 17 October.

Cohen, Philip. 2013. "The 'End of Men' is Not True: What is not and What Might Be on the Road to Gender Equality." *Boston University Law Review* 93:1159–1181.

Coleman, Daniel, and Smaro Kamboureli (eds.). 2011. *Retooling the Humanities.* Edmonton: University of Alberta Press.

Community Foundations of Canada. 2012. #Generation Flux: Understanding the Seismic Shifts That are Shaking Canadian Youth. *Vital Signs.* Prepared by Dominque O'Rourke. October.

Conference Board of Canada. 2010. Gender Income Gap. Retrieved 5 August 2010 from www.conferenceboard.ca .

Conference Board of Canada. 2011a. Society: Child Poverty. Available at www.conferenceboard.ca .

Conference Board of Canada. 2011b. World Income Inequality. September. Available at www.conferenceboard.ca .

Conference Board of Canada. 2012. Education and Skills Overview. Retrieved from www.conferenceboard.ca .

Conference Board of Canada. 2013a. High Consumption and Throwaway Habits Make Canada an Environmental Laggard. News Release. 17 January.

Conference Board of Canada. 2013b. How Canada Performs: Society. February.

Conference Board of Canada. 2014. The Buck Stops Here: Trends in Income Inequality between Generations. September.

Conference Notes. 2015. Racialization at Canadian Universities. Presentation to the Centre for Ethnicity and Racism Studies, University of Leeds. Presenters: Frances Henry, Carl James, Ena Dua, Audrey Kobayashi, and Malinda Smith. 21 April.

Connell, R.W. 1996. "Politics of Changing Men." *Socialist Review* 25(1).

Connell, Raewyn. 2011. *Confronting Inequality: Gender, Knowledge, and Global Change.* Malden MA: Polity.

Cooke, Martin, and Jennifer McWhirter. 2010. Public Policy and Aboriginal Peoples in Canada: Taking a Life Course Perspective. Canadian Public Policy.

Cooke, Martin and David Long. 2016. "Moving Beyond the Politics of Aboriginal Well-Being, Health, and Healing," in *Visions of the Heart*. D. Long and O.P. Dickason (eds.), pp. 292–327. Toronto: Oxford.

Cooke, Martin, Francis Mitrou, David Lawrence, David Povah, Elina Mobilia, Eric Guimond, and Stephen Zubrik. 2014. Gaps in Indigenous Disadvantage Not Closing: A Census Cohort Study of Social Determinants of Health in Australia, Canada, and New Zealand from 1981–2006. BMC (BioMed Central) Public Health 14:201–210.

Coontz, Stephanie. 2012. "The Myth of Male Decline." *The New York Times*. 29 September.

Coontz, Stephanie. 2013. "Why Gender Equality Stalled." *The New York Times*. Opinion. 16 February.

Coontz, Stephanie. 2015. The Tricky Business of Sorting Out Sexual Assaults: An Introduction to the Council of Contemporary Families Conference Online Symposium on Intimate Partner Violence. Convened by Stephanie Coontz, University of Miami. 20 April.

Cooper, Barry. 2010. Book Review: "Uprising, 'White' Indians, and a Crack Shot." Retrieved from http://c2cjournal.ca .

Cooper, Glenda. 2014. "Dear Disney, Stop Telling My Six-year-old Girl the 'Princess' Look Includes Pin-up-girl Cleavage." *National Post*. 26 August.

Cooper, Jamie, and Tanisha Salomons. 2009/10. Addressing Violence against Aboriginal Women. Prepared for the Battered Women's Support Services. October to February.

Corak, Miles. 2010. Chasing the Same Dream, Climbing Different Ladders. Economic Mobility in the United States and Canada. Economic Mobility Project. January.

Corak, Miles. 2012. Is the U.S. Still a "Land of Opportunity?": The Canada We Want in 2020. 10 January. Available at http://canada2020.ca .

Corak, Miles, and Mark Stabile. 2013. "How to Stay Ahead of the Gatsby Curve." *The Globe and Mail*. 18 October.

Cornell, Stephan, and Joseph P. Kalt. 2003. "Sovereignty and Nation-building: The Development Challenge in Indian Country Today." Joint Occasional Papers on Native Affairs No. 2003-03. Originally published in the *American Indian Culture and Research Journal*, 1998.

Corntassel, Jeff. 2008. "Toward Sustainable Self-Determination: Rethinking the Contemporary Indigenous-Rights Discourse." *Alternatives* 33:105–132.

Cote, James, and Anton Allahar. 2007. *Ivory Tower Blues: A University System in Crisis*. Toronto: University of Toronto Press.

Cote-Meek, Sheila. 2014. *Colonized Classrooms: Racism, Trauma, and Resistance in Postsecondary Education*. Halifax: Fernwood Publishing.

Cottle, Simon, ed. 2005. *Ethnic Minorities and the Media: Changing Cultural Boundaries*. Philadelphia: Open U Press.

Coulthard, Glen. 2014. *Red Skins, White Masks: Rejecting the Colonial Politics of Recognition*. Minneapolis: University of Minnesota Press.

Council of Canadian Academies. 2012. Strengthening Canada's Research Capacity: the Gender Dimension. The Expert Panel on Women in University Research.

Courchene, Thomas J. 2011. Rekindling the American Dream: A Northern Perspective. Policy Horizons Essay. Institute for Research in Public Policy.

Coyne, Andrew. 2012. "The Problem Isn't Giving People Money When They Don't Work . . . It's Taking It Away When They Do." *National Post*. 16 November.

Crompton, Rosemary. 2008. *Class and Stratification*. 3rd ed. Polity.

Crooks, Harold. 2014. *The Price We Pay*. Documentary.

Cross, Philip. 2014. Cross in the National Post. Canadians are Not Undertaxed. Macdonald-Laurier Institute. 8 April.

Cross, Philip. 2015. Economic Growth, not Wealth Transfer, Should be Focus of 2015 Budget. Cross on CTV. Macdonald-Laurier Institute. 25 April.

Cross, Philip, and Munir A. Sheikh. 2015. Caught in the Middle: Some in Canada's Middle Class are Doing Well; Others Have Good Reason to Worry. The School of Public Policy Research Paper. University of Calgary. Vol. 8, Issue 12. March.

Croteau, David, and William Hoynes. 2003. *Media/Society: Industries, Images, and Audiences*. 3rd ed. Thousand Oaks: Sage.

Croteau, David, William Hoynes, and Stephanie Milan. 2012. *Media/Society*. Thousand Oaks: Sage.

Crouch, Carl 2011. *The Strange Non-Death of Neo-Liberalism*. Polity.

Cunningham, Brent. 2004. "Across the Great Divide: Class." *Columbia Journalism Review* 43 (1):31–38.

Curtice, John. 2012. The Uphill Battle Ahead for "Responsible Capitalism." Institute Public Policy Research. IPPR 19(2).

Curtis, James, and Lorne Tepperman. 2004. *Social Problems. A Canadian Perspective*. Toronto: Oxford University Press.

Cushen, J. 2013. "Financialization in the Workplace." *Organization and Society* 38 (4):314–331.

Czyzewski, Karina. 2011. "Colonialism as a Broader Social Determinant of Health." *International Indigenous Policy Journal* 2(1). Article 5.

Dale, Roger. 2010. The Dark Side of the Whiteboard. Education, Poverty, Inequalities, and Exclusion. Paper at the Belgian EU Presidency Conference on Education and Social Inclusion. Ghent, 28–29 September.

Daschuk, James. 2013. *Clearing the Plains: Disease, Politics of Starvation, and the Loss of Aboriginal Life*. Regina, SK: University of Regina Press.

Das Gupta, Tania. 2009. *"Real" Nurses and Others: Racism in Nursing*. Halifax: Fernwood.

Davey, Joseph Dillon. 2012. *The Shrinking American Middle Class: The Social and Cultural Implications of Growing Inequality*. New York: Palgrave Macmillan.

Davies, Scott, and Neil Guppy. 2010. *The Schooled Society*, 2nd ed. Vancouver: UBC Press.

Davies, Scott, Vicky Maldonado, and David Zarifa. 2014. "Effectively Maintaining Inequality in Toronto: Predicting Student Destinations in Ontario Universities." *Canadian Review of Sociology* 51(1):22–53.

Davin, Nicholas Flood. 1879. Report on Industrial Schools for Indians and Half Breeds. Submission to the Minister of the Interior.

Davison, Ryan C. 2012. "Literature Review: Critically Thinking about Brain and Gender Differences," in *Apply Research to Practice (ARP) Resources*. B. Bogue and E. Cady (eds.). Retrieved from www.engr.psu.edu .

De Leeuw, Sarah, and Margo Greenwood. 2011. "Beyond Borders and Boundaries: Addressing Indigenous Health Inequities in Canada through Theories of Social Determinants of Health and Intersectionality," in *Health Inequalities in Canada: Intersectional Frameworks and Practices*, O. Hankivsky (ed.), pp. 53–70. Vancouver: UBC Press.

Dean, Jodi. 2009. *Democracy and Other Neoliberal Fantasies: Communicative Capitalism and Left Politics*. Duke University Press.

DeAngelis, Tori. 2009. "Unmasking 'Racial Micro Aggressions.'" *American Psychological Association* 40(2):42–46.

Deane, Art. 2012. Workplace Safety: Innovative Practices and Strategies for Critical Safety Thinking. Speaking Notes, University of Alberta. 29 March.

Deaton, Angus. 2013. *The Great Escape: Health, Wealth, and the Origins of Inequality*. Princeton University Press.

deBoer, Kaila, David Rothwell, and Christopher Lee. 2013 Child and Family Poverty in Canada: Implications for Child Welfare Research. Canadian Child Welfare Research Portal Information Sheet #123.

DeCellis, Katherine and Michael Norton. 2016. "Physical and Situational Inequality on Airplanes Predicts Air Rage." *Proceedings of the National Academy of Sciences of the United States of America* 113(20).

Dechief, Diane, and Philip Oreopoulos. 2012. Why Do Some Employers Prefer to Interview Matthew but Not Samir: New Evidence from Toronto, Montreal, and Vancouver. Canadian Labour Market and Skills Researcher Network. Working Paper No 95. February.

Deckha, Maneesha. 2010. "Gender, Culture, and Violence: Toward a Paradigm Shift?" *Equity Matters*. Fedcan Blog. Retrieved from http://blog.fedcan.ca/2010/02/18/ .

DeKeseredy, Walter. 2011. *Violence against Women: Myths, Facts, Controversies*. Toronto: University of Toronto Press.

DeKeseredy, Walter S., and Molly Dragiewicz. 2007. "Understanding the Complexities of Feminist Perspectives on Women Abuse: A Commentary on Donald Dutton's Rethinking Domestic Violence," in *Violence against Women* 13(8): 874–884.

Delic, Senada, and Francis Abele. 2010. "The Recession and Aboriginal Workers," in *How Ottawa Spends, 2010/2011*. G.B. Doern and C. Stoney (eds.), pp. 187–216. Montreal and Kingston: McGill-Queen's University Press.

Deloitte. 2011. *Welcome to Canada: Now What? Unlocking the Potential of Immigrants for Business Growth and Innovation*. White paper summary of Deloitte's Dialogue on Diversity. November.

Denis, Ann. 2008. "Intersectional Analysis: A Contribution of Feminism to Sociology." *International Sociology* 23(5):677–694.

Denis, Claude. 1997. *We Are Not You: First Nations and Canadian Modernity*. Peterborough: Broadview Press.

Denis, Jeffrey S. 2012. "Bridging Understandings: Anishinaabe and White Perspectives on the Residential School and Prospects for Reconciliation," in *Reading Sociology: Canadian Perspectives*, L. Tepperman and A. Kalyta (eds.). pp. 257–262. Toronto: Oxford University Press.

Denney, Justin, R. McNown, R. Rogers, and S. Doubilet. 2012. "Stagnating Life Expectancies and Future Prospects in an Age of Uncertainty." *Social Science Quarterly* 43.

Dent, Tamsyn. 2008. Women and the Media: What do They Want? Polis and the Gender Institute Seminar. March.

Department of Justice Canada. 2012. Family Violence Initiatives. Retrieved from www.justice.gc.ca .

Deschamps, Marie. 2015. External Review of Sexual Misconduct and Sexual Harassment in the Canadian Armed Forces. 27 March.

Deveau, Denise. 2013. "Engineering Struggling to Bring Women into the Profession." *National Post*, 7 May.

Deveaux, Monique. 2006. *Gender and Justice in Multicultural Liberal States*. New York: Oxford University Press.

DeVega, Chauncey. 2014. The "Niggerization" of Michael Brown by the Ferguson Police Department and the Right Wing Media. 18 August. Retrieved from www.alternet.org/speakeasy/chaunceydevega/niggerization-michael-brown-ferguson-police-department-and-right-wing-media .

Dey, Anouk. 2012. The Global Village, Circa 2012. 17 January. Available online at www.opencanada.org/features/mcluhan-jane-jacobs/.

Dhamoon, Rita Kaur. 2009. *Identity/Difference Politics: How Difference is Produced and Why It Matters*. Vancouver: UBC Press.

Dhamoon, Rita Kaur, and Olena Hankivsky. 2011. "The Theory and Practice of Intersectionality Matter to Health Research and Policy," in *Health Inequalities in Canada: Intersectional Frameworks and Practices*. O. Hankivsky, ed. pp. 16–52. Vancouver: UBC Press.

Dharssi, Alia. 2015. "Deconstructing Development." *National Post*, 2 November.

Diamond, Peter, and Emmanuel Saez. 2011. "The Case for a Progressive Tax: From Basic Research to Policy Recommendations." *Journal of Economic Perspectives* 25 (4):165–190.

Diamandis, Peter, and Steven Kotler. 2012. *Abundance: The Future is Better than You Think*. New York: Free Press.

Dick, Kirby, and Ava Ziering. 2015. *The Hunting Ground*. Documentary.

Dickinson, Tim. 2015. "Canada's Crude Awakening." *Rolling Stone*, Issue 1230, pp 32–35. 12 March.

Dobbin, Murray. 2013a. "Canada's Reckless Banks Inflate House Price Bubble." *The Tyee*, 11 March.

Dobbin, Murray. 2013b. "The Power of Idle No More's Resurgent Radicalism." *The Tyee*. 14 January.

Dobbin, Murray. 2015. "Austerity or Prosperity? Canada's $626 Billion Question." *The Tyee*. 12 January.

Doctors for Fair Taxation. 2012. "Raise Taxes to Roll Back Inequality." *Toronto Star*. 2 April.

Dodd, Douglas. 2013. "Growing Poverty Among Canadian Immigrants Could Explode: Study." *Vancouver Sun*. 28 June.

Dogan, Recep. 2011. "Is Honor Killing a 'Muslim Phenomenon'? Textual Interpretations and Cultural Representations." *Journal of Muslim Minority Affairs* 31(3).

Dooley, Chris. 2013. Review of *Healing Stories*. By L.M. Drees. *Oral History* 33.

Dorling, Danny. 2010. *Injustice: Why Social Inequality Persists*. Polity Press.

Dorling, Danny. 2011. "Underclass, Overclass, Ruling Class, Supernova Class," in *Fighting Poverty, Inequality, and Injustice*. A. Walker, A. Sinfield, and C. Walker (eds.). pp. 153–163. Polity Press.

Dorling, Danny. 2012. The Case for Austerity among the Rich. Institute for Public Policy Research. Discussion Paper. March.

Dorling, Danny. 2013. "The No-Nonsense Guide to Equality." *New Internationalist*.

Dorling, Danny. 2014. *Inequality and the 1%*. Brooklyn: Verso.

Douglas, Debbie, Avvy Go, Margaret Parsons, and Deep Mattoo. 2014. "Election Must Address Diversity." *Toronto Star*. 2 August.

Douglas, Stacy, and Suzanne Lenon. 2014. "Introduction." *Canadian Journal of Law and Society* 29(2):141–143.

Douglas, Susan. 1994. *Where the Girls Are: Growing Up Female with the Mass Media*. New York: Random House.

Drees, Laurie Meijers. 2013. *Healing Stories: Stories from Canada's Indian Hospitals*. Edmonton: University of Alberta Press.

Drummond Don, and Francis Fong. 2010. The Changing Canadian Workplace. Special Report, TD Economics. March 8.

Dufraiment, Lisa. 2002. "Continuity and Modification of Aboriginal Rights in the Nisga'a Treaty." UBC *Law Review* 35(2):455–477.

Dullien, Sebastian, Hansjorg Herr, and Christian Kellerman. 2011. *Decent Capitalism: A Blueprint for Reforming Capitalism*. London: Pluto Press.

Dungan, Peter, Tony Fang, and Morley Gunderson. 2012. Macroeconomic Impacts of Canadian Immigration: Results from a Macro Model. Discussion Paper No. 6743. July. Bonn: IZA (Study of Labour).

Dutton, Donald G. 2006. *Rethinking Domestic Violence*. Vancouver: UBC Press.

Duxbury, Linda, and Christopher Higgins. 2012. Revisiting Work-Life Issues in Canada: The 2012 National Study on Balancing Work and Caregiving in Canada. Ottawa: Carleton University.

Economist, The. 2013. "Towards the End of Poverty." 1 June.

Economist, The. 2014. "The Final Frontier." 19 July.

Economist Intelligence Unit. 2014. Global Liveability Ranking and Report. August. Retrieved from www.eiu.com/public/topical_report.aspx?campaignid=Liveability2014 .

Economist Intelligence Unit. 2015. Assessing Urban Security in the Digital Age. The Safe Cities Index 2015.

Economist 2015. Travelling Light. 29 August

Editorial, 2015. "Unsafe to Drink? Hard to Swallow." *The Globe and Mail*, 14 September.

Edwards, Sherri. 2011. Age Discrimination in the Workplace: Is it Ageism or your Attitude? Retrieved from www.forbes.com/sites/moneywisewomen/2011/03/02/age-discrimination-in-the-workplace-is-it-ageism-or-your-attitude/#2d-7d7e797b83 .

Eggins, Heather. 2011. *Access and Equity: Comparative Perspectives*. Boston: Sense Publishers.

Eichler, Leah. 2012. "Breaking the Boardroom Gender Barrier." *The Globe and Mail*, 3 March.

Ehrenreich, Barbara. 2009. "Rich Get Poorer, Poor Disappear." *Current Affairs*, 12 January. Available at http://ehrenreich.blogs.com .

Ehrenreich, Barbara. 2014. "It is Expensive to be Poor." *The Atlantic*. 13 January.

Eisenkraft, Harriet. 2013. "Aren't We There Yet?" *University Affairs*. November, pp 22–26.

EKOS Politics. 2013a. Immigration, Diversity, and the Political Landscape. 19 April.

EKOS Politics. 2013b. Choosing a Better Future? 26 July.

EKOS Politics. 2013c. What is the Greatest Canadian Achievement? 26 February.

Elder-Vass, Dave. 2010. *The Causal Power of Social Structures: Emergence, Structure, and Agency*. Cambridge: Cambridge University Press.

Elinder, Mikael, and Oscar Erixson. 2012 Gender, Maritime Norms, and Survival in Maritime Disasters. PNAS [Proceedings of the National Academy of Science] Early Edition. July 30, pp 1-5.

El-Naggar, Mona, 2012. "Family Life According to the Brotherhood." *The New York Times*. 4 September.

Employment and Social Development Canada. 2013. Snapshot of Racialized Poverty in Canada. Government of Canada.

Engler, Gary. 2013. *New Commune-ist Manifesto. Workers of the World, It Really is Time to Unite*. Halifax: Fernwood.

Engler, Gary. 2014. Ten Ways We Can Build a Better Economic System. Rabble.ca. 25 August.

Engler, Yves. 2016. *Canada in Africa: 300 Years of Aid and Exploitation*. Halifax: Fernwood.

Environics. 2016. Survey of Muslims in Canada 2016. April

Epperson, Brent. 2014. "Universities are Ill-Served by a Corporate Governance Model." *University Affairs*. 20 August.

Esmail, Nadeem. 2013. "Free Health in Canada Costs More than it's Worth." *Huff Post Politics* Canada. 9 October.

Esmail, Nadeem, and Bacchus Barua. 2013. Waiting Your Turn: Wait Times for Health Care in Canada, 2013 Report. Fraser Institute. Studies on Health Policy. October.

Essed, Philomena. 1991. Understanding Everyday Racism: An Interdisciplinary Theory. Newbury Park, CA: Sage.

EUAFFR [European Union Agency for Fundamental Rights]. 2014a. Being Trans in the European Union. Comparative Analysis of EU LGBT Survey Data.

EUAFFR. 2014b. Violence against Women: An EU-wide Survey. Main Results Report. March.

Evans, Geoff, and James Tilley. 2015. The New Class War: Excluding the Working Class in 21st Century Britain. IPPR, 30 March.

F.A.C.E.S. of Peel Collaborative. 2015. The Black Community in Peel. Summary. Research Findings from Four Reports. Prepared by the Social Planning Council of Peel. 4 May.

FAFIA [Canadian Feminist Alliance for International Action]. 2008. Submission to the United Nations Committee on the Elimination of Discrimination Against Women.

FAFIA. 2009. No Progress, No Action. Response to Canada's Report Back to the UN Committee on the Elimination of Discrimination against Women. Published by the Canadian Women's Health Network

FAFIA/CLC [Canadian Feminist Alliance for International Action/Canadian Labour Congress]. 2010. Reality Check: Women in Canada and the Beijing Declaration and the Platform for Action Fifteen Years On. A Canadian Civil Society Response. 22 February.

Fallis, George. 2013. "Canada's Surprising One Percent." *Literary Review of Canada*. March.

Faludi, Susan. 1999. *Stiffed. The Betrayal of the American Man.* New York, NY: Perennial (an imprint of Harper Collins).

Fanelli, Carlo, Chris Hurl, Priscilla Lefebvre, and Gulden Ozcan. 2011. "Introduction: Saving Global Capitalism; Interrogating Austerity and Working Class Responses to Crises." *Alternative Routes: A Journal of Critical Social Research*. pp. 1–6.

Farrell, Diana. 2004. "Beyond Cheap Labor: Lessons for Developing Economies." *McKinsey Quarterly*, 21 December.

Farrugia, David, and Jessica Gerrard. 2015. "Academic Knowledge and Contemporary Poverty: The Politics of Homeless Research." *Sociology*, pp. 1–18.

Feagin, Joe. 2010. *The White Racial Frame. Centuries of Racial Framing and Counter-Framing*. New York: Routledge.

Feagin, Joe. 2011. "Introduction," in *Everyday Forms of Whiteness. Understanding Race in a "Post Racial World."* Melanie Bush. 2nd ed. Lanham, MD: Rowman & Littlefield.

Feree, Myra Marx. 2008. Inequality, Intersectionality, and the Politics of Discourse: Framing Feminist Alliances. In *The Discursive Politics of Gender Equality: Stretching, Bending, and Policy-Making*. E. Lombardo, P. Meier, and M. Verloo (eds.). New York: Routledge.

Ferguson, David. 2014. Louisiana's Gov. Jindal Prayer Rally Handouts Blame Gays and Abortion for Hurricane Katrina. *US News*. Retrieved from www.alternet.org/louisiana-gov-jindals-prayer-rally-handouts-blame-gays-and-abortion-hurricane-katrina.

Ferguson, Susan J. 2012. *Race, Gender, Sexuality, and Social Class. Dimensions of Inequality*. Thousand Oaks: Sage.

Field, C.C., G.A. Jones, G. Karram Stephenson, and A. Khoyetsyan. 2014. *The "Other" University Teachers: Non-Full-Time Instructors at Ontario Universities*. Toronto: Higher Education Quality Council of Ontario.

Finn, Ed. 2011. No Excuse for Inequality. Canadian Centre for Policy Alternatives. 1 March.

Finnie, Ross, Richard E. Mueller, Arthur Sweetman, and Alex Usher (eds.). 2008. *Who Goes, Who Stays, What Matters? Accessing and Persisting in Post-Secondary Education in Canada*. Montreal and Kingston: Queen's School of Policy Studies/McGill-Queen's University Press.

Finnie, Ross, Stephen Childs, Dejan Pavlic, and Nemanja Jevtovic. 2014. How Much Do University Graduates Earn? Education Policy Research Initiative. Research Brief No. 3 (Version 14-11-21). University of Ottawa.

Fiorito, Joe. 2013. "Poverty Costs us Billions." *Toronto Star*, 17 April.

Fischer, Karin. 2016. "Engine of Inequality." *The Chronicle of Higher Education*. 17 January.

Fiske, Susan T., and Hazel Rose Markus. 2012. *Facing Social Class. How Societal Rank Influences Interaction*. New York: Russell Sage Foundation.

Fiss, Tanis. 2004. Apartheid: Canada's Ugly Secret. Centre for Aboriginal Policy Change. Canadian Taxpayer Federation. Calgary.

Fiss, Tanis. 2005. Dividing Canada. The Pitfalls of Native Sovereignty. Centre for Aboriginal Policy Change. Canadian Taxpayers Federation. Calgary.

Fister, Emily. 2014. "What Makes Us Unequal? Being a Mom." *The Tyee*. 6 September.

Flanagan, Tom. 1999. *First Nations? Second Thoughts*. Montreal and Kingston: McGill-Queen's University Press.

Flanagan, Tom, C. Alcantara, and A. Le Dressay. 2009. *Beyond the Indian Act: Restoring Aboriginal Property Rights*. Montreal and Kingston: McGill Queen's University Press.

Flanagan, Tom, and Katrine Beauregard. 2013. The Wealth of First Nations: An Exploratory Study. Centre for Aboriginal Policy Studies. Fraser Institute. June.

Flavelle, Dana. 2014. "Top 100 CEOs Pay Booming, Report Finds." *Toronto Star*. 2 January.

Fleras, Augie. 1996. "Behind the Ivy Walls: Racism/Anti-racism on Campus," in *Racism in Education*. I. Alladin (ed.), pp. 134–177. Toronto: Harcourt Brace.

Fleras, Augie. 2003. *Mass Communication in Canada*. Toronto: Nelson.

Fleras, Augie. 2005. *Social Problems in Canada*, 4th ed. Toronto: Pearson.

Fleras, Augie. 2009. *The Politics of Multiculturalisms: Multicultural Governances in Comparative Perspectives*. New York: Palgrave Macmillan.

Fleras, Augie. 2011a. *The Media Gaze: Representations of Diversities in Canada*. Vancouver: UBC Press.

Fleras, Augie. 2011b. From Multiculturalism to Multiversality. Paper presented to the Conference on 40th Anniversary of Canadian Multiculturalism. Ottawa, September.

Fleras, Augie. 2012. *Unequal Relations: Race, Ethnic, and Aboriginal Relations in Canada*. 7th ed. Toronto: Pearson Education.

Fleras, Augie. 2014a. *Racisms in a Multicultural Canada*. Waterloo, ON: Wilfrid Laurier Press.

Fleras, Augie. 2014b. *Immigration Canada*. Vancouver: UBC Press.

Fleras, Augie. 2014c. Mainstream Media as White Ethnic Press. Paper delivered to the Media and Minority Conference. Jewish Museum. Berlin. November.

Fleras, Augie. 2015. "Beyond Multiculturalism: Managing Complex Diversities in a Postmulticultural Canada," in *Revisiting Multiculturalism in Canada*. L. Wong and S. Guo (eds.), pp 297–321. Rotterdam: Sense Publishers.

Fleras, Augie. 2016. *Unequal Relations. A Critical Introduction to Race, Ethnic, and Aboriginal Relations*. 8th ed. Toronto: Pearson Education

Fleras, Augie, and Paul Spoonley. 1999. *Recalling Aotearoa*. Auckland: Oxford University Press.

Fleras, Augie, and Jean Lock Kunz. 2001. *Media and Minorities*. Toronto: Thompson Publishing.

Fleras, Augie, and Roger Maaka. 2005. *The Politics of Indigeneity*. Dunedin, NZ: Otago University Press.

Fleras, Augie, and Roger Maaka. 2009a. "Mainstreaming Indigeneity, Indigenizing Policymaking." *Indigenous Policy Journal*. October.

Fleras, Augie, and Roger Maaka. 2009b. "Towards an Indigenous Grounded Analysis Policymaking Framework". *International Indigenous Policy Journal* (online), Vol. 1.

Fleras, Augie, and Shane Dixon. 2011. "Re-masculinizing the Working Class Heroic." *Canadian Journal of Communication* 38(4):579–599.

Florby, Gunilla, Mark Shackleton, and Katri Suhonen. 2009. *Canada: Images of a Post/National Society*. New York: Peter Lang.

Fobister, Simon. 2013. "Logging Plans Would Deepen the Tragedy at Grassy Narrows." *Toronto Star*. 3 November.

Fobister, William. 2003. A Message from Chief William Fobister. November 11. Retrieved from www.envirowatch.org .

Foley, Jonathan 2014. "Feeding Nine Billion." *National Geographic* 225(5):26–57.

Foley, Kelly, and David A. Green. 2015. "Why Education Will Not Solve Rising Inequality (and May Make it Worse)," in *Income Inequality: The Canadian Story*, Vol. V., David A. Green, W. Craig Riddell, and Frances St-Hilaire (eds.). Institute for Research on Public Policy.

Fontaine, Phil, and Bernie Farber. 2013. "What Canada Committed against First Nations was Genocide: The UN Should Recognize It." *The Globe and Mail*. 14 October.

Food Banks Canada. 2014. HungerCount Survey Reveals Alarmingly High Needs. 4 November.

Ford, Martin. 2015. *Rise of the Robots: Technology and the Threat of a Jobless Future*. Basic Books.

Fortin, Nicole, D.A. Green, T. Lemieux, K. Milligan, and W.C. Riddell. 2012. Canadian Inequality: Recent Developments and Policy Options. Prepared for the Canadian Labour Market and Skills Research Network. Canadian Public Policy xxxviii (2). Published as well in *Canadian Public Policy* 38(2):121–145.

Foster, John Bellamy, and Fred Magdoff. 2009. "The Great Financial Crisis: Causes and Consequences." *Monthly Review Press*.

Foucault, M. 1991. *Discipline and Punish. The Birth of Prison*. London: Penguin.

Foucault, M. 1998. *The History of Sexuality*. London: Penguin.

Frank, Kristyn. 2013. "Immigrant Employment Success in Canada: Examining the Rate of Obtaining a Job Match." *International Migration Review* 47(1):76–105.

Frank, Kristyn, Feng Hou, and Grant Schellenberg. 2014. Life Satisfaction among Recent Immigrants in Canada: Comparison with Source-Country Populations and the Canadian Born. Publication 11F0019M, No 363. Statistics Canada.

Frank, Lesley. 2013. The Nova Scotia Child Poverty Report Card. Canadian Centre for Policy Alternatives. 26 November.

Frank, Robert H. 2007. *Richistan: A Journey through the American Wealth Boom and the Lives of the New Rich*. New York: Crown Publishing.

Frank, Robert H. 2011. *The Darwin Economy. Liberty, Competition, and the Common Good*. Princeton University Press.

Fraser, Nancy. 1997. *Justice Interruptus*. Routledge.

Fraser, Nancy. 2008. *Adding Insult to Injury: Nancy Fraser Debates Her Critics*. London and New York: Verso.

Fraser, Nancy, and Axel Honneth. 2003. *Redistribution or Recognition? A Political-Philosophical Exchange*. London and New York: Verso.

Freeland, Chrystia. 2011. "The Rise of the New Global Elite." *The Atlantic*. Jan./Feb.

Freeland, Chrystia. 2012a. "Two New Guilded Ages Create Global Stress." *The New York Times*. 19 February.

Freeland, Chrystia. 2012b. *Plutocrats: The Rise of the New Global Super-Rich and the Fall of Everyone Else*. Penguin.

Freeland, Chrystia. 2013. "The New Capitalism: Make Money, Do Good." *The Globe and Mail*. 17 July.

Freeman, Sunny. 2015. "Canada's 6 Biggest Banks Earned $96M a Day in 2015." *Toronto Star*. 4 December.

Frenette, Marc. 2014. An Investment of a Lifetime? The Long-Term Labour Market Premiums Associated with a Postsecondary Education. Publication 11F0019M, No. 359. Statistics Canada.

Frenette, Marc, and Ping Ching Minnie Chan. 2015. "Why Are Academic Prospects Better for Private High School Students? Economic Insights," published by Statistics Canada. March.

Freshley, Zach. 2014. "Racism 2.0: Living in a Post-Racial America." *Bedlam Magazine*. 21 April.

Frey, Bruno, David Savage, and Benno Torgler. 2011. "Behavior under Extreme Conditions: The *Titanic* Disaster." *Journal of Economic Perspectives* 25(1):209–222.

Frey, Carl, and Michael Osborne. 2013. The Future of Employment: How Susceptible are Jobs to Computerisation? 17 September. Paper presented at the Machines and Employment Workshop, hosted by Oxford University. Retrieved from www.oxfordmartin.ox.ac.uk .

Friday, Terrine, and Toby Cohen. 2010. "'Fork-Tongued' Governments to Blame for Passport Issue, Mohawk Leader Says." *National Post*. July 15.

Fridell, Gavin. 2010. The Case against Cheap Bananas: Lessons from the EU-Caribbean Banana Agreement. Cerlac Working Paper Series. March.

Frideres, James S., and René R. Gadacz. 2012. *Aboriginal Peoples in Canada*, 9th ed. Scarborough, ON: Pearson Education Canada.

Friedman, Sarah. 2015. "Still a 'Stalled Revolution'? Work/Family Experiences, Hegemonic Masculinity, and Moving Toward Gender Equality." *Sociology Compass* 9(2):140–155.

Friedman, Thomas. 2005. *The World is Flat: A Brief History of the Twenty-First Century*. New York: Picador.

Friesen, Joe. 2015. "StatsCan Jobless Figures Exclude Reserves." *The Globe and Mail*. 23 January.

Frketich, Joanna. 2015. "More Aboriginal Children Expected to Quit Chemo, Says Researcher." *Toronto Star*, 28 February.

Furstenau, Sonia. 2010. "The High Price of Cheap Bananas." *Toronto Star*. 5 June.

Gaetz, Stephen. 2010. "The Struggle to End Homelessness in Canada: How We Created the Crisis and How We Can End It." *The Open Health Services and Policy Journal*, 3:21–26.

Gaetz, Stephen. 2012. At Home/Chez Soi. Interim Report for the Mental Health Commission of Canada. Calgary. September.

Gaetz, Stephen. 2014. "Coming of Age: Reimagining the Response to Youth Homelessness in Canada." Canadian Homelessness Research Network. Toronto: York University.

Gaetz, Stephen, Jesse Donaldson, Tim Richter, and Tanya Gulliver. 2013. "The State of Homelessness in Canada

2013." Homeless Hub Paper No 4. Canadian Homelessness Research Network/Canadian Alliance to End Homelessness.

Gardiner, Laura. 2015. "Does the Gig Economy Revolutionise the World of Work, Or is it a Storm in a Teacup?" *The Economist*, 23 October.

Gerber, Linda. 2014. "Education, Employment, and Income Polarization among Aboriginal Men and Women in Canada." *CES* 46(1):121–144.

Galabuzi, Grace-Edward. 2006. *Canada's Economic Apartheid: The Social Exclusion of Racialized Groups in the New Century*. Toronto: Canadian Scholars Press.

Galabuzi, Grace-Edward, Amy Casipullai, and Avvy Go. 2012. "The Persistence of Racial Inequality in Canada." *Toronto Star*. 20 March.

Galbraith, James K. 2014. "Kapital for the Twenty-first Century?" *Dissent*, Spring, 1–7.

Galea, Sandro, Melissa Tracy, Katherine J. Hoggatt, Charles DiMaggio, and Adam Karpati. "2011 Estimated Deaths Attributable to Social Factors in the United States." *American Journal of Public Health*. June.

Gallagher, Bill. 2012. *Resource Rulers: Fortune and Folly on the Way to Canada's Road to Resources*. Self-published.

Gandy, Jr. Oscar. 2007. Minding the Gap: Covering Inequality in *The New York Times* and *The Washington Post*. Paper prepared for the IAMCR section on Political Communication. Paris, July

Gandy Jr., Oscar, and Jonathan Baron. 1998. "Inequality: It's All in the Way You Look at It." *Communication Research* 25:505–519.

Gates, Bill. 2008. Speech at the World Economic Forum, Davos Switzerland. Reported in the *Wall Street Journal*, 24 January.

Gauntlett, David. 2008. *Gender, Media, and Identity*, 2nd ed. New York: Routledge.

Gauthier, Carol-Ann. 2016. "Obstacles to Socioeconomic Integration of Highly Skilled Immigrant Women: Equality, Diversity, and Inclusion." *An International Journal* 35(1):17–30.

Gavron, Kate. 2009. "Foreword," in *Who Cares About the White Working Class?* K.P. Sveinson (ed.). London: Runneymede Perspectives. January.

Gazso, Amber. 2004. "Women's Inequality in the Workplace as Framed in News Discourse: Refracting from Gender Ideology." *Canadian Review of Sociology and Anthropology* 41(4):450–462.

Gebhard, Amanda. 2012. Pipeline to Prison. *Briarpatch Magazine*. 1 September.

Gee, Ellen M., Karen M Kobayashi, and Steven G. Prus. 2007. "Ethnic Inequality in Canada: Economic and Health Dimensions," in *Dimensions of Inequality in Canada*. D. Green and J. Kesselman (eds.). Vancouver: UBC Press.

Gee, Marcus. 2013. "Markham's Rapid Change into Canada's Most Diverse City." *The Globe and Mail*. 26 October.

Geiger, John. 2012. "A Matter of Class." *The Globe and Mail*. 13 April.

Gemi, E., I. Ulasiuk, and A. Triandafyllidou. 2013. "Migrants and Media Newsmaking Practices." *Journalism Practices* 7(3):266–281.

George, Usha, and Fernana Chaze. 2014. "Discrimination at Work: Comparing the Experiences of Foreign-Trained and Locally Trained Engineers in Canada." *Canadian Ethnic Studies* 46(1):1–21.

Gerth, Hans, and C. Wright Mills, 1958. *From Max Weber: Essays in Sociology*. Oxford University Press.

Ghosh, Ratna. 2011. The Liberating Potential of Multiculturalism in Canada: Ideals and Realities. *Canadian Diversities*. Spring, pp. 3–8.

Giddens, Anthony. 1998. *The Third Way*. Malden, MA: Blackwell.

Giddens, Anthony. 1999. "Giddens Defends Third Way Politics." *Times Higher Education*. 1 November.

Gilchrist, Kristen. 2010. "'Newsworthy' Victims? Exploring Differences in Canadian Local Press Coverage of Missing/Murdered Aboriginal and White Women." *Feminist Media Studies*.

Gilens, Martin, and Benjamin I. Page. 2014. "Testing Theories of American Politics: Elites, Interest Groups, and Average Citizens; Perspective on Politics." *American Political Science Association* 12(3):564–581.

Gillard, Spring. 2011. "Secrets of the Banana." *The Tyee*. 28 December.

Gillespie, Kerry. 2012. "OHL Threatened with Legal Action over Pay." *Waterloo Region Record*. 27 October.

Gilmour, R.J., D. Bhandar, J. Heer, and M.C.K. Ma (eds.). 2012. *"Too Asian?" Racism, Privilege, and Post-Secondary Education*. Toronto: Between the Lines.

Ginsburgh, Nicola. 2012. "'Chav,' Class, and Representation." *International Socialism*, Issue 136. 8 October.

Gladwell, Malcolm. 2000. *The Tipping Point*. Little Brown and Company.

Glennie, Alex. 2012. Globalisation 3.0 can "Raise Living Standards across the World." IPPR. 31 January.

Global Slavery Index. 2014. Hope for Children Organisation Australia.

Goar, Carol. 2015. "Canada Needs a New Tax Bracket for the Hyper-rich." *Toronto Star*. 12 January.

Goar, Carol. 2016. "Life on the Streets Quickly Turns Sour." *Toronto Star*, 3 February.

Godlewska, Christina, and Jeremy Webber. 2007. "The Calder Decision: Aboriginal Title, Treaties, and the Nisga'a," in *Let Right Be Done*. H. Foster, H. Raven and J. Webber (eds.), p. 1–36. Vancouver: UBC Press.

Goldberg, Jonah. 2012. "Which Kind of Capitalism?" *The Washington Times*. 22 May.

Goldberg, Michael, Steve Kerstetter, and Scott Klein. 2012. "Erasing a Good Poverty Line." *Toronto Star*. 20 February.

Goldfarb, D. and J. Palladini. 2015. Becoming a Services Superpower: Tapping into the Global Appetite for High Values Services. Conference Board of Canada. 16 December.

Goldin, Ian. 2013. *Divided Nations: Why Global Governance is Failing and What We Can Do About It*. Oxford University Press.

Goldstone, Jack A. 2010. "The New Population Bomb: The Four Megatrends that will Change the World." *Foreign Affairs*. January/February.

Gonick Cy. 2011. "Precarious Labour." *Canadian Dimension*. 11 May.

Gonick, Cy, and Andrea Levy. 2013. "Canadian Dimension Interviews Linda McQuaig." *Canadian Dimension*. 27 September.

Goodyear-Grant, Elizabeth. 2013. *Gendered News: Media Coverage and Electoral Politics in Canada*. Vancouver: UBC Press.

Gordon, Larry. 2011. "Where's Canada, Warren Buffett?" *Toronto Star*. 26 August.

Gordon, Stephen. 2015. "What is Income Inequality?" *National Post*. 10 March.

Gornick, Janet, and Markus Jantti. 2013. *Income Inequalities: Economic Disparities and the Middle Class in Affluent Countries*. Stanford University Press.

Gorski, Paul. 2008. "The Myth of the 'Culture of Poverty.'" *Educational Leadership* 65(7):32-36. April.

Goswami, Namita, Maeve M. O'Donovan, and Lisa Yount. 2014. *Why Race and Gender Still Matter: An Intersectional Approach*. London: Pickering & Chatto Publishers.

Gould, J.J. 2012. "Slavery's Global Comeback." *The Atlantic*. 19 December.

Grabb, Edward. 2006. *Theories of Social Inequality*. 5th ed. Toronto: Nelson.

Grabb, Edward, and Neil Guppy. 2009. *Social Inequality in Canada: Patterns, Problems, and Policies*, 5th ed. Toronto: Pearson Education Canada.

Grady, Patrick. 2011. How Are the Children of Visible Minority Immigrants Doing in the Canadian Labour Market? Global Economics Working Paper No. 2011-1. 27 January.

Graham, John, and Francois Levesque. 2010. First Nations Communities in Distress: Dealing with Causes, Not Symptoms. Institute on Governance. April.

Graham, Yao. 2012. "The Roots of Inequality: Mining Profits Soar, But Africans are Still Poor." *Embassy Magazine*. 19 August.

Graham-Leigh, Elaine. 2012. *Counterfire* Review of "Too Many People?" *Counterfire*. 27 September.

Grant, Karen, and Janice Drakich. 2011. "When Women are Equal: The Canada Research Chair Experience." *Canadian Journal of Higher Education* 41(1): 61–73.

Grant, Tavia. 2011. "Stretching Food Banks a Measure of Canada's Frail Recovery." *The Globe and Mail*, 1 November.

Grant, Tavia. 2012. "The Caterpillar Shutdown's Stark Warning for the Industrial Heartland." *The Globe and Mail*, 22 February.

Grant, Tavia. 2013. "Canada a Good, Not Great, Place to Live." *The Globe and Mail*, 4 February.

Grant, Tavia. 2014. "Canada's Top Earners See Share of Income Shrink, Unlike U.S." *The Globe and Mail*, 18 November.

Grant, Tavia. 2015. "Companies Squeamish on Hiring." *The Globe and Mail*. 23 March.

Grant, Tavia. 2016. "Human Trafficking: Why Indigenous Women are More Likely to be Victims; Missing and Murdered; Search for the Lost Series." *The Globe and Mail*, 13 February.

Gratton, Lynda. 2010. "The Future of Work." *Business Strategy Review*, Q 3, pp. 16–23.

Gratzer, David. 2015. "Our Next Great National Project." *National Post*. 3 December.

Graves, Frank. 2013. The Trust Deficit: What Does it Mean? EKOS Politics. 14 May.

Graves, Frank. 2014a. From the End of History to the End of Progress. EKOS Politics. 19 September. Retrieved from www.ekospolitics.com .

Graves, Frank. 2014b. Rethinking the Public Interest: Evolving Trends in Values and Attitudes. Presentation at the Canada 2020 Conference, Ottawa, 2 October.

Graves, Frank. 2015. "The Ekos Poll: Are Canadians Getting More Racist?" *iPolitics*, 12 March.

Gray, John. 1998. *False Dawn: The Delusions of Global Capitalism*. London: Granta Publications.

Graydon, Shari. 2001. "The Portrayal of Women in the Media: The Good, the Bad, and the Beautiful," in C. McKie and B. Singer (eds.) *Communication in Canadian Society*, 5th ed. Toronto: Thompson Publishing.

Green, David A., and Jonathan R. Kesselman. 2006. *Dimensions of Inequality in Canada*. Vancouver: UBC Press.

Green, David, W. Craig Riddell, and France St. Hilaire (eds.). 2015. Income Inequality: the Canadian Story. Institute for Research on Public Policy.

Green, Duncan. 2012. *From Poverty to Power: How Active Citizens and Effective States Can Change the World*, 2nd ed. Rugby, UK: Practical Action Publishing, and Oxford: Oxfam International.

Green, Joyce. 2004. "Equality Quest: It's Time to Undermine the Institutional and Cultural Foundations that Support Inequality." *Briarpatch Magazine*. November.

Green, Joyce (ed.). 2007. *Making Space for Indigenous Feminism*. London: Zed Books.

Greenwald, Richard. 2013. "Dying for the Shirt on Your Back." *Los Angeles Times*, 7 May.

Grossman, Lawrence. 1998. *The Political Economy of Bananas: Contract Farming, Peasants and Agrarian Change in the Eastern Caribbean*. University of North Carolina Press.

Grusky, David B. and Tamar Kricheli-Katz (eds.). 2012. *The New Gilded Age: The Critical Inequality Debates of our Times*. Stanford: Stanford University Press.

Gulliver-Garcia, Tanya. 2016. Putting an End to Child and Family Homelessness. Report by Raising the Roof.

Gunstone, Andrew. 2009. "Whiteness, Indigenous Peoples, and Australian Universities." *Australian Critical Race and Whiteness Studies Association* 5(1).

Guo, Shibao, and Zenobia Jamal. 2007. "Nurturing Cultural Diversity in Higher Education: A Critical Review of Select Models." *Canadian Journal of Higher Education* 37(3):27–49.

Gustafson, Mark. 2007. Addressing Indian Residential Schools in the U.S. and Australia. Memorandum. University of Toronto Faculty of Law, International Human Rights Clinic. Retrieved from www.claihr.ca .

Gutstein, Donald. 2014. *Harperism: How Stephen Harper and His Think Tank Colleagues Have Transformed Canada*. Toronto: James Lorimer & Company.

Gwin, Peter. 2014. "The Ship-breakers." *National Geographic* 225(5):80–95.

Gwyn, Richard. 2012. "Old-style Class System Resurfaces." *Toronto Star*, 10 September.

Hacker, Jacob S. and Paul Pierson. 2010. *Winner-Take-All Politics: How Washington Made the Rich Richer and Turned Its Back on the Middle Class*. New York: Simon and Schuster.

Hafner-Burton Emilie. 2013. *Making Human Rights a Reality*. Princeton University Press.

Hackett, Robert A. et al. 2000. *The Missing News. Filters and Blindspots in Canada's Press*. Aurora ON: Canadian Centre for Policy Alternatives/Garamond Press

Halikiopoulou D. and S. Vasilopoulou. 2011. "Introduction: Bridging the Gap Between Nationalism and Globalisation." D. Halikiopoulou and S. Vasilopoulou (eds.), pp. 1–14. New York: Routledge.

Hall, Stuart. 1997. "Racist Ideologies and the Media," in *Media Studies: A Reader*. P. Marris and S. Thornham (eds.). pp. 271–282. New York University Press

Halli-Vedanand, Shiva S. 2007. "The Problem of Second-Generation Decline: Perspectives on Integration in Canada." *International Migration and Integration* 8: 277–287.

Hamilton, Tyler. 2013. "Clean Capitalism Superheroes Lead Evolution of Free Enterprise." *Corporate Knights*. Winter, p. 8.

Hankivsky, Olena, and Renee Cormier. *2009 Intersectionality: Moving Women's Health Research and Policy Forward*. Vancouver: Women's Health Research Network.

Hankivsky, Olena (ed.). 2011. *Health Inequalities in Canada: Intersectional Frameworks and Practices*. Vancouver: UBC Press.

Harada, M. et al. 2011. "Mercury Pollution in the First Nations Group in Ontario, Canada: 35 Years of Canadian Minamata Disease." *Journal of Minamata Studies* 3:3–30.

Harari, Yuval Noah. 2014. *Sapiens: A Brief History of Human Kind*. Signal Publishing.

Harding, Robert. 2010. "The Demonization of Aboriginal Child Welfare Authorities in the News." *Canadian Journal of Communication* 35(1) 85–108.

Harman, Bryan. n.d. Inclusion/Integration? Is There a Difference? Retrieved from http://www.cdss.ca.

Harris, John. 2012. "The End of Men? Cardboard Man is Dead: Now Let's Redefine Masculinity." *The Guardian*. 30 September.

Harris, Peter. 2014. The University Degrees that Earn the Highest Salaries. Workopolis Study. 6 August. Retrieved from www.workopolis.com .

Harris, Scott. 2001. "What Can Interactionism Contribute to the Study of Inequality? The Case of Marriage and Beyond." *Symbolic Interaction* 24:445–480.

Harris-Short, Sonia. 2007. "Self-Government in Canada: A Successful Model for the Decolonisation of Aboriginal Child Welfare," in *Accommodating Cultural Diversity*. S. Tierney (ed.). Hampshire, UK: Ashgate Publishing.

Harvey, David. 2005. *A Brief History of Neoliberalism*. Oxford University Press.

Harvey, David. 2007. "Neoliberalism as Creative Destruction." *Annals*, AAPSS, 610: 22–35.

Harvey, Simon-Pierre, and Richard Y. Bourhis. 2013. "Discriminations between the Rich and the Poor under Contrasting Conditions of Wealth Stratification." *Journal of Applied Social Psychology* 43:351–366.

Hatton, Erin E. 2011. *The Temp Economy: From Kelly Girls to Permatemps in Postwar America*. Philadelphia: Temple University Press.

Hay, David. 2009. Poverty Reduction Policies and Programs. Canadian Council on Social Development.

Health Canada. 2013. Drinking Water and Wastewater—First Nations and Inuit Health. Retrieved from www.hc-sc.gc.ca .

Heath, Joseph. 2009. *Filthy Lucre*. Toronto: HarperCollins.

Heath, Anthony, and Sin Yi Cheung. 2007. "The Comparative Study of Ethnic Minority Disadvantage," in *Unequal Chances: Ethnic Minorities in Western Labour Markets*. A. Heath and S.Y. Cheung (eds.), pp. 1–44. New York: Oxford University Press.

Hedges, Chris, and Joe Sacco. 2012. *Days of Destruction, Days of Revolt*. New York: Nation Books.

Hedican, Edward J. 2013. *Ipperwash: The Tragic Failure of Canada's Aboriginal Policy*. Toronto: University of Toronto Press.

Heffernan, Tracy, Mary Todorow, and Helen Luu. 2015. Why Housing First Won't End Homelessness. Rabble.ca. 7 July.

Heisz, Andrew, and Brian Murphy. 2015. The Role of Taxes and Transfers in Reducing Income Inequality. Institute for Research on Public Policy. 4 June.

Helin, Calvin. 2006. *Dances with Dependency*. Orca Publishing.

Helin, Calvin. 2010. *The Economic Dependency Trap*. Ravencrest Publisher.

Heller, Zoë. 2015. "Rape on the Campus." *The New York Review of Books*, pp. 1–13. 5 February.

Helmes-Hayes, Rick, and James Curtis (eds.). 1998. *The Vertical Mosaic Revisited*. Toronto: University of Toronto Press.

Henderson, Peter. 2016. "Workplaces Shifting in 2016." *Waterloo Region Record*, 2 January.

Hennebry, Jenna. 2010. "Who Has Their Eye on the Ball? 'Jurisdictional Futbol' and Canada's Temporary Foreign Worker Program." *Policy Options*. July/August.

Hennebry, Jenna, and Bessma Momani. 2013. "Introduction: Arab Canadians as Targeted Transnationals," in *Targeted Transnationals: The State, the Media, and Arab Canadians*, Jenna Hennebry and Bessma Momani (eds.), pp. 1–14. Vancouver: UBC Press.

Henry, Frances. 2006. "A Response to Hier and Walby's Article: 'Competing Analytical Paradigms in the Sociological Study of Racism in Canada.'" *Canadian Ethnic Studies* 38(2).

Henry, Frances. 2004. Understanding the Experiences of Visible Minority and Aboriginal Faculty Members at Queen's University. Report submitted to Queens University, Kingston, ON.

Henry, Frances, and Carol Tator. 2002. *Discourses of Domination*. Toronto: University of Toronto Press.

Henry, Frances, and Carol Tator (eds.). 2009. *Racism in the Canadian University: Demanding Social Justice, Inclusion, and Equity*. Toronto: University of Toronto Press.

Henry, Frances, and Carol Tator. 2010. *The Colour of Democracy: Racism in Canada*, 3rd ed. Toronto: Thomson/Nelson.

Hensler Ben. 2013. Global Wage Trends for Apparel Workers, 2001-2011. Published by Center for American Progress and Workers Right Coalition. July.

Hepburn, Bob. 2013. "Urgent Call for More Women in Politics." *Toronto Star*, 10 October.

Hernandez-Ramdwar, Camille. 2009. "Caribbean Students in the Canadian Academy: We've Come a Long Way?" in *Racism in the Canadian University*. F. Henry and C. Tator (eds.), pp. 106–127. Toronto: University of Toronto Press.

Hertz, Noreena. 2012. Towards a Theory of Co-op Capitalism. IPPR. 15 February.

Heyninck, Emanuela. 2014. "Women's Day in Canada: Much to Celebrate, Much More Work to Do." *The Globe and Mail*. 8 March.

Hier, Sean, and Kevin Walby. 2006. "Competing Analytical Paradigms in the Sociological Study of Racism in Canada." *Canadian Ethnic Studies* 38(1).

Hier, Sean, and Joshua Greenberg. 2002. "News Discourse and the Problematization of Chinese Migration to Canada," in *Discourses of Domination: Racial Bias in the Canadian English-Language Press*. Frances Henry and Carol Tator, eds., pp. 138–62. Toronto: University of Toronto Press.

Hill, Steve. 2010. *Europe's Promise: Why the European Way is the Best Hope in an Insecure Age*. Berkeley: University of California Press.

Himmelfarb, Alex. 2013. "Canada Passes the Mean Test." *Toronto Star*, 3 January.

Hobsbawn, Eric. 2011. *How to Change the World: Reflections on Marx and Marxism*. New Haven: Yale University Press.

Hodgson, Godfrey. 2010. America Divided: The Politics of Inequality. Available online at www.opendemocracy.net .Posted 16 July.

Hoehn, Felix. 2012. *Reconciling Sovereignties: Aboriginal Nations and Canada*. Saskatoon: Native Law Centre: University of Saskatchewan.

Hoffman, Reid, Ben Casnocha, and Chris Yeh. 2013. "Tours of Duty: The New Employer–Employee Compact." *Harvard Business Review*. June.

Hoffman, Steve G. 2012. "Academic Capitalism." *Contexts* 11(4):12–13.

Hogarth, Kathy. 2013. "Contested Belonging: The Experiences of Racialized Immigrant Women in Canada." *International Journal of Diversity in Organizations, Communities, and Nations* 10(5):63–74.

Holton, Robert J. 2011. *Globalization and the Nation-State*, 2nd ed. New York: Palgrave Macmillan.

Homans, Jennifer. 2012. "Review of *The End of Men*." *The New York Times*. 16 September.

Homeless Hub 2015. Housing First. Retrieved from http://homelesshub.ca .

Hopper, Tristin. 2014. "Critics Complain of Qualification Inflation as More Canadians Hold University Degrees—and Low-Paying Jobs." *National Post*. 3 January.

Hough, Jennifer. 2014. "Canadians Pay 42% of Income in Tax." *National Post*. 12 August.

HRSDC [Human Resources and Skills Development Canada]. 2011. Understanding Homelessness. Available online at www.hrsdc.gc.ca .

HRSDC. 2012a. Work—Work Related Injuries. Retrieved from www4.hrsdc.gc.ca .

HRSDC. 2012b. Live-in Caregiver Program. Retrieved from www.hrsdc.gc.ca .

Huber, Lindsay Perez, and Daniel D. Solorzano. 2015. "Visualizing Everyday Racism: Critical Race Theory, Visual Microaggressions, and the Historical Image of Mexican Banditry." *Qualitative Inquiry* 21(3):223–238.

Hugill, David. 2010. *Missing Women, Missing News: Covering Crisis in Vancouver's Downtown Eastside*. Winnipeg: Fernwood.

Hulchanski, J.D. 2009 Homelessness in Canada: Past, Present, and Future. Keynote Address to Growing Home: Housing and Homelessness in Canada Conference. University of Calgary, 18 February.

Hulchanski, J.D. 2010. Three Cities within Toronto: Income Polarization among Toronto's Neighbourhoods, 1970–2005. University of Toronto.

Hulchanski, J. David. 2011. "The 99% Know All About Inequality." *Toronto Star*, 26 October.

Human Rights Watch. 2012. Discrimination, Inequality, and Poverty—A Human Rights Perspective. Retrieved from www.hrw.org .

Human Rights Watch. 2013. Those Who Take Us Away: Abusive Policing and Failures in Protection of Indigenous Women and Girls in Northern British Columbia. New York.

Human Rights Watch. 2015a. "Work Faster or Get Out." Labor Rights Abuses in Cambodia's Garment Industry. March.

Human Rights Watch. 2015b. Bangladesh: 2 Years After Rana Plaza, Workers Denied Rights. 22 April

Human Rights Watch. 2015c. Worker's Rights in Bangladeshi Garment Factories. 22 April

Hume, Christopher. 2014. "How Can a City So Rich Have So Many Poor?" *Toronto Star*. 19 December.

Hunnicutt, Gwen. 2009. "Varieties of Patriarchy and Violence against Women: Resurrecting Patriarchy as a Theoretical Tool." *Violence against Women* 15 (5):553–573.

Hunter, Justine. 2013. "PM's Envoy Warns of Troubles with First Nations over Energy." *The Globe and Mail*, 9 October.

Hurtig, Mel. 2015. *The Arrogant Autocrat: Stephen Harper's Takeover of Canada*. Hurtig-Books.

Huseman, Jennifer, and Damien Short. 2012. "'Slow Industrial Genocide': Tar Sands and the Indigenous Peoples of Northern Alberta." *The International Journal of Human Rights* 16(1):216–237.

Hussain, Murtaza. 2013. "Of Persian Snake Charmers: Racism and Global Hegemony; Opinion." *Al Jazeera* English. 10 October.

Hutchinson, Brian 2016. "Victoria's Fight over Treating its Sewage—Or Keep Pushing it Raw into Ocean as it has for Decades." *National Post*, 25 February.

Hyslop, Katie. 2012. "Finishing the Fight on Poverty." *The Tyee*. 27 August.

Ibbitson, John. 2012. "New Canada: Land of Immigrants with Many Families under the Same Roof." *The Globe and Mail*. 19 September.

Ibbitson, John. 2015. "The Harper Effect." *The Globe and Mail*. 7 February.

Iceland, John. 2012. *Poverty in America: A Handbook*. Berkeley: University of California Press.

Iceland, John, and Gregory Sharp. 2013. "White Residential Segregation in the U.S. Metropolitan Areas." *Population Research and Policy Review* 32:663–686.

Ignatius, Adi. 2013. "From the Editor: Where Are All the Women?" *Harvard Business Review*. April.

Ilcan, Suzan, and Anita Lacey. 2011. *Governing the Poor: Exercises in Poverty Reduction, Practices of Global Aid*. Montreal and Kingston: McGill-Queen's University Press.

Intergovernmental Panel on Climate Change. 2014. Climate Change 2014: Impacts, Adaptation, and Vulnerability. United Nations.

International Labour Organization. 2013. *Domestic Workers across the World: Global and Regional Statistics and the Extent of Legal Protection*. New York: ILO Publication.

Ivanova, Iglika. 2011. The Cost of Poverty in BC. Canadian Centre for Policy Alternatives, BC Office. July.

Ivanova, Iglika. 2014. "How Have Taxes Changed Over the Last Century?" CCPA *Monitor*. September, p. 10.

IWGIA [International Working Group for Indigenous Affairs]. 2015. The Indigenous World 2015. Copenhagen.

Jackson, Andrew. 2013. Racial Discrimination and the Economic Downturn. *The Broadbent Blog*. Broadbent Institute. 26 June.

Jackson, Andrew. 2014a. "Canadian-born Visible Minority Youth Facing an Unfair Job Future." *The Globe and Mail*. 29 May.

Jackson, Andrew. 2014b. A New Gilded Age Ahead: Thomas Piketty's *Capital in the Twenty-First Century*. Rabble.ca. 8 May.

Jackson, Andrew. 2015 Quebec Model Balances Greater Inequality with Economic Progress. Broadbent Institute. 21 March.

Jackson, Andrew. 2016. "Ottawa Should Reconsider Seniors Poverty." *The Globe and Mail*. 7 January.

Jackson, Margaret A. 1999. "Canadian Aboriginal Women and Their 'Criminality': The Cycle of Violence in the Context of Difference." *The Australian and New Zealand Journal of Criminology* 32(2) pp. 197–208.

Jackson, Tim. 2009. Prosperity without Growth: Economics for a Finite Planet. Report for the Sustainable Development Commission. London. March.

Jackson, Robert Max. 2010. *Destined for Inequality: The Inevitable Rise of Women's Status*. Harvard University Press.

Jahan, Selim. 2015. Working for Human Development. Human Development Report 2015. Selim Jahan, lead writer. New York: United Nations.

James, Carl. 2009. "'It Will Happen without Putting in Place Special Measures': Racially Diversifying Universities," in *Racism in the Canadian University*. F. Henry and C .Tator (eds.), pp. 128–159. Toronto: University of Toronto Press.

James, Carl. 2011. "Paradoxes of 'Visible Minorities' in Job Ads." *University World News*. 15 May.

James, Carl. 2012. "Making It, But Still 'Working Twice as Hard to Get Half as Far.'" *Canadian Diversity*, Winter, pp. 44–47.

Janoski, Thomas, David Luke, and Christopher Oliver. 2014. *The Causes of Structural Unemployment*. Polity.

Janzen, Ed. 2009. "Television with Class." *Canadian Dimension*, November/December, p. 42.

Jedwab, Jack, and Vic Satzewich. 2015. "Introductory Essay," in *The Vertical Mosaic: An Analysis of Social Class and Power in Canada. 50th Anniversary Edition*, by John Porter, pp. xvii-xxxvii. Toronto: University of Toronto Press.

Jiang, Jess. 2013. "The Deadliest Jobs in America." *NPR Planet Money*. Retrieved from www.npr.org .

Jiwani, Yasmin. 2006. *Discourses of Denial. Mediations on Race, Gender, and Violence*. Vancouver: UBC Press.

Jiwani, Yasmin. 2010. "Erasing Race: The Story of Reena Virk," in *Reena Virk: Critical Perspectives on a Canadian Murder*, M. Rajiva and S. Batacharya (eds.), pp. 82–121. Toronto: Canadian Scholars Press.

Jiwani, Yasmin. 2011. "Hierarchies of Worthiness: Women and Victimhood in the Canadian Media." *Briarpatch Magazine*, 6 May.

Jiwani, Yasmin. 2012. "Racism and the Media." Stop Racism and Hate Collective. www.stopracism.ca .

Johnson, Kerri L., Kristin Pauker, and Jonathan B Freeman. 2012. "Race is Gendered: How Covarying Phenotypes and Stereotype Bias Sex Categorization." *Journal of Personality and Social Psychology* 102(1):116–131.

Johnson, Allan. 1997. *The Gender Knot: Unravelling our Patriarchal Legacy*. Philadelphia: Temple University Press.

Johnson, Boris. 2013. "May the Smartest Cornflake Triumph." Printed in the *National Post*. 29 November. Speech available at cps.org.uk .

Johnson, Heather Beth. 2015. *The American Dream and the Power of Wealth*. 2nd ed. New York: Routledge.

Johnson, Richard. 2013. "Canadian Aid Spending." *National Post*. 11 January.

Johnson, Richard, Mike Faille, and Andrew Barr. 2013. Aboriginal Canada. *National Post*. 13 May.

Jones, Owen, 2011. *CHAVS: The Demonisation of the Working Class*. Verso.

Jones, Owen. 2012. "Introduction: Why Inequality Matters," in *Why Inequality Matters*. Produced by members of My Fair London in Association with the Equality Trust. Centre for Labour and Social Studies.

Journalists for Human Rights. 2013. "'Buried Voices': Media Coverage of Aboriginal Issues in Ontario." *Media Monitoring Report*, 2010–2013. August.

Justice Canada. 2012. An Estimation of the Economic Impact of Spousal Violence in Canada. Ottawa. Author.

Justice Centre for Constitutional Freedoms. 2012. Campus Freedom Index. Calgary.

Kanellakis, Abigail. 2007. Women through the Eyes of the Mainstream Media. Available online at www.associated-content.com .

Kanter, Rosabeth, 1997. *Men and Women of the Corporation*. New York: Basic Books.

Kantor, Jodi. 2014. "Working Anything But 9 to 5." *The New York Times*. 13 August.

Kantor, Jodi, and David Streitfeld. 2015. "Inside Amazon: Wrestling Big Ideas in a Bruising Workplace." *The New York Times*, 15 August.

Karim, Karim. 2010. "Re-viewing the 'National' in 'International Communication': Through the Lens of Diaspora," in *International Communication: A Reader*. D.K. Thussu (ed.). pp. 393–409. New York: Routledge.

Kasperkevic, Jana 2014. "Walmart Workers Increasingly Rely on Food Banks, Report Says." *The Guardian*, 21 November.

Kaur, H. 2011. Income Gap Between Rich and Poor Immigrants a Lesson For All Canadians—Study. Canada Updates. 25 January.

Kay, Barbara. 2013. "Book Review: *Uprising* by Douglas L. Bland." *The Huffington Post*. Posted 19 January.

Kay, Jonathan. 2014. "Spare a Tear for the 'Clopeners.'" *National Post*. 22 August.

Kay, Jonathan, 2015. "Diversity's Final Frontier." *The Walrus*, 3 November.

Kazemipur, A. 2014. *The Muslim Question in Canada: A Story of Segmented Integration*. Vancouver: UBC Press.

Keenan, Greg. 2012. "Caterpillar Pulls Plug on London Plant." *The Globe and Mail*, 3 February.

Keister, Lisa A., and Darby E. Southgate. 2012. *Inequality. A Contemporary Approach to Race, Class, and Gender*. New York: Cambridge University Press.

Kelly, Cathal. 2014. "Female Athletes Cast in Disney Roles." *The Globe and Mail*. 26 August.

Kelly, Marjorie. 2002. *The Divine Right of Capital. Dethroning the Corporate Aristocracy*. San Francisco: Berrett-Koehler.

Kendall, Diane. 2005/2010. *Framing Class. Media Representations of Wealth and Poverty in America*, Maryland: Rowman & Littlefield.

Kennedy, Mark. 2015. "Canadians Need Conversation about Residential Schools: Murray Sinclair." *Ottawa Citizen*. 15 April.

Kerbo, Harold R. 2012. *Social Stratification and Inequality*, 8th ed. New York: McGraw Hill.

Kerstetter, Steve. 1999. The Affordability Gap. Canadian Centre for Policy Alternatives. September.

Khanna, Parag. 2010. "The Age of Nations is Over: The New Urban Era has Begun." *Foreign Policy*. September/October.

Khan, Sheema. 2013. "Coming Together to Prevent Crimes of 'Honour.'" *The Globe and Mail*, 30 January.

Khazan, Olga. 2014. "How Being Poor Makes You Sick." *The Atlantic*. 21 May.

Khondker, H.H. 2004. "Glocalization as Globalization: Evolution of a Sociological Concept." *Bangladeshi e-Journal of Sociology* 1(2):1–14.

Khoo, S.-E., E. Ho, and C. Voigt-Graf. 2008. "Gendered Migration in Oceania: Trends, Policies, and Outcomes," in *New Perspectives in Gender and Migration*. N. Piper (ed.), pp. 101–136. New York: Routledge.

Kilbourne, Jean. 1990. "Beauty and the Beast of Advertising." *Media & Values*, No. 49. Winter.

Kilbourne, Jean. 2010. *Can't Buy My Love: How Advertising Changes the Way We Think and Feel*. New York: Simon & Schuster.

Killian, Crawford. 2007. "Rich as Hell." *The Tyee*, 9 October.

Killian, Crawford. 2013. "Media Elders Failed Us by Sneering at Idle No More." *The Tyee*. 16 January.

Killian, Crawford. 2015. "How Harper Turned Canada into a Rogue State." *The Tyee*. 26 March.

Kimeldorf, H., R. Meyer, M. Prasad, and I. Robinson. 2006. "Consumers With a Conscience: Will They Pay More?" *Contexts* 5(1): 24–29.

Kimes, Mina. 2013. "King Cat." *Bloomberg Businessweek*. 20–25 May.

Kimmel, Michael. 2000. *The Gendered Society*. New York: Oxford University Press.

Kimmel, Michael. 2008. *The Gendered Society*, 3rd ed. New York: Oxford University Press.

Kimmel, Michael. 2009. *Guyland: The Perilous World Where Boys Become Men*. Harper Perennial.

Kimmel, Michael. 2013. *Angry White Men: American Masculinity at the End of an Era*. Nation Books.

Kimmett, Colleen. 2012. "The Problem with Food Banks." *The Tyee*, 25 April.

Kingston, Anne. 2016. "What's Really on Trial in the Ghomeshi Case." *Maclean's*, pp. 40-42, 8 February.

Kino-nda-niimi Collective. 2014. *The Winter We Danced: Voices from the Past, the Future, and the Idle No More Movement*. Arbeiter Ring Publishing.

Kirby, Jason. 2011. "The Great White Tax Haven: How Canada Has Quietly Emerged as a Go-To Destination for the World's Ultra-Rich." *Maclean's, 19 July*.

Kirby, Michael. 2002. The Health of Canadians—the Federal Role. Vol. 6: Recommendations for Reform. Published by the Standing Senate Committee on Social Affairs, Science, and Technology Study on the State of the Health Care System in Canada. Ottawa.

Klees, Steven. 2014. "How the Rhetoric and Reality of Privatization Distorts Education." *CCPA Monitor*. November: 24–27.

Klein, Naomi. 2014. *This Changes Everything*. Toronto: Knopf.

Klein, Seth. 2011. From the Missing Election File: Poverty Reduction. Canadian Centre for Policy Alternatives. 27 April.

Kobayashi, Audrey. 2009. "Now You See Them, How You See Them: Women of Colour in Canadian Academia." *Racism in the Canadian University*. F. Henry and C. Tator (eds.), pp. 60–75. Toronto: University of Toronto Press.

Kollmeyer, Christopher J. 2004. "Corporate Interests: How the News Media Portray the Economy." *Social Problems*, 51(3), 432–452.

Korteweg, Anna C., and G. Yurdakul. 2010. Religion, Culture, and the Politicization of Honour-Related Violence. Gender and Development Programme Paper No. 12. October. UN Research Institute for Social Development.

Korzeniewicz, Roberto Patricio, and Timothy Patrick Moran. 2009. *Unveiling Inequality: A World-Historical Perspective*. New York: Russell Sage Foundation.

Kovach, Margaret. 2009. Being Indigenous in the Academy: Creating Space for Indigenous Scholars. In *First Nations, First Thoughts*. Annis May Timpson, (ed.), pp.51–76. Vancouver: UBC Press.

Krahn, Harvey, Graham S. Lowe, and Karen Hughes. 2010. *Work, Industry, and Canadian Society*, 6th ed. Toronto: Nelson.

Kraus, Krystalline. 2013. Grassy Narrows Wants Justice for Destructive Logging and Mercury Poisoning. Rabble.ca. 5 November. Retrieved from http://rabble.ca .

Kraus, Krystalline. 2016. Deadly Water Still Haunts Grassy Narrow. Rabble.ca. 27 May.

Kristof, Nicholas D., 2013. "Slavery Isn't a Thing of the Past." *The New York Times*, 17 November.

Kristof, Nicholas. 2015. "U.S.A., A Land of Limitations." *The New York Times*, 15–16 August.

Kristof, Nicholas. 2016. "America's Aristocracy." *National Post*, 22 January.

Kristof, Nicholas, and Sheryl WuDunn. 2009. *Half the Sky: Turning Oppression into Opportunity for Women Worldwide*. Random House.

Krugman, Paul. 2013. "Why Inequality Matters." *The New York Times*, 22 December.

Kubes, Danielle. 2014. "Not Super Rich or Super Smart? Well Then, Don't Major in Arts." *Financial Post*. 20 August.

Kulchyski, Peter. 2013. *Aboriginal Rights are Not Human Rights: In Defence of Indigenous Struggles*. Arbeiter Ring Publishing.

Kunz, Jean Lock, Ann Milan, and Sylvain Schetagne. 2001. Unequal Access: A Canadian Profile of Racial Differences in Education, Employment and Income. Prepared for the Canadian Race Relations Foundation by the Canadian Council for Social Development. Ottawa.

Kuokkanen, Rauna. 2007. *Reshaping the University: Responsibility, Indigenous Epistemes, and the Logic of the Gift*. Vancouver: UBC Press.

Kurlantzick, Joshua. 2012. *Democracy in Retreat*. Yale University Press.

Kuran, Kent. 2012. "Well-educated Canadians Struggle with Student Debt." *Toronto Star*. 3 November.

Labonte, Ronald, Abdullahel Hadi, and Xaxier E. Kauffmann. 2011. Indicators of Social Exclusion and Inclusion: A Critical and Comparative Analysis of the Literature. Globalization and Health Equity Research Unit, Institute of Population Health. University of Ottawa.

Lamman, Charles, Amela Karabegovic, and Niels Veldhuis. 2012. Measuring Income Mobility in Canada: Studies in Economic Prosperity. Fraser Institute, November.

Lamman, Charles, and Milagros Palacios. 2013. Canadians Celebrate Tax Freedom Day on June 10. Fraser Institute.

Lamman, Charles, and Hugh Macintyre. 2016. An Introduction to the State of Poverty in Canada. Fraser Institute, 25 January.

Lamont, Michele, and Peter Hall (eds.). 2013. *Social Resilience in the Neo Liberal Age*. Cambridge University Press.

Lankin, Frances, and Munir Sheikh. 2012. Brighter Prospects: Transforming Social Assistance in Ontario. Available at www.mcss.gov.on.ca/documents/en/mcss/social/publications/social_assistance_review_final_report.pdf .

Lansley, Stewart. 2012. *The Cost of Inequality*. UK: Gibson Square Books.

Lardner, James, and David A. Smith. 2007. *Inequality Matters*. Perseus Distribution Services.

Lareau, Annette. 2002. "Invisible Inequality: Social Class and Childrearing in Black Families and White Families." *American Sociological Review* 67:747–776.

Lareau, Annette, and Dalton Conley. 2010. Social Class: How Does It Work? Russell Sage Foundation.

Larking, Emma. 2014. *Refugees and the Myth of Human Rights*. Ashgate.

Larrazet, Christine, and Isabelle Rigoni. 2014. "Media and Diversity: A Century-Long Perspective on an Enlarged and Internationalized Field of Research." inMedia, 17 September. Retrieved 4 November 2014 from http://inmedia.revues.org/749 .

Lasn, Kalle. 2012. *Meme Wars: The Creative Destruction of Neoclassical Economics*. New York: Seven Stories Press.

Laurin, Alexander, and Finn Poschmann. 2013. Treading Water: The Impact of High Marginal Effective Tax Rates on Working Families in Canada. C.D. Howe Institute. July.

Law Commission of Ontario. 2009. Addressing Ageism and Advancing Substantive Equality: Developing a Principles Based Approach.

Law Commission of Ontario. 2012. Vulnerable Workers, Interim Report. Retrieved from www.lco-cdo.org .

Lawrence, Regina, and Melody Rose. 2009. *Hilary Clinton's Race for the White House*. Boulder, CO: Lynne Rienner Publishing.

Lebowitz, Michael A. 2008. "Building Twenty-First Century Socialism." *Canadian Dimension*. September 6.

Lee, Marc, Iglika Ivanova, and Seth Klein. 2011. BC's Regressive Tax Shift: A Decade of Diminishing Tax Fairness, 2000–2010. Canadian Centre for Policy Alternatives, BC Office.

Leech, Garry. 2012. *Capitalism: A Structural Genocide*. New York: Zed Books.

Legal Strategy Coalition [LSC] 2015. Violence against Aboriginal Women. Review of Reports and Recommendations. 26 February.

Lehrman, Sally. 2014. Creating an Inclusive Public Commons: Values and Structures in Journalism that can Promote Change. Paper presented to the Media and Minorities Conference sponsored by the Academy of the Jewish Museum Berlin and Council of Migration, Berlin, 27 November.

Leigh, Darcy. 2009. "Colonialism, Gender, and the Family in North America: For a Gendered Analysis of Indigenous Struggles." *Studies in Nationalism and Ethnicity* 9(1):70–88.

Leisinger, K., K.M. Schmitt, and R. Pandya-Lorch. 2002. *Six Billion and Counting*. Washington DC: International Food Policy Research Institute.

Leistyna, Pepi, and Debra Mollen. 2008. Teaching Social Class through Alternative Media and By Dialoguing across Disciplines and Boundaries. *Radical Teacher* 81(1), 20–27.

Lemieux, Thomas, and Brahim Boudarbat. 2010. Why are the Relative Wages of Immigrants Declining? A Distributional Approach. Canadian Labour Market and Skills Researcher Network. Working paper No. 65, September.

Lemieux, Thomas, and W. Craig Riddell. 2015. Who Are Canada's Top 1 Percent? Institute for Research on Public Policy. 9 July.

Leslie, Keith. 2012. "Caterpillar Shuts Locked out Plant in London, Ont." Canadian Press, printed in the *Waterloo Region Record*. 4 February.

Levinson, J.D., H. Cai, and D. Young. 2010. "Guilt by Implicit Racial Bias: The Guilty/Not Guilty Implicit Association Test." *Ohio State Journal of Criminal Law* 8:187–206.

Levitas, Ruth. 2005. The Imaginary Reconstitution of Society, or Why Sociologists and Others Should Take Utopia More Seriously. Inaugural Lecture, University of Bristol. 24 October.

Levitas, R., C. Pantazis, K.E. Fahmy, D. Gordon, E. Lloyd, and D. Patsios. 2007. The Multi-Dimensional Analysis of Social Exclusion. University of Bristol. January.

Levrau, Francois, and Patrick Loobuyck. 2013. "Politics of Redistribution and Recognition." *The Political Quarterly* 84(1):95–108.

Levy, Daniel, and Natan Sznaider. 2006. "Sovereignty Transformed: A Sociology of Human Rights." *British Journal of Sociology* 57(4).

Levy, Jacob T. 2012. "The High Cost of Low Tuition in Quebec." *Academic Matters*. November, pp. 12–15.

Lewchuk, Wayne et al. 2013. It's More Than Poverty: Employment Precarity and Household Well-Being. Prepared by PEPSO, McMaster University Social Sciences, and Toronto United Way.

Lewenza, Ken. 2012. "How to Prevent another Caterpillar." *Toronto Star*, 14 February.

Lewis, Oscar. 1959. *Five Families: Mexican Case Studies in the Culture of Poverty*. New York: BASIC Books.

Lewis, Oscar. 1964. *Pedro Martinez—A Mexican Peasant and His Family*. New York: Random Books.

Lin, Ann Chih, and David R. Harris. 2012. "Why is American Poverty Still Colored in the Twenty-First Century?" in *The Colors of Poverty: Why Racial and Ethnic Disparities Exist*. A.C. Lin and D.R. Harries eds., pp. 1–12. Russell Sage Foundation.

Lindsay, Colin. 2008. Are Women Spending More Time on Unpaid Domestic Work Than Men in Canada? Statistics Canada.

Linkon, Sherry. 2012. Beyond Stereotypes: What Makes a Good Representation of the Working Class? Working Class Perspectives, 20 February. Retrieved from http://working-classstudies.wordpress.com .

Linneman, Thomas J. 2012. "The Rich and the Rest." *Contexts* 11(3):66–67.

Livingston, Anne-Marie, and Morton Weinfeld. 2015. "Black Families and Socio-Economic Inequality in Canada." *Canadian Ethnic Studies* 47(3).

Llewellyn, Jennifer. 2002. "Dealing with the Legacy of Native Residential School Abuse in Canada," (subsequently published in revised form as "The Relationship between Truth and Reconciliation: Bridging the Gap"), in *From Truth to Reconciliation: Transforming the Legacy of Residential Schools*. M. Castellano, L. Archibald, and M. Degagne (eds.), pp. 183–203. Ottawa: Aboriginal Healing Foundation.

Long, David. 2011. "Preface and Acknowledgements," in *Visions of the Heart*. D. Long and O.P. Dickason (eds.), pp. xvi–xx. Toronto: Oxford University Press.

Long, David, and Olive Patricia Dickason (eds.). 2011. *Visions of the Heart*. Toronto: Oxford University Press.

Longoria, Richard T. 2006. Meritocracy and Americans' Views on Redistributive Justice. Poster Presentation Midwest Political Science Association Annual Meeting. April. Retrieved from http://citation.allacademic.com .

Lopez, Ricardo. 2013. "Most U.S. Workers Dislike Jobs, Poll Says." *Toronto Star*. 24 June.

Louie, Clarence, and Dawn Matahbee. 2015. "Economic Development for Aboriginal People Still Not on Track." Op-ed, *Ottawa Citizen*, 17 June.

LSC [Legal Strategy Coalition on Violence against Indigenous Women]. 2015. Review of Reports and Recommendations, Executive Summary. 26 February.

Lukes, Steven. 2005. *Power: A Radical View*. New York: Palgrave Macmillan.

Lukes, Steven. 2007. Power. *Contexts* 6(3):59–61.

Lutz, Helma. 2011. *The New Maids: Transnational Women and the Care Economy*. New York: Palgrave.

Lyder, Roisin. 2012. "Fight For Equality, Down with Tuition Fees." *The Peak* 52(1):35–38.

Lyons, Sean, Linda Schweitzer, and Ed Ng. 2011. *Industrial Relations*. Cheltenham, UK: Edward Elgar Publishing.

Maaka, Roger, and Augie Fleras. 2005. *The Politics of Indigeneity*. Dunedin, NZ: University of Otago Press.

Macdonald, David. 2012. The Rich Stay Rich: Fraser Institute. Behind the Numbers, 20 November. Retrieved from http://behindthenumbers.ca .

Macdonald, David. 2014. Outrageous Fortune: Documenting Canada's Wealth Gap. CCPA, 3 April.

Macdonald, David. 2015a. The Wealth Advantage. The Growing Gap between Canada's Affluent and the Middle Class. CCPA, June.

Macdonald, David, and Erika Shaker. 2011. The Impact of Rising Tuition Fees on Ontario Families. CCPA, 31 August.

Macdonald David, and Daniel Wilson. 2013. Poverty or Prosperity: Indigenous Children in Canada. CCPA and Save the Children Canada.

Macdonald, David and Daniel Wilson. 2016. Shameful Neglect. Indigenous Child Poverty in Canada. CCPA and Save the Children. May.

Macdonald, David, Michael Dan, and Bernie M. Farber. 2015. "John A. Macdonald Was a Near Genocidal Extremist Even for His Time." *National Post*. 11 January.

MacDonald, Jake. 2014. "Clarence Louie and the Man behind Clarence Louie." *Report on Business Magazine*, pp. 42–54. June.

MacDonald, Moira. 2013. Sessionals, Up Close. *University Affairs*. 9 January.

Macionis, John, and Ken Plummer. 2008. *Sociology: A Global Introduction*. Essex, UK: Pearson Education Limited.

Macionis, John, and Linda Gerber. 2010. *Sociology*, 7th Canadian ed. Toronto: Pearson.

Macklin, Audrey. 1999. "Women as Migrants in National and Global Communities." *Canadian Woman Studies* 19(3): 24–32.

Mackenzie, Hugh. 2012. "Inequality Frays the Ties that Bind." *Toronto Star*. 31 December.

Mackenzie, Hugh. 2014. All in a Day's Work? CEO Pay in 2012. CCPA, 2 January.

Mackenzie, Hugh. 2015. Glory Days. CEO Pay in Canada Soaring to Pre-Recession Highs, CCPA, January.

Mackenzie, Hugh. 2016. Staying Power: CEO Pay in Canada. CCPA, 4 January.

MacKinnon, Mary Pat. 2004. Citizens' Values and the Canadian Social Architecture: Evidence from the Citizens' Dialogue on Canada's Future. Research Report F/42 Ottawa: Canadian Policy Research Networks.

MacKinnon, Shauna. 2008. Poverty and Social Exclusion. CCPA, Economic and Social Trends, September.

MacKinnon, M., and M. Strauss. 2013. "Spinning Tragedy: The True Cost of a T-Shirt." *The Globe and Mail*, 12 October.

Maclean's Magazine. 2013. "Who Earns What," 2 September.

Macleod, Andrew. 2015. *A Better Place on Earth*. Madeira Park, BC: Harbour Publishing.

Magdoff, Fred. 2012. Saving Resources and the Environment: A Modest Proposal. Retrieved from http://climateandcapitalism.com/2012/03/29/a-modest-proposal/ .

Mahtani, Minelle. 2002. "Representing Minorities: Canadian Media and Minority Identities." *Canadian Ethnic Studies* xxxiii(3):99–131.

Mainwaring, Simon. 2011. *We First*. New York: Palgrave Macmillan.

Maioni, Antonia. 2015. Canadian Universities Need to Connect Themselves to Their Students and the World. *The Globe and Mail*. 18 March.

Maitland, Alison, and Peter Thomson. 2011. *Future Work: How Businesses Can Adapt and Thrive in the New World of Work*. New York: Palgrave Macmillan.

Mani, A., S. Mullainathan, E. Shafir, and J. Zhao. 2013. "Poverty Impedes Cognitive Function." *Science* 341(6149):976–980.

Mann, Ruth. 2012. "Invisibilizing Violence against Women," in *Power and Resistance: Critical Thinking about Canadian Social Issues*, 5th ed. L. Samuelson and W. Antony (eds.), pp. 48–71. Halifax: Fernwood.

Manyika James, S. Lund, B. Auguste, and S. Ramaswamy. 2012. Help Wanted: The Future of Work in Advanced Economies. McKinsey Global Institute, March.

Manzoor, Safras. 2008. "The Forgotten People." *The Guardian*, 12 December.

Marche, Steve. 2013. "The Case for Filth." *The New York Times*. 8 December.

Marfelt, M.M. 2016. "Grounded Intersectionality: Equality, Diversity, and Inclusion." *An International Journal* 35(1):31–47.

Marginson, Simon. 2016. "Higher Education and Growing Inequality." *Academic Matters*, pp. 7–12, January.

Markovich, Steven J. 2014. The Incoming Inequality Debate. Council on Foreign Relations. 3 February. Retrieved from www.cfr.org .

Markus, Hazel Rose, and Susan T. Fiske. 2012. "Introduction: A Wide-Angle Lens on the Psychology of Social Class," in *Facial Social Class: How Societal Rank Influences Interaction*. S.T. Fiske and H.R. Marcus (eds.). New York: Russell Sage Foundation.

Marlein, Mary Beth. 2015. "Corporatisation 'Threatens Academic Freedom'—AAUP." *University World News*, Issue No. 358, 13 March.

Marsh, John. 2011. *Class Dismissed*. New York: Monthly Review Press.

Marsden, Lorna. 2012. *Canadian Women & the Struggle for Equality*. Toronto: Oxford University Press.

Marshall, Katherine. 2011. "Generational Change in Paid and Unpaid Work." *Canadian Social Trends*, Winter.

Marston, Greg. 2003. Rethinking Social Inequality: The Case of "Illegal Refugees." CRSI 2003 Conference Proceedings, Social Inequality Today, Macquarie University, 12 November.

Martin, Roger, and John Milway. 2012. Canada: *What it is, What it can be*. Toronto: University of Toronto Press.

Mathieson, Jane, J. Popay, E. Enoch, S. Escorel, M. Hernandez, H. Johston, and L. Rispel. 2008. "Social Exclusion: Meaning, Measurement and Experience and Links to Health Inequalities," WHO Social Exclusion Knowledge Network Background Paper No 1. September.

Matthews, Chris. 2016. The Gig Economy Shows How Desperate American Workers Are. Fortune.com., 19 February.

Mazurkewich, Karen, and David Pett. 2010. "Women in the Workforce . . . But Their Kids Put Them Behind." *The Globe and Mail*, 13 October.

McAlaster, Trish. 2013. "Gender Divide." *The Globe and Mail*, 5 June.

McCarthy, Shawn. 2016. "UN Holds Up Canada as Global Touchstone." *The Globe and Mail*, 16 February.

McChesney, Robert W. 2014. Blowing the Roof off the Twenty-First Century: Media, Politics, and the Struggle for Post-Capitalist Democracy. Published by *Monthly Review*, New York.

McCracken, Carrie. 1998. The Impacts of Banana Plantation Development in Central America. Available online at http://members.tripod.com .

McDonald, David. 2013. "The Future of Work." *Carleton University Magazine*. Spring: 24–29.

McDonald, Ted et al. (eds.). 2010. Canadian Immigration: Economic Evidence for a Dynamic Policy Environment. *Queen's Policy Studies Series*. Montreal and Kingston: McGill-Queen's University Press.

McGavock, Jon. 2016. "Linking Culture and Health for First Nations." *Toronto Star*, 28 May.

McGowan, William. 2001. *Coloring the News: How Political Correctness Has Corrupted American Journalism*. New York: Encounter Books.

McGrane, David. 2015. Could a Progressive Platform Capture Canada's Youth Vote? Broadbent Institute. March.

McInturff, Kate. 2013a. Closing Canada's Gender Gap. CCPA, April.

McInturff, Kate. 2013b. The Gap in the Gender Gap. CCPA, July.

McInturff, Kate. 2015. The Best and the Worst Places to be a Woman in Canada 2015. CCPA, July.

McInturff, Kate, and Paul Tulloch. 2014. Narrowing the Gap: The Difference that Public Sector Wages Make. CCPA, 29 October.

McIntyre, Sheila. 1994. "Backlash against Equality: The 'Tyranny' of the 'Politically Correct.'" *McGill Law Journal* 38(1):3–63.

McKenna, Barrie. 2014. "Canada Failing in Governance Rankings Because of Harper Majority, Report Finds." *The Globe and Mail*, 8 May.

McKinsey & Company. 2013. Women Matter 2013. Gender Diversity in Top Management: Moving Corporate Culture, Moving Boundaries.

McLeod, Andrew. 2015. *A Better Place on Earth: The Search for Fairness in a Super Unequal British Columbia*. Madeira Park, BC: Harbour Publishing.

McMahon, Paul. 2015. *Feeding Frenzy*. Vancouver: Greystone Books.

McMahon, Tamsin. 2012. "State of the Anti-Union." *Maclean's*, pp. 54–58, 16 April.

McMahon, Tamsin. 2013. "Land of Misfortune." *Maclean's*, pp. 41–43, 29 April.

McMahon, Tamsin. 2014. "Second Class Children." *Maclean's*, pp. 16–21, 21 July.

McMullin, Julie. 2010. *Understanding Social Inequality: Intersections of Class, Age, Gender, Ethnicity and Race in Canada*. Toronto: Oxford University Press.

McMullin, Julie Ann, and Victor W. Marshall (eds.). 2010. *Aging and Working in the New Economy*. Northampton, MA: Edward Elgar.

McMurtry, John. 2013. *The Cancer State of Capitalism*. 2nd ed. Halifax: Fernwood.

McNally, David. 2012. "Power, Resistance, and the Global Economic Crisis," in *Power and Resistance: Critical Thinking about Canadian Social Issues*. 5th ed. L. Samuelson and W. Antony (eds.), pp.126–145. Halifax: Fernwood.

McNamee, Stephen J. 2014. *The Meritocracy Myth*, 3rd ed. Lanham, MD: Rowman & Littlefield Publishing.

McPherson, Dennis H., and J. Douglas Rabb. 2013. "Prolegomena to Any Further Discussion of Rights That May be Considered Aboriginal," in *Philosophy and Aboriginal Rights: Critical Dialogues*. S. Tomsons and L. Mayer (eds.). Toronto: Oxford University Press.

McQuaig, Linda, and Neil Brooks. 2010. *The Trouble with Billionaires*. Viking.

McWhorter, John. 2014. "'Microaggression' is the New Racism on Campus." *TIME*, 21 March. Retrieved from http://time.com.

Meili, Ryan. 2012. *A Healthy Society: How a Focus on Health Can Revive Canadian Democracy*. Saskatoon, SK: Purich.

Meltzer, Kimberly. 2010. "A Different Sort of Reality TV Hero: Extreme Fishermen, Loggers and Truckers on the Edge," in *Reel Politics: Reality Television as a Platform for Political Discourse*. Lemi Baruh and Ji Hoon Park (eds.), pp. 249–264. Cambridge, UK: Cambridge Scholars Publishing.

Memon, Nadeem. 2010. "Social Consciousness in Canadian Islamic Schools?" *International Migration and Integration* 11:109–117.

Mendelson, Michael. 2006. Aboriginal Peoples and Postsecondary Education in Canada. Published by the Caledon Institute of Social Policy. July.

Mertens, Richard. 2013. "Poverty Changes its Address." *Christian Science Monitor Weekly*, 16 September.

Metis Nation of Ontario. 2013. *Selected Demographics: Aboriginal and Metis Populations of Canada*. Ottawa: Author.

Michael, Christopher. 2012. "Follow the Bouncing Theories." *The Globe and Mail*, 13 August.

Milanovic, Branko. 2011. *The Haves and the Have-Nots: A Brief and Idiosyncratic History of Global Inequality*. New York: Basic Books.

Milanovic, Branko (ed.). 2012. *Globalization and Inequality*. Northampton, MA: An Elgar Research Collection.

Milke, Mark. 2012. Corporate Welfare Bargains at Industry Canada. Fraser Institute. September.

Milke, Mark. 2013. *Tax Me, I'm Canadian*. Thomas & Black Publishers.

Milke, Mark. 2014a. Government Subsidies in Canada: A $684 Billion Price Tag. Fraser Institute, June.

Milke, Mark. 2014b. "Chrysler's $700 Million Ask is Troubling." *Waterloo Region Record*, 22 February.

Miller, J.R. 1996. *Shingwauk's Visions: A History of Indian Residential Schools*. Toronto: University of Toronto Press.

Miller, Richard W. 2011. "How Global Inequality Matters." *Journal of Social Philosophy* 42(1):88–98.

Miller, Matthew G. and Peter Newcomb. 2013. "World's Rich Got Richer in 2012." Bloomberg. Reprinted in the *Waterloo Region Record*, 3 January.

Mills, Edward J. et al. 2011. "The Financial Cost of Doctors Emigrating From Sub-Saharan Africa: Human Capital Analysis." *British Medical Journal*, pp. 1–13.

Mills, Mary Lou. 2011. "Let's Rethink Poverty to Change Minds, Lives: Social Policy in Ontario." Reprinted in *The Lindsay Post*, 4 October.

Miranda, Veerle. 2011. Cooking, Caring, and Volunteering: Unpaid Work around the World. OECD Report, 20 September.

Mirtle, James. 2013. "The Great Offside: How Canadian Hockey is becoming a Game Strictly for the Rich." *The Globe and Mail*, 8 November.

Mitchell, Alanna. 2013. "An Inconvenient Truth." *The Globe and Mail*, 3 August.

Mitra, Debashish. 2014. "Microaggression is the New Face of Racism." *Times of Oman*, 3 May.

Modood, Tariq. 2011. Post-Immigration "Difference" and Integration: The Case of Muslims in Western Europe. A Report Prepared for the British Academy, Policy Centre.

Moellendorf, Darrell. 2009. *Global Inequality Matters*. New York: Palgrave Macmillan.

Moffatt, Mike. 2012a. "The $5 Million Electro-Motive Subsidy That Wasn't." *The Globe and Mail*, 7 February.

Moffatt, Mike. 2012b. "Electro-Motive Patents Overwhelmingly American." *The Globe and Mail*. 10 February.

Mohammed, Sara. 2010. "Historicizing Health Inequities: Healing and Vestiges of Residential Schooling." *Indigenous Policy Journal* xxi (3).

Monbiot, George. 2012a. "Corporate Power Grips Us All by the Throat." *The Guardian Weekly*, 14 December.

Monbiot, George. 2012b. "Must the Poor Starve so the Rich Can Drive?" *The Guardian Weekly*, 24 August.

Monchalin, Lisa. 2016. "The Failed Foreign Justice System and the Problem with Canada," in *Visions of the Heart*, 4th ed. David Long and Olive Dickason (eds.), pp. 351–373. Toronto: Oxford University Press.

Monck, Adrian. 2012. To Serve Society Better, Capitalism Needs a Redesign. News Release by the World Economic Forum Annual Meeting. Davos. 25 January.

Monsebraaten, Laurie. 2013. "Well-being of Canadian Children Lags Other Nations." *Toronto Star*. 10 April.

Monsebraaten, Laurie. 2014. "City Faces 'Epidemic' of Child Poverty." *Toronto Star*. 27 August.

Monsebraaten, Laurie. 2016. "Internet Takes a Big Bite out of Food Budget." *Toronto Star*. 2 February.

Monster-GfK. 2013. Monster Survey Reveals International Work Attitudes Gap. 18 November. Retrieved from www.about-monster.com .

Monture, Patricia. 2009. "Doing Academy Differently: Confronting 'Whiteness' in the University," in *Racism in the Canadian University*. F. Henry and C. Tator (eds.), pp. 76–105. Toronto: University of Toronto Press.

Monture, Patricia A. 2011. "The Need for Radical Change in the Criminal Justice System: Applying a Human Rights Framework," in *Visions of the Heart*. D. Long and O.P. Dickason (eds.), pp. 238–257. Toronto: Oxford University Press.

Morrow, Adrian. 2010. "Canadians among the Best Educated in the World: Report." *The Globe and Mail*. 7 September.

Mosby, Ian. 2013. "Administering Colonial Science: Nutrition Research and Human Biomedical Experimentation in Aboriginal Communities and Residential Schools, 1942–1952." *Social History* 46(91):145–172.

Mouawad, Jad, and Martha C. White. 2013. "As Airlines Need to Fill up All Their Seats, Customers are Getting Packed in Like Sardines." *The New York Times*. Reprinted in the *National Post*, 23 December.

Moynihan, Daniel Patrick. 1965. The Negro Family: The Case for National Action. US Department of Labor, Office of Policy Planning and Research. Washington, DC.

Moyo, Dambisa. 2012. *Winner Take All: China's Race for Resources and What It Means for the World*. Basic Books.

Moyo, Dambisa. 2016. Why Haven't We Cracked the Inequality Puzzle? World Economic Forum Agenda, 19 February.

Mukherjee, Ananya, and Darryl Reed. 2014. "After Rana Plaza, What Can We Do For Workers?" *Toronto Star*, 8 September.

Mukherjee, Arun, Alok Mukherjee, and Barbara Godard. 2006. "Translating Minoritized Cultures: Issues of Class, Caste, and Gender." *Postcolonial Text* 2(3).

Mullen, Ann. 2012. "The Not-So-Pink Ivory Tower." *Contexts* 11(4):34–39.

Mullen, Ann. 2013. *Degrees of Inequality: Culture, Class, and Gender in American Higher Education*. Baltimore: Johns Hopkins University Press.

Mullings, Leith. 2013. "Inequality Within." *Anthropology News*. Published by American Anthropological Association, May/June.

Mundy, Liza. 2012. *The Richer Sex: How the New Majority of Female Breadwinners is Transforming Sex, Love, and Family*. New York: Simon & Schuster.

Murray, Charles. 2012. *Coming Apart: The State of White America, 1960-2010*. Crown Forum.

Nakhaie, M. Reza. 1999. *Debates on Social Inequality: Class, Gender and Ethnicity in Canada*. Toronto: Harcourt Brace.

Nakhaie, M. Reza, and A. Kazemipur. 2013. Social Capital, Employment and Occupational Status of the New Immigrants in Canada. *International Migration & Integration* 14:419–437.

National Aboriginal Economic Development Board. 2015. *The Aboriginal Economic Progress Report*. Gatineau, June.

National Council of Welfare. 2011. The Dollars and Sense of Solving Poverty. 28 September.

National Council of Welfare. 2012. Poverty Profile. Special Edition. Ottawa.

National Women's Law Center. 2013. Closing the Wage Gap is Crucial for Women of Color and Their Families. Fact Sheet. November.

Naylor, Tom. 2011. *Crass Struggle: Greed, Glitz, and Gluttony in a Wanna-Have World*. Montreal and Kingston: McGill-Queen's University Press.

Nazroo, James, and Saffron Karlson. 2002. "Relationship between Racial Discrimination, Social Class, and Health Among Ethnic Minorities." *American Journal of Public Health* 92(4):624–632.

Neeganawedgin, Erica. 2012. "'Chattling the Indigenous Other': A Historical Examination of the Enslavement of Aboriginal Peoples in Canada." *AlterNative* 8(1).

Nel, Philip. 2008. *The Politics of Economic Inequality in Developing Countries*. New York: Palgrave Macmillan.

Nelson, Adie. 2010. *Gender in Canada*. 4th ed. Toronto: Pearson.

Nelson, Jacqueline. 2014. "The Changing Face of Wealth." *The Globe and Mail*, 9 August.

Nestel, Sheryl. 2012. Colour Coded Health Care: The Impact of Race and Racism on Canadians' Health. Wellesley Institute, Toronto, January.

New Zealand Listener. 2011. "Commentary: Life-span Discrepancies between Rich and Poor," July 31.

Newcomb, Peter, and Alex Sazonov. 2014. "2014: The Year the Richest 400 People on Earth Got $US92 Billion Richer." *Bloomberg News*. 30 December. Reprinted in *Financial Post*.

Newhouse, David, and Yale Belanger. 2011. "The Canada Problem in Aboriginal Politics," in *Visions of the Heart*. D. Long and O.P. Dickason (eds), pp. 352–380. Toronto: Oxford University Press.

Newhouse, David, Kevin FitzMorris, Tricia McGuire-Adams, and Daniel Jette. 2012. *Well-Being in the Urban Aboriginal Community*. Toronto: Thompson Publishing.

Newman, David M. 2011. *Identities and Inequalities. Exploring the Intersections of Race, Class, Gender, and Sexuality*. 2nd ed. McGraw Hill.

Newsom, Jennifer Siebel. 2011. *Miss Representation*. http://ther-epresentationproject.org/film/miss-representation .

Ng, Winnie, A. Sundar, G.-E. Galabuzi, S. Arat-Koc, S. Khan, and S. Serajelahi. 2013. *An Immigrant All Over Again? Recession, Plant Closures, and Older Racialized Immigrant Workers: A Case Study of the Workers of Progressive Moulded Products*. June. Toronto: Ryerson University.

Nicoll, Doreen. 2016. There is No Gender Symmetry When It Comes to Domestic Violence. Rabble.ca. 1 February.

Niezen, Ronald. 2013. *Truth and Indignation: Canada's Truth and Reconciliation Commission on Indian Residential Schools*. Montreal and Kingston: McGill-Queen's University Press.

Noah, Timothy. 2012. "The Mobility Myth." *The New Republic*. 8 February.

Noel, Alain, 2012. Fighting Poverty, Inequalities, and Social Exclusion. Conference Report. QICSS and CRDCN, Montreal.

Noisecat, Julian Brave. 2015. "Voting, Not Just Protest, Is Essential for Survival." *The Guardian Weekly*. 18 September.

Noland, Marcus, and Tyler Moran. 2016. "Study: Firms with More Women in the C-Suite Are More Profitable." Peterson Institute for International Economics. Published by *Harvard Business Review*, 8 February.

Noland, Marcus, Tyler Moran, and Barbara Kotschwar. 2016. "Is Gender Diversity Profitable? Evidence from a Global Survey." Peterson Institute for International Economics. Working Paper Series 16-3. February.

Nolen, Stephanie. 2013. "More Disasters, Greater Unease." *The Globe and Mail*, 27 April.

Nordstrom, Louise. 2012. "*Titanic* an Exception: 'Women and Children' on Sinking Ship a Myth, Say Researchers." *Toronto Star*, 12 April.

Northrup, David, and Lesley Jacobs. 2014. The Growing Income Inequality Gap in Canada: A National Survey. Institute for Social Research, York University, 31 January.

Nutt, Samantha. 2011. *Damned Nations: Greed, Guns, Armies, and Aid*. Toronto: McClelland & Stewart.

NWAC [Native Women's Association of Canada]. 2014. Sexual Exploitation and the Trafficking of Aboriginal Women and Girls. Literature Review and Key Informant Interviews. Final Report, October.

Nye, Joseph. 2012. "Even in a 'Woman's World', Gender Doesn't Matter." *The Globe and Mail*, 3 March.

O'Connor, L.J., and Morgan O'Neil. 2010. *Dark Legacy: Systemic Discrimination against Canada's First Peoples*. Vancouver: Totem Publications.

OECD 2012 Education at a Glance. OECD Indicators, OECD Publishing.

OECD. 2013a. Crisis Squeezes Income and Puts Pressure on Inequality and Poverty. Results from the OECD Income Distribution Database, May 2013.

OECD. 2013b. OECD Skills Outlook 2013. First Results from Survey of Adult Skills, November.

OECD. 2014a. Education at a Glance. OECD Indicators, OECD Publishing.

OECD. 2014b. Focus on Inequality and Growth, December.

OECD. 2014c. Top Incomes and Taxation in OECD Countries: Was the Crisis a Game Changer? 24 May.

OECD. 2015a. In It Together: Why Less Inequality Benefits Us All. Paris: OECD Publishing.

OECD. 2015b. Employment Outlook. How Does Canada Compare? Paris: OECD Publishing, July.

OECD. 2015c. Canada—Economic Forecast Summary. Paris: OECD Publishing, June.

OHCHR [Office of the High Commissioner for Human Rights]. 2013. Combatting Discrimination Based on Sexual Orientation and Gender Identity.

Okri, Ben. 2015. "The Spirit of its People Will Transform Africa." *The Guardian Weekly*, 9 November.

Olive, David. 2012. "Capitalism's Ugly Face." *Toronto Star*. 6 February.

Olive, David. 2013a. "Consumers Can Help Avert Another Rana." *Toronto Star*, 18 May.

Olive, David. 2013b. "Past Yellen and Lagarde, Women Still Have a Long Way to Go." *Toronto Star*, 7 December.

Olsen, Gregg M. 2011. *Power & Inequality: A Comparative Introduction*. Toronto: Oxford University Press.

Olson, Alexandra. 2013. "Canada Faces 'Crisis' over Aboriginal Issues, Anaya Tells the UN." *The Globe and Mail*, 22 October.

Olua, Ijeoma. 2015. What's Left Out of the "Gender in the Workplace" Debate: The Race Factor. The Lind Initiative, 29 October.

Omidvar, Ratna. 2014. "Don't Throw the Nanny out with the Bathwater." *The Globe and Mail*, 13 August.

Omidvar, Ratna, and John Tory. 2012. "New Glass Ceiling for Minorities." *Toronto Star*, 20 March.

ONPHA [Ontario Non Profit Housing Association] and CHF [Cooperative Housing Federation of Canada, Ontario Region]. 2013. *Where's Home?* Retrieved from http://www.chfcanada.coop

O'Neill, June. 2012. *The Declining Importance of Race and Gender in the Labor Market: The Role of Employment Discrimination Policies*. Lanham, MD: Rowman & Littlefield.

Ontario. 2013. Breaking the Cycle: Ontario's Poverty Reduction Strategy; The Fifth Progress Report. Toronto: Author.

Ontario College of Physicians and Surgeons of Ontario (2014). Registering Success: 2013. Retrieved from http://www.cpso.on.ca

OPHI [Oxford Poverty and Human Development Index]. 2015. Index Identifies Poorer Countries Where Poverty is "Shrinking." Oxford Poverty and Human Development Initiative. Oxford University.

Oreopoulos, Philip. 2009. Why Do Skilled Immigrants Struggle in the Labour Field? A Field Experiment with Six Thousand Resumes. Working Paper Series No. 09-03. Metropolis British Columbia, May.

Oreopoulos, Philip. 2011. Why Do Skilled Immigrants Struggle in the Labour Market? A Field Experiment with Thirteen Thousand Resumes. *American Economic Journal: Economic Policy* 3 (November):148–171.

Ornstein, Michael. 2006. *Ethno-Racial Groups in Toronto, 1971–2001: A Demographic and Socio-Economic Profile*. Toronto: Institute for Social Research.

Osberg, Lars. 2007. Reality Check—Economic Inequality in Canada. Why Inequality Matters in 1000 Words or Less: Growing Gap. CCPA, December, pp. 25–27.

Osberg, Lars. 2012. Instability Implications of Increasing Inequality: Growing Gap. CCPA, May.

Oxfam. 2013. The Cost of Inequality: How Wealth and Income Extremes Hurt us All. Oxfam Media Briefing, 18 January.

Oxfam. 2015. Wealth: Having It All and Wanting More. Oxfam Issue Briefing. Available at www.oxfam.org/sites/www.oxfam.org/files/file_attachments/ib-wealth-having-all-wanting-more-190115-en.pdf .

Oxfam International. 2016. An Economy for the 1%. 18 January.

Owram, Kristine. 2015. "Ottawa, Ontario Ante up $100M for Toyota." *National Post*, 31 July.

Packer, George. 2011. "The Broken Contract. Inequality and the American Dream." *Foreign Affairs*. November, pp. 20–31.

Palmater, Pam. 2013. "Why Idle No More Matters to Us All." *Now Magazine*. 17 January.

Palmeter, Pamela. 2015. *Indigenous Nationhood: Empowering Grassroots Citizens*. Halifax: Fernwood.

Pankin, Robert, and Carla Weiss. 2011. Part-Time Faculty in Higher Education: A Selected Annotated Bibliography. Faculty Publications Paper 276. Rhode Island College.

Papp, Aruna. 2010. Culturally Driven Violence Against Women: A Growing Problem in Canada's Immigration Communities. Frontier Centre for Public Policy.

Parcels, Jim. 2013. *Selling the Dream: How Hockey Parents and Their Kids are Paying the Price for our National Obsession*. Toronto: Penguin.

Parenti, Michael. 1977. *Democracy for the Few*. St Martin's Press.

Parker, Kim 2013. *Modern Parenthood*. Pew Research: Social & Demographic Trends, 14 March.

Parkin, Andrew. 2015. International Report Card on Public Education: Key Facts on Canadian Achievement and Equity. Final Report for the Environics Institute, June.

Parks, Robert H. 2011. *The End of Capitalism: Destructive Forces of an Economy Out of Control*. Amherst NY: Prometheus Books.

Paterson, Alex. 2012. Opinion: Inequality at the Top of Everyone's Agenda; The Canada We Want in 2020. Retrieved from http://canada2020.ca .

Patriquin, Martin. 2012. "Canada, Home to the Suicide Capital of the World." *Maclean's*, 30 March.

Paul, Daniel. 2012. "'We Were Not the Savages.' Indian Residential Schools," in *Power and Resistance: Critical Thinking about Canadian Social Issues*. 5th ed. L. Samuelson and W. Antony (eds.), pp. 146–166. Halifax: Fernwood.

Pauktuutit. 2006. *National Strategy to Prevent Abuse in Inuit Communities*, and *Sharing Knowledge, Sharing Wisdom: A Guide to the National Strategy*. Nunavut: Pauktuutit Inuit Women of Canada.

Peace, Robin. 2001. "Social Exclusion: A Concept in Need of Definition?" *Social Policy Journal of New Zealand*, Issue 16: July, pp. 17–32.

Peach, Ian. 2005. "The Politics of Self-Government." *SIPP News* (Spring): 4–6.

Peck Don. 2010. "How a New Jobless Era will Transform America." *The Atlantic*, March.

Peck, Don. 2011. "Can the Middle Class Be Saved?" *The Atlantic*, September.

Pegoraro, Leonardo. 2015. "Second Rate Victims: The Forced Sterilization of Indigenous Peoples in the USA and Canada." *Settler Colonial Studies* 5(2): 161–173.

Pendakur, Krishna, and Ravi Pendakur. 2008. Aboriginal Income Disparity in Canada. Metropolis British Columbia. Working Paper Series, December.

Pendakur, Krishna, and Ravi Pendakur. 2011. Colour by Numbers: Minority Earnings in Canada 1996–2006. Metropolis British Columbia. Working Paper Series. No. 11-05, May.

Penner, A.M., and A. Saperstein. 2013. "Engendering Racial Perceptions." *Gender & Society* 27(3): 319–344.

Pennisi, Elizabeth. 2014. "Our Egalitarian Eden." *Science* 344(6186):824–825.

Perception. 2007. "Defining and Re-defining Poverty in Canada." *Perception* 29(1/2):406.

Percy-Smith, Janie (ed.). 2000. *Policy Responses to Exclusion. Towards Inclusion?* Philadelphia: Open University Press.

Perreault, Samuel. 2011. Violent Victimization of Aboriginal People in the Canadian Provinces, 2009. Statistics Canada. Publication 85-002-x.

Perreaux, Les. 2015. "Montreal Controversy Shows Cities Regularly Dump Sewage into Rivers." *The Globe and Mail*. 9 October.

Perucci, Robert, and Earl Wysong. 2008. *The New Class Society: Goodbye American Dream?* Lanham, MD: Rowman & Littlefield.

Peters, Katie. 2013. Garment Worker Wages Declined in Majority of Top-Apparel-Exporting Countries Over the Last Decade, New Study Reveals. Center for American Progress, 11 July.

Petersen, John L. 2009. "A New End, a New Beginning." *Reality Sandwich*. Retrieved from http://realitysandwich.com/13018/new_end_new_beginning/ .

Petersen, John L. 2012. *A Vision for 2012: Planning for Extraordinary Change*. Golden, CO: Fulcrum Publishing.

Petoukhov, Konstantin. 2013. "Recognition, Redistribution, and Representation: Assessing the Transformative Potential of Reparations for Indian Residential Schools Experience." *McGill Sociological Review* 3(February):73–91.

Pettigrew, Todd. 2014. "McGill Students Apologize for Forcing Farnan to Say Sorry." *Maclean's*, 10 March.

Pew Charitable Trusts. 2010. Pew Finds Economic Mobility Rates Differ for Canadians and Americans. Economic Mobility Project, January.

Pew Charitable Trusts. 2011. Does America Promote Mobility as Well as Other Nations? Economic Mobility Project, November.

Phelps, Edmund S. 2006. Capitalism and Keynes: From the Treatise on Probability to the General Theory. Conference Commemorating Keynes 1883-1946. Santa Columba (Siena), Italy, 4–6 July.

Picard, Andre. 2000. "Homeless Men Die Young, Study." *The Globe and Mail*, 25 April.

Picard, Andre. 2004. "The Rich Are Healthier, Live Longer Report Says." *The Globe and Mail*, 26 February.

Picard, Andre. 2005. "Native Health Care is a Sickening Disgrace." *The Globe and Mail*, 3 November.

Picard, Andre. 2012. "Tories 'Want Out of the Aboriginal Business.'" *The Globe and Mail*, 10 April.

Picard, Andre. 2013. "Wealth as a Matter of Health." *The Globe and Mail*, 4 June.

Picard, Andre. 2014. "Seniors on Stretchers: A Health Care Disgrace." *The Globe and Mail*, 23 September.

Picot, G., F. Hou, and S. Coulombe. 2007. "Chronic Low Income and Low-Income Dynamics among Recent Immigrants." *Analytical Studies Branch Research Paper Series* 2007(294). Statistics Canada.

Picot, G., and F. Hou. 2011. Seeking Success in Canada and the United States: The Determinants of Labour Market Outcomes among Children of Immigrants. *Analytical Studies Branch Research Paper Series*. Catalogue No. 11F0019M–No. 331. Statistics Canada.

Picot, Garnett, and Feng Hou, 2014. Immigration, Poverty, and Inequality in Canada: What is New in the 2000s. Statistics Canada, December.

Pierce, Chester. 1974. "Psychiatry Problems of the Black Minority," in *American Handbook of Psychiatry*. S. Arieta (ed.), pp. 512–523. New York: Basic Books.

Pietersee, Jan Nederveen. 2002. "Global Inequality: Bringing Politics Back In." *Third World Quarterly* 23(6):1–12.

Piketty, Thomas. 2014. *Capital in the Twenty-first Century*. Cambridge, MA: Belknap Press.

Pilon, Mary. 2016. "Aristocracy Revisited." *Bloomberg Business*, 28 December to 10 January.

Pimlott, Herbert. 2015. "WLU Faculty Pinched While Bureaucracy Grows." *Waterloo Region Record*, 26 February.

Pinder, Sherrow O. 2013. "Introduction: The Concept and Definition of American Multicultural Studies," in

American Multicultural Studies: A Diversity of Race, Ethnicity, Gender, and Sexuality. S.O. Pinder (ed.), pp. ix–xxii. Thousand Oaks: Sage.

Pinker, Susan. 2008. *The Sexual Paradox: Extreme Men, Gifted Woman and the Real Gender Gap.* Random House.

Piper, Nicola. 2008. "International Migration and Gendered Axes of Stratification: Introduction," in *New Perspectives on Gender and Migration.* N. Piper (ed.), pp. 1–18. New York: Routledge.

Pirkle, Catherine M. 2014. "Food Insecurity and Nutritional Biomarkers in Relation to Stature in Inuit Children in Nunavik." *Journal of the Canadian Public Health Association* 105(4):213–218.

Piven, Frances Fox, and Richard A. Cloward (eds.). 1974. *Regulating the Poor: The Functions of Public Welfare.* New York: Vintage.

Plan International. 2013. "In Double Jeopardy: Adolescent Girls and Disasters." Published in the Series *Because I am a Girl: State of the World's Girls*, 2013.

Plender, John. 2012. "Capitalism in Crisis: The Code that Forms a Bar to Harmony." *Financial Times.* 8 January.

Pocklington, Tom, and Allan Tupper. 2002. *No Place to Learn: Why Universities Aren't Working.* Vancouver: UBC Press.

Poelzer, Greg, and Ken Coates. 2015. *From Treaty Peoples to Treaty Nation.* Vancouver: UBC Press.

Pogatchnik, Shawn. 2013. "165 Million Children Stunted From Malnutrition, UN Says." *Toronto Star*, 16 April.

Polanyi, M., L. Johnston, A. Khanna, S. Dirie, and M. Kerr. 2014. The Hidden Epidemic: A Report on Child and Family Poverty in Toronto. Children's Aid Society of Toronto and Children's Aid Foundation Community Initiatives Program, November.

Polster, Claire, and Janice Newson. 2015. A Penny for Your Thoughts. CCPA.

Polushin, William. 2012. "Electro-Motive Closure: The Game Has Changed." *The Globe and Mail*, 8 February.

Pomfret, Richard. 2011. *The Age of Equality: The Twentieth Century in an Economic Perspective.* Cambridge, MA: The Belknap Press of Harvard University.

Popay, Jennie, S. Escorel, M. Hernandez, H. Johnston, J. Mathieson, and L. Rispel. 2008. *Understanding and Tackling Social Exclusion: Final Report to the WHO Commission on Social Determinants of Health, From the Social Exclusion Knowledge Network.* Lancaster UK, February.

Porter, Catherine. 2013. "Food Policy Truly Shameful." *Toronto Star*, 5 March.

Porter, John. 1965. *The Vertical Mosaic: The Analysis of Social Class and Power.* Toronto: University of Toronto Press.

Postmedia News. 2011. "Canada Ranks Third-best Country in the World to be a Woman," 21 September.

Pottie-Sherman, Yolande, and Rima Wilkes. 2014. Good Code, Bad Code: Exploring the Immigration-Nation Dialectic Through Media Coverage of the Herouxville "Code of Life" Document. Migration Studies.

Power, Jonathan. 2007. *Conundrums of Humanity: The Quest for Global Justice.* Leiden, the Netherlands: Martinus Nijhoff Publishers.

Public Safety Canada. 2014. National Forum on Human Trafficking—Summary Report 2014. Retrieved from www.publicsafety.gc.ca .

Puffer, Sheila M. 2004. "Introduction: Rosabeth Moss Kanter's 'Men and Women of the Corporation and the Change Masters,'" *The Academy of Management Executives* 18(2):92–95.

Pupo, Norene, and Mark Thomas (eds.). 2009. *Interrogating the New Economy.* Toronto: University of Toronto Press.

Pupo, Norene, Dan Glenday, and Ann Duffy. 2011. *The Shifting Landscape of Work.* Toronto: Nelson.

Putnam, David. 2011. Healthy, Wealthy, and Happy. David Putnam on AustralianRadio, 25 April. Retrieved from http://socialcapital.wordpress.com .

Putnam, David. 2015. *Our Kids: The American Dream in Crisis.* New York: Simon & Schuster.

Pyatt, Graham. 2003. "Development and the Distribution of Living Standards: A Critique of the Evolving Data Base." *Review of Income and Wealth* 49(3):333–358.

Quesnel, Joseph, and Conrad Winn. 2011. The Nisga'a Treaty: Self Government and Good Governance; The Jury is Still Out. Frontier Centre for Public Policy. Policy Series No 108. June.

Race Forward. 2014. How the Media Covers Racism and Other Barriers to Productive Racial Discourse. Part 1. January.

Raine, Adrian. 2013. *The Anatomy of Violence: The Biological Roots of Crime.* New York: Pantheon Books.

Rainer, Rob. 2007. "Toward a National Ideal: Canada without Poverty by 2020." *Perception* 29 (1/2):7–9.

Rajotte, James. 2013. Income Inequality in Canada: An Overview. Report of the Standing Committee on Finance. House of Commons, 41st Parliament, 2nd Session. December.

Rajiva, Mythili, and Sheila Batacharya (eds.). 2010. *Reena Virk: Critical Perspectives on a Canadian Murder.* Toronto: Canadian Scholars Press.

Ramos, Howard. 2012. "Does How You Measure Representation Matter? Assessing the Persistence of Canadian Universities' Gendered and Colour Coded Vertical Mosaic." *Canadian Ethnic Studies* 44 (2).

Randstad Institute. 2014. Women Shaping Business: Challenges and Opportunities 2014.

Rank, Mark Robert. 2004. *One Nation, Underprivileged: Why American Poverty Affects Us All.* New York: Oxford University Press.

Rank, Mark R. 2011. "Rethinking American Poverty." *Contexts* 10(2):16–21.

Raphael, Dennis. 2002. Poverty, Income Inequality, and Health in Canada. The CSJ Foundation for Research and Education, June.

Raphael Dennis. 2004. *Social Determinants of Health: Canadian Perspectives*, 2nd ed. Toronto: Canadian Scholars Press.

Raphael, Dennis. 2011. "Mainstream Media and the Social Determinants of Health in Canada: Is it Time to Call it a Day?" *Health Promotion International* 26(2):220–229.

Ravitch, Diane. 2009. *The Death and Life of the Great American School System.* Basic Books.

Raymond, Susan, and Mary Beth Martin. 2012. "The End of Geography." *Currents* 38(6):9–12.

RBC [Royal Bank of Canada]. 2011a. Immigrant Wage and Employment Gaps Persist. RBC Economics.

RBC Economics. 2011b. Immigrant Labour Market Outcomes in Canada: The Benefits of Addressing Wage and Unemployment Gaps. Current Analysis, December.

RCMP. 2014. Murdered and Missing Aboriginal Women: A National Operational Overview. Ottawa.

Reading, Charlotte Lopie, and Fred Wien. 2009. Health Inequalities and Social Determinants of Aboriginal Peoples' Health. National Collaborative Centre for Aboriginal Health.

Readings, Bill. 1997. *The University in Ruins.* Harvard University Press.

Reay, Diane. 1998. "Rethinking Social Class: Qualitative Perspectives on Class and Gender." *Sociology* 32(2):259–275.

Rebick, Judy. 2013a. 2012: A Year of Activism From Maple Spring to Idle No More. Blog Canadian Dimension, 1 January.

Rebick, Judy. 2013b. Idle No More: A Profound Social Movement That is Already Succeeding. Blog Canadian Dimension, 12 January.

Rebick Judy. 2014. December 6: A Reminder to Uproot Our Culture of Misogyny. Rabble.ca. 5 December.

Redden, Joanna. 2014. *The Mediation of Poverty: The News, New Media, and Politics.* Toronto: Lexington Books.

Redeaux, Monique. 2011. "The Culture of Poverty Reloaded." *Monthly Review* 63(3).

Redfern, Catherine, and Kristin Aune. 2010. *Reclaiming the F Word: The New Feminist Movement.* London and New York: Zed Books.

Reeves, Richard V., and Kimberly Howard. 2013. The Parenting Gap. Center on Children and Families, Brookings Institute, 9 September.

Reich, Robert. 2012. *Beyond Outrage: Expanded Edition.* New York: Vintage.

Reich, Robert. 2013. *Inequality for All.* DVD documentary.

Reich, Robert. 2015. *Saving Capitalism: For the Many, Not the Few.* New York: Knopf.

Reichel, Justina. 2013. "Women Passed Over for Top Positions in Canada's Best Companies." *Epoch Times,* 21–27 February.

Reid, Erin. 2015. "Embracing, Passing, Revealing, and Ideal Worker Image: How People Navigate Expected and Experienced Professional Identities." *Organizational Science,* published online, 20 April.

Reist, Michael. 2011. *Raising Boys in a New Kind of World.* Toronto: Dundurn.

Reist, Michael. 2012. "Why Schools are a Target of Choice." *The Globe and Mail,* 17 December.

Reitz, Jeffrey. 2012. "The Distinctiveness of Canada's Immigrant Experience." *Patterns of Prejudice* 46 (5): 518–538.

Reitz, Jeffrey, and Rupa Banerjee. 2007. "Racial Inequality, Social Cohesion, and Policy Issues," in *Belonging?* K. Banting et al. (eds.), pp. 489–546. Montreal: IRPP.

Reitz, Jeffrey, Mai B. Phan, and Rupa Banerjee. 2015. "Gender Equity in Canada's Newly Growing Religious Minorities." *Ethnic and Racial Studies* 38(5):681–699.

Reliefweb. 2012. Slow Progress in Closing Global Economic Gender Gap, New Major Study Finds. World Economic Forum, Global Gender Gap Report 2012. Retrieved from http://reliefweb.int/report/world/global-gender-gap-report-2012 .

Renzetti, Elizabeth. 2012. "Warning: The Icebergs of *Titanic* Ethnic Stereotypes are Dead Ahead, Old Bean." *The Globe and Mail,* 14 April.

Report. 2014a. Gap between Rich and Poor. Toronto Vital Signs Report.

Report. 2014b. Murdered and Missing Aboriginal Women in British Columbia, Canada. Inter-American Commission on Human Rights. Washington DC, 21 December.

Reputation Institute. 2012. Canada is the Country with the Best Reputation in the World According to Reputation Institute. New York, 27 September.

Reputation Institute. 2015. The World's Most Reputable Countries. New York, July.

Revera Report. 2013. *Revera Report on Ageism: A Look at Gender Differences.* Revera Inc. and the International Federation on Ageing. A Look at Gender Differences.

Rhoads, R.A. and C.A. Torres (eds.). 2006. *The University, State, and Market: The Political Economy of Globalization in the Americas.* Palo Alto, CA: Stanford University Press.

Richards, John. 2014. "Are We Making Progress? New Evidence on Aboriginal Education Outcomes in Provincial and Reserve Schools." Commentary No 408. C.D. Howe Institute. Toronto, April.

Richmond, Ted, and Anver Saloojee. 2005. *Social Inclusion: Canadian Perspectives.* Halifax: Fernwood.

Rider, David. 2015. "City's Income Gap Keeps Widening." *Toronto Star,* 29 January.

Ridgeway, Cecilia. 2011. *Framed by Gender: How Gender Inequality Persists in the Modern World.* Toronto: Oxford University Press.

Ridgeway Cecilia. 2014. "Why Status Matters for Inequality." *American Sociological Review* 79(1):1–16.

Riggins, Stephen (ed.). 1992. *Ethnic Minority Media: An International Perspective.* Newbury Park: Sage.

Rifkin, Jeremy. 2004. *The European Dream: How Europe's Vision of the Future is Quietly Eclipsing the American Dream.* New York: Tarcher/Penguin.

Rifkin, Jeremy. 2005. American Capitalism vs. European Social Markets. Spiegel Online International, August 1.

Rifkin, Jeremy. 2011. *The Third Industrial Revolution: How Lateral Power is Transforming Energy, the Economy, and the World.* New York: Palgrave Macmillan.

Riley, Jason L. 2014. *Please Stop Helping Us.* New York: Encounter Books.

Riseboro, Caroline. 2010. "8.8 Million Children Die as World Spends Billions on Pet Food." *Toronto Star,* 2 April.

Ritchie, Justin. 2012. "Idea #1: 'MOOC'; Saviour of Higher Ed?" *The Tyee,* 19 December.

Ritzer, George. 2015. *The McDonaldization of Society,* 8th ed. Pine Ridge, CA: Sage.

Roberts, Steve, Will Atkinson, and Mike Savage (eds.). 2012. *Class Inequality in Austerity Britain: Power, Difference, and Suffering.* Palgrave Macmillan.

Robinson, William I., and Mario Barrera. 2012. "Global Capitalism and Twenty-First Century Fascism: A US Case Study." *Race & Class* 53(3):4–29.

Robson, John. 2015. "The Academic Upper Crust." *National Post.* 20 March.

Robson, Karen L. 2013. *Sociology of Education in Canada.* Toronto: Pearson.

Rogers, Elizabeth. 2012. Ageism in the Workplace Remains an Issue. Retrieved from www.50plus.com .

Rohac, Dalibor. 2012. Does Inequality Matter? Adam Smith Institute (the Free Market Thinktank). London.

Rolfe, Gary. 2013. *The University in Dissent.* New York: Routledge.

Rolfsen, Catherine. 2008. "After the Apology." *This Magazine,* September/October.

Rollo, Tobold. 2013. I Am Canadian (Because of Treaties with Indigenous Nations). Rabble.ca. 3 January.

Romanow, Roy J. 2012. "Foreword," in Ryan Meili (ed.), *A Healthy Society.* Saskatoon, SK: Purich.

Root, Jesse, Erika Gate-Gasse, John Shields, and Harald Bauder. 2014. Discounting Immigrant Families: Neoliberalism and the Framing of Canadian Immigration Policy Change. RCIS Working Paper No. 2014/7, October, Ryerson University.

Roscigno, Vincent J. 2010. "Ageism in the American Workplace." *Contexts* 9(1):16–21.

Rosenblum, Simon, and Sid Frankel. 2011. "Canadian Corporate Tax Policy Sustains Child Poverty." *Toronto Star,* 6 May.

Rosen, Ruth. 2012. "Women Never Said 'We Wanted it All.'" *The Tyee,* 8 August.

Rosin, Hanna. 2012. *The End of Men: And the Rise of Women.* New York: Riverhead Books.

Rothkopf, David. 2013. "The Balance of Power." *Foreign Policy,* May/June, pp. 103–104.

Rotman, Leonard Ian. 1996. *Parallel Paths: Fiduciary Doctrine and the Crown–Native Relationship in Canada.* Toronto: University of Toronto Press.

Roy, Alice. 1995. "The Grammar and Rhetoric of Inclusion." *College English* 57(2):182–195.

Royal Commission. 1996. "People to People, Nation to Nation: Highlights From the Report on the Royal Commission on Aboriginal Peoples." Ottawa: Minister of Supply and Services Canada.

Royce, Edward. 2015. *Poverty and Power. The Problem of Structural Inequality.* 2nd ed. Rowman & Littlefield Publishers.

Ryan, Sid. 2015. "Seeking Justice for Fallen Workers." *Toronto Star.* 28 April.

Ryerson, James. 2015. "All Things Being Unequal." Sunday Book Review, *The New York Times,* 15 December.

Sakamoto, I., D. Jeyapal, R. Bhuyan, J. Ku, L. Fang, H. Zhang, and F. Genovese. 2013. *An Overview of Discourses of Skilled Immigrants and "Canadian Experience": An English-Language Print Media Analysis.* CERIS Working Paper No. 98. Toronto: Ontario Metropolis Centre.

Sale, Peter F. 2012. *Our Dying Planet.* Berkeley: University of California Press.

Saloojee, Anver. (n.d.) Social Inclusion, Citizenship, and Diversity. Published by the Canadian Council of Social Development. Retrieved from www.ccsd.ca .

Saloojee, Anver. 2003. Social Inclusion, Anti-racism and Democratic Citizenship. Perspectives on Social Inclusion. Laidlaw Foundation.

Saltmarsh, Sue. 2005. "'White Pages' in the Academy: Plagiarism, Consumption, and Racist Rationalities." *International Journal for Educational Integrity* 1(1):1–11.

Samli, A. Coskun. 2008. *Globalization from the Bottom Up.* Jacksonville, FL: Springer.

Samson Natalie. 2014. "New CRC Guidelines Aim To Reduce Unconscious Hiring Bias Against Women." *University Affairs,* 3 December.

Samuel, Edith, and Shehla Burney. 2003. "Racism, eh? Interactions of South Asian Students with Mainstream Faculty in a Predominantly White Canadian University." *The Canadian Journal of Higher Education* xxxiii (2):81–114.

Sandborn, Tom. 2014. "Our Tarnished Maple Leaf." *The Tyee,* 15 December.

Samuelson, Les. 2012. "Crime as a Social Problem: From Definition to Reality," in *Power and Resistance: Critical Thinking about Canadian Social Issues* 5th ed. L. Samuelson and W. Antony (eds.), pp. 373–404. Halifax: Fernwood.

Sanchez, Peter M., and Kathleen M. Adams. 2007. "The Janus Faced Character of Tourism in Cuba." *Annals of Tourism Research* 35(1):27–76.

Sandberg, Sheryl. 2013. *Lean In: Women, Work, and the Will to Lead.* New York: Knopf.

Sandborn, Tom. 2013. "Big Firms Hoard Tax Cut Riches While Economy Drags, CLC." *The Tyee,* 31 January.

Sandercock, Leonie. 2003. Rethinking Multiculturalism for the 21st Century. Working Paper No. 3-14, Research on Immigration and Integration in the Metropolis. Vancouver Centre of Excellence.

Sapers, Howard. 2013a. Spirit Matters: Aboriginal People and the Corrections and Conditional Release Act. Report Office of the Correctional Investigator.

Sapers, Howard. 2013b. Annual Report of the Office of the Correctional Investigator 2012–2013. Ottawa.

Sapers, Howard. 2016. "Prison Watchdog Says More Than a Quarter of Federal Inmates are Aboriginal People." CBC *News.* Posted 16 January.

Sarkar, Saral. 2011. *The Crisis of Capitalism: A Different Study of Political Economy.* Berkeley, CA: Counterpoint.

Sarlo, Christopher. 2013. Poverty: Where Do We Draw the Line? Fraser Institute, November 14.

Sarlo, Christopher. 2016. Our Continuing Obsession with Inequality. Fraser Institute article. Posted 29 January.

Sarlo, Christopher, and Suzanne Walters. 2001. Measuring Poverty in Canada. Fraser Institute, 23 July.

Sarlo, Christopher, Jason Clemens, and Joel Emes. 2015. Income Inequality Measurement Sensitivities. Fraser Institute, July.

Satzewich, Vic, and Nikolaos Liodakis. 2013. *"Race" and Ethnicity in Canada: A Critical Introduction,* 3rd ed. Toronto: Oxford University Press.

Saul, John Ralston. 2014. *The Comeback: How Aboriginals are Reclaiming Power and Influence.* Toronto: Viking.

Saul, Nick. 2013. "The Hunger Game." *The Walrus.* April 17–19.

Saunders, Doug. 2013. "Is Your Wardrobe Killing Bangladeshis or Saving Them?" *The Globe and Mail,* 27 April.

Saunders, Doug. 2014. "Why the Last Mile is Always the Hardest." *The Globe and Mail*, 29 November.

Saunders, Doug. 2015. "Hasta La Vista Employment." *The Globe and Mail*, 2 May.

Saunders, Peter. 2011. *The Rise of the Equalities Industry*. London: Civitas: Institute for the Study of Civil Society.

Savage, Mike, and Fiona Devine. 2013. *Survey Charts the Emergence of a New Class System*. London School of Economics and Political Science.

Savage, Mike, Fiona Devine, Niall Cunninghum, Mark Taylor, Yaojun Li, Johs Hjellbrekke, Brigitte Le Roux, Sam Friedman, and Andrew Miles. 2013. "A New Model of Social Class? Findings from the BBC's Great British Class Survey." *Sociology* 47(2): 219–250.

Save the Children Report. 2012. A Life Free From Hunger. London.

Sayenga, Kurt (director). 2014. *Is Poverty Genetic? Through the Wormhole*. Discovery Science Channel. Season 5, Episode 4. Released 4 June.

Scheff, T., and C. Poulson. 2013. "Dangerous Shame." *Contexts* 12(2):5.

Scheurich, J.J., and M.D. Young. 2002. "White Racism among White Faculty," in *The Racial Crisis in American Higher Education*. W.A. Smith, P.G. Altbach, and K. Lomotey (eds.), pp. 221–239. Albany: State University of New York.

Scheurkens, Ulrike. 2010. "Introduction." In *Globalizations and Transformations of Social Inequality*. New York: Routledge.

Schiller, Bradley R. 2004. *The Economics of Poverty and Discrimination*, 9th ed. Upper Saddle Creek, NJ: Prentice Hall.

Schliesman, Paul. 2012. *Honour on Trial: The Shafia Murders and the Culture of Honour Killing*. Fitzhenry and Whiteside.

Schmidt, Volker H. 2013. "Gradual and Categorical Inequalities," in *Worlds of Difference*. S.A. Arjomand and E. Reiss (eds.), pp. 252–268. Thousand Oaks CA: Sage.

Schutz, Eric A. 2011. *Inequality and Power: The Economics of Class*. New York: Routledge.

Schwalbe, Michael. 2008. *Rigging the Game: How Inequality is Reproduced in Everyday Life*. New York: Oxford University Press.

Schwanen, Daniel. 2014. Tradeable Services: Canada's Overlooked Success Story. C. D. Howe Institute, January.

Schwartz, Zane. 2015. "Do the Math." *Maclean's*, pp. 40–41. 27 April.

Schweickart, David. 2011. *After Capitalism*, 2nd ed. Lanham: Rowman & Littlefield Publishers.

Scoffield, Heather. 2013. "National Household Survey: Richest are Middle-aged White Men." *National Post*, 11 September.

Scott, Tracie Lea. 2012. *Postcolonial Sovereignty? The Nisga'a Final Agreement*. Saskatoon: Purich.

Seabrook, Jeremy. 2014. *The Song of the Shirt: Cheap Clothes across Continents and Centuries*. Navayana Publishers.

Sekharan, V. 2015. Infographic: *Canadian Women in Poverty*. Produced by the Canadian Women's Foundation. Hosted by The Homeless Hub/Canadian Observatory on Homelessness, 25 March.

Selley, Chris. 2012. "A Dark Spin on Poverty." *National Post*, 23 November.

Senate. 2013. Reducing Barriers to Social Inclusion and Social Cohesion. Report of the Standing Senate Committee on Social Affairs, Science and Technology. K.K. Ogilvie and A. Eggleton. June.

Sernau, Scott. 2011. *Social Inequality in a Global Age*, 4th ed. Sage.

Shafir, Eldar, and S. Mullainathan. 2013. *Why Having Too Little Means So Much*. Time Books.

Shah, Anup. 2010. "The Banana Trade War." *Global Issues*. Retrieved from www.globalissues.org/article/63/the-banana-trade-war .

Shah, Anup. 2011. Poverty around the World—Global Issues. Available online at www.globalissues.org .

Shaker, Erica, and David Macdonald. 2014. Tier for Two: Managing the Optics of Provincial Tuiition Fees Policies. CCPA, 10 September.

Shantz, Jeff, and José Brendan Macdonald (eds.). 2013. *Beyond Capitalism: Building Democratic Alternatives for Today and the Future*. New York: Bloomsbury Academic.

Shapcott, Michael. 2012. Universal Periodic Review—Canada 2013. Wellesley Institute, 2 October.

Sharpe, Andrew, and Jill Hardt. 2006. Five Deaths a Day: Workplace Fatalities in Canada, 1993–2005. Centre for the Study of Living Standards. Ottawa, December.

Sharpe, Andrew, and Christopher Ross. 2011. Living Standards Domain of the Canadian Index of Wellbeing. CSLS Research Report 2022-17. Ottawa, November.

Shecter, Barbara. 2014. "Gender Gap on Boards Narrows." *Financial Post*, 19 November.

Sheehy, Elizabeth. 2010. Misogyny is Deadly: Inequality Makes Women More Vulnerable to Being Killed. CCPA, July/August newsletter.

Sheikh, Munir. 2015. Great Gatsby v. Zero Dollar Linda. McDonald-Laurier Institute. April.

Sherman, Jennifer, and Elizabeth Harris. 2012. "Social Class and Parenting: Classic Debates and New Understandings." *Sociology Compass* 6(1):60-71.

Sheppard, Colleen. 2010. *Inclusive Equality: The Relational Dimensions of Systemic Discrimination in Canada*. Montreal and Kingston: McGill-Queen's University Press.

Shillington, Richard, and John Stapleton. 2010. Cutting Through the Fog: Why is it so Hard to Make Sense of Poverty Measures? Metcalf Foundation. May.

Shkilnyk, Anastasia. 1985. *Poison Stronger Than Love*. Princeton: Yale University Press.

Siebold, Steve. 2010. *How Rich People Think*. London House Press.

Siemiatycki Myer. 2012. The Diversity Gap. The Electoral Underrepresentation of Visible Minorities in the GTA. Commissioned by DiverseCity. The Greater Toronto Leadership Project. Published by the Ryerson Centre for Immigration and Settlement.

Signs. 2013. "Intersectionality: Theorizing Power, Empowering Theory." Vol. 38, No 4.

Silk, Mark. 2008. "Islam and the American News Media Post September 11," in *Mediating Religion*. J. Mitchell and S. Marriage (eds.), pp. 73-88. New York: T. and T. Clark, a Continuum Imprint.

Silver, Jim. 2012. "Persistent Poverty in Canada: Causes, Consequences, Solutions," in *Power and Resistance: Critical Thinking About Canadian Social Issues*, 5th ed. L. Samuelson and W. Antony (eds.), pp. 98–125. Halifax: Fernwood.

Silver, Jim. 2015. *About Canada: Poverty*. Halifax: Fernwood.

Simmons, Alan. 2010. *Immigration to Canada*. Toronto: Canadian Scholars Press.

Simpson, Leanne. 2013. "Another Story from Elsipogtog." *The Tyee*, 21 October.

Simpson, Timothy (ed.). 2013. *The Relevance of Higher Education: Exploring a Contested Nation*. Lanham, MD: Lexington Books.

Singer, Natasha. 2012. "Boardroom Bonanza." *The New York Times*, 15 April.

Singh, Rashmee. 2014. "Stephen Harper is Wrong: Crime and Sociology are the Same Thing." *The Globe and Mail*, 4 September.

Singh, Renu. 2012. "The Reality of Honour Killings in Canada." *Darpan Magazine*. March. Retrieved from www.darpan-magazine.com .

Sinha, Maire. 2012. Violence against Intimate Partners. Statistics Canada. Retrieved from www.statcan.gc.ca .

Sinha, Maire. 2013. "Measuring Violence against Women: Statistical Trends." *Juristat* article. Component of Statistics Canada catalogue No. 85–002–x., 25 February.

Sinha, V., and A. Blumenthal. 2014. "From the House of Commons Resolution to Pictou Landing Band Council and *Maurina Beadle v. Canada*: An Update on the Implementation of Jordan's Principle." *First Peoples Child & Family Review* 9(1).

Sirin, S.R., and L. Sirin-Rogers. 2015. The Educational and Mental Health Needs of Syrian Children. Migration Policy Institute, October.

Sivanandan, A. 2010. Fighting Anti-Muslim Racism. An Interview with A. Sivanandan. Institute for Race Relations. March. Available at www.irr.org.uk/news/fighting-anti-muslim-racism-an-interview-with-a-sivanandan/ .

Sivanandan, A. 2013. "The Market State vs the Good Society." *Race & Class* 54(3):1–9.

Skaggs, Sheryl, and Jennifer Bridges. 2013. "Race and Sex Discrimination in the Employment Process." *Sociology Compass* 7(5):404–415.

Skeggs, Beverley, and Helen Wood. 2012. "Introduction: Real Class," in *Reality Television and Class*. H. Wood and B. Skeggs (eds.), pp. 1–17. New York: Palgrave Macmillan.

Skidelsky, Robert, and Edward Skildesky. 2012. *How Much is Enough? Money and the Good Life*. New York: Random House.

Slaughter, Anne-Marie. 2012. "Why Women Still Can't Have It All." *The Atlantic*, July/August.

Slaughter, Anne-Marie. 2015. *Unfinished Business: Women Men Work Family*. Random House.

Smith, Malinda. 2016. "Words are not Enough." Comment/Analysis, CAUT Bulletin. February, p. A5.

Smith, Miriam. (ed.). 2007. *Group Politics and Social Movements in Canada*. Peterborough: Broadview.

Smith, Sharon. 2008. "The Politics of Identity." *International Socialist Review*, Issue 57. January–February.

Smith, Stacy L. 2010. Gender Oppression in Cinematic Context? A Look At Females On-Screen and Behind the Cameras in Top-Grossing 2007 Films. Retrieved from http://annenberg.usc.edu/pages/~/media/MDSCI/Gender%20Inequality%202007.ashx .

Smith, Taigi. 2003. *Sometimes Rhythm, Sometimes Blues: Young African Americans on Love, Relationships, Sex, and the Search for Mr. Right*. Seal Press.

Smith, Yves. 2012. Austerity Kills: How the Eurocrisis is Being Used to Break the Social Contract. Naked Capitalism. Retrieved from www.nakedcapitalism.com/2012/06/austerity-kills-how-the-eurocrisis-is-being-used-to-break-the-social-contract.html .

Smith, Ekuwa. 2004. "Nowhere to Turn? Responding to Partner Violence against Immigrant and Visible Minority Women." Canadian Council of Social Development. Submitted to the Department of Justice.

Smith, Richard. 2013. "Sleepwalking to Extinction: Capitalism and the Destruction of Life and Earth." *Adbusters*, 14 November.

Smith, Joanna, and Bruce Campion-Smith. 2013. "Chiefs Threaten to Pull Cord." *Toronto Star*, 11 January.

Snider, Laureen. 2015. *About Canada: Corporate Crime*. Halifax: Fernwood.

Social Progress Index. 2015. Social Progress Index 2015 Report. Social Progress Imperative, 8 April.

Sopinski, John. 2014. "On the Heels of Apple Report, A Look at Diversity in the Tech Sector." *The Globe and Mail*, 13 August.

Somerville, Kara, and Scott Walsworth. 2010. "Admission and Employment Criteria Discrepancies: Experiences of Skilled Immigrants in Toronto." *International Migration and Integration* 11:341–352.

Sorrenson, Chris, and Charlie Gillis. 2013. "The New Underclass." *Maclean's*, 21 January.

Spafford, M.M., V.I. Nygaard, F. Gregor, and M.A. Boyd. 2006. "Navigating the Different Spaces: Experiences of Inclusion and Isolation among Racially Minoritized Faculty in Canada." *Canadian Journal of Higher Education* 36(1):1–27.

Spears John. 2013. "Caterpillar Plant Closes, 330 Toronto Jobs Lost." *Toronto Star*, 4 May.

Spector, Malcolm, and John Kitsuse. 1977. *Constructing Social Problems*. Menlo Park CA: Cummings.

Spence, Michael. 2011. "Globalization and Unemployment." *Foreign Affairs*.

Spence, Nicholas 2011. "Introductory Essay: An Rx for Indigenous Health Inequality; The Social Determinants of Health." *The International Indigenous Policy Journal* 2(1). Article 12.

Spence, Michael, and Sandile Hlatshwayo. 2011. The Evolving Structure of the American Economy and the Employment Challenge. Council on Foreign Relations, March.

Spoonley, Paul, and Andrew Butcher. 2009. "Reporting Superdiversity: The Mass Media and Immigration in New Zealand." *Journal of Intercultural Studies* 30(4):355–372.

Srivastava, Sarita. 2008. "A 'Culture of Whiteness' (Is Change Possible?)". *The Ardent Review* 1(1):23–25.

Standing, Guy. 2012. *The Precariat: The New Dangerous Class*. Bloombury.

Stanford Center on Poverty & Inequality. 2014. The Poverty and Inequality Report. State of the Union.

Stanley, Timothy J. 2011. *Contesting White Supremacy: School Segregation, Anti-Racism and the Making of Chinese Canadians*. Vancouver: UBC Press.

Stanley Timothy J. 2012. "Analyzing Racisms in the Workplace." *Canadian Diversity* 9(1):53–57.

Stapleton, John. 2011. Trading Places: Single Adults Replace Lone Parents as the New Face of Social Assistance. With assistance from Vass Bednar, Mowat Centre Task Force.

Stapleton, John. 2013. A Ball Player, a Cop, a Janitor, and a Welfare Recipient. Broadbent Institute Blog, 16 January.

Stapleton, John. 2015. The Working Poor in the Toronto Region. Metcalfe Foundation, 20 April.

Stapleton, John, Brian Murphy, and Yue Xing 2012. The Working Poor in the Toronto Region. Summary Report for the Metcalf Foundation, February.

Stasiulis, Daiva K. 1999. "Feminist Intersectional Theorizing," in *Race and Ethnic Relations in Canada*, 2nd ed. Peter Li (ed.), pp. 347–397. Toronto: Oxford University Press.

Stasiulis, Daiva K., and Abigail B. Bakan. 1997. "Negotiating Citizenship: The Case of Foreign Domestic Workers in Canada." *Feminist Review* 57: 112–139.

Statistics Canada. 2010. "Women in Canada: Paid Work." *The Daily*, 9 December.

Statistics Canada. 2012a. Education Indicators in Canada: Fact Sheets. February.

Statistics Canada. 2012b. Persons in Low Income before Tax.

Statistics Canada. 2012c. Persons in Low Income after Tax.

Statistics Canada. 2013a. "High Income Trends Among Canadian Taxfilers, 1982-1-2010." *The Daily*, 28 January.

Statistics Canada. 2013b. 2011 National Household Survey: Aboriginal Peoples in Canada: First Nations People, Metis, and Inuit. Catalogue No. 99-011-x2011001. May.

Statistics Canada. 2013c. "Labour Force Survey: October." *The Daily*. 8 November.

Statistics Canada. 2013d. Portrait of Canada's Labour Force. Catalogue No. 99-011-x2011002. June.

Statistics Canada. 2013e. The Educational Attainment of Aboriginal Peoples in Canada. National Household Survey 2011. Catalogue No. 99-012-x2011003.

Statistics Canada. 2014. Median Total Income by Family Type, By Province, and Territory. 23 July.

Statistics Canada. 2015a. Payroll Employment Earnings and Hours, December 2014. 26 February.

Statistics Canada. 2015b. "Homicide in Canada 2014." *The Daily*, 25 November.

Staton, Michael. 2014. "The Degree is Doomed." *Harvard Business Review*. Blog Network, 8 January.

Status of Women Canada. 2015. Fact Sheet: Economic Security. Government of Canada.

Steckley, John, and Guy Kirby Letts. 2007. *Elements of Sociology: A Critical Canadian Introduction*. Toronto: Oxford University Press.

Steffen, Will, W. Broadgate, L. Deutsch, O. Gaffney, and C. Ludwig. 2015. "The Trajectory of the Anthropocene: The Great Acceleration." *The Anthropocene Review*, 16 January.

Steinmetz, Katy. 2016. "Exclusive: See How Big the Gig Economy Really Is." *Time Magazine*, 6 January.

Stewart Kirstine. 2015. *Our Turn*. Random House.

Stewart, Anthony. 2009. *You Must be a Basketball Player: Rethinking Integration in the University*. Halifax: Fernwood Publishing.

Stewart, Heather. 2012. "Wealth Doesn't Just Trickle Down—It Just Floods Offshore, Research Reveals." *The Guardian*, 21 July.

Stiglitz, Joseph. 2012. *The Price of Inequality: How Today's Divided Society Endangers Our Future*. New York: W.W. Norton.

Stock, Shayna. 2012. "Beyond Inclusivity." Letter from the Editor. *Briarpatch Magazine*, 1 January.

Stockdill, Brett, and Mary Yu Danico (eds.). 2012. *Transforming the Ivory Tower: Challenging Racism, Sexism, and Homophobia in the Academy*. Honolulu: University of Hawaii Press.

Stote, Karen. 2015. *An Act of Genocide: Colonialism and the Sterilization of Aboriginal Women*. Halifax: Fernwood.

Stout, Lynn A. 2012. *The Shareholder Value Myth: How Putting Shareholders First Harms Investors, Corporations, and the Public*. San Francisco: Berrett-Koehler Publishers.

Strauss, Marina, and Joanna Slater. 2013. "A Retailer's Dilemma: The Line between Cost and Safety." *The Globe and Mail*, 4 May.

Straw, Will, and Alex Glennie. 2012. "The Third Wave of Globalisation." IPPR, 26 January.

Stuart Elizabeth. 2015. "China Has Almost Wiped out Urban Poverty: Now it must Tackle Inequality." *The Guardian*, 19 August.

Sue, Derald Wing. 2010. *Microaggressions in Everyday Life: Race, Gender, and Sexual Orientation*. Hoboken, NJ: Wiley.

Sue, Derald Wing. 2011. "Microaggressions and Marginality: Manifestations, Dynamics, and Impact." Hoboken, NJ: Wiley.

Sue, Derald Wing, Christina M. Capodilupo, Gina C. Torino, Jennifer M. Bucceri, Aisha M.B. Holder, Kevin L. Nadal, and Marta Esquilin. 2007. "Racial Microaggressions in Everyday Life: Implications for Clinical Practice." *American Psychologist* 62(4):271–286.

Sundararajan, Arun. 2015. "The 'Gig Economy' is Coming: What Will It Mean for Work?" *The Guardian*, 26 July.

Suzuki, David. 2011. "Overconsumption, Not Overpopulation, is the Biggest Problem." *Georgia Strait*, 1 November.

Suzuki, David, and Ian Hanington. 2012. *Everything under the Sun: Toward a Brighter Future on a Small Blue Planet*. Vancouver: Greystone Books, D&M Publishers.

Swartz, D.L., 2007. "Recasting Power in its Third Dimension: Review of Steven Luke's, *Power: A Radical View*." *Theoretical Sociology*.

Symes, Jean. 2012. "Promoting Social and Economic Justice for All." *Inter Pares*, February.

Symes, Jean. 2013. Open for Justice: Campaign for Corporate Accountability. Newsletter, Inter Pares. November.

Taber, Jane. 2012. "Re-Paving the Way for Women on the Hill . . . Yet Again." *The Globe and Mail*, 3 February.

Tal, Benjamin. 2014. Canada's Employment Quality Index. CIBC Economics Report, 5 May.

Tal, Benjamin. 2015a. Employment Quality—Trending Down. Canadian Employment Quality Index. CIBC Economics, 5 March.

Tal, Benjamin. 2015b. Higher Levels of Profit Margins are here to Stay. CIBC Economics, 31 March.

Tal, B., and E. Enenajor. 2013. "Degrees of Success: The Payoff to Higher Education in Canada," in *Focus* (CIBC World Markets Report), 26 August.

Tamburri, Rosanna. 2015. "New Study Shows Strong Labour-Market Outcomes for University Grads." *University Affairs*, 21 January.

Tang, Sannie Y. and Annette J. Browne. 2008. "'Race' Matters: Racialization and Egalitarian Discourses Involving Aboriginal People in the Canadian Health Care Context." *Ethnicity & Health* 13(2):109–127.

Tanovich, David. 2015. "'Whack' No More: Infusing Equality in the Ethics of Defence Lawyering in Sexual Assault Cases." *Ottawa Law Review.* 45(3):495–525.

Tanovich, David, and Elaine Craig. 2016. "Whacking the Complainant: A Real and Current Systemic Problem." *The Globe and Mail*, 10 February.

Tapscott, Don. 2012. "Discovery Learning is the New Higher Learning." *The Globe and Mail*, 15 October.

Tarasuk, Valerie, Andy Mitchell, and Naomi Dachner. 2013. *Household Food Insecurity in Canada, 2011. Research to Identify Policy Options to Reduce Food Insecurity (PROOF).* Toronto: University of Toronto.

Tarkan, Laurie. 2012. Is Ageism Widespread in the Workplace? Fox News, 7 June.

Tatia, Sandeep. 2010. Diversity Will Change the Face of the Workplace. *Financial Post*, 18 March.

Taylor, Jillian. 2015. "Shamattawa Suicides Shake Northern Manitoba Reserve." CBC *News*, 26 March.

Taylor, Peter Shawn. 2005. "Help Wanted." *Canadian Business.* March, pp. 29–34.

Taylor-Gooby, Peter. 2013. "Why Do People Stigmatise the Poor at a Time of Rapidly Increasing Inequality, and What Can Be Done about It?" *The Political Quarterly* 94(1):31–39.

TD Economics. 2011. Post-Secondary Education is the Best Investment You Can Make. September 12.

TD Economics. 2012. Income and Income Inequality: A Tale of Two Countries. Special Report, 11 December.

TD Economics. 2013. Get on Board Corporate Canada. Special Report, 7 March.

Teelucksingh, Cheryl, and Grace-Edward Galabuzi. 2005. Working Precariously: The Impact of Race and Immigrant Status on Employment Opportunities and Outcomes in Canada. Report for the Canadian Race Relations Foundation. Toronto.

Teelucksingh, Cheryl, and Grace-Edward Galabuzi. 2010. Social Cohesion, Social Exclusion, Social Capital. Region of Peel Immigration Discussion Paper. February. Region of Peel Human Services.

Tendoh, Constance Inju. 2009. "Immigrants' Perspectives about Home and the Politics of Return." 4 August. http://www.articlesbase.com

Tepper, Elliot L. 1988. *Changing Canada: The Institutional Response to Polyethnicity: The Review of Demography and Its Implications for Economic and Social Policy.* Ottawa: Carleton University.

Tepperman, Lorne. 2012. Habits of Inequality. A New Approach to Sociology's Oldest Problem. Presentation at the James E. Curtis Memorial Lecture, University of Waterloo, 27 February.

The Lancet. 2014. *Violence against Women and Girls: Special Issue.* 21 November. Retrieved from www.thelancet.com .

Therborn, Goran. 2013. *The Killing Fields of Inequality.* Thousand Oaks: Sage.

Thibault, Eric. 2014. "Federal Inmate Cost Soars to $117Gs Each Per Year." *Edmonton Sun*, 18 March.

Thielen-Wilson, Leslie. 2014. "Troubling the Path to Decolonization: Indian Residential School Case Law, Genocide, and Settler Illegitimacy." *Canadian Journal of Law and Society* 29(2):181–199.

Thobani, Sunera. 2007. *Exalted Subjects: Studies in the Making of Race and Nation in Canada.* Toronto: University of Toronto Press.

Thomson-Reuters Foundation and the Rockefeller Foundation. 2015. Canada. The Five Key Issues Facing Women Working in the G20. Key Findings. October. Retrieved from www.trust.org .

Thornett, Alan. 2012. "Ecosocialists Debate 'Too Many People?'" *Socialist Resistance*, 2 January.

Tibaijuka, Anna. 2009/10. "Opinion: Message from the Executive Director." *Urban World.* December/January, p. 4.

Tieleman, Bill. 2015. "Is Stephen Harper a Social Progressive?" *The Tyee*, 10 February.

Tiessen, Kaylie. 2014. Seismic Shift: Ontario's Changing Labour Market. CCPA, March.

Tiessen, Kaylie. 2016. Ontario's Social Assistance Poverty Gap. Canadian Centre for Policy Alternatives. 9 May.

Tilly, Charles. 2005. "Rethinking Inequality." *Polish Sociological Review* 3(151).

Timson, Judith. 2011. "Women, Please Don't Shut Up, Whatever You Do." *The Globe and Mail*, 10 March.

Tjepkema, Michael, Russell Wilkins, and Andrea Long. 2013. *Cause-Specific Mortality by Income Adequacy in Canada: A 16-Year Follow-Up Study.* Statistics Canada.

Todd, Nicolas. 2012. Income Inequality: A Top Global Risk. Canada 2020. Available online at http://canada2020.ca .

Toller, Carol. 2013. "Different can be Better." *Canadian Business*, 13 May.

Tolley, Erin. 2016. *Framed: Media and the Coverage of Race in Canada.* Vancouver: UBC Press.

Tomsons, Sandra, and Lorraine Mayer. 2013. General Introduction, in *Philosophy and Aboriginal Rights: Critical Dialogues.* S. Tomsons and L. Mayer (eds.). Toronto: Oxford University Press.

Town Hall Report. 2013. Health Care in Canada: What Makes us Sick. Canadian Medical Association, July.

Tripp, Rob. 2012. *Without Honour: The True Story of the Shafia Family and the Kingston Canada Murders.* Toronto: HarperCollins.

True, Jacqui. 2012. *The Political Economy of Violence against Women.* Toronto: Oxford University Press.

Truth and Reconciliation Commission Report. 2015. *Honouring the Truth, Reconciling for the Future.* Summary of the Final Report.

Tsaparis, Paul. 2013. "The Business Case for Responsible Capitalism." *The Globe and Mail*, 10 July.

Tungohan, Ethel et al. 2015. "After the Live-in Caregiver Program: Filipina Caregivers' Experiences of Graduated and Uneven Citizenship." *Canadian Ethnic Studies* 46(2).

Trovato, Frank, and Anatole Romaniuk. 2014. "Introduction, Aboriginal Populations: Social, Demographic, and Epidemiological Perspectives," in *Aboriginal Populations: Social, Demographic, and Epidemiological Perspectives*. F. Trovato and A. Romaniuk (eds.), xiii–xxix. Edmonton: University of Alberta Press.

Trypuc, Bri, and Jeffrey Robinson. 2009. Homeless in Canada. Charity Intelligence Canada. October.

Tully, James. 2000. "The Struggles of Aboriginal Peoples for and of Freedom," in *Political Theory and the Rights of Indigenous Peoples*. D. Ivison et al. (eds.), pp. 39–56. Cambridge: Cambridge University Press.

Turcotte, Martin. 2010. Women and Education. Statistics Canada. Publication No. 89-503-x.

Tuhiwai Smith, Linda. 1998. *Decolonizing Methodologies: Research and Indigenous Peoples*. London: Zed Books.

Tuhiwai Smith, Linda. 2012. *Decolonizing Methodologies: Research and Indigenous Peoples*, 2nd ed. London: Zed Books.

Turpel-Lafond, Mary Ellen. 2014. "Put Native Women on the Agenda." *The Globe and Mail*, 21 August.

Ubelacker, Sheryl. 2010. "Accessing Care a Challenge for Minority Women." *The Globe and Mail*, March 30.

Ucarer, Emek M. 1997. "Introduction: The Coming of an Era of Human Uprootedness: A Global Challenge," in *Immigration into Western Societies: Problems and Policies*. E.M. Ucarer and D.J. Puchala, (eds.), pp. 1–16. London: Cassells.

UN. 2009. Rethinking Poverty: Report on the World Social Situation 2010. Department of Economics and Social Affairs.

UN. 2014. World Urbanization Prospects. Department of Economic and Social Affairs (DESA) Population Division.

UN Commission on the Status of Women. 2015. Political Declaration on the Occasion of the Twentieth Anniversary of the Fourth World Conference on Women. 59th Session, 9–20 March.

UN News. 2015. Gender Equality—Still a Long Way to Go. 9 March.

UN Women [United Nations Entity for Gender Equality and the Empowerment of Women]. 2011. In Pursuit of Justice: Progress of the World's Women 2011–2012. New York.

UN Women. 2015. Progress of the World's Women 2015–2016: Transforming Economies, Realizing Rights. United Nations, 27 April.

Unger, David. 2013. "Europe's Social Contract Lying in Pieces." Editorial Observer. *The New York Times*, 13 June.

UNICEF. 2012. "Measuring Child Poverty." *Innocenti Report Card 10*. Florence

UNICEF Office of Research. 2013. "Child Well-Being in Rich Countries: A Comparative Overview." *Innocenti Report Card 11*. Florence.

UNICEF Office of Research. 2014. "Children of the Recession." *Innocenti Report Card 12*. Florence.

United Way. 2015. The Opportunity Equation: Building Opportunity in the Face of Growing Income Inequality. With Ekos and Neighbourhood Change Research Partnership, University of Toronto: February.

UNODC. [United Nations Office on Drugs and Crime]. 2014. Global Report on Trafficking in Persons 2012.

Upadhayaya, Venus. 2012. "Indian Quarry Workers Break Out of Bondage." *Epoch Times*, 17 August. Available at www .theepochtimes.com/n3/1482591-indian-quarry-workers-break-out-of-bondage/ .

Urbina, Ian, and Darren Winter. 2015. Forced Labor, To Catch Cheap Fish. Solarglide, 29 July. Retrieved from www .solarglide.com/blog/forced-labour-for-cheap-fish?utm_content=bufferba8a7&utm_medium=social&utm_source=plus.google.com&utm_campaign=buffer .

US News and World Report, Wharton School of Business, and BAV Consulting. 2016. Best Countries Report. Retrieved from http://www.usnews.com

Usher, Alex. 2015. Setting Tuition Fees. Posted 27 January. Retrieved from http://higheredstrategy.com .

Usher, Alex. 2016a. Two Simple Reasons Tuition Rises Have Little Effect on Access. Posted 16 February. Retrieved from http://higheredstrategy.com .

Usher, Alex. 2016b. Some Curious Student Loan Numbers. Posted 17 February. Retrieved from http://higheredstrategy.com .

Valaskakis, Gail, Madeleine Dion Stout, and Eric Guimond (eds.). 2009. *Restoring the Balance: First Nations*. Winnipeg: University of Manitoba Press.

Vale, Brenda, and Robert Vale. 2009. *Time to Eat the Dog? The Real Guide to Sustainable Living*. Thames and Hudson Publishers.

Vallas, Steven Peter. 2011. *Work: A Critique*. Polity Press.

Vallis, Mary. 2009. "Why Ads Paint Dads as Buffoons." *National Post*, June 20.

Valpy, Michael. 2013. "What Binds Us Together, What Pulls Us Apart? The 2013 Atkinson Series, Me You Us." *Toronto Star*, 5 December.

Van der Gaag, Nikki. 2014. *Feminism & Men*. London: Zed Books.

Vecsey, Christopher. 1987. "Grassy Narrows Reserve: Mercury Pollution, Social Disruption, and Natural Resources: A Question of Autonomy." *American Indian Quarterly* 11(4):287–314.

Vedder, Richard. 2012. "In Praise of Profit." *Contexts* 11(4):19–20.

Veenstra, Gerry. 2011. Race, Gender, Class, and Sexual Orientation: Intersecting Axes of Inequality and Self-related Health in Canada. *International Journal for Equity in Health* 10(3).

Veldhuis, Niels, and Charles Lammam. 2012. "The 'Poor' are Getting Significantly Richer, Study Concluded." *Waterloo Region Record*, 24 November.

Vincent, Donovan. 2013. "Grassy Narrows First Nations Anti-Logging Battle with Province Heats Up." *Toronto Star*. 30 October.

Vose, Robin. 2015a. "The Great Austerity Swindle." CAUT *Bulletin*, April.

Vose, Robin. 2015b. "The Political Challenge of Academic Commitment." *Academic Matters*: Spring-Summer Issue.

Voyageur, Cora. 2011. "First Nations Women in Canada," in *Visions of the Heart*. D. Long and O.P. Dickason (eds.), pp. 213–237. Toronto: Oxford University Press.

Voyageur, Cora J. 2016. "First Nations Women in Canada," in *Visions of the Heart*, 4th ed. David Long and Olive Dickason (eds.), pp. 127–151. Toronto: Oxford University Press.

Voyageur, Cora, Laura Brearley, and Brian Calliou (eds.). 2015. *Restoring Indigenous Leadership: Wise Practices in Community Development*, 2nd ed. Banff Centre Press.

Wagamese, Richard. 2013. "Native Despair: Face to Face With Ennui on a Reserve." *The Globe and Mail*, 24 August.

Walby, Sylvia. 2009. *Globalization and Inequalities*. Thousand Oaks, CA: Sage.

Waldie, Paul. 2013. "The British Class System: Needs a Makeover, Innit." *The Globe and Mail*, 3 April.

Walker, Alan, and Carol Walker. 2011. "Conclusion: Building on the Legacy of Peter Townsend," in *Fighting Poverty, Inequality, and Injustice: A Manifesto Inspired by Peter Townsend*. W. Walker, A. Sinfield, and C. Walker (eds.), pp. 275–291. Polity Press.

Walker, James W. St. G. 1997. *"Race," Rights and the Law in the Supreme Court of Canada*. Waterloo, ON: Wilfrid Laurier Press.

Wallis, Maria, and Augie Fleras. 2009. *The Politics of Race in Canada*. Toronto: Oxford University Press.

Wallis, Maria, and Siu-Ming Kwok. 2008. *Daily Struggles: The Deepening Racialization and Feminization of Poverty in Canada*. Toronto: Canadian Scholars' Press.

Wallis, Maria, Lina Sunseri, and Grace-Edward Galabuzi. 2010. *Colonialism and Racism in Canada: Historical Trace and Contemporary Issues*. Toronto: Nelson.

Walters, Richard. 2014. Overcoming Persistent Stereotypes: The Battle against LGBT Discrimination. International Public Relations Association. June.

Ward, Olivia. 2013. "Revisiting the Price of Cheap." *Toronto Star*, 5 May.

Warren, Michael. 2013. "Why Capitalism Has Time to Save Itself." *The Globe and Mail*, 14 August.

Warry, Wayne. 2009. *Ending Denial: Understanding Aboriginal Issues*. Toronto: University of Toronto Press.

Warwick-Booth, Louise. 2013. *Social Inequality*. Thousand Oaks: Sage.

Watson, Paul. 2013. "This is Not Planet Earth, it's Planet Ocean," in *22 Ideas to Fix the World*. P. Dutkiewicz and R. Sakwa (eds.), pp. 95–110. New York: New York University Press.

Watson, Stephanie. 2015. Students Unhappy in School, Survey Finds. Yale Center for Emotional Intelligence. Posted October 25, WebMD Health News.

Watson, William. 2015. *The Inequality Trap: Fighting Capitalism Instead of Poverty*. University of Toronto Press.

Wayland, Sarah V. 2006. "Unsettled: Legal and Policy Barriers for Newcomers to Canada: Literature Review." Law Commission of Canada/Community Foundations of Canada.

Weaver, Sally M. 1993. "First Nations Women and Government Policy 1970–1992: Discrimination and Conflict," in *Changing Patterns: Women in Canada*, 2nd ed. Sandra Burt et al. (eds.). Toronto: McClelland and Stewart.

Webb, Jack. 2013. The Burden of Being Bright: Academic Achievement among African American Males. Retrieved from www.examiner.com.

Weber, Bob. 2013a. "Government Ran Experiments on Hungry People on Reserves." *The Globe and Mail*, 17 July.

Weber, Bob. 2013b. "TB Vaccine Tested on Reserves in 1930s." *Toronto Star*, 28 July.

Weber, Max. 1958. *From Max Weber: Essays in Sociology*. New York: Oxford University Press.

Weber, Tim. 2012. "World Economic Forum: Stark Inequality 'Top Global Risk.'" *BBC News Business*, 11 January.

Weinberg, Merlinda. 2008. "Structural Social Work: A Moral Compass for Ethics in Practice." *Critical Social Work* 9(1).

Weisman, Alan. 2013. *Countdown: Our Last Best Hope for a Future on Earth*. New York: Little Brown & Co.

Weil, David. 2014. *The Fissured Workplace*. Cambridge, MA: Harvard University Press.

Wells, Jennifer. 2016. "Little Has Changed Since Bangladesh Factory Collapsed." *Toronto Star*, 23 April.

Wente, Margaret. 2012. "Our School System is So Last Century." *The Globe and Mail*, 3 March.

Wells, Jennifer. 2012. "Caterpillar Cunning Yields London Showdown." *Toronto Star*, 4 February.

Wesley, Dana, and Shauna Shiels. 2007. "'Everyday Racism' is No Less Violent." *The Journal*. Queen's University, 26 October.

Westheimer, Joel. 2010. "Higher Education or Education for Hire?" *Academic Matters*: April–May Issue.

Westwood, Rosemary. 2013. "What Does that $14 Shirt Really Cost?" *Maclean's*, 13 May.

Wheeler, Jessica. 2015. A Review of National Crime Victim Victimization Findings on Rape and Sexual Assault. Council of Contemporary Families. 20 April.

White Gillian B. 2015. "The Invisible Work that Women Do around the World." *The Atlantic*, 14 December.

Widdowson, Frances, and Albert Howard. 2009. *Disrobing the Aboriginal Industry*. Montreal and Kingston: McGill-Queen's University Press.

Widdowson, Frances, and Albert Howard. 2013. *Approaches to Aboriginal Education in Canada: Searching for Solutions*. Brush Education Inc.

Wienstock, Daniel. 2012. "Equality of Opportunity, Equality of Means: An Argument for Low Tuition and the Student Strike." *Academic Matters*, pp. 16–18. November.

Wilk, Piotr, and Martin Cooke. 2015. "Collaborative Public Health System Interventions for Chronic Disease Prevention among Urban Aboriginal Peoples." *The International Indigenous Policy Journal* 6(4).

Wilkes, Rima, Catherine Corrigall-Brown, and Danielle Ricard. 2010. "Nationalism and Media Coverage of Indigenous People's Collective Action in Canada." *American Indian Culture and Research Journal* 34, 4: 41–59.

Wilkinson, Richard, and Kate Pickett. 2009. The Spirit Level: Why Equality is Better for Everyone. Equality Trust.

Wilkinson Richard, and Kate Pickett. 2010. "Inequality: The Enemy between Us? Why Inequality Matters." *Kosmos ix* (1):5–8.

Williams, Ross. 2012. "Canada Places Third in New International Ranking of Higher-Ed Systems." *University Affairs*, 11 May.

Willow, Anna J. 2012. "Strong Hearts, Native Lands: The Cultural and Political Landscape of Anishinaabe

Anti-Clearcutting Activism." *SUNY Series.* State University of New York.

Wilson, Daniel, and David Macdonald. 2010. The Income Gap between Aboriginal Peoples and the Rest of Canada. CCPA.

Winckler, Victoria, and Michael Trickey. 2014. Rethinking Poverty. Implications for Action. 4 November, Bevan Foundation.

Winlow, Simon, and Steve Hall. 2013. *Rethinking Social Exclusion: The End of the Social?* Thousand Oaks: Sage.

Winson, Anthony. 2006. "EcoTourism and Sustainability in Cuba: Does Socialism Make a Difference?" *Journal of Sustainable Tourism* 14(1):6–19.

Winter, James. 2001. *Media Think.* Montreal: Black Rose Books.

Working-Class Perspectives. 2008. Stereotyping the Working Class. Posted 8 September. Available online at http://work-ingclassstudies.wordpress.com .

Wolf, Alison. 2013. *The XX Factor: How the Rise of Working Women Has Created a Far Less Equal World.* Crown Publishing.

Wolf, Naomi. 2013. "Twenty Years On, Women Still Looking at Lookism." *The Globe and Mail*, 17 August.

Wolfe, Barbara, William Evans, and Teresa E. Seeman (eds.). 2012. *The Biological Consequences of Socioeconomic Inequalities.* New York: Russell Sage Foundation.

Wolff, Richard. 2012. *Democracy at Work: A Cure for Capitalism.* Chicago: Haymarket Books.

Wolff, Richard. 2013. "Capitalism Becomes Questionable." *Canadian Dimension*, 21 February.

Women's Media Center. 2015. The Status of Women in the U.S. Media 2015. Retrieved from www.womensmediacenter.com .

Woods, Michael. 2013. "Canada's One Percenters Earn at Least $191,000 a Year, Most are Likely Male, Live in Toronto." *National Post*, 13 September.

Woolford, Andrew. 2013. "Ethnic Cleansing, Canadian Style." *Literary Review of Canada.* October, pp. 1–10.

Woolfson, Michael, Michael Veall, and Neil Brooks. 2014. Piercing the Veil—Private Corporations and Income of the Affluent. Retrieved from http://igopp.org/wp .

Woolley, Frances. 2012. "Employment Equity Policy: One Size Doesn't Fit All." *The Globe and Mail*, 12 September.

Workers' Action Centre. 2015. Still on the Edge: Building Decent Jobs from the Ground Up. Toronto. March.

Workman, Bruce. 2011. The New Robber Barons. LaborNET. Retrieved from www.labornet.org/news/0000/workman.html .

World Bank. 2015. Electricity Power Consumption (KWh) Per Capita.

World Economic Forum [WEF]. 2012. Global Risks 2012.

World Economic Forum. 2013. Global Gender Gap Report.

World Economic Forum. 2015. Deepening Income Inequality. Report on the Outlook on the Global Agenda. August.

World Health Organization [WHO]. 2012. Violence against Women. Fact Sheet No. 239. November.

World Health Organization. 2013. Global and Regional Estimates of Violence against Women: Prevalence and Health Effects of Intimate Partner Violence and Non-Partner Sexual Violence.

World Meteorological Organization. 2014. Annual Report.

Wormer, Katherine van, Laura Kaplan, and Cindy Juby. 2012. *Confronting Oppression, Restoring Justice: From Policy Analysis to Social Action*, 2nd ed. Alexandria, VA: Council of Social Work Education Press.

Wotherspoon, Terry. 2009. *The Sociology of Education in Canada.* Toronto: Oxford University Press.

Wotherspoon, Terry, and Bernard Schissel. 2003. *The Legacy of School for Aboriginal People: Education, Oppression, Emancipation.* Toronto: Oxford University Press.

Wotherspoon, Terry, and John Hansen. 2013. "The 'Idle No More' Movement: Paradoxes of First Nations Inclusion in the Canadian Context." *Social Inclusion* 1(1):21–36.

Wright, Erik Olin. 1994. *Interrogating Inequality.* London: Verso.

Wu, Zheng, Christoph M. Schimmele, and Feng Hou. 2012. "Self-Perceived Integration of Immigrants and Their Children." *Canadian Journal of Sociology* 37: 381–409.

Wynne, Ashley, and Cheryl L. Currie. 2011. "Social Exclusion as an Underlying Determinant of Sexually Transmitted Infections among Canadian Aboriginals." *Pimatisiwin: A Journal of Aboriginal and Indigenous Community Health* 9(1):113–129.

Yakabuski, Konrad. 2013a. "Inequality Yes, But Canada's in a Sweet Spot." *The Globe and Mail*, 16 October.

Yakabuski, Konrad. 2013b. "Youth Unemployment is a Global Crisis." *The Globe and Mail*, 3 June.

Yakabuski, Konrad. 2013c. "Left Behind? That's Oh So Canadian." *The Globe and Mail*, 7 November.

Yakabuski, Konrad. 2013d. "Income Inequality in Canada: What's the Problem?" *The Globe and Mail*, 13 December.

Yakabuski, Konrad. 2015. "On a New Road, With Uber at the Wheel." *The Globe and Mail*, 20 July.

Yalnizyan, Armine. 2010. The Rise of the Richest 1%. CCPA, December.

Yalnizyan, Armine. 2011. Canadian Income Inequality. Published by the Conference Board of Canada.

Yalnizyan, Armine. 2012. "Why We're Seeing the Ugly New Face of Capitalism." *The Globe and Mail.* 14 February.

Yang, Jennifer. 2013. "Why Girls Are More At Risk During Natural Disasters." *Toronto Star*, 10 October.

Yardley, Jim. 2013. "Bangladeshi's Empire Built on Hate and Fear." *The New York Times*, 12 May.

Yardley, Jim, and Binyamin Applebaum. 2015. "Harsh Words for Capitalism." *The New York Times*, 18/19 July.

Yoder, Janice D. 1991. "Rethinking Tokenism: Looking Beyond Numbers." *Gender & Society* 5(2):178–192.

Yu, Soojin, and Anthony Heath. 2007. "Inclusion for All but Aboriginals in Canada," in *Unequal Chances: Ethnic Minorities in Western Labour Markets.* A. Heath and S.Y. Cheung (eds.), pp. 181–220. New York: Oxford University Press.

Zawilski, Valerie. 2016. *Inequality in Canada: A Reader in the Intersections of Gender, Race, and Class*, 3rd ed. Toronto: Oxford University Press.

Zingales, Luigi. 2012. *A Capitalism for the People: Recapturing the Lost Genius of American Prosperity.* New York: Basic Books.

Zlomislic, Diana. 2013. "New MDs Can't Find Work in Specialties." *Toronto Star*, 10 October.

Zuckerman, Seth. 2010. "Lessons From Cuba: What Can We Learn from Cuba's Two Tier Economy?" *Travel Outward.* Retrieved from http://traveloutward.com .

Index

pets, 268–9

physicians, immigrant accreditation, 171–3

Pickett, Kate, x

Pikangikum community, MB, 40, 182

Piketty, Thomas, 302–3

politics in Canada: gender involvement, 125, 136–8; and inequality, 9–10; and poverty, 97, 107–8, 113–14; racialized minorities, 155

poor class, 90–1, 101–2

population, globally, 270–1

Porter, John, ix, 176

post-Fordism, 209, 213, 214, 217–18

post-secondary education. *see* universities

poverty: Aboriginal peoples, 180; absolute *vs.* relative, 104–8; blame-the-system model, 102–4; blame-the-victim model, 57, 112, 113–14; in Canada, 94–6, 98–107, 309; as category, 97; and children (*see* child poverty); distribution, 100–2; and foodbanks, 106, 162; and globalization, 269–70; and health, 39; immigrants, 162; levels of, 99–100, 112; low income measure and cut-off line, 106–7, 108; meaning and measurement, 96, 99, 100, 104–8, 112; politics of, 97, 107–8, 113–14; racialization, 101; racialized minorities, 156, 161–2; reduction strategies, 114–15; reframing, 112–14; social exclusion, 97–8; sociological lens on, 97–8; street-level, 108–11; and women, 101; working poor, 101–2

power: in corporate world, 61–2; and inequality, 44–6; of language, 48; Marx and Weber's views of, 45, 48–9; media representations, 46–8

precarious work, 208, 220–3

prime minister of Canada, salary, 4–5

prisons, Aboriginal peoples in, 40, 183

problem–solution nexus, 22–3

production and productivity: food, 271, 274–6; and globalization, 283; in new economy, 212, 217

proportional equality, 294–7

psychology, and blame-the-victim model, 57

quick-service industry, 217–18

racialized minorities: bias and stereotypes, 159–60; and child poverty, 101; diversity in workplace, 161; domestic violence, 149–50, 181–2; and education, 237; employer discrimination, 160; ethnicity *vs.* critical race models, 174–7; exclusion in inclusive society, 162–74; in government, 40; historical treatment, 154; income and earnings, 139, 156, 157–8, 159, 169; inequalities in Canada, 153–62, 310; inequalities overview, 153–6, 313; integration, 165–6; in management, 64–5; media representation, 46–8, 155; names of job seekers, 159–60; in politics, 155; poverty, 101, 156, 161–2; structural inequality, 60; unemployment, 156–7, 158–61; and university, 252–5; vertical hierarchy, 11–13; women, 140, 142–51; work, 154, 156–7, 227; *see also* immigrants; minorities

racism, 66–9, 253, 256–7

radical conflict, 54, 55, 58–60, 69–70

Rajiva, Mythili, 149, 167

Rana Plaza disaster, 20

Reay, Diane, 80

reform, and inequality as social, 36

refugees, 142, 166

Reiter, Ester, 218

representation. *see* media representation

reserve lands in Canada, 50, 51

residential school system, 239–43

responsible capitalism, 294, 303–5

Rosin, Hanna, 121–2

Rousseau, Jean-Jacques, 53, 54, 55

salary. *see* wages

sameness, and equality, 294–5

Samuel, John, 172

Sanchez, Peter, 266

Sarlo, Christopher, 99–100, 108

schooling. *see* education

Schwalbe, Michael, 24

scientific management of workplace, 217–18

self-determining autonomy models, 192–3

sexual orientation, and human rights, 279–80

sexual violence, 122–3, 138, 144–5, 147–51, 181–2

situational model, 54, 55, 65, 198, 199

Smith, Ekuwa, 149–50

"social", in social inequality, 35–9

social class. *see* class

social construction, 17, 29, 86–8, 97

social contract, at work, 215

social determinants of health, 37–9

social dimensions, 29–30

social equality: attainment and hope for, 289–90, 291–3, 297, 312, 313–14; in Canada, 290–1, 292–3, 309, 314; and capitalism, 294; definition, 30; hybrid model, 304

social exclusion: components, 30–1; definition and concept, 30, 31; as framework, 31; and poverty, 97–8; and social inequality, 18, 30–2, 313, 318; structural dimensions, 31–2; as topic in sociology, 16

social inequality: in Canada, 14–16, 293, 308–11, 313, 314; deconstruction, 19, 35–46; as defining issue, 307–8; definition and conceptualization, 27–8, 30, 311–12; and exclusion, 30–2, 35, 313; explanatory models, 54, 55–60, 65, 69–70; global aspect, 19; and inclusiveness, 32; "inequality" in, 39–46; and institutions, 205–6; as interplay of Agency + Structure + Context, 18, 312; normalization, 17–18; parameters of study, 26–8; points of contention, 15–16; polite fictions and inconvenient facts, 308–11; prioritization of, 23–4; as a problematic, 18; reconstruction, 19, 311–12; social construction, 17; and social exclusion, 18, 30–2, 313, 318; "social" in, 35–9; and social location, 19, 27; and social stratification, 27; and society, 27–8; and sociology, 2, 16, 28–30, 53–5; themes and assumptions, 16–19; universality of, 17

social institutions, 9

socialism, 303–4

social location, 19, 27, 60, 63, 75–6

social market model, 302–3

social mobility, and income in Canada, 33–4

social movements, 49, 50–1, 313

social power, 44–6

social reforms, 49

social stratification, 27, 32–5

social structures, 59–60

society, 27–8, 146

socio-economic inequality, overview, 73–4

socio-economic ladder, mobility, 33–4

sociological imagination, 29

sociology: assumptions about inequality, 16–19; criteria for analysis of inequality, 35–6; critical orientation, 29; of exclusion, 2, 16,